MULTIMEDIA SYSTEMS

John F. Koegel Buford

University of Massachusetts Lowell

Contributing Editor

ACM Press • SIGGRAPH Series
New York, New York

ADDISON-WESLEY PUBLISHING COMPANY

Reading, Massachusetts • Menlo Park, California • New York
Don Mills, Ontario • Wokingham, England • Amsterdam • Bonn
Sydney • Singapore • Tokyo • Madrid • San Juan • Milan • Paris

This book is published as part of the SIGGRAPH Books Series with ACM Press Books, a collaborative effort among ACM SIGGRAPH, ACM Press, and Addison-Wesley Publishing Company. The SIGGRAPH Books Series publishes books on theory, practice, applications, and imaging in computer graphics and interactive techniques, some developed from courses, papers, or panels presented at the annual ACM SIGGRAPH conference.

Library of Congress Cataloging-in-Publication Data

Multimedia systems / John F. Koegel Buford, contributing editor.
p. cm.
Includes bibliographical references and index.
ISBN 0-201-53258-1
1. Multimedia systems. I. Koegel Buford, John F.
QA76.575.M85 1994
006.6--dc20 93-19184
CIP

1 2 3 4 5 6 7 8 9 10—MA—9897969594

Contents

MEDIA AND TIME

FUTURE DIRECTIONS

Preface

The multimedia revolution has become the latest cultural phenomenon, changing vocabularies and everyday concepts of work and life. Government and industry leaders from telecommunications, entertainment, and computing promote the information superhighway. Billions of dollars are being staked as companies and industries bet that a high-speed connection to every home and business can open large and lucrative markets. The ideas presented by technology visionaries decades ago now seem realizable.

New developments in computing and communications technologies are at the forefront of the multimedia revolution. There has been a surge of research related to the many significant technical issues involved in the development of large-scale multimedia computing and communications systems. This book brings many of these ideas together and provides an organizing framework by which recent results can be put into focus.

As recently as five years ago, only a small number of industry and university research groups working in multimedia technologies existed. Those of us wishing to join these technology trailblazers soon encountered the problem of following an uncharted course: few maps and landmarks to reference. Additionally, important interdisciplinary aspects of multimedia, including sound and video recording, television engineering, and digital signal processing, have their own specialized literature not particularly geared towards the development of digital multimedia systems.

Today, a large and growing interest in the technical community is leading to significant new results in multimedia systems architectures, user interfaces, algorithms, and technology. Because this research crosses traditional demarcations of computer science, the results are dispersed throughout literature, difficult to access, and not coherently treated. *Multimedia Systems* was conceived to fill these varied needs:

- ☐ a clear statement as to the rationale, issues, and directions facing the development of global multimedia information and communication systems,
- ☐ a single source for basic information on digital media and fundamental multimedia concepts,
- ☐ a unified survey of current results and research directions in the field of multimedia systems, and
- ☐ an assessment of open issues and future directions.

To accomplish these goals, *Multimedia Systems* includes contributed chapters which were specifically developed or edited to fit into the overall organization of the book. The contributors are recognized experts in the areas in which they write. Each chapter provides a comprehensive treatment of a given area of multimedia systems and should be accessible for a broad technical audience.

The availability of multimedia systems and services depends upon advances in system architecture, operating systems and services, network communications, information systems, and user interface technology. Design issues, including temporal modeling, synchronization, quality of service, and performance, are common across all these areas. Additionally, the functions of the elements of multimedia systems are interrelated. Bringing these topics together in one volume recognizes that multimedia systems have become a significant area of specialization, which can be treated in a unified manner.

The development of multimedia systems is currently an active research area and commercial endeavor. While the major design issues are well understood, a consensus on the design of multimedia systems is still emerging, and much of the activity is still at the prototype stage. While theory and practice will undoubtedly continue to evolve over the next several years, it is possible today to provide a detailed discussion of the technical issues, principles, current results, and likely directions, drawing upon the research literature and activity in industry and in the standards community. Such a discussion will contribute to and accelerate the development of multimedia systems.

This book will be useful to those who wish to have a technical introduction to the issues of multimedia systems as well as those who need a single reference source for the central topics. It is comprehensive in that it covers the major areas but is not intended to be encyclopedic. As a collection of contributed chapters it offers the benefit of specially written articles by experts in the given topics. Because it is not an anthology of papers, the chapters are coordinated and provide general coverage of the topics.

1.1 ORGANIZATION

The organization of the book is based on the widespread recognition that personal communications and computing are converging. In the framework introduced in Chapter 3, this convergence is represented by the intersection of multimedia information systems and multimedia communications systems. This leads naturally to sections that deal with each of these areas. The other sections of the book provide complementary material.

The book is composed of five sections. The first section provides an overview of multimedia systems from various perspectives. Section 2 presents background information on the fundamental concepts of media and time. Section 3 presents a sequence of chapters that covers topics in multimedia information systems, ranging from real-time kernel support to multimedia authoring. Section 4 provides a similar sequence for multimedia communications systems, ranging from BISDN architecture to groupwork. Section 5 examines two high definition television and knowledge-based multimedia systems.

Acknowledgments

The fields of multimedia computing and communications are moving forward at a fast pace. New international conferences, journals, and books are appearing constantly. Writing timely descriptions that will not be outdated by the next conference or journal issue (or tomorrow's newspaper!) is a challenging task. I would like to express my personal appreciation to each of the contributors for their effort in preparing material for this book. I also thank Arch Luther for allowing republication of his work in Chapters 5 and portions of Chapter 6, Brian Marquardt and the Interactive Multimedia Association for permission to publish the material in Chapter 9, and Hiroshi Ishii and Naomi Miyake for allowing republication of their work as Chapter 16.

This book draws on a significant body of research. Care has been taken to cite the referenced work where it has been used in each chapter. Not all important work could be discussed or cited in this book, but those who have contributed to the research literature have produced the results that make a book like this possible.

The editor wishes to thank those who reviewed the book for their helpful comments on improving its overall quality, including Andrew Davidson of Philips Interactive Media, Edward Fox of Virginia Polytechnic Institute, Walter L. Hill, Thomas Little of Boston University, Arch C. Luther, Fillia Makedon of Dartmouth College, and Chris Sherman of Logical Insight Multimedia. Gina S. Lee produced artwork for Chapters 3, 10, 11, 14 and 15. I am grateful to Alan Rose of Intertext Publications, Nhora Cortes-Comerer of ACM Press, and Helen Goldstein of Addison-Wesley for their help throughout the process of creating the book.

The editor can be reached at buford@cs.uml.edu to report errors, comments, and suggestions.

John F. Buford

CONTRIBUTORS

David Backer, Ph.D.
Course Technology
Cambridge, MA

John F. Koegel Buford, Ph.D.
Dept. of Computer Science
University of Massachusettts Lowell
Lowell, MA

Rita Brennan
Apple Computer
Cupertino, CA

Walter L. Hill, Ph.D.
San Francisco, CA

Hiroshi Ishii, Ph.D.
NTT Human Interface Laboratories
Kanagawa, Japan

Thomas D. C. Little, Ph.D.
Dept. of Elec., Comp., and
Systems Engr.
Boston University
Boston, MA

Arch C. Luther
Luther Associates
Merchantville, NJ

Naomi Miyake, Ph.D.
School of Computer and
Cognitive Sciences
Chukyo University
Toyota, Japan

Jeannette G. Neal, Ph.D.
Calspan Corporation
Buffalo, NY

Jeffrey S. Porter
Commodore International
Westchester, PA

Charles Poynton
Sun Microsystems Computer Corp.
Mountain View, CA

Prodip Sen, Ph.D.
NYNEX Science and Technology
White Plains, NY

Stuart Shapiro, Ph.D.
State Univ. of New York at Buffalo
Buffalo, NY

John Strawn, Ph.D.
S Systems
Larkspur, CA

Hideyuki Tokuda, Ph.D.
Carnegie Mellon University
Pittsburgh, PA
and
Faculty of Environmental
Information
Keio University
Kanagaw, Japan

CHAPTER 1

USES OF MULTIMEDIA INFORMATION

John F. Koegel Buford
University of Massachusetts Lowell

1.1 INTRODUCTION

A complex weave of communications, electronics, and computer technologies is emerging to create a new multimedia fabric for the next decade. The nature of this cloth is still evolving as an assortment of industries—telecommunications, consumer electronics, computers, cable and broadcast television, and information providers—compete for the emerging market. The potentially biggest near-term market will be the home and consumer, as recent developments such as consumer-oriented computer products, interactive television, and video-on-demand suggest. However, in time many expect the new technologies to be as pervasive as today's television and telephone and the impact to reach to the sum of computers, telecommunications, and electronics, touching all parts of society from industry to government, education to recreation.

The widespread interest in multimedia is largely based on the perception that computer control of digital multimedia forms provides a low-cost easy accessibility to multimedia information that so far has been limited to specialists and production houses with million dollar equipment budgets. If the computer-integrated version of multimedia can be made as approachable as today's word processor, then digital multimedia technology becomes the Gutenberg press for visual forms of communication media.

At the same time, the convergence of multimedia technology with the telecommunications industry is creating a scenario with similar impact. If the features of the telephone and television are combined, the resulting visually enriched communication makes applications such as home shopping, distance learning, remote collaboration with specialists, and interactive access to live and stored video sources around the world possible.

These two technology revolutions are underway and are synergistic. The resulting development and realignment of industries, products, and infrastructure is creating many technical challenges, which are compounded by the scope and interdisciplinary aspects of multimedia information processing. The design of new *multimedia systems* to support these applications will lead to changes in the architecture of today's computers, networks, operating systems, user interfaces, and public communications systems. Because of the scope of these changes and the expected pervasiveness of the technology, the full impact is yet to be determined. The remainder of this chapter addresses this issue by examining some of the applications that have been demonstrated so far.

1.2 WHAT IS MULTIMEDIA?

"Multimedia: An application requiring more than two trips to the car to operate."
—Interactive Multimedia Association

The concepts behind what is emerging today date back to over four decades to a series of visionary thinkers who foresaw the evolution of computers towards richer personalized devices that would become an extension of the individual. In 1945 Vannevar Bush, then the Director of the Office of Scientific Research and Development in the U.S. government, suggested [1] that one of the future devices available for individuals would be a memex, "a device in which one stores all his books, records, and communications, and which is mechanized so that it can be consulted with exceeding speed and flexibility. It is an enlarged intimate supplement to his memory." The memex would additionally be an associative device, so that related items could be easily located.

Today, the linking of associated data for easy access is called hypertext, a term coined by Ted Nelson [2], or hypermedia, when any type of media form can be linked. It is the simultaneous use of data in different media forms (voice, video, text, animations, etc.) that is called multimedia. Digital video and audio media are the most demanding of the new media that are being added to the repertoire of computing and communications systems.

Because of their time-sampled nature, these types of media are frequently referred to as continuous media (CM). The term multimedia computing commonly refers to the use of multimedia data types in computer applications and systems, and multimedia communications denotes communications systems which support the real-time transmission of continuous media.

1.3 EARLY HYPERTEXT AND COLLABORATIVE RESEARCH

The idea of linking related information gave impetus to Ted Nelson and Doug Englebart, who separately conceived and developed the first computerized versions of hypertext-style editing systems. In 1968 Englebart demonstrated the NLS system developed at SRI [3,4], which had interactive multiperson editing, branching to different files, text search facilities, and outline processing. In the late 1960s, Ted Nelson and Andries van Dam collaborated at Brown University to develop a hypertext editing system on an IBM 360 [4,5]. A fourth-generation system developed at Brown, Intermedia, has continued this research and includes animation and video tools.

1.4 MULTIMEDIA AND PERSONALIZED COMPUTING

In 1967, Nicholas Negroponte formed the Architecture Machine Group in the Architecture Department at MIT. Although the initial goal was to use computers for architectural design [6], a new focus developed: that of making computers easier to use.

1.4.1 Spatial Data Management System

In early 1976, the Architecture Machine Group proposed a research program to the U.S. Defense Advanced Research Projects Agency (DARPA) entitled "Augmentation of Human Resources in Command and Control through Multiple Media Man-Machine Interaction." A basic precept of the project would be the use of spatial cues to aid in task performance and memory. Information organization would be tied to locality, and the user interface would include a large wall-size display and an octaphonic sound system to provide spatial audio cues. The user would access a data item by traveling to it in a virtual space as opposed to referencing it by name. Objects in the space could be text, graphics, videos, or active procedures.

The Spatial Data Management System (SDMS) was a major step toward moving the computer interface away from the conventional video display terminal to one which was close to human perceptual space. The SDMS

Figure 1.1 SDMS media room with instrumented Eames chair, large screen display, and side touch screen monitors (Reproduced courtesy of the MIT Media Laboratory, © MIT Media Laboratory 1978)

media room contained an instrumented Eames chair, large projection screen, and side view video screens (Figure 1.1). While seated in the chair, the user could use joysticks, a touch screen, or stylus. These controls were used to navigate through the information space viewed on the large screen (Figure 1.2), which acted as a window to the data space. One of the side view monitors provided a continuous top-level view of the information landscape.

The first version of the system organized the space hierarchically, with lower levels reachable via ports. SDMS II used a single global space and zooming could be used to inspect an object in greater detail. While navigating the space, auditory cues provided a sense of direction and distance from an object. Later, voice-based navigation and control were added to the system [7].

1.4.2 Movie Maps and Surrogate Travel

In the late 1970s, the theme of spatially organized data continued with the work of researcher Andy Lippman [8] and doctoral student Robert Mohl [9]. In what came to be known as the Aspen project, film shots taken from a moving vehicle traveling through the town of Aspen, Colorado, were stored

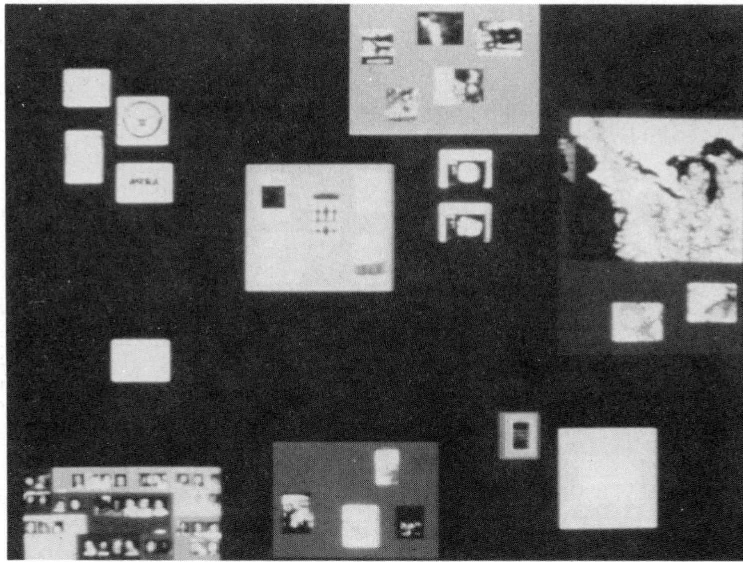

Figure 1.2a Top-level view of DataLand in SDMS (Reproduced courtesy of the MIT Media Laboratory, © MIT Media Laboratory 1978)

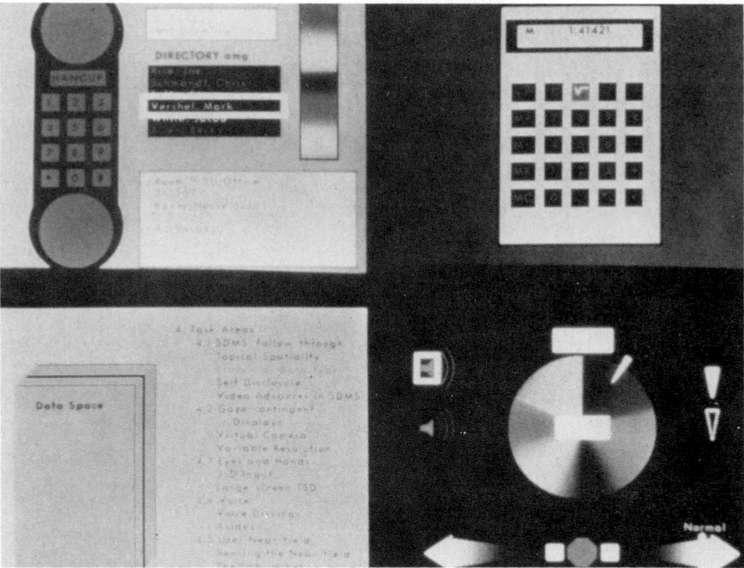

Figure 1.2b SDMS monitor interface showing various tools available (Reproduced courtesy of the MIT Media Laboratory, © MIT Media Laboratory 1978)

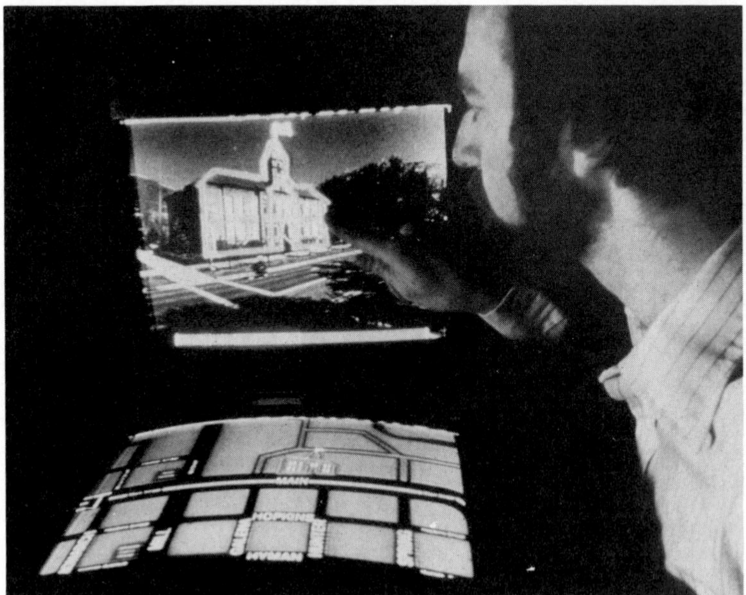

Figure 1.3a Surrogate travel using movie maps sample interface from the MIT Aspen project (Reproduced courtesy of the MIT Media Laboratory, © MIT Media Laboratory 1978)

on videodiscs. These were then accessed interactively to simulate driving through the town. A touch screen or joystick interface allowed the user to control the speed and direction of travel (Figure 1.3).

Images of the facade of significant buildings in the town were stored on videodisc as well. The driver could stop at any of these buildings and access data associated with the building. For example, the town records were accessed from the town hall.

Mohl's work added a simultaneous aerial view of the town. Different techniques for zooming, which maintained constant position of the target, were tried. Aerial views could be annotated to include landmarks of places of interest or to identify where the user had traveled. Experiments with users indicated that spatial context is a significant aid to memory; users of the system upon a later visit to the town reported complete comfortability in finding their way. Further, the use of spatial reference points as a contextual aid for data navigation could apply to any domain with a spatial topography, from molecular chemistry to socio-economic patterns [9].

1.4.3 The Electronic Book

From 1980 to 1983, a demonstration system combining features of print, broadcast, and computer media was developed by Dave Backer for his

Figure 1.3b Moving video view of Aspen streets with control interface (top) and aerial view (bottom) for top-level navigational control (Reproduced courtesy of the MIT Media Laboratory, © MIT Media Laboratory 1978)

doctoral dissertation on a prototype of the electronic book [10]. The project used automobile repair as its theme, and is significant both for its book-like user interface as well as the underlying authoring environment. From the users' perspective, a sophisticated multimedia book was literally at their

Figure 1.3c Entering the Aspen courthouse (top) and then court clerk's office (bottom) for access to town records (Reproduced courtesy of the MIT Media Laboratory, © MIT Media Laboratory 1978)

fingertips because of the touchscreen interface (Figure 1.4). Pages turned like ordinary books, but searching and indexing had the added benefit of the computer. The material could be personalized by annotations and the addition of new material. The underlying authoring system was available to the user, and anticipated today's authoring tools by providing an object-oriented storage model and a scripting language.

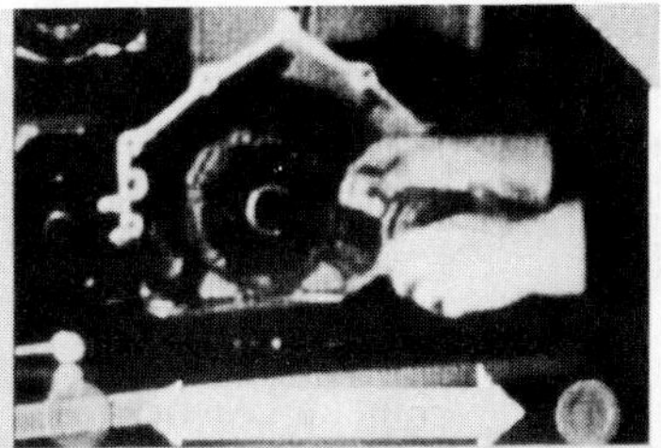

REMOVAL OF OIL PUMP
The oil pump is removed by removing the seven (7) retaining bolts. The bolts may need to be started with the socket wrench, but can then be removed by hand. After the bolts are removed, a slide hammer is used to pull the pump out by screwing it into two of the cover holes. Alternate from hole to hole until the pump is freed. Do not try to remove the pump by pulling on just one of the holes, or it may become wedged.
Remove the pump from the case by sliding it off the input shaft. On the outside diameter of the pump, there is a seal that holds the pump to the case. The gasket on the top surface of the pump is used because hydraulic pressure passes from the pump to the case.

Figure 1.4 Screen from Dave Backer's prototype electronic book showing how to repair an automobile transmission. Video controls are overlaid on the image in the right-hand corner. As the video plays, the accompanying text changes in step. (Reproduced courtesy of the MIT Media Laboratory, © MIT Media Laboratory 1978)

The prototype workstation integrated sound, data, images, and video presentation. The first use of coordinated access to synchronized media appears here. Video and accompanying text were synchronized in time. If the user changed the position of either text or video during presentation, both streams repositioned automatically.

1.4.4 Formation of the MIT Media Lab

"The future of videodiscs is situated at the intersection of three previously distinct industries: television, publishing, and computers. As such, a new medium must emerge, characterized by the auditory and visual richness of television, the accessibility and personal quality of books, and the interactivity and expressive potential of computers."
—Nicholas Negroponte, Intelligent Videodiscs and Their Applications, 1980.

"Some terminals of the future will be all-knowing rooms without walls. Others will be flat, thin, flexible touch-sensitive displays. And others will be wrist watches and cuff links with the right hand talking to the left by satellite."
—Nicholas Negroponte

As these research projects proceeded, Negroponte was developing a vision of the future uses of multimedia technology and an agenda to pursue it. Together with Jerome Wiesner, president of MIT at the time, Negroponte raised \$40 million for facilities for a new Media Lab. More than 40 corporate sponsors picked up the startup tab and the \$4 million annual operating

Table 1.1 MIT Media Lab (circa 1985)

Group	*Investigator(s)*	*Interests*
Electronic Publishing	Walter Bender	On-line, personalized multimedia newspapers/magazines
Film and Video	Ricky Leacock	Convergence of film production and presentation with computer technology
Visual Language Workshop	Muriel Cooper, Ron McNeil	New user interface and authoring techniques
Electronic Music	Barry Vercoe	Computer composition, synthesis, and performance of music
Spatial Imaging and Photography	Steve Benton	Technolgy for holograms and holgraphic movies
Learning and Epistemology	Seymour Papert	Deconstructible computer-based learning environments
Movies of the Future	Andy Lippman	Digital video as media; hierarchical coding of video
Advanced Television Research	William Schreiber	High-definition and digital television coding techniques
Speech Processing	Chris Schmandt	Uses of audio and speech recognition in the user interface; computer-based telephony
Human-Machine Interface Group	Dick Bolt	Development and use of new input devices such as gloves and eye-trackers

expenses. After more than five years of fund raising, the lab opened in 1985 with ten research groups (Table 1.1).

1.5 MULTIMEDIA ON THE MAP

During the 1980s, other multimedia research groups were being formed as well. Two notable ones were:

- ☐ Olivetti Research Lab

  The Cambridge, England, research group had two multiyear multimedia projects. Pandora, a joint effort with Cambridge University, focused on developing a peripheral box for creating a multimedia workstation testbed. The second project developed a dynamic locator system called Active Badge. By using sensors located throughout the building and sensor badges carried by each individual, anyone could be located.

The California research group's focus was desktop audio. Some of the earliest work in combining telephony functions with workstations resulted. A server architecture called VOX was developed for managing audio and is discussed in Chapter 15.

- ☐ Apple Computer Multimedia Lab

  The Apple Multimedia Lab, directed by Kristina Hooper Woolsey, carried out a large number of innovative multimedia projects, particularly focusing on the area of education as discussed later in this chapter.

1.6 A TOUR OF EMERGING APPLICATIONS

As the technology has moved to the mainstream, applications in many areas have appeared. Entertainment, home shopping, education, health care, and engineering are a few examples.

1.6.1 Entertainment: Growing Interactivity and Group Participation

The use of interactive media for entertainment is no new phenomenon, yet the scale and sophistication of games and movies will dramatically advance in three stages. First, the amount of programming available to audiences will increase in a drive to video-on-demand services. Second, the use of interactive television facilities for video-on-demand will make it possible to incorporate audience participation into existing programming. Third, participation will move from a highly controlled audience mode to open-ended group collaboration and teaming, from many-to-one to many-to-many.

The size of the entertainment market will be a significant force in creating the economies of scale necessary for other applications of the technology to emerge. Further, the evolution of multimedia computer hardware could be determined by the success of multimedia consumer products.

Video-on-Demand

The first stage is developing as an effort by the cable television industry, the telephone industry, and broadcasters to provide greater flexibility in what programming is shown when. The video-on-demand model [11] takes advantage of some form of two-way communication between the home and the video source, which could be a low-bandwidth back channel on a CATV path or a phone line with sufficient bandwidth to carry a compressed video signal. The home may be furnished with a low-cost box, which accepts signals from a hand-held control and which transmits the appropriate status to the video control center. The viewer uses the hand-held control to navigate a selection menu and choose a program. Shortly after the selection is made, the program begins playing. During the course of the movie the viewer is able to pause, reposition, and use other VCR-like controls.

Interactive Cinema

In what is billed as the first interactive cinema, a New York production company hopes to usher audiences toward a day when the next step of the hero or heroine is in the hands of movie watchers. The company, Controlled Entropy Entertainment, uses low-cost technology, which allows the audience to vote on the direction of the plot. Their first film, *I'm Your Man*, has three principal characters. About every 90 seconds during the drama the audience is given a three-way branch in the plot. They register their votes using a three-button pistol grip on the armrest of each seat (Figure 1.5), the choice of the majority being taken.

Unpredictability of the film after repeated showings appears to be part of the attraction. The production has 68 scene variations for a total of about 90 minutes of footage, though a given showing lasts only 20 minutes. Whether the audience feels more in control or more involved in the creative process may depend on how frequently their votes coincided with the

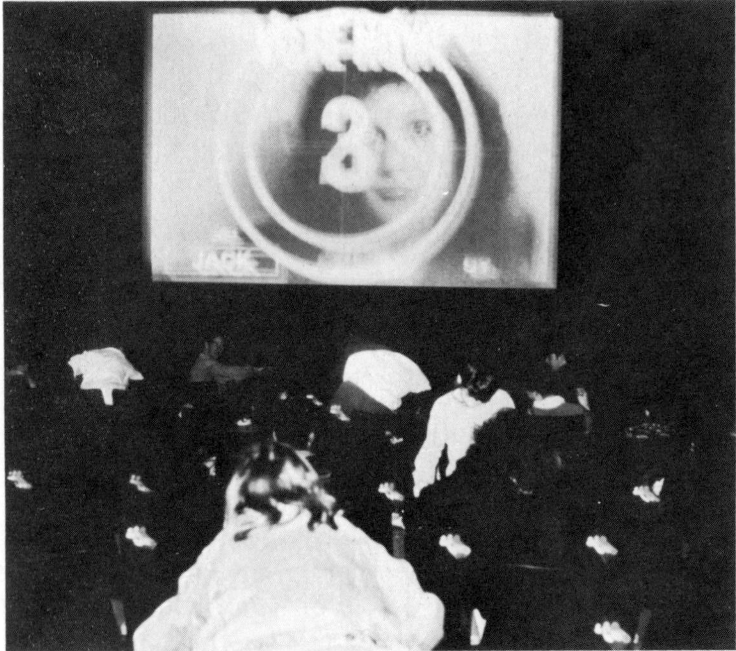

Figure 1.5 Scene from the interactive film *I'm Your Man*, in which the audience votes to control the direction of the plot (Reproduced with permission of Controlled Entropy Entertainment)

majority. In the context of home viewing, this aspect might be more evident.

While the videodisc technology used to deliver the film appears conventional, the scripting of interactive movies is more challenging. The script writer must ensure that every path connects in a coherent way to the previous scenes.

Collaborative Computer-Supported Games

During the 1992 presidential campaign, the computer service Prodigy initiated a collaborative on-line game called The Next President, which let thousands of users participate in a simulated election campaign (Figure 1.6). The game paralleled the real campaign, closely following the primary and convention process, but used fictitious candidates who campaigned on platforms determined by their supporters. Each week the game creators would marshall the candidates through press conferences, elections, campaign crises, and rumors, using the messages and votes of the game's players. Unlike the typical computer game that sets player against the computer, The Next President illustrates the evolution of entertainment towards participation and collaboration.

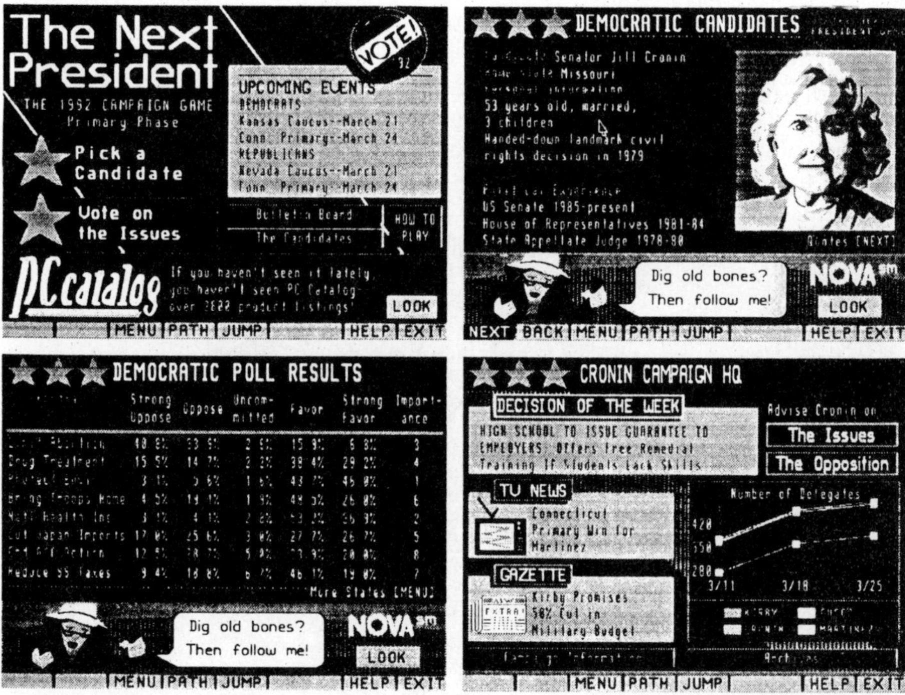

Figure 1.6 The Next President, an on-line game in which hundreds of participants compete and collaborate to determine the fate of their favorite fictitious presidential aspirant. (Reproduced with permission of Prodigy Services Company, © 1992 Prodigy Services Company; game designed and developed by Crossover Technologies)

1.6.2 Home Shopping

Today, upwards of 60 million U.S. homes have access to cable television channels in which a variety of retail goods are marketed. Potential customers can make a purchase by dialing their telephone and using their credit card. Two possible directions that this application might take are:

- ☐ Interactive television: In the model based on the convergence of TV and the computer, greater interactivity and an increase in the number of available channels will permit home shopping to be conducted to many retailers throughout the community.
- ☐ Video-telephony: In the model based on the convergence of the TV and the telephone, subscribers would dial the retailer of interest, but would connect to a live video salesperson or a prerecorded video showcase.

Home shopping is currently a $2 billion industry. It offers greater convenience but restricts the buyer to a limited seller-conducted test drive. However, home shopping can work for buyer preparation even if the final sale must be conducted in person.

In another type of home shopping, touchscreen kiosks have entered the business of residential real-estate sales. Developed by a company in Denmark, Home-Vision™ allows buyers to interactively browse a photo database of homes, seeing different views and the rooms of the property (Figure 1.7). The interface is visually oriented and entirely screen-based. The buyer selects price range and geographic area of interest. The system then presents a collage of properties matching the specification. From there the buyer can choose any house for a visual tour. The interface includes an accompanying audio track, which can be enabled or disabled by the viewer.

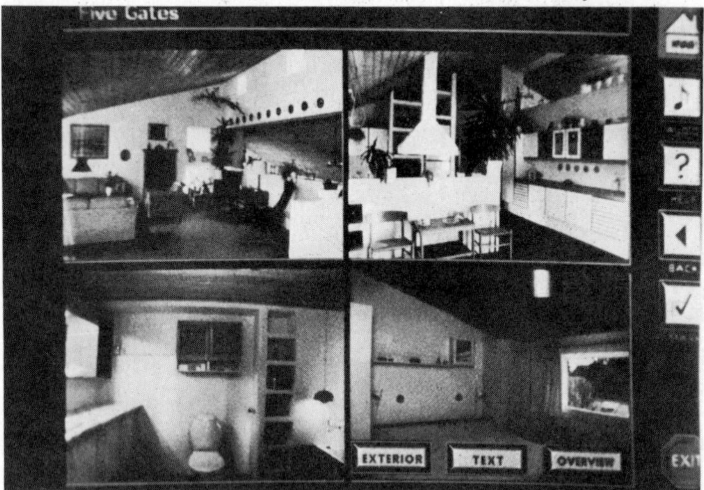

Figure 1.7 User interface of Home-Vision™, a multimedia kiosk application that uses an IBM PS/2® running OS/2® and was developed by the Danish company Multimedia Management

Figure 1.8 Demonstration of a multimedia inventory management interface, designed by GainTechnology and created using the GainMomentum authoring environment (Courtesy of GainTechnology, Inc.)

The Home-Vision system reduces the number of homes that agents must take a buyer to see by 50 percent. An added benefit is the transparent tracking of buyers as they browse the database. These statistics can be used by real-estate agencies to generate marketing reports to the seller and to better understand the buyer.

A crucial advantage of multimedia technology is the shift to a visually-oriented interface. The Home-Vision system is one illustration of this. Replacing tables and text with pictures can make the information and the interaction process more direct for users. For example, the mock-up pharmacy inventory interface (Figure 1.8) developed by GainTechnology shows a section of the store shelf. Store personnel and customers can point at the items as if browsing through a store catalog.

1.6.3 Multimedia Communications for Healthcare

Environments in which imaging applications are prominent are good candidates for the use of multimedia technology, since the technology permits visual data to be more easily viewed, shared, and processed. Certain segments of the health-care industry are examples of this, and several systems involving multimedia communications and computers have been tested [12–16].

In a recent multiyear Media Broadband Services (MBS) study involving four Boston-area hospitals, the regional Bell operating company NYNEX provided broadband interconnections to field test the benefits of high-bandwidth communications. NYNEX and the hospitals also collaborated on developing applications software needed for medical specialists to perform workstation-based video conferencing and image retrieval.

In their assessment of the case for multimedia communications in healthcare, NYNEX observed the following:

- One hospital has a staff of 59 people to maintain and transport hardcopy imaging between different hospital facilities. The MBS facilities permit the hospital to use electronic transfer for these images.
- Access to specialists is a frequent problem, leading to delays in diagnosis or requiring the specialist to travel from hospital to hospital. MBS provides multimedia workstations for the home of the specialists, from which they can review computer tomography (CT) and magnetic resonance imaging (MRI) images and consult with attending physicians.
- One hospital's on-line medical record system is text-based; by adding imaging and multimedia communications, a more complete record is available that can be shared on-line by collaborating physicians.

While acknowledging the potential substantial costs of providing multimedia communications, NYNEX expects benefits in three areas:

1. Reduced cost of delivering healthcare

   Although a typical 500-bed hospital creates over two million paper record documents annually, less than 1 percent of health-care facilities with more than 300 beds have systems for storing paper documents on optical disks, despite the potential savings. Additionally, on-line storage of reports would permit remote access, saving the costs of moving records between the storage facility and the hospital.

2. Increased revenue opportunities

   Major hospitals can use high-bandwidth communications from smaller hospitals to increase referrals for complex procedures and attract wider usage of advanced facilities. The communication facilities act to strengthen the relationship between the teaching hospital and the client hospitals, which become more dependent on the higher-quality service.

3. Improved patient care

   Multimedia communications can provide significantly greater access to specialists, particularly valuable for complex treatments. Information sharing and video conferencing are key components of multimedia communications.

The use of imaging techniques (X-rays, CT, MRI, etc.) is growing in healthcare. The collection, maintenance, processing, and distribution of

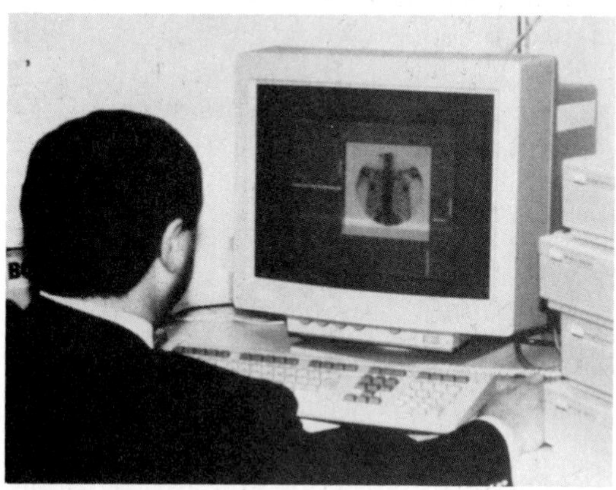

Figure 1.9 Multimedia communications for a radiology application (Reproduced with permission of NYNEX Science and Technology)

these records can be significantly improved by using computer-based storage and high-bandwidth communications. Once these records are integrated with the on-line patient information and easily shared by both local and remote physicians, a large number of benefits in reduced costs and improved care result.

1.6.4 Geographic Information Systems

The management of facilities such as buildings, roads, power lines, and railroad tracks is a problem that concerns government offices, utilities, and many industries. Specially designed computer database management systems called geographic information systems (GIS) are available to provide on-line support for these types of applications. Such systems typically offer a storage model for spatially organized data so that queries based on area or location can be quickly answered. Frequently, the user interfaces of such applications are visually oriented, showing maps or blueprints of the facility and allowing fast zooming and panning.

With the addition of multimedia information, visual and audio data can be associated with landmarks and other points of interest. The map acts as the spatial context for organizing the multimedia information for easy access. A recent survey of multimedia GIS [16] lists a number of existing uses, including:

- The National Capital Planning Commission (NCPC) in Washington, DC, uses on-line video clips and images of buildings and intersections as an aid in park planning and maintenance. Significant time is saved by having all the site information immediately available to the decision makers, who are able to quickly compare different areas and alternatives.

- ☐ Union Pacific Railroad used on-line video records in a pilot project in which right-of-way images for 1600 miles of track were captured. The on-line system permits users to interactively evaluate crossings where accidents have occurred, and can significantly reduce the need for time-consuming field visits.
- ☐ Jefferson County Property Valuation Administration in Kansas City, Missouri links a videodisc record of over 200,000 properties to its property database for use in assessments and hearings. The system reduces the need for field trips when properties are reassessed.

Georgia Power Company has developed a multimedia GIS for the Georgia Resource Center (GRC) presentation system. GRC is used as an information resource for business executives who are considering locating or expanding in the state (Figure 1.10). The use of multimedia GIS is beneficial both as a promotional tool and for quickly navigating the various sites of interest.

The system contains information on 250 communities, 500 industrial parks, and 550 available industrial facilities. The user of the system enters the specifications for his/her project, such as:

Building and site parameters
Community demographics
Labor, wage, and tax criteria
Educational statistics and institutions
Transportation services

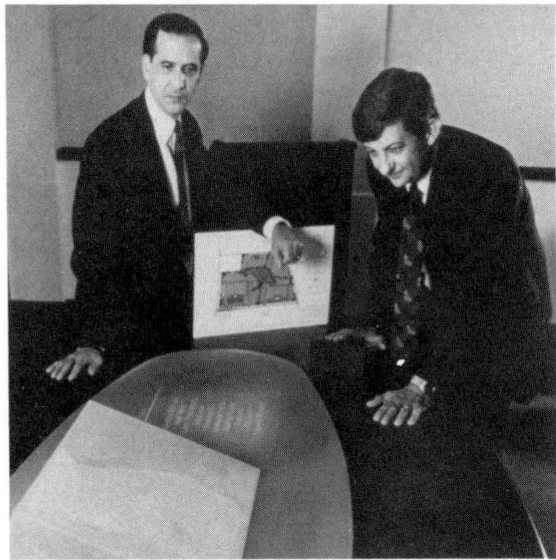

Figure 1.10 The Georgia Power Company's multimedia GIS for the Georgia Resource Center's business locator presentation system. (Reproduced with permission of Georgia Power Company)

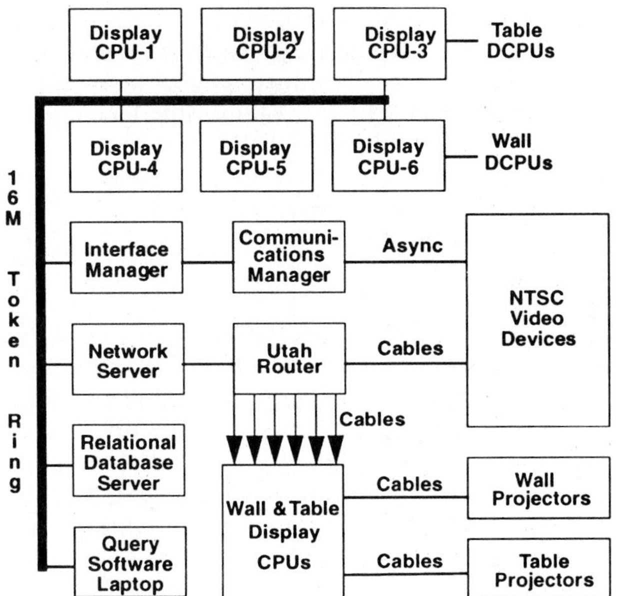

Figure 1.11 Architecture of the multimedia presentation system developed by the Georgia Power Company. (Reproduced with permission of Georgia Power Company)

Sites which meet the given requirements are highlighted on a 3-D map of Georgia. Sites can be accessed in any order to view images of buildings or community video clips illustrating quality of life and business highlights. Once the sites of interest are identified, arrangements for site visits are made.

The underlying system (Figure 1.11) uses a distributed set of computers to control six independent video projectors for three wall screens and three monitors built into the navigation table. A table-mounted laptop computer has custom software for user queries. Queries are sent to the relational database that contains the indices for maps, device controls, and reports stored on the network server. Once the query is completed, the interface manager is notified. The interface manager tells each display CPU to present specific parts of the data on the corresponding screen. Control of videodiscs and other devices is handled by the communications manager, which has 32 serial interfaces for communicating with devices. The interface manager handles user input, in particular allowing the user to move the pointer from screen to screen in one continuous virtual coordinate system.

1.6.5 Education

The ability of multimedia materials to convey by picture, sound, animation, or movie what is otherwise hard to express, to capture for reuse on any occasion remote lands and singular events, and, with the use of the computer, to provide this information in a form that can be engagingly interactive and easily recast by any aspiring communicator is the explanation for the popularity and particularly long history of multimedia technology's role in education. For many years educational titles have been one of the dominant product areas for multimedia computing, surpassed only by entertainment. A view of some of the innovative uses that have been produced for education purposes can be obtained from a sampling of the projects and products developed by Apple Computer's Multimedia Lab, directed by Kristina Hooper Woolsey.

The Visual Almanac is an ambitious early project [17] that created a large audiovisual database (stored on videodisc), a set of HyperCard-based multimedia tools, and a number of sample activities for educators to use as models. The audiovisual database is organized as twelve collections having a variety of cultural, historical, and scientific themes; the total database consists of over 7000 media objects, with accompanying keywords, citations, and descriptive material. Specific tools for searching, editing, and composing, with the media objects as the raw materials, are included with the software.

The Visual Almanac has been a resource for many subsequent efforts, both within and external to the Apple Multimedia Lab. One interesting effort, Beyond the Desktop [18], provides students with picture cards of objects in the visual database. Each card has a barcode, which, when scanned by the student, will call up the corresponding media object on the computer. The card becomes a tangible reminder, like a baseball card, that can be carried around and referred to by the child. Everyday objects like pages of a book, pencils, and rocks can be barcoded and used in the same way. This allows familiar objects and experiences to be tightly associated with the information in the computer.

The Classroom Multimedia Kiosk project [18] uses a kiosk equipped with video and computer presentation and a barcode scanner and printer as a centerpiece for class discussion. In a U.S. history scenario (based on a Geography Television videodisc), students use the kiosk to view a video segment on a historical topic and to make small printed History Cards. The cards are barcoded and are associated with a specific video sequence selected by the student. The student can later scan the card to replay the video sequence. The card also contains an image taken from the video sequence. Collections of history cards can be used by the students to collaboratively create timelines, maps, and other compositions.

In 101 Activities [18], the computer becomes an advisor, suggesting interesting and creative recreational activities at home. Following *My First Activity Book* by Angela Wilkes, the child first goes on a treasure hunt to find as many items as possible needed for the activity. After the collection step is completed, the child selects the What Can I Do? button. Given the available items, the computer then lists possible activities, their complexity, and duration. For any selected activity, the computer provides a guided tour

Table 1.2 Survey of Selected Apple Multimedia Lab Projects/Products (1987–1992)

Project	*Description*
Visual Almanac	A videodisc collage of audiovisual materials for educators, organized in 12 collections. Over 7000 media objects, 5000 from external sources.
GTV: A Geographical Perspective on American History	Combines still images and music in an MTV-style presentation popular with middle school age group.
Interactive NOVA: Animal Pathfinders	Supplements the NOVA movie about animal migration with additional documentation and three activities that involve the students in the subject matter.
Life Story	Supplements BBC's movie about the discovery of DNA with accessory materials including documentary interviews, text transcriptions, simulations, references, and navigational tools.
Mystery of the Disappearing Ducks	Using raw footage from a TV documentary on wetlands, provides an interactive means to explore the ecological controversy. Includes a mystery game about disappearing ducks developed by high school students and professional designers.

with pictures of intermedia steps of the projects and video clips of complicated tasks.

The Apple Multimedia Lab is noteworthy not only for the varied educational titles that it has produced (Table 1.2), but also for the rich set of ideas that have come from its quarters regarding the shape and direction of the technology [18,19]. During its six-year history, over 100 individuals participated in its projects.

1.6.6 Multimedia Communications: An Enabling Technology for Concurrent Engineering and Manufacturing

The Institute for Defense Analysis [20] has identified various practices, known as concurrent engineering, which organizations have adopted in order to accelerate the design and manufacture of complex systems and products. One of the key precepts of these practices is the coordinated activity of engineering, manufacturing, and management activities of a project through all phases of its development. The benefits of this approach are reduced time-to-market and improved product quality.

The concurrent engineering methodology accelerates product development by incorporating more parallelism between what are conventionally serial phases of a project. This parallelism, however, requires closer coordination between the different functions within the organization, with correspondingly increased group communication requirements. The use of multimedia communications tools is one of two uses of multimedia technology that play an enabling role for concurrent engineering. These tools permit product groups to communicate in distributed environments, sharing applications and data, using on-line group decision support tools, and interacting in group conference calls.

Engineering and manufacturing groups rely increasingly on CAD and CAM software to design, manufacture, and maintain their products. Together with technical publishing software, these tools permit design specifications and technical documentation to be created and accessed on-line. The second enabling role of multimedia technology is to supplement these existing tools with a richer information processing environment. For example, audiovisual product information, voice annotations of design documentation, and on-line interactive help manuals can be supported by the availability of on-line multimedia information. The richer information content indirectly enables the concurrent engineering process by providing a more effective and direct form for expressing an idea.

The practice of concurrent engineering can be enhanced by use of computer and communication technologies. In particular, multimedia technologies permit work groups to collaborate in a richer information environment. Researchers at the Center for Productivity Enhancement (CPE) at the University of Massachusetts Lowell, funded by NYNEX, have developed a demonstration system for the use of multimedia technology for concurrent engineering. The project extends an existing factory-of-the-future prototype robotic workcell with a distributed multimedia workstation environment.

The CPE Factory-of-the-Future system (Figure 1.12) was designed in the late 1980s to demonstrate a number of advanced manufacturing concepts, including:

Integrated design and manufacturing software environments

Flexible robotic workcell techniques, including coordination between robots during subsystem errors

Automatic generation of manufacturing instructions from the engineering design

Intelligent application of design rules during the design process

The distributed multimedia workstation environment, developed in 1990, combines a cross-campus video network, existing applications software, and shared applications to allow multimedia documents to be shared during group video conferences (Figure 1.13). Using the Factory-of-the-Future as a backdrop, group discussions on common engineering/manufacturing issues such as design reviews, remote diagnosis of equipment failures, and change orders were enacted and various multimedia design materials

Figure 1.12 The University of Massachusetts Lowell Factory-of-the-Future as used for demonstration of multimedia technology in concurrent engineering and manufacturing

were provided in on-line manuals. These experiences demonstrated the two roles of multimedia technology in concurrent engineering:

- Engineering and manufacturing as a visually rich domain is a natural beneficiary of multimedia information processing
- Group communications, when conducted via the computer workstation, allows the participants to refer to and share any on-line materials that might be appropriate to the discussion

Figure 1.13 Video conferencing tool used as part of the multimedia communications environment in the University of Massachusetts Lowell concurrent engineering demonstration

1.6.7 The Impact of Ubiquitous Multimedia Services

There is an impressive range of applications of multimedia technology, some of which may not have been conceived of yet. Independently, each one offers testimony to the potential benefits of multimedia systems. However, a greater impact will result when the parts are knit into the whole, when multimedia computing and communications become as widely available as today's telephone and television. Then multimedia documents, presentations, mail, games, and other applications will be the common denominator by which people and organizations communicate, work, and play together. This prospect is one that will be the most socially transforming not only because of enriched modes of expression, greater information access, and more accessible tools, but because of the potential for greater involvement of the individual on the creation side of the media content.

1.7 MULTIMEDIA SYSTEMS: THE CHALLENGES

The challenges ahead to developing ubiquitous multimedia systems include solving a gamut of technical problems that are discussed in the remainder of the book:

Temporal and intermedia synchronization within the operating system, network architecture, and presentation system

Higher performance networking of time-based media

On-line storage, access, and interchange of multimedia content

New user interface paradigms

New tools for authoring and using multimedia information

Widely adopted standards, many of which are underway, will be a significant asset to the development of the market. The cooperation of information providers, system integrators, communications and computer companies, and application developers are likewise essential to the direction of the technology and the pace of its growth.

1.8 ACKNOWLEDGMENTS

I appreciate the assistance of the following individuals in providing information used in the preparation of this chapter:

Dave Backer (Course Technology)

Diane Blackman (Entropy Entertainment)

Valerie Eames (MIT Media Lab)

Andy Hopper (Olivetti Research Lab)
Eric Koskoff (Multi Media Management, Inc.)
Michael Massimilla (Crossover Technologies)
Joyce McGuire and Kristina Hooper Woolsey (Apple Computer)
Ray Plott (Georgia Resource Center)
James Robinson (Nynex Science and Technology)
Pierre Scaruffi (Olivetti)
Hank Stewart (Prodigy Services Company

1.9 REFERENCES

1. Bush, V. As We May Think. *The Atlantic Monthly*. vol. 1. July 1945. pp. 101–108.
2. Nelson, T. The Hypertext. *Proc. of the World Documentation Federation*. 1965.
3. Englebart, D. C., and English, W. K. A Research Center for Augmenting Human Intellect. *AFIPS Conf. Proceedings*. 1968 Fall Joint Computer Conference. 1968. pp. 395–410.
4. van Dam, A. Hypertext '87: Keynote Address. *Communications of the ACM*. vol. 7. July 1988. pp. 887–895.
5. Carmody, S., W. Gross, T. Nelson, D. Rice, and A. van Dam. A Hypertext Editing System for the 360. In Faiman and Nievergelt (eds.), *Pertinent Concepts in Computer Graphics*. University of Illinois Press. 1969.
6. Negroponte, N. *The Architecture Machine*. MIT Press. 1970.
7. Bolt, R. Put-That-There: Voice and Gesture at the Graphics Interface. *ACM Computer Graphics 14*, vol. 3. July, 1980. pp. 262–270.
8. Lippman, A. Movie Maps: An Application of the Optical Videodisc to Computer Graphics. *ACM Computer Graphics 14*, vol. 3. July 1980. pp. 32–42.
9. Mohl, R. The Interactive Movie Map: Surrogate Travel with the Aid of Dynamic Aerial Overviews. *1980 Midcon Professional Program*. November 1980. pp. 1–7.
10. Backer, D. Prototype for the Electronic Book. In M. Greenberger (ed.), *Media for a Technological Future—Electronic Publishing Plus*. Knowledge Industry Publications. 1985.
11. Sell, C. Switched "Video On Demand" Trial Control and Resource Management. *SPIE Proceedings*. vol. 1786. September 1992.
12. Reis, H., Brenner, D., and J. Robinson. Multimedia Communications in Healthcare. *New York Academy of Sciences Conference on Extended Clinical Consulting by Hospital Computer Networks*. March 1992.
13. Sclabassi, R. et al. The Multi-Media Medical Monitoring, Diagnosis, and Consultation Project. *Proceedings of HICSS-24*. January 1991. pp. 717–728.
14. Chipman, K. et al. Medical Applications in a B-ISDN Field Application. *IEEE J. Sel. Areas in Comm*. vol. 10, no. 7. September 1992. pp. 1173–1186.
15. Karmouch, A. et al. A Multimedia Medical Communications System. *IEEE J. Sel. Areas in Comm*. vol. 8, no. 3. April 1990. pp. 325–339.
16. Lang, L. GIS Comes to Life. *Computer Graphics World*. October 1992. pp. 27–36.
17. Apple Computer, Inc. *Visual Almanac Technical Report*. 1991.
18. Apple Computer, Inc. *The Apple Multimedia Laboratory (1987–1990)*. February 1992.
19. Woolsey, K. H. Multimedia Scouting. *IEEE Computer Graphics and Applications*. July 1991.
20. Winner, R., Pennel, J. P., Bertrand, H. E., and Slusarczuk, M. M. G. *Concurrent Engineering for Weapons System Acquisition*. Institute for Defense Analysis, IDA Report R-338, Alexandria, Virginia. June 1991.

CHAPTER 2

THE CONVERGENCE OF COMPUTERS, COMMUNICATIONS, AND ENTERTAINMENT PRODUCTS

Jeffrey S. Porter
Commodore International

Multimedia technology is breaking down the traditional boundaries between devices for computing, personal communications, and consumer entertainment. Major industries are rethinking their market strategy and forming a web of new alliances connecting entertainment, telecommunications, computing, publishing, and other global enterprises. Multimedia devices are expected to replace ubiquitous appliances such as the telephone and television and change many of the activities associated with them. The large scale of these trends and the many participants in these developments have added to the complexity of the possibilities. This chapter provides a contemporary account of the major technology forces affecting this convergence and identifies the significant near-term issues that lie ahead.

2.1 A BRIEF LOOK AT THE PAST DECADE

2.1.1 Computers

The past ten years have brought much change to the world of computers, communications, and consumer products. Let's review how far we've come.

In 1980, personal computers were Apple IIs, Radio Shack TRS80s, Commodore Pets, and perhaps lesser known SOL20s and Exidy Sorcerers. Mini-computers were PDP 11/70 and VAX 11/780. Remarkably, punch cards were still around for those "big jobs." The Commodore 64 appeared in 1981 and eventually won the home computer war against the likes of game machines such as the Atari 2600 VCS and Atari 5200, Mattel Intellivision, and others because it was a "real" computer instead of just a game machine. The C64 and its successor, the C128, also won over other similar home computers such as the Atari 400/800 and the various flavors of Radio Shack TRS80 models. This was a crazy time for the birth of the home computer. Many companies came and went in an attempt to provide the next hot consumer product.

On the business computer forefront there were CP/M machines like Osborne and Kaypro. Osborne-1 was the first portable computer, taking up the size of a large suitcase and including floppy drives and a monochrome monitor. The Osborne shall be best remembered in the annals of computer history for announcing the Osborne Executive, a follow-on product, before its time. The announcement caused sales of the original Osborne-1 to dry up seemingly overnight. The company went out of business before it could bring out its new model and hence this tragedy has been immortalized as the "Osborne Syndrome."

The IBM PC appeared in 1981, was built like a tank, and went all of 4.77 MHz with a monochrome display. Since the technology that was in an IBM PC was mostly off-the-shelf ICs, the hardware was easy to clone. IBM even gave out full schematics and technical documentation on their new computer, a first for IBM. The PC, expandable with card slots and drive bays, was a third-party developer's dream come true. Soon people were making plug-in cards of all types. The software field was also wide open. But this was not enough. Some wanted to make the computer as well. A company called Phoenix Technologies was the first to develop a "clean room" legal version of the PC's BIOS, and, since Microsoft was free to sell MS-DOS, anyone could get into the clone business. Later, semiconductor startup companies made turn-key PC clone kits available to all and a huge market was born. In 1988, VGA was created, which, when married with increasingly more powerful CPUs from Intel and many more megabytes of RAM than anyone ever thought they would ever need, has finally given the PC a reasonable amount of horsepower.

Like the IBM PC, the Apple computer with its built-in expansion slot capability was welcomed by third-party developers and became a huge success. Whatever the base machine lacked could be put on an inexpensive plug-in card. The follow-up to the Apple would not be easy. After failing with the Lisa and Apple III computers, Apple introduced the Macintosh (a cost-reduced Lisa) in 1984 with its famous lemmings Super Bowl commercial, which commercialized and legitimized pointing and clicking based on technology originally developed at Xerox PARC. Apple's greatest impact on society in the last decade is probably the credit for commercializing desktop laser printer technology that was developed by Canon and for defining a new tool for businesses called desktop publishing. Apple has continually enhanced and improved the Macintosh with a very broad product offering, including a continuous stream of new operating system software features to refine ease-of-use to an art form.

In 1985, Commodore introduced the Amiga. At the time, most other computers were monochrome; the Amiga was color, and fast at that. The Amiga also offered—for the first time in a desktop system—multitasking. Today both Apple and IBM are still struggling to provide true pre-emptive multitasking in their systems. The Amiga was an immediate success with artists, but certainly did not set the business world on fire. In 1986, Commodore expanded its first Amiga 1000 with a lower-cost home version called the Amiga 500 and a business version called the Amiga 2000. To date Commodore has sold over 4 million Amigas worldwide.

In what might be a repeat of the home computer wars of the early 1980s, there is a new revolution going on for home communications products in the early 1990s. In 1991, Commodore introduced CDTV. Also in 1991, Philips introduced the long awaited CD-I player. Both machines are black boxes that connect to a TV set and stereo system, have infrared remote controls, and play "5-inch round shiny things." CDTV is based on Amiga technology. CD-I is based on technology developed by Philips and Microware's OS-9 operating system.

In 1992, Tandy introduced a similar system (called VIS) based on a subset of PC technology, namely a 1 MB, 12.5 MHz 80286 running a stripped-down version of Microsoft Windows, called Modular Windows. Kodak introduced its PhotoCD players in 1992, which store up to 100 film images on a CD for display on a TV set.

In 1993, a new contender, 3DO, entered the race. 3DO is yet another attempt to do what CD-I, CDTV, and VIS have failed to do in setting a standard for home multimedia players. 3DO was founded by Trip Hawkins, chairman of Electronic Arts, and is backed by Matsushita, Time Warner, and AT&T. They have designed a new RISC-based CD game machine. Unlike its competitors, 3DO is not manufacturing the hardware; instead, they are licensing the technology to a variety of manufacturers and collecting a nominal royalty on each software disc sold. It has yet to be seen which of these black boxes that connects to the TV set will be the next VHS or IBM PC.

In the late 1980s, the PC chipset semiconductor companies managed to miniaturize things so much that portable PCs were possible. Although their battery life is still not what consumers expect it should be, the portable PC segment is one of the fastest growing today. The first laptops were introduced in the early eighties by Radio Shack with their Model 100. Although this was not MS-DOS based, as a portable word processor at a $500 price, it was reasonably successful. By the mid-eighties Toshiba had introduced MS-DOS PC compatible laptops, which today nearly every company has cloned. The next wave is likely to be subnotebooks or micro-notebooks and a somewhat confused category called palmtops.

In 1988, Sharp introduced an electronic organizer call the Wizard. With application programs on solid-state "credit cards," the Wizard was basically an electronic address book and appointment scheduler. Palmtop computers were introduced in 1990 by Atari with the Portfolio and in 1991 by Hewlett-Packard with the 95LX. These were intended to take the Wizard concept one step further by adding a bigger display, a mini-QWERTY keyboard, and MS-DOS compatibility. Heading more towards the ultimate "file-a-fax," Apple, at the 1992 Summer Consumer Electronics Show in Chicago, previewed its Newton Technology, which may do to the Sharp Wizard what the Macintosh has done to the IBM PC. Many Newton-like devices are already being marketed in Japan by the likes of Sony and Sharp. In fact, in 1993, Sharp introduced a touch screen Wizard in the United States prior to Apple launching the Newton. Also in 1993 Hewlett-Packard upped the ante with a newer palmtop called the 100LX and a subnotebook called the Omnibook 300.

The Newton and CD-I concepts are the first generation of the new convergence of computers, communications, and consumer products. They are not traditional televisions or phones or computers, but a hybrid of each. As new technologies become available, the fine line between these products gets even fuzzier. We've taken a look at the evolution of computers into this convergence, but let's review where the phone has been in the last decade.

2.1.2 Communications

In 1980, the Bell System in the United States was still a monopoly. On January 1, 1982, Judge Harold Green dissected the Bell System into Regional Bell Operating Companies (RBOCs), commonly referred to as "Baby Bells." Bell Labs and Western Electric were also restructured (as American Bell and later renamed AT&T Consumer Products) so as not to have an unfair advantage with the Bell name. With deregulation in place, any number of companies could sell a telephone or provide long-distance service. Years later, most of the cheap $5 phones are a thing of the past. After the FCC opened up the 46-MHz band, as well as the 49-MHz band, use of cordless phones has grown significantly. The FCC has now also opened up a new 900-MHz band for cordless phones, which has extended range and less interference with radio-controlled toys than the 49-MHz band.

Deregulation also led to changes in modem and fax technology. Single-chip 300-baud modems were new in the early 1980s. Twelve hundred-baud modems were still technology only offered by companies such as Hayes or US Robotics. After deregulation, semiconductor companies were offering turn-key solutions for 1200 baud and later 2400 baud and higher. Fax machines in the early 1980s were still something of a speciality item. After deregulation, semiconductor companies provided fax chipsets, making the fax machine business a commodity business. These chipsets have given way to faxcards for PCs that allow paperless faxes from the comfort of your laptop PC.

In the rest of the world, most countries still have a government monopoly on the phone system, though this is changing because of influence from the U.S. market. The United Kingdom is probably the most progressive non-U.S. market. Cellular phones have been tariffed so inexpensively in the United Kingdom that most people own cellular phones. Many U.S. companies, such as US West, have set up U.K. subsidiaries to sell cable TV and phone service at 15 percent lower rates than the local monopoly. The monopoly position does have its advantages however. For new technology to take hold in the United States, each of the RBOCs must endorse the new technology and the market must show a need. In other countries, the PTT may proclaim that a certain technology will be adopted (like Integrated Services Digital Network [ISDN] for instance), and there is a government mandate to make it happen. For this reason, Europe is much farther ahead in deploying ISDN than the United States.

In the United States, the Federal Communications Commission (FCC) has a reasonable scope of influence to open doors for multimedia communications. In 1992, the FCC allocated a new frequency band at 218–219 MHz for interactive video applications. This new band will be used for a nationwide interactive TV service called TV-Answer, which is based on a radio frequency (RF) cellular-like modem. Since most cable networks today are transmit-only, this new RF channel can provide the return communications path for these new services. Home shopping is one obvious use of this technology.

The FCC has also made it possible for phone companies to offer "video dialtone" by distinguishing between broadcast video and video transmitted on demand during a phone connection. Since Bellcore has demonstrated 1.5-Mbps transmission across the existing twisted-pair wiring the phone companies already have in place, the RBOCs may be able to avoid rewiring to get digital video dialtone started.

Some RBOCs are even going as far as buying cable companies to hedge their bets. In 1993, US West, the RBOC serving many mid-western states, purchased 25 percent of Time Warner, the country's second largest cable company. While US West is currently prevented from getting into the cable business in their territory by the U.S. government, they are free to offer these services outside of their region. Time Warner services areas nearly completely outside of US West's region, thus making it a legal marriage. Don't be surprised if Time Warner offers cable TV and telephone service through the same coax wire in the near future. The US West/Time Warner deal is especially interesting since Time Warner is also the world's largest media company. Also in 1993, Bell Atlantic has agreed to acquire TCI, the country's largest cable operator, and NYNEX has invested in Viacom, a large cable operator.

With this many developments appearing on the horizon, an information war may emerge between the cable companies, the phone companies,

Direct Broadcast Satellite (DBS) companies, and now RF modem companies, all vying to become the de facto information provider of choice in the home of tomorrow. Many of these companies could bring fiber to the doorstep (or the curb), gaining a technical advantage over the other competitive media because of fiber's huge bandwidth and two-way capability. The winner could be a hybrid of these, and, in fact, due to deregulation, different schemes may be adapted in different locations. Without a "Communications Czar," there is not likely to be a standard very quickly.

The telecommunications equipment suppliers have not set the world on fire towards a convergence of computers, communications, and consumer products, but there will be a few entrepreneurs that will add Newton-like features to telephones today or provide inexpensive video teleconferencing in home or office or make fax modem/data modem/voice mail/answering machines in the future. The technology is there. To really take it to the limit requires the RBOCs to move together.

2.1.3 Consumer Entertainment

When the average person talks about consumer electronics, TV is what first comes to mind. Television is a very young industry. The first black and white broadcasts started in 1941. Color TV sets were not available at consumer prices until 1964. Cable TV was not widely available in most areas of the United States until the 1980s. Today, the average cable system has more than forty channels to choose from. CNN, MTV, HBO, and the like were not available in the 1960s and only just started in the 1970s. MTS stereo television broadcasts and stereo TV sets have only been available in the 1990s. In Europe and Japan commercial and cable TV has not flourished the way it has in the United States due to regulatory constraints and language barriers. Most countries have fewer than five TV channels.

Consumer electronics in the early 1980s introduced inexpensive home VCRs. The war between Beta and VHS was hot and heavy. Eventually VHS won due to JVC's aggressive licensing and VHS's eight-hour capability. The picture quality was poor, and the technology was inferior, but strong marketing won out. Camcorders, another recent innovation, have replaced the 8 mm and Super8 movie cameras in a very few years. The compact disc (CD) was introduced by Philips and Sony in 1981. Today, it's almost impossible to get a real record (as in LP). Similar changes have occurred in tape recording technology and electronic musical synthesizers.

In the United States, there are really only two companies that control the design of set top boxes that connect TV sets to cable: General Instruments (Jerrold Division) and Scientific Atlanta. General Instruments has over 60 percent of the U.S. cable set top converter market. Scientific Atlanta has a 25 percent market share. Zenith and others make up the rest. General Instruments has been working with Tele-Communications, Inc., the world's largest cable company, and Scientific Atlanta has been working with Time Warner Cable to provide a field trial of 4000 homes in Orlando with an R4000 MIPS RISC-based set top box that is being designed in conjunction with Silicon Graphics. Although this is not low-cost, it will be an interesting test of what services will and won't work in a real-life situation.

If there is one theme of the last ten years, it is that the consumer has grown to have high expectations for future technology. Some items perhaps did not quite happen the way they were supposed to, however. Consider video phones. These electronic marvels were first demonstrated at the 1964 World's Fair in New York, but now nearly thirty years later we still don't really have them. Only recently has AT&T shown an expensive video phone with poor picture quality, which, as it is now offered, is not a consumer product because it is not at a consumer price. I'm still not sure I want to be forced to get dressed before answering the phone, but I'm sure a computer simulation in the future will help me with this.

The computing, communications, and consumer entertainment industries are now undergoing a transformation from three well-defined markets (Figure 2.1) to a convergence of sorts (Figure 2.2). This convergence is occurring at both the device level and the communications infrastructure

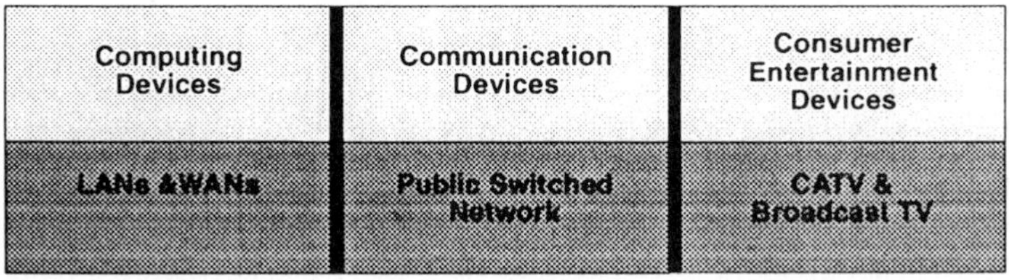

Computing Devices	Communication Devices	Consumer Entertainment Devices
LANs & WANs	Public Switched Network	CATV & Broadcast TV

Figure 2.1 During the past decade the boundaries between computing, communications, and entertainment markets have been well defined, both for devices and communications.

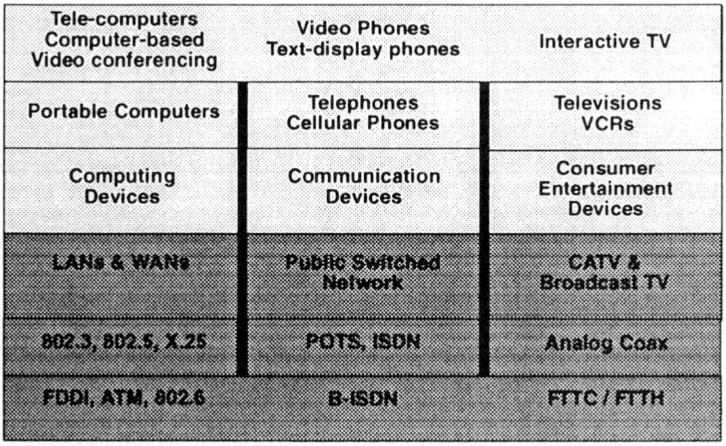

Tele-computers Computer-based Video conferencing	Video Phones Text-display phones	Interactive TV
Portable Computers	Telephones Cellular Phones	Televisions VCRs
Computing Devices	Communication Devices	Consumer Entertainment Devices
LANs & WANs	Public Switched Network	CATV & Broadcast TV
802.3, 802.5, X.25	POTS, ISDN	Analog Coax
FDDI, ATM, 802.6	B-ISDN	FTTC / FTTH

Figure 2.2 Multimedia technology is fueling the convergence of these three domains, as shown by this extension to Figure 2.1. The convergence is occurring in both devices (the top half of the diagram) and communications (the bottom half of the diagram).

level. Next we will consider some of the basic technologies that are behind this convergence.

2.2 TECHNOLOGY TRENDS

Multimedia devices and communications are becoming practical because of trends in electronics, telecommunications, and displays. The continued progression of these technologies will play a determining role in what can be achieved in the next decade.

2.2.1 Electronics: Increasing Circuit Density

Besides co-founding Intel with Robert Noyce, Gordon Moore is probably best known in the semiconductor world for his profound prediction in 1964 of the growth rate of semiconductors. Mr. Moore predicted that the number of transistors on a chip will double every three years. While I can remember many years where I was sure that Moore's Law would fail, it rarely has. Andrew Rappaport of the Technology Research Group at the 1990 Microprocessor Forum took this one step further. Mr. Rappaport stated that silicon is free. While many semiconductor vendors may disagree with this comment (others may say that the silicon is free, but the package the silicon goes into is not!), Mr. Rappaport's claim is that technology has progressed so far that instead of being limited by the technology, we are limited by our ability to fill all of the available silicon with good ideas.

2.2.2 Communications: Increasing Bandwidth and Switching Speed

Due to the advances in digital signal processing techniques, it is possible to produce low-cost 9600-baud V.32 modems. What is perhaps silly about this is that modem technology is trying to cope with phone lines from the 1950s, when in actuality the Bell System has not been standing still all these years. If the phone company's trunks are already digital, why not tap into them directly?

One way is with a technology called DataKit developed at Bell Labs. With a more appropriate (and lower tech) modem, it is possible to get 9600 baud (or better) full duplex data on the same twisted pair of phone wire and have this data be completely independent of the phone voice signal. It's a low-end ISDN. The proposed ADSL "Video Dialtone" service should work in a similar way, but at much higher bit rates and with modems that are much more expensive.

The largest leap forward in communications bandwidth, though, is available with fiber optics, which, while requiring the replacement of the existing wiring, will lead to orders of magnitude more data capacity. A switching fabric for fiber optic data rates, Asynchronous Transfer Mode

(ATM), is making gigabit rate packet switched fiber optic networks feasible. ATM is the basis for Broadband ISDN (B-ISDN) discussed in Chapter 13 and has also been proposed as the basis for future fiber optic CATV networks.

2.2.3 Presentation Technology

The applications for video will be expanding in the next decade due to its digital future, and hence will create the necessity for improved presentation technology. Color LCD displays from postage stamp size to 13" diagonal screens are available today. Although CRT technology is much more mature and less expensive, LCDs will have their day. From Dick Tracy TV watches to home projection TV theaters to Star Trek-like touchscreen notebooks, it's all coming.

The CRT technology contained in most color TV sets and computer monitors is fairly well known. There are red, green, and blue dots, slots, or stripes (depending on the tube manufacturer) that are modulated in an analog fashion to give the desired color picture. TV sets usually have a dot pitch of approximately 0.6 mm. Cheap computer monitors will have a dot pitch of 0.42 mm or 0.39 mm. Standard grade VGA monitors usually have a dot pitch of 0.31 mm or 0.28 mm. Some expensive monitors have even finer dot pitch. The smaller the dot pitch the higher the resolution.

For instance, a TV set can only display an image of 320 × 200, whereas a VGA monitor can display 640 × 480 and large 21" monitors with 0.28 dot pitch can display images as large as 1280 × 1024. This is fairly well established technology and it is not likely to change drastically in the years ahead. Making large tubes with small dot pitches is a fairly tricky business, similar to silicon wafer fabrication. The yield must be very high. If just one pixel is bad on a CRT, the entire tube must be scrapped. In the years ahead, the major R&D investment in CRTs will be in improving yields of large CRTs in anticipation of a market for wide-screen HDTV TV sets. From a CRT point of view, HDTV changes the aspect ratio of 4:3 to 16:9, but the underlying process technology is the same.

Color LCDs are fairly new. Digital watches and calculators were the first commercial use of LCDs in large volume. Calculators and watches require displays with very few segments, which are easy to make. For TV or computer displays, a dot matrix display is needed. Dot matrix displays require a much larger number of segments or pixels. To keep the electronics economical, each dot must be multiplexed at 100:1 or 200:1. This multiplexing of dots has the result of lowering the contrast of the display, since each dot is not individually driven. To improve contrast, LCD manufacturers have devised ways of improving the liquid crystal materials.

In a normal LCD, the liquid crystal material is placed between two planes of glass (one etched with row conductors, the other etched with column conductors) rotated 90 degrees against a polarizing film to cause a black and white difference. Different polarizing films can be used to get different color LCDs. In Super Twist LCDs, the liquid crystal material rotates 270 degrees.

In Double Super Twist displays, two layers of liquid crystal material rotate 270 degrees between three planes of glass or sometimes plastic.

This trick improves the contrast, but at the expense of response time. In a computer application, this gives the effect of a long persistence phosphor, or a smearing effect. In some cases, the response time is so long that fast-moving elements (like a cursor) will completely disappear, until they stop moving. To combat this effect, the active matrix display was developed.

In an active matrix display, a thin film transistor is actually deposited on the glass, thereby providing an individual driver transistor for each pixel. This improves contrast and response time dramatically at the expense of a more complicated glass process.

By far the most expensive element of an LCD display is not the cost of the glass but the cost of the driver chips. A monochrome 640 × 480 display may have as many as 28 driver chips, each with 100 leads. Extrapolate this to color LCDs: Now you need three times the number of pixels—one each for red, green, and blue. Next add a tremendously bright back light to be able to see through all the layers. Then add active matrix circuitry to prevent smearing of the video. Making color LCDs is no simple process.

In the late 1980s, the first commercial use of color active matrix LCDs in a consumer product was for a small 2" to 3" portable color TV set. Because the resolution was low and size was small, the yields were sufficient to allow a cost-effective display for a consumer-priced portable TV comparable to CRTs.

Laptop computers have had a major impact on the development of larger LCDs. In this case the displays must have a resolution of at least 640 × 480 with at least a 9" diagonal size. Strictly black and white displays are generally considered insufficient. A gray scale monochrome display is required as a minimum. New LCD controller ICs were developed to achieve this gray scale performance by tightly controlling the linear region of the display segments (which are inherently nonlinear). More recently, there has been a drive to bring down the price of VGA sized color LCDs, but they are still quite pricey and power hungry compared to monochrome displays. If the technology becomes cost competitive with CRTs, then we will see the market for color LCDs explode. Until that time, they will be relegated to products where people will pay a premium price for a small package such as a laptop computer.

2.2.4 Input Technology: Portability and New Interaction Modes

People are always looking for a better user interface to new technology—a user interface that will be intuitive to the average person. The trick is that the definition of the average person is changing. People are being exposed to computer technology at a younger age. Telephone answering machines, fax machines, infrared remote controls, home computers, calculators, bar code scanners in the supermarket, 24-hour automated teller machines, and credit cards, to name a few, have daily impact on our lives as we grow more and more accustomed to new technology.

Pointing and clicking has revolutionized PCs and will likely continue to be the preferred human interface for PCs for some time to come. Digital signal processing (DSP) technology, besides bringing excellent computational power for compression and decompression, can also provide voice processing, such as voice synthesis and voice recognition. The kind of voice interaction with computers that you night see in a Star Trek movie may not be that far from the truth in the future.

Companies like AT&T Bell Laboratories are already well on their way to providing this raw capability in everyday applications. The key needed to open this technology to everyday applications is in designing the right software model for DSP. AT&T has developed a DSP operating system called VCOS. VCOS is a real-time multitasking kernel with a full complement of high-level DSP algorithms for speech recognition, speech synthesis, modems, audio compression, video compression, music synthesizers, and many others.

Touch screens have been around for some time, but have not really been widely accepted except in kiosk applications. Pen computing is a new type of application for touch screens with portable LCD devices. In these applications, the user writes on the LCD with a stylus. The touch screen digitizes this writing, and the computer attempts to recognize the writing and convert it to letters, numbers, or even graphics. The traditional use of this sort of device is in the "form-fill-er-in-er" application. Someone doing a survey could more quickly gather information, or your local delivery person might ask for an electronic signature.

Infrared devices in conjunction with interactive television devices will most likely expand to make searching and retrieving easier. They will probably resemble mouse pointing and clicking, but with fewer choices. As technology progresses, voice input in the home will become more common, but it will be some time before it becomes inexpensive enough for the average consumer electronics product.

2.3 MULTIMEDIA APPLIANCES: HYBRID DEVICES

As the lines blur between devices, we will find that hybrid devices emerge to find their niche in our lives. Will the TV just be a TV in the future? Will the phone remain just a phone, or do the appliances of today get morphed into something else? The first stage is the development of hybrid devices (Table 2.1) which combine two or more existing ones.

2.3.1 Computer-Based Video Phones

The telephone is easily incorporated into many different devices. We already have answering machines, fax machines, and computers that all

Table 2.1 Examples of the Hybrid Approach

Conventional Devices	*Portable Versions*	*Hybrid Function*
Telephone	Cellular phones	Video phones
Computers	Laptops, palmtops	Computer-based telephony
Televisions	TV Walkmans	Interactive TV

connect to the phone line. Video phones are already on the horizon. AT&T offers a video phone today that works over conventional telephone lines. This relies heavily on real-time encoding (compression) and decoding (decompression) of the audio and video as well as sophisticated modem technology to make this product happen.

Similar capability is now being offered on plug-in boards to provide video conferencing from the computer desktop. The next step is to build this functionality into portable computers and add the software services to provide personal communications management.

2.3.2 Computer-Based Consumer Entertainment Products

When it comes to entertainment products, the lines get very blurry. Is it a computer, a TV, a VCR, a game machine, or all of the above? Entertainment will come in many different forms, but will revolve around what we now consider to be the TV set. Interactive TV products could play a pivotal role in bringing all of these technologies together.

Until the technology is more economically priced, it appears that the end user will want to do more with these devices. Exposing the underlying computer technology to the user, who then can add applications software for education, personal management, or many other uses, is one way to increase its utility. Having these boxes communicate with other appliances in the home provides additional utility, but we are just seeing the beginning of this. A box such as CD-I or CDTV will allow your TV to become an information terminal into the world, assuming that it has the connections to the outside world.

2.3.3 Some More Hybrid Examples

Apple has listed a few ideas regarding their Newton technology, which may bring some additional insight about hybrid devices. The traditional Newton is a Sharp Wizard-like device. A "Speak and Spell" Newton could be used for children. A "refrigerator magnet" Newton could be used to leave messages to other members of the family. A "Dick Tracy" Newton might be built into a future watch. A "white board" Newton might be used in a classroom or a conference room to communicate ideas to those in attendance either in person or remotely.

AT&T has recently shown an LCD touchscreen phone. This could be a home banking terminal or a way to get home e-mail, and perhaps names, addresses and telephone numbers and a note pad function could be built into this as well.

Some years ago, Zenith introduced a TV set with a speakerphone built in. This concept may have been a bit ahead of its time, but it definitely is possible. The real integration of phone and TV set will be when home video teleconferencing is possible. From a design space point of view, the TV set can easily be the centerpiece of home video teleconferencing.

2.4 A DESIGNER'S VIEW OF MULTIMEDIA APPLIANCES

The hybrid approach is only the first step in creating new multimedia devices. More innovative devices may result by taking a bigger view of the technological possibilities.

2.4.1 Industrial Design Considerations

It's important to remember that the industrial design of an appliance must make sense for people to use it. Form must follow function.

For example, it doesn't make sense to have your desktop PC in your living room. It doesn't attach to your TV set. Even if you could, the user interface of a PC is not meant to be used at a distance of 12 feet. The keyboard and mouse cables don't make sense from your easy chair. If you wanted a PC-compatible computer in your living room, you would either redesign it to be a laptop computer, or redesign both the box and the software much like Tandy has done with their VIS.

2.4.2 Human Factors and the Design of New Products

Human factors is a very important part to any new product design. Traditionally, most product development people will look at what products are already in existence that seem to work and sell well when designing a new product. For example, every car has four wheels and is generally the same shape. You don't need a lot of market research to determine basics for designing a new automobile: You start with four wheels. The existence theorem works. This is merely the rehashing of old proven ideas.

When we set off to make a new category of product, things are not so easy. The first home computers (such as the MITS Altair 8800) were about the size of a bread box (Do people still have bread boxes? How about, "As big as a toaster oven"?). The front of this box had many toggle switches and LEDs. There was no floppy, no keyboard, no mouse, and no display. Everything that we take for granted today was not there, but you must remember who designed these things. Companies like Apple did not even exist at that time. It didn't take long for people to understand that toggle switches and LEDs were not going to cut it.

As the lines blur into the future of computers, communications, and consumer products, it may take manufacturers some time to figure out what works. Will the TV set of tomorrow absorb this new intelligence, or will it merely remain a dumb display device? Will the computer remain a shrine, or will its usefulness get distributed among many dedicated portable devices like Newton? Will CD-I, CDTV, VIS, or 3DO survive, or do they get absorbed into the cable box? Will there even be a cable box? Will the phone still have wires, or will everything be cellular? There is no single answer for any of this. It depends on the ability of a few key companies to bring the requisite technology together in a user-friendly manner.

2.5 INDUSTRY PERSPECTIVES FOR THE NEXT DECADE

As the technology pieces come into the focus, the industries that are creating these new markets will likely undergo major changes. These changes will depend in part on the technology that each brings to the table.

2.5.1 Telecommunications

Telecommunications in the 1990s may not be strictly limited to what we think of as the telephone company today. Telephone services may be offered by what are now the cable companies, and video services may be offered by what are today the telephone companies. In essence, each industry is afraid that each will take over communications in the home of the future. There may be a war in the home of the future between the cable companies and the phone companies. The war is not strictly limited to cable or the phone line. New information channels may grow out of new technology such as fiber, DBS, and RF modems.

To try and pick a winner in all of this is quite difficult and involves technical, regulatory, and market issues. With independent phone companies and cable companies throughout the United States, the winner may not be the winner everywhere. Further, the war may be resolved through alliances, mergers, and acquisitions. Let's examine each of the competitive media.

Cable is unidirectional today but needs to be bidirectional. In order to do this, much of the installed equipment will have to be replaced. Cable companies have no competitive pressures today, other than the fear that the phone companies will beat them to the next technology revolution. The cable industry is not accustomed to transaction-based services such as the phone service, nor is it accustomed to individual communications. Cable companies usually send the same signal to everyone. This inexperience is likely to be their downfall versus the other possible media for telecommunications.

DBS, like cable, is not bidirectional and must rely on the phone or other RF communications for a back channel. On the other hand, DBS does not actually have to bring a *wire* to the home and can beam its signal to anyone anywhere in a relatively large and unrestricted area, provided a receiving dish is installed.

Tip and ring (i.e., the two wires of the conventional phone line) are too low bandwidth for the quality and volume of services that the cable companies are planning. However, we only need to see one thing at a time, whereas the cable would send everything all the time. The phone line is an individual bidirectional transaction-based service, but without a higher bandwidth channel from the central office to the home, its days are numbered. The ADSL "Video Dialtone" is the one hope with the existing infrastructure. If both cable and phone systems go to a fiber optic infrastructure, then bandwidth is no longer an issue and services become the key.

2.5.2 Entertainment

Entertainment will always be a key market. Dedicated boxes to provide entertainment will exist as well. These might be vastly different from the Sega or Nintendo box of today, but in essence they will fill the same need. The difference in the next decade is that the computer hackers of yesteryear will not be providing the computer games of tomorrow: Hollywood will be. As computer technology and graphics technology allow for digital full-motion video, the picture of Mario will look more like live TV—a real picture of a guy named Mario.

Now we are talking about actors and actresses, shooting films, and editing sequences digitally to provide a true interactive TV experience from a CD-ROM containing the footage. Today you can't do this sort of thing on a small budget. This is big business. Although it will probably start off like the music video business, it will soon get swallowed into the kinds of things that Hollywood does. It will be much less important who the computer programmer is that puts the pieces together. That will be the easy part. The computer programmers of today do not have the resources to put a high-budget production together. That will revolutionize the video game market and the entertainment market.

2.5.3 Information Services

Entertainment will not be the only driver for the development of video dialtone infrastructure. A strong market for home shopping already exists, and its leaders are part of the push towards interactive TV. Pilot projects to distribute newspapers electronically are also underway.

On the business front, Dow Jones and NYNEX have developed a prototype distribution system for business news in multimedia format. Dow Jones developed a multimedia production studio to generate the outgoing news materials. NYNEX wideband transmission lines carry the stories to a distribution server.

To adapt to the multimedia news market, the information industry will have to change its system for collection and production of multimedia content. Customers will demand faster access to information, and the ability to filter in real time these new media for the content of interest. Will the multimedia information industry be dominated by a few global players, or will the availability of low-cost computer-based production and distribution create an industry of smaller niche information providers? Will media production services be limited to specialized studios or will a cottage industry equivalent to desktop publishing emerge?

2.5.4 Computer Industry

The low-cost portable computer technology has led computer companies such as Apple, IBM, and H-P closer and closer to the consumer marketplace. This trend is likely to continue as digital video and phone functionality become a standard part of the computer. The intersection of consumer HDTV and high-end workstations (see Chapter 17) is also coming, though probably closer to the end of the decade. How these companies will compete in the consumer marketplace with consumer electronics giants remains to be seen.

2.6 A FORWARD VIEW

The key to new services in the next decade is software, but I don't mean Lotus 1-2-3. The information providers of the future will become the new software developers. The actual programming in the computer-science sense of the word will become secondary to the information. Companies with databases of reference material will need to connect with the technologists to bring new services to the home. In fact, this has already started. Sony has acquired one of the leading developers of entertainment software for the Amiga: Psygnosis—the people who brought us those lovable Lemmings. Sony has also previously acquired Columbia Pictures, TriStar Studios, and CBS Records. Companies such as Sony have the big budgets and the rights to use the footage from TV, movies, and music videos. Put these all together with the software companies of today, and you have the software companies of the future.

Service providers like the cable companies and telephone companies will link up with information providers like CNN or ESPN and possibly join forces with CompuServe or Prodigy, which have large databases of text-based information. Information is the new software.

There may well be nontechnical issues involved with the coming information age. Will government regulation encourage or discourage any particular industry? For instance, there are many regulations regarding the phone companies, but few regulations regarding the cable companies. Will service providers be allowed to get into the equipment business? Will everyone be able to afford these new services? What responsibility, if any, does the government have to make these services affordable? Will access to information become a class distinction in the world? Will this create an "information elite" society? Access to information may likely become as second nature as a TV set or a telephone or an automobile. The need for information will pervade all aspects of society from work to school, home, finance, entertainment, social, medical, and even transportation.

Will any of these new technologies have as much impact on society as the automobile or television or telephone? These are all very good questions that I am afraid we can only speculate about. Because there are many industries that must cooperatively develop each of the pieces of this puzzle, it may be a long time before the puzzle is complete.

The key links to the chain start with the authors of information. The authors then must get their information produced, which is in turn sold to distribution companies who market the goods to information carriers in your neighborhood. Finally, there needs to be a receiver or black box, which the end user can buy for a modest amount of money, that is compatible with the information being offered. Each one of these links must be compatible, technology-wise, with each other in order for the system to work.

The key technologies needed to allow this to happen include providing powerful computers in the home that get embedded in what most people will simply use as an appliance. I'm not saying that your refrigerator needs a 486, but your TV might need a 68020. Software and hardware standards will be important to make sure that the information can be shared by all. Compression standards such as MPEG are important, but this needs to be taken a step further to ensure compatibility. DSPs will have increasing performance as user interfaces take the next step with voice recognition.

2.7 KEY CHALLENGES AHEAD: TECHNICAL, REGULATORY, SOCIAL

The key technical challenge in the years ahead begins with process technology for integrated circuits. We wouldn't be able to do half of what we take for granted today without process technology allowing dies to shrink on integrated circuits, which allows us to be somewhat casual with throwing more and more technology at a problem until the problem is solved. The next technical challenge will be in manufacturing technology to fit these more complex chips into cost-effective products. It's wonderful to say that you have solved a problem, but if everyone in the world needs to buy a Cray supercomputer to use it, you've missed the point. Technical compatibility with the entire industry is the only other technical hurdle. After this, it's all "trickle-down" technology to a real solution.

This industry-wide compatibility and trickle-down technology is no small order. As I mentioned before, different government programs could expedite or retard our growth. We've managed to get a worldwide telephone network together, but it may take considerable effort to take that to the next step.

Even if you assume that the technology problems are solved and that governments around the world cooperate like they have never cooperated before and actually encourage growth in high-tech fields, we may have social obstacles to the acceptance of new technology as fast as it could become available. What if people just don't want it? Will people feel that their privacy is being jeopardized and that the information providers know more about you than you do? Will there be a technology Bill of Rights where people are able to enjoy life, liberty, the pursuit of happiness, and a fast data line without Big Brother peeking in?

These are all good questions that we really haven't needed to face yet, but we will, and it's coming faster than you can imagine. It's an exciting time ahead. We've just skimmed the beginning of the next generation. The mind boggles sometimes when you start to think about what the future might be, but it's worth the trip, and I, for one, can't wait to see it.

2.8 ACKNOWLEDGMENTS

Figures 2.1 and 2.2 and Table 2.1 were provided by John Buford.

2.9 FOR FURTHER READING

1. Chia, S. The Universal Mobile Telecommunication System. *IEEE Communications*. (30) 12. 1992. pp. 54–63.
2. Clark, J. A TeleComputer. *SIGGRAPH '92 Conference Proceedings*. 1992. pp. 19–23.
3. Fox, E. Advances in Interactive Digital Multimedia Systems. *IEEE Computer*. October 1991. pp. 9–19.
4. Koegel, J. A Design Space Perspective on the Evolution of Multimedia Technology. *The Challenge of Multimedia*. Trinity College at Dublin. March 1993.
5. Koegel, J. The Advent of (Standardized) Integrated Multimedia Environments. (invited paper). *Proc. ED-MEDIA '93*. AACE. 1993. pp. 294–301.
6. Miller, G., Baber, G., and Gilliland, M. News On-Demand for Multimedia Networks. *Proc. ACM Multimedia '93*. August 1993. pp. 383–392
7. Sheng, S., Chandrakasan, A., and Brodersen, R. A Portable Multimedia Terminal. *IEEE Communications Magazine*. (30) 12. 1992. pp. 64–72.
8. Sutherland, J., and Litteral, L. Residential Video Services. *IEEE Communications*. (30) 7. pp. 36–41.

CHAPTER 3

ARCHITECTURES AND ISSUES FOR DISTRIBUTED MULTIMEDIA SYSTEMS

John F. Koegel Buford
University of Massachusetts Lowell

The need for multimedia data types in existing computing and communications systems is leading to a rethinking of the design of these systems to accommodate new requirements for performance and application abstractions. Further, the scope of distributed systems is no longer focused on the LAN topology; instead, global scale networks are envisioned which connect nodes with telephony as well as computing functionality. The structure of these multimedia computing and communication systems is complicated by the range of system facilities that are impacted. A partial list includes: distributed object management facilities, hypermedia document architectures, multimedia interchange formats, scripting languages, media formats, application toolkits, operating system services, and network protocols and architectures. This chapter presents a framework for organizing and interrelating these activities. The framework is a high-level model. It is used here to discuss current status, direction, and open issues as a precursor to the remaining chapters in the book. The chapter includes a summary of the multimedia technology standards that relate to this framework.

3.1 DISTRIBUTED MULTIMEDIA SYSTEMS

The value of multimedia information and communication increases with the number of potential consumers of the information and users of the connectivity. It is widely expected that multimedia systems will provide large-scale access and distribution functions similar to the global telephone network and the Internet. The design of such systems is a distributed systems problem. However, distributed multimedia systems require special consideration of the requirements for continuous media.

3.1.1 Supporting Continuous Media

The term *continuous media* refers to the temporal dimension of media such as digital video and audio in that at the lowest level, the data are a sequence of samples—each with a time position. The timing constraints are enforced during playback or capture when the data are being viewed by humans. In addition to the time dimension, continuous media data are typically of large volume. These two factors impact the design of the core facilities of multimedia computing systems, as shown in Table 3.1. Table 3.1 summarizes resource management in multimedia computing systems in three areas: process, file system, and network.

General-purpose computing systems have been optimized for interactive use. File systems use layout policies that maximize use of disk space. Network protocols are designed for bursty traffic. Real-time operating systems exist, but flexible mechanisms for dynamically changing service levels are not available.

Resource management, the key responsibility of the operating system, must now account for a new class of service in which time constraints and negotiable service levels must be satisified. The existing interactive applications must continue to be serviced as well. For many continuous media applications there is flexibility in the required level of service. Missed deadlines are not necessarily terminal conditions. During heavy load, bandwidth requirements could be reduced by decreasing resolution of one or more continuous media streams.

These types of scenarios require a negotiation process between application and local resource managers. The term *quality of service* (QOS) is used to represent the application requirements for a given resource. Standard QOS definitions have not been defined, but typical QOS parameters are minimum and maximum resolution, allowed error rate, and acceptable jitter and delay bounds.

The paradigm for resource management in the context of continuous media is based on the realization that some applications will require hard or deterministic guarantees of service. These strong guarantees can be given as long as certain factors such as load, buffer space, and schedule can be monitored and controlled. Other applications will need only statistical

Table 3.1 Summary of Resource Management in Multimedia Computing and Communication Systems

	Processor	*File System*	*Network Architecture*
Conventional systems	Optimized for interactive processes RT is hard RT Large interrupt latency	Large access latencies No service guarantees Low storage capacity	Performance No timing guarantees
Resource	RT-Thread	RT-Session	RT-Channel
Admissibility factors	Schedulability Processor load	Consumption rate Buffer requirements Storage system load	Average data rate Peak data rate QOS Network load
Design parameters	Scheduling policies Classes of RT-threads	File layout Scheduling algorithm Buffering requirements Storage architecture	QOS parameter selection Isochronous versus nonisochronous network Use existing or create new protocol stack
Sample current work	Various RT scheduling policies Use of micro-kernel architecture Recovery of missed deadlines	Deterministic guarantees Arbitrary layout versus constrained layout and merging Various scheduling policies	Reservation-based service model Real-time protocols Intermedia synchronization Policing Call models Multicast support
Outstanding issues	More experimental data needed	Statistical guarantees Multiple service categories	QOS negotiation Dynamic QOS management

guarantee of some range of performance, that is, performance with some probability *p*. These two categories may be further subdivided based on more detailed service requirements. Applications which require minimal performance guarantees can be serviced on a *best effort* basis.

For a given service class, the resource manager will perform an *admissibility* test when the resource is requested. The test determines whether a service schedule, which satisfies the requirements of the existing and new clients, can be constructed. If so, the request can be granted. If the request is refused, the resource manager might recommend lower-level service classes that might be available. The resource manager maintains a *scheduling function* in which currently admitted clients are serviced. During service cycles, the resource manager must monitor the application's use of the resource so that unexpected overloading does not cause service deterioration for other clients.

The time-sampled nature of digital video and audio, referred to as *isochronous* data, requires that delay and jitter be tightly bounded from the point of generation or retrieval to the point of presentation. This requirement is referred to as *intramedia synchronization*. If several continuous media streams are presented in parallel, potentially from different points of generation or retrieval, constraints on their relative timing relationships are referred to as *intermedia synchronization*. Both types of synchronization require coordinated design of the resource managers so that end-to-end synchronization can be met.

3.1.2 Distributed Systems and Multimedia Systems

Multimedia computing and communication systems provide mechanisms for end-to-end delivery and generation of multimedia data that meet QOS requirements of applications. Distributed multimedia systems add capabilities such as global name spaces, client/server computing, global clocks, and distributed object management. Such facilities enable the sharing of resources over a larger population of users. With the technology for multimedia computing, distributed services will be feasible over a wide area using broadband networks.

Design issues for distributed systems and multimedia issues are to a large extent complementary. For example, distributed scheduling research focuses on load balancing and load sharing [1], whereas multimedia systems have been concerned with real-time scheduling and QOS guarantees. An approach to integrating distributed computing facilities with continuous media services is discussed in Chapter 9.

3.2 SYNCHRONIZATION, ORCHESTRATION, AND QOS ARCHITECTURE

A fundamental requirement for multimedia systems is to provide intramedia and intermedia synchronization. The intermediate subsystems involved in delivering a stream may introduce delay, jitter, and errors. Along any path these values are cumulative, and it is the cumulative delay, jitter, and error rate that must be managed to achieve the end-to-end QOS requirements. The management of collections of resource managers to achieve end-to-end synchronization is referred to as *orchestration*. QOS parameters are considered to be a basic tool in orchestration. The definition of QOS parameters which permit system-wide orchestration is referred to as a *QOS architecture*.

3.2.1 Synchronization

Synchronization is the coordinated ordering of events in time, and various mechanisms and formalisms for synchronization have been developed, ranging from low-level hardware-based techniques to abstractions for concurrent programming languages. Systems using continuous media data do not require fundamentally new synchronization primitives, but do require consideration of two aspects of multimedia applications [2]: 1) synchronization events have real-time deadlines, and 2) failure to synchronize can be handled using techniques such as frame repetition or skipping such that the application can still continue to execute.

Because of the layered design of multimedia systems, the granularity of synchronization events is generally coarser at the application level, becoming more detailed at the lower levels of the system. For example, an application might be concerned with synchronization points such as the beginning and end of a video segment, the presentation system might be concerned with frame synchronization, and the network over which the video is transmitted might be concerned with packet-level or cell-level synchronization. Consequently, the representation of synchronization requirements might vary from layer to layer as well as between different applications. Temporal relationships for representing synchronization are discussed in Chapter 7.

For a single media element which has a presentation deadline t_p, if the maximum end-to-end delay due to retrieval, generation, processing, transmission, etc., is D_{max}, then the scheduling of the presentation steps must begin by time t_p-D_{max}. If the media object is a stream of elements, not necessarily isochronous, with deadlines $\{t_{p1}, t_{p2}, t_{p3}, \ldots\}$, then the scheduling problem becomes meeting the sequence of deadlines $\{t_{p1}-D_{max}, t_{p2}-D_{max}, t_{p3}-D_{max}, \ldots\}$ for each object being presented. Any admissibility test which is to satisfy the synchronization requirement must consider the delay requirements of the application, i.e., $D_{req} \leq D_{max}$. If the average delay experienced per media element, D_{avg}, is less than D_{max}, then additional capacity exists to schedule other media objects, though with increased probability of failure.

If elements arrive prior to the presentation deadline D_{max}, due to variations in system latencies, buffering is required to hold the element in reserve until time t_{pi}. Due to the deadline specification, data errors in retrieval or transmission may not be correctable via re-retrieval or retransmission. Acceptable error rates are application and media dependent.

In order to meet the requirements of schedulability of a continuous media stream, each subsystem must provide a maximum delay with some probability p. Further, in order to limit buffering requirements, the variation in delay, referred to as *jitter*, must also be bounded.

Media elements from two or more objects may need to be synchronized, for example, for presentation of a video object and an associated audio object. This requires that each element from the synchronized objects arrive in time to meet the presentation deadline t_p. In general, each media object will have separate scheduling requirements due to media-specific delay and jitter characteristics resulting from different sampling rates and resolutions. Additionally, acceptable error rates are media dependent. Variation in delay between corresponding elements of two or more synchronized media objects is referred to as *skew*. Skew results when errors or delays in one media stream prevent the system from meeting the presentation schedule for that stream. When the skew exceeds the application's skew tolerance, then the streams must be resynchronized. Techniques for allowing the slow stream to catch up (e.g., skipping) or delaying the fast streams can be used, but the result must meet the application's requirements.

The concepts of synchronization, delay, jitter, and skew are discussed further in Chapter 7.

Synchronization in multimedia systems has received a significant amount of attention. Steinmetz [2] provides a categorization for analyzing synchronization requirements and uses this categorization to discuss unique aspects of synchronization in multimedia systems. Little and Ghafoor discuss temporal composition and low-level synchronization in [3]. In [4], they present a theoretical framework for application synchronization over a network, including scheduling algorithms and network protocols. Transport-level synchronization protocols are evaluated in [5]. Synchronization of streams in a joint-viewing (group work) environment is discussed in [6]. Techniques for intermedia and intramedia synchronization are presented in [7,8,9]. A distributed network protocol for jitter control is described in [10].

3.2.2 Orchestration or Meta-Scheduling

Each resource manager includes a scheduling function which orders the current requests for servicing so as to meet the required performance bounds. For example, a continuous media file system schedules storage system access operations, and the network layer schedules traffic to the transport layer. An application requires the coordinated operation of these scheduling functions if end-to-end performance bounds are to be met. An approach to coordinating resource scheduling of the various systems is to add a layer between the application and the resource managers for orchestration [11,12] or meta-scheduling [13].

Nicolau [11] introduced the orchestration layer in his architecture for real-time multimedia systems (Figure 3.1). The orchestration layer provides overall synchronization and scheduling functions as required by the application.

3.2.3 QOS Architecture

Quality of service (QOS) is used in the OSI reference model [14] to allow service users to communicate with network service regarding data transmission requirements. In OSI, QOS is specified using a number of parameters which can be grouped into three sets: single transmission, multiple transmission, and connection mode. QOS parameters include transit delay,

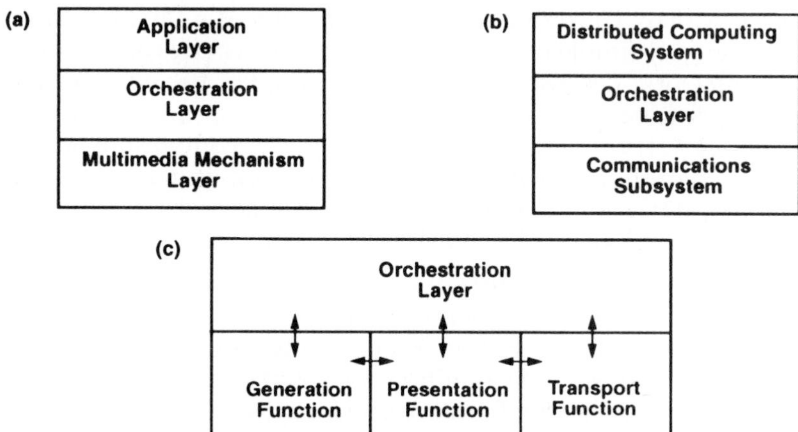

Figure 3.1 Nicolau's [11] real-time multimedia system architecture: (a) the orchestration layer as a middle layer between the application and multimedia system services, (b) the orchestration layer as a service for providing synchronization for a distributed computing system, and (c) the orchestration function, with vertical arrows indicating control paths and horizontal arrows indicating data paths.

residual error rate, and throughput. For connection-oriented service, the QOS parameters required by the network service user are specified in the request for connection. The network service provider determines whether the requested service parameters can be provided. If so, the request is forwarded to the called party, possibly with different parameter values. The called party can either accept or reject the request. If not, the network provider will reject the request. If the connection is confirmed, the actual QOS parameter values are returned to the network user.

The QOS parameters are passed down the OSI stack during the connection establishment phase for negotiation and configuration of the connection. Some parameters are only available to the upper levels. For connectionless service, the QOS parameters are passed with the data transmission request.

Although there is wide agreement that the OSI parameterization of QOS must be extended to support multimedia communications, the selection of the specific extensions and how these parameters will be used within the network architecture remains a topic of research. Additionally, efficient negotiation of QOS for multipoint connections deserves study (OSI provides only point-to-point services). Kurose [15] surveys work in QOS and identifies four approaches to providing QOS guarantees in high-speed networks:

1. **Tightly controlled:** The traffic patterns of a stream are preserved at each switching point in the network. This simplifies computation of performance bounds for admission tests, but the queuing discipline can be complex to implement and the network can be significantly underutilized.

2. **Approximate:** The traffic patterns of data sources are approximated using relatively simple models at both the network edge and internal to the network. Because the models are simpler, the approximate approach is more suited to implementation of a real-time admissibility algorithm. Further, because worst-case traffic assumptions are not made at the internal switching points, network utilization can be improved. However, the models are approximate and, as yet, do not provide formal deterministic guarantees of service.
3. **Bounding:** A bound (statistical or fixed) is specified for traffic on the edge of the network. Bounds are recomputed for each session along the route of the session. Issues in the use of this approach include the tightness of the resulting bounds and the extent to which traffic can be modeled by the statistical bounds.
4. **Observation-based:** Measurements of actual data sources are used to define different service classes. An arriving call specifies its expected service class. The current set of calls and the service class assignments are used to determine admissibility. The dependence of this approach on traffic measurement parameters, number of active calls, and the size of the network requires further study.

In addition to the use of QOS for service-level negotiation at the network interface, the use of QOS as a unifying resource management principle has been proposed based on research at Lancaster University [16]. The service guarantees of interest to the application refer to the end-to-end configuration. In the case of distributed multimedia systems, this includes not only

Table 3.2 Lancaster University's QOS Architecture [16]

	Per Connection QOS Characteristics					*Multiconnection QOS Characteristics*		
	Setup QOS	*Jitter*	*Delay*	*Through-put*	*Error Rate*	*Sync*	*Multicast*	*QOS Mgmt Planes*
Appl. Platform and OS		Sched-uling	Sched-uling	Sched-uling			Message-Ordering Semantics	
Orchestration (multiple connection synchronization)		Jitter correction		Rate regulation		Multi-Session Rate Regulation		Negotiation/ Resource Allocation
Transport Subsystem				Flow control	FEC/ Selec. Ret./ ARQ/ etc.		Multicast Error Control	Monitoring/ Policing
ATM Network		Jitter bounding (sched-uling)	Sched-uling	Congestion control (sched-uling)	Network error bound			

the communications system but also the operating system and storage system. As discussed previously, resource management of each subsystem involves an admissibility test and a scheduling function. The system-wide use of QOS parameters has the advantages of providing applications with a unified high-level view of its resource requirements as well as offering a common paradigm for resource management.

In the Lancaster model, system-wide QOS is defined using a QOS architecture such as that shown in Table 3.2. The use of QOS in the transport and network layers is shown in the lower half of the diagram. The orchestration layer sits on top of the transport layer and provides multichannel synchronization. The platform layer includes the real-time thread scheduling of the operating system. Once QOS is established, the QOS management functions on the right of the diagram perform the monitoring and renegotiation tasks.

Since QOS parameters at different levels are not necessarily the same (being optimized for the given layer), mapping of QOS parameters from one level to the next is required. At the interface for each level some subset of the following elements would be provided:

A notation for QOS characteristics

A notation for commitment specification, as in deterministic or statistical with some probability p

A notation for cost specification

A protocol for QOS negotiation

3.2.4 Summary

In order to meet the strict synchronization requirements of multimedia information presentation, real-time scheduling of multimedia transmission, retrieval, processing, and presentation requests are required. This scheduling must take into account the latencies, delay variations, and error rates of the systems involved in providing the end-to-end service. Because multimedia presentation scheduling requirements can typically be characterized as soft real-time, resource managers may provide statistical as well as deterministic guarantees of performance. Statistical guarantees permit the resource manager to admit a larger amount of traffic, leading to greater system utilization, with the possibility that system overloading may cause curtailment of full service to some clients.

The resource management paradigm in multimedia systems involves an admissibility test and a scheduling function. The application requests resources in order to meet a combined end-to-end schedule of presentation events. The coordinated management of resource managers to achieve end-to-end scheduling is referred to as orchestration or meta-scheduling. The orchestration function is a key part of the architecture for distributed multimedia systems and can be seen as a new layer between applications and traditional operating system and network functions.

A QOS architecture can offer a unified view of resource management to the application and the various resource managers. Consequently a detailed specification of a QOS architecture will be a significant step in the development of distributed multimedia systems.

3.3 THE ROLE OF STANDARDS

The goal of universal access and distribution using distributed multimedia systems technology requires a significant amount of interoperability of the components and exchanged information. The interoperabilty requirement depends upon standards for communication, information formats, and system services. The development of standards for multimedia technology is an area of great activity. Recent reviews of multimedia standardization activities are given in [17,18].

The diversity of standardization requirements is illustrated in Figure 3.2 and Table 3.3. Figure 3.2 shows some of the components of the future global telecommunications infrastructure, and suggests possible interconnection points. Table 3.3 presents multimedia standards organized by use and defining body. As can be seen from the table, the scope of standardization activities is broad. Additionally, competing standards are being produced by standards bodies, trade groups, and vendors with significant market presence.

Standards are a means of satisfying the interoperability requirement. Compatible standards lead to interoperability at the next level. Compatibility is a significant issue facing the development of standards specifica-

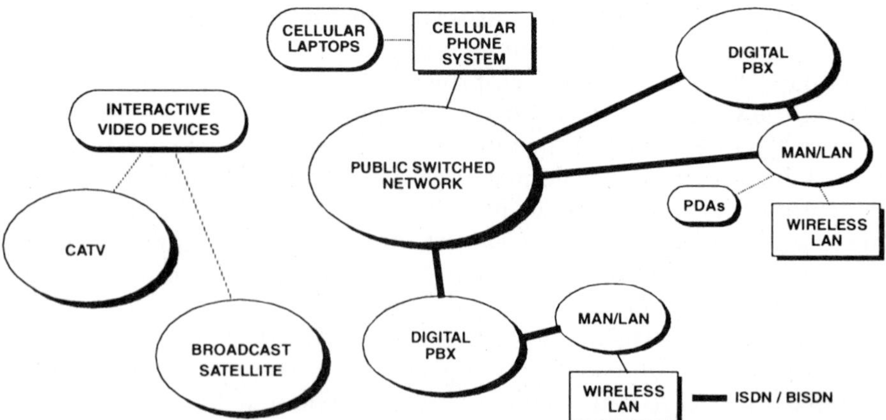

Figure 3.2 Intersection of telephony with computer communications and television networks will involve both ISDN and BISDN standards as well as new technologies for mobile computing.

Table 3.3 Categorization of Multimedia Standards

User	*Function*	*ISO/ITU*	*Trade Group*	*Vendor*
AUTHOR	Scripting Language	SMSL	IMA RFT	Kaleida Labs ScriptX GainMomentum GEL
	Hypermedia Document Architecture	SGML/HyTime ODA/HyperODA		
DEVELOPER	Distributed Object Arch.	ODP/ANSA	OMG CORBA	Microsoft OLE
	UI Toolkits	PIKS	X Consortium XIE	Apple QuickTime
		PREMO	COSE	Microsoft MME
SYSTEM VENDOR	Multimedia System Services		IMA RFT COSE UNIX Intl	
	Multimedia Mail		IETF MIME	
	Interchange Format	MHEG	IMA RFT OMFI	Apple QuickTime Movie File Format Microsoft AVI
NETWORK PROVIDER	Multiservice Network	ATM FDDI-II	IEEE 802.6	
	Protocol Stack	OSI	IETF RTP	
PUBLISHER	Storage Formats	9660	Rock Ridge	Kodak PhotoCD Philips CD-I
	Media Formats	MPEG,MPEG-2,-4 JPEG H.261	MMA MIDI	Intel DVI

tions that will have system-wide use. Compatibility can be best examined in the context of overall system architecture.

3.4 A FRAMEWORK FOR MULTIMEDIA SYSTEMS

The framework presented here provides an overall picture of the development of distributed multimedia systems from which a system architecture can be developed. The framework highlights the dominant feature of multimedia systems: the integration of multimedia computing and communications, including traditional telecommunications and telephony functions.

Low-cost multimedia technology is evolving to provide richer information processing and communications systems (Figure 3.3). These systems, though tightly interrelated, have distinct physical facilities, logical models, and functionality. Multimedia information systems extend the processing, storage, and retrieval capabilities of existing information systems by introducing new media data types, including image, audio, and video. These new data types offer perceptually richer and more accessible representations for many kinds of information. Multimedia comunication systems extend existing point-to-point connectivity by permitting synchronized multipoint group communications. Additionally, the communication media

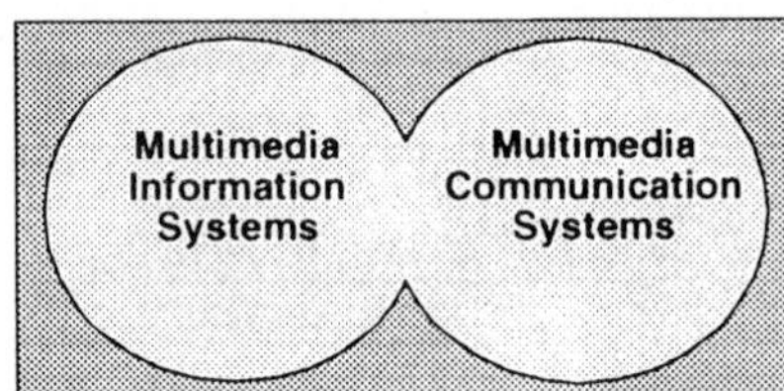

Figure 3.3 Multimedia technology is facilitating the convergence of multimedia information processing systems and multimedia communications systems.

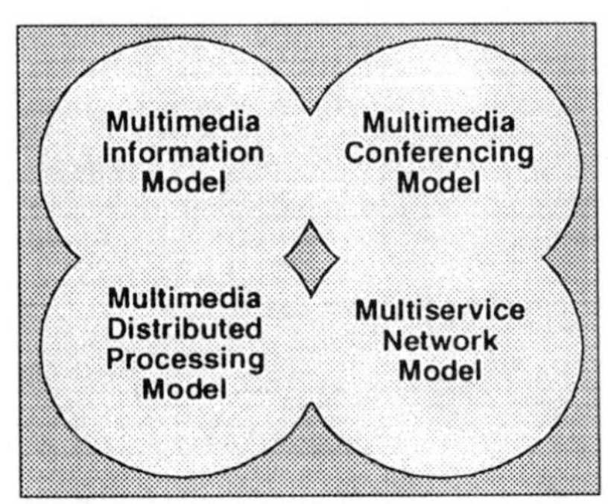

Figure 3.4 The framework consists of four interrelated models. The information and distributed processing models constitute the Multimedia Information System (MMIS). The conferencing and multiservice network models form the Multimedia Communications System (MCS).

include time-dependent visual forms as well as computer application conferencing.

This view can be further decomposed into the four parts shown in Figure 3.4. The information model and distributed processing model are the two components of the MMIS. The multimedia information model includes data modeling for storage, retrieval, and processing. The multimedia distributed processing model includes system services, application toolkits, and application frameworks. The multimedia conferencing and multiservice network models are the two components of the MCS. The conferencing model provides abstractions for multiparty communication, real-time interchange, electronic mail, and telephony. The multiservice network model supports the communication model with a network architecture, network protocols, and interfaces.

Sample elements of each model are shown in Figure 3.5. Aspects of each model are discussed in the following subsections.

3.4.1 Multimedia Distributed Processing Model

A layered view of the multimedia distributed processing model is shown in Figure 3.6. Models similar to this have been published by the Interactive Multimedia Association in its Architecture Reference Model [19] and UNIX International's Open Distributed Multimedia Computing model [20]. Each layer provides services to the layers above. Significant additions to the facilities of traditional computing environments include (from the top):

Scripting languages: Special-purpose programming languages for controlling interactive multimedia documents, presentations, and applications. Scripting languages are dicussed further in Chapter 12.

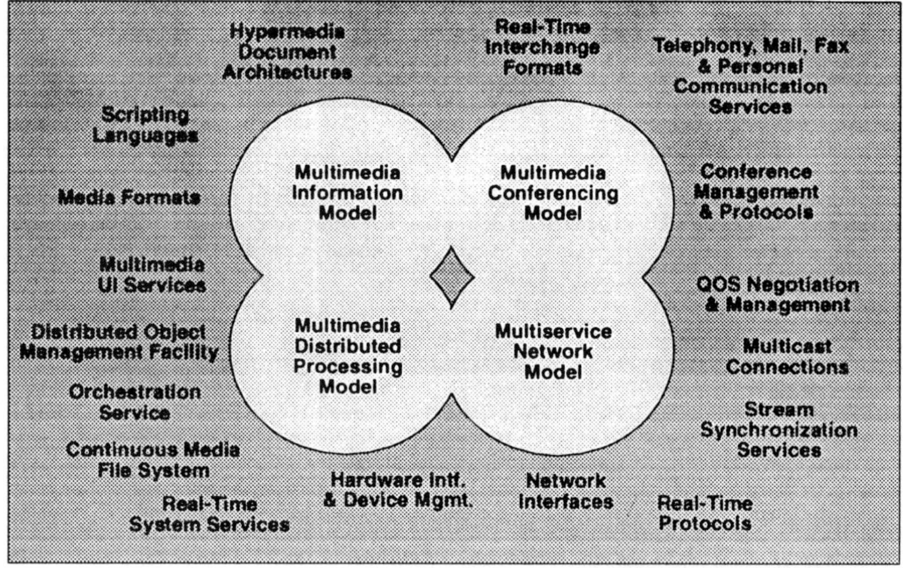

Figure 3.5 Each of the four models of the distributed multimedia systems framework specifies various components. Example components, which might be services, formats, and/or APIs are shown in the periphery of the corresponding models.

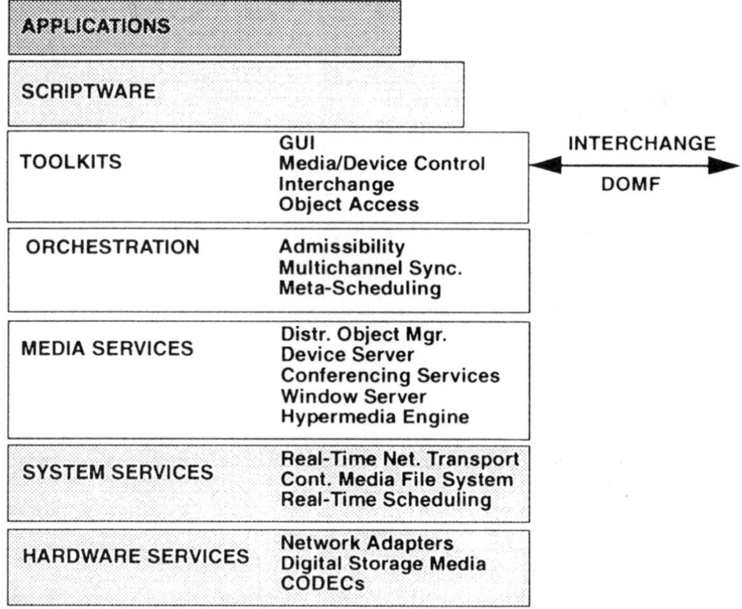

Figure 3.6 Multimedia distributed processing model: a layered view of a distributed environment

Media device control: A combination of toolkit functions, programming abstractions, and services which provide application programs access to multimedia peripheral equipment. Several architectures are discussed in Chapter 10.

Interchange: Multimedia data formats and services for interchange of multimedia content. Interchange formats are discussed in Chapter 14.

Conferencing services: Facilities for managing multiparty communications using high-level call model abstractions. Multimedia conferencing is the topic of Chapter 15.

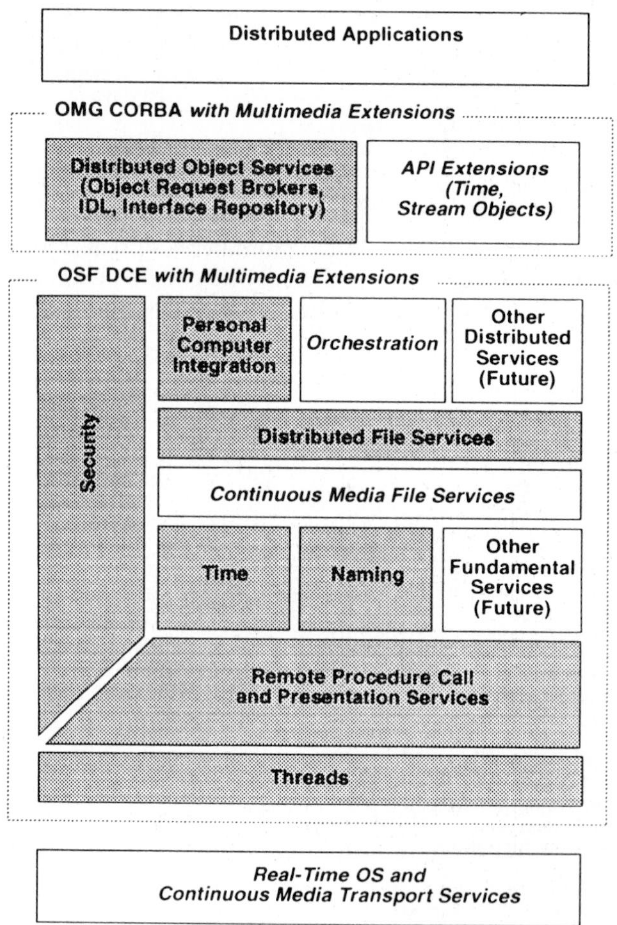

Figure 3.7 The integration of multimedia technology and distributed systems technology by extensions to the Open Software Foundation's Distributed Computing Environment (DCE) and the Object Management Group's Common Object Request Broker Architecture (figure based on [21]).

Hypermedia engine: A hypermedia object server that stores multimedia documents for editing and retrieval. Hypermedia models and continuous media file systems are discussed in Chapter 15.

Real-time scheduler: Operating system process or thread scheduling so as to meet real-time deadlines. Real-time scheduling is discussed in Chapter 8.

Figure 3.7 shows another model based upon extending the Open Software Foundation's Distributed Computing Environment (DCE) and the Object Management Group's Common Object Request Broker Architecture (CORBA) with facilities for multimedia [21]. The DCE and OMG specifications have been widely adopted by workstation vendors to support distributed computing and a distributed object application framework. Chapter 9 describes a proposed design which provides multimedia service abstractions through CORBA.

3.4.2 Multimedia Information Model

The second component of the framework relates to the abstractions and data models for organizing multimedia documents, presentations, and other information. While there is no universal hypermedia document model, the ability to include multimedia content and describe associations between document components (hyperlinking) is considered basic. Support for temporal relationships between components, interactivity, and components with active behavior is also considered important.

While several hypermedia document models exist, further work is needed in characterizing the logical structure of multimedia documents (Figure 3.8). This issue is related to the authoring process for creating multimedia information, a process which has many forms and tools. The related issues of hypermedia document models and multimedia authoring are discussed in Chapters 11 and 12, respectively.

Text Document	*Multimedia Document*
Book	?
Chapter	?
Section	?
Paragraph	?

Figure 3.8 Logical models for text documents are well understood; standards such as SGML and ODA provide languages for specifying such models. By comparison, multimedia documents have a relatively short history and small population by which to define logical models.

3.4.3 Multiservice Network Model

Networks for distributed multimedia systems must support a wide range of traffic requirements, including traffic with real-time requirements. Such networks are described as *multiservice.* The requirements for the network architecture include QOS guarantees that are sufficient for real-time transport, multiway connections, and high performance. Existing network architectures such as OSI and TCP/IP do not satisfy these requirements. Efforts in designing multiservice networks are being carried out for both the public switched network and the Internet.

Public Switched Network

During the past decade, the telecommunications industry has developed a roadmap for the evolution of digital switched communication services based on ISDN (Integrated Services Digital Network) [14,22]. ISDN standardizes connection interfaces, transmission protocols, and services. More recently, initial recommendations for Broadband ISDN (BISDN) have been adopted [14]. Unlike ISDN, which is a digital circuit switching network, BISDN uses cell relay or asynchronous transfer mode (ATM) [23]. ATM is suitable for very high speed switching of fiber optic transmission networks. BISDN will be upwardly compatible with ISDN, leading to a global high-speed network suitable for high-speed multimedia traffic with common service definitions throughout the switching components.

Chapter 13 examines protocols and architecture issues for multimedia communications over BISDN.

Internet

Early experimental work on supporting real-time traffic for multimedia conferencing over the Internet included the development of a revised experimental Internet Stream Protocol commonly called ST II [24,25]. ST II creates simplex tree reserved-bandwidth connections from an origin to the specified destinations. It is at the same protocol level as IP. ST II has been used for experiments in video conferencing over the Internet.

More recently, several Internet working groups have been formed to address the requirements of multimedia conferencing and real-time traffic. The Audio-Video Transport Working Group is developing a transport protocol for real-time applications, RTP [26,27]. RTP uses the end-to-end transport services such as TCP, UDP, or ST II (Figure 3.9). RTP uses timestamps to provide playout synchronization between a source and a set of destinations. Multiple media and conferences can be multiplexed over one connection and demultiplexed at a destination. RTP is intended for use by conference control protocols such as CCP [28].

The Internet work is still in the experimental stages. Issues which will be of interest in the near future include scalability of current research systems,

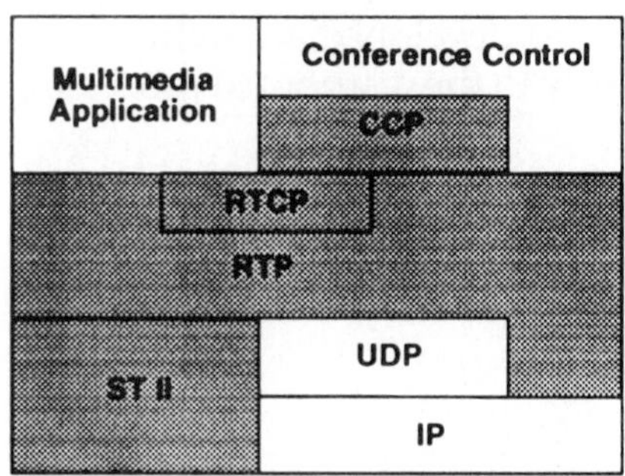

Figure 3.9 Experimental Internet protocol stack for real-time transport and multimedia multiparty conferencing

accounting mechanisms based on usage, and general use of the Internet for telephony [29].

3.4.4 Multimedia Conferencing Model

Trends in communications and computing are leading to convergence of computer-based telephony and communications functions. Existing network architectures such as the OSI reference model and TCP/IP were not designed with the intent of supporting real-time multiparty conferencing. Today's computer-based communications applications, such as mail systems and shared windowing systems, are typically monolithic entities that are not designed to be integrated with other applications. New software architectures for computer-based applications, such as those described in Chapter 15, will enable applications generally to access and control communications services. In contrast to traditional telecommunications where communications services are accessed separately, it is expected that in the future the majority of computer applications will support communications access, and the dedicated communication application will be the exception rather than the rule.

3.5 RELATED WORK

The development of a multimedia and hypermedia reference model (MHRM) is currently being studied within ISO [30]. The approach taken so far consists of two parts: 1) a model of information models and multimedia and hypermedia service areas, and 2) identification of the relationship between MHRM and four other ISO reference models: Open Distributed Processing (ODP), Computer Graphics (CGRM), Open Systems Environment (OSE RM), and Open Systems Interconnect (OSI RM).

The Interactive Multimedia Association has developed an architectural reference model that corresponds most closely to the distributed processing model of the framework presented here.

Researchers at Lancaster University have developed a distributed multimedia computing and communications testbed. Their architecture is being integrated with the ISO ANSA model (part of ODP) [31–33].

3.6 SUMMARY

There are significant technical, regulatory, and market issues facing the arrival of integrated multimedia environments, but the frameworks for multimedia computing and multimedia communications are well understood. The process by which these systems are realized will be evolutionary, and various multimedia computing and communications standards will play an important role in the pace of market growth because of the importance of interchangeability to multimedia information use. There are a number of competing trends which are yet to be resolved. However, the two major functions enabled by multimedia systems are unambiguous: richer information processing and delivery and real-time multimedia-based multiway communication.

In this chapter the common issues related to the design of distributed multimedia systems have been presented, including synchronization, quality of service, and orchestration. A framework for providing a unified picture of multimedia communication and information processing systems has been described. This framework consists of four models which can be used to organize more detailed architectures for the components of distributed multimedia systems.

3.7 REFERENCES

1. Goscinski, A. *Distributed Operating Systems: The Logical Design*. Addison-Wesley. 1991.
2. Steinmetz, R. Synchronization Properties in Multimedia Systems. *IEEE J. on Sel. Areas in Comm*. vol. 8, no. 3. April 1990. pp. 401–412.
3. Little, T. D. C., and Ghafoor, A. Network Considerations for Distributed Multimedia Object Composition and Communication. *IEEE Network Magazine*. November 1990. pp. 32–48.
4. Little, T. D. C., and Ghafoor, A. Multimedia Synchronization Protocols for Broadband Integrated Services. *IEEE J. on Sel. Areas in Comm*. vol. 9, no. 9. December 1991. pp. 1368–1381.
5. Ravindran, K., and Bansal, V. Delay Compensation Protocols for Synchronization of Multimedia Data Streams. *IEEE Trans. on Knowledge and Data Engineering*. vol. 5, no. 4. August 1993. pp. 574–589.
6. Rothermel, K., and Dermler, G. Synchronization of Joint-Viewing Environments. *Third Intl. Workshop on Network and Operating System Support for Digital Audio and Video*. November 1992. pp. 97–109.

7. Anderson, D., and Homsy, G. A Continuous Media I/O Server and Its Synchronization Mechanism. *IEEE Computer*. vol. 24, no. 10. October 1991. pp. 51–57.
8. Little, T. D. C., and Kao, F. An Intermedia Skew Control System for Multimedia Data Presentation. *Third Intl. Workshop on Network and Operating System Support for Digital Audio and Video*. November 1992. pp. 121–132.
9. Ramanathan, S., and Rangan, P. V. Feedback Techniques for Intra-Media Continuity and Inter-Media Synchronization in Distributed Multimedia Systems. *The Computer Journal*. vol. 36, no. 1. 1993. pp. 19–31.
10. Ferrari, D. Design and Applications of a Delay Jitter Control Scheme for Packet-Switching Internetworks. In R. Herrtwich (ed.) *Proc. Second Intl. Workshop on Network and Operating System Support for Digital Audio and Video*. Springer-Verlag LNCS No. 614. November 1991.
11. Nicolaou, C. An Architecture for Real-Time Multimedia Communication Systems. *IEEE J. on Sel. Areas of Comm*. vol. 8, no. 3. April 1990. pp. 391–400.
12. Campbell, A., Coulson, G., Garcia, F., and Hutchison, D. A Continuous Media Transport and Orchestration Service. *Proc. SIGCOMM '92*. 1992. pp. 99–110.
13. Anderson, D., Osawa, Y., and Govindan, R. A File System for Continuous Media. *ACM Trans. on Computer Systems*. vol. 10, no. 4. November 1992. pp. 311–337.
14. Stallings, W. *Networking Standards: A Guide to OSI, ISDN, LAN, and MAN Standards*. Addison-Wesley. 1993.
15. Kurose, J. Open Issues and Challenges in Providing Quality of Service Guarantees in High-Speed Networks. *Computer Communication Review*. June 1993. pp. 6–15.
16. A Suggested QOS Architecture for Multimedia Communications. ISO/IEC JTC 1/SC 21/WG 1 (Source: United Kingdom). September 1992.
17. Fox, E. A. Advances in Interactive Digital Multimedia Systems. *IEEE Computer*. vol. 24, no. 10. October 1991. pp. 9–22.
18. Koegel, J. The Advent of (Standardized) Multimedia Environments. (invited paper). *World Conference on Educational Multimedia and Hypermedia,* AACE. June 1993. pp. 294-301.
19. *IMA Compatibility Project: Request for Technologies*. Interactive Multimedia Association. December 1992.
20. *Open Distributed Multimedia Computing*. UNIX International. 1993. *Also:* Buford, J., Doran, M., and Bornfreund, J. Open Distributed Multimedia Computing in *Handbook of Multimedia* (ed. J. Keyes), McGraw-Hill (to appear).
21. Diaz-Gonzalez, J. Broadband Network Computing. In M. Hodges and R. Sasnett (eds.), *Multimedia Computing*. Addison-Wesley. 1993.
22. Roca, R. ISDN Architecture. *AT&T Technical Journal*. 1985. pp. 5–15
23. Le Boudec, J.-Y. The Asynchronous Transfer Mode: A Tutorial. *Computer Networks and ISDN Systems*. vol. 24. May 1992. pp. 277–310.
24. Topolcic, C. ST II. *First Intl. Workshop on Network and Oper. Sys. Support for Digital Audio and Video*. November 1990.
25. Partridge, C., and Pink, S. An Implementation of the Revised Internet Stream Protocol (ST-2). *Second Intl. Workshop on Network and Oper. Sys. Support for Digital Audio and Video*. Heidelberg, Germany. November 1991.
26. Schulzrinne, H. Issues in Designing a Transport Protocol for Audio and Video Conferences and Other Multiparticipant Real-Time Applications. *IETF Audio-Video Transport Working Group*. Working Draft. October 1993.
27. Schulzrinne, H., and Casner, S. RTP: A Transport Protocol for Real-Time Applications. *IETF Audio-Video Transport Working Group*. Working Draft. September 1993.
28. Schooler, E. Case Study: Multimedia Conference Control in a Packet-Switched Teleconferencing System. *Internetworking: Research and Experience*. vol. 4. 1993. pp. 99–120.
29. *Working Draft of the Technical Report on Multimedia and Hypermedia Model and Framework (Version 2.0)*. ISO/IEC JTC 1/SC 18. N 4199. June 1993.

30. Casner, S. Multimedia Abstractions and the Internet. *Proc. ACM Multimedia '93 Workshop: Programming Abstractions for Distributed Multimedia Applications*. August 1993.
31. Ruston, L., Blair, G., Coulson, G., and Davies, N. Integrating Computing and Telecommunications: A Tale of Two Architectures. *Second Intl. Workshop on Network and Oper. Sys. Support for Digital Audio and Video*. Heidelberg, Germany. November 1991.
32. Coulson, G., Blair, G. S., Davies, N., and Williams, N. Extensions to ANSA for Multimedia Computing. *Computer Networks and ISDN Systems*. vol. 25. September 1992, pp. 305–323.
33. Blair, G., Campbell, A., Coulson, G., Garcia, F., Hutchison, D., Scott, A., and Shepherd, D. A Network Interface Unit to Support Continuous Media. *IEEE J. on Sel. Areas in Communications*. vol. 11, no. 2. February 1993. pp. 264–275.

CHAPTER 4

Digital audio representation and processing

John Strawn
S Systems

This is the first of several chapters to provide important background information on basic media. This chapter is devoted to audio, with specific discussion of music and speech, and reviews fundamentals necessary for developing tools, applications, and interfaces involving audio. The survey includes physical aspects of sound, psychoacoustics, the nature of musical sound, stereophonic and quadrophonic sound, and audio processing building blocks. Standard formats for digital audio are described, as well as the MIDI protocol for music synthesizers. Algorithms and architectures for data compression, music synthesizers, speech recognition, and speech generation are reviewed.

4.1 USES OF AUDIO IN COMPUTER APPLICATIONS

The initial interfaces to digital data processing equipment were visually oriented. The operator turned switches or fed punched cards; audio interfaces came later. Early anecdotal references can be found to late-night researchers playing songs using the bells and whistles on teletypes and printers of a mainframe. Others used radio frequency static generated by digital equipment to drive radios placed on the top of the computer cabinet.

The first serious work involving the computer and sound came at Bell Labs, where John Pierce and Max Mathews [1] pioneered digitized speech work that evolved into computer-generated sound. Computers have been adopted in the music community for composition, printing, and data processing (e.g., insipid catalogs), but those applications are not discussed here. In the music industry, digital technology has all but supplanted analog technology for synthesis and is making major inroads in sound storage and processing. Meanwhile, the loudspeaker and microphone remain analog.

Outside the music and audio industries, audio has been increasingly associated with digital technology; a few examples are given here. Rosenberg [2] discusses the computer-supported cooperative work environment, including teleconferencing. Voice mail is now a common adjunct to electronic mail. The popularization of multimedia brings with it the embedding of audio information in hyperdocuments, supported by storage media such as CD-ROM. With optical character recognition now commonplace on personal computers for encoding incoming faxes, one can envision faxes read aloud by the computer. Telephone voice-response systems allow those in the field to retrieve or modify information in a database at the home office. Speaker recognition and identification provides a new level of security for access to sites, equipment, and data. Digit recognition systems are now widely used by telephone companies to help with automating information requests or collect call billing.

Sonification is a relatively new and relevant field that deserves some explanation even in this brief introduction. Sonification involves mapping the parameters of sound to one or more variables of a set of data [3]. In one implementation, an independent variable is treated as musical time. As the independent variable increases in value, the data points indexed by the independent variables are performed, so to speak [4]. In another implementation [5], the user sweeps the mouse over a graphic representation of the data points. That graphic representation may itself incorporate information about more than one variable. But as the mouse is swept, a more or less musical note is sounded for each data point encountered. The parameters of the note, including attack time, decay time, spectrum, amplitude, frequency, amount of reverberation, apparent elevation, and left-right mix can be varied. In some cases, each parameter in the data space is mapped onto a different attribute of sound. In other cases, several attributes of sound are mapped onto the same parameter of the data space on purpose. The interplay of redundant parameters helps make it possible for human perceptual and cognitive mechanisms to find structure in the data. Several studies discussing the effectiveness of sound for representing data are discussed in [5].

One of the disadvantages of audio compared with other media is the ephemeral nature of sound. A painting by Cézanne or a pie graph showing profit and loss for each corporate division can be placed on the wall for enjoyment and/or study. The eye can wander over the image at will, easily revisit those parts already viewed, and in general choose freely between a micro and macro view. The visual mode also allows the viewer to integrate large amounts of data into a whole. With music as an art form and with sound as a communications medium, the listener must pay attention and remember what has already passed. The implications of this in using sound to represent data are discussed in [5]. For example, with audio as a component of the user interface, the alternative to relying on memory is to keep resounding background information. But if too many things are constantly in the audio background, cacophony results. For most people, fatigue sets in as well; a constant background sound is no longer consciously perceived.

Audio is an important communication channel and, in some cases (e.g., involving human emotions), the most appropriate and efficient. We all know the richness of the subtle cues transmitted by inflection in the voice. Audio provides three-dimensional cues (e.g., in the back of the head) that are not available to other human sensory systems.

This chapter concentrates on certain important aspects of audio as related to digital technology. The selection of topics is motivated by relevance to implementation of audio in digital systems, especially workstations, multimedia systems, and computer-based conferencing systems. On the other hand, topics such as memory of auditory experiences or speaker identification by humans are largely ignored.

4.2 PSYCHOACOUSTICS

We first turn to the interaction between physical stimuli and the human nervous system. Some good recent books on hearing and related topics include [6,7,8].

For this discussion, audio is defined as a disturbance in air pressure that reaches the human eardrum. In terms of frequency, amplitude, time, and other parameters, there are limits to the kinds of air pressure disturbance that will evoke an auditory percept in humans. The development of the human ear's limitations and capabilities was undoubtedly motivated by evolutionary necessity. Survival is granted to those who can distinguish the rustle of an attacker in a forest, for example, from a babbling brook nearby. As we design multimedia systems, the limitations of the auditory channel need to be respected.

4.2.1 Frequency Range of Human Hearing

As the frequency of periodic disturbances in the air increases, the human ear starts hearing sound when the disturbances are in the region of about 20 cycles per second, or 20 Hz. When we are first born, the upper range of audibility lies around 20,000 Hz, or 20 kHz, and usually declines with increasing age. It is important to distinguish between the *frequency* of a tone, which is a physical measure, and the percept of *pitch,* which the tone evokes. There is a close but not always exact relationship between frequency and pitch.

4.2.2 Dynamic Range of Human Hearing

The lower limit of the dynamic range of human hearing is at the threshold of audibility, and the upper limit is the threshold of pain (or damage). The audibility threshold for a 1-kHz sinusoidal wave is generally set at 0.000283 dyne per square centimeter. (A sinusoidal waveform, a fundamental building block of audio waveforms, is shown in Figure 4.1.) As with pitch, it is important to distinguish between *amplitude* as a physical measure and *loudness* as a percept.

The amplitude of the sinusoidal waveform can be increased from the threshold of audibility by a factor of approximately 1,000,000 until the threshold of pain is reached. Working with such a large range of numbers is not convenient. To characterize the range from the threshold of hearing to the threshold of pain, it is more convenient to define the unit *decibel*, which results in a range of numbers that can be easily managed. Also, our general impression is that the loudness of a sound increases logarithmically with the power of the sound, rather than linearly.

For two waveforms with peak amplitudes A and B, the decibel measure of the difference in their amplitudes is given by

$$dB = 20 \log_{10} (A/B)$$

If the value of 0.000283 dyne per square centimeter (for a 1-kHz signal) given above is used as a reference value for 0 dB, then the threshold of pain is reached at a sound pressure level (SPL) somewhere between 100 and 120 dB for most individuals.

There are complex interactions between the frequency and amplitude of a signal. For example, the perceived pitch of a tone can be modified by changing its amplitude. Consider further a plot of frequency as the x-axis and sound pressure level in dB as the y-axis, as shown in Figure 4.2. The threshold of audibility, the lowest curved line in the figure, is not a

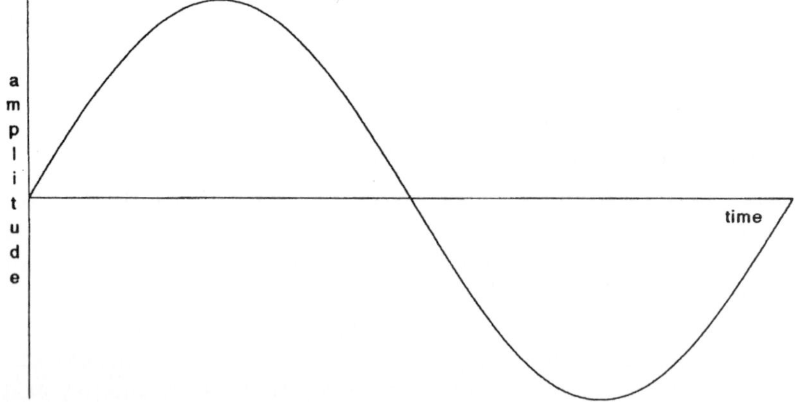

Figure 4.1 Sinusoidal waveform

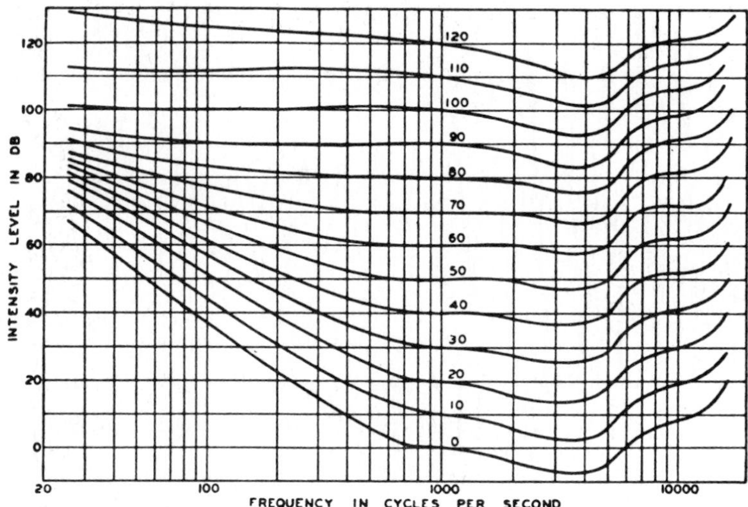

Figure 4.2 Perceived loudness. Each line shows a contour of equal loudness. (From Olson [9], p. 253, with permission)

horizontal line. Instead, the threshold of audibility is higher at low and high frequencies than in the middle.

Furthermore, the perceived loudness of a tone is not constant if the frequency of the tone changes. Put another way, a tone at some frequency may need to have a larger or smaller amplitude than a tone at some different frequency, if both tones are to be perceived as having the same loudness. Figure 4.2 shows contours of equal loudness, known as Fletcher-Munson curves. On the thick curve that passes through the 1000 Hz/40 dB point, a tone at, say, 10,000 Hz would need an amplitude of more than 50 dB to be perceived at the same loudness.

4.2.3 Spectral Characteristics in Human Hearing

Figure 4.3 shows a section of the waveform of a musical note. Clearly this waveform does not match the sinusoidal waveshape of Figure 4.1. Using the mathematical techniques of Fourier analysis, one can break such a waveform down into its spectral components. The spectral components for a more or less constant waveshape are often graphed as in Figure 4.4. For waveforms from wind, brass, and string instruments and from vowels in speech, the frequencies at which spectral components occur are given by more or less whole-number multiples of the lowest, or fundamental, frequency. In Figure 4.4, the vertical bars are thus more or less evenly spaced. The spectral components for percussion instruments often occur at nonintegral multiples of the fundamental.

The ear is sensitive to peaks and valleys in the overall shape of the spectral components. A *formant* is a frequency region in which the amplitudes of the spectral components are significantly raised or lowered; such regions

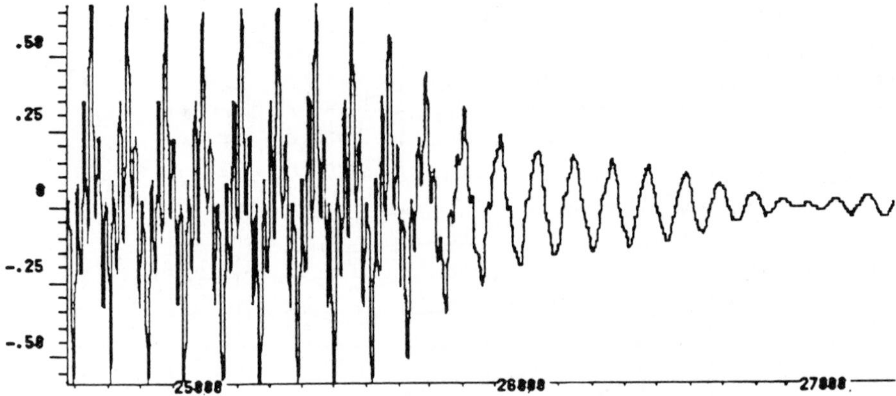

Figure 4.3 Time-varying waveform from the end of a clarinet note—x-axis: time, y-axis: amplitude

can be seen in Figure 4.4. In human speech, the vowels are distinguished by having a few marked formant regions. In musical instruments, formant effects are often given by the shape of the resonating body (such as the tube of a woodwind instrument). As the fundamental frequency changes, fixed formants affect spectral components at different distances from the fundamental. The ear is quite sensitive to unnatural changes in the relationship between fundamental frequency and formant structure. Consider the chipmunk effect, when audio recordings are played more quickly than normal. Both the pitch and the formants are transposed, whereas the ear usually expects the pitch to be transposed independently of the formants.

The spectrum and other parts of an auditory event give rise to the percept labeled timbre. Timbre perception is complicated and not yet well understood [6,10]. One way of treating timbre is to say that timbre allows us to identify the source of a sound. The timbre of a trumpet is said to be different from that of a trombone. Another aspect of timbre lies in the subjective qualities associated with a sound. One speaks of a piercing piccolo or a

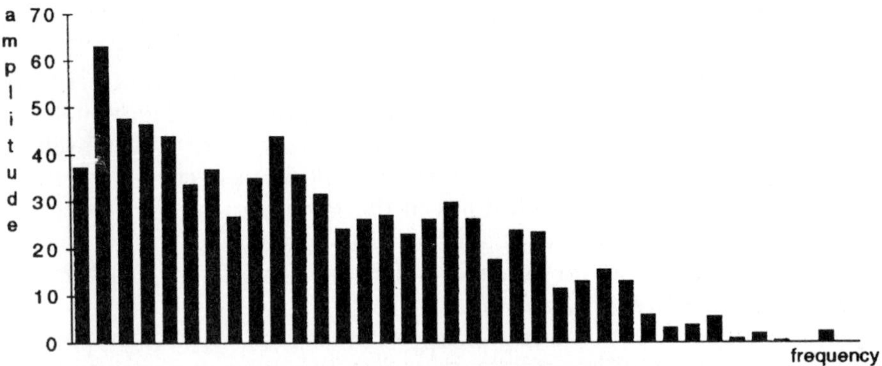

Figure 4.4 Spectrum of a portion of the steady state from a musical tone

boomy bass drum. Unfortunately, in music, there is as yet no simple way to move from the physical waveform, or even the spectrum of a musical instrument tone, to a generalized framework for treating either source identification or the quality of a sound. (Some possibilities in speech are discussed below.)

This has implications for multimedia systems. Suppose one wants to use an attention-grabbing sound from a sound database as part of a presentation. What makes a sound attention-grabbing? Or suppose one wants to search a sound track for relaxing sounds. In a written article, one can search for words and phrases; or if an author sprinkles labels in the text, it is easy to do a keyword search. There is no equivalent in dealing with an audio signal. At best, textual descriptions can be recorded in parallel to recorded audio segments. In building a sound effects library, the sound editor in a film or video studio can supply subjective text labels. Fortunately, the labels can themselves be entered into a database to simplify retrieval of sounds. But new sounds entered into the system must still be classified subjectively, by hand. The work of Loeb et al. [11] on classifying musical examples with a user-supplied set of characteristics and preferences may be applicable to future databases of musical sounds.

4.2.4 Time-Varying Aspects of Natural Sound

In the past century, sound has come to be generated by nontraditional means, many of them electric and electronic. Traditionally, musical tones were divided into three regions in time, called attack, steady-state, and decay (Figure 4.5). In the steady-state region, it is supposed that the spectrum remains fixed. The simplest synthesis model calls for generating a waveform with fixed components, such as those of Figure 4.4, and applying an amplitude envelope, such as in Figure 4.5.

Almost everyone can tell the resulting sound from the richer sound of an orchestral instrument. Research has shown [12] that there are significant changes in the spectral components of a musical tone in time. Figure 4.6 shows the time-varying amplitude spectrum of the attack of a musical tone. By studying such plots, we have learned that the spectral components vary in time with respect to each other, both in frequency and in amplitude. The frequencies are almost never in exact integer ratios, but instead vary in the region of 0.999 to 1.001 (see discussion in [14]).

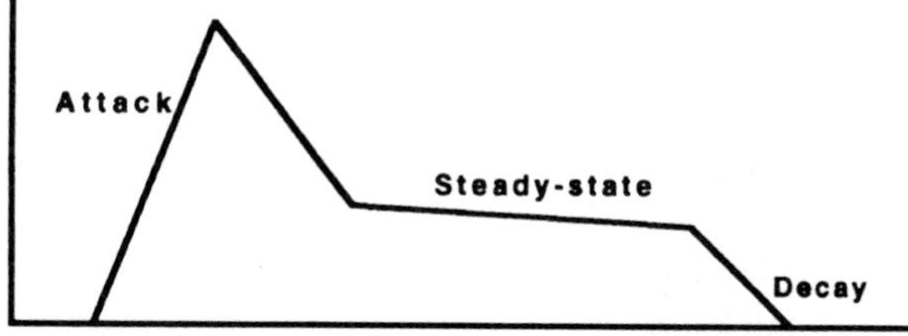

Figure 4.5 Simplified amplitude evolution of a musical note

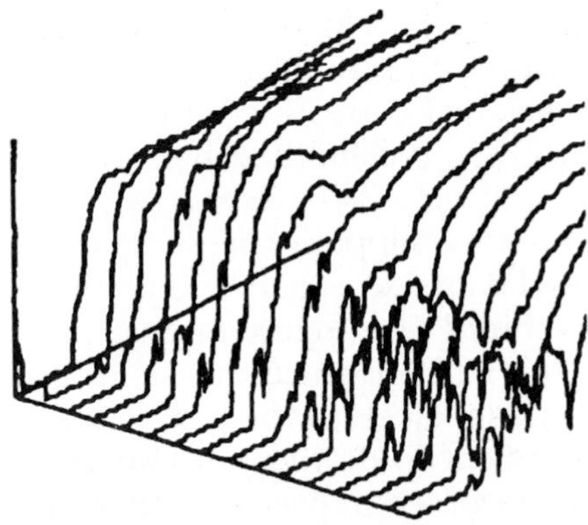

Figure 4.6 Time-varying amplitude of the first 16 harmonics of the attack of a trumpet tone. The fundamental is at the back. Amplitude is the vertical axis. Time runs from lower left to upper right. (Reprinted from [13] with permission)

Closely related to this is the realization [15] that the attack portion of natural sounds is crucial for identification. In an experimental setting, subjects were asked to identify musical instruments after hearing short sections spliced from tones. Experiments show that it is far easier to identify a musical instrument from its attack than from its steady-state. Thus, the time-varying parts of the attack spectrum are often crucial for maintaining musical quality. (This again probably has an evolutionary motivation.)

It is important to mention in passing the time-resolution capabilities of the human ear. At one level, it is possible for the ear to detect changes at the level of a few milliseconds. For example, if one uses the data of Figure 4.6 to resynthesize a tone, a careful listener can discern the absence of the small "blips" in the attack. If these are left out, many listeners discern the difference and complain about the blatty quality of the brass tone as well.

These phenomena have implications for the design of audio in digital systems. Mistakes can be disruptive. If your operating system has swapped out during a multimedia presentation when the synthesizer needs some new parameters, the attention of the listener in the audience will suddenly be drawn instinctively to the resulting disturbance in the sound effects, even if the listener does not consciously notice a mistake in the sound. To avoid such mistakes in synthesizing high-quality sound, one might like to calculate the data rate for parameter updates to a synthesizer. However, since detail in the attack portion of sounds can be so important, one cannot get by with a calculation of throughput rate for parameter updates; one needs to take the burst rate into account. Of course, some parameters can be preloaded (see [16] p. 7, for one example) to accommodate the bursts. Or, if the system is just playing back prerecorded sounds, they too can be preloaded for playback. There is another problem with that approach, however. Consider a multimedia conferencing system. In natural human communication, it must be possible for one speaker to interrupt another. Likewise, in real-time music making, the performance needs to be modified as it happens because of adjustments made by the skilled performer. If too much audio data or parameters are enqueued, then one needs a mechanism to "jump to the head of the queue" [17].

4.2.5 Masking

Masking may be easier to explain in the visual domain. We all know that if a bright light is shining in our eyes, such as headlights from an oncoming car, then other dimmer lights are impossible to see. There are similar phenomena in the auditory world. One sound can make it impossible to hear another, or one sound may shift the apparent loudness of another. The masking of one sound may be total or partial. Also, parts of one sound can mask parts of another sound, even if we cannot consciously detect such masking in normal circumstances. Auditory masking effects can die away in a matter of milliseconds.

If one tone is masking another, the effect depends on the separation in frequency. Figure 4.7 shows a typical plot of the masking effect (see [18], for example, for plots of maskers at different frequencies). The solid black line is the threshold of audibility. A spectral component on the left causes the threshold of audibility to be shifted upward, shown by the dotted line.

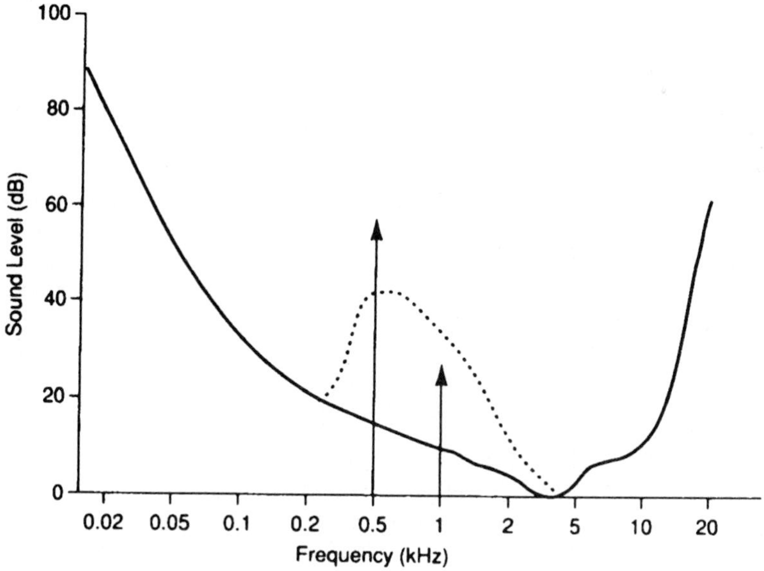

Figure 4.7 The threshold of audibility (solid line) shifted in the presence of a masker (left arrow). (Reproduced with permission from [19], p. 264)

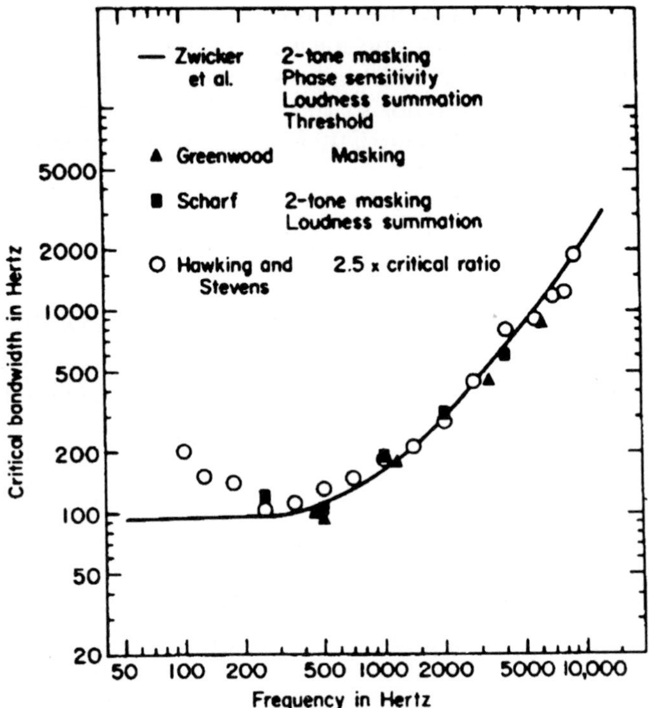

Figure 4.8 Critical bandwidth (y-axis) as a function of the frequency at the center of the critical band (x-axis). The solid line, circles, triangles, and squares are based on various measurements. (Reproduced from [20], vol. 1, p. 161, with permission of *Journal of the Acoustical Society of America*)

A second spectral component, shown by the arrow on the right, is masked. Notice that the masking effect falls off more steeply to the right of the curve, that is, toward higher frequencies. Thus, a low tone can effectively mask more high frequencies, but a high tone affects relatively fewer lower frequencies. Masking can also happen if the tones do not happen simultaneously; that is, if a masking tone is short but occurs before another tone, the masked tone can still be obscured. Masking effects happen whether the masker is a single tone or a broader band of noise.

Laboratory studies of such masking effects led to the notion of critical band; that is, a given frequency is surrounded by a band of frequencies within which various auditory phenomena can be shown to occur. For example, consider the loudness percept evoked when two tones are at the same frequency. Now move the tones apart. As the frequency between the tones increases, experimental evidence shows that the perceived loudness does not increase until the distance between the tones exceeds a critical band. A critical band is characterized by a center frequency and by a bandwidth. The bandwidth is approximately one-third of an octave above, perhaps, 300 Hz. Below that, the bandwidth is more or less fixed (see

Figure 4.8). The theory does not state that the ear has fixed bands; rather, the theory says that the band within which certain phenomena occur increases in size (frequency) as frequency increases. This property can be closely matched to physiological properties of the human ear. The implications of masking and critical band phenomena for communications technology are discussed below, especially in the section on MPEG.

4.2.6 Phase

One of the characteristics of a waveform not yet discussed here is its phase. Two waves with the same waveform are said to be in phase if they start at the same point and move in the same direction. For sinusoidal waveforms, such as in Figure 4.1, the waveform is said to be 180 degrees out of phase when the illustration is flipped top-to-bottom. There is some controversial evidence that humans can hear absolute phase [21,22]. More importantly, phase problems occur in stereo transmission. If two signals are exactly out of phase, they cancel, resulting in the sound of silence. For normal listening, this rarely occurs. But consider the case when a stereo soundtrack from a movie is mixed to mono for transmission to conventional, monophonic televisions. It can and does happen that some sound engineer somewhere mixed up the phase relations on some sound effect or two. There are true stories of the network executive heating up the telephone after the machine gun on his television suddenly spoke silently. Phase continues to be a practical problem in broadcast and will undoubtedly creep into, for example, multichannel conferencing systems.

4.2.7 Binaural Hearing and Localization

In most normal listening situations, we hear sounds coming from all directions around us, including above and below. The ear uses various factors to determine sound location [23]. These include intensity (if the sound is louder on the left, it probably came from the left); timing (if the sound hits the right ear first, it probably came from the right); and spectrum (the head imposes filtering effects as sound wraps around from one ear to the other). It is now known that the outer ear imposes certain filter characteristics as well, depending on the direction and elevation of the sound (see, for example, [24]).

The distance of a sound to the listener is affected by the reverberant field. In any enclosed room, the sound from the original source bounces off the walls, ceiling, and floor. Within a few tens of milliseconds after the sound starts, there can be literally thousands of these mini-echoes, especially in a good concert hall. It is now well understood how to make artificial reverberation [25].

The effects of sound in space are subtle but important. In a teleconferencing system (or on a movie screen), if the speaker's head is shown in one position and the sound of the speaker's voice comes from another position, then the listener can be confused. For a discussion of the importance of this when the speaker is moving in a teleconferencing system, see [2], p. 26.

4.3 DIGITAL REPRESENTATIONS OF SOUND

4.3.1 Time-Domain Sampled Representation

Sound in the analog world is said to be continuous in both time and amplitude. The sound's analog amplitude can be measured to an arbitrary degree of accuracy, and measurements can be taken at any point in time. A digital signal is different; the signal is defined only at certain points in time, and the signal may take on only a finite number of values.

To sample a signal means to examine it at some point in time. Sampling usually happens at equally separated intervals, at a rate called the *sample frequency*, determined by the Sampling Theorem. If a signal contains frequency components up to some frequency f, then the sample frequency must be at least $2f$ in order to reconstruct the signal properly. In practical systems, the sample frequency must be higher than $2f$. In the early days of digital audio, sample frequencies at 44.1 kHz and 48 kHz were adopted to handle the full 20-kHz range of human hearing. The sample frequency of 32 kHz is also common. In multimedia systems for the PC market, submultiples of 44.1 (22.05 kHz, 11.025 kHz) are often found. The highest frequency that can be handled (i.e., one-half the sample rate) is often called the *Nyquist frequency*.

To quantize a signal means to determine the signal's value to some arbitrary degree of accuracy. Figure 4.9a shows an analog waveform (solid line) and the representation of that waveform as quantized samples (vertical bars). The digital signal is defined only at the times where the vertical bars occur. The height of each vertical bar can take on only certain values, shown by dashed lines, which are sometimes higher and sometimes lower than the original signal. If the height of each bar is translated into a digital number, then the signal is said to be represented by pulse-code modulation, or PCM. Pohlmann ([19], p. 37) gives a good overview of other digital representations of sampled signals. (In the world of digital music, a sampled and quantized signal shown by the vertical bars in Figure 4.9a is called simply a *sampled* signal, to distinguish it from signals synthesized, for example, with frequency modulation; this is discussed below in more detail.)

The difference between a quantized representation and an original analog signal is called the *quantization noise*. Figure 4.9b shows the quantization noise for the signal in Figure 4.9a. Quantization noise differs from analog tape hiss. Quantization noise can be present only when there is some audio signal to be quantized, whereas tape hiss is always present. Basically, quantization noise follows the signal like a halo. With more bits for quantization of a PCM signal, the signal sounds cleaner. Each additional bit of accuracy improves the signal-to-noise ratio by about 6 dB. This is

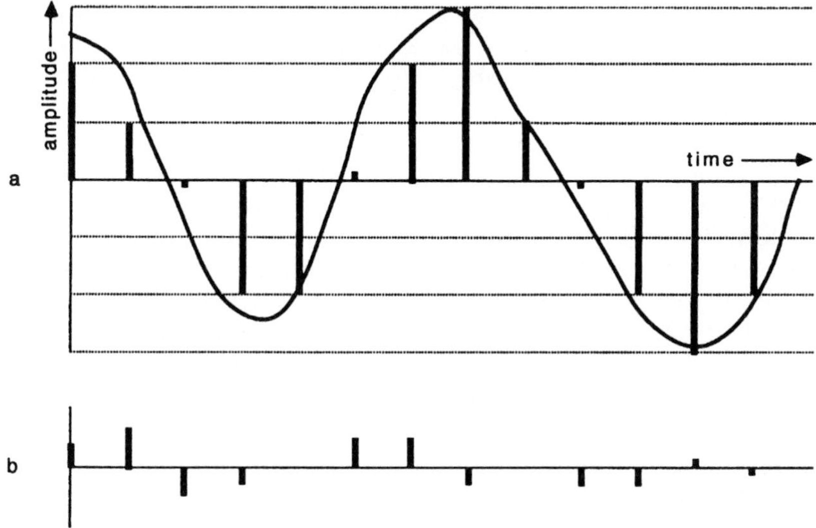

Figure 4.9 (a) A sampled and quantized signal (vertical bars) compared with an analog original signal (solid line), (b) the quantization error.

because each bit represents a factor of 2, and 20 log 2 approximately equals 6 dB. For 8-bit systems, the quantization noise is quite audible. Early digital audio systems operated on 16 bits, given in part by the 16-bit word length common in computers and digital hardware. Audio CDs store 16 bits of data. As discussed above, the human ear can hear a wider range (perhaps 120 dB) than the 16 bits × 6 dB/bit = 96 dB maximum range provided by a 16-bit system. One obvious solution is to use more bits, such as 20.

There are hardware devices called digital-to-analog converters (DACs) and analog-to-digital converters (ADCs) for moving between the analog and digital domains. The hardware in and around an ADC follows the input analog signal; takes a snapshot of its value at the sample time; holds onto that value until conversion is finished; and outputs a number. The opposite happens in analog-to-digital conversion. The DAC accepts a number; hangs onto that value until the value is converted to some electrical signal (such as current or voltage); and sends that signal to the outside world. If the converted signal is fed to a loudspeaker, for example, then the loudspeaker cone is made to move in a way that causes us to believe that we are hearing a recorded signal.

There is a filter, called the anti-alias filter, involved with the ADC. As required by the sampling theorem, this filter removes components above the Nyquist frequency. There is a corresponding filter, often called a reconstruction filter, associated with the DAC.

The filtering associated with DACs and ADCs can itself introduce unwanted distortions into the signal. Although these are often subtle, for high-quality work they should be minimized. One solution is to use so-called oversampling DACs. The DAC operates at four, eight, or some other multiple of the sample frequency. The requirements on the associated filter are not so stringent in the audio band. In effect, the problems associated with the filtering are pushed into higher-frequency ranges, where they become inaudible.

Since we are working with the transition from the analog to the digital world, it is important to mention in passing that the digital world is often unfriendly to analog signals. For example, the radio frequency signals bouncing around inside a PC leak easily into analog lines coming in from the outside. Also, the usual variations in manufacturing, temperature, and line voltage can lead to nonlinearities in DACs and ADCs, so that a 16-bit system is not really a 16-bit system after all. Another problem worth mentioning has to do with interrupting the digital stream on its way to the outside world. The loudspeaker cone protests vigorously if several samples are inadvertently skipped. It can and does happen, even on the floors of professional audio trade shows, that someone has made an implementation mistake. Suddenly the loudspeaker cone is trying to move from its extreme inward position to its extreme outward position. The result is a big bang. Those debugging digital audio in the early stages of algorithm development are advised to keep the volume on their audio gear turned down.

Other Methods of Encoding the Analog Signal

Real-world requirements may make it impossible to handle the full bit stream of, for example, CD-quality audio. One solution (*delta modulation*) is to encode not the value of each sample, but the difference between one sample and the next. In most cases, fewer bits per sample need to be transmitted, but delta modulation has problems. A more practical variant is called *adaptive delta pulse code modulation*, or ADPCM. In order to handle both signals that change quickly as well as signals that change slowly, the step size encoded between adjacent samples varies according to the signal itself. In other words, if the waveform is changing rapidly, large steps can be quantized. This is the method used in CD-I (compact disc-interactive), discussed below.

For speech signals, a widely used system works with a quantization step size that increases logarithmically with the level of the signal. This means that the quantization levels are closest together when the signal is quiet and spaced further apart when the signal is louder [26]. CCITT Recommendation G.711 codifies the A-law and μ-law encoding scheme whereby speech is transmitted at 8 kHz. For A-law transmission, the signal is encoded according to

$$y = \begin{cases} \dfrac{Ax}{1 + \ln A} & \left(0 \le x \le \dfrac{1}{A}\right) \\[2ex] \dfrac{1 + \ln(Ax)}{1 + \ln A} & \left(\dfrac{1}{A} \le x \le 1\right) \end{cases}$$

For μ-law encoding, the formula is

$$y = \frac{\ln(1 + \mu x)}{\ln(1 + \mu)} \qquad (0 \le x \le 1)$$

In standard telephone work, μ is set to 255 and *A* is set to 87.6. The result in either case is an 8-bit signal that produce the dynamic range approximately associated with 12-bit PCM. Details of implementing these two encoding schemes are given in [27].

CD-Audio, CD-ROM, CD-I

CD-audio is one full name for the CD that you buy in a local store. CD-ROM uses the same data format as CD-audio to store arbitrary data; the data bytes are simply interpreted differently. CD-ROM can address data through bits available in the Q subcode channel defined in the CD-audio format [19]. The CD-ROM specification does not by itself guarantee that audio will be available. But many CD-ROM players include some form of D/A converter and associated circuitry so that they can also play CD-audio discs.

CD-I, or CD-interactive, is a specific application of CD-ROM. In the data fields, audio, video, and text/binary data are interleaved to allow for synchronized presentation. For audio data, there are five kinds of storage available, varying in quality (Table 4.1). The CD-DA quality is effectively the same as CD-audio. ADPCM, discussed above, is used for three levels. Level A is about the same in quality as vinyl LP records, level B is similar to FM broadcast, and level C is similar to AM broadcast. The quality of phonetic encoding is similar to that on the telephone. Modes A, B, and C can be encoded mono or stereo. For mono encoding, the playing times shown in the table are doubled. The amount of video and text data that can be stored is tightly coupled with the amount of audio stored.

There is a further version of the CD-I known as full-motion video (FMV). In this format, audio and video are encoded using the MPEG standard to be discussed below. This means that full-motion video with high-quality stereo can be output from a CD. More information on CD-ROM, CD-I, and other CD variants can be found in [19].

Table 4.1 Five Audio Formats Available in CD-I

Level	*Encoding*	*Bandwidth (kHz)*	*Word Length*	*Playing Time (hours, stereo)*
CD-DA	PCM	20	16	1
A	ADPCM	17	8	2
B	ADPCM	17	4	4
C	ADPCM	8.5	4	8
Information	phonetic	N/A	N/A	10,000

4.3.2 Transform Representations

A sampled and quantized signal such as shown in Figure 4.9a can be *transformed* into another representation. Such transforms have been extensively studied. A primary motivation comes from communications channels with narrow bandwidths. Even in the early days of analog communications, researchers explored whether a transformed signal might be easier or more robust to transmit than the original signal. The signal would be transformed at the sender, the transform parameters would be transmitted at a lower bandwidth, and the receiver would reconstruct the signal.

Fourier Methods

One of the most common methods is to use a digital form of the Fourier transform. The PCM signal is referred to as the time-domain signal, and the Fourier coefficient representation is referred to as the frequency-domain signal. For a stationary time-domain signal lasting an infinite amount of time, a single set of Fourier coefficients is adequate to represent and reconstruct the signal. For real-world musical and speech signals that vary in time, as we have seen, we are technically dealing with the discrete short-time Fourier transform, popularly known as the phase vocoder [28,29]. In the world of digital music, this corresponds to additive synthesis [30].

The phase vocoder and its close relatives have proven to be an invaluable tool for research into the nature of speech and sound. One simple example was given in Figure 4.6. Nonetheless, there are problems with the phase vocoder. Depending on the parameters, there can be an explosion of data by a factor of 10 to 100 or more. Only recently, with the advent of systems such as the Silicon Graphics Indigo or the NeXT, has it become fairly easy to deal with these amounts of data.

There are other transform domains to be mentioned in passing. One of the closest to the digital world is the Walsh transform [31] which has not yet, to my knowledge, been exploited in any commercial musical system. The problem with the Walsh representation is that there is no intuitive relationship between changing one of the Walsh coefficients and the auditory results of the change.

Subband Coding and MPEG Audio

Another clever method for compacting the required data stream is to exploit the masking properties of the ear discussed earlier. One way to do this involves subband coding, in which the signal is broken into bands which can be transmitted as a group at lower data rates than required for the original signal. There are many subband coding schemes for audio, such as the ATRAC scheme used in Sony's Mini Disc format ([19], pp. 263–265, [32]) or the Digital Compact Cassette (DCC) introduced by Philips [33]. Subband coding has been studied extensively in the speech community [34].

A standard known popularly as MPEG (Motion Picture Experts Group) Audio is given in the document ISO/IEC DIS 11172 promulgated jointly by the international standards organizations ISO and IEC. The MPEG group is officially known as ISO-IEC/JTC1/SC29/WG11. The video encoder and decoder, which form part of the theoretical basis of the video portion, are given in full in the ISO/IEC document and are also discussed in [35] and Chapter 6 of this book. For more information on MPEG audio, see also [36,37,38]. We now discuss MPEG in some detail, since MPEG provides a good example of subband coding theory and practice.

A full MPEG system includes an encoder and a decoder. As with MPEG video, the audio encoder is not strictly defined in the document, but functionality of the decoder is tightly specified. Some sample audio encoders are given in the document; they are briefly reviewed here. Some companies are working on chip implementations of MPEG coder/decoders (CODECs), such as the C-Cube CL450. Proprietary implementations of MPEG audio encoders are being patented and will be brought to the marketplace as well.

The MPEG audio standard is closely bound to the arena of mono and stereo audio to accompany images, as opposed to professional and consumer audio electronics. (A standard tied to professional audio would have envisioned an escape mechanism for more than two channels, for example.) There are four modes:

single channel

dual channel (two independent channels, for example in two languages, coded in one bitstream)

stereo (two stereo channels coded in one bitstream)

joint stereo (stereo pair coded exploiting redundancy between right and left channels)

There are three possible *layers*, or degrees, of processing. Regardless of which layer of coding is used, an audio frame consists of a header, optional bits for cyclic redundancy (CRC) error check, the audio data itself, and (in layers 1 and 2) optional ancillary data. The header contains a synchronization word, identification of the layer (1, 2, or 3), sample frequency (32, 44.1, or 48 kHz), a padding bit (to help with 44.1-kHz sample frequency), a bit for private use, some bits for emphasis, and copy protection bits.

The encoder for layer 1 (Figure 4.10) maps the digital audio input into 32 subbands; that is, the available frequency range is divided into 32 bands. The conversion to subbands is done for a *frame* of 384 audio samples. During each frame, the subbands are sampled 12 times. But not every subband is actually encoded.

Instead, a psychoacoustic model (three top right-hand boxes in the figure) determines allocation of the available bits to the perceptually strongest bands. A new allocation of bits among the subbands is determined for every frame. Actually, two psychoacoustic models are available in the specifica-

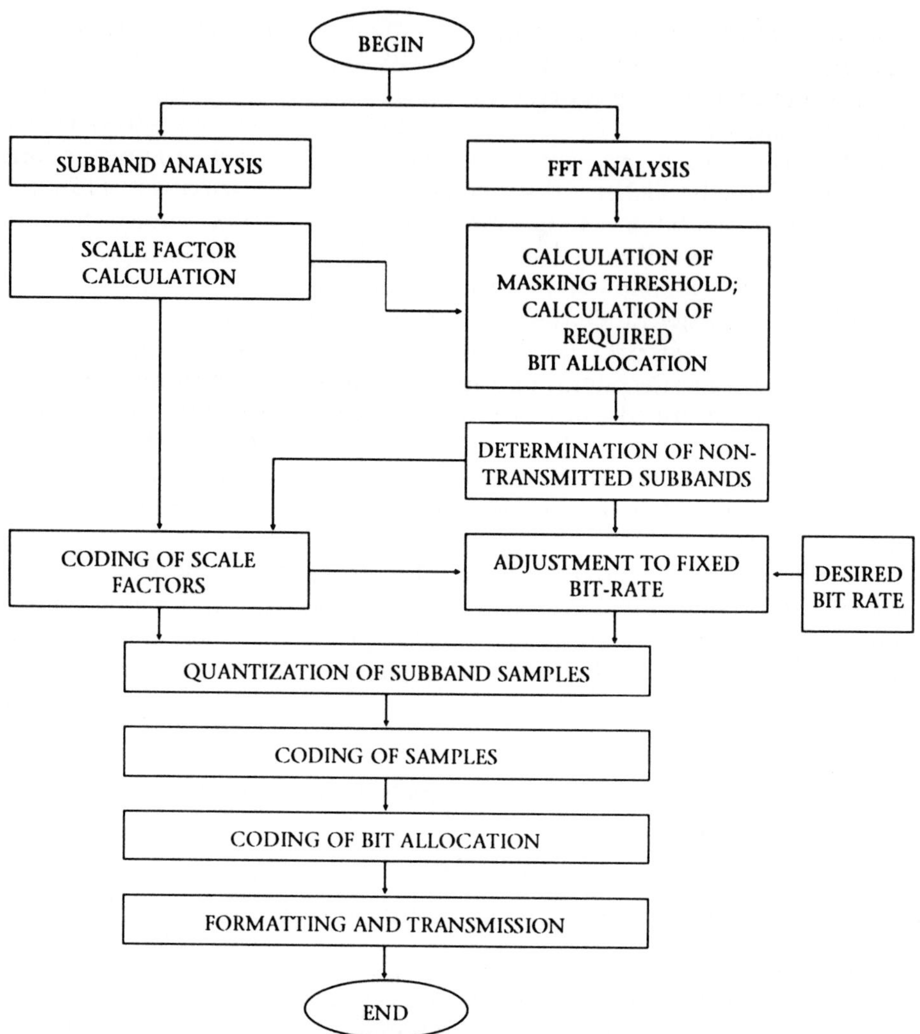

Figure 4.10 The structure of the encoder for MPEG layers 1 and 2. (Reproduced with permission from ISO/IEC DIS 11172, Figure 3-C.2)

tion. Only the first is described here. The first model separates the bands output by fast Fourier transform (FFT) analysis into those that are more sinusoidal (called *tonal* in the specification) and those that are more noise-like. The model determines which bands are masked by others, based on critical bands. The model removes bands that are irrelevant, that is, bands which fall below the *absolute threshold*, which is similar to the lower line in Figure 4.2. Then the model calculates the masking threshold for each band, based on the surviving maskers. In each band, the model further compares the signal in the band with the calculated masker. Using the resulting signal-to-mask ratio, the model determines the mask-to-noise ratio (MNR) in each band. An iterative procedure uses the MNR to assign coding bits to the bands with the lowest MNR. As long as bits are available, more subbands are encoded.

This means that some subbands remain uncoded, in which case a zero is transmitted as the bit allocation. A scale factor is also transmitted for each band when the number of bits is not zero, since the bands are scaled before quantization. Finally, for nonzero subbands, 2 to 15 data bits per subband are transmitted. One advantage of this scheme, by the way, is that noise in one band is independent of noise in another band.

User-defined ancillary data can also be transmitted. Since the ancillary data consume some bits that would otherwise be available for audio itself, using ancillary data could possibly degrade the audio quality.

Decoding, shown in Figure 4.11, is the opposite of encoding. The decoder determines from the bitstream which subbands have nonzero data. The data

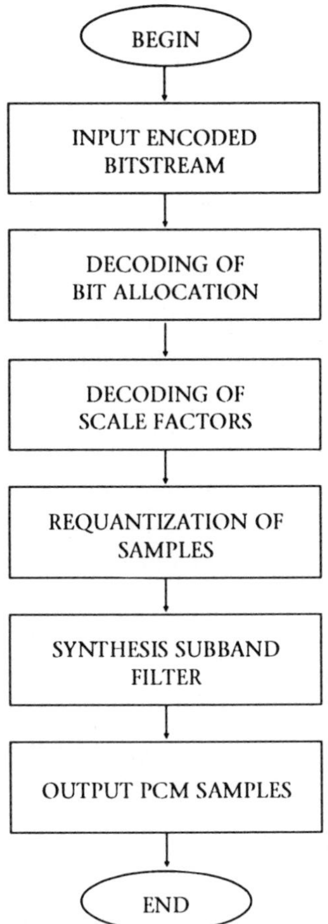

Figure 4.11 The structure of the MPEG decoder for layers 1 and 2. (Reproduced with permission from ISO/IEC DIS 11172, Figure 3-A.1)

from those bands are read, and the bands are rescaled according to scale factors. A resynthesis filter creates an output PCM stream.

Layer 2 features additional coding of bit allocation, scale factors, and samples. There is a different frame rate of 1152 input samples in one frame. As many as three scale factors are transmitted for each frame, for 36 subband samples per frame. If the differences between successive scale factors are very small, only one scale factor needs to be transmitted, freeing up bits for encoding the subbands.

In level 3, there are 1152 input samples per encoded frame, and the encoder is much more complicated. One difference is that a "hybrid" filter bank is used to increase frequency resolution. More precisely, the available frequency range is divided into two parts. The higher-frequency components above a certain point can be encoded with better time resolution. The lower-frequency components are encoded with better frequency resolution. Level 3 also has a nonuniform quantizer and adaptive segmentation of data; that is, if there is a peak demand for bits in a given frame, the number of bits available for coding can be temporarily increased. The frame header mentioned above occurs at regular intervals, but the data for a frame of input samples can occur before and after the header corresponding to that frame.

4.3.3 Subtractive-Based Representations

Another popular approach is to model the signal as a spectrally rich source followed by one or more filters. The most popular implementation of this model in the speech community is called *linear prediction*, discussed below. The linear predictor has found wide application in the computer music community [39,40,41]. The advantage of the linear predictor for music composition and performance is that the fundamental frequency can be separated from the spectral characteristics. Still, the linear predictor is not a high-quality system in terms of musical quality. One reason is that the all-pole model used in traditional linear prediction cannot model closely the spectral shape of musical instrument tones.

4.3.4 Parametric Representations

Another class of representations has nothing to do with models of hearing or acoustics in particular, but exploits some numerical properties to achieve high-quality audio results. The first major breakthrough in this arena was *frequency modulation*, developed at Stanford by John Chowning [42,43]. FM had been used for several decades for radio transmission. Chowning discovered that certain combinations of carrier and modulator frequencies could produce waveforms that mimicked the properties of musical waveforms. FM was used in digital synthesizers and other musical devices, mostly by Yamaha. Many PC plug-in cards also use FM chips for sound synthesis.

Other techniques such as granular synthesis [44], waveshaping [45], Chant [46], or the Karplus-Strong algorithm [47] have been investigated in the computer music community and implemented in some synthesizers such as the Korg 01/2 Series (waveshaping). Techniques in the speech community such as vector quantization are discussed below.

4.4 TRANSMISSION OF DIGITAL SOUND

When one is sending signals from one piece of digital equipment to another, many problems can be encountered. There is always the fallback position of connecting the analog output of one digital machine to the analog input of another digital machine. A copy made in this manner will still sound very clean. But often in real-world work, several generations of copies must be made. If the signal is converted to the analog domain for every copy, unacceptable amounts of noise are gradually introduced.

One problem in connecting digital equipment is that there are several standard combinations of sample rate, number of channels, bit and byte order, and number of bits per channel used in digital audio recording. Some are intended for professional recording studios, other strictly for consumers, and some are called "semiprofessional." For example, the compact disc nominally stores stereo 16-bit signals at a 44.1-kHz sample rate; this consumer format is acceptable for semiprofessional use. Another format is the Digital Compact Cassette (DCC), which uses a different form of encoding, with sample rates of 32, 44.1, and 48 kHz.

Other kinds of problems occur in recording studios, for example, where equipment with noisy fans must be isolated from the recording studio itself. A digital signal can degrade when transmitted over some kinds of long cables.

To solve the problem of differing sample rates, one uses a sample-rate converter. This process can also introduce subtle amounts of noise if the implementation is not handled properly. Chips have been introduced recently to simplify implementation [48].

Several formats have been standardized for connecting digital audio equipment. One basic format is known as the AES/EBU format (Audio Engineering Society/European Broadcast Union) [49]. The AES/EBU format transmits at least 16 bits of PCM audio, and can easily transmit up to 20 bits. Two channels are always transmitted at once. Clock information is encoded with the data, so no extra connectors need to be provided for a clock signal, as is the case with some formats. Several "status" bits are transmitted as well. These can include the sample rate as well as user-programmed information. For work in large recording studios, the AES/EBU format has been generalized to the multichannel audio digital interface (MADI) format [50], which handles 56 channels of audio and up to 24 bits of audio data per sample. Some companies have introduced their own formats, such as Sony-Philips digital interface format (SPDIF), Sony digital interface format (SDIF), Yamaha, and Mitsubishi Electric Company (Melco). A good overview is in [51,52].

4.5 DIGITAL AUDIO SIGNAL PROCESSING

Digital Signal Processing (DSP) treats a signal as a series of numbers. Regardless of the content implied by the numbers, the numbers (the signal) can be treated (processed) in many ways. For example, if every number is replaced by the average of itself and its neighbor, the graph of the sequence of numbers is smoothed out. In the audio domain, this creates a low-pass filter.

Traditional digital audio signal processing is based on linear systems theory; that is, if you insert a signal with certain spectral components into the input of the system, the output has spectral components at the same frequencies, possibly delayed in time—no new frequencies are introduced. The limitations of linear theory become evident when one strives to characterize, for example, the behavior of a clarinet reed. For many years there have been simple but practical uses for nonlinear systems, such as in the "fuzz box" (nonlinear circuit to enrich sound) popular with guitar players. With recent advances, nonlinear theory and practice are becoming more and more important [53].

Another characteristic of traditional digital signal processing is that it deals with causal systems; that is, there can be no output that happens before an input. Put another way, causal digital signal processing cannot "look ahead into the future." However, this causal nature is often thwarted in real-world applications. For example, in nonreal-time systems for cleaning up tape hiss or background noise, the software "looks ahead" to see if it can characterize the background sound more precisely. Another example is in the side chain of audio compressors, discussed below.

In hardware and software, DSP is used to implement the usual functions needed to modify sound for recording and playback. Simple DSP algorithms can be chained together to create filters (high-pass, low-pass, bandpass, band-reject). Everyone knows some such controls from home entertainment equipment. Professional recording engineers use these filters for more subtle effects, such as making the singer "stand out" from the background by changing the equalization on the singer's voice. Such filters can be grouped into equalizer banks. More sophisticated uses of DSP include time-warping signals, such as in the WordFit system [54]. Briefly, in re-recording spoken passes for redubbing telephone and movie sound, it is necessary to make the re-recorded sound match in time the original spoken dialogue. WordFit finds the words in two sets of recordings based on the same text and then maps the timing of one recording to fit the timing of another.

For modifying level, gain control in DSP is a simple multiplication. More complicated level modification is given by a compressor, which reduces the dynamic range of a signal. In such a unit, the output level is equal to the input level until the input level reaches a certain threshold. Above that threshold, the output level increases by smaller amounts as the input level increases. If the signal is first compressed and then the whole signal is amplified, the result is a signal which sounds louder overall. This can be useful in automobiles, for example, where the quiet parts of symphonic music get lost in traffic noise. A variant on the compressor is the limiter, which tries to limit the signal's output level to some more or less hard level. In devices such as compressors and limiters, the input signal can be delayed before being processed. This allows the unit to "look ahead," circumventing causality. For example, if a loud drum strike is coming soon, it may make musical sense to start lowering the level of the output signal now rather than later. If the amplitude is reduced only when the drum hits, the listener may hear an unnatural result.

If a signal is delayed and added back into itself, an echo can result. If many such echoes are generated at the right time and scaled at the right amplitudes, the effect of reverberation can be generated. Digital reverberators were the first commercially available digital audio units on the market.

There have been significant advances in DSP in general with tracking and identification of arbitrary signals. Submarine warfare is one hot topic. One wants to know from the acoustic signature of a submarine whether it is friend or foe. The concept of friend or foe is rarely encountered in musical structure, but tracking musical performances would be a useful aid to computer-based musicians. Unfortunately, a seemingly simple problem such as pitch tracking turns out to be difficult. For example, if the musician connects two notes with a glissando, where does one note end and another note begin? Even when the pitches of two successive notes are distinct, it is hard to know for certain when a new pitch has been reached. (Endpoint detection is more advanced for word recognition in speech [55] than in music.) Musicians performing with pitch trackers practice hard and learn to avoid the pitfalls. As for identification of instruments, even to identify accurately a solo instrument recorded separately is considered a difficult task today. A more complex problem, such as separating musical instruments from the total symphonic signal, is barely in its infancy. The DSP solutions to speaker identification in speech are mentioned below.

To prepare the sound track for a movie, video, or presentation, it is necessary to assemble sounds in sequence. In decades past this kind of work was done in professional and semiprofessional studios with audio tape. Recently, hard disk systems have become common in the professional and semiprofessional audio industry. For PCs, inexpensive boards are available for individual users that have the same capabilities. This brings the world of "desktop audio" (I stole the term from [56]) one step closer to the kinds of gains that desktop publishing has achieved in the past 20 years. In hard systems, sampled sound is stored as files on a hard disk (as opposed to tape, the previous working medium in the audio industry). The sounds can be spliced together in a given sequence under software control. Often the begin and end of a sound must be trimmed to remove, for example, unneeded silence. To chain two sounds, it is usually necessary to perform a crossfade across some number of milliseconds. Again, if two sounds are simply abutted, then it can easily happen that the digital sample values at the join have an unexpectedly large difference in amplitude, causing a very unpleasant pop.

As an aside, it deserves to be mentioned that the sophisticated notions developed for client/server relations in graphics have barely been extended to audio [57]. Some audio and DSP resources are often expensive. Also, audio hardware resources are rarely needed for, say, hours at a time. It makes sense in many settings to have the audio resources centrally located. One implementation involves a large $N \times M$ switch, with N the number of inputs and M the outputs. Under computer control, the switch sends outputs to individual workstations as needed. A mixer at the user's station, possibly computer-controlled as well, can set final output levels. A written description of one such setup, similar to those which have been used in computer music centers for many years, is given in [56].

Returning, then, to the world of DSP, it is possible for add-in boards for even the Macintosh or the PC to perform significant signal processing with current digital signal processing chips, such as the Motorola DSP 56001 family or the Texas Instruments TMS 320 family. The NoNoise System from Sonic Solutions, for example, which runs on a Macintosh, can perform click removal and background noise cleanup.

4.5.1 Stereophonic and Quadrophonic Signal Processing Techniques

The first known stereo transmission of sound occurred more than 100 years ago, when the Paris opera could be heard in stereo over headphones at a remote site [58]. The fundamental principle of most modern stereo recording and reproduction systems is to record the natural sound field with two microphones and reproduce those signals from two loudspeakers. For signals recorded with just one microphone, or for synthesized signals, it is possible to "pan" the signal from left to right simply by changing the relative amplitudes of the signals going to the left and right speakers. To make the sound appear more distant, reverberation can be added, and the ratio of direct to reverberant sound is an important control. For sound in motion, Doppler shift is also needed. To synthesize elevation, the filter response of the outer ears of test subjects can be averaged so that the frequency response corresponding to a given elevation can be added. All of these algorithms can be implemented on commercially available processor cards. There are also commercially available (sometimes proprietary) systems such as the Roland Sound Space (RSS) that add location information to a signal. For a quick review of recent 3-D developments in the commercial audio industry, see [59].

Adding location information is more than just a game. For example, fighter pilots often listen to three or four continuous streams at once. If the *perceived* location of each stream can be separated in 3-D perceptual space, then it is easier for the pilot to separate which stream to pay attention to. Similarly, in audio augmentation of a computer graphic system, suppose that there is a sound associated with each window. As discussed by Ludwig et al. [60], it makes sense for the apparent location of each sound to match the position of its associated window on the screen. When a new window pops up, say with a video image of another participant in teleconferencing, the sound should seem to come from the position of the speaker's head. More importantly, sounds can be processed so that they are treated hierarchically. If the window disappears, the sound can be turned off. If the user selects the window, the sound can be made to jump "into the foreground."

4.5.2 Architecture of an Audio Signal Processing Library

Various researchers in the digital signal processing, speech, and computer music communities have dealt with the problem of sound representation during the past 20 years or so. Some of the efforts have fortunately been standardized and released for general use.

In dealing with audio signals, there is first the problem of storage. (We ignore tape solutions here, such as DAT players.) It may seem odd to discuss file formats here, but disk access speed and DSP chip bandwidth are still such that one quickly comes up against real-world constraints. Typically, for a signal stored in PCM format, one wants random access to permit editing, and one wants real-time playback. Until recently, playback from disk was a difficult problem that required careful planning and possibly even specially formatted disks. For a signal stored in the transform domain, one wants easy access for editing, but high throughput for possible real-time resynthesis. For time-varying Fourier analysis, editing is easier when each channel's Fourier representation is stored as one unit on the disk. For real-time resynthesis, such a format results in a high number of disk seeks, so a format in which all channels in each time slice are stored together is more convenient. One would also like to regularize the storage format so that ideally one editing program can read and edit sampled data, LPC, time-varying Fourier coefficients, and the like. The ESPS system by Entropic Systems Laboratories is typical. The file header, stored on disk with the data, specifies the format for storage. In practice, one format for sound files and another for data files typically becomes standard practice.

We now turn to components of signal processing libraries. The components obviously depend on the application. Perhaps the first main software signal processing library was put together by IEEE. The IEEE FORTRAN library [61] contains implementations of Fourier transforms, linear prediction, and filter design, among others. The Numerical Recipes volumes (such as [62]) were another big step, containing implementations of interpola-

Table 4.2 Example Functions from the NeXT Signal Processing Library

Function	*Description*
cvconjugate	form a complex vector from the elementwise conjugate of a complex vector
cvtcv	pointwise multiplication of two complex vectors
fftr2a	radix 2 decimation-in-time FFT, complex input and output, in-place, output shuffled
mtm	multiply two two-dimensional matrices, creating an output matrix
sumvsq	sum squares of vector elements to a scalar
vmovebr	vector move, bit reversed
vramp	fill a vector with a ramp function
vtvmvtv	pointwise multiplication of two vectors, subtract pointwise multiply of two vectors

tion, linear equations, FFTs, random number generators, and the like (see also [63]). For the Motorola DSP 56001 chip included in the NeXT computer, there is a library of hand-coded routines, most of which operate on vectors. Some examples of the contents of the library are given in Table 4.2.

At another level, the VCOS operating system from AT&T includes a Multimedia Module Library (MML) containing these components [64]:

generate and decode TouchTone® dual-tone multifrequency tones

CCITT G.722 standard audio compression and decompression

MPEG audio encoder and decoder

subband encoder and decoder, compressing 8-kHz sampled speech to 16 or 24 kb/sec

sample rate conversion at ratios of 1:3 and 3:1

JPEG decoder

In other libraries one finds modules for music synthesis algorithms, standard filter structures, reverberators, time delays, implementations of vocoders, and the like.

4.5.3 Editing Sampled Sound

Hardware and software systems for editing digital audio have existed for several decades. Some started in the commercial world, especially with the Fairlight synthesizer. Others, often discussed in the pages of *Computer Music Journal* and the *Proceedings of the International Computer Music Conference,* were developed in academia. A good overview of the current state of affairs for Macintosh-based software in the music world is in Chapter 13 of [65]. One typical package for Sun workstations is in the ESPS system, available from Entropic and mentioned in the previous section.

Certain basic capabilities can be found in any sound editing system. One needs to see the waveform, sometimes up close (short time resolution), sometimes far away (overview). Figure 4.12 shows a typical editing window. Time runs from left to right. The top layer of icons allows for operations such as playback, zoom, and cursor movement. Other options are available from menu items. The gray horizontal graph shows an overview of the recording, which lasts approximately two minutes. Below that are two large windows, each showing one channel of the stereo file. The highlighted areas in the stereo detail match one of the small outlined rectangles in the overview.

The user wants to see the values of the sound file, listen to parts of a file, and perform operations (fade-in, fade-out, FFT, and the like). In the music world, composers and performers need to mark sections of a sound file for synchronization with video, using SMPTE code, for example. Cut, duplicate, and paste operations are often important. In speech processing, most systems allow the user to mark symbols from the international phonetic alphabet. Many systems allow other arbitrary text labels to be associated with given points on the waveform. It is useful to be able to compare several

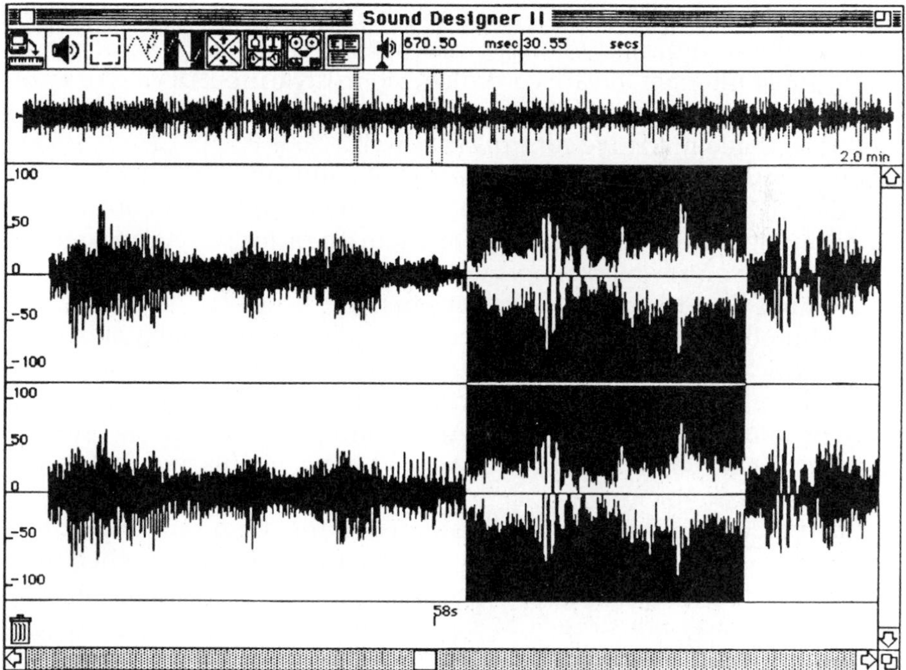

Figure 4.12 Typical sound display, taken from DigiDesign's Sound Designer II. (Courtesy of Toby Richards, DigiDesign)

sound files at once, optionally forcing them all to follow the same time scale. Many systems allow the user to redraw the waveform by hand on the screen. The sound file can be played back transposed in frequency or faster and slower than normal. Sound files need to be converted from one format to another. If the sound is transformed, then the transform data can be shown on the screen, with the cursor of the sound file tied to the cursor in the transformed data.

4.6 DIGITAL MUSIC-MAKING

4.6.1 Musical Instrument Synthesizers

The core of a digital music synthesizer [66] is some hardware for creating sound. This may be concentrated in a special-purpose chip set; it may be a general-purpose DSP chip running special software; or it may be a board containing several chips, each of which implements one or more "voices."

The earliest digital synthesizers were usually built as a single unit with a keyboard interface controlling the sound generator. In current single-unit keyboard synthesizers, the hardware enclosure typically features an LCD screen, switches, knobs, sliders, a joystick, track ball, and a "pitch bend wheel" or two, used for creating life-like effects such as glissando. Nowadays, it is common to have a musical controller separate from the tone-generation unit, which can be relegated to a backstage location or a different room in the recording studio. Typical controllers include a separate keyboard, guitar interface, breath controller, violin-style input device, or woodwind controller, to name the most common. Virtual reality research is producing some inventive controllers as well.

Some synthesizers, especially those from Roland, offer a video connector. At this writing, graphic user interfaces for the complicated controls of a digital music synthesizer unfortunately remain primitive. Almost all synthesizers now on the market operate on a MIDI network, explained below, so one finds one or more MIDI connectors.

The line between the disk-based audio systems mentioned above and boards which can generate music with personal computers is now blurred. Boards from companies such as Turtle Beach, Ariel, or DigiDesign can be used for sound editing or music synthesis and performance. The personal computer with add-on board and associated software thus serves as a digital synthesizer as well.

A *sampler* is a synthesizer that uses stored (rather than synthesized from scratch) sounds. Some samplers only play back stored sounds; others allow the user to record new sounds. The sampler may encode sound in some fashion, so it may not store PCM samples directly. Still, in *sampling* (used here in the music industry sense), the sounds are basically recorded by the musician and stored in the synthesizer. There are now fine sets of sampled sounds available on CDs, such as Denny Jaeger's CDs or the set from McGill.

In the narrow sense, a synthesizer uses a synthesis technique to generate sound (although people commonly speak of a sampling synthesizer). A *synthesis technique* is an algorithm for generating digital samples which, when played through appropriate conversion hardware and loudspeakers, sound more or less like the desired musical sounds. Techniques such as additive synthesis, FM, waveshaping, and granular synthesis were mentioned earlier in this chapter.

One view of the synthesizer hardware developed in the 1970s and early 1980s is that manufacturers competed to find new, unusual (and patentable) synthesis techniques that allowed for musical control while still offering low-cost implementation in hardware. Typical for this era, the Yamaha DX-7 was a pure FM synthesizer and a great commercial success in part because of its "FM" sound. Nowadays, it is more common for a synthesizer to create a sound by overlaying several sounds or by chaining parts of sounds to make one note. Each layer or each chained part may come from a different synthesis technique.

Whether the synthesizer is based on sampling or on one or more synthesis techniques, it is a nontrivial task to "voice" a synthesizer. One starting point is steady-state or time-varying (Fourier) analysis of recorded waveforms. Another way to work is to study the physical properties of, say, the bowed string or the clarinet reed. Another is to explore parameter settings to find some interesting sounds which are then refined. Much trial and error is involved, with repeated listening (and/or comparison with recorded sounds) as settings are changed. Synthesizer manufacturers sometimes develop an in-house development system for voicing. For everyday musicians to voice a synthesizer using the LCD on the front panel of the synthesizer case is a frustrating experience, due to the small size of the LCD and the primitive user interface design usually found. Many of the software packages available for the Macintosh and PC computers now allow the user to voice a synthesizer on the screen.

4.6.2 MIDI Protocol

In the early 1980s, several music instrument manufacturers agreed on a networking standard for musical instruments called MIDI, the Music Instrument Digital Interface. The standard is now maintained by MMA, the MIDI Manufacturer's Association and disseminated by the International MIDI Association (IMA) [67]. The specification is also reproduced in whole or in part in references such as [65,68,69]. The specification calls for certain hardware connections, using a 5-pin DIN connector. There are three kinds of connections allowed: in, out, and "thru." A thru connector provides a direct copy of the input signal. I would like to mention in passing that the MIDI network, although it has been made to work, is not the computer scientist's model of a well-designed network [70,71]. It is to be expected that some super-set of MIDI will appear on the market. Already companies like

Lone Wolf have attempted to bring to the market an optical network which includes MIDI as a subset.

The MIDI software specification involves 8 data bits, a start bit, and a stop bit, for a total of 10 bits transmitted at a rate of 31.25 kbaud. A message consists of one Status byte followed by zero or more Data bytes.

MIDI devices, such as tone generators, can be connected in networks such as chains or trees. Each device can listen to one or more MIDI channels. All data and mode messages are sent to all receivers, but the messages include a channel number so that only some receivers may act on specific messages. The messages defined for musical events, such as note on, note off, and pitch bend change, are summarized in Table 4.3. The key number represents keys from the bottom of the keyboard range to the top. Velocity means the speed with which the key is struck and generally controls attack characteristics, overall amplitude, and spectrum of the note. The polyphonic key pressure message is sent by devices such as keyboards that can measure the pressure applied as each key is held. The pressure for each key can be sent separately so that individual notes can be modified in performance. A channel pressure message comes from a device that can measure the pressure from its sensors, but can send only one pressure detected (usually the maximum).

A program change message causes the synthesizer to select one of 128 voices. In the early years of MIDI, each manufacturer assigned arbitrary voices to these program numbers. The recent General MIDI specification includes a 128-voice Instrument Pitch Map. A melody recorded on one

Table 4.3 MIDI Channel Voice Messages

Status Byte (hex)	*Data Byte 1*	*Data Byte 2*	*Meaning*
8n	0k	0v	Note Off
9n	0k	0v	Note On
An	0k	0v	Polyphonic Key Pressure (aftertouch)
Bn	0c	0v	control change
Cn	0p		program change
Dn	0v		Channel pressure (aftertouch)
En	0v	0v	Pitch changes, LSB + MSB

Notes:
n: Voice Channel Number (1–16)
k: Note Number (0–127, from bottom of the keyboard range to the top)
v: Velocity (0–127), or pressure value, or control value
c: Controller, such as breath controller, soft pedal, or sustain pedal
p: Program Number (0–127)

General MIDI synthesizer's xylophone sound, for example, will also be played back using a xylophone, and not a tuba, on some other General MIDI synthesizer.

Four Mode messages (not shown in the table) determine, among other things, whether the instruments' voices will be assigned to incoming notes in a monophonic (single melody) or polyphonic (several voices at once) fashion.

There is also provision for common messages (sent to all receivers), real-time messages (for synchronization), and for system exclusive (sysex) messages. System exclusive is essentially a generalized escape mechanism for messages of arbitrary length.

MIDI is not limited to hardware systems. Indeed, the acceptance of MIDI made possible the proliferation of software programs running on the Amiga, Macintosh, Atari, and PC. MIDI software includes sequencer programs, with which the musician can record, play back, view, and alter musical events, working with music notation, piano-roll notation, text displays of MIDI commands, and the like. Figure 4.13 shows a simple melody. Table 4.4 shows the basic MIDI messages for playing back the melody from a synthesizer. In the figure, all of the messages are sent out over channel 0. The note numbers and velocities are given in decimal representation. A note-on message with a velocity of 0 is the same as a note-off message. Time in the first column is in milliseconds, with 90 quarter notes to the second. Note that the first note occurs after a 3-second delay from the start of playback.

The original MIDI specification dealt primarily with real-time music performance. To store a performed or composed sequence, the programmer must implement a representation of time. To represent time in music, there are basically two possibilities—absolute time and delta time. With delta time, the time interval elapsed since the previous event is recorded. With absolute time, time elapsed since the beginning of the composition is represented. In the most general terms, both kinds of time are identical. But in practical implementation, delta time has the advantage that a whole sequence can be moved as one unit; only the start time of the unit must be changed. The disadvantage of delta time is that it can lead to incremental errors. Suppose the composer specifies three notes, which together should occupy 1 second. An integer representation of 1/3 second is rounded off. After three such delta units, there is a small time discrepancy, which can build up in a composition lasting 10 or 15 minutes. Absolute time coding avoids those errors, but makes editing harder. (The proposed MHEG stand-

Figure 4.13 A short musical example ("Justin's Lullaby," © 1990 John Strawn). Notation produced with the Finale program, courtesy of Robert Duisberg. Table 4.4 gives the corresponding MIDI messages.

Table 4.4 MIDI Messages for Figure 4.13

Time	*MIDI Status Byte*	*MIDI Pitch Byte (Data Byte 1)*	*Velocity (Data Byte 2)*	*Meaning*	*Pitch*
3642	9	74	49	note on	D
4149	9	74	0	note off	
4222	9	72	49	note on	C
5307	9	72	0	note off	
5380	9	69	49	note on	A
5549	9	69	0	note off	
5573	9	72	49	note on	C
5742	9	72	0	note off	
5765	9	69	49	note on	A
5934	9	69	0	note off	
5958	9	67	49	note on	G
7045	9	67	0	note off	
7117	9	65	49	note on	G
7286	9	65	0	note off	
7310	9	67	49	note on	G
7478	9	67	0	note off	
7503	9	65	49	note on	F
7672	9	65	0	note off	
7696	9	62	49	note on	D
8783	9	62	0	note off	
8856	9	60	49	note on	C
9362	9	60	0	note off	
9435	9	60	49	note on	C
10520	9	60	0	note off	

ard for multimedia and hypermedia objects also allows for time to be represented in what are essentially absolute and delta times, see [72] and Chapter 14.) Some way of representing time with rational numbers is also needed, as the example of three notes in 1 second shows. Early software sequencers stored the recorded data in proprietary file formats. Ultimately, an extension to the MIDI specification called Standard MIDI Files was established. The Standard Midi File format adopted a delta time representation, with time specified for each MIDI event. The file header effectively specifies the tempo. The delta time is a variable-length number between 0 and 0xFFFFFFF that specifies the number of time units given in the file header.

MIDI has also been extended to control theater lighting (MIDI Show Control). Yavelow's "bible" [65] is the best current source of information on MIDI, computers, and (Macintosh) software. To follow the current scene, one should consult magazines such as *Keyboard*, *MIX*, and *Electronic Musician*.

4.7 BRIEF SURVEY OF SPEECH RECOGNITION AND GENERATION

Speech is one of the main channels for human communication [73] and thus must be handled carefully in any multimedia communications system. In contrast to what has been discussed thus far about music, a major criterion in speech is intelligibility; the various measures are discussed in [74,75]. For example, "telephone-quality" speech has a bandwidth limited to around 200–3400 Hz. An 8-kHz sample rate results in a 68 kb/sec bit rate for PCM speech, far smaller than required for music PCM.

4.7.1 Speech Production

The organs involved in speech include the larynx, which encloses loose flaps of muscle called vocal cords. The puffs of air that are released create a waveform which can be approximated by a series of rounded pulses. The waveform created by the vocal cords propagates through a series of irregularly shaped tubes, including the throat, the mouth, and the nasal passages. At the lips and other points in the tract, part of the waveform is transmitted further, and part is reflected. The flow can be significantly constricted or completely interrupted by the uvula, the teeth, and the lips.

A voiced sound occurs when the vocal cords produce a more or less regular waveform. The less periodic, unvoiced sounds involve turbulence in which some part of the whole tract is tightened.

Vowels are voiced sounds produced without any major obstruction in the vocal cavity. In speech, formants (introduced above) are created by the position of tongue and jaw, for example. In separating vowels, the first three formants are the most significant. In the male, the fundamental frequency of voiced sounds is around 80 –160 Hz, with three formants around 500, 1500, and 2500 Hz. The fundamental of the female is around 200 Hz and higher, with the formants perhaps 10 percent higher than those of the male. Consonants arise when the vocal tract is more or less obstructed. Sounds at the level of consonants and vowels are collectively known as phonemes, the most basic unit of speech differentiation, analysis, and synthesis. The next level up from phonemes is the diphthong and the syllable, then the word.

Figure 4.14b shows a sonogram, a time-varying representation of a speech signal. The regions of high energy appear dark. The vertical stripes in the dark region correspond to individual pulses from the vocal cords. The

a)

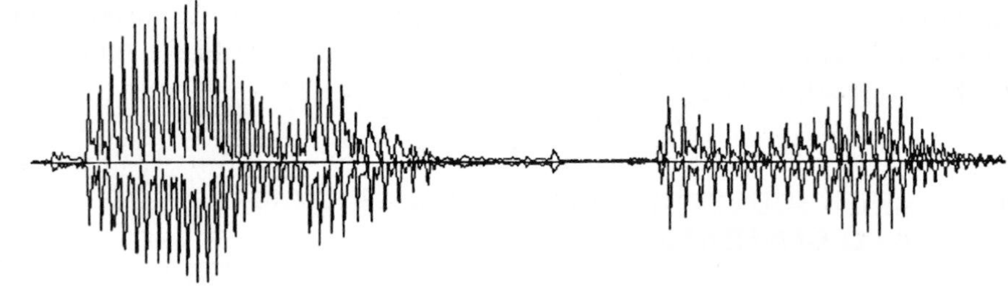

b)

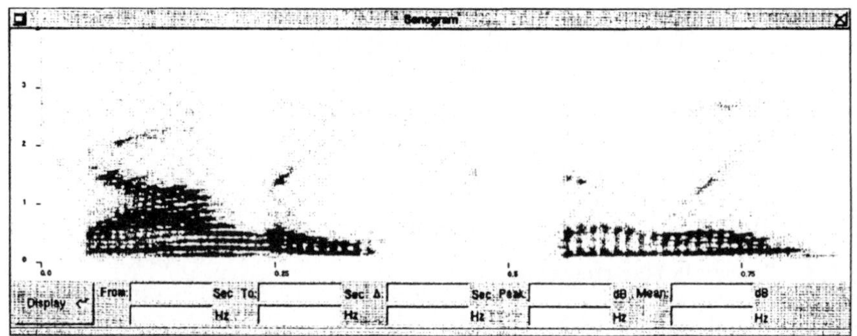

Figure 4.14 (a) The utterance "Golly, Scully," (b) A sonogram of the same utterance, prepared using the program Sonogram by Hiroshi Momose. (Both figures courtesy of Perry Cook)

change in the position of the darkest areas from left to right corresponds to the changes in formants.

The SPASM system developed by Cook [76] combines models of the glottal waveform and noise sources in the vocal tract with modeling of the tubes and obstructions in the vocal tract. The resulting articulatory model is implemented with a GUI, including cross-section of the head, to permit synthesis of spoken and singing voice.

4.7.2 Encoding and Transmitting Speech

The simplest way to encode speech is to use PCM, discussed above. The 8-bit, 8-kHz standard for speech is of significantly lower quality than what is required for music. Still, at the nominal 64-kb/sec rate for speech, if one bit per sample can be saved, then the total saving is 8 kb/sec. Methods for lowering the bit rate thus remain an active area of research. The ADPCM method discussed above can easily save 2 to 4 bits per sample.

PCM, ADPCM, and related methods attempt to describe the waveform itself. There are other methods, such as the subband coding discussed above under MPEG. We now turn to another class of methods, called voice coders, or vocoders.

The human vocal tract can be simplified by assuming, for example, that the source of vibration for voiced sounds is not affected by the rest of the vocal tract. The series of filters that model the vocal tract can be modeled such that if one filter changes, there is no effect on the others. Under such conditions, we can calculate the voice model coefficients independently of the fundamental frequency or the voiced/unvoiced decision. We can also reasonably assume that formants change quite slowly compared to the rate of individual pulses from the vocal tract and transmit the filter coefficients at a slower rate.

The channel vocoder pioneered by Dudley [77] analyzes speech as a bank of filters. The driving function for synthesis is noise or a series of pulses like those generated by the vocal cords. The filter coefficients, the fundamental frequency, and the voiced/unvoiced decision are transmitted. Research on the channel vocoder ultimately led to the phase vocoder implementation mentioned above.

Linear prediction, also mentioned above, models the vocal tract as a source followed by a series of filters [78]. Those filters can be modeled as a series of tubes, and the tube parameters can be transmitted. There is, unfortunately, no intuitive relationship between tube parameters and, say, the spectrogram representation, but LPC is certainly adequate for compressing speech for reproduction in chips. One transmits the pitch period, gain, the voice/unvoiced decision, and a dozen or so filter coefficients.

In a different kind of system, both encoder and decoder can contain a lookup table. Each table entry is a vector containing a series of samples. Rather than transmit the samples, one can transmit just the index into the table. If the exact sequence of samples cannot be found, the closest vector is transmitted. This method can be used to transmit the waveform itself or sequences of coefficients for a vocoder [79].

As we have seen, the basic data rate is 64 kb/sec (CCITT G.211) for 8-bit PCM. With ADPCM, 4 to 6 bits per sample are transmitted, for 32 to 48 kb/sec; there is a 32 kb/sec CCITT standard G.721 for ADPCM. Some subband coding systems operate as low as 16 kb/sec. For higher-quality speech with subband coding, there is CCITT G.722 for 50–7000 Hz at a 64-kb/sec rate. For various methods of coding, bit rates can fall as low as 2400-bit/s, but with a corresponding reduction in quality. There is a good discussion of the various CCITT standards in [80,81]. Improvements in quality and lowering bit rate are being driven (as always) by military research and the usual telephone companies, but also by factors such as the desire to incorporate voice with other data, such as in ISDN, or the need to scrunch more channels from cellular networks.

4.7.3 Speech Synthesis

A major driving force in speech synthesis has come from text-to-speech (TTS). A brief overview can be found in [82]. A more extensive introduction is in [83,84].

A TTS system assumes that the text already exists in machine-readable form, such as an ASCII file. The machine-readable form is possibly obtained from optical character recognition. TTS converts the text symbols to a parameter stream representing sounds. This includes expanding common abbreviations, such as "Pres.," and symbols like "&." Also, the system figures out how to handle numbers: 1492 can be read as a date, and even the dollar amount $1492.00 could be read starting with "fourteen hundred . . ." or "one thousand four hundred. . . ." After creating a uniform symbol stream, the system creates initial sound parameter representation, often at the word level—some words may simply be looked up in a dictionary.

Other parts of the stream are broken down into morphemes, the syntactic basic units of the language. With luck, a group of text symbols corresponds to one morpheme. It is often the case that there is a regular mapping between the symbols of such a group and some sound, in which case the group can be turned into sound. As a last resort, the system converts individual text symbols to sound using rules. The system synthesizes sounds from the parameter string based on an articulatory model [85], or using sampled sounds, LPC, or formants. The synthesis system may store units at the level of phonemes, diphthongs, syllables, or words.

The sounds are concatenated. Then higher-level elements of speech such as prosody (the rise and fall of pitch), overall emphasis (e.g., whisper, shout), and glottal stops are added. Syntactical analysis provides the basis for adjustments in clause ends or sentence ends, e.g., the rise in pitch for a question.

4.7.4 Speech Recognition

A speech recognition system starts by breaking speech down into a parametric representation. The first step is to isolate speech segments in time. (One big problem, as in music, lies in the fact that in the acoustic signal, there are no discrete units.) The speech signal is parameterized as the outputs of a bank of bandpass filters, or as LPC coefficients, or some form derived from LPC coefficients, such as cepstral coefficients (the log of the transform of the spectrum). Individual frames of data typically last on the order of 10–30 msec. The frames are matched against a template, using some measure of goodness of fit between input and template. The template typically contains raw spectral data or vector quantized spectral data. The measure of fit can be improved by dynamic time warping, in which the time-varying input signal is measured against several time-varying templates. The time scale of the input is modified nonmonotonically so that the representation of the input best matches the representation of the template. In this manner, subtle differences in timing that would otherwise throw off template matching can be removed ([86], p. 28). This is similar to the WordFit time adjustment scheme discussed in digital signal processing, above.

Another algorithm for improving identification involves Hidden Markov Models (HMM) [87]. The core of an HMM identification system is a finite-state machine, with probabilities associated with the transition from one state to another. But the states of the machine cannot be directly observed. Instead, a finite number of observations can be made about the current state of the state machine. The observations are stochastically related to the actual states. There is an algorithm for deriving the probability that a given sequence of observations was generated by a given sequence of states. In an HMM-based system, each element (e.g., phoneme) has one model representing it, that is, one state machine with associated probable initial state, transition probabilities, and observation probabilities. There is also an algorithm for deciding which of a set of models produced the speech being analyzed. Recently, neural networks have come to be used for speaker identification and speaker verification. Chapter 10 of [88] discusses other applications of neural nets in speech.

Obviously, speech recognition systems have an easier job if all speakers speak the same text. Isolated words are easier, connected speech is harder. Handling any arbitrary speaker from the general population is harder. Allowing an arbitrary vocabulary makes the task harder still. Currently, typical systems achieve an accuracy in the mid 90 percent range for dictionaries of several hundred words spoken by different speakers. For further information, see [55,89].

4.8 DIGITAL AUDIO AND THE COMPUTER

It is now common to find audio capabilities in many computers, large and small. In this last section, we review the capabilities for audio and music at various levels of quality.

One fundamental capability is audio storage: 8-bit audio at an 8-kHz sample rate consumes 1 KB for 1 second of sound. CD-quality audio (stereo, 16-bit linear PCM, 44.1-kHz sample rate) consumes 176 KB per second, and stereo sound at the professional rate of 48 kHz eats almost 200 kbytes per second. Sound storage on disk thus requires large disks.

Sound playback and recording require a DAC and ADC, respectively. The 8-bit hardware on many computers is adequate for speech and basic algorithm testing, but not for professional music or recording. Plug-in boards with 16-bit DACs and ADCs are the solution if such hardware is not provided as part of the basic system. Even better audio quality can be had with external conversion units, using, for example, a SCSI connector.

For digital input and output, a connector for AES/EBU transmission and/or an SPDIF connector is required. Often, the DACs and ADCs on an external DAT player with an appropriate interface can be used instead of dedicated hardware.

For real-time processing of sound, plug-in cards and external units are available with commercially available DSP chips. With a single chip, typically a stereo stream can be input, processed, and output. In such a scheme, the sound does not necessarily go to disk. Such systems can also generate three-dimensional audio, for example. There is a tendency nowadays to use

RISC or CISC chips instead of DSP chips for dedicated processing. In some systems, a single RISC chip is fast enough to provide the generalized compute power as well as extra cycles for sound processing. Using two RISC chips in parallel, one for general computing and one for real-time applications, has the advantage that the software development is the same for both. (When a DSP chip is used, the software environment is usually radically different from that for the computer's CPU.) For music synthesis, there are also plug-in cards currently available implementing FM synthesis, sampling, and other synthesis techniques.

Editing sound requires a good graphics system; for editing transform data, graphics accelerators are often recommended, as the amount of data can be enormous. Sound can be edited on the screens of portable computers, but a large crisp color monitor is to be preferred.

Given all the power in and fanfare surrounding UNIX workstations, such as the Sun or SPARC, one would expect them to support music easily. But UNIX is not a real-time operating system, and musicians complain when their music stops dead while the operating system services something else.

Finally, a remark about sound in personal computers and multimedia is in order. For many years, the basic capabilities implied in this chapter have been included in plug-in boards for the PC, such as the SoundBlaster. With the release of documents such as Multimedia PC Specification Version 1.0 (Microsoft), we can expect the computer industry to follow a path well known to digital audio and computer music specialists. The software protocols will become standardized, as will music and sound exchange formats. The quality of the sound coming into and out of the system will improve. The capabilities of the system will be expanded to include more and more sophisticated techniques.

4.9 CLOSING REMARKS

First, a comment is in order about the relative difficulty of implementing audio versus video/graphics in a multimedia system. Audio is often considered as easier than video or graphics, perhaps because the bandwidth is smaller. But audio imposes significant design constraints which must be handled by themselves. At the same time, Loeb [11] makes the interesting argument that audio provides a good platform for prototyping generalized applications with continuous data streams, precisely because the data rates in audio are lower.

Second, I would like to provide a gentle warning for those coming to audio from other domains. It is tempting to take some of the implications of the theory given above and to implement them in hardware, expecting a system to fall in place. In the music world, we have seen this happen time and time again, with almost predictable results. Consider the developers of the ill-fated Synthia synthesizer (ca. 1980) who implemented Fourier analysis and synthesis. After months of work in their garage, they came up with a synthesizer that had a beautiful graphics user interface, one that has rarely been equaled since in an integrated graphics user interface on a synthesizer. But this was a synthesizer that sounded awful (I heard it myself). The developers had assumed that the theory would give them good orchestral sounds, and it didn't. Or consider the hardware card discussed in [90]. It became the hardware basis for the commercial synthesizer called GDS and Synergy [91] still used by Wendy Carlos [92]. But the software and musical sound development by far exceeded the cost and time needed for the hardware. Ultimately, the project failed. In working with musical systems, it is necessary to plan for more than just the hardware necessary to take the physical characteristics of sound into account.

I close with a remark about the relative importance of audio in digital systems (see also [93]). Historically, starting perhaps with the invention of cuneiform, the act of committing data to a permanent medium required, for the most part, the use of the hands and eyes. The invention of the typewriter led to the QWERTY keyboard being identified with the permanent recording of data. As data processing machinery and computers were developed, it was natural that the QWERTY keyboard would be a standard feature of the hardware, just as a musical keyboard was a standard feature of early music synthesizers. The recent pen operating system loosens the connection between the QWERTY keyboard and the computer, but still requires use of the hand and the eye. With audio inputs and outputs such as speech and sound synthesis, text-to-speech, audio window systems, and speech recognition, one can conceive of a computer with an entirely audio interface. For the first time in several millennia, the act of recording data can be freed from the necessity of using the hand and the eye. Indeed, perhaps for the first time since cuneiform, the medium of communication reverts to (recorded) human speech, not just icons representing human communication. I do not advocate the development of a purely audio-based computer (would the audio user interface be an AUI?). Rather, I wish to point out that audio as a computer I/O channel has reached a level of development where it is strong enough to serve as a full-fledged part of generalized I/O. We know that human communication works at its fullest when the various perceptual modes are working together. (After all, the telephone does not match the tête-à-tête.) I feel that the most effective systems of tomorrow will include audio (music and speech) at least on equal footing with other modes of interaction.

4.10 ACKNOWLEDGMENTS

I appreciate the assistance of Thom Blum, Jeff Barish, Marina Bosi, Perry Cook, Robert Currie, Robert Duisberg, Robert Gross, John Buford, Shoshana Loeb, Mike Minnick, Ken Pohlmann, Toby Richards, Curtis Roads, Bill Schottstaedt, John Snell, and Julius O. Smith III as I was preparing this chapter.

4.11 REFERENCES

1. Mathews, Max V., Miller, Joan E., Moore, F. Richard, Pierce, John R., and Risset, Jean-Claude. *The Technology of Computer Music.* MIT Press. 1969.
2. Rosenberg, Jonathan, Kraut, R., Gomez, L., and Buzzard, C. Multimedia Communications for Users. *IEEE Communications Magazine.* vol. 30. 1992. pp. 20–36.
3. Kramer, G., (ed.). Proceedings of ICAD '92 (International Conference on Auditory Display). *Proceedings of the Santa Fe Institute Science Board #18.* Addison-Wesley. 1993.
4. Kramer, G., and Ellison, S. Audification: The Use of Sound to Display Multivariate Data. *Proceedings of the 1991 International Computer Music Conference.* Computer Music Association. 1991. pp. 214–221.
5. Smith, Stuart, Grinstein, G. G., and Bergeron, R. D. Stereophonic and Surface Sound Generation for Exploratory Data Analysis. *Conference Proceedings, CHI 90.* 1990. pp. 125–132. Reprinted in M. M. Blatter and R. Dannenberg (eds.), *Multimedia Interface Design.* ACM Press. New York. 1992. pp. 73–182.
6. Handel, S. *Listening.* MIT Press. 1989.
7. Buser, H. *Audition.* Éditeurs des science et des arts. Paris. 1987. Translated by R. H. Kay. MIT Press. 1992.
8. Carterette, E. C., and Friedman, M. P. *Handbook of Perception.* Academic Press. 1978.
9. Olson, H. F. *Music, Physics, and Engineering.* 2nd ed. Dover. 1967.
10. Plomp, Reinier. *Aspects of Tone Sensation: A Psychophysical Study.* Academic Press. 1976.
11. Loeb, Shoshana, Hill, R., and Brinck, T. Lessons from LyricTime: A Prototype Multimedia System. *Proceedings of Multimedia '92, Fourth IEEE ComSoc International Workshop on Multimedia Communications.* 1992. pp. 106–110.
12. Grey, John M. An Exploration of Musical Timbre. Ph.D. diss. Department of Psychology. Stanford University. Department of Music Report STAN-M-2. 1975.
13. Strawn, J. Editing Time-Varying Spectra. *Journal of the Audio Engineering Society,* vol. 35, no. 5. pp. 337–351. 1987.
14. Strawn, J. Modeling Musical Transitions. Ph.D. diss. Department of Music. Stanford University. Department of Music Report STAN-M-26. 1985.
15. Saldanha, E. L., and Corso, John F. Timbre Cues and the Identification of Musical Instruments. *Journal of the Acoustical Society of America* 36. 1964. pp. 2021–26.
16. Binding, Carl, Schmandt, C., Lantz, K. A., and Arons, B. Workstation Audio and Window-Based Graphics: Similarities and Differences. *IFIP Working Conference on Engineering for Human-Computer Interaction.* 1989.
17. Loy, D. G. Notes on the Implementation of MUSBOX: A Compiler for the Systems Concepts Digital Synthesizer. *Computer Music Journal* 5,1. 1981. pp. 34–50.
18. Fielder, L., and Davidson, G. A. AC-2: A Family of Low Complexity Transform Based Music Coders. *Proceedings of the 10th International AES Conference: Images of Audio.* Audio Engineering Society. 1992. pp. 57–70.
19. Pohlmann, K. *The Compact Disc Handbook.* 2nd ed. A-R Editions (Computer Music and Digital Audio Series). 1992.
20. Tobias, J. V. *Foundations of Modern Auditory Theory.* Academic Press. 1970.
21. Greiner, R. A., and Melton, D. E. Observations on the Audibility of Acoustic Polarity. Paper presented at the 1991 Audio Engineering Society Convention, New York. Preprint no. 3170. 1991.
22. Johnsen, Clark. Proofs of an Absolute Polarity. Paper presented at the 1991 Audio Engineering Society Convention, New York. Preprint no. 3169. 1991.
23. Blauert, J. *Rumliches Hören.* Hirzel. 1974. Translated by J. Allen as *Spatial Hearing: The Psychophysics of Human Sound Localization.* MIT Press. 1983.
24. Kendall, G. S., and Rodgers, C. A. Puddie. The Simulation of Three-Dimensional Localization Cues for Headphone Listening. In L. Austin and T. Clark (comps.), *Proceedings, 1981 International Computer Music Conference.* Computer Music Association. 1983. pp. 225–243.

25. Moorer, James A. About This Reverberation Business. *Computer Music Journal* 3,2. 1979. pp. 13–28. Reprinted in C. Roads and J. Strawn (eds.), *Foundations of Computer Music*. MIT Press. 1985. pp. 605–639.
26. Brierley, H. G. *Telecommunications Engineering*. Edward Arnold. 1986.
27. Cheval, E. Logarithmic/Linear Conversion Routines for DSP56000/1 (Application Note ANE408/D). Motorola Literature Distribution. 1990.
28. Portnoff, Michael R. Time-Scale Modification of Speech Based on Short-Time Fourier Analysis. Ph.D. diss. Department of Electrical Engineering and Computer Science. MIT. 1978.
29. Strawn, J. Analysis and Synthesis of Musical Transitions Using the Discrete Short-Time Fourier Transform. *Journal of the Audio Engineering Society*, 35(1/2):3–14. 1987.
30. Roads, Curtis, with Strawn, J., Abbott, C., and Gordon, J. *Computer Music Tutorial*. MIT Press. (in press)
31. Rozenberg, M. Microcomputer-Controlled Sound Processing Using Walsh Functions. *Computer Music Journal* 3,1. 1979. pp. 42–47.
32. Tsutsui, K., Suzuki, H., Shimoyoshi, O., Sonohara, M., Akagiri, K., and Heddle., R. M. ATRAC: Adaptive Transform Acoustic Coding for MiniDisc. Paper presented at the 1992 Audio Engineering Society Convention, San Francisco. Preprint no. 3456. 1992.
33. Wirtz, G. C. Digital Compact Cassette: The Audio Coding Technique. Paper presented at the 1991 Audio Engineering Society Convention, New York. Preprint no. 3216. 1991.
34. Crochiere, R. E. Real-Time Speech Coding. *IEEE Transactions on Communication COM-30*. 1982.
35. LeGall, Didier. MPEG: A Video Compression Standard for Multimedia Applications. *Communications of the ACM* 34,4. 1991. pp. 46–63.
36. Brandenburg, K., and Stoll, G. The ISO/MPEG-Audio Codec: A Generic Standard for Coding of High Quality Digital Audio. Paper presented at the 1992 Audio Engineering Society Convention, Vienna, Austria. Preprint no. 3336. 1992.
37. Herre, J., and Eberlein, E. Combined Stereo Coding. Paper presented at the 1992 Audio Engineering Society Convention, San Francisco. Preprint no. 3369. 1992
38. Wiese, D. Optimization of Error Detection and Concealment for ISO/MPEG/AUDIO CODECs Layers I and II. Paper presented at the 1992 Audio Engineering Society Convention, San Francisco. Preprint no. 3368. 1992.
39. Cann, R. An Analysis/Synthesis Tutorial. In C. Roads and J. Strawn (eds.), *Foundations of Computer Music*. MIT Press. 1985. pp. 114–144.
40. Dodge, C., and Jerse, T. A. *Computer Music Synthesis, Composition, and Performance*. Schirmer. 1985.
41. Lansky, P., and Stieglitz, K. Synthesis of Timbral Families by Warped Linear Prediction. *Computer Music Journal* 5,3. 1981. pp. 45–49.
42. Chowning, J. The Synthesis of Complex Audio Spectra by Means of Frequency Modulation. *Journal of the Audio Engineering Society*. 21(7):526–534. 1973.
43. Roads, C., and Strawn, J. (eds.). *Foundations of Computer Music*. MIT Press. 1985.
44. Roads, C. Granular Synthesis of Sound. In C. Roads and J. Strawn (eds.), *Foundations of Computer Music*. MIT Press. 1985. pp. 145–159.
45. LeBrun, M. Digital Waveshaping Synthesis. *Journal of the Audio Engineering Society* 27. 1977. pp. 250–266.
46. Rodet, Xavier, Potard, Y., and Barrire, J.-B. The CHANT Project: From Synthesis of the Singing Voice to Synthesis in General. *Computer Music Journal* 8(3):15–31. 1984.
47. Karplus, K., and Strong, A. Digital Synthesis of Plucked-String and Drum Timbres. *Computer Music Journal* 7,2. 1983. pp. 43–55.
48. Adams, R., and Kwan., T. VLSI Architecture for Asynchronous Sample-Rate Conversion. Paper presented at the 1992 Audio Engineering Society Convention, San Francisco. Preprint no. 3348. 1992.
49. Finger, R. A. AES3-1992: The Revised Two-Channel Digital Audio Interface. *Journal of the Audio Engineering Society* 40,3. 1992. pp. 107–116.

50. AES Recommended Practice for Digital Audio Engineering—Serial Multichannel Audio Digital Interface (MADI). *Journal of the Audio Engineering Association* 39,5. May 1991. pp. 368–377.
51. Rumsey, F. *Digital Audio Operations*. Focal Press. 1991.
52. Watkinson, J. *The Art of Digital Audio*. Focal Press. 1988.
53. Lindemann, E. Routes to Chaos in a Non-Linear Musical Instrument Model. Paper presented at the 1988 Audio Engineering Society Convention, Paris. Preprint no. 2621. 1988.
54. Bloom, P. J. Use of Dynamic Programmming for automatic Synchronization of Two Similar Speech Signals. *ICASSP Proceedings*. vol. 1. 1984. pp. 2.6.1–2.6.4.
55. Rabiner, L. R., and Levinson, S. E. Isolated and Connected Word Recognition Theory and Selected Applications. *IEEE Transactions on Communications* COM-29,5. 1981. pp. 621–659.
56. Arons, Barry, Binding, C., Lantz, K. A., and Schmandt, C. The VOX Audio Server. *Second IEEE International Workshop on Multimedia Communications*. 1989.
57. Reichbach, J. D., and Kemmerer, R. A. SoundWorks: An Object-Oriented Distributed System for Digital Sound. In D. Baggi (ed.), *Readings in Computer-Generated Music*. IEEE Computer Society Press. 1992. pp. 161–180.
58. 100 Years with Stereo: The Beginning. *Journal of the Audio Engineering Society* 29,5. May 1981. pp. 368-372.
59. Goldberg, Ron. 3-D Audio. *Electronic Musician* 8,10. October 1992. pp. 38–47.
60. Ludwig, L., Pincever, N. and Cohen, M. Extending the Notion of a Window System to Audio. *IEEE Computer* 23,8. 1990. pp. 66–72.
61. Digital Signal Processing Committee. IEEE Acoustics, Speech, and Signal Processing Society. *Programs for Digital Signal Processing*. IEEE Press. 1979.
62. Press, W. H., Flannery, B., Teukolsky, S., and Vetterling, W. *Numerical Recipes in C*. Cambridge University Press. 1988.
63. Embree, P. M., and Kimble, B. *C Language Algorithms for Digital Signal Processing*. Prentice-Hall. 1991.
64. AT&T. *VCOS Multimedia Development Kit Technical Reference Manual, Version 1.0.*
65. Yavelow, C. *Macworld Music and Sound Bible*. IDG Books. 1992.
66. Pressing, J. *Synthesizer Performance and Real-Time Techniques*. A-R Editions (Computer Music and Digital Audio Series). 1992.
67. International MIDI Association, 5316 W. 57th Street, Los Angeles CA 90056.
68. Rothstein, J. *MIDI: A Comprehensive Introduction*. A-R Editions (Computer Music and Digital Audio Series). 1992.
69. DeFuria, S., and Scacciaferro, J. *MIDI Programming for the Macintosh*. M&T Publishing. 1988.
70. Loy, G. Musicians Make a Standard: The MIDI Phenomenon. *Computer Music Journal* 9,4. 1985. pp. 8–26.
71. Moore, F. R. The Dysfunctions of MIDI. *Computer Music Journal* 12,1. 1988. pp. 19–28.
72. Kretz, Francis, and Colatis, F. Standardizing Hypermedia Information Objects. *IEEE Communications Magazine*. 1992. pp. 60–70.
73. Cherry, Colin. *On Human Communication: A Review, a Survey, and a Criticism*. Science Editions. 1961.
74. Logan, John S., Greene, B. G., and Pisoni, D. B. Segmental Intelligibility of Synthetic Speech Produced by Rule. *JASA* 86,2. 1989. pp. 566–581.
75. Steeneken, Herman J. M. Quality Evaluation of Speech Processing Systems. In A. N. Ince (ed.), *Digital Speech Processing: Speech Coding, Synthesis and Recognition*. Kluwer. 1992, pp. 127–159. TK 7882 S65 D54 1992.
76. Cook, P. R. *Identification of Control Parameters in an Articulatory Vocal Tract Model, With Applications to the Synthesis of Singing*. Ph.D. diss. Department of Music. Stanford University. Dept. of Music Report STAN-M-68. 1990.
77. Dudley, H. The vocoder. *Bell Labs Record* 17. 1939. pp. 122–126.
78. Markel, J. D., and Gray, A. H. *Linear Prediction of Speech*. Springer-Verlag. 1976.
79. Gersho, A., Wang, S., and Zeger, K. *Vector Quantization Techniques in Speech Coding*. Marcel Dekker. 1992.

80. Ince, A. N. Speech Processing Standards. In A. N. Ince (ed.), *Digital Speech Processing: Speech Coding, Synthesis and Recognition*. Kluwer. 1992. pp. 161–188.
81. Jayant, N. High-Quality Coding of Telephone Speech and Wideband Audio. In S. Furui and M. Sondhi (eds.), *Advances in Speech Signal Processing*. Marcel Dekker. 1992. pp. 85–108. Eng TK 7882 S65 A29 1992.
82. O'Malley, Michael H. Text-to-Speech Conversion Technology. *IEEE Computer*. 1990. pp. 17–23.
83. Klatt, D. H. Review of Text-to-Speech Conversion for English. *Journal of the Acoustical Society of America* 82,3. 1987. pp. 737–793.
84. Allen, Jonathan. Overview of Text-to-Speech Systems. In S. Furui and M. Sondhi (eds.), *Advances in Speech Signal Processing*. Marcel Dekker. 1992. pp. 741–790.
85. Cook, P. R. LECTOR: An Ecclesiastical Latin Control Language for the SPASM/Singer Instrument. *Proceedings of the International Computer Music Conference, Montreal*. Computer Music Association. 1991. pp. 319–321.
86. Peacocke, Richard D., and D. H. Graf. An Introduction to Speech and Speaker Recognition. *IEEE Computer* 23,8. 1990. pp. 26–33.
87. Juang, B.-H., and Rabiner, L. R. Issues in Using Hidden Markov Models for Speech Recognition. In S. Furui and M. Sondhi (eds.), *Advances in Speech Signal Processing*. Marcel Dekker. 1992. pp. 509–553.
88. Morgan, D. P., and Scofield, C. L. *Neural Networks and Speech Processing*. Kluwer. 1991.
89. Rosenberg, A. E., and Soong, F. K. Recent Research in Automatic Speaker Recognition. In S. Furui and M. Sondhi (eds.), *Advances in Speech Signal Processing*. Marcel Dekker. 1992. pp. 701–738.
90. Alles, H. G. An Inexpensive Digital Music Synthesizer. *Computer Music Journal* 3,3. 1979. pp. 28–37.
91. Kaplan, S. J. Developing a Commercial Digital Sound Synthesizer. *Computer Music Journal* 5,3. 1981. pp. 62–73.
92. Milano, D., and Doerschuk, R. L. Back to Bach—After 25 Years, Wendy Carlos Remakes "Switched-on Bach," the Album That Made Synthesizers Famous. *Keyboard* 18,8. August 1992. pp. 88–110.
93. Buxton, W., Gaver, W. and Bly, S. *Auditory Interfaces: The Use of Non-Speech Audio at the Interface. Cambridge. Tutorial 10 CHI '89. ACM Press. 1989.*

CHAPTER 5

VIDEO TECHNOLOGY[1]

Arch C. Luther
Luther Associates

In order to pursue the discussion of multimedia, we need to understand the principles of analog video as they exist in the television industry. In most cases we will be using standard television equipment and systems to originally produce our video—converting it to digital video will be a later step. Therefore, a good knowledge of analog video nomenclature, characteristics, performance, and limitations will be essential to our appreciation of the overall video system. This chapter will explain analog video fundamentals as they relate to the uses of video in digital formats. It presents a simplified model of an analog video system, which will probably seem elementary to readers who are already familiar with video; however, this chapter is intended for a reader who does not have a video background. You will be introduced to a lot of video and television terminology, which will be particularly useful in other portions of this book that discuss digital video and HDTV.

Most things in nature are analog—real images and sounds are based on light intensity and sound pressure values, which are continuous functions in space and time. For television we must convert images and sounds to electrical signals. That is done by appropriate use of sensors, also called

[1] This chapter is reprinted from Chapter 2, *Analog Video Fundamentals in Digital Video in the PC Environment*, 2nd ed., by Arch C. Luther, McGraw-Hill, 1991. Reprinted by permission of McGraw-Hill.

transducers. Sensors for converting images and sounds to electronic signals are typically analog devices, with analog outputs. The world of television and sound recording is based on these devices. Video cameras and microphones (the sensors) are familiar objects to almost everyone, and their purpose is generally well understood. Here, however, we will concentrate on how they work. This chapter is concerned with video.

5.1 RASTER SCANNING PRINCIPLES

The purpose of a video camera is to convert an image in front of the camera into an electrical signal. An electrical signal has only one value at any instant in time—it is one-dimensional, but an image is two-dimensional, having many values at all the different positions in the image. Conversion of the two-dimensional image into a one-dimensional electrical signal is accomplished by *scanning* that image in an orderly pattern called a *raster*. With scanning, we move a sensing point rapidly over the image—fast enough to capture the complete image before it moves too much. As the sensing point moves, the electrical output changes in response to the brightness or color of the image point beneath the sensing point. The varying electrical signal from the sensor then represents the image as a series of values spread out in time—this is called a *video signal*.

Figure 5.1 shows a raster scanning pattern. Scanning of the image begins at the upper left corner and progresses horizontally across the image, making a scanning line. At the same time, the scanning point is being moved down at a much slower rate. When the right side of the image is reached, the scanning point snaps back to the left side of the image. Because of the slow vertical motion of the scanning point, it is now a little below the starting point of the first line. It then scans across again on the next line, snaps back, and continues until the full height of the image has been scanned by a series of lines. During each line scanned, the electrical output from the scanning sensor represents the light intensity of the image at each position of the scanning point. During the snap-back time (known as the *horizontal blanking interval*) it is customary to turn off the sensor so a zero-output (or blanking level) signal is sent out. The signal from a complete scan of the image is a sequence of line signals, separated by horizontal blanking intervals. This set of scanning lines is called a *frame*.

5.1.1 Aspect Ratio

An important parameter of scanning is the *aspect ratio*—it is the ratio of the length of a scanning line horizontally on the image, to the distance covered vertically on the image by all the scanning lines. Aspect ratio can also be thought of as the width-to-height ratio of a frame. In present-day television,

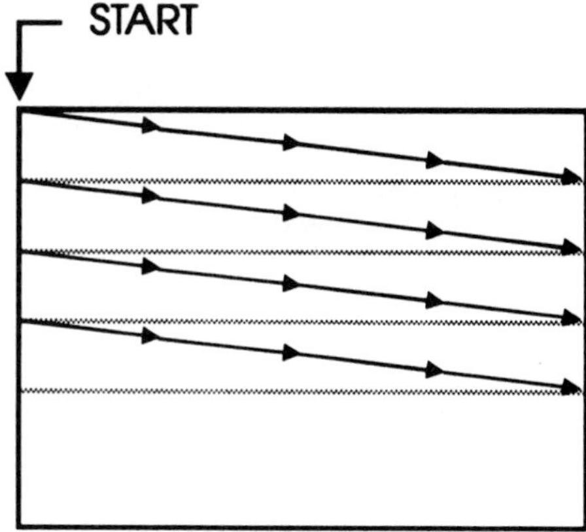

Figure 5.1 Raster scanning

aspect ratio is standardized at 4:3. Other imaging systems, such as movies, use different aspect ratios ranging as high as 2:1 for some systems.

5.1.2 Sync

If the electrical signal from a scanning process is used to modulate the brightness of the beam in a cathode-ray tube (CRT) that is being scanned exactly the same way as the sensor, the original image will be reproduced. This is what happens in a television set or a video monitor. However, the electrical signal(s) sent to the monitor must contain some additional information to ensure that the monitor scanning will be in synchronism with the sensor's scanning. This information is called sync information, and it may be included within the video signal itself during the blanking intervals, or it may be sent on a separate cable (or cables) just for the sync information.

5.1.3 Resolution

Resolution is the ability of a television system to reproduce fine detail in the scene. It is expressed separately for horizontal and vertical directions.

Horizontal Resolution

As the scanning point moves across one line, the electrical signal output from the sensor changes continuously in response to the light level of the part of the image that the sensor sees. One measure of scanning performance is the *horizontal resolution* of the pickup system, which depends on the size of the scanning sensitive point. A smaller sensitive point will give higher resolution. Figure 5.2 shows the result of scanning across a sharp vertical edge in an image using scanning sensors of different sizes. Note that the electrical output is zero while the scanning sensor is looking at the black

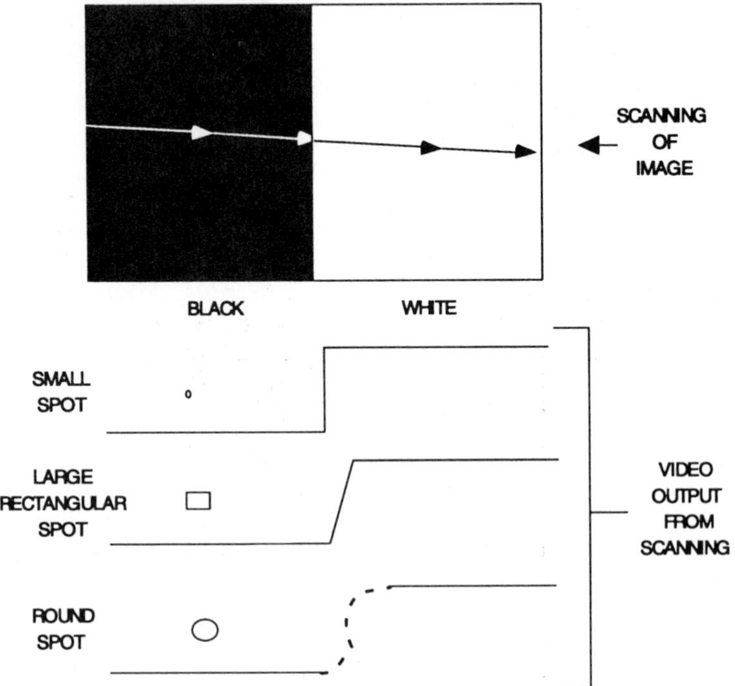

Figure 5.2 Scanning across a vertical edge with different sizes and shapes of scanning spots

area, and the output begins to rise as the sensor moves partially onto the white area. Full output (100) is reached when the sensor is completely on the white area.

To test the horizontal resolution performance of a system, which also measures the capability to reproduce horizontal fine detail, we place closely spaced vertical lines in front of the camera. If the sensor area is smaller than the space between the vertical lines, the lines will be reproduced, but when the sensor is too large, the lines will average out under the sensor and will not be seen in the output signal. In the television business, horizontal resolution is measured by counting the number of black and white vertical lines that can be reproduced in a distance corresponding to the raster height. (The raster height was chosen as the standard basis for specifying television resolutions, both horizontal and vertical.) Thus, a system that is said to have a horizontal resolution of 400 lines can reproduce 200 white and 200 black lines alternating across a horizontal distance corresponding to the height of the image.

Scanning across a pattern of vertical black and white lines produces a high-frequency electrical signal. It is important that the circuits used for processing or transmitting these signals have adequate bandwidth for the signal. Without going into the details of deriving the numbers, broadcast television systems require a bandwidth of 1 MHz for each 80 lines of horizontal resolution. The North American broadcast television system is designed for a bandwidth of 4.5 MHz, and this has a theoretical horizontal resolution limit of 360 lines. Bandwidth considerations affect the choice of scanning parameters, as we will see later.

Vertical Resolution

The vertical resolution of a video system depends on the number of scanning lines used in one frame. The more lines there are, the higher is the vertical resolution. Broadcast television systems use either 525 lines (North America and Japan) or 625 lines (Europe, etc.) per frame. In a sense, the vertical resolution response of television is not an analog process because a discrete number of samples are taken vertically—one for each scanning line. The result is that the vertical resolution response of television often displays sampling artifacts such as aliasing.

A small number of lines out of each frame (typically 40) are devoted to the vertical blanking interval. Both blanking intervals (horizontal and vertical) were originally intended to give time for the scanning beam in cameras or monitors to retrace before starting the next line or the next frame. However, in modern systems they have many other uses, since these intervals represent nonactive picture time where different information can be transmitted along with the video signal.

5.1.4 Frame Rates for Motion

For motion video, many frames must be scanned each second to produce the effect of smooth motion. In standard broadcast video systems, normal frame rates are 25 or 30 frames per second, depending on the country you are in. However, these frame rates—although they are high enough to deliver smooth motion—are not high enough to prevent a video display from having flicker. In order for the human eye not to perceive flicker in a bright image, the refresh rate of the image must be higher than 50 per second. However, to speed up the frame rate to that range while preserving horizontal resolution would require speeding up of all the scanning, both horizontal and vertical, therefore increasing the system bandwidth. To avoid this difficulty, all television systems use *interlace*.

Interlace in a television system means that more than one vertical scan is used to reproduce a complete frame. Broadcast television uses 2:1 interlace—2 vertical scans (fields) make up a complete frame. Larger interlace numbers have also been used in some special-purpose television systems. With 2:1 interlace, one vertical scan displays all the odd lines of a frame, and then a second vertical scan puts in all the even lines. At 30 frames per second (North America and Japan), the vertical rate is 60 scans per second. Since the eye does not readily see flickering objects that are small, the 30 per second repetition rate of any one line is not seen as flicker, but rather the entire picture appears to be being refreshed at 60 per second.

Although interlace improves large-area flicker, it introduces some other artifacts that are the reason it is not often used with computer systems. One of these is *gear-toothing*, a motion artifact that shows jagged edges on moving vertical objects. This occurs because the two fields of a frame are effectively captured at different times, 1/60 second apart. If the image moves significantly in that time, the edges do not line up between the odd and even lines. This problem may be visually masked by the motion in the image, but if you try to capture a still frame from a moving scene, it will be obvious in the still frame. Therefore, still frames from a television system are usually taken from only one field, and the odd and even lines are generated from only one field.

Another interlace artifact is *interline flicker*, a problem in stationary images which have sharp, high-contrast horizontal edges or fine horizontal (or near-horizontal) lines. This is not usually a problem with natural images, but it is serious with computer-generated images, where small high-contrast objects often occur in text characters or graphics. Therefore, computer displays do not often use interlace. Sometimes you want to convert a computer image or screen to television format to display it on a TV system; you have to use larger text and graphics in order to avoid interline flicker in the result.

5.2 SENSORS FOR TV CAMERAS

It is possible to make a television camera as described above with a single light-sensitive element; however, that proves not to be an effective approach because the sensor only receives light from a point in the image for the small fraction of time that the sensor is looking at that point. Light coming from a point while the sensor is not looking at that point is wasted, and this is most of the time. The result is that this type of video sensor has extremely poor sensitivity—it takes a large amount of light to make a picture. All present-day video pickup devices use an *integrating* approach to collect all the light from every point of an image all the time. The use of integration in a pickup device increases the sensitivity thousands of times compared to nonintegration pickup. With an integrating pickup device, the image is optically focused on a two-dimensional surface of photosensitive material, which is able to collect all the light from all points of the image all the time, continuously building up an electrical charge at each point of the image on the surface. This charge is then read out and converted to a voltage by a separate process which scans the photosensitive surface.

Without going into all possible kinds of pickup devices, there are two major types in use today which differ primarily in the way they scan out the integrated and stored charge image. Vacuum-tube pickup devices (vidicon, saticon, etc.) collect the stored charge on a special surface deposited at the end of a glass vacuum tube. An electron beam scans out the signal in this kind of device. The other type of pickup device is solid-state, where the stored charge image is developed on a silicon chip, which is scanned out by a solid-state array overlaid on the same chip. The solid-state devices are known by names like CCD, MOS, etc. Both kinds of devices can have excellent performance, but there are many detail differences including cost, size, and types of supporting electronics required to interface them into a camera system.

5.3 COLOR FUNDAMENTALS

The previous discussion assumed that the image being scanned was monochrome. However, most real images are in color, and what we really want is to reproduce the image in color. Color video makes use of the tri-stimulus theory of color reproduction, which says that any color can be reproduced by appropriate mixing of three primary colors. In grade school we learned to paint colors by doing just that—mixing the three colors: "red," "blue," and yellow. (The use of quotes on "red" and "blue," but not yellow, is deliberate and will be explained below.) These paint colors are used to create all possible colors by mixing them and painting on white paper. This process is known technically as subtractive color mixing—because we are starting with the white paper, which reflects all colors equally, and we are adding paints whose pigments filter the reflected white light to subtract certain colors. For example, we mix all three paint primaries to make black—meaning that we have subtracted all the reflected light (the paper looks black when no light at all is being reflected).

There is a different system of primary colors that is used when we wish to create colors by mixing colored lights. This is the additive primary system, and those colors are red, green, and blue. If we mix equal parts of red, green, and blue lights, we will get white light. Note that two of the additive primary color names seem to be the same as two of the subtractive primaries—"red" and "blue." This is not the case—red and blue are the correct names for the additive primaries, but the subtractive paint primaries "red" and "blue" should technically be named, respectively, magenta, which is a red-blue color, and cyan, which is a blue-green color.

The relationship of these two systems of primary colors can be somewhat confusing. Figure 5.3 shows how overlapping circles of color interact for both additive and subtractive systems. The left part of Figure 5.3 shows that white light consists of an equal mixture of the three additive primaries—red, green, and blue—and the right part of the figure shows that an equal mixture of subtractive primaries produces black. The subtractive relationships are easily related to the additive situation by thinking in terms of what the subtractive primaries do to the light reflected off the white paper. The subtractive "blue" primary prevents reflection of red light, and it can therefore be called minus red—it filters out red light. If you look through a

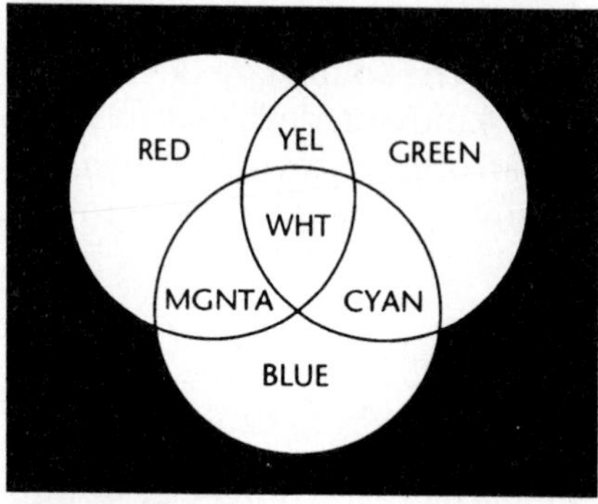

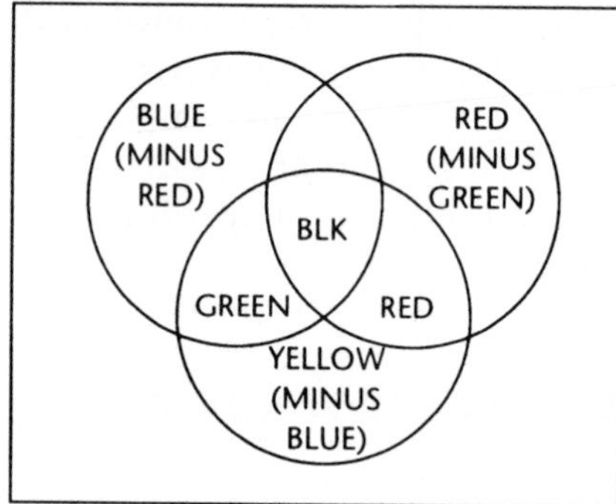

Figure 5.3 Additive and subtractive color mixing

subtractive "blue" filter, anything red will appear black—it has been filtered out. Similarly, the subtractive "red" removes green light, and the subtractive yellow removes blue light. Therefore, when we mix two subtractive colors, such as "blue" and yellow, we have removed both the red and the blue from the reflected light—leaving the green light—so mixing "blue" and yellow paint makes green. You can try the other combinations yourself to convince you that it agrees with what you learned in grade school.

5.4 COLOR VIDEO

Let's return to the additive system, because that is the basis for color video systems. Video is an additive color system because the color CRT used for display creates three light sources which are mixed to reproduce an image. A color CRT mixes red, green, and blue (RGB) light to make its image. The colors are produced by three fluorescent phosphor coatings, which are on the faceplate of the CRT. Typically, these are scanned by three electron guns, which are arranged so that each of them impinges on only one of the phosphors. (There are many ways to do this.) The intensity of each of the guns is controlled by an electrical signal representing the amount of red, green, or blue light needed at each point of the picture as the scanning progresses.

So a color video camera needs to produce three video signals to control the three guns in a color CRT. A conceptually simple way to do this is to split the light coming into a color video camera into three paths, filter those paths to separate the light into red, green, and blue, and then use three video pickup devices to create the necessary three signals. In fact, many video cameras do exactly that, as shown in Figure 5.4. This kind of camera, known as a three-tube or three-sensor camera, is complicated and expensive because of the three parallel paths. A lot of the difficulty arises because the

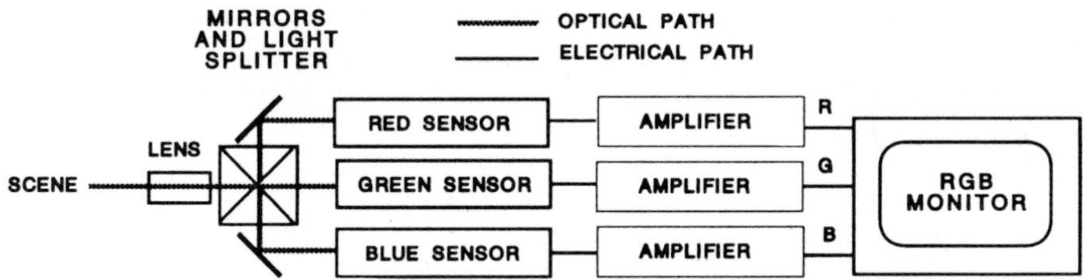

Figure 5.4 Block diagram of a three-sensor RGB color video camera

three sensors must be scanned in exact synchronism and exact physical relationship so that at any instant of time the three output signals represent the color values from exactly the same point in the image. This calls for extremely demanding electrical and mechanical accuracy and stability in a three-sensor camera design. The process for obtaining these exact relationships is known as *registration*. If a camera is not in exact registration, there will be color fringes around sharp edges in the reproduced picture. In spite of these difficulties, three-sensor cameras produce the highest quality images, and this approach is used for all the highest performance cameras.

There also are single-sensor color cameras, as shown in Figure 5.5. These use a system of filtering that splits the incoming light into spots of colored light, which appear side by side on the surface of the sensor. When the sensor is scanned in the normal way, the electrical output for each spot in the image will consist of three values coming in sequence, representing the red, green, and blue values for that point. Because of the critical relationship required between the sensor and the color filter, it is customary to build the color filter right on top of the sensor's storage layer. Electronic circuits are then used to separate the sequential output from the sensor as it is scanned into the required three separate signals. This approach is effective if the three spots of color can be small enough that they will not reduce the resolution of the final reproduction. Because that requires a threefold increase in the resolution of the sensor used (and that is difficult to come by), single-sensor cameras often are a compromise with respect to resolution. However, they are still the simplest, lowest cost, and most reliable cameras, and therefore single-sensor color cameras are widely used. All

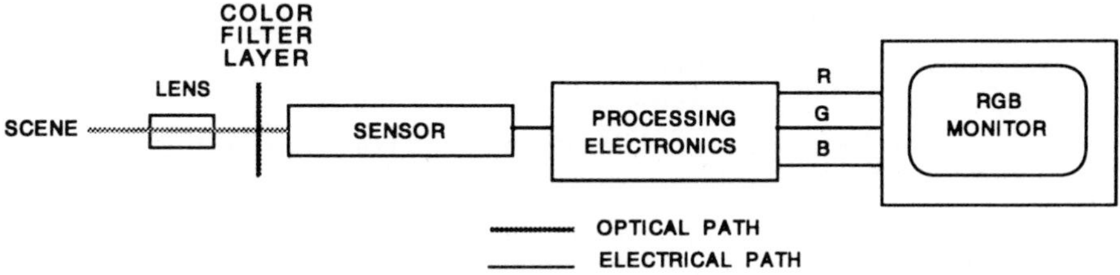

Figure 5.5 Single-sensor color video camera

home video cameras are of the single-sensor type. Solid-state sensors are particularly suited to making single-sensor cameras. Because the resolution capability of solid-state sensors is steadily improving, single-sensor cameras are getting better.

5.4.1 Color Television Systems—Composite

The color cameras just described were producing three output signals—red, green, and blue. This signal combination is called RGB. Most uses of video involve more than a single camera connected to a single monitor, as we had in Figures 5.4 and 5.5. The signal probably has to be recorded; we may wish to combine the outputs of several cameras together in different ways, and almost always we will want to have more than one viewing monitor. Therefore, we will usually be concerned with a color video system, containing much more than cameras. In RGB systems, all parts of the system are interconnected with three parallel video cables, one for each of the color channels. However, because of the complexities of distributing three signals in exact synchronism and relationship, most color TV systems do not handle RGB (except within cameras), but rather the camera signals are encoded into a *composite* format which may be distributed on a single cable. Such composite formats are used throughout TV studios, for video recording, and for broadcasting. There are several different composite formats used in different countries around the world—NTSC, PAL, SECAM—and they will be covered specifically in the next section. Here we will concentrate on some of the conceptual aspects of composite color video systems.

Composite color systems were originally developed for broadcasting of color signals by a single television transmitter. However, it was soon found that the composite format was the best approach to use throughout the video system, so it is now conventional for the composite encoding to take place inside the camera box itself before any video signals are brought out. Except for purposes such as certain video manipulation processes, RGB signals do not exist in modern television plants.

All composite formats make use of the *luminance/chrominance* principle for their basic structure. This principle says that any color signal may be broken into two parts—luminance, which is a monochrome video signal that controls only the brightness (or luminance) of the image, and chrominance, which contains only the coloring information for the image. However, because a tri-stimulus color system requires three independent signals for complete representation of all colors, the chrominance signal is actually two signals, called color differences.

Luminance and chrominance are just one of the many possible combinations of three signals which could be used to transmit color information. They are obtained by a linear matrix transformation of the RGB signals created in the camera. The matrix transformation simply means that each of the luminance and chrominance signals is an additive (sometimes with negative coefficients) combination of the original RGB signals. In a linear transmission system there are an infinity of possible matrix transformations that might be used; we just need to be sure that we use the correct inverse transformation when we recover RGB signals to display on a color monitor. Psychovisual research (research into how images look to a human viewer) has shown that by carefully choosing an appropriate transformation, we can generate signals for transmission which will be affected by the limitations of transmission in ways that will not show as much in the reproduced picture.

The color printing world uses another version of the luminance/chrominance system that has many similarities to that used in color television. That is called the *hue-saturation-value* (HSV) system or the *hue-saturation-intensity* (HSI) system. In these systems, value or intensity is the same as luminance—it represents the black and white component of the image, and hue and saturation are the chrominance components. Hue refers to the color being displayed, and saturation describes how deep that color is. In a black and white image, saturation is zero (and hue is meaningless), and as the image becomes colored, saturation values increase. The same terms, hue and saturation, are used with the same meaning in color television.

In a composite system, the luminance and chrominance are combined by a scheme of *frequency-interleaving* in order to transmit them on a single channel. The luminance signal is transmitted as a normal monochrome signal on the cable or broadcast channel, and then the chrominance information is placed on a high-frequency subcarrier located near the top of the channel bandwidth. If this carrier frequency is correctly chosen, very little interference will occur between the two signals. This interleaving works because of two facts:

1. The luminance channel is not very sensitive to interfering signals that come in near the high end of the channel bandwidth. This is especially effective if the interfering signal has a frequency that is an odd multiple of half the line scanning rate. In this case, the interfering frequency has the opposite polarity on adjacent scanning lines, and visually the interference tends to cancel out. The selection of carrier frequency for the chrominance ensures this interlace condition.

2. The eye is much less sensitive to color edges than it is to luminance edges in the picture. This means that the bandwidth of the chrominance signals can be reduced without much visual loss of resolution. Bandwidth reductions of 2 to 4 for chrominance relative to luminance are appropriate.

Thus, a composite system is able to transmit a color signal on a single channel that has the same bandwidth as each of the three RGB signals we started with. The transmission is not perfect, but it is good enough to be the basis of our worldwide television systems. This packing of the three RGB signals into the same bandwidth we once used for only one (black and white) signal may seem like we are getting something for nothing, but that's not true. What is really happening is that we are utilizing the spaces in the channel which are unused when transmitting only a single television signal, and we are also making compromises in the reproduction of the color information based on knowing what the viewer can and cannot see in the final image. Together, these two features allowed the development of the color TV system as we know it today.

5.4.2 Color Video Formats—NTSC

The NTSC color TV system is the standard broadcasting system for North America, Japan, and a few other countries. NTSC is an acronym for National Television Systems Committee, a standardizing body which existed in the 1950s to choose a color TV system for the United States. The NTSC system is a composite luminance/chrominance system as described above, and its key numbers are given in the tables at the end of this chapter. An important objective for the NTSC system was that it had to be compatible with the monochrome color system which was in place with millions of receivers long before color TV began. This objective was met by making the luminance signal of NTSC be just the same as the previous monochrome standard—existing monochrome receivers see the luminance signal only. Furthermore, the color signal present at the top of the bandwidth does not show up very much on monochrome sets because of the same frequency-interleaving that reduces interference between luminance and chrominance.

In NTSC the luminance signal is called the Y signal, and the two chrominance signals are I and Q. I and Q stand for in-phase and quadrature, because they are two-phase amplitude-modulated on the color subcarrier signal (one at 0 degrees, and one at 90 degrees—quadrature). The color carrier frequency is 3.579545 MHz, which must be maintained very accurately. (The reasons for the funny number and the accuracy are beyond the scope of this discussion—see the references at the end of this chapter if you are interested.) The tables at the end of this chapter give the matrix transformation for making Y, I, and Q from RGB. As already explained, the I and Q color difference signals have reduced bandwidths. While the luminance can utilize the full 4.5-MHz bandwidth of a TV channel, the I bandwidth is only 1.5 MHz, and the Q signal is chosen so that it can get away with only 0.5 MHz bandwidth. (In fact, pretty good results are obtained if both I and Q only use 0.5 MHz—most TV receivers and VCRs in the United States have 0.5-MHz bandwidth in both chrominance channels.)

When the I and Q signals are modulated onto the color subcarrier of the NTSC system, they result in a color subcarrier component whose amplitude represents the saturation values of the image, and the phase of the color subcarrier represents the hue values of the image. NTSC receivers usually have controls to adjust these two parameters in the decoding of the NTSC color signal. (On NTSC receivers, the hue control is often called tint, and the saturation control is called color.)

It should be pointed out that the NTSC system was designed to deliver satisfactory performance with the kind of signals created by TV cameras looking at real scenes. Today, we also can generate video signals with computers, and there can be problems if a computer-generated signal does not follow the rules when it is expected to be passed through an NTSC system.

5.4.3 Color Video Formats—PAL and SECAM

The PAL and SECAM systems, which originated in Europe, are also luminance/chrominance systems. They differ from NTSC primarily in the way in which the chrominance signals are encoded. In PAL, chrominance is also transmitted on a two-phase amplitude-modulated subcarrier at the top of the system bandwidth, but it uses a more complex process called Phase Alternating Line (PAL), which allows both of the chrominance signals to have the same bandwidth (1.5 MHz). Because of the different bandwidths, a different set of chrominance components is chosen, called U and V instead of I and Q. In addition, PAL signals are more tolerant of certain distortions that can occur in transmission paths to affect the quality of the color reproduction. The tables at the end of this chapter give numbers for the PAL system.

The SECAM system (*Sequentiel Couleur avec Memoire*), developed in France, uses an FM-modulated color subcarrier for the chrominance signals, transmitting one of the color difference signals on every other line, and the other color difference signal on alternate lines. Like the PAL system, SECAM is also more tolerant of transmission path distortions.

Most television production and broadcasting plants are concerned primarily with the composite standard of the country in which they are located. However, it is now common for programs to be produced for distribution to locations anywhere in the world, regardless of the different standards in different countries. This has led to the development of equipment for conversion between different composite standards. Such equipment does a remarkable job, but it is complex and expensive, and even so it has performance limitations.

There is an effort in standardizing circles to develop a worldwide program-production standard that is not necessarily the same as any of the composite standards, but would allow easy and nearly transparent conversion to any of the world's composite standards for local distribution. This goal will probably be achieved by the use of digital video technology.

Because the television standards in use are more than 30 years old, it is not surprising that the industry is also considering possible new standards for a much higher-performance television system, usually referred to as High Definition Television (HDTV). Chapter 17 discusses the current status of HDTV standards.

5.5 VIDEO PERFORMANCE MEASUREMENTS

Analog television systems cause their own particular kinds of distortion to any signal passing through. Remember, analog systems are never perfect. Analog distortions also accumulate as additional circuits are added, and in a large system all the parts of the system must be of higher quality if the picture quality is to be maintained. A single component intended for a large system has to be so good that its defects become extremely difficult to observe when the component is tested by itself. However, when the component is used repeatedly in cascade in a large system, the accumulation of small distortions becomes significant. Many sophisticated techniques have been developed for performance measurement in analog television systems.

All analog video measurements depend on either looking at images on a picture monitor or making measurements of the video waveform with an oscilloscope or waveform monitor (which is just a special oscilloscope for television measurements). Because monitors also have their own distortions, looking at images on picture monitors tends to be suspect. Image-based measurements also involve judgment by the observer and therefore are subjective. On the other hand, oscilloscopic evaluation of waveforms can be more objective and therefore waveform-based approaches have been developed for measuring most parameters. However, picture monitors are good qualitative tools for performance evaluation, particularly when the characteristics of the monitor being used are well understood and the observer is skilled. Of course, the fundamental need for picture monitors in a TV studio is artistic—there is no other way to determine that the correct scene is being captured with the composition and other features desired by the producer and director.

One measurement on video waveforms that must always be done is the measurement of video levels. The television system is designed to operate optimally when all video signals are kept to a particular amplitude value or level. If signals get too high, serious distortions will occur and display devices may become overloaded. Similarly, if levels are too low, images will be faded out and the effect of noise in the system will become greater. Most video systems are designed for a standard video voltage level, such as 1 volt peak-to-peak, and all level-measuring equipment is calibrated for that level. To simplify going between different systems that have different actual voltage standards, most oscilloscopes and other level indicators are calibrated in IRE levels. (IRE is an acronym for Institute of Radio Engineers, one of the forerunners of today's worldwide electrical engineer's professional society, the Institute of Electrical and Electronics Engineers.) This refers to a standard for video waveforms which specifies that blanking level will be defined as 0 IRE units and peak white will be 100 IRE units. Other aspects of specific signals can then be defined in terms of this range.

Most video performance measurements are based on the use of test patterns. These are specialized images which show up one or more aspects of video performance. Test patterns may be charts, which are placed in front of a camera, or they may be artificially generated signals, which are introduced into the system after the camera. Because a camera has its own kinds of impairment, a camera usually cannot generate a signal good enough for testing the rest of the system. Therefore, a camera is tested by itself with test charts, and then the rest of the system is tested with theoretically perfect signals, which are electronically generated by test signal generators.

5.5.1 Measurement of Resolution

Let's begin with the characterization of resolution. One test pattern for resolution is the multiburst pattern—it can be either artificially generated or made into a test chart, and it is used to test horizontal resolution of a system. A multiburst pattern is shown in Figure 5.6. It consists of sets of vertical lines with closer and closer spacing, which give a signal with bursts of higher and higher frequency. Figure 5.6 also shows a line waveform for correct reproduction of a multiburst pattern and another waveform from a system that has poor high-frequency response. This latter system would

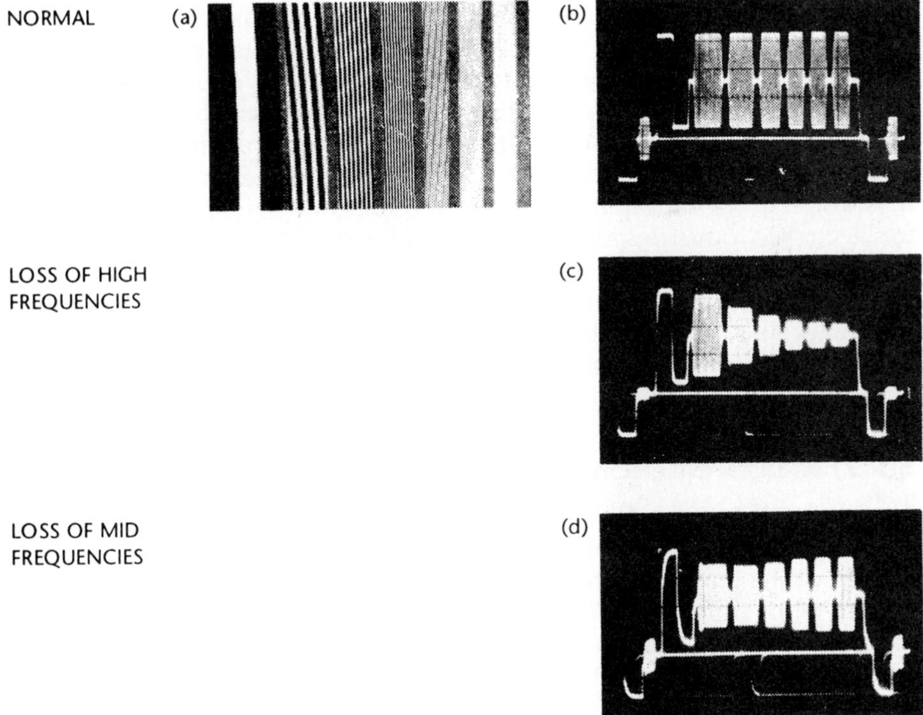

Figure 5.6 Testing frequency response with a multiburst pattern

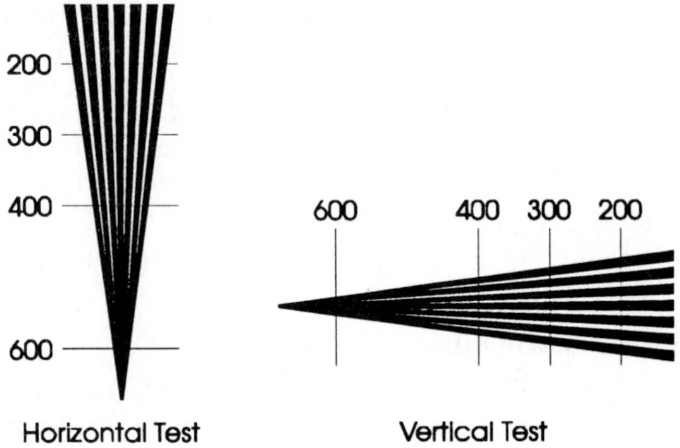

Figure 5.7 Resolution wedge patterns

cause vertical lines to appear fuzzy in an image. Another more subtle impairment is shown by the third waveform in Figure 5.6—in this case there is a mid-frequency distortion, which would make images appear smeared.

The multiburst pattern only tests horizontal resolution. To test vertical resolution as well, a resolution wedge test pattern is used. Figure 5.7 shows some resolution wedge patterns for testing both horizontal and vertical resolution. A resolution wedge is used by observing where the lines fade out as the wedge lines become closer together. The fadeout line number can be estimated from the numbers beside the wedge—this would be the resolution performance of the system or camera being tested. A common resolution test chart is the EIA Resolution Test Chart, designed to test many parameters in addition to resolution. It is usually placed in front of a camera. (EIA stands for Electronic Industries Association, an industry group in the United States which is very active in standards for television in that country.) There are wedges for both horizontal and vertical resolution at different locations in the image and various other blocks and circles to test camera geometric distortion (linearity) and gray scale response.

5.5.2 Measurement of Gray Scale Response

The gray scale test has its own special pattern, called the stairstep. This may be either a camera chart or an electronic generator. Figure 5.8 shows one version of the gray scale chart, with examples of the signals created by the pattern going through various systems. An important consideration regarding gray scale reproduction in TV systems is that an equal-intensity-step gray scale test chart should not produce an equal-step electrical signal. The reason for this is that the electrical signal will ultimately drive a CRT display, and the brightness versus voltage characteristic of a CRT is not linear. Therefore, television cameras include *gamma correction* to modify the volt-

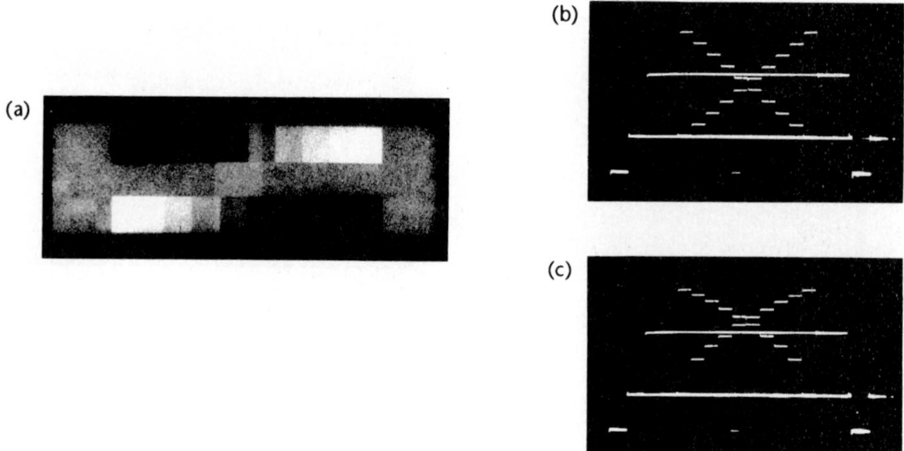

Figure 5.8 (a) Gray scale test chart, (b) normal waveform, (c) distorted waveform showing black stretch

age transfer characteristic of the signal to compensate for an average CRT's brightness versus voltage behavior. This is written into most television standards because the CRT was the only type of display that existed at the time of standardization. New-type displays such as LCDs may have different gamma characteristics for which they must include their own correction if they are to properly display standard television signals.

A typical CRT has a voltage-to-intensity characteristic close to a power of 2.2. To correct for this CRT gamma characteristic, a signal from a camera sensor having a linear characteristic (gamma of 1.0, which is typical for sensors) must undergo gamma correction by a circuit which takes the 2.2 root of its input signal. If gamma correction is left out of a system, the effect is that detail in the black regions of the picture will be lost, and pictures appear to have too much contrast regardless of how you adjust the display. In dealing with computer-generated images, it is important to provide for the gamma characteristic to create realistic looking pictures on CRT displays.

5.5.3 Measurement of Noise

Measurement of noise in a television system is an art in itself. Most specifications are in terms of signal-to-noise ratio (S/N), which is defined as the ratio between the peak-to-peak black-to-white signal and the *rms value* (rms means root-mean-square—a kind of averaging) of any superimposed noise.

S/N numbers are commonly given in decibels (dB), which are logarithmic units specifically designed for expressing ratios. The bel represents a power ratio of 10:1, the decibel is one-tenth of that. Since signal-to-noise ratios

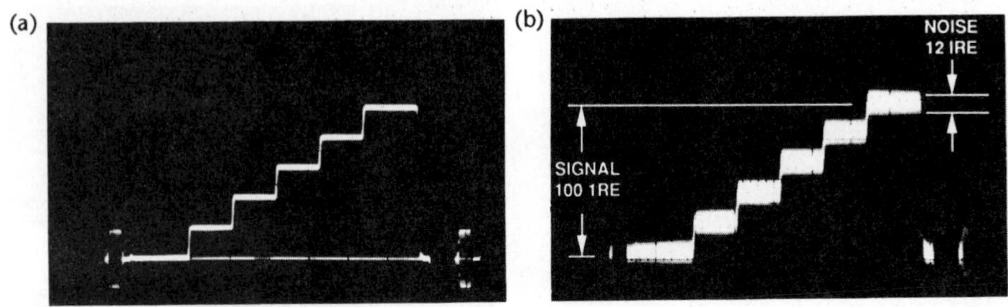

Figure 5.9 Noise measurement using an oscilloscope: (a) signal without noise, (b) signal with noise. S/N ratio = 600/12 = 50:1 = 34 dB.

are usually voltage ratios, not power, a 10:1 signal-to-noise ratio is 20 decibels because the power ratio goes as the square of voltage ratio. Because the decibel is logarithmic, doubling the dB value is the same as squaring the ratio—thus, 40 dB would be a signal-to-noise ratio of 100:1. A good S/N ratio for a system is around 200:1 (46 dB), which means that the rms noise in that system is 200 times less than the maximum black-to-white video level the system is designed to handle. Note that the measurement of rms noise requires an integrating kind of meter, and for this purpose there needs to be a region of the image for measurement that does not have any other signal present. There are many different kinds of test patterns for noise measurements.

It is also possible to get an approximate S/N measurement by looking at video signals with a waveform monitor or oscilloscope, as shown by Figure 5.9. Noise appears on a video waveform as a fluctuating fine grain fuzz, which is usually evident on all parts of the active picture area of the waveform. (Noise usually does not appear during the blanking intervals because video equipment often regenerates the blanking interval, replacing sync and blanking—which may have gotten noisy in transmission or recording—with clean signals.) The peak-to-peak value of the noise fuzz can be estimated as a percentage of the total video black-to-white range. Then an approximate S/N ratio may be calculated by dividing 600 by the percentage of noise fuzz. This is based on the assumption that typical noise has an rms value six times less than its peak-to-peak value. Therefore, a 46-dB system would show about 3 percent peak-to-peak noise fuzz on its signals.

5.5.4 Measurement of Color Performance

Another class of measurement is involved with the color performance of a system. Measurement of color rendition of cameras is beyond our scope here, but there are simple means to test the NTSC parts of the system. This is most often done with an electronically generated signal called a color bar

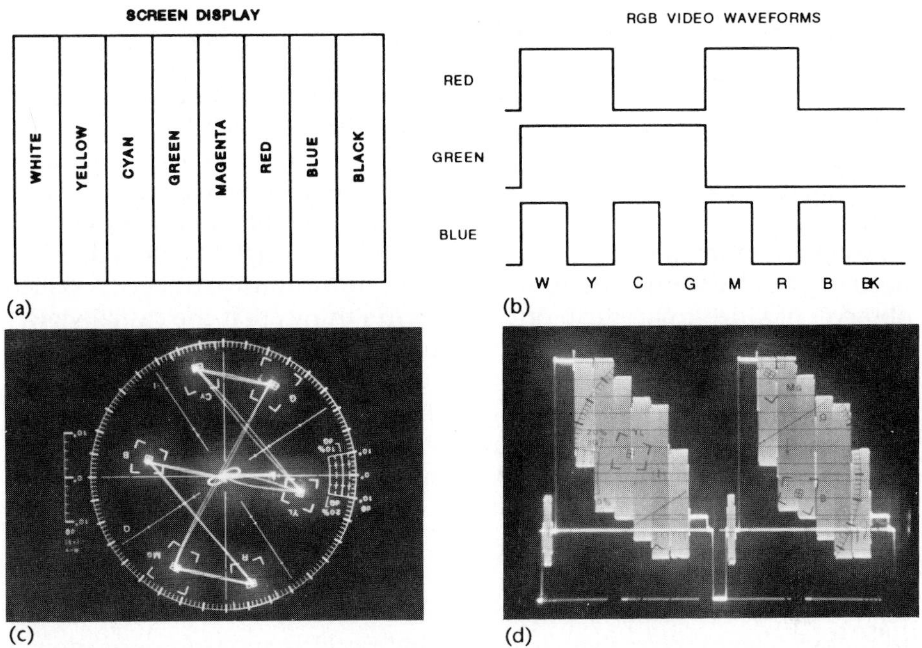

Figure 5.10 (a) Color bar test pattern, (b) RGB video waveforms, (c) NTSC video waveform, (d) NTSC vectorscope display

test pattern. Figure 5.10 shows a color bar pattern and the resulting waveform display used widely in NTSC systems. The particular bar sequence chosen arranges the colors in order of decreasing luminance values, which makes an easy-to-remember waveform. The color bar signal can also be examined with a special oscilloscope made for studying the chrominance components—this instrument is called a vectorscope. Figure 5.10 also shows what an NTSC color bar signal looks like on a vectorscope. There are also split-field versions of the color bar pattern, which put the bar pattern at the top of the screen and a different pattern (such as a stairstep pattern) at the bottom. With this arrangement, several different tests can be made using only one test signal. Available test signal generators provide many combinations of the test signals, to be used individually or simultaneously in split-field combinations.

Color distortions in NTSC systems can occur as the result of amplitude shifts or phase shifts in the chrominance components of the signal. Amplitude changes the saturation (intensity) of the color, and phase shifts change the hue (tint) of the colors. Both of these distortions can be observed by the proper use of a vectorscope.

There are many other kinds of video performance measurements. For our purpose in understanding the interfaces between analog and digital video, the few that are covered in the foregoing paragraphs are sufficient.

5.6 ANALOG VIDEO ARTIFACTS

Archaeologists use the word artifact to refer to an unnatural object which has been found in nature—thus it is presumably manmade. In the video world, artifacts are unnatural things which may appear in reproduction of a natural image by an electronic system. In order to appreciate the vagaries of analog video, and particularly to appreciate the different things which an analog system does to video compared to what a digital system does, we need to give attention to these analog image distortions—artifacts. A skilled observer of video images can often recognize things that the casual viewer will never notice—but being able to recognize them is important when you are responsible for the system. Often the artifacts are clues to something that is starting to go wrong, recognizable before it becomes catastrophic. So, at the risk of destroying your future enjoyment of television images that may be less than perfect, let's look at analog video artifacts.

5.6.1 Noise

As we have already said, the most common form of noise is what we refer to on our television receiver as snow. The speckled appearance of snow is caused by excessive amounts of noise rather uniformly distributed over the bandwidth of the video signal, which is often called white noise or flat noise. Flat noise is readily observable when the signal-to-noise ratio falls below about 40 dB. A good three-sensor camera will generate a signal where the S/N is nearer to 50 dB. However, this signal may be subsequently degraded by various transmission paths or by video recording (see later discussion on recorders).

There are other types of noise which look quite different. For example, noise that is predominantly low-frequency (in the vicinity of the line frequency or lower) will appear as random horizontal streaks in the picture. The eye is quite sensitive to this kind of noise, but fortunately it is unusual in properly operating systems. When this kind of noise is seen, something in the system may have become intermittent or is about to fail catastrophically. Another noise phenomenon that looks different from snow is color noise. This is noise in the transmission path for a composite signal which appears in a frequency band close to the color subcarrier. Because of the relatively narrow bandwidth of the chrominance channels, color noise appears as moderately large streaks of varying color. Color noise is primarily an artifact of video recording.

5.6.2 RF Interference

Various kinds of coherent (not random) interferences can creep into video signals from other sources. The appearance of these interferences will depend on the exact frequency relationship they have to the scanning frequencies and to the color subcarrier. The degree to which they produce moving patterns depends on whether (or how closely) they are synchronized with the main signal. You have probably seen the interference which consists of two vertical bars spaced about 10 percent of the picture width which move slowly across the picture, taking several seconds to go all the way across. This is interference from another color television signal on the same standard but not synchronized with the main signal. It is quite common in signals received over the air, and it also may be a problem in a television studio system that has several sources of signals that are not synchronized.

Interference from single-frequency nontelevision signals will produce diagonal- or vertical-line patterns, either stationary or moving. The relationship to the horizontal scanning frequency controls the exact pattern produced. Interference from multifrequency sources will produce more complex patterns. For example, interference getting into video from an audio signal will produce a pattern of horizontal bars which changes in size and position with the sound. The relationship is obvious if you are able to hear the sound while you watch the patterns in the video.

Interference from coherent sources is much more visible than is random interference or noise. This is because the coherent interference creates some kind of pattern, which repeats over and over in the same (or a slowly moving) location. Patterns of bars may have any spacing and may range from vertical bar patterns through diagonal patterns to horizontal bar patterns. Coherent interferences are often visible if they exceed about 0.5 percent peak-to-peak relative to the black-to-white video range.

5.6.3 Loss of High Frequencies

In a composite color television system, the first effect of loss of high frequencies is that the color saturation (vividness of color) will be reduced, or color may be lost entirely. (Except in the SECAM system: In SECAM the FM nature of the color subcarrier will retain color saturation. The effect becomes one of increasing color noise, or finally loss of color.) More severe loss of high frequencies will noticeably affect the sharpness of vertical edges in the image. In an RGB system, loss of high frequency will only affect sharpness, although if the loss is not the same in all three channels, it will also show as color fringes on vertical edges.

5.6.4 Smear

Smear shows up as picture information which is smeared to the right (usually). Figure 5.11 shows an image with smear. It is caused by a loss of amplitude or a phase shift at frequencies near or somewhat above the

Figure 5.11 Image showing the smear artifact

horizontal line frequency. Many tube-type cameras have a high-peaker adjustment, which can cause this kind of distortion if not properly set. It is also caused by long video cables which are not properly equalized.

5.6.5 Streaking

Streaking is present when a bright object in the image causes a shifting of brightness all the way across the image at the vertical location of the bright object. Figure 5.12 shows what it looks like. Streaking is usually caused by video information which gets into the blanking interval and then interferes with the level-setting circuits (called clamps) present in many pieces of video equipment. It may occur when a signal with an extreme case of smear passes through equipment containing clamps, or it can happen due to loss of frequency response at frequencies below the line frequency. The latter is usually caused by a component failure somewhere in the system.

5.6.6 Color Fringing

Color fringing is present when edges in the picture have colors on them that were not in the original scene. This may be over all of the picture, or it may be confined to only one part of the picture. The principal cause of color fringing is registration errors in cameras. However, there are some less

Figure 5.12 Image showing analog streaking artifact.

frequent kinds of distortions in the frequency domain or in recording systems which will cause similar effects. In these cases the entire picture is usually affected, and it will most likely occur only on vertical edges.

5.6.7 Color Balance Errors

In an RGB system, the most likely color errors are those caused by the video levels not being the same in the three channels. This is a color balance error, and it shows up as a constant color over the entire image. It is independent of what colors are in the scene. For example, if the red level is too low, white areas in the image will have a minus red cast—that is, they will appear cyan. All parts of the image will have cyan added to the correct color. Correct reproduction of white areas is a good test for color balance. In a composite system, color balance errors usually originate at the camera, where they may be caused by balance errors in the RGB circuits of the camera or errors in the composite encoder built into the camera. In NTSC and PAL systems, the subcarrier output goes to zero in white areas of the picture, so looking for zero subcarrier on a white bar is the test for proper balance of an NTSC or PAL signal. There are more subtle color balance errors where the color balance varies as the brightness level of the image changes. This is tested by observing the color balance on all the steps of a gray scale test pattern or test signal. The most common source of this kind of error is the camera.

5.6.8 Hue Errors

In RGB systems, hue errors are unusual if the color balance is correct. However, in composite systems, particularly NTSC, hue errors are caused by improper decoding of the color subcarrier; in particular, the phase of the color subcarrier controls hue in an NTSC system. NTSC television receivers have a hue control which adjusts this parameter. In a color origination system, however, the signals must all be set to a standard, so that the viewer will not feel that the hue control has to be readjusted every time a different camera is used. In the PAL system, the phase-alternating line-encoding approach makes the hue much less sensitive to the phase of the color subcarrier, and PAL receivers usually do not have a hue control.

5.6.9 Color Saturation Errors

It has already been explained that in composite systems, color saturation errors are most commonly caused by incorrect high-frequency response, which leads to incorrect color subcarrier amplitude.

5.6.10 Flag-Waving

In low-cost video recorders, there can be a problem of synchronization instability at the top of the picture called flag-waving. It shows up as vertical edges at the top of the screen moving left to right from their correct position. In the recorder it is caused when the video playback head of the recorder has to leave the tape at one edge and come back onto the tape at the other edge (which happens during the vertical blanking interval, so this itself is not seen). If the tape tension is not correctly adjusted, flag-waving may appear. Some video recorders have a control called skew, which is an adjustment to minimize this effect.

5.6.11 Jitter

If the entire picture shows random motion from left to right (called jitter), the motion usually is caused by time-base errors from video recorders. In a video recorder the smoothness of the mechanical motion of the recorder's head drum is very critical in order to reproduce a stable picture. Higher-priced recorders contain a time base corrector (TBC) to correct this problem, but TBCs are expensive, and it costs less in a low-priced recorder to try to make the mechanical motion stable enough without a TBC. Occasionally, jitter effects will be caused by other kinds of defects or interferences getting into the synchronizing signals or circuits.

5.7 VIDEO EQUIPMENT

The video business is a mature, fully developed industry around the world. There are many manufacturers selling competitively to worldwide markets and because there are good standards for video signals and broadcasting, there is a wide range of equipment made for every imaginable purpose in video production, recording, postproduction, broadcasting, and distribution. The markets for video equipment range from the most sophisticated network or national broadcasting companies through industrial and educational markets, to the home (consumer) market. In the discussion that follows, we will simplify the market structure to just three categories:

1. **Broadcast:** Equipment used by large-market TV broadcast stations and networks. This equipment has the highest performance, is intended for large system application, and is the most expensive.
2. **Professional:** Equipment for use in educational and industrial applications (and smaller broadcasters) who cannot afford full broadcast-level equipment but still need a lot of performance and features.
3. **Consumer:** Home equipment where price is the first consideration. Must have simple operation and high reliability for use by a nontechnical user. The intended system application is very simple—usually one-camera, one-recorder systems.

5.7.1 Live-Pickup Color Cameras

Broadcast-level video cameras for live pickup are generally of the three-sensor variety. The highest performance cameras are large units for studio use, and they have large-format sensors. They also support a very wide range of lenses for extreme zoom range, wide angle, very long telephoto, etc. These cameras can also be taken in the field when the highest possible performance is needed, but their large size hampers portability. There are smaller broadcast cameras, which are designed to be truly portable, and no expense is spared to keep the performance as high as possible. Broadcast cameras today generally contain computers which control their setup adjustments and many features of operation. However, the signal processing is usually analog.

Professional-level video cameras are also of the three-sensor type, but they typically use smaller sensors and smaller optics to reduce the cost. They usually have a simpler system design with fewer special features; therefore, they are lower in cost and easier to operate and maintain. The compromises in picture quality and flexibility resulting from these changes have been chosen to be acceptable to the markets for this class of equipment. Applications are in education, training, and institutional uses.

Consumer-level video cameras go to the ultimate in cost reduction. They use the single-sensor format, which is a compromise in resolution performance compared to the other cameras, but it yields a small, reliable, low-cost unit. Consumer cameras are designed for high-volume production and do not have a lot of special features. Very simple system application is intended. However, their performance and features have been good enough to create a mass consumer market, and they are an outstanding value in terms of what you get for the price.

In the consumer market, you can no longer find video cameras by themselves—they are all combined with video recorders as *camcorders*. This is a great convenience and also a cost saving, so camcorders have replaced separate cameras. Camcorders are also available in the broadcast and professional categories; however, they have not completely replaced separate equipment in these fields, primarily because broadcast and professional users often will use several cameras with a single recorder, or maybe with no recorder at all if they are broadcasting live. Therefore, there will always be separate cameras for these uses.

5.7.2 Color Cameras for Pickup from Film

Cameras specifically designed for television pickup from motion picture film or slides are called telecine cameras. Getting good television pictures from film is not as simple as it sounds because of two key problems. The first is that the frame rate for film is usually 24 frames per second, whereas television frame rates are 25 or 30 Hz. In the parts of the world where television frame rate is 25 Hz, film is shown on television simply by speeding the film frame rate up to match the television frame rate—a 4 percent increase. This amount of speedup is usually acceptable. However, for 30-Hz television systems, the 20 percent speedup required would be unacceptable. In these systems, an approach called 3:2 *pulldown* is used to resolve the different frame rates. In the 3:2 approach, one film frame is scanned for three television fields and the next film frame is scanned for only two television fields; that is, two film frames are shown in five television fields, which is 2.5 television frames. This ratio of 2.5:2 is exactly the same as the 30:24 frequency ratio, so the average film frame rate can be the correct value. There are artifacts from 3:2 pulldown, such as a certain jerkiness in motion areas of the image—most television viewers in North America have become used to this effect and accept it. Another 3:2 pulldown artifact is the wheels appearing to turn backwards on a car or wagon. When you see this effect, you can be sure that the program or commercial was originally shot on film.

The second film-television problem is a mismatch between film and television with regard to color reproduction capability. This arises because television is an additive color system, whereas film is a subtractive color system. Film images typically have more contrast than a television system can handle, and film shows its best colors in dark parts of the image (where the dye concentrations are the highest). Television gives its best colors in bright regions where the CRT is turned on fully and can overcome the effect of stray ambient light on the tube face. Both of these effects may be mostly overcome by using excess gamma correction (much more than is needed to correct for the CRT characteristic) to bring up the dark areas of the image from film. Telecine cameras have elaborate gamma circuits to provide this feature. In addition, since high gamma correction tends to also bring up sensor noise effects, telecine cameras need to start with a higher signal-to-noise ratio from the sensors in order to withstand the high gamma correction.

There are other problems of color rendition in reproducing film, which lead to a need in telecine cameras for much more flexible color adjustment circuits as well. It is common for telecine systems to contain very elaborate color correctors to deal with faded film, incorrect color balance, and other kinds of color errors. Because of the complexities of television from film, there is not much telecine equipment on the market outside of the broadcast field. Even in the broadcast field, telecine has become a specialized capability—used only for film-to-tape transfer. That is because videotape is much easier than film to deal with in a broadcast operation. Most film you see on television was transferred to tape some time before it is broadcast, often immediately after the film was processed.

5.7.3 Video Recording Equipment

For our use in digital video systems we will almost always be dealing with recorded video as the input to the digital system. Video will be shot with analog cameras, recorded, and often processed extensively before it is digitized. A whole industry, referred to as video postproduction, has grown up to take recorded video material and put it together into finished programs. Techniques and facilities for postproduction are highly developed and are serving large markets for television and other video production. We can expect that for some time these approaches will be the best way to create video for any use, including digital video.

Analog video recording is mostly based on magnetic technology. (An exception is the laser videodisc, which is optical.) Magnetic recording is not a good medium for use directly in analog recording, because it is highly nonlinear. Magnetic recording is in fact better as a digital medium, where a domain of magnetic material can be considered either magnetized or not magnetized. In video recording systems, this is dealt with by modulating the video signal onto an FM carrier before recording. The FM carrier is very well matched to the characteristics of magnetic recording, because it does not require sensitivity to different levels of magnetization; rather, it depends on the size and location of magnetized regions.

One of the considerations of video recording for producing a program is that creation of the finished program requires going through the recording system several times. Original video is shot by using a camera with one recorder to get each of the scenes separately. A SMPTE time code signal is also recorded with all the material for use in controlling later processes. Recording scenes one at a time is done because it is much more efficient from the staging and talent viewpoint to not try to put scenes together in real time. This process of capturing the scenes one at a time is called production. To put together a program involving scenes from several cameras and often several locations, all the original tapes will be taken to a postproduction studio where the desired shots will be selected for assembly into the final program. Time code locations of all critical points will be tabulated. Then each of the scenes is run from its original tape under time code control and re-recorded in the proper sequence on a new tape to create an edited master. In that process various transition effects between scenes can also be introduced, such as dissolves, fades, wipes, etc. The edited master is usually backed up by making another edited master (called a protection master) or, more commonly, by re-recording copies from a single edited master (called a protection copy). Re-recording of videotape is called dubbing, and the resulting tape is called a dub.

If the dub from the edited master is the copy we use to digitize, you can see that we have gone through the analog recording process at least three times—once in original production, again in making the edited master, and a third time to back up the edited master. This is referred to as three generations. Since analog distortions will accumulate, a recording system that will deliver good pictures after three generations must have considerably higher performance than a recorder we will only go through once. In fact, three generations is almost a minimum number—there are often additional steps of video postproduction which can lead to needing five or six generations before the final copy is made.

Most video recorders are designed to record the composite video signal—NTSC, PAL, or SECAM. However, there are several new systems that use an approach called component recording. In a component recorder, the signal is recorded in two parallel channels, usually with luminance on one channel and chrominance on the other channel. Some of the recording artifacts can be reduced by this approach. If a component recorder is used with a composite camera, the composite signal must be decoded at the input of the recorder to create the component format. In this case, there is little performance advantage for a single generation because both component and composite signal degradations will be present. However, if the component recorder is either combined with a camera or used with a camera having component outputs, then the composite encoding does not have to occur until after recording, and the system performance can be improved. There are even some attempts to build component postproduction facilities where composite encoding does not occur until after postproduction. Such a facility is able to go through more generations and therefore can perform fancier postproduction effects.

Because of the need for multiple generations in video recording, there is a move in the television industry to develop digital video recorders. A digital recorder and a digital postproduction system could use unlimited generations, just as we are used to doing with computer recording devices. (In a computer we never worry about repeated loading and saving of data because we have confidence that the digital system will make no errors.) There are digital video recorders coming out in the broadcast field in both composite and component formats. The composite recorders use the same analog formats we have been talking about—they digitize the analog composite signal at their input. However, the digital component recorder takes a digitized YUV input format.

The standard of broadcast-level analog composite video recorders is the Type C recorder, using one-inch videotape in a reel-to-reel format. This equipment is the workhorse of broadcast television around the world and delivers the best analog recording performance available today. The basic Type C machine is a large unit weighing somewhat more than 100 pounds and intended for fixed or transportable use. Type C recorders will deliver good performance after three generations and are usable up to five or six generations. Another broadcast-level format, which is somewhat less used in the United States but is found extensively in Europe is the Type B system. The Type B recorders also use one-inch tape, but their format is different in a way which allows smaller machines to be built. Type B performance is equivalent to Type C.

The two broadcast-level component recording formats, mentioned earlier, are the Betacam format and the Type MII format. Both of these use half-inch tape in a cassette and have performance that is close to Type C level. Because of the small tape size, very compact machines can be built, including a camcorder format, which combines camera and VCR in one hand-held unit.

In professional-level recording, the three-quarter-inch U-Matic format is the workhorse. This format uses a cassette with three-quarter-inch tape, and machines come in rack-mounted, tabletop, and portable configurations. The three-quarter-inch system uses a different way of getting the composite signal onto the tape, which requires that the luminance and chrominance be taken apart and then put back together inside the recorder. Doing that to a composite signal introduces some inherent degradations so that the picture quality of the three-quarter-inch system is not as good as Type C, particularly with respect to color sharpness and luminance bandwidth. The three-quarter-inch system typically can go only two generations with acceptable pictures.

Recently, two other formats for the professional market have been introduced. These are the S-VHS and the Hi-8 formats, derived from the VHS and 8-mm consumer formats. These are component formats whose performance is highly competitive with U-Matic, the equipment is smaller, and they will probably take over the market in the future.

In the consumer-level recording field we have the familiar VHS and 8-mm formats. These systems all use a method of recording similar to the three-quarter-inch systems, in which separating of luminance and chrominance is required inside the recorder. However, because of the smaller tape sizes and lower tape speeds, bandwidths are much lower, and the pictures are noticeably impaired by the recorder. However, they have proven themselves to be good enough for consumer entertainment use—witness the proliferation of consumer VCRs around the world. As a medium for input to a digital system, however, the consumer equipment is not very satisfactory. The reason is that these VCRs introduce artifacts that are different from the digital artifacts, and, therefore, when their signal is digitized by a low-cost digital system, both kinds of artifacts can appear. That is usually just too much. Note, however, that broadcast- and professional-level component systems (Betacam, Type MII, S-VHS, or Hi-8) are based on the same consumer half-inch or 8-mm tape technologies, but the component recording technique allows much better performance—at a higher price, of course. The component systems generally are quite satisfactory for recording source material for digital systems.

5.7.4 Video Monitoring Equipment

Monitoring equipment for analog television includes picture monitors and waveform monitors, which also come in various price/performance levels. Broadcast-level video monitors cost several thousand dollars and come as close as possible to being transparent, which means that the picture you see depends on the signal and not the monitor. Broadcast monitors will also include various display modes, which allow different aspects of the signal (in addition to the picture content) to be observed. One common feature is the pulse-cross display, which shows the synchronizing signal part of a composite video signal. Broadcast monitors are designed to be capable of being matched, so that a group of monitors will show the same signal the same way. Matching is important when several monitors are going to be used to set up signals that may eventually be combined into the same program. In such a case, it is important that the color reproduction of all signals match as closely as possible. Broadcast monitors always have inputs for composite signals. Some monitors also have RGB inputs, but this is unusual, because RGB signals seldom exist today in broadcast studios or postproduction facilities.

Professional-level monitoring equipment is designed to a slightly lower price/performance point—pictures are still very good but some features may be sacrificed in the interest of price.

Consumer-level monitoring is mostly done with the ubiquitous television receiver. All TV receivers have an antenna input for receiving the composite signal in RF form as it is broadcast on a TV channel. Recently, TV sets are also adding video inputs for a baseband composite signal, which may come from a consumer camera, VCR, or home computer. (A baseband composite signal is a video signal that has not been modulated up to a TV channel.) More rare is the RGB input, although this will appear in more televisions as the use of computers grows in the home.

Broadcasting of the composite video signal also introduces some characteristic performance problems, which we sometimes observe on our TV sets. In a wired system, it is unusual to get extremely noisy (snowy) signals or signals containing ghost images; however, these are common defects in over-the-air transmission. TV receivers are designed to deal as well as possible with these problems and still make an entertaining picture. Because broadcasting in a fixed channel bandwidth puts an absolute limit on the bandwidth for the video signal, pictures received on a TV set will not look as good as they do in the studio. Also, there is a lot of competition in TV receiver manufacturing, and they are available at several points on the price/performance curve.

5.8 WORLDWIDE TELEVISION STANDARDS

This section presents a summary of the major parameters of the principal television systems in the world—NTSC, PAL, and SECAM. For more information about these standards, consult *Television Engineering Handbook*, Chapter 21 [1]. That reference will also lead you to the formal standards publications for many of the countries.

There are minor differences between the same system implemented in different countries. The information given here is for NTSC-M (United States), PAL-B (West Germany), and SECAM-L (France).

Scanning Parameters

Scanning	**NTSC**	**PAL**	**SECAM**
Lines/frame	525	625	625
Frames/second	30	25	25
Interlace ratio	2:1	2:1	2:1
Aspect ratio	4:3	4:3	4:3
Color subcar. (Hz)	3,579,545	4,433,619	Note 1
sc/h ratio	455/2	1135/4	Note 1

Sync Waveforms: Horizontal Timing

Refer to Figure 5.13 for nomenclature. All values given are nominal. Horizontal sync values are in microseconds.

Horizontal Timing (μsec)	**NTSC**	**PAL**	**SECAM**
Line period (H)	63.55	64.0	64.0
Blanking width	10.9	12.0	12.0
Sync width	4.7	4.7	4.7
Front porch	1.2	1.2	1.2
Burst start	5.1	5.6	Note 2

Horizontal Timing (μsec)	**NTSC**	**PAL**	**SECAM**
Burst width	2.67	2.25	Note 2
Equalising width	2.3	2.35	2.35
Vert. sync width	27.1	27.3	27.3

Sync Waveforms: Vertical Timing

Vertical Sync	**NTSC**	**PAL**	**SECAM**
Blanking width	20H	25H	25H
Num. equalizing	6	5	5
Num. vert. sync	6	5	5
Burst suppression	9H	Note 3	Note 4

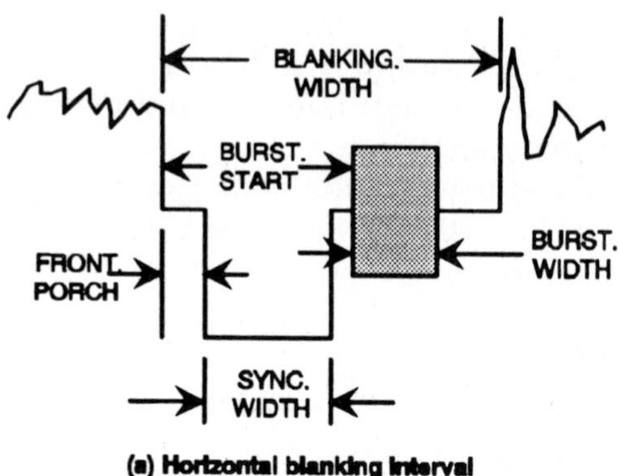

(a) Horizontal blanking interval

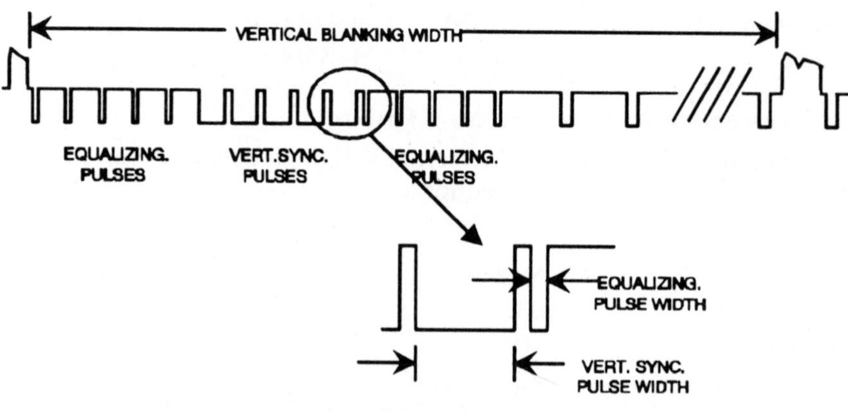

(b) Vertical blanking interval

Figure 5.13 Sync waveform nomenclature

NTSC

Color Matrix Equations	Chrominance Bandwidth (-3 dB)
$Y = 0.30\,R + 0.59\,G + 0.11\,B$	
$I = 0.60\,R - 0.28\,G - 0.32\,B$	1.3 MHz
$Q = 0.21\,R - 0.52\,G + 0.31\,B$	0.45 MHz

PAL

Color Matrix Equations	Chrominance Bandwidth (-3 dB)
$Y = 0.30\,R + 0.59\,G + 0.11\,B$	
$U = 0.62\,R - 0.52\,G - 0.10\,B$	1.3 MHZ
$V = -0.15\,R - 0.29\,G + 0.44\,B$	1.3 MHz

SECAM

Color Matrix Equations	Chrominance Bandwidth (-3 dB)
$Y = 0.30\,R + 0.59\,G + 0.11\,B$	
$DR = -1.33\,R + 1.11\,G + 0.22\,B$	1.3 MHz
$DB = -0.45\,R - 0.88\,G + 1.33\,B$	1.3 MHz

5.8.1 Sync Waveform Nomenclature

Color Modulation Parameters

NTSC The chrominance subcarrier is suppressed-carrier amplitude modulated by the I and Q components, with the I component modulating the subcarrier at an angle of 0 degrees, and the Q component at a subcarrier phase angle of 90 degrees. The reference burst is at an angle of 57 degrees with respect to the I carrier.

PAL The chrominance subcarrier is suppressed-carrier amplitude modulated by the U and V components, with the U component modulating the subcarrier at an angle of 0 degrees, and the V component at a subcarrier phase angle of 90 degrees. The V component is alternated 180 degrees on a line-by-line basis. The reference burst also alternates on a line-by-line basis between an angle of +135 degrees and –135 degrees relative to the U carrier.

SECAM The chrominance subcarrier is frequency modulated by the D_R and D_B signals on alternate lines. At the same time, the subcarrier frequency changes on alternate lines between SC_R and SC_B (see Note 1). The color burst also alternates between the two frequencies, as explained in Note 2.

5.8.2 Notes

Note 1: SECAM uses two FM-modulated color subcarriers transmitted on alternate horizontal lines. SC_R is 4.406250 MHz ($282{*}f_H$), and SC_B is 4.250000 MHz ($272f_H$).

Note 2: SECAM places a burst of SC_R or SC_B on alternate horizontal back porches, according to the subcarrier being used on the following line.

Note 3: Because the PAL burst alternates by 90 degrees from one line to the next, the 8.5-line burst suppression during vertical sync must be shifted according to a four-field sequence (called meandering) in order to ensure that each field begins with the burst at the same phase.

Note 4: SECAM color burst is suppressed during the entire vertical blanking interval. However, a different burst (called the bottle signal) is inserted on the 9 lines after vertical sync.

5.9 SUMMARY

There are many other kinds of video equipment in use today for production and postproduction. The points to remember from this chapter are:

- ☐ All video begins as analog (continuous values).
- ☐ Analog systems are never perfect.
- ☐ Analog distortions accumulate as you go through the system.
- ☐ You get what you pay for in video equipment.

5.10 REFERENCES

1. Benson, K. Blair (ed.). *Television Engineering Handbook*. McGraw-Hill. 1986.

5.11 FOR FURTHER READING

1. Brown, G. H. The Choice of Axes and Bandwidth for the Chrominance Signals in NTSC Color Television. *Proc. IRE* 42,1. January 1964. pp. 58–59.
2. Hunt, R. W. G. *The Reproduction of Color in Photography, Printing and Television*. John Wiley and Sons. 1975.

CHAPTER 6

DIGITAL VIDEO AND IMAGE COMPRESSION[1]

Arch C. Luther
Luther Associates

Reducing the amount of data needed to reproduce images or video (compression) saves storage space, increases access speed, and is the only way to achieve digital motion video on personal computers. This chapter surveys general techniques for video and image compression, and then it describes several standardized compression systems, including JPEG, MPEG, p*64, and DVI Technology. If you need more detailed or specific information, you can consult the references at the end of the chapter.

6.1 EVALUATING A COMPRESSION SYSTEM

In order to compare video compression systems, one must have ways to evaluate compression performance. Three key parameters need to be considered:

Amount or degree of compression
Image quality
Speed of compression or decompression

---

1 Material in sections 6.1–6.3.5 and 6.8 is based on material from Chapter 11, *Video Compression Technology in Digital Video in the PC Environment*, 2nd ed., by Arch C. Luther, McGraw-Hill, 1991. Reprinted by permission of McGraw-Hill.

In addition, we must also look at the hardware and software required by each compression method.

6.1.1 How Much Compression?

Compression performance is often specified by giving the ratio of input data to output data for the compression process (the compression ratio). This measure is a dangerous one unless you are careful to specify the input data format in a way that is truly comparable to the output data format. For example, the compressor might have used a 512 × 480, 24 bits-per-pixel (bpp) image as the input to the compression process, which then delivered a bitstream of 15,000 bytes. In that case, the input data was 737,280 bytes, and this would give a compression ratio of 737,280/15,000 = 49. However, the output display has only 256 × 240 pixels, so we achieved 4:1 of that compression by reducing the resolution. Therefore, the compression ratio with equal input and output resolutions is more like 12:1. A similar argument can be made for the bpp relationship between input and output—the output quality may not be anything near 24 bpp!

A much better way to specify the amount of compression is to determine the number of bits per displayed pixel needed in the compressed bitstream. For example, if we are reproducing a 256 × 240 pixel image from a 15,000-byte bitstream, we are compressing to

(bits) / (pixels)
(15,000 × 8) / (256 × 240) = 2 bits per pixel

The rest of this chapter will use this method to specify degree of compression.

6.1.2 How Good Is the Picture?

In talking about picture quality performance of a compression system, it is helpful to divide the world of compression into two parts—lossless compression and lossy compression. Lossless compression means that the reproduced image is not changed in any way by the compression/decompression process; therefore, we do not have to worry about the picture quality for a lossless system—the output picture will be exactly the same as the input picture. Lossless compression is possible because we can use more efficient methods of data transmission than the pixel-by-pixel PCM format that comes from a digitizer.

On the other hand, lossy compression systems by definition do make some change to the image—something is different. The trick is making that difference hard for the viewer to see. Lossy compression systems may introduce any of the digital video artifacts, or they may even create some unique artifacts of their own. None of these effects is easy to quantify, and final decisions about compression systems, or about any specific compressed image, will usually have to be made after a subjective evaluation—

there's not a good alternative to looking at test pictures. The various measures of analog picture quality—signal-to-noise ratio, resolution, color errors, etc., may be useful in some cases, but only after viewing real pictures to make sure that the right artifacts are being measured.

6.1.3 How Fast Does It Compress or Decompress?

In many applications, compression and decompression will be done at different times; they may even be done with totally different systems at different locations. The reason for this is that there is usually storage or transmission of the image in between the two processes—storage or transmission is why we need compression in the first place. Therefore, we must evaluate the speeds of compression or decompression separately.

In most cases of storing still images, compression speed is less critical than decompression speed—since we are compressing the image ahead of time to store it, we can usually take our time in that process. On the other hand, decompression usually takes place while the user is waiting for the result, and speed is much more important. With motion video compression there is a need for fast compression in order to capture motion video in real time as it comes from a camera or VCR. In any case, compression and decompression speed is usually easy to specify and measure.

6.1.4 What Hardware and Software Does It Take?

Some amount of compression and decompression can be done in software using standard PC hardware. Except with very simple algorithms, this approach quickly runs into speed problems—the process takes too long, and simple algorithms do not provide the best compression. This is a moving target with time because of the continued advance in the processing power of PCs. However, at present, most systems will benefit from some special hardware to speed up or accelerate compression/decompression.

Complex algorithms performing tens, hundreds, or even thousands of operations relative to every input pixel will require proportionally more powerful hardware, or they will become extremely slow. The trade between speed and hardware processing power is an important choice in designing a compression/decompression system.

One can also choose between general-purpose or special-purpose acceleration hardware. A single algorithm can usually be implemented more economically in special-purpose hardware which has the algorithm built right in (called hard-wired) to the circuits. On the other hand, this kind of system may be more expensive to design compared to utilizing general-purpose hardware already available off the shelf, where the algorithm is implemented in software. Also, the hard-wired system is limited to the one algorithm and any options which were designed initially. Improvements will not be possible without changing the hardware design and possibly obsoleting all existing equipment. Because of this, it is important that the algorithm be standardized before designing hard-wired compression or decompression equipment.

6.2 REDUNDANCY AND VISIBILITY

Redundancy in a digital video image occurs when the same information is transmitted more than once. For example:

- ☐ In any area of the picture where the same color spans more than one pixel location, there is redundancy between pixels, since adjacent pixels will have the same value. This applies both horizontally and vertically.
- ☐ When the scene or part of the scene contains predominantly vertically oriented objects, there is a possibility that two adjacent lines will be partially or completely the same, giving us redundancy between lines. These two types of redundancy (pixel and line) exist in any image and are called spatial redundancy.
- ☐ When a scene is stationary or only slightly moving, there is a further possibility of redundancy between frames of a motion sequence—adjacent frames in time are similar, or they may be related by a simple function such as translation. This kind of redundancy is called temporal redundancy.

Compression schemes may exploit any or all of these aspects of redundancy.

Another consideration in image reproduction is that we do not need to display more information than our viewer will be able to see. The best example of this arises from the human eye's poor spatial acuity for certain colors. Because of this characteristic of the viewer, it is not necessary to provide independent color values for every pixel. The color information can be transmitted at lower resolution than the luminance or black and white portion of the image. This principle, called color subsampling, is used successfully in NTSC and PAL color television, and it can be implemented in a digital video system as well.

6.3 VIDEO COMPRESSION TECHNIQUES

A great deal of research has been done in image and video compression technology, going back more than 25 years. The references at the end of this chapter will lead you into the voluminous literature of this research. Many powerful techniques have been developed, simulated, and fully characterized in the literature; in fact, today it is quite difficult to invent something new in this field—it has been so well researched.

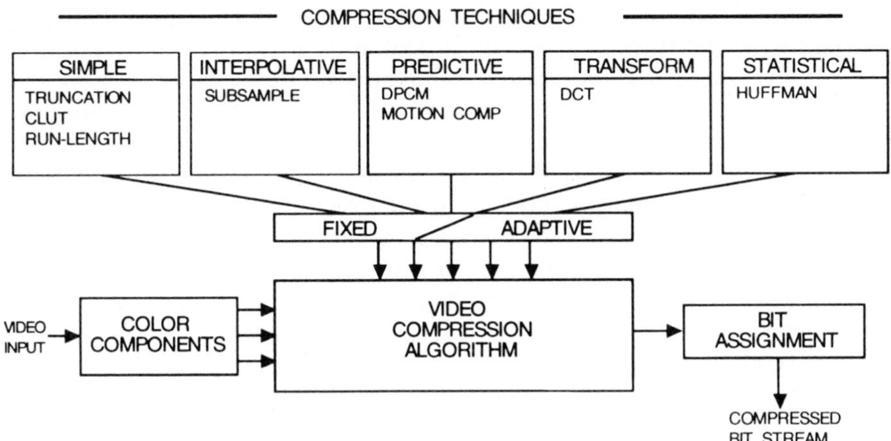

Figure 6.1 Compression techniques

However, broad application of the more sophisticated video compression approaches has not been practical because of the cost of the hardware required. That is now changing because of the power of high-performance digital signal processing chips and custom VLSI devices.

In this discussion, we will use the word technique to refer to a single method of compression—usable by itself, but possibly also used in combination with other techniques. On the other hand, an algorithm refers to the collection of all the techniques used by any particular video compression system. Figure 6.1 is a block diagram of how techniques are used to create an algorithm.

We will assume that the input to the compression system is always a PCM digitized signal in color component (RGB, YUV, etc.) form. Most compression systems will deal with the color components separately, processing each one by itself. In decompression, the components similarly are separately recovered and then combined into the appropriate display format after decompression. Note, however, that there is nothing that requires that the individual color components be processed in the same way during compression and decompression—in fact, there are sometimes significant advantages to handling the components of the same image by different techniques. This brings up immediately that we must choose the color component format to use, and that choice could make a big difference in what performance is achieved by the system. Two obvious choices that we have already discussed are RGB components or luminance/chrominance components. Where it is relevant, the significance of the color component choice will also be covered.

Similarly, there is always a possibility of making any technique adaptive, which means that the technique can change as a function of the image content. Adaptivity is not a compression technique itself; rather, it is a way to cause any given technique to be more optimized locally in the image or temporally in the frame sequence. Almost all the compression techniques we will be discussing can be made adaptive, but of course this adds complexity. Where adaptivity is an important aspect, it will be discussed with each technique.

The output of a compression process is a bitstream—it is usually no longer a bitmap and individual pixels may not be recognizable. The structure of the bitstream is important, however, because it can also affect the compression efficiency and the behavior of the system when errors occur in transmission or storage. Therefore, Figure 6.1 shows a separate box called bit assignment—this is where the bitstream structure is imposed on the compressed data. It may be a task which is subsumed in the algorithm, or it may be a separate step in the process.

6.3.1 Simple Compression Techniques

A good example of simple compression is truncation—reducing data through arbitrary lowering of the bits per pixel. This is done by throwing away some of the least significant bits for every pixel. If we go too far with truncation, we will begin to see contouring, and our image will start looking like a cartoon. However, many images can stand this up to a point; so, for example, we can usually truncate to 16 bpp with good results on real images. 16 bpp is usually done by assigning bits to color components such as R:G:B 5:5:5 or Y:V:U 6:5:5. In the R:G:B 5:5:5 case, the 16th bit could be used as a flag for some other purpose, such as a keying signal. Truncation is attractive because its processing is extremely simple.

Another simple compression scheme, which creates a different kind of artifact, is the color lookup table (CLUT) approach. With a CLUT, the pixel values in the bitmap represent an index into a table of colors, but the table of colors will have much greater bpp than the pixel values. It is usually done with pixels having no more than 8 bpp, which means that the entire picture must be reproduced with 256 or fewer colors at a time. The colors in the CLUT are chosen from a palette represented by the color depth in the lookup table. For some kinds of images, that is not as bad as it sounds—if the 256 colors are carefully chosen. However, that means each image must be processed ahead of time to choose the 256 best colors for that image (a unique CLUT must be created for each image), and that is a nontrivial amount of preprocessing. Going higher than 8 bpp with CLUT (more colors) will of course give better results, but by the time we get to 16 bpp, it will probably be better to simply use the truncation approach of the previous paragraph because the processing for truncation is much simpler.

A third simple technique is run-length (RL) coding. In this technique, blocks of repeated pixels are replaced with a single value and a count of how many times to repeat that value. It works well on images which have areas of solid colors—for example, computer-generated images, cartoons, or CLUT images. Depending entirely on the kind of image, RL coding can achieve large amounts of compression—well below 1 bpp. However, its effectiveness is limited to images (or other data streams) that contain large numbers of repeated values, which is seldom the case for real images from a video camera.

6.3.2 Interpolative Techniques

Interpolative compression at the pixel level consists of transmitting a subset of the pixels and using interpolation to reconstruct the intervening pixels. Within our definition of compression, this is not a valid technique for use on entire pixels because we are effectively reducing the number of independent pixels contained in the output, and that is not compression. The interpolation in that case is simply a means for reducing the visibility of pixellation, but the output pixel count is still equal to the subset. However, there is one case where interpolation is a valid technique. It can be used just on the chrominance part of the image while the luminance part is not interpolated. This is called color subsampling, and it is most valuable with luminance-chrominance component images (YUV, YIQ, etc.).

The color components I and Q of the YIQ format (in NTSC color television) were carefully chosen by the developers so that they could be transmitted at reduced resolution. This works because a viewer has poor acuity for color changes in an image, so the lower resolution of the color components really is not noticed. The same is true for YUV components, which are used in PAL television systems.

For example, in a digital system starting with 8 bits each of YUV (24 bpp total), we can subsample the U and V components by a factor of 4 both horizontally and vertically (a total ratio of 16:1). The selected U and V pixels remain at 8 bpp each, so we still are capable of the full range of colors. When the output image is properly reconstructed by interpolation, this technique gives excellent reproduction of real pictures. The degree of compression works out to 9 bpp:

bpp = (luminance) 8 + (UV) 16/(subsamp. ratio) 16 = 9

Please note that we have used the term "real" images when talking about the advantages of color subsampling and interpolation. It is not as effective on "nonreal," i.e., computer-generated images. Sometimes a computer-generated image using color subsampling and interpolation will have objectionable color fringes on objects, or thin colored lines may disappear. This is inherent in the technique.

Interpolation can also be applied between frames of a motion sequence. In this case, certain frames are compressed by still compression or by predictive compression; the frames between these are compressed by doing an interpolation between the other frames and sending only the data needed to correct the interpolation. This will be covered further when discussing motion video compression algorithms.

6.3.3 Predictive Techniques

Anyone who can predict the future has a tremendous advantage—that applies to video compression as much as it applies to the stock market. In video compression, the future is the next pixel, or the next line, or the next frame. We said earlier that typical scenes contain a degree of redundancy at all these levels—the future is not completely different from the past. Predictive compression techniques are based on the fact that we can store the previous item (frame, line, or pixel) and use it to help build the next item. If we can identify what is the same from one item to the next, we need only transmit the part that is different because we have predicted the part that is the same.

DPCM

The simplest form of predictive compression operates at the pixel level with a technique called differential PCM (DPCM). In DPCM, we compare adjacent pixels and then transmit only the difference between them. Because adjacent pixels often are similar, the difference values have a high probability of being small and they can safely be transmitted with fewer bits than it would take to send a whole new pixel. For example, if we are compressing 8-bit component pixels, and we use 4 bits for the difference value, we can maintain the full 8-bit dynamic range as long as there is never a change of more than 16 steps between adjacent pixels. In this case, the DPCM step size is equal to one quantization step of the incoming signal.

In decompression, the difference information is used to modify the previous pixel to get the new pixel. Normally the difference bits would represent only a portion of the amplitude range of an entire pixel, meaning that if adjacent pixels did call for a full-amplitude change from black to white, the DPCM system would overload. In that case, it would take a number of pixel times (16, for the example of the last paragraph) before the output could reach full white, because each difference pixel only represents a fraction of the amplitude range. This effect is called slope overload, and it causes smearing of high-contrast edges in the image.

ADPCM

The distortion from slope overload may be reduced by going to adaptive DPCM (ADPCM). There are many ways to implement ADPCM, but one common approach is to adapt by changing the step size represented by the difference bits. In the previous example, if we knew that the black-to-white step was coming, we could increase the step size before the b-w step came, so that when we got there, the difference bits would represent full range, and a full-amplitude step could then be reproduced. After the step had been completed, the adaptive circuit would crank the step size back down in order to better reproduce fine gradations. This changes the artifact from slope overload's smearing to edge quantization—an effect of quantization noise surrounding high-contrast edges. You might have a hard time deciding which is better.

In the previous example of ADPCM, we glossed over the problem of how the decompression system knows what step size to use at any time. This information must somehow be coded into the compressed bitstream. There are lots of ways for doing that (which we will not go into here) but you should be aware that using adaptation with any algorithm will add the problem of telling the decompression system how to adapt. A certain amount of overhead data and extra processing will always be required to implement adaptation.

The DPCM example also highlights a problem of predictive compression techniques in general. What happens if an error creeps into the compressed data? Since each pixel depends on the previous pixel, one incorrect pixel value will tend to become many incorrect pixel values after decompression. This can be a serious problem. A single incorrect pixel would normally not be much of a problem in a straight PCM image, especially a motion image; it would just be a fleeting dot that a viewer might never see. However, if the differential system expands a single dot error into a line that goes all the way across the picture (or maybe even into subsequent lines), everyone will see it. Therefore, predictive compression schemes typically add something else to ensure that recovery from an error is possible and that it happens quickly enough that error visibility will not be objectionable. A common approach is to make a differential system periodically start over, such as at the beginning of each scanning line or at the beginning of a frame.

After all the previous discussion, it shouldn't be a surprise to say that DPCM or ADPCM are not widely used by themselves for video compression. The artifacts of slope overload and edge quantization become fatal as we try to achieve more than about 2:1 compression. The techniques, however, do find their way into more complex compression algorithms that combine other more powerful techniques with some form of differential encoding. (DPCM and ADPCM are widely used for audio compression, as discussed in Chapter 4.)

Other Predictive Techniques

Continuing with predictive compression schemes and moving to the next higher level, we should talk about prediction based on scanning line redundancy. However, line-level prediction is not often used by itself; rather, it tends to be subsumed in the two-dimensional transform techniques which very neatly combine pixel and line processing in one package.

Prediction is also a valuable technique at the frame level for motion video compression. We will discuss it later.

6.3.4 Transform Coding Techniques

A transform is a process that converts a bundle of data into an alternate form which is more convenient for some particular purpose. Transforms are ordinarily designed to be reversible—that is, there exists an inverse transform which can restore the original data. In video compression, a "bundle of data" is a group of pixels—usually a two-dimensional array of pixels from an image, for example, 8 x 8 pixels. Transformation is done to create an alternate form which can be transmitted or stored using less data. At decompression time, the inverse transform is run on the data to reproduce the original pixel information.

6.3.5 A Simple Transform Example

In order to explain how a transform works, we will make up a very simple example. Consider a 2 × 2 block of monochrome (or single-color component) pixels, as shown in Figure 6.2.

We can construct a simple transform for this block by doing the following:

1. Take pixel A as the base value for the block. The full value of pixel A will be one of our transformed values.
2. Calculate three other transformed values by taking the difference between the three other pixels and pixel A.

Figure 6.2 shows the arithmetic for this transformation, and it also shows the arithmetic for the inverse transform function. Note that we now have four new values, which are simply linear combinations of the four original pixel values. They contain the same information.

Now that we have made this transformation, we can observe that the redundancy has been moved around in the values so that the difference values may be transmitted with fewer bits than the pixels themselves would

2 x 2 ARRAY OF PIXELS

A	B
C	D

TRANSFORM	INVERSE TRANSFORM
X0 = A	A_n = X0
X1 = B - A	B_n = X1 + X0
X2 = C - A	C_n = X2 + X0
X3 = D - A	D_n = X3 + X0

Figure 6.2 Example of simple transform coding

have required. For example, if the original pixels were 8 bits each, the 2 × 2 block then used 32 bits. With the transform, we might assign 4 bits each for the difference values and keep 8 bits for the base pixel—this would reduce the data to only 8 + (3 × 4) or 20 bits for the 2 × 2 block (resulting in compression to 5 bits/pixel). The idea here is that the transform has allowed us to extract the differences between adjacent pixels in two dimensions, and errors in coding of these differences will be less visible than the same errors in the pixels themselves.

This example is not really a useful transform—it is too simple. Useful transforms typically operate on larger blocks, and they perform more complex calculations. In general, transform coding becomes more effective with larger block sizes, but the calculations also become more difficult with larger blocks. The trick in developing a good transform is to make it effective with calculations that are easy to implement in hardware or software and will run fast. It is beyond our scope here to describe all the transforms that have been developed for image compression, but you can find them in the literature. The Discrete Cosine Transform (DCT) is especially important for video and image compression and is covered in detail below.

The Discrete Cosine Transform

The DCT is performed on a block of horizontally and vertically adjacent pixels—typically 8 × 8. Thus, 64 pixel values at a time are processed by the transform; the output is 64 new values, representing amplitudes of the two-dimensional spatial frequency components of the 64-pixel block. These are referred to as DCT coefficients. The coefficient for zero spatial frequency is called the DC coefficient, and it is the average value of all the pixels in the block. The remaining 63 coefficients are the AC coefficients, and they represent the amplitudes of progressively higher horizontal and vertical spatial frequencies in the block.

Since adjacent pixel values tend to be similar or vary slowly from one to another, the DCT processing provides opportunity for compression by forcing most of the signal energy into the lower spatial frequency components. In most cases, many of the higher-frequency coefficients will have zero or near-zero values and can be ignored.

A DCT decoder performs the reverse process—spatial frequency coefficients are converted back to pixel values. Theoretically, if DCT encoding and decoding is done with complete precision, the process of encoding followed by decoding would be transparent. However, in a real system there will be slight errors because the signals have been quantized with finite numbers of bits, and the DCT algorithm involves transcendental mathematical functions, which can only be approximated in any real system. Thus, the process will not be perfectly transparent. The trick is to choose the quantizing parameters so that the errors are not visible in the reproduced image. This is successfully done in the standards discussed later, but the small remaining errors explain why DCT cannot be used for lossless compression.

6.3.6 Statistical Coding

Another means of compression is to take advantage of the statistical distribution of the pixel values of an image or of the statistics of the data created from one of the techniques discussed above. These are called statistical coding techniques, or sometimes entropy coding, and they may be contained either in the compression algorithm itself, or applied separately as part of the bit assignment following another compression technique. The usual case for image data is that all possible values are not equally probable—there will be some kind of nonuniform distribution of the values. Another way of saying that is: Some data values will occur more frequently than other data values. We can set up a coding technique which codes the more frequently occurring values with words using fewer bits, and the less frequently occurring values will be coded with longer words. This results in a reduced number of bits in the final bitstream, and it can be a lossless technique. One widely used form of this coding is called Huffman coding.

The above type of coding has some overhead, however, in that we must tell the decompression system how to interpret a variable-word-length bitstream. This is normally done by transmitting a table (called a code book) ahead of time. This is simply a table which tells how to decode the bitstream back to the original values. The code book may be transmitted once for each individual image, or it may even be transmitted for individual blocks of a single image. On the compression side, there is overhead needed to figure out the code book—the data statistics must be calculated for an image or for each block.

6.3.7 Motion Video Compression Techniques

In the still-image compression techniques that we discussed above, we gave little consideration to the matter of compression or decompression speed. With still images, processing only needs to be fast enough that the user does not get bored waiting for things to happen. However, when one begins to think about motion video compression systems, the speed issue becomes overwhelming. Processing of a single image in one second or less is usually satisfactory for stills. However, motion video implies a high enough frame rate to produce subjectively smooth motion, which for most people is 15 frames per second or higher. Full-motion video as used here refers to normal television frame rates—25 frames per second for European systems, and 30 frames per second for North America and Japan. These numbers mean that our digital video system must deliver a new image every 30–40 milliseconds. If the system cannot do that, motion will be slow or jerky, and the system will quickly be judged unacceptable.

At the same time that we need more speed for motion compression, we also need to accomplish more compression. This comes about because of data rate considerations. Storage media have data rate limitations, so they cannot simply be speeded up to deliver data more rapidly. For example, the CD-ROM's continuous data rate is fixed at 153,600 bytes per second—there is no way to get data out faster. If CD-ROM is being used for full-motion video at 30 frames per second, we will have to live with 5,120 bytes per frame. Therefore, we face absolute limits on the amount of data available for each frame of motion video (at least on the average); this will determine the degree of compression we must achieve.

For CD-ROM at 5,120 bytes of data per frame (40,960 bits per frame) and at a resolution of 256 × 240 pixels, the required compression works out to be 0.67 bits per pixel. Some still compression systems can work down to this level, but the pictures are not very good, and 256 × 240 already is a fairly low pixel count. Therefore, we should look at motion video to see if there are possibilities for compression techniques which can be used in addition to the techniques we discussed for stills.

Fortunately, motion video offers its own opportunities to achieve additional compression. There is the redundancy between adjacent frames—a motion video compression system can (or must) exploit that redundancy. Techniques for dealing with this are prediction and interpolation or a special technique called motion compensation. We will discuss motion compensation shortly.

Another concept that comes into play with motion video systems is the idea of symmetry between compression and decompression. A symmetric compression/decompression system will use the same hardware for both compression and decompression and perform both processes at roughly the same speed. Such a system for motion video will require hardware that is too expensive for a single-user system, or else it will have to sacrifice picture quality in favor of lower-cost hardware. The reason is that a symmetric system must digitize and compress motion video in real time, which implies that the system must process data rates that can exceed 20 Mb per second.

However, this problem can be effectively bypassed by the use of an asymmetric system where the compression is performed on expensive hardware, but the decompression is done by low-cost hardware. This works in situations where the single-user system needs only to play back compressed video which has been prepared ahead of time—it will never have to do compression.

In fact, most interactive video applications do not require that the end-user system contains a compression capability—only decompression. Motion video for this class of application can be compressed (once) during the application design process, and the final user only plays back the compressed video. Therefore, the cost of the compression process is shared by all the users of the application. This concept can lead to the establishment of a centralized compression service which performs compression for many application developers, thus sharing the costs even further.

Motion Compensation

Consider the case of a motion video sequence where nothing is moving in the scene. Each frame of the motion video should be exactly the same as the previous one. In a digital system, it is clear that all we need to do is transmit the first frame of this scene, store that and simply display the same frame until something moves. No additional information needs to be sent during the time the image is stationary. However, if now a dog walks across our scene, we have to do something to introduce this motion. We could simply take the image of the walking dog by itself, and send that along with the coordinates of where to place it on the stationary background scene—sending a new dog picture for each frame. To the extent that the dog is much smaller than the total scene, we are still not using much data to achieve a moving picture.

The example of the walking dog on a stationary background scene is an overly simplified case of motion video, but it already reveals two of the problems involved in motion compensation:

How can we tell if an image is stationary?

How do we extract the part of the image which moves?

We can try to answer these questions by some form of comparison of adjacent frames of the motion video sequence. We can assume that both the previous and the current frames are available to us during the compression process. If we do a pixel-by-pixel compare between the two frames, the compare should produce zero for any pixels which have not changed, and it will be nonzero for pixels which are somehow involved in motion. Then we could select only the pixels with nonzero compares and send them to the decompressing system. Of course, we would have to also send some information which tells the decompressing system where to put these pixels.

However, this very simple approach, which is a form of frame-to-frame DPCM, is really not too useful because of several problems. First, the pixel compare between frames will seldom produce a zero, even for a completely stationary image, because of analog noise or quantizing noise in the system. This could be alleviated by introducing a threshold that would let us accept small comparison values as zero, but there is a more serious problem—images from video or film cameras are seldom stationary. Even if the scene itself contains no motion (which is unusual in natural scenes) the camera may be moving slightly, causing all pixel compares to fail. Even partial pixel movements will create changes large enough to upset the comparison technique.

Therefore, more sophisticated techniques are needed to do the motion detection for the purpose of motion compensation. This problem is usually addressed by dividing the image into blocks, just as we did with still images for transform coding. Each block is examined for motion, using approaches which consider all of the pixels in the block for motion detection of that block. If the block is found to contain no motion, a code is sent to the decompressor to leave that block the way it was in the previous frame. If the block does have motion, a transform may be performed and the appropriate bits sent to the decompressor to reproduce that block with the inverse transform.

If enough computing power is available for the compression process, still more sophisticated approaches can be pursued. For example, blocks which contain motion can be further examined to see if they are simply a translation of a block from the previous frame. If so, only the coordinates of the translation (motion vectors) need to be sent to tell the decompressor how to create that block from the previous frame. A variation of this approach is used in the MPEG video compression standard (Figure 6.3). Even more elaborate techniques can be conceived to try to create the new frame using as much as possible of the information from the previous frame instead of having to send new information.

6.4 STANDARDIZATION OF ALGORITHMS

The preceding discussion of techniques introduced the building blocks available for creating algorithms. An actual algorithm consists of one or more techniques which operate on the raw digitized image to create a compressed bitstream. The number of algorithm possibilities is nearly infinite. However, practical applications require that all users who wish to interchange compressed digital images or video must use exactly the same algorithm choice. Further, sophisticated algorithms will benefit from the development of special hardware or processing chips, where the algorithm and its options may be cast in the silicon. All this expresses the need for a standard to allow the orderly growth of markets which utilize image or video compression technology.

A successful example of a digital imaging market that took off once a standard was developed is the Group 3 facsimile machine, which is standardized under CCITT Recommendation T.4.1980. However, this Recommendation applies only to bilevel images (one bit per pixel), whereas here we are interested in continuous-tone images, typically represented by 8 bits per pixel or more, and often in color. Applications such as desktop publishing, graphic arts, color facsimile, wirephoto transmission, medical imaging, computer multimedia, and others, have a serious need for a continuous-tone image compression standard.

Driven by these needs, there has been a strong effort to develop international standards for still image and motion video compression algorithms, under way for several years in the International Organization for Standardization (ISO) and the International Electrotechnical Commission (IEC). There are two working parties for algorithm standardization in a joint ISO/IEC Committee (called JTC1). These working parties are the Joint Photographic Expert Group (JPEG), which considers still image standards

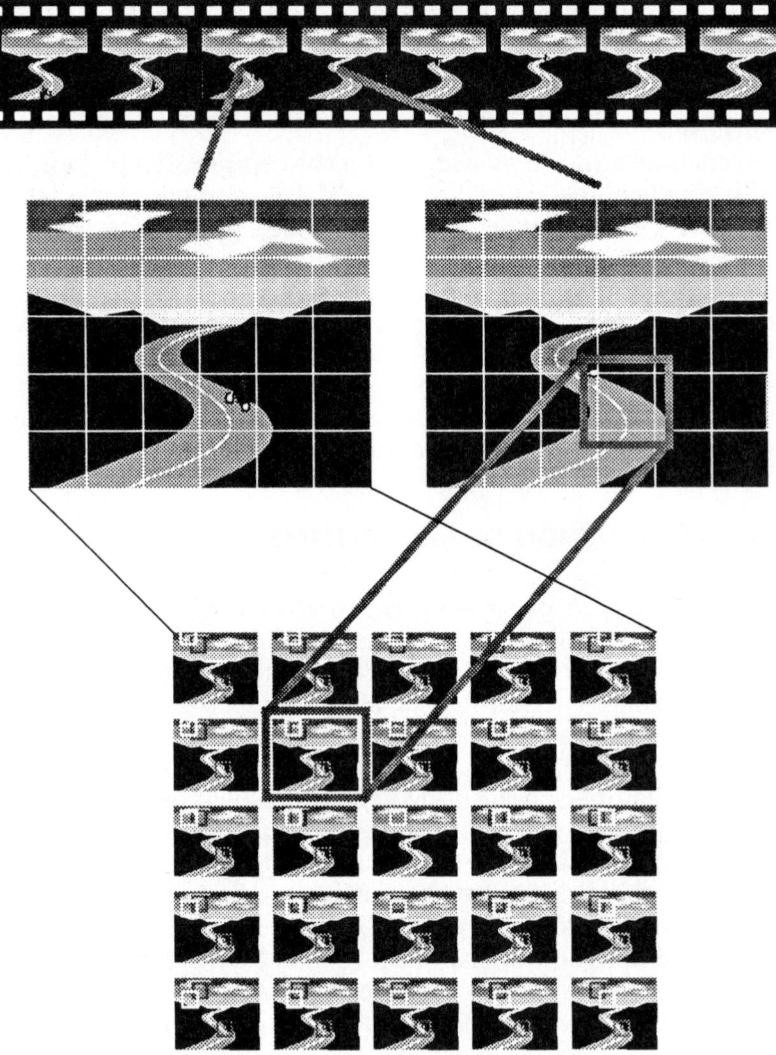

Figure 6.3 An example of motion estimation for a block video sequence. If the receiver buffers the previous frame, then the transmitter can send either the transformed block or the coordinates of a closely matching block in the buffered frame. If the match isn't exact, then the vector might be accompanied by a correction block so that the receiver can reproduce the block with higher fidelity.

in several categories, and the Motion Picture Coding Expert Group (MPEG), which considers algorithms for motion video compression. These groups have both produced standards documents which are described in detail below.

Standardization of image or video compression can be done at several levels. It can be based on special hardware, which is the case for DVI Technology; it can be based on special software; or it can be done at the level of a bitstream, which is the case for JPEG and MPEG. Each of these approaches has advantages and disadvantages, but a bitstream-level standard will have the broadest applicability because no special hardware or software is inherently required. However, a bitstream standard does not provide a complete system for compression or decompression—it becomes the task of the system vendor, the software supplier, and the user to assemble the pieces which will actually put the standard into use. But this situation has the opportunity for innovation, competition, and enhancement in implementation of the standard, while protecting the feature that image or video data can be exchanged between systems or users.

6.5 THE JPEG IMAGE COMPRESSION STANDARD

6.5.1 JPEG—Objectives

JPEG undertook to develop a single standard [1] applicable to the still-imaging needs of a wide range of applications in all the different industries that might use digital continuous-tone imaging. The scope of this is best seen by listing the objectives in detail:

1. To be at or near the state of the art for degree of compression versus image quality,
2. To be parameterizable so that the user can select the desired compression versus quality tradeoff,
3. To be applicable to practically any kind of source image, without regard to dimensions, image content, aspect ratio, etc.,
4. To have computational requirements that are reasonable for both hardware or software implementations, and
5. To support four different modes of operation:
   (a) sequential encoding, where each image component is encoded in the same order that it was scanned;
   (b) progressive encoding, where the image is encoded in multiple passes so that a coarse image is presented rapidly, followed by repeated images showing greater and greater detail;
   (c) lossless encoding, where the encoding guarantees exact reproduction of all the data in the source image;
   (d) hierarchical encoding, where the image is encoded at multiple resolutions.

These objectives were extremely ambitious, yet they are largely met by the completed standard, which is testimony to the excellent work of the

JPEG committee. The four modes of operation and the options within them cause the complete standard to be quite complex. However, most implementations will not use them all, but rather they will focus on the choices that are relevant to the intended application(s). In this way, the standard is more like a shopping list of algorithms, from which you can select the approach which best suits your purpose. The JPEG standard defines a Baseline sequential coder, which will be sufficient for a wide range of applications. Many early implementations are only supporting the Baseline.

6.5.2 JPEG—Architectures

The lossy modes of operation (a, b, d) are implemented with DCT encoding of 8 x 8 pixel blocks, followed by one of two statistical coding methods, while the lossless option (c) is implemented with simple predictive coding followed by statistical coding. This is shown in Figure 6.4.

The architectures shown in Figure 6.4 apply to a single gray scale image or to one of the components of a color image. To compress a color image, the color components can be either completely compressed one after another, or the three components can be interleaved for each block of the image. In the case of sequential-mode encoding, DCT encoding is done on the blocks of the image as they are scanned, and the DCT coefficient output is transmitted block by block in the same order. For progressive-mode encoding, an image buffer is added after the DCT encoding step. The progressive-mode behavior is obtained by reading out different portions of the DCT coefficients to achieve progressively improved quality over several scans. For hierarchical-mode encoding, processing is added ahead of the DCT encoder to filter and subsample the source image before encoding. This subsampling and encoding is done repeatedly with progressively less subsampling to transmit images of increasing resolution one after another.

6.5.3 JPEG—DCT Encoding and Quantization

The output of the DCT encoder (the DCT coefficients) is shown in Figure 6.5a as a 2-D array with the DC coefficient in the upper left corner, and the AC coefficients arranged with increasing spatial frequency horizontally and vertically. These components are quantized according to a 64-entry table, which must be specified to the encoder by the application. The quantization table has 8 bits per entry and specifies the step size of quantizing for each DCT coefficient. This allows each coefficient to be represented with no more precision than is necessary to achieve the desired image quality. The standard does not specify any quantization tables; these must be provided by the application and will become part of the data stream, so the decoder knows what table was used. Therefore, modification of the quantization table specified during encoding is one way to vary the degree of compression.

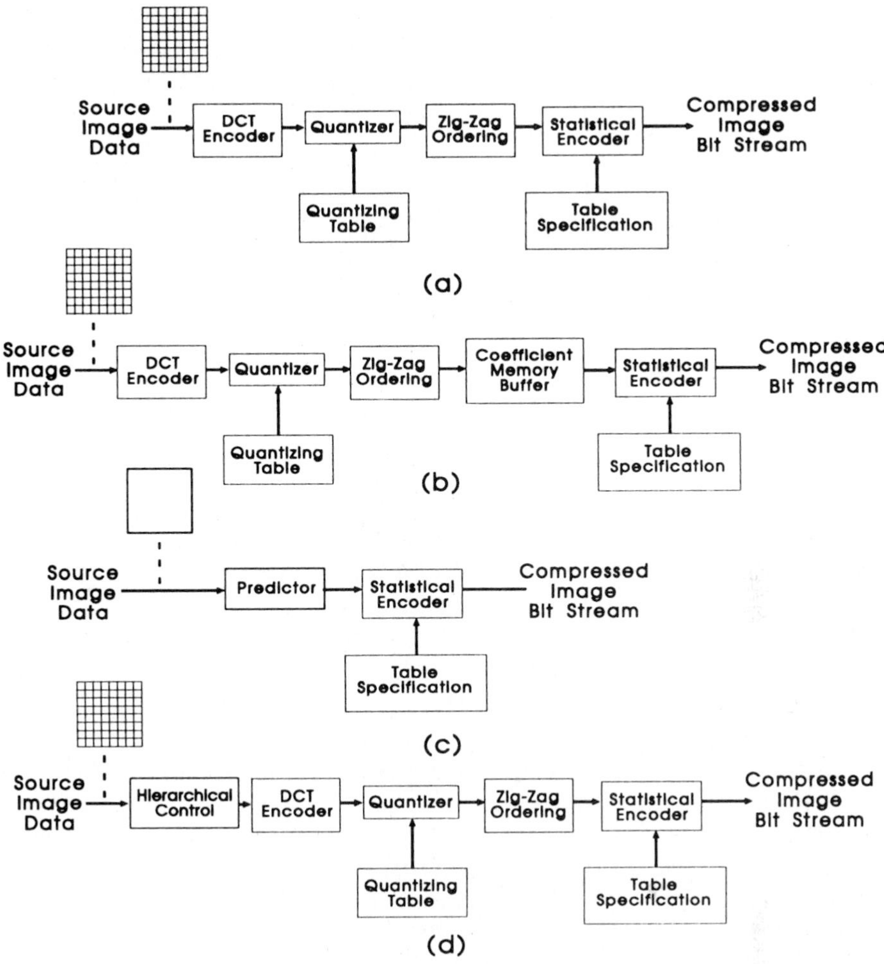

Figure 6.4 (a) sequential coding block diagram, (b) progressive encoding block diagram, (c) lossless coding block diagram, (d) hierarchical coding block diagram

After quantization, the DC coefficient is treated differently from the AC coefficients. Because there is usually a strong correlation between DC coefficients of adjacent 8 × 8 blocks, the DC coefficient is encoded as the difference from the previous block in the encoding sequence.

Figure 6.4a also shows a step called zig-zag ordering between the quantizer and the statistical coder. This is an important step, which arranges the DCT coefficients so that the statistical coding will be more effective. It is diagrammed in Figure 6.5b.

In order to create a bitstream where coefficients that are more likely to be nonzero (low-frequency ones) are placed before coefficients that are more likely to be zero (high-frequency ones), the zig-zag sequence shown by Figure 6.5b is used to read the coefficients into the bitstream. The result

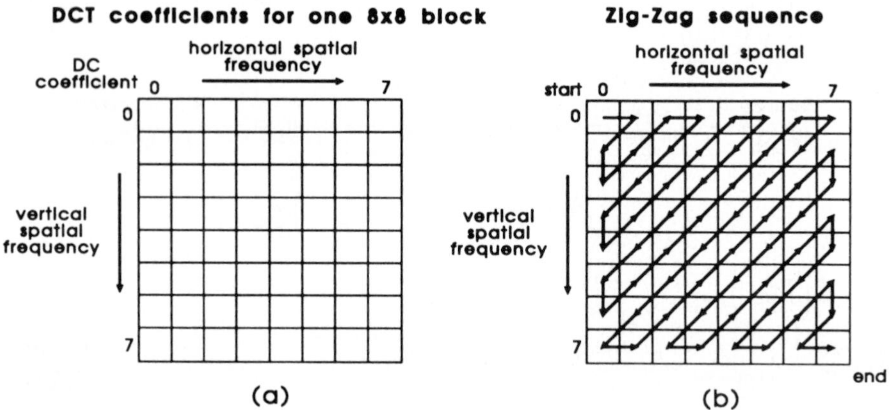

Figure 6.5 (a) 2-D matrix of DCT coefficients, (b) zig-zag ordering

is that all the zero-value coefficients tend to be together at the end of the block and can be transmitted with very few bits using a simple run-length code.

6.5.4 JPEG—Statistical Coding

The final encoder processing step is statistical coding. It achieves lossless compression by encoding the quantized DCT coefficients more efficiently based on their statistical characteristics. The JPEG standard allows two types of statistical coding—Huffman coding or arithmetic coding. The Baseline sequential coder uses only Huffman statistical coding.

Huffman coding requires specification of the Huffman table or code book; this is the job of the application, the standard does not specify a table, except for the Baseline coder. The Huffman tables also become part of the image bitstream; the standard supports up to four Huffman tables per image, to provide for different tables for each component of a multicomponent image.

The arithmetic statistical coding option does not require a separate table to be provided, but it does require a little more processing for implementation. However, it results in a little better compression (5 to 10 percent) for many images.

6.5.5 JPEG—Predictive Lossless Coding

The lossless compression option, Figure 6.4c, does not use DCT. Instead, a simple predictor is used, but there is a choice of seven different kinds of prediction available. The different predictor choices specify how many and which adjacent pixels are used to predict the next pixel. The statistical coding in the lossless mode can use either of the two methods specified for the DCT modes, and is similar to what is specified for the DC coefficient of the DCT modes.

The lossless compression will work with source images having from 2 to 16 bpp, and typically deliver around 2:1 compression for photographic color images.

6.5.6 JPEG—Performance

Compression performance is best specified by relating image quality to bits per pixel in the compressed data stream. This relationship depends to some degree on the characteristics of the source image—some images are harder to compress successfully than others. With this in mind, here are some figures for "typical" source images [2]:

0.25–0.5 bpp: moderate to good quality, sufficient for some applications;

0.5–0.75 bpp: good to very good quality, sufficient for many applications;

0.75–1.5 bpp: excellent quality, sufficient for most applications;

1.5–2.0 bpp: undistinguishable from the original, sufficient for the most demanding applications.

6.6 ITU-T RECOMMENDATION H.261 (p*64)

Digital video compression was first used commercially in the teleconferencing and video phone fields. Both of these services transmit video over digital telephone channels, which offer data rates at integral multiples of 64 kb/sec. ITU-T undertook to develop video compression standards for these services, resulting in ITU-T Recommendation H.261 [3], completed in 1990. This standard is often referred to as p*64, because of the integer channel data rate multiplier (p), which can have values between 1 and 30.

6.6.1 Objectives

H.261 was developed for video and audio transmission over digital telephone channels worldwide. More specific objectives are:

1. The source video may be either a 525-line or a 625-line television signal. The application must convert the source video to a common intermediate format (CIF—part of the standard) that is independent of the source video format. This permits standard coders and decoders to communicate between regions that have different television formats.

2. The bitstream produced by a standard coder is self-contained and may be combined with other signals during transmission (audio, for example).
3. The Recommendation is intended to be used at video bit rates between 40 kb/sec and 2 Mbps. The standard will deliver acceptable video quality for teleconferencing or visual telephone at these data rates, but recognizing that the lower data rates will cause slower transmission.
4. Bidirectional and unidirectional visual communications are both supported.
5. The bitstream shall include error-correction capabilities, which are optionally used by decoders.
6. Features necessary to support switched multipoint operation must be included.

6.6.2 Common Intermediate Format

The CIF specifies a luminance-chrominance component format (Y, CB, CR) with 8 bits/sample for all components and operating at 30 frames/second. Luminance sampling for the CIF is 352 pixels per line and 288 lines per picture. Sampling of the two color-difference components is 172 × 144 (2:1 subsampling in each direction). A second format, called quarter-CIF (QCIF), cuts all the numbers above in half. The QCIF format is supported by all coders and decoders, the CIF format is optional. This is consistemt with the emphasis on the lower data rates in the standard.

6.6.3 Coding Algorithm

H.261 uses interpicture prediction to exploit temporal redundancy and DCT transform coding of the prediction correction signal to reduce spatial redundancy. Motion compensation can also be incorporated as an option. Two modes are available on a per-picture basis: INTRA mode, where the input picture is DCT coded independent of any other picture; and INTER mode, where prediction is used from the previous picture.

In all cases, pictures are divided into 16 × 16 macroblocks, containing four 8 × 8 blocks of luminance and two 8 × 8 blocks of color-difference information. The data structure also contains a subpicture element called a Group of Blocks (GOB), which contains 33 adjacent macroblocks. The numbers work out so that the CIF and QCIF formats generate integral numbers of GOBs, as shown in Figure 6.6.

The standard supports dropping of entire frames when needed to reduce the data rate. 0, 1, 2, or 3 frames can be dropped between transmitted

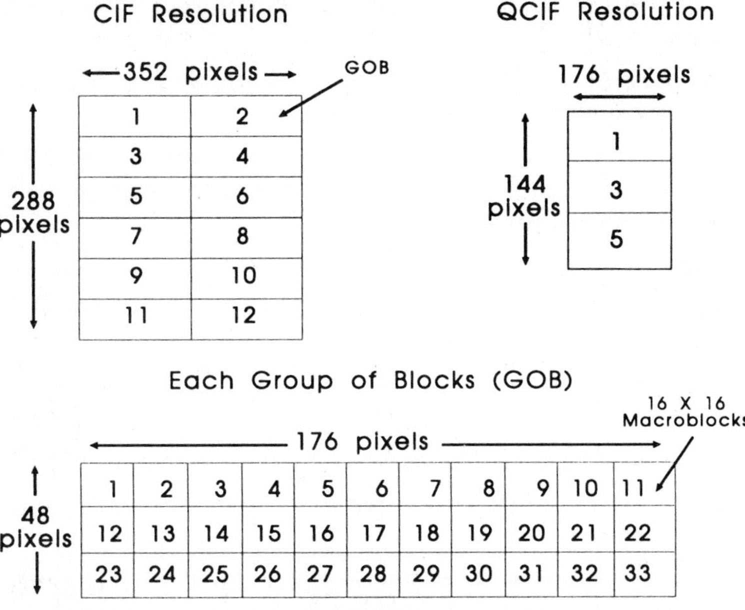

Figure 6.6 GOB layout for CIF and QCIF

frames. This, of course, introduces motion artifacts (slowness), but it is considered to be the best tradeoff to make for the lowest data rates.

6.7 THE MPEG MOTION VIDEO COMPRESSION STANDARD

Digital motion video can be accomplished with the JPEG still-image standard if you have fast enough hardware to process 30 images per second. However, the maximum compression potential cannot be achieved because the redundancy between frames is not being exploited. Furthermore, there are many other things to be considered in compressing and decompressing motion video, as indicated in the objectives below.

6.7.1 Objectives

As with the JPEG standard, the MPEG standard [4] is intended to be generic, meaning that it will support the needs of many applications. As such, it can be considered as a motion video compression toolkit, from which a user selects the particular features that best suit his or her application. More specific objectives are:

1. The standard will deliver acceptable video quality at compressed data rates between 1.0 and 1.5 Mbps.

2. It will support either symmetric or asymmetric compress/decompress applications.
3. When compression takes it into account, random-access playback is possible to any specified degree.
4. Similarly, when compression takes it into account, fast-forward, fast-reverse, or normal-reverse playback modes can be made available in addition to normal (forward) playback.
5. Audio/video synchronization will be maintained.
6. Catastrophic behavior in the presence of data errors should be avoidable.
7. When it is required, compression-decompression delay can be controlled.
8. Editability should be available when required by the application.
9. There should be sufficient format flexibility to support playing of video in windows.
10. The processing requirements should not preclude the development of low-cost chipsets which are capable of encoding in real time.

As you can see, some of these objectives are conflicting, and they all conflict with the objectives of cost and quality. In spite of that, the proposed standard provides for all of the objectives, but of course not all at once. A proposed application has to make its own choices about which features of the standard it requires and accept any tradeoff that this may cause.

6.7.2 Architecture

The MPEG standard is primarily a bitstream specification, although it also specifies a typical decoding process to assist in interpreting the bitstream specification. This approach supports data interchange, but it does not restrict creativity and innovation in the means for creating or decoding that bitstream. The bitstream architecture is based on a sequence of pictures, each of which contains the data needed to create a single displayable image. Note that the order of transmission of pictures in the data stream may not be the same as the order in which pictures will be displayed—this will be evident shortly.

There are four different kinds of pictures, depending on how each picture is to be decoded:

I pictures are intracoded, meaning that they are coded independent of any other picture. An I picture must exist at the start of any video stream and also at any random-access entry point in the stream.

P pictures are predicted pictures, which are coded using motion compensation from a previous I or P picture.

B pictures are interpolated pictures, which are coded by interpolating between a previous and a future I or P picture. This process is sometimes referred to as bidirectional prediction.

D pictures are a special format that is only used for implementing fast search modes.

An I picture requires the most data; it is similar to a JPEG image. It is structured into 8 × 8 blocks that are DCT coded, quantized, and statistically encoded. A P picture requires about one-third of the data of an I picture; it consists of 16 × 16 macroblocks, which have motion compensation vector values, and 8 × 8 blocks, which are DCT coded motion correction values. A B picture takes 2:1 to 5:1 less data than a P picture; it also has macroblocks and blocks containing interpolation parameters and DCT coded correction values. The most compression is obtained by using as many B pictures as possible. However, to perform B decoding, the "future" I or P picture involved must be transmitted before any of the dependent B pictures can be processed. This inherently means that there is a delay in the decoding proportional to the number of B pictures in series.

Because of the delay issue, the considerations of random access, and the effectiveness of the interpolation technique, a typical displayed picture sequence would be of the form (the numbers are the order of display):

I B B B P B B B I B B B P ...
1 2 3 4 5 6 7 8 9 10 11 12 13

This picture sequence is diagrammed in Figure 6.7 showing the dependencies of pictures on each other. The standard, however, is completely flexible with regard to the picture sequence, and an application can (if it wishes) tailor it to optimize any situation.

As mentioned before, when B pictures are used, the reference I and P pictures must be transmitted before any dependent B pictures. This means

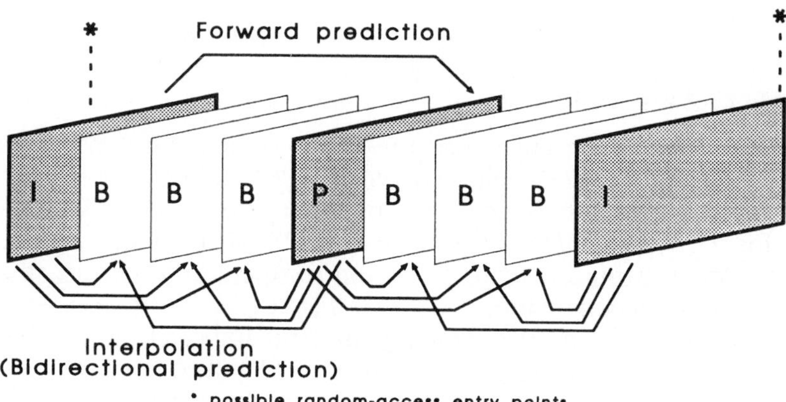

Figure 6.7 A typical MPEG picture sequence showing interframe dependencies.

that the order of transmission for the sequence above is (the numbers are still the order of display):

I P B B B I B B B P B B B ...
1 5 2 3 4 9 6 7 8 13 10 11 12

6.7.3 Bitstream Syntax

The bitstream is structured at six levels of hierarchy in order to support all of the features of MPEG video. These are:

Sequence layer—an independent video stream.

Group of pictures layer—this is a clip of video that begins with a random-access entry point and has uniform video parameters within it.

Picture layer—represents one displayable image.

Slice layer—a variable-size subpicture group that provides for resynchronizing of the decoder in the event of an error.

Macroblock layer—the 16 × 16 pixel motion compensation unit.

Block layer—an 8 × 8 pixel block that can be intracoded, motion compensated, or interpolated.

The syntax levels are diagrammed in Figure 6.8.

6.7.4 Performance

MPEG provides for a wide range of video resolutions and data rates. One set of choices that has been widely researched is optimized for data rates of about 1.2 Mbps (CD-ROM data rate). For 30 frames/second video at a display resolution of 352 × 240 pixels, the quality of compressed and decompressed video at this data rate is often expressed as similar to VHS recording. Most scenes do not exhibit compression artifacts, but the most demanding material may require resolution or frame rate tradeoffs to obtain visually acceptable results.

6.7.5 MPEG-2 and MPEG-4

The ISO committee which developed the MPEG standard is currently at work specifying a successor standard known as MPEG-2. The video component is targeted for bit rates in the range of about 2 to 15 Mbps, which is sufficient for supporting HDTV. Additionally, MPEG-2 includes a number of new features with the intent of providing compatibility with existing standards such as terrestrial video, MPEG, and H.261.

Compatible transmission is conceptually similar to today's TV broadcasts, which can be received by both color and black and white television sets. The MPEG-2 encoding is intended to allow a single transmission to be received by a range of digital televisions, from small portable units that might only support NTSC resolution to HDTV receivers. Scalable digital

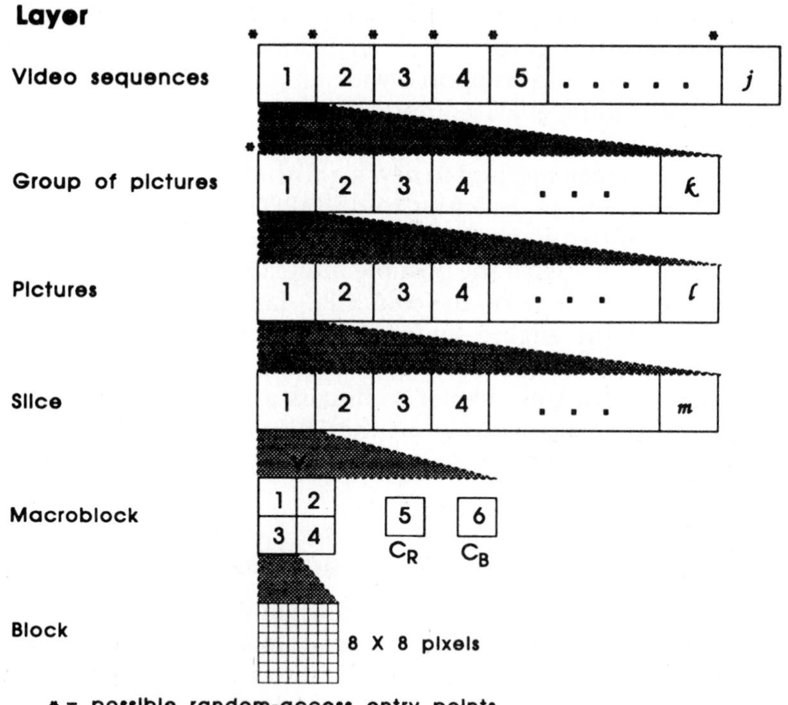

Figure 6.8 MPEG layered bitstream structure

video is also critical to transmission over packet switching networks. As the load on the network increases, the transmitting node adjusts by decreasing the quality of the transmitted video.

The audio encoding for MPEG-2 is also being extended. MPEG-2 audio will encode up to five full bandwidth channels (left, right, center, and two surround channels), an additional low-frequency enhancement channel, and up to seven commentary or multilingual channels. Several improvements on the MPEG audio format are planned for lower sample rates.

More recently, another digital video encoding standard effort known as MPEG-4 is underway. This new initiative is for very low bitrate coding of audiovisual programs, with particular application to mobile multimedia communications. Although MPEG-2 and MPEG both use a DCT algorithm, it is anticipated that MPEG-4 will be based on a new algorithm, which, though computationally more expensive, results in significantly higher compression.

6.8 DVI TECHNOLOGY

DVI technology is different from the other standards discussed here because it is specifically based on the use of special hardware. Intel Corporation and

IBM Corporation have developed a programmable chipset which implements the technology in a co-processor environment on any type of computer platform. These chips support a wide range of multimedia functions in software, including JPEG compression and several DVI-unique compression algorithms for stills or motion video. Because of the programmability of the chipset, it can respond to new algorithm developments—for example, the programming of the chips to do MPEG processing is being explored. Intel is committed to producing higher-speed DVI processors in the future and has even discussed the possible integration of DVI functionality with a future generation of the x86 CPU family. Thus, the DVI hardware is an important engine for present and future compression developments.

It is beyond the scope of this chapter to discuss all the features of DVI Technology; we will concentrate only on the DVI-unique motion video compression systems of PLV and RTV.

6.8.1 DVI Technology Motion Video Compression

DVI Technology can do both symmetric and asymmetric motion video compression/decompression. The asymmetric approach is called Production-Level Video (PLV). Video for PLV must be sent to a central compression facility, which uses large computers and special interface equipment, but any DVI system is capable of playing back the resulting compressed video. The picture quality of PLV is the highest that can currently be achieved. The other DVI compression approach is called Real Time Video (RTV). It is done on any DVI system that has the ActionMedia Capture Board installed. Playback of RTV is on the same system or any other DVI system. Because RTV is a symmetric approach, which requires that compression be done with only the computing power available in a DVI system, RTV picture quality is not as good as PLV picture quality.

6.8.2 DVI Production-Level Compression

PLV is an interframe compression technique; the algorithm details are proprietary, and we can only say that it is block-oriented and that it involves multiple compression techniques. Since it was designed specifically for the DVI chipset, it is optimized for that environment, and it probably would not make much sense to run it on different hardware.

PLV compression is an asymmetric approach where a large computer does the compression and the DVI hardware in the PC does the decompression. It takes a facility costing several hundred thousand dollars to perform PLV compression at reasonable speeds. Since this cost is too much for a single application developer to bear, centralized facilities are provided where developers can send their video to be compressed for a fee. We will discuss what such facilities involve and how they are made available to developers.

High-quality motion video compression has difficulties right from the start. The data rates created by the initial digitizing are high, even for large computers. This happens because the initial digitizing really has to be done in real time to obtain the best quality. In most cases, the input video medium for compression will be an analog videotape—for best results, it will be one-inch broadcast quality tape. Although one-inch tape machines can play at slow speeds, they do it by introducing frame storage and processing, which would interfere with the quality of the compressed result. The only way to get around that processing is to run the VTR at normal play speed (30 frames per second). Therefore, for best quality, we must invest in digitizing and interface hardware, which will let the VTR run at normal speed and capture the digital data on computer disk.

For PLV compression, the real-time video from the VTR is digitized, filtered, and chrominance subsampled by special hardware before storage on digital disk. Such storage still requires a data rate of about 2 megabytes per second—substantially higher than the storage data rate of a typical PC—and a 1.2-gigabyte digital disk only holds 10 minutes of this partially compressed digital video. Then, in nonreal time, the data is taken frame by frame from the digital disk and run through the PLV compression algorithm.

The compression algorithm typically runs on a parallel processor CPU. Compression takes about 3 seconds per frame on a 250-MIPS machine—still about 90 times slower than real time. (A minute of final compressed video will take 90 minutes to compress.) Of course, compression speed is proportionally faster on an even larger parallel machine.

PLV Performance

The DVI PLV compression algorithm is proprietary and will not be described here. Its performance is also difficult to describe or show here, because it does not make sense to show still frames from a motion sequence. That is because an individual frame from motion video may contain artifacts which are not visible when those frames are delivered to a viewer at 30 frames per second. There is a significant degree of visual averaging taking place when viewing 30 frames per second video. This is also true for normal analog television—noise artifacts become highly visible in a single still frame, whereas the averaging between frames in a motion sequence makes noise much less visible. You can observe this problem if you experiment with a VCR which has slow-motion or still-frame features. A stopped picture looks much worse than normal-motion pictures. Anyway, PLV compressed video delivers full-screen, full-motion pictures at a quality subjectively competitive with half-inch VCR pictures.

The PLV compression algorithm must be given goals for the data rate of the compressed bitstream and for the amount of DVI processor chip time per frame which will be devoted to decompression. Even when working with CD-ROM, we will often want to use fewer than 5120 bytes per frame for the average data rate of the video because we want to leave space in the

CD-ROM rate for audio or possibly other data. We also may wish to display the motion video at less than full-screen in order to save data so that more than 72 minutes could be on one CD-ROM disc. In that case, we would specify a cropped picture to be compressed to fewer bytes per frame.

Another way to effectively reduce the compressed data rate is to lower the video frame rate. In some cases, 15 frames per second is fast enough. This can be used either to cut the video data rate in half or to allow more than 5120 bytes per frame to achieve somewhat higher video quality.

In the case of the DVI processor decompression time, there are 33 milliseconds per frame available at 30 frames per second (40 milliseconds per frame at 25 frames per second), but we may not want to let all of that time be used for decompression because we need the processor to perform some other processes on each frame, such as drawing graphics over the motion image or scaling the image to a different size.

You can see that there is a multidimensional tradeoff here involving four interacting parameters, which together will determine the resulting picture quality:

Image cropping (pixel count)

Compressed data bytes per frame

Video frame rate

Decompression processing time

The PLV compression software takes all of these parameters as input, and it will try to produce the best-quality pictures within these constraints.

Because PLV is a frame-to-frame compression scheme, there are some special considerations involved in starting up playback of a scene or in starting a scene in the middle. The first frame of a motion sequence must be treated as a still image (called a reference frame); additional time is required to send all the data for a reference frame—about three times the data of an average motion video frame. (If we are using motion video at 5120 bytes average per frame, a reference frame will require around 15,000 bytes of data.) If it is intended that a scene will be started by the application at several different points, it is necessary to introduce reference frames at those points. This can usually be done without causing any noticeable interruption of motion when the scene is played from end to end, because the DVI decompression software uses multiple frame buffers in VRAM so that variations in the input compressed data rate are accommodated without affecting the displayed frame rate. In any case, if you have special needs for reference frames in your video, they have to be expressed at the time you order PLV compression.

6.8.3 DVI Real-Time Compression

The use of a centralized compression service that is remote from the developer of an application introduces delay and expense into the application development process. It also precludes any application that needs to do real-time compression. In creating an application, a developer needs a way to experiment with the video and audio in the context of the application without incurring this delay and expense. This need is filled by DVI's Real-Time Video (RTV), which is a compression process that is done in real time on a DVI development system. With RTV, the developer may compress his or her video and audio to the same file size as from the PLV service, and then use those files in the application under development in exactly the same way that the final PLV files will be used. By this means the developer may experiment as much as needed and actually try out the complete application before sending any video out for PLV compression.

The tradeoff in RTV is picture quality. To accomplish motion video compression with only the resources of a DVI development system means that RTV is lower in resolution and frame rate than PLV. Compression is done with the DVI processor chips and, while these chips are very powerful among their peers, in the milliseconds available to compress a frame in real time the processors do not compare with the computer cycles available in 3 seconds on a large parallel machine. Therefore, the algorithm must be simplified. However, the results produced are good enough to fill most needs for application development and testing. For some applications which do require real-time compression within the application, RTV may completely fill the bill.

RTV compression allows the user to make some trades of compression versus picture quality if the RTV-compressed code will never have to be stored on a CD-ROM. By allowing the data rate to go higher than 153,600 bytes per second using fast hard disk storage, the RTV frame rate can be increased to 30 frames per second. Most DVI capture software provides for user choice of these parameters.

Communication between RTV and PLV occurs through the medium of SMPTE time code. The original one-inch videotape which will eventually go to PLV compression must have SMPTE time code on it. When this tape is compressed by RTV for development purposes, the time code is captured for storage with the video frames. RTV is not frame-to-frame compression, so an RTV file can be started or stopped at any point. In the RTV mode, decisions about in and out cut points for the displayed video can be made and the time code values may be read from the RTV file data to create the edit list which will be used for the PLV compression. After all decisions about video material have been made, the master one-inch tapes and the edit list go to the PLV compression facility for final compression of exactly and only the selected scenes.

6.9 ACKNOWLEDGMENTS

Section 6.7.5 and Figure 6.3 provided by John Buford.

6.10 REFERENCES

1. ISO/IEC 10918-1. Digital Compression and Coding of Continuous-Tone Still Images. (Also ITU-T Rec. T.81) 1993.
2. Wallace, G. K. The JPEG Still Picture Compression Standard. *Communications of the ACM*. vol. 34, no. 4. April 1991. pp. 30–44.
3. ITU-T Rec. H.261. Codec for Audiovisual Services at px64 kbit/s. Geneva. 1990.
4. ISO/IEC 11172. Coding of Moving Pictures and Associated Audio for Digital Storage Media at up to about 1.5 MBit/s. 1993.

6.11 FOR FURTHER READING

1. Feig, E., and Winograd, S. Fast Algorithms for Discrete Cosine Transform. *IEEE Trans. on Signal Proc.* 40,9. September 1992.
2. Gaggioni, H., and Le Gall, D. Digital Video Transmission and Coding for Broadband ISDN. *IEEE Trans. Consumer Electronics*. vol. CE-34. February 1988. pp. 16–35.
3. Le Gall, D. MPEG: A Video Compression Standard for Multimedia Applications. *Communications of the ACM*. vol. 34, no. 4. April 1991. pp. 46–58.
4. Liou, M. L. Visual Telephony as an ISDN Application. *IEEE Commun. Magazine* 28. February 1990. pp. 30–38.
5. Lippman, A., and Butera, W. Coding Image Sequence for Interactive Retrieval. *Comm. ACM* 32,7. July 1989. pp. 852–860.
6. Netravali, A., and Limb, J. Picture Coding: A Review. *Proceedings of the IEEE*. vol 68, no. 3. March 1980. pp 366–406.
7. Patel, K., Smith, B. C., and Rowe, L. A. Performance of a Software MPEG Video Decoder. *Proc. ACM Multimedia* 93. August 1993. pp. 75–82.
8. Pennebaker, W. B., and Mitchell, J. L. *JPEG Still Image Data Compression*. Van Nostrand Reinhold. 1993.
9. Rao, K. R., and Yip, P. *Discrete Cosine Transform: Algorithms Advantages, Applications*. Academic Press. 1990.
10. Special Issue on Digital Multimedia Systems. E. Fox, ed. *Commun. ACM* 34,4. April 1991.
11. Urabe, T., et al. MPEGTool: An X Window Based MPEG Encoder and Statistics Tool. *Proc. ACM Multimedia* 93, August 1993. pp. 259–266.

CHAPTER 7

TIME-BASED MEDIA REPRESENTATION AND DELIVERY

Thomas D. C. Little
Boston University

Temporal relationships are a characteristic feature of multimedia objects. Continuous media objects such as video and audio have strict synchronous timing requirements. Composite objects can have arbitrary timing relationships. These relationships might be specified to achieve some particular visual effect of sequence. Several different schemes have been proposed for modeling time-based media. These are reviewed and evaluated in terms of representational completeness and delivery techniques.

7.1 INTRODUCTION

Multimedia refers to the integration of text, images, audio, and video in a variety of application environments. These data can be heavily time-dependent, such as audio and video in a motion picture, and can require time-ordered presentation during use. The task of coordinating such sequences is called multimedia *synchronization* or *orchestration*. Synchronization can be applied to the playout of concurrent or sequential streams of data and also to the external events generated by a human user. Consider the following illustration of a newscast (adapted from Kipp [1]), shown in Figure 7.1. In this illustration multiple media are shown versus a time axis in a *timeline* representation of the time-ordering of the application.

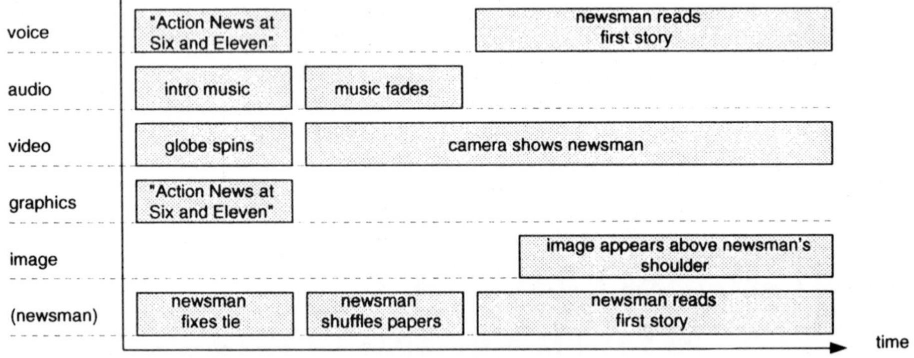

Figure 7.1 "Action News" timeline representation

Temporal relationships between the media may be implied, as in the simultaneous acquisition of voice and video, or may be explicitly formulated, as in the case of a multimedia document which possesses voice annotated text. In either situation, the characteristics of each medium and the relationships among them must be established in order to provide coordination in the presence of vastly different presentation requirements.

In addition to simple linear playout of time-dependent data sequences, other modes of data presentation are also viable and should be supported by a multimedia information system (MMIS). These include reverse, fast-forward, fast-backward, and random access. Although these operations are quite ordinary in existing technologies (e.g., VCRs), when nonsequential storage, data compression, data distribution, and random communication delays are introduced, the provision for these capabilities can be very difficult.

In this chapter, we describe time-based media representations with respect to specification, user interaction, and system timing enforcement. The primary issues deal with the *physical level*, the *service level*, and the *human interface level* [2]. At the physical level, data from different media are multiplexed over single physical connections or are arranged in physical storage. The service level is concerned with the interactions between the multimedia application and the various media, and among the elements of the application. This level deals primarily with intermedia synchronization necessary for presentation or playout. The human interface level describes the random user interaction with a multimedia information system such as viewing a succession of database items, also called *browsing*. We also overview important temporal models necessary to describe time-dependent media and survey various approaches for their specification. Furthermore, we describe the implications of time-dependent data retrieval in a real system.

The remainder of this chapter is organized as follows. In Section 7.2 we describe basic models of time. Section 7.3 describes representations of time with respect to multimedia timing specification and delivery. Section 7.4 describes the data presentation or delivery problem. Section 7.5 concludes the chapter.

7.2 MODELS OF TIME

A significant requirement for the support of time-dependent data playout in a multimedia system is the identification and specification of temporal relations among multimedia data objects. In this section we introduce models of time that can be applied to multimedia timing representations and introduce appropriate terminology.

As a multimedia author, we seek to specify the relationships between the components of this application. The service provider (the multimedia system) must interpret these specifications and provide an accurate rendition. The author's view is abstract, consisting of complex objects and events that occur at certain times. The system view must deal with each data item, providing abstract timing satisfaction as well as fine-grained synchronization (lip sync) as expected by the user. Furthermore, the system must support various temporal access control (TAC) operations such as reverse or fast playout.

Time-dependent data are unique in that both their values and times of delivery are important. The time dependency of multimedia data is difficult to characterize since data can be both static and time-dependent as required by the application. For example, a set of medical cross-sectional images can represent a three-dimensional mapping of a body part, yet the spatial coordinates can be mapped to a time axis to provide an animation allowing the images to be described with or without time dependencies. Therefore, a characterization of multimedia data is required based on the time dependency both at data capture and at the time of presentation (see Table 7.1) [3].

Time dependencies present at the time of data capture are called *natural* or *implied* [3] (e.g., audio and video recorded simultaneously). These data

Table 7.1 Definitions of Time Dependencies

Static	no time dependency
Discrete	single element
Transient	ephemeral
Natural or Implied	real-world time dependencies
Synthetic	artificially created time dependencies
Continuous	playout is contiguous in time
Persistent	maintained in a database
Live	data originate in real time
Stored Data	data originate from prerecorded storage

streams often are described as continuous because recorded data elements form a continuum during playout, i.e., elements are played out contiguously in time. Data can also be captured as a sequence of units which possesses a natural ordering but not neccessarily one based on time (e.g., the aforementioned medical example). On the other hand, data can be captured with no specific ordering (e.g., a set of photographs). Without a time dependency, these data are called *static*. Static data, which lack time dependencies, can have synthetic temporal relationships (e.g., Figure 7.1). The combination of natural and synthetic time dependencies can describe the overall temporal requirements of any preorchestrated multimedia presentation. At the time of playout, data can retain their natural temporal dependencies or can be coerced into synthetic temporal relationships. A synthetic relation possesses a time-dependency fabricated as necessary for the application. For example, a motion picture consists of a sequence of recorded scenes, recorded naturally, but arranged synthetically. Similarly, an animation is a synthetic ordering of static data items. A live data source is one that occurs dynamically and in real time, as contrasted with a stored data source. Since no reordering or look-ahead to future values is possible for live sources, synthetic relations are only valid for stored data.

Data objects can also be classified in terms of their presentation and application lifetimes. A persistent object is one that can exist for the duration of the application. A nonpersistent object is created dynamically and discarded when obsolete. For presentation, a transient object is defined as an object that is presented for a short duration without manipulation. The display of a series of audio or video frames represents transient presentation of objects, whether captured live or retrieved from a database. Henceforth, we use the terms static and transient to describe presentation lifetimes of objects while persistence expresses their storage life in a database.

In the literature, media are often described as belonging to one of two classes: continuous or discrete [4,5,6]. This distinction is somewhat confusing since time ordering can be assigned to discrete media, and continuous media are time-ordered sequences of discrete ones after digitization. We use a definition attributable to Herrtwich [7]: Continuous media are sequences of discrete data elements that are played out contiguously in time. However, the term *continuous* is most often used to describe the fine-grain synchronization required for audio or video.

7.2.1 Conceptual Models of Time

In information processing applications, temporal information is seldom applied towards synchronization of time-dependent media; rather, it is used for maintenance of historical information or query languages [8,9]. However, conceptual models of time developed for these applications also apply to the multimedia synchronization problem. Two representations are indi-

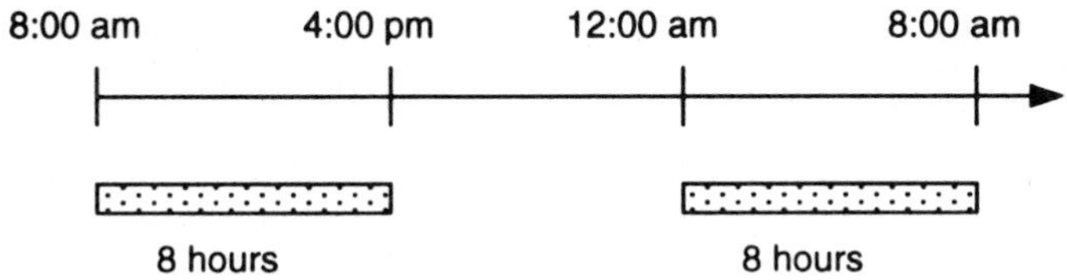

Figure 7.2 Instants versus intervals

cated. These are based on instants and intervals (see Figure 7.2 and [10]), described as follows.

A time instant is a zero-length moment in time, such as "4:00 P.M." By contrast, a time interval is defined by two time instants and, therefore, their duration (e.g., 100 minutes or 9 to 5). Intervals are formally defined as follows: let $[S, \leq]$ be a partially ordered set, and let a, b be any two elements of S such that $a \leq b$. The set $\{ x \mid a \leq x \leq b\}$ is called an interval of S denoted by $[a,b]$. Time intervals are described by their endpoints (e.g., a and b as defined above). The length of such an interval is identified by $b - a$. The relative timing between two intervals can be determined from these endpoints. By specifying intervals with respect to each other rather than by using endpoints, we decouple the intervals from an absolute or instantaneous time reference, leading us to temporal relations.

There are thirteen ways in which two intervals can relate in time [11], whether they overlap, abut, precede, etc. These relations are indicated graphically by a timeline representation shown in Figure 7.3 [12]. The thirteen relations can be represented by seven cases because six of them are inverses. For example, after is the inverse relation of before, or, equivalently, *before* $^{-1}$ is the inverse relation of *before* (*a equals b* is the same as *b equals a*). For inverse relations, given any two intervals, it is possible to represent their relation by using the noninverse relations only by exchanging the interval labels. The equality relation has no inverse.

Temporal intervals can be used to model multimedia presentation by letting each interval represent the presentation time of some multimedia data element, such as a still image or an audio segment. These intervals represent the time component required for multimedia playout, and their

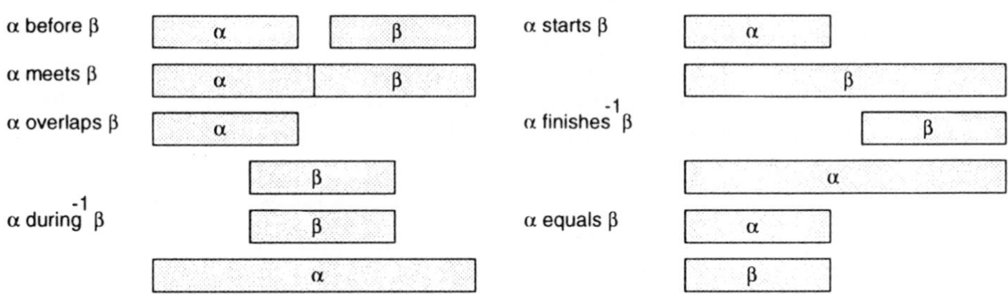

Figure 7.3 Binary temporal relations

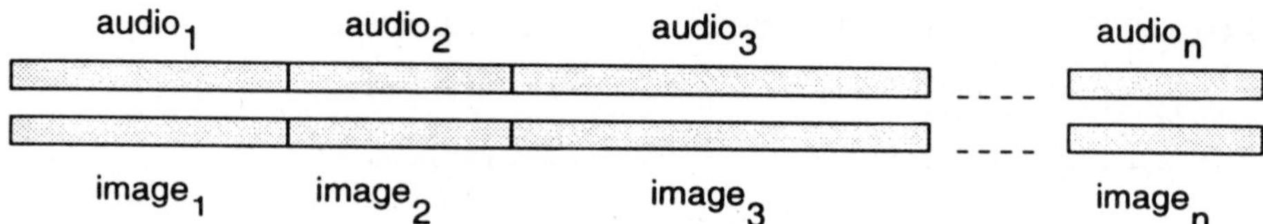

Figure 7.4 Temporal interval representation of audio and video

relative positioning represents their time dependencies. Figure 7.4 shows audio and images synchronized to each other using the *meets* and *equals* temporal relations. For continuous media such as audio and video, an appropriate temporal representation is a sequence of intervals described by the *meets* relation. In this case, intervals abut in time, and are nonoverlapping, by definition of a continuous medium. With a temporal-interval-based (TIB) modeling scheme, complex timeline representations of multimedia object presentation can be delineated.

7.3 TIME AND MULTIMEDIA REQUIREMENTS

The problem of synchronizing data presentation, user interaction, and physical devices reduces to satisfying temporal precedence relationships under real timing constraints. In this section, we introduce conceptual models that describe temporal information necessary to represent multimedia synchronization. We also describe language- and graph-based approaches to specification and survey existing methodologies applying these approaches.

The goal of temporal specification is to provide a means of expressing temporal relationships among data objects requiring synchronization at the time of their creation, in the process of orchestration. This temporal specification ultimately can be used to facilitate database storage and playback of the orchestrated multimedia objects from storage.

To describe temporal synchronization, an abstract model is necessary for characterizing the processes and events associated with presentation of elements with varying display requirements. The presentation problem requires simultaneous, sequential, and independent display of heterogeneous data. This problem closely resembles that of the execution of sequential and parallel threads in a concurrent computational system, for which numerous approaches exist. Many concurrent languages support this concept, for example, CSP [13] and Ada; however, the problem differs for multimedia data presentation. Computational systems are generally interested in the solution of problems which desire high throughput, such as the parallel solution to matrix inversion. On the other hand, multimedia presentation is concerned with the coherent presentation of heterogeneous media to a user. Therefore, there exists a bound on the speed of delivery beyond which a user cannot assimilate the information content of the presentation. For computational systems it is always desired to produce a solution in minimum time. An abstract multimedia timing specification concerns presentation rather than computation.

To store control information, a computer language is not ideal; however, formal language features are useful for the specification of various properties for subsequent analysis and validation. Many such languages or varying capabilities exist for real-time systems [14], (e.g., RT-ASLAN, ESTEREL, PEARL, PAISLey, RTRL, Real-Time Lucid, PSDL, Ada, HMS Machines, COSL, RNet, etc.). These systems allow specification and analysis of real-time specifications but not guaranteed execution under limited resource constraints. Providing guaranteed real-time service requires the ability to either formally prove program correctness, demonstrate a feasible schedule, or both. In summary, distinctions between presentation and computation processing are found in the time dependencies of processing versus display and the nature of the storage of control flow information.

Timing in computer systems is conventionally sequential. Concurrency provides simultaneous event execution through both physical and virtual mechanisms. Most modeling techniques for concurrent activities are specifically interested in ordering of events that can occur in parallel and are independent of the rate of execution (i.e., their generality is independent of CPU performance). However, for time-dependent multimedia data, presentation timing requires meeting both precedence and timing constraints. Furthermore, multimedia data do not have absolute timing requirements (some data can be late).

A representation scheme should capture component precedence, real-time constraints, and provide the capability for indicating laxity in meeting deadlines. The primary requirements for such a specification methodology include the representation of real-time semantics and concurrency and a hierarchical modeling ability. The nature of multimedia data presentation also implies further requirements including the ability to reverse presentation, to allow random access (at a start point), to incompletely specify timing, to allow sharing of synchronized components among applications, and to provide data storage of control information. Therefore, a specification methodology must also be well suited for unusual temporal semantics as well as be amenable to the development of a database for timing information.

In the next section we investigate the requirements of multimedia data types with respect to time. The important requirements include the ability to specify time in a suitable manner for authoring, the support of temporal access control (TAC) operations, and suitability for integration with other models (e.g., spatial organization, document layout models). In Section 7.4 we describe related requirements with respect to enforcing temporal specifications and delivery.

7.3.1 Relative versus Absolute Timing Specification

Timing relationships can be described using relative or absolute timing. In this section we describe the limitations of these two representations.

Temporal Instants

An instant-based temporal reference scheme has been extensively applied in the motion picture industry, as standardized by the Society of Motion Picture and Television Engineers (SMPTE). This scheme associates a virtually unique sequential code to each frame in a motion picture [15]. By assigning these codes to both an audio track and a motion picture track, intermedia synchronization between streams is achieved. This absolute, instant-based scheme presents two difficulties when applied to a computer-based multimedia application. First, since unique, absolute time references are assumed, when segments are edited or produced in duplicate, the relative timing between the edited segments becomes lost in terms of playout (see Figure 7.5). Furthermore, if one medium, while synchronized to another, becomes decoupled from the other, then the timing information of the dependent medium becomes lost. This scenario occurs when audio and image sequences are synchronized to a video sequence with time codes. If the video sequence is removed, the remaining sequences do not have sufficient timing information to provide intermedia synchronization. Instant-based schemes have also been applied using MIDI (Musical Instrument Digital Interface) time instant specification [16] as well as via coupling each time code to a common time reference [17]. Other work using instant-based representation includes [18] for editing multimedia presentations using timelines.

Temporal Intervals

Temporal intervals can be used to model multimedia presentation by letting each interval represent the presentation of some multimedia data element, such as a still image or an audio segment using TIB modeling. TIB repre-

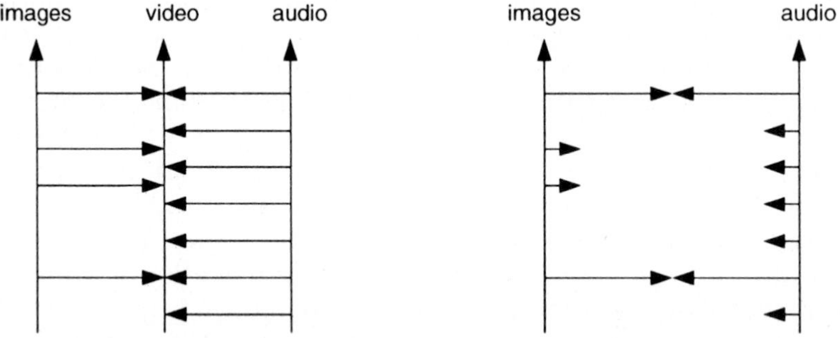

Figure 7.5 Decomposition anomalies in an instant-based representation

sentations are fundamental to the study of time and temporal logic [12]. TIB representations using temporal relations applied to multimedia include HyTime [19], ODA [20] and ODA extensions [4], the work of Little and Ghafoor [21,22], and Dimitrova and Golshani [23] for supporting temporal queries.

Standardization activities have resulted in several approaches to synchronization for electronic documents, including hypermedia. For electronic document representation and interchange, the Office Document Architecture (ODA) [20] describes parallel, sequential, and independent temporal control [24,25] but does not support synchronization for continuous types. However, there are proposals to extend the ODA model for this purpose [4].

Other existing approaches to timing specification for multimedia either rely on simple time precedence relationships or are based on temporal intervals. Of the ones based on intervals, most only provide support for the simple parallel and sequential relationships. Synchronization can be accomplished using a purely TIB representation, with explicit capture of each of the thirteen temporal relations [26], or with additional operations to facilitate incomplete timing specification [4] .

The notion of temporal intervals can also support reverse and partial playout activities. For example, a recorded stream of audio or video can be presented in reversed order. For this purpose, reverse temporal relations can be defined. These relations, derived from the forward relations, define the ordering and scheduling required for reverse playout. Furthermore, partial interval playout is defined as the playout of a subset of a TIB sequence [22].

Parallel and Sequential Relations

A common representation for time-dependent media relies on a subset of the thirteen temporal relations by using only the parallel (*equals*) and sequential (*meets*) relations. By restricting temporal composition operations to these relations, most temporal interactions can be specified. This approach has been used by Poggio et al. in the development of the Command and Control Workstation Project (CCWS) [27], by Postel [28] (also including an independent relationship), and by Ravindran [29] using AND-OR graphs and an *occurs–after* relation to specify timing precedence.

This definition also requires uniform represenation of data elements to eliminate overlap in time. Conversion from aperiodic representations can be achieved by decomposing larger intervals into a uniform size, as shown in Figure 7.6 [4].

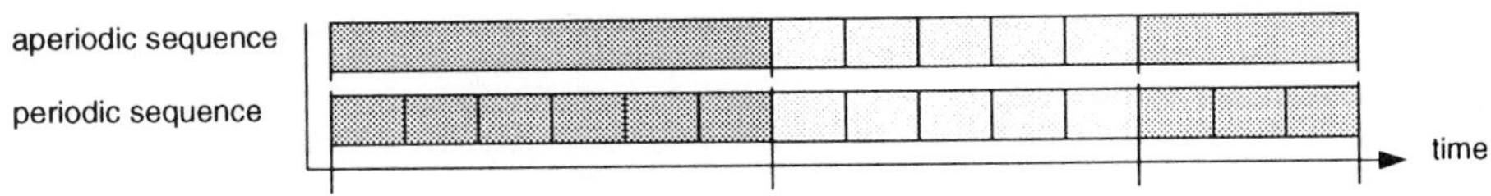

Figure 7.6 Aperiodic interval conversion

7.3.2 Temporal Access Control

A significant requirement for a media representation is the support of TAC operations. These operations provide the base functionality on which time-based multimedia applications can be built, including the system support (delivery) described in Section 7.4. Clearly there are common characteristics required by the media authoring system, the user TAC functionality, and the system support primitives. Here we introduce and identify the following TAC operations:

- reverse
- fast-forward
- fast-backward
- midpoint suspension
- midpoint resumption
- random access
- looping
- pseudo-sequential access (browsing)

These operations can be implemented in various ways. For example, fast-forward can be provided either by skipping video frames or by doubling the rate of playout. Therefore, these operations can imply vastly different data structures and system delivery functionality.

7.3.3 Incomplete Timing

Under some conditions, it may be desirable to introduce incomplete timing specifications, as can often arise when time-dependent data are to be played out in parallel with static ones [4] (Figure 7.7). For example, if an audio segment is presented in synchrony with a single still picture, the time duration for image presentation could be unspecified and set to the duration of the audio segment. Incomplete specification can allow the static medium to assume the playout duration of the continuous medium. It is always possible to incompletely specify the timing for the parallel *equals* relation when only one medium is not static. For other types of relations, more information is required to describe the desired temporal result.

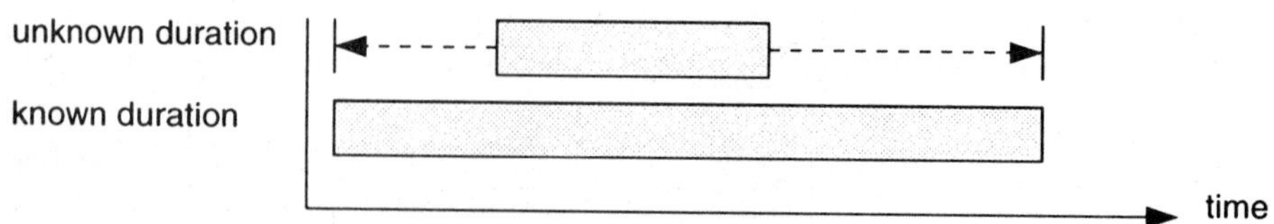

Figure 7.7 Incomplete timing specification

If both media have preassigned but unequal time durations, synchronous playout requires forcing one medium to alter its timing chraracteristics by time compression/expansion or data dropping/duplication. This kind of timing coercion is straightforward in theory [4,21] but has limited applicability to some media (e.g., music).

7.3.4 Temporal Transformations

Temporal transformations change one frame of time reference to another, as illustrated in Figure 7.8. These transformations can meet the conceptual TAC operation requirements, although they can also be restricted by limitations of system delivery mechanisms. Temporal transformations include

- scaling
- cueing
- inverting
- translation (shifting)

Temporal transformations can be applied to many time-based representations. If a time-based representation expresses precedence and ordering, or relative timing, temporal transformations can provide a mapping from the representational domain to a playout time coordinate system. This approach is used by the Athena Muse system [17], HyTime [30], Herrtwich [7], Gibbs et al. [31], Dannenberg [32], and many others. For example, the relative timing of video frames as described by sequence numbers ($i = 1, 2, 3, \ldots$) can be mapped to real-time units of 15, 30, or n frames/s, as illustrated in Figure 7.9. In the Athena Muse system [33], time is described as a dimension that can be manipulated apart from real time and is treated as a virtual dimension. The system must provide support for any transformation or manipulation of this dimension (a virtual time coordinate system).

Some of the requirements for time-dependent data are not well described by either the graph or language-based specifications. For example, to reduce (slow motion) or increase (fast-forward) the speed of a multimedia presen-

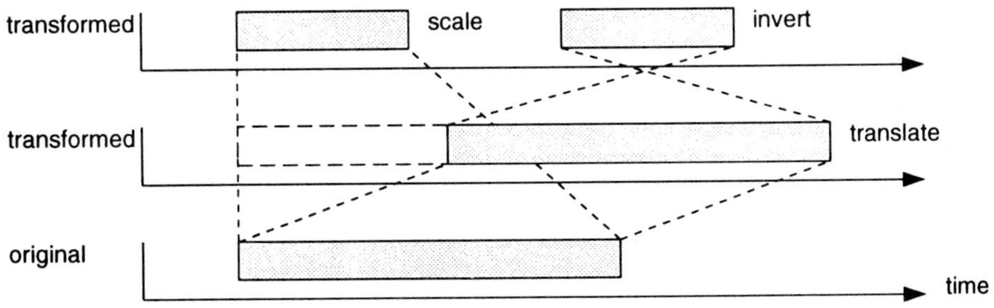

Figure 7.8 Common temporal transforms

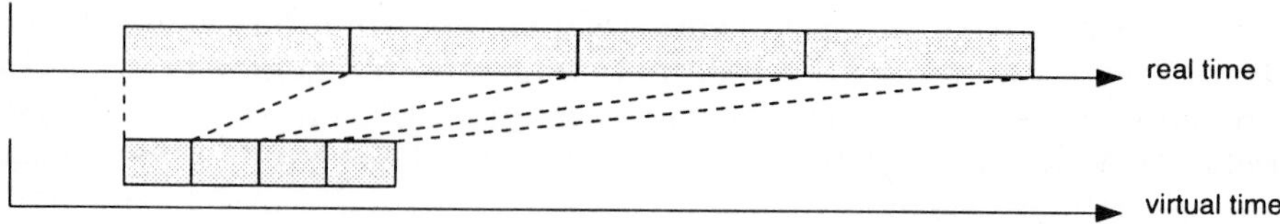

Figure 7.9 Projection of virtual time to playout (real) time

tation via temporal transformation, these temporal models are deficient. These requirements can be addressed by temporal abstractions, which are means to manipulate or control the presentation of a temporal specification via time reference modification.

Various virtual time abstractions have been described in the literature [7,19,34]. These describe the maintenance of a time reference that can be scaled to real time and adjusted to appropriate playout speeds (e.g., Figure 7.9). If real time is defined as nominal clock time as we perceive it, then virtual time is any other time reference system suitable for translation to real time. For example, a unitless reference can be converted, or projected [19], to a real-time system by any scaling or offsetting operations. In this manner, the output rate and direction for a sequence of data elements can be changed by simply modifying this translation, i.e., an entire temporal specification, language- or graph-based, can track a specific time reference or translation process.

For continuous data, temporal information can be encapsulated in the description of the data using the object-oriented paradigm [7]. Using such a scheme, temporal information—including a time reference, playout time units, temporal relationships, and required time offsets—can be maintained for specific multimedia objects.

A timed data stream $s = \{m_i\}$ where $m = (\textit{data value, timestamp, duration})$. This is combined with an access modifier called *clock*, which acts upon the encapsulated data:

$$\text{clock} = (R, S, V_0, T_0)$$

where R is the clock rate ($1/R$ is its period), S is the speed (nominally of unit value—similar to utilization), V_0 is the initial clock value, and T_0 is the absolute start time of the clock. The clock provides a time reference system to the timed data stream. Using the clock, the ith item is defined as

$$m_i = (V_0 + iS/R, T_0 + i/R, 1/R)$$

i.e., the time capsule can define the behavior of a periodic stream and also provide various TAC operations through transformations.

If the data are periodic, this approach can define the time dependencies for an entire sequence by defining the period or frequency of playout (e.g., 30 frames/s for video). Similarly, for mixed-type time-dependent data, there have been several proposals for their conceptual modeling, most based on TIB schemes [4,26,35].

Another scheme, used in the Etherphone environment [36], defines abstractions for continuous media of audio and video. Here samples and frames describe the basic audio and video data unit sizes, respectively. Strands are defined as sequences of either audio samples or video frames. When strands become aggregated or interleaved, they become ropes.

7.3.5 Nontemporal Transformations

Another important requirement of a temporal representation scheme is the ability to indicate nontemporal transformations of data. These transformations include the fading of audio and video signals, mixing of channels, color enhancement of images, generation of fonts, etc. To distinguish these from temporal transformations we call these spatial operations [37]. A number of time-based data representations have been proposed to capture both spatial and temporal transformations. These include the work of Herrtwich [7] and Gibbs et al. [31].

Typically both a time-based representation and a spatial transformation model are required to describe a complex multimedia orchestration. Figure 7.10 illustrates this point. Here, two video scenes are synchronized with a soundtrack (music) but overlap during a fade interval. Over this interval the visual effect is one of a fading of one scene to the other. This activity can be described as a spatial transformation or process applied to the video data. Few representational schemes have an appropriate means of representing this time-dependent transformation in a uniform data model (i.e., video is not preprocessed to provide the fading effect).

7.3.6 Abstractions for Authoring and Visualization

Multimedia authoring (discussed in Chapter 12) of time-dependent multimedia presentations requires some means of abstracting the final product via a representational scheme. Both language-based (including scripting) and flow graph- (or icon-) based approaches have been proposed. In each

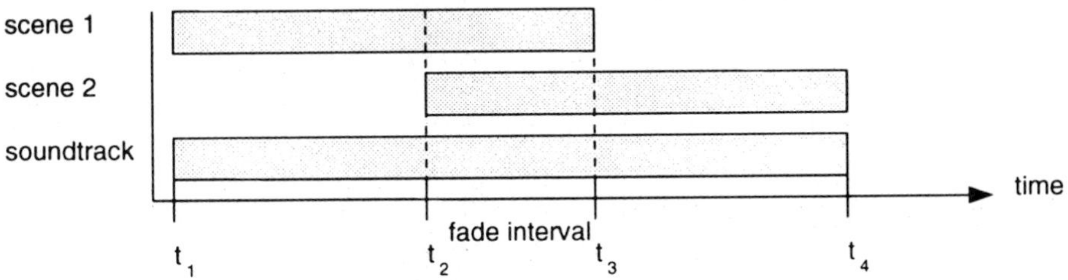

Figure 7.10 Fading interval

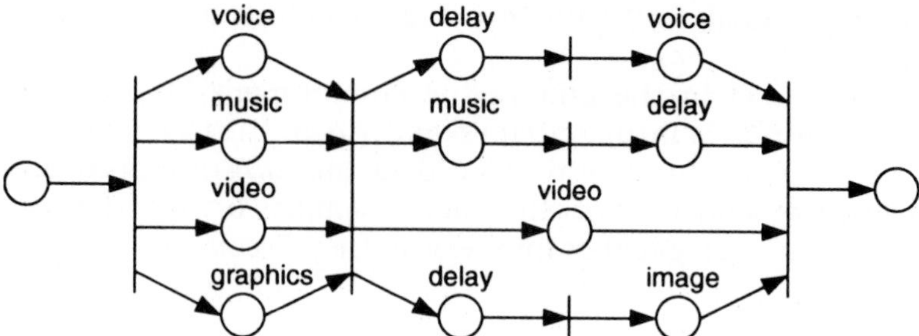

Figure 7.11 OCPN for the "Action News" example

case, the significant requirement is the ability to represent concurrency and to specify real-time presentation timing.

Graph-Based Representations

Although some language-based or script-based representations satisfy these requirements, graphical models have the additional advantage of pictorially illustrating synchronization semantics and are suitable for visual, icon-based orchestration of multimedia presentations. Graph-based representations satisfying these requirements include timelines, flow graphs, the Timed Petri net [21,38,39,40], and temporal hierarchies [22,29].

For example, Figure 7.11 represents an OCPN (object composition petri net—a TPN derivative [21]) of the "Action News" example of Figure 7.1. This TPN explicitly captures any of the temporal relations and can provide simulation in both the forward and reverse directions. Each place in this TPN represents the playout of a multimedia object while transitions represent synchronization points. In contrast, the TPNs of Stotts and Furuta [39] and Fujikawa [40] are designed to capture the nondeterministic actions introduced by a user through browsing.

Script-Based Representations

There are a number of language-based temporal representation schemes generally formulated on parallel and sequential programming language features. *Scripts* represent a subset of this classification, but are derived from the scripting of theatrical works.

For language-based schemes, an extension for the language CSP has been proposed to support multimedia process synchronization, including a resolution of the synchronization blocking problem for continuous media [5]. Various other language-based approaches have also been proposed, e.g., a specification using Language of Temporal Ordering Specification (LOTOS) [41] and process-oriented synchronization in CCWS [27].

HyTime (Hypermedia/Time-based Structuring Language) [19,30] and the HyTime application SMDL (Standard Music Description Language) [35] are language-based approaches to synchronization based on SGML (Standard

Generalized Markup Language). The HyTime language is discussed in Chapter 11.

Scripting is another possibility. Scripts are used in the description of music (e.g., Dannenberg [42,43,44]) as well as for indicating "paths" through documents [45]. Rennison et al. present a scripting language for multimedia (MuXScript) [46]. Tsichritzis et al. describe a representative scripting language [47] for multimedia time dependencies using sequential, parallel, and looping operations. For sequential operations, a_1 occurring before a_2 is specified as

$$a_1 >> a_2$$

Similarly, parallel operations such that a_1 occurs simultaneously with a_2 can be specified as

$$a_1 \,||\, a_2$$

Furthermore, iteration of n times is specified with $n{*}a$.

Some of the requirements for multimedia presentation are not well described by either the graph- or language-based specifications as described previously. To provide temporal transformations such as playout rate changes, additional abstractions can be used as modifiers to either a language-based or graph-based representation.

Additional requirements for authoring include support for spatial transformations, composition of composite orchestrations, relative timing management, recursion, encapsulation (hierarchy), iteration (looping), incomplete timing specification, and support for user input (discussed next).

With respect to relative timing management, media editing operations such as cutting and pasting result in segments of time-dependent data that must be repositioned in a multimedia orchestration. Timing of individual data elements must be maintained with respect to the selected elements rather than some absolute time.

7.3.7 Interaction and Synchronization

When a human user interacts with a multimedia system, the application must synchronize the user and the external world. This can take the form of starting or stopping the presentation of an object, posing queries against the database, browsing through objects, or other inherently unpredictable user- or sensor-initiated activities. For continuous-media systems, user interaction also implies random access to a sequential form of information. Consider a database of video stills representing scenes from an automobile, shot while looking out at a city's streets [48]. If the scenes are recorded at regular intervals, then a virtual drive down the street is possible through animation. When the database contains images from all possible orientations (e.g., all streets of a city), driving may include turns and corresponding

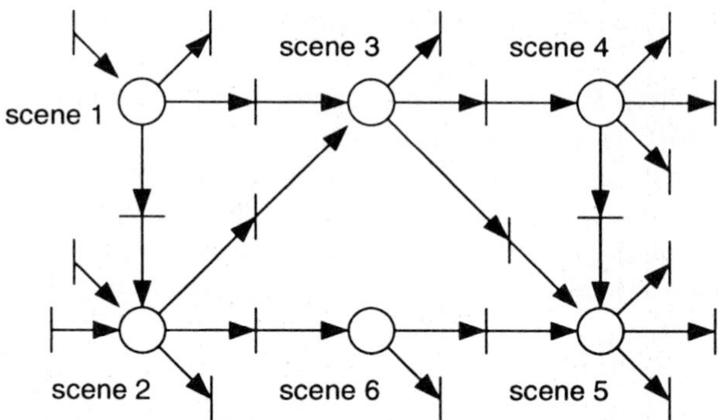

Figure 7.12 PNBH for representing relationships between scenes of a motion picture

jumps out of the sequential nature of the sequence of images corresponding to a street. Synchronization in this case requires coordination of the multimedia presentation with random external events created by the user. This application has been implemented [49] for interactive movies by using the hypertext paradigm.

The essence of the hypertext paradigm is the nonlinear interconnection of information, unlike the sequential access of conventional textual information. Information is linked via cross-referencing between keywords or subjects to other fragments of information. It is possible to represent this interaction using a graph-based model such as the Petri net [39,50] and also relying on a detailed time-based representation for individual data objects. Such a Petri-Net-Based-Hypertext (PNBH) expresses information units as net places and links as net arcs. Transitions in PNBH indicate the traversal of links or the browsing of information fragments. For example, in Figure 7.12 we show a PNBH network consisting of segments of an interactive movie (such as Lippman's [48]). These segments can be played out in a random order, as selected by the user and restricted by the semantics of the net.

Unlike the OCPN, which is a form of *marked graph* [38], net places in PNBH can have multiple outgoing arcs, and therefore can represent nondeterministic and cyclic browsing. Instead, the OCPN specifies exact presentation-time playout semantics, useful in real-time presentation scheduling. Clearly these two models complement each other for specifying both user interaction and presentation orchestration.

Other important time ordering in multimedia includes the coordination of multiple users in computer-supported collaborative work (CSCW) or group work technology. Important considerations here are concurrency control for shared objects and the management of distributed data sources. Time management in CSCW is beyond the scope of this chapter; however, some recent work on this topic includes Ravindran and Prasad [51], Ramanathan et al. [52], and Yavatkar [53].

7.4 SUPPORT FOR SYSTEM TIMING ENFORCEMENT — DELIVERY

Temporal intervals and instants provide a means for indicating exact temporal specification. However, the character of multimedia data presentation is unique, since catastrophic effects do not occur when data are not available for playout, i.e., deadlines are soft in contrast to specification techniques which are designed for real-time systems with hard deadlines [54].

Time-dependent data differ from historical data, which do not specifically require timely playout. Typically, time-dependent data are stored using mature technologies possessing mechanisms to ensure synchronous playout (e.g., VCRs or audio tape recorders). With such mechanisms, dedicated hardware provides a constant rate of playout for homogeneous, periodic sequences of data. Concurrency in data streams is provided by independent physical data paths. When this type of data is migrated to more general-purpose computer data storage systems (e.g., disks), many interesting new capabilities are possible, including random access to the temporal data sequence and time-dependent playout of static data. However, the generality of such a system eliminates the dedicated physical data paths and the implied data structures of sequential storage. Therefore, a general MMIS needs to support new access paradigms, including a retrieval mechanism for large amounts of multimedia data, and must provide conceptual and physical database schemata to support these paradigms. Furthermore, an MMIS must also accommodate the performance limitations of the computer.

Once time-dependent data are effectively modeled, an MMIS must have the capability for storing and accessing these data. This problem is distinct from historical databases, temporal query languages [8,9], or time-critical query evaluation [55]. Unlike historical data, time-dependent multimedia objects require special considerations for presentation due to their real-time playout characteristics. Data need to be delivered from storage based on a prespecified schedule, and presentation of a single object can occur over an extended duration (e.g., a movie). In this section we describe database aspects of synchronization including conceptual and physical storage schemes, data compression, operating system support, and synchronization anomalies. Physical storage schemas are described in Chapter 11.

7.4.1 Synchronization

The term *synchronization* defines the occurrence of simultaneous events. By using dedicated devices and complete parallelism (e.g., the sound and image tracks of a motion picture) synchronization can be achieved. In a more

Table 7.2 Synchronization Tolerances for Various Media

Medium	*Maximum Delay (sec)*	*Maximum Jitter (msec)*
voice	0.25	10
video (TV quality)	0.25	10
compressed video	0.25	1
text	1	not applicable
data (file transfer)	1	not applicable
image	1	not applicable

general-purpose computer system, it is more difficult to attain this goal. Instead, storage devices, the network, the system bus, and dynamic memory must be carefully reserved and scheduled to provide similar but more flexible functionality. At each component and at different levels of system abstraction the synchronization requirements differ in character and control.

For multimedia data, the absolute synchronization requirement can be relaxed to different degrees for each medium without adversely affecting their presentation quality. For example, Table 7.2 shows the synchronization tolerances for various media (adapted from [56]).

We define timing parameters characterizing intermedia and real-time synchronization for the delivery of periodic (e.g., audio and video) and aperiodic data (e.g., text and still images). Parameters applicable to aperiodic data are maximum delay, minimum delay, and average delay as measured with respect to real time or with respect to other aperiodic data [57] (Table 7.2). For periodic data, maximum, minimum, and average delay are also applicable to individual data elements, but, in addition, instantaneous delay variation or jitter is important for characterizing streams. These parameters can describe time skew with respect to real time as well as to other periodic streams in an manner analogous to a phase angle.

Synchronization implies the occurrence of multiple events at the same instant in time. If they occur at different instants they are *skewed* in time (Figure 7.13). For two sequences of events (e.g., sequences of audio and video data frames) individual differences between corresponding events are

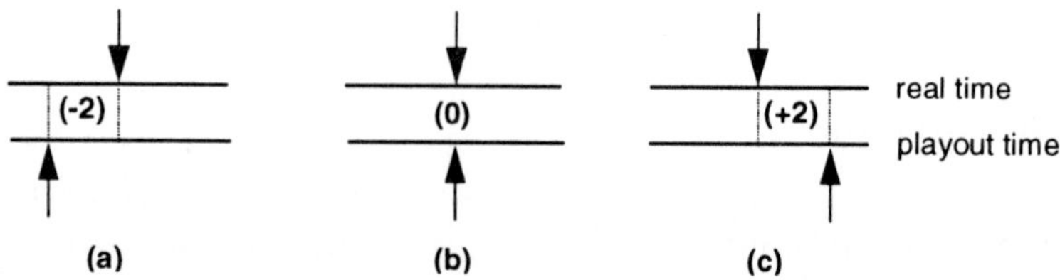

Figure 7.13 Skew: (a) lagging, (b) none, (c) leading

called *jitter*, whereas the average difference over some n interval of frames is called *skew*.

For periodic data such as audio and video, data can be lost, resulting in *dropouts* or gaps in playout. Such losses cause the stream of frames to advance in time or cause a stream lead. Similarly, if a data frame is duplicated, it causes the stream to retard in time or a stream lag.

Because many streams are possible, we characterize both intermedia and real-time reference skew for k streams using a matrix representation as,

$$skew = \begin{bmatrix} 0 & sk_{2,1} & sk_{1,3} & sk_{1,k+1} \\ sk_{2,1} & 0 & sk_{2,3} & sk_{2,k+1} \\ sk_{3,1} & & 0 & sk_{3,k+1} \\ & & & \\ sk_{k+1,1} & sk_{k+1,2} & sk_{k+1,3} & 0 \end{bmatrix}$$

where $sk_{p,q}$ describes the skew from stream p to stream q (q to p is negative) and the k+1th element corresponds to a real-time reference. We also define a target skew matrix $\Theta_{p,q}$ (similar to Ravindran's divergence vector [29]), which indicates target values which can be interpreted by a skew control function. Related to skew is data utilization [58]. Utilization U describes the ratio of the actual presentation rate to the available delivery rate of a sequence of data. Frame drops will decrease utilization whereas duplicates will increase utilization from its nominal unit value.

We define three measures of synchronization. The first defines single event synchronization (see Figure 7.14). The second is a generalization of the event synchronization, and the third is specific to periodic stream data characteristics of audio and video data and is more practical to implement. In each case, synchronization depends on multiple event occurrences including a reference event and a synchronized event.

Definition 1: A data item (object) with actual playout time ρ is synchronized with playout reference time π *iff*

$$|\rho - \pi| \leq \theta$$

where θ is the synchronization tolerance. Note that the units and time reference are arbitrary as long as they are consistent.

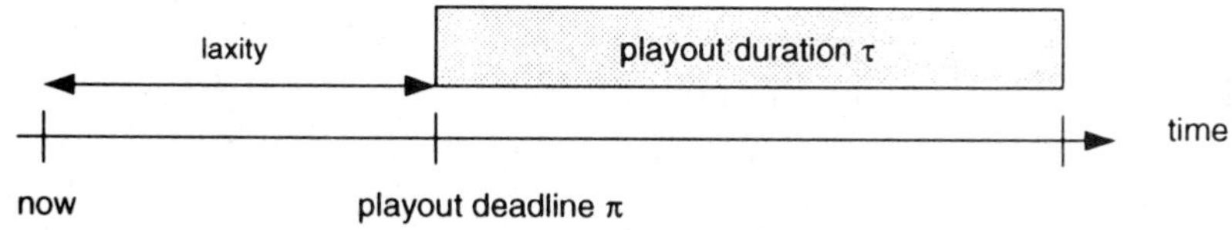

Figure 7.14 Single event synchronization

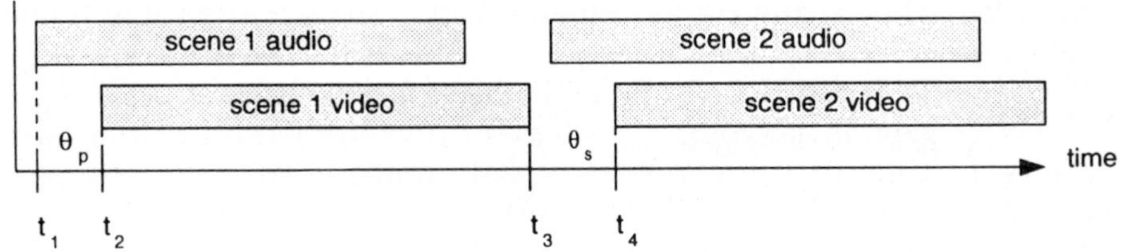

Figure 7.15 Synchronization tolerance

Definition 2: A composite object with actual playout times $P = \{\rho_i\}$ is synchronized with playout reference times $\Pi_i = \{\pi_i\}$ *iff*

$$\forall i, \mid \rho_i - \pi_i \mid \leq \theta_i$$

where $\Theta = \{\theta_i\}$ are the synchronization tolerances between each element and the reference.

This definition is similar to Ravindran's divergence vector [29] and Gibbs' definition of synchronization [31].

Definition 3: A continuous, periodic data stream comprised of n elements with actual playout times $P = \{\rho_i\}$ is synchronized with respect to a playout reference time π and period τ *iff*

$$\forall i, 0 \leq i < n, \mid \rho_i - \pi - i(\tau + \varepsilon) \mid \leq \theta_i$$

where θ is the synchronization tolerance for the stream and ε is the clock drift tolerance.

This definition allows for a drift in the actual playout times with respect to the reference. Furthermore, this tolerance can be described as a maximum or a statistical value.

The synchronization tolerance can also be defined with respect to sequential and parallel events, as shown in Figure 7.15, where θ_p describes the timing tolerance between parallel events and θ_s describes the tolerance between sequential events.

In each definition of synchronization, the reference and actual playout times can be in any consistent frame of reference or coordinate system and therefore can be applied in conjunction with the aforementioned (linear) temporal transformations.

Definition 3 is intended for continuous audio and video for which cumulative error can be more significant than the relative error. The cumulative error is associated with the ε in the aforementioned definition. *Relative* timing refers to the θ in the previous definitions whereas *absolute* timing refers to the θ_i. For these data, sample rates and frame rates define the playout times for individual data elements. For aperiodic data, the simplicity of Definition 3 can be applied by conversion to a periodic stream [7], as illustrated in Figure 7.6.

7.4.2 Data Structures for Temporal Representation

To support a time-based representation, an MMIS must capture the representation using an appropriate data structure that is suitable for subsequent application and TAC functionality and is also appropriate for object evolution through object editing. Because multimedia data are large with respect to data storage, a data structure supporting a temporal representation must be suitable for efficient data retrieval via database indexing and query.

Few language- or graph-based representation techniques specify appropriate data structures that support subsequent TAC operations on a database schema. One such approach provides mapping from a specification methodology to a database schema using the TPN and the relational database model [22]. In this case, temporal intervals and relationships are described by a timeline representation in an unstructured format or by a TPN in a structured format. Using a TPN, temporal hierarchy can be imparted to the conceptual schema as sets of intervals bound to a single temporal relation are identified and grouped. For example, this process is applied to the TPN of Figure 7.11, resulting in the conceptual schema of Figure 7.16.

With this approach, the time-based representation can be translated to a conceptual schema in the form of a temporal hierarchy representing the semantics of the specification approach. Subsets or subtrees of this hierarchy represent subsets of the specification, illustrating the capability of composing complex multimedia presentations. Leaf elements in this model indicate base multimedia objects (audio, image, text, etc.), and additional attributes can be assigned to nodes in the hierarchy for conventional DBMS access. Timing information is also captured with node attributes, allowing the assembly of component elements during playout.

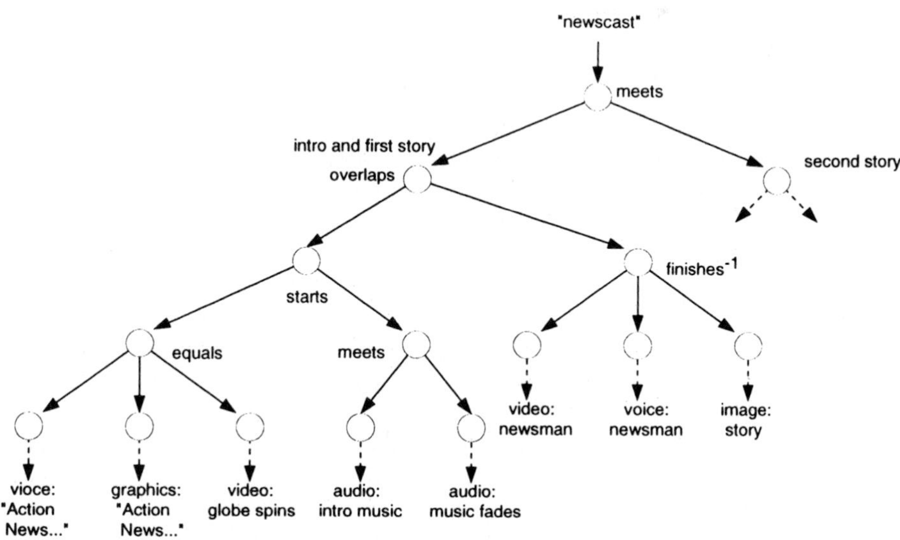

Figure 7.16 Temporal hierarchy for the "Action News"

7.4.3 Data Compression

Since multimedia data types have enormous storage and communications requirements, data compression is desirable, if not essential, to enable multimedia applications. In this section, some of the implications of data compression on continuous-mode data are discussed.

The advantage of compressed data is clearly the savings in storage space and communication bandwidth. However, it becomes more difficult to identify points of synchronization between streams requiring synchronization when variable bit rate (VBR) compression is applied. The reason is as follows. Compression schemes use both intra- and interframe coding. Intraframe coding applies compression schemes within a single time-dependent frame. Therefore, a timing specification can apply to the self-contained frame before, during, and after compression. For interframe coding, compression schemes apply across a sequence of frames. For the proposed MPEG coding scheme, differential values are generated for sequences of frames between interframe coded ones. This approach presents several problems for synchronization. First, it is desirable to have the ability to start at an arbitrary point in the continuous stream. With inter-frame coding this is not possible without first regenerating intermediate frames. Second, in order to provide reverse presentation, differential values must be available in both directions. The ability to begin presentation at an arbitrary point in a stream or to choose direction is part of the larger problem of providing random access or random insertion points into a stream-type object. These problems are approached in the MPEG scheme. To provide random insertion points, intraframe coding is used at intervals as often as required for access as specified by the application. Reverse playout is accommodated by bidirectional differential frames.

7.4.4 System Support for Synchronization

For supporting time-dependent media, an MDBMS must deal with storage device latencies, including ones due to data distribution across a network. Providing a transport mechanism for time-dependent data requires managing the resources of a computer network. For delay-sensitive media, these resources are communication bandwidth and end-to-end delay. The problem of synchronization across a network is most acute when providing intermedia synchronization for multiple independent stored-data sources. In this case, to achieve intermedia synchronization, random network delays on each connection must be overcome, in spite of variations in clock rates at each remote data source. Typically, the delay variations on each channel are estimated during connection setup, and an end-to-end delay, called a *control time*, is introduced, representing an interval over which buffering is applied. The result of this buffering is a reshaping of the channel delay distribution to reduce variance.

7.4.5 Synchronization Anomalies

When data are delayed and are not available for playout, a synchronization anomaly occurs. At the output device, this can result in a gap in the sequence of presented elements or a shortage of data to present per unit time. Policies for handling late-arriving data include discarding them or changing the playout rate to maintain a constant number of buffered elements. When data are lost or discarded, reconstruction can also be used. Steinmetz [5] proposes performing some alternate activity when a data element is not available, such as extending the playout time of the previous element. Generally, when gaps in a data sequence are ignored with respect to the playout rate, the loss of data elements when subsequent data are available advances the sequence in time and can be corrected by slowing the playout rate until the schedule is correct. Approaches to synchronization of received packets include varying the playout rate and the utilization of received data [59]. The expansion method lets each packet be played out even if late. The result is the delay of all successive packets and an accumulation of skew with time. Another approach is to ignore some data since much redundant information is contained in the data streams, thereby preserving the duration of the overall sequence. This is analogous to a reduction in packet utilization [58]. One further gap-compensating technique for continuous media reconstructs the missing data elements. This approach is to substitute alternate data for the missing data in the stream. The data are chosen as null or non-null values (zero amplitude and waveform stuffing) or are interpolated from previous values [60].

7.5 CONCLUSION

We presented a review of temporal representations for time-dependent multimedia data and their suitability for supporting data by means of various delivery operations including presentation. Significant issues remain for providing time-dependent delivery of multimedia data in a general multimedia information system. The primary issues are specification and storage of temporal information describing the time dependencies of multimedia data, provision of an enforcement mechanism for temporal specifications, and accommodation of the latency in the retrieval of time-dependent data when they are not available for playout.

7.6 REFERENCES

1. Kipp, N., Newcomb, V. and Newcomb, S. *Hytime Review*. TechnoTeacher Inc. 1990.
2. Sventek, J. S. An Architecture for Supporting Multi-Media Integration. *Proc. IEEE Comp. Soc. Office Automation Symposium*. April 1987. pp. 46–56.

3. Little, T. D. C., Ghafoor, A., Chen, C. Y. R., Chang, C. S., and Berra, P. B. Multimedia Synchronization. *IEEE Data Engineering Bulletin*. vol. 14, no. 3. September 1991. pp. 26–35.
4. Herrtwich, R. G., and Delgrossi, L. ODA-Based Data Modeling in Multimedia Systems. *International Computer Science Institute Tech. Rept. TR-90-043*. August 1990.
5. Steinmetz, R. Synchronization Properties in Multimedia Systems. *IEEE J. Selected Areas in Comm*. vol. 8, no. 3. April 1990. pp. 401–412.
6. Nicolaou, C. An Architecture for Real-Time Multimedia Communication Systems. *IEEE J. Selected Areas in Comm*. vol. 8, no. 3. April 1990. pp. 391–400.
7. Herrtwich, R. G. Time Capsules: An Abstraction for Access to Continuous-Media Data. *Proc. 11th Real-Time Systems Symp*. December 1990. pp. 11–20.
8. Snodgrass, R. The Temporal Query Language TQuel. *ACM Trans. on Database Systems*. vol. 12, no. 2. June 1987. pp. 247–298.
9. Tansel, A. U., Arkun, M. E., and Ozsoyoglu, G. Time-by-Example Query Language for Historical Databases. *IEEE Trans. on Software Engineering*. vol. 15, no. 4. April 1989. pp. 464–478.
10. Anderson, T. L. Modeling Time at the Conceptual Level. In P. Scheuermann (ed.), *Improving Database Usability and Responsiveness*. Academic Press. 1982. pp. 273–297.
11. Hamblin, C. L. Instants and Intervals. In J. T. Fraser, et al. (ed.), *Proc. of the 1st Conf. of the Intl. Society for the Study of Time*. Springer-Verlag. 1972. pp. 324–331.
12. Allen, J. F. Maintaining Knowledge about Temporal Intervals. *Comm. of the ACM*. vol. 26, no. 11. November 1983. pp. 832–843.
13. Hoare, C. A. R. Communicating Sequential Processes. *Communications of the ACM*. vol. 21, no. 8. August 1978. pp. 666–677.
14. Wirth, N. Toward a Discipline of Real-Time Programming. *Comm. of the ACM*. vol. 20, no. 8. August 1977. pp. 577–583.
15. SMPTE Recommended Practice: RP 136-1986 Time and Control Codes for 24, 25, or 30 Frame-Per-Second Motion Picture Systems. *SMPTE J*. August 1986. pp. 862–864.
16. Moore, D. J. Multimedia Presentation Development Using the Audio Visual Connection. *IBM Systems J*. vol. 29, no. 4. 1990. pp. 494–508.
17. Hodges, M. E., Sasnett, R. M., and Ackerman, M. S. A Construction Set for Multimedia Applications. *IEEE Software*. January 1989. pp. 37–43.
18. Toshiharu, T., Shinju, H., and Takashi, O. Multi-Media Visual Information Editing Techniques. *Globecom '87 (IEEE/IEICE Global Telecommunications Conference Record 1987*. November 1987. pp. 1192–1196.
19. Committee Draft International Standard—Information Technology Hypermedia/Time-based Structuring Language (HyTime). ISO/IEC CD 10743. April 1, 1991.
20. International Organization for Standardization. *ISO Document no. 8613*. ISO. March 1988.
21. Little, T. D. C., and Ghafoor, A. Synchronization and Storage Models for Multimedia Objects. *IEEE J. on Selected Areas in Comm*. April 1990, pp. 413–427.
22. Little, T. D. C., Ghafoor, A., and Chen, C. Y. R. Conceptual Data Models for Time-Dependent Multimedia Data. *Proc. 1992 Workshop on Multimedia Information Systems (MMIS '92)*. February 1992. pp. 86–110.
23. Dimitrova, H., and Golshani, F. EVA: A Query Language for Multimedia Information Systems. *Proc. 1992 Workshop on Multimedia Information Systems*. February 1992. pp. 1–20.
24. Garcia-Luna-Aceves, J. J., Poggio, A. Multimedia Message Content Protocols for Computer Mail. In Hugh Smith (ed.), *Proc. IFIP WG 6.5 Working Conf. on Computer-Based Message Services*. May 1984. North-Holland. pp. 87–98.
25. Postel, J. A Structured Format for Multimedia Documents. Report RFC767, DDN Network Information Center, SRI International, Menlo Park, CA, 94025, USA. August 1980.
26. Schramm, C., and Goldberg, M. Multimedia Radiological Reports: Creation and Playback. *Proc. SPIE Medical Imaging III: Image Capture and Display*. vol. 1091, January 1989. pp. 191–201.
27. Poggio, A., Garcia-Luna-Aceves, J. J., Craighill, E. J., Moran, D., Aguilar, L., Worthington, D., and Hight, J. CCWS: A Computer-Based Multimedia Information System. *Computer*. October 1985. pp. 92–103.

28. Postel, J., Finn, G., Katz, A., and Reynolds, J. An Experimental Multimedia Mail System. *ACM Trans. on Office Information Systems.* vol. 6, no. 1. January 1988. pp. 63–81.
29. Ravindran, K. Real-Time Synchronization of Multimedia Data Streams in High Speed Networks. *Proc. 1992 Workshop on Multimedia Information Systems.* February 1992. pp. 164–188.
30. Newcomb, S. R., Kipp, N. A., and Newcomb, V. T. The "HyTime" Hypermedia/Time-based Document Structuring Language. *Comm. of the ACM.* vol. 34, no. 11. November 1991. pp. 67–83.
31. Gibbs, S., Dami, L. and Tsichritzis, D. An Object-Oriented Framework for Multimedia Composition and Synchronisation. *Object Composition, Tech. Rept.* University of Geneva. June 1991. pp. 133–143.
32. Dannenberg, R. B. Remote Access to Interactive Media. *Proc. SPIE Symposium OE/FIBERS '92 (Enabling Technologies for Multi-Media, Multi-Service Networks).* September 1992.
33. Hodges, M. E., and Sasnett, R. M. Plastic Editors for Multimedia Documents. *Proc. Summer 1991 Usenix Conf.* June 1991. pp. 563–573.
34. Anderson, D. P., Tzou, S. Y., Wahbe, R., Govindan, R., and Andrews, M. Support for Continuous Media in the Dash System. *Proc. 10th Intl. Conf. on Distributed Computing Syst.* May 1990. pp. 54–61.
35. Committee Draft International Standard—Information Technology—Standard Music Description Language (SMDL). ISO/IEC CD 10743. April 1, 1991.
36. Vin, H. M., Zellweger, P. T., Swinehart, D. C., and Rangan, P. V. Multimedia Conferencing in the Etherphone Environment. *Computer.* October 1991. pp. 69–79.
37. Little, T. D. C. and Ghafoor, A. Spatio-Temporal Composition of Distributed Multimedia Objects for Value-Added Networks. *Computer* (Special Issue: Multimedia Information Systems). vol. 24, no. 10. October 1991. pp. 42–50.
38. Peterson, J. L. Petri Nets. *Computing Surveys.* vol. 9, no. 3. September 1977. pp. 225–252.
39. Stotts, P. D., and Furuta, R. Petri-Net-Based Hypertext: Document Structure with Browsing Semantics. *ACM Trans. on Office Automation Systems.* vol. 7, no. 1. January 1989. pp. 3–29.
40. Fujikawa, K., Shimojo, S., Matsuura, T., Nishio, S., Miyahara, H. Multimedia Presentation System "Harmony" with Temporal and Active Media. *Proc. Summer 1991 Usenix Conf.* June 1991. pp. 75–93.
41. Weiss, K. H. Formal Specification and Continuous Media. *Proc. 1st Intl. Workshop on Network and Operating Support for Digital Audio and Video.* November 1990.
42. Dannenberg, R. B., et al. Arctic: A Functional Approach to Real-Time Control. *Computer Music Journal* 10(4). Winter 1986. pp. 67–78.
43. Dannenberg, R. B. Arctic: A Functional Language for Real-Time Control. *Conference Record of the 1984 ACM Symposium on LISP and Functional Programming.* August 1984. pp. 96–103.
44. Dannenberg, R. B. Expressing Temporal Behavior Declaratively. *CMU Tech Report.* (in press)
45. Zellweger, P. T. Toward a Model for Active Multimedia Documents. In M. M. Blattner and R. B. Dannenberg (eds.), *Multimedia Interface Design.* ACM Press. 1992. pp. 39–52.
46. Rennison, E., Baker, R., Kim, D. D., and Lim, Y. H. MuX: An X Co-Existent, Time-Based Multimedia I/O Server. *The X Resource: A Practical Journal of the X Window System (Proc. 6th Annual X Technical Conf.)* no. 1. Winter 1992. pp. 213–233.
47. Tsichritzis, D., Gibbs, S., and Dami, L. Active Media *Object Composition.* Tech. Rept. University of Geneva. June 1991. pp. 115–132.
48. Lippman, A. Movie-Maps: An Application of the Optical Videodisc to Computer Graphics. *Computer Graphics.* July 1980. pp. 32–42.
49. Sasnett, R. M. Reconfigurable Video. Master's thesis. MIT. 1986.
50. Stotts, P. D., and Furuta, R. Temporal Hyperprogramming. *J. of Visual Languages and Computing.* vol. 1. 1990. pp. 237–253.
51. Ravindran, K. and Prasad, B. Communication Structures and Paradigms for Multimedia Conferencing Applications. Tech. Rept. Dept. Computing and Information Sciences. Kansas State University. January 1991.

52. Ramanathan, S., Rangan, P. V., Vin, H. M., and Kaeppner, T. Optimal Communications Architectures for Multimedia Conferencing in Distributed Systems. *Proc. 12th Intl. Conf. on Distributed Computing Systems (ICDCS)*. June 1992.
53. Yavatkar, R. Issues of Coordination and Temporal Synchronization in Multimedia Communication. *Proc. 4th IEEE ComSoc Intl. Workshop on Multimedia Communications (Multimedia '92)*. April 1992. pp. 286–293.
54. Faulk, S. R., and Parnas, D. L. On Synchronization in Hard Real-Time Systems. *Comm. of the ACM*. vol. 31, no. 3. March 1988. pp. 274–287.
55. Hou, W. C., Ozsoyoglu, G., and Taneja, B. K. Processing Aggregate Relational Queries with Hard Time Constraints. *Proc. ACM SIGMOD Intl. Conf. on the Management of Data*. June 1989.
56. Hehmann, B. B., Salmony, M. G., and Stuttgen, H. J. Transport Services for Multimedia Applications on Broadband Networks. *Computer Communications*. vol. 13, no. 4. May 1990. pp. 197–203.
57. Little, T. D. C., and Gibbon, J. F.Management of Time-Dependent Multimedia Data. *Proc. SPIE Symposium OE/FIBERS'92, (Enabling Technologies for Multi-Media, Multi-Service Networks)*. September 1992.
58. Little, T. D. C., and Ghafoor, A. Network Considerations for Distributed Multimedia Object Composition and Communication. *IEEE Network*. November 1990. pp. 32–49.
59. Naylor, W. E., and Kleinrock, L. Stream Traffic Communication in Packet Switched Networks: Destination Buffering Considerations. *IEEE Trans. on Communications*. vol. COM-30, no. 12. December 1982. pp. 2527–2524.
60. Suzuki, J., and Taka, M. Missing Packet Recovery Techniques for Low-Bit-Rate Coded Speech. *IEEE J. on Selected Areas in Comm*. vol. 7, no. 5. June 1989. pp. 707–717.

CHAPTER 8

OPERATING SYSTEM SUPPORT FOR CONTINUOUS MEDIA APPLICATIONS

Hideyuki Tokuda
Carnegie Mellon University and Keio University

8.1 INTRODUCTION

Many modern workstations are equipped with specialized hardware capable of producing digital audio and displaying high-resolution graphics. The current trend in multimedia computing is toward incorporating full-motion digital video and audio into many types of applications. Such applications range from multimedia mail, hypermedia, conferencing systems, remote teleprocessing, and virtual reality. We call these *continuous media applications*.

Although continuous media applications are becoming very popular in workstation environments, current workstation operating systems face many problems in supporting multiple instances of continuous media applications. For instance, we often encounter a jitter problem while we are reading video mail whenever a background file transfer program starts. A music play program often accelerates its speed when the contending programs terminate.

Similarly, running many video phone programs often places the system into an overload situation. However, the current systems do not provide an intelligent overload control or management scheme. Instead of having every program suffer from the overload, a user may want to maintain the quality of service (QOS) of only the current important sessions.

These problems originate from two factors: the lack of real-time support from the operating system, which can provide better time-driven computation, and the lack of QOS-based resource management where the system can guarantee the quality of service of the active applications.

In a QOS-based resource management scheme, it is not sufficient to simply specify a QOS level at session creation time which statically remains in force for the life of the session. Instead, we have proposed and implemented a dynamic QOS control scheme with CBSRP (Capacity-Based Session Reservation Protocol) for real-time communications [1]. Other researchers also have proposed dynamic QOS control schemes [2,3,4].

In our QOS model, a QOS level for continuous media objects can be expressed with temporal and spatial resolutions. The temporal resolution can be expressed by the number of frames per second (fps) or sampling rate. The spatial resolution can be expressed by data size, the number of bits per pixel (bpp), compression scheme, compression ratio, and so on. For a simple digital video session, a user task may choose an acceptable range of fps for its temporal resolution and a range from the image size and the bpp, such as 8, 16, or 24 bpp for the spatial resolution. By specifying these ranges, the system or user will be able to change QOS of existing sessions during the course of the session.

In this chapter, we describe new operating system support for continuous media applications with a case study we have been experimenting with using the Real-Time Mach microkernel [5]. In Section 8.2, we discuss the limitations in the current workstation operating systems, and Section 8.3 describes new operating system support based on our experience using Real-Time Mach for digital video and audio applications. We show some experimental results using Real-Time Mach in Section 8.4, and we make a few concluding remarks in Section 8.5.

8.2 LIMITATIONS IN WORKSTATION OPERATING SYSTEMS

Since many workstation operating systems (such as UNIX) are designed to offer fair use of system resources among competing programs, it is not easy to maintain timely system response to continuous media applications. The system does not have any mechanism to maintain a specified QOS level for such applications. Similarly, the current systems do not provide any overload prevention or management scheme when the system encounters a transient overload situation. Every program, then, will slow down and a user may end up with unpredictable delay and jitter problems.

We also face a problem with lack of real-time services. For instance, from a programming point of view, UNIX's "process" abstraction is a very useful concept; however, its context switching costs are unacceptable for many continuous media applications. It often forces us to choose a user-level "thread" package that provides much lighter context switching. Thread packages often also have a shortcoming, namely the lack of the first-class treatment of user-level threads, including the lack of support for preemptable threads.

In this section, we review the basic issues for supporting distributed continuous media applications in traditional workstation operating systems.

8.2.1 Interrupt Latency and Throughput

The large interrupt latency is another reason that UNIX does not support real-time activities well. In continuous media applications such as the handling of a MIDI data stream, the application produces a frequent number of interrupts to the kernel. The resulting heavy context switching cannot keep up with the highly demanding event stream.

Like the UNIX kernel, all non-preemptable kernels provide very poor interrupt latency. Processing of a real-time event that wakes up a new thread may be deferred until the current processing of the kernel primitive completes. It may take as long as several milliseconds in the worst case.

There are three approaches to reducing kernel interrupt latency. The first approach is to make the kernel highly preemptable by changing its internal structure. The second scheme is to add a set of safe preemption points to the existing kernel. The third scheme is to convert the current kernel to be one of the user programs and run it on top of a microkernel. This chapter discusses the third approach.

8.2.2 Priority Inversion Management

When a real-time program shares the same resource in the system with non real-time programs, there are cases where the real-time program must wait for the completion of the non real-time programs. In fact, if many applications share the same system server, such as a network server, then a high-priority task's video stream's packet must wait for the completion of all previously queued low-priority packets.

This type of priority inversion caused by the nonpreemptive server often causes unpredictable delay and jitter problems. The structure of the server, which is shown below, will cause the problem, since the body of the server (i.e., `do_service`) is simply executed one message at a time and the message queuing is done in a FIFO order.

```
server( ) {
 while(1){
     receive_msg( );
     do_service( );
```

```
        reply( );
    }
}
```

To avoid priority inversion in a client/server environment, at a minimum, better operating system support is needed. Priority inheritance and priority hand-off mechanisms are two techniques that are used in real-time operating systems.

8.2.3 Periodic Activity

Continuous media require periodic service activities for transmission or presentation. The simplest way of manipulating a periodic data stream is to use a loop construct for handling the sequence of data images as follows.

```
while(1) {
    get_cm_object(. . .);
    draw_cm_object(. . .);
}
```

In this scheme, the user does not have any control over the drawing rate of the continuous media objects. In a multiprogrammed environment, the drawing rate (i.e., temporal resolution) may vary depending on the workload of the system. When the system encounters an overload situation, the drawing may stop momentarily. When the other task terminates, the drawing may even speed up. We refer to this type of control scheme as an *implicit binding* of a timing constraint on the code.

On the other hand, in a traditional operating system like UNIX, we can provide more explicit timing control by using a `sleep` function for regulating the drawing rate as follows.

```
start time = get_current_time();
while(1){
    get_cm_object(. . .);
    draw_cm_object(. . .);
    start_time = start_time + period;
    duration = start_time - get_current_time();
    sleep(duration);
}
```

In this scheme, if the execution of the program is suspended after `get_cm_object()` is evaluated and the execution is later resumed, duration is calculated with the incorrect value of the current time. So the program might be delayed too long in the `sleep()` statement. As shown in this example, the preemption of the program often interferes with the timing control logic. It is well known that this type of relative temporal synchronization is a poor mechanism in a multiprogrammed environment. Either absolute time specification or operating system support for periodicity is necessary to overcome this problem.

8.2.4 Deadline and Recovery Management

Unlike hard real-time systems, many continuous media application programs have inherently soft deadlines. For instance, we are typically able to continue a video conference even if the most recent video image could not be processed in time. Missing a single deadline may not cause total chaos; however, the deadline-missed notification to the application is important information. Based on this information, the applications may want to change the QOS level for video or audio sessions.

The basic issues are related to deadline control, notification, and recovery schemes the system can support. When the program misses a deadline due to overload or hardware/software errors, the user program should be able to decide the counteractions.

In order to discuss the issues in deadline and recovery management, let us use a modern real-time programming language, such as RTC++ [6]. In RTC++, a simple deadline handler **q** can be expressed in **within t do s except q** as follows.

```
within (dead_line_duration) do {
    get_cm_object(. . .);
    draw cm object(. . .);
} except {
    recovery_action;
}
```

In this example, the recovery action always will be running with the same priority of the main activity. However, it is often necessary to execute the action in a higher priority than the main activity. So the recovery action should take place after bumping up its priority first:

```
within (dead_line_duration) do {
    get_cm_object(. . .);
    draw_cm_object(. . .);
} except {
    bump_up_priority(high);
    recovery_action;
}
```

However, again, due to a multiprogramming environment, before executing `bump_up_priority(high)`, this task could be preempted. In other words, in order to provide such semantics, we need to treat the exception notification and bump-up operation as an atomic action.

8.2.5 QOS Management and Admission Control

QOS management for continuous media applications can be classified into two types of QOS control schemes: *static* and *dynamic*. With a static control scheme, a user simply specifies a QOS level at session creation time. The specified QOS level will be maintained during the lifetime of the session.

A dynamic control scheme, on the other hand, allows the system or a user program to change the initial QOS level during the course of the session. It can be initiated in two ways: one is from a QOS manager when the availability of system resources becomes very low, and the other is from the user task when it wants to degrade the initial QOS level gracefully or improve the QOS level. In general, static and dynamic QOS control schemes are not well supported in workstation operating systems yet.

A simple skeleton of an admission control for the QOS manager can be expressed as follows.

```
qos_manager( )
        ...
        accept_request( );
        switch(msg)
                case admission_test:
                        estimate_resource_req( );
                        buffer_check( );
                        schedulability_check( );
                        network_capacity_check( );
                        if (is_request_acceptable)
                              qos_level = determine_qos_init_level( );
                        reply(requester, qos_level)
...
```

In this example, the QOS manager can return an initial value of the QOS level to the client if all resource checks can be passed. Current systems, however, do not provide any mechanism to perform such admission control for avoiding potential overload situations.[1] A resource enforcement mechanism, which prevents unexpected excess use of processor cycles, is also lacking for processor resources.

8.3 NEW OS SUPPORT

Many workstations are now offering multimedia computing support; however, we do lack a comprehensive software standard or common operating system support functions. Various types of operating system support have been discussed, ranging from a very simple real-time scheduler to sophisti-

---

[1] Even in traditional real-time systems, many systems did not have any overload control mechanism.

cated modification to device drivers. Although operating system supports alone cannot create distributed continuous media applications, fundamental changes are needed in the traditional operating systems.

New operating system supports for continuous media applications can be classified into three categories: *architectural support, resource management support,* and *programming support.* In this section, we will describe these categories based on our experience on extending Real-Time Mach for continuous media applications.

8.3.1 Architectural Support

The basic structure of traditional operating systems has been dominated by a monolithic kernel architecture. However, new types of applications such as continuous media applications, mobile computing, personal digital assistance, and wireless networking are demanding not only advanced operating system services but also better, flexible operating systems architectures.

8.3.2 Microkernel Architecture

A microkernel architecture is becoming very popular among the next generation workstation operating systems. A *microkernel* is an operating system kernel which is only responsible for manipulating low-level (or meta-level) system resources, and is independent from any specific user-level computational paradigm. Examples of such low-level system resources are address spaces, processor cycles, interrupt, and trap-handling mechanisms.

For instance, the Mach microkernel [7,8,9] only includes interrupt, trap, scheduler, device servers, virtual memory, and interprocess communication facilities. However, even a traditional device driver can be implemented as a user-level task.

In the microkernel-based architecture, traditional system components such as file system and network protocol modules reside outside of the kernel. A system scheduler can also be outside the traditional kernel.

There are several ways of placing new operating system functions on top of the microkernel (Figure 8.1). A new system service can be realized as a service by library routines (SL), by a server or servers (SS), and by microkernel functions (SK). While the SK scheme can provide easy sharing of system resources between a new system service and the microkernel, the SS and SL schemes provide better extensibility of the microkernel. However, tradeoff among these schemes must be examined carefully.

8.3.3 Resource Management Support

A new resource management scheme should be adopted to provide necessary system resources such as processor cycles, memory and network

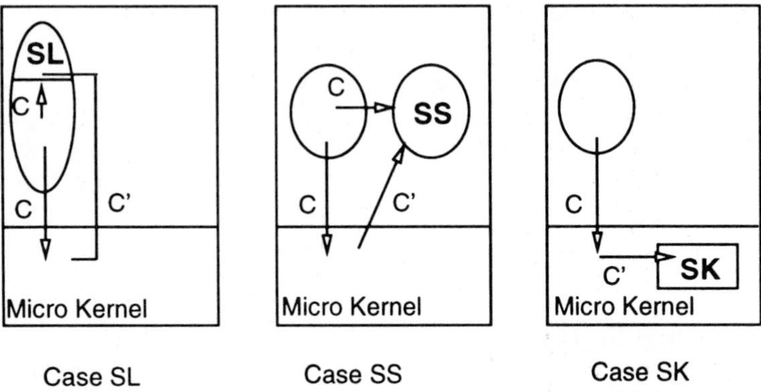

Figure 8.1 Placement of system functions: SL, SS, and SK schemes

bandwidth, so that the application can maintain the requested QOS level without encountering unpredictable delay and jitter while reproducing the video display and audio sound. We discuss several resource management techniques for continuous media applications.

QOS-Based Resource Control

A new approach is to manage continuous media applications based on their QOS requirements. QOS in continuous media can be expressed in terms of temporal and spatial characteristics. Although the temporal and spatial characteristics of periodic and aperiodic data streams are mostly application dependent, the system must maintain users' requested QOS level.

One paradigm change is that the system may accept a user's request if, and only if, there are enough system resources available to maintain the requested QOS levels. The system may negotiate with application programs or a user to reduce its QOS levels so that it can be accommodated under the current resource constraint. In other words, the system will have an admission control mechanism to avoid unexpected overload or interference to ongoing QOS guaranteed activities.

In a dynamic control scheme, a user program or the system's QOS manager may change the initial QOS level during the course of the session. For instance, we can show the following case as an example of dynamic QOS change in the program.

```
main ( ) {
    main_thread_body;
    . . .
    session_create (qos_mgr, qos_req);
    . . .
    session_control(qos_mgr, qos_change);
    . . .
}
```

```
9. session_call_back_stub(session, qos level) {
10.    adjust qos(session, qos level);
11.}
```

After creating a session (line 4), the user program may be able to submit a request for degrading the initial QOS level explicitly (line 6). On the other hand, the QOS manager may be able to invoke a call-back function such as `session_call_back_stub()` (line 9) for restoring or degrading the QOS of the ongoing session.

Real-Time Scheduler

A real-time scheduler offers better processor scheduling support among time constrained continuous media application programs. The traditional real-time scheduling policy, such as fixed preemptive (FP), rate monotonic (RM), and earliest deadline first (EDF), should be incorporated with the admission control and enforcement mechanism for the QOS-based paradigm.

An enhanced version of the real-time scheduler should be able to control and enforce a minimum and maximum execution rate of continuous media applications in order to maintain the requested QOS level during the course of the session.

The notion of *schedulability analysis* is important in hard/soft real-time systems, whereas the QOS-based system requires *playability analysis* under the range of the given QOS levels.

QOS-Based Memory Management

In traditional real-time systems, memory management avoids using virtual memory with a demand paging scheme since it may not bound the worst case paging-in/out time. However, the volume of continuous media objects (such as digital video objects) is very large, and without using a kind of shared memory management scheme, the system will be very slow due to excess amount of data copying.

In a QOS-based approach, the system should be able to prefetch the continuous media objects in a timely fashion. It is effective to use such time-driven prefetching policy; however, it is very difficult to access the right pages in the continuous media object if a user starts requesting a video frame randomly by pointing at its location in the video stream.

Timed I/O Management

The primary concern of real-time system designers is improving the processing speed of incoming I/O events. However, for continuous media applications, the temporal correctness of the I/O request is very important since the system must support the synchronization of multiple data streams, such as audio and video sessions.

One approach is to attach a timestamp at which the actual processing of the I/O data should take place. For instance, in Real-Time Mach, our audio driver can accept a request such as playing audio data at time *t*. In this way, the driver can preprocess the data before time *t*; then we can reduce the delay at the driver level.

8.3.4 Programming Support

Traditional abstraction of concurrent processes is very useful for continuous media applications. However, additional features such as proper time management, real-time threads, synchronization, and real-time IPC are often missing. In this section, we discuss these programming supports in Real-Time Mach.

Real-Time Threads

A real-time thread in Real-Time Mach can be created and killed using the rt and thread system calls.[2] Unlike non real-time threads, a real-time thread is defined with its timing constraint. As shown in a C-like pseudo-language in the following example, a real-time thread, `f()` is created with its thread attributes `{f, Si, Ti, Di}`. `f` indicates its thread's function `f()`; `Si`, `Ti`, and `Di` indicate thread `f`'s start time, period, and deadline, respectively.

```
root( )
{
    thread id f id;

    f_attr = {f,Si,Ti,Di}; /* set thread attribute of f */
    thread_create(f_id,f_attr); /* creating f() as a thread */
}

f(arg) {
        f's body
}
```

Note that if thread `f` is periodic, then it will automatically restart, or reincarnate, when it reaches the end of its function body.

Deadline Management

When a thread generates a bad memory reference, or commits a floating point error, this is seen as a logical correctness error and is flagged by the operating system as an exception. A real-time thread can also suffer from errors in temporal correctness, or *timing faults*. A timing fault is a failure mode which arises from a failure to meet user-specified timing constraints.

---

2 Unlike the C-thread [10] package, the current implementation of the real-time thread is based on a kernel thread.

To a real-time program this can be as disastrous as a bad memory reference. For this reason we provide an interface to catch timing faults like other exceptions and to allow users to dispose of them in an application-specific fashion.

For instance, when a periodic thread misses a deadline, its deadline handler must decide whether it is meaningful to continue or whether it should simply abort. Furthermore, if a periodic thread is delayed more than one additional period, it must also decide whether the main thread should catch up with all skipped instances or simply discard them.

The scheduling priority of the timing fault handler is an important issue. If we use a language construct, like **within (t) do s except q**, then the execution of **q** would be treated as the same priority as **s**. However, it is often necessary to change **q**'s priority based on the nature of the timing fault.

We support both methods by decoupling the timing fault mechanism from the scheduling context of the faulting thread. Instead, a timing fault causes the faulting thread to be suspended and a message to be sent to a user-specified port. A separate thread, with user-selectable scheduling precedence, waits on this port and takes action only when a timing fault occurs. Below is a simple example of how this works.

```
root( ) {

    f_attr = {f,Si,Ti,Di}; /* set thread attribute of f */
    rf_attr = {rf,Si,Ti,Di}; /* set thread attribute of rf */
    thread_create(rf_id, rf_attr); /* creating rf thread */
    thread_create(f_id, f_attr); /* creating f thread */
}

f(arg) {
    f's body
}

rf(time, thread, message)
{
     wait_for_notification( ); /* waiting for a deadline-miss
                                  notice */
     rf's body
}
```

In this example, the `rf` thread is created before the main thread starts, and it immediately waits for a timer notification indicating that thread `f` has missed its deadline. After receiving the notification, it can execute the proper recovery action against this timing fault.

This mechanism easily generalizes typical hard and soft real-time responses. A soft real-time application might ignore the error by executing `thread_resume(f)` while a hard real-time application might terminate the offending thread with `thread_terminate(f)`.

Real-Time Synchronization

For real-time synchronization support, the system should at least provide a fast event notification mechanism and a real-time mutual exclusion mechanism. For both mechanisms, the queueing policy for waiting threads should be based on their priority instead of a FIFO ordering. Traditional (non real-time) synchronization primitives use a FIFO-based queuing for avoiding the starvation problem among waiting threads. However, for real-time programs, FIFO ordering often causes the priority inversion problem [11]. One way of avoiding the priority inversion problem is to use priority-based queuing with the priority inheritance protocol [11,12].

In Real-Time Mach, for example, a critical section can be implemented by using the following `rt_mutex_lock` and `rt_mutex_unlock` primitives [13].

```
1. mutex_attr.mutex_policy = PRI_BPI
         /* setting a mutex policy */
2. ret = rt_mutex_allocate( mutex, mutex_attr)
         /* allocating a mutex variable */
3. ret = rt_mutex_lock(mutex);
4.       /* body of critical section */
5. ret = rt_mutex_unlock(mutex);
```

As shown in line 1, a user can choose a synchronization policy for a critical section by setting an attribute of the mutex variable. In Real-Time Mach, kernelized monitor (KM), basic policy (BP), basic priority inheritance protocol (BPI), priority ceiling protocol (PCP), and restartable critical region (RCS) are supported.

In the KM protocol, if a thread enters the kernelized monitor region, all preemption is prevented. Thus, the duration of the critical section must be shorter than any real-time thread's deadline. The BP policy, on the other hand, simply enqueues waiting threads in the lock variable based on the thread's priority. BPI provides the inheritant function that a lower-priority thread executing the critical section inherits the priority of the higher-priority thread when the lock is conflicted. In the PCP protocol, the ceiling priority of the lock is defined as the priority of the highest priority thread that may lock the lock variable.

The underlying idea of PCP is to ensure that when a thread *T* preempts the critical section of another thread *S* and executes its own critical section *CS*, the priority at which *CS* will be executed is guaranteed to be higher than the inherited priorities of all the preempted critical sections. For the RCS policy, a higher-priority thread is able to abort the lower-priority thread in the critical section and put it back to the waiting queue while recovering the state of the shared variable. After this recovery action, the higher-priority thread can enter the critical section without any waiting in the queue. A user program must be responsible to recover the state of shared variable.

8.3.5 Real-Time IPC

Similar to the original synchronization primitives, the queuing policy of the message is in a FIFO ordering. Thus, a user cannot avoid the priority inversion problem within a nonpreemptive server. In Real-Time Mach, we have extended the original IPC by providing priority-based queuing, priority hand-off, and priority inheritance mechanisms [14]. The programming interface is almost identical to the original IPC except that proper port attributes must be set when it is allocated. The following attributes for the communication port are provided.

- **Message Queuing:** It specifies the message queue ordering. FIFO and priority-based ordering policies can be used.
- **Priority Hand-off:** Priority hand-off manipulates the receiver's priority when a message is transferred. If this attribute is set, the priority of the receiver is propagated from that of the sender or given priority according to the selected policy. If it is disabled, the priority of the receiver is not changed.
- **Priority Inheritance:** It executes the priority inheritance protocol [11]. If it is activated, the server inherits the priority of the sender thread which sent the highest priority message.
- **Message Distribution:** It selects a proper receiver thread when two or more receivers are running. Arbitrary or priority-based (WORK) selection can be specified as a policy. When the arbitrary policy is specified, a receiver thread is chosen in FIFO order. The priority-based policy selects a receiver thread according to a given priority.

Since the server's service time seems much longer than a critical section, a user must be concerned with these priority inversion problems in distributed multimedia applications. In particular, we have implemented an integrated priority inheritance mechanism between the synchronization and IPC domains [15].

8.4 EXPERIMENTS USING REAL-TIME MACH

To demonstrate the effectiveness of operating systems support described in Section 8.3, we show the experimental results using Real-Time Mach 3.0, which has been in use for development of distributed real-time applications. Real-Time Mach is a real-time version of the Mach microkernel [8] developed at CMU.

We evaluate three programs in this section. The first program is a QuickTime [16] movie player program, which displays QuickTime movie files on a X11/R5 window system using real-time threads. The use of real-time threads and dynamic rebinding of timing attributes are demonstrated. The second program is a part of a new Real-Time Mach microkernel feature, processor reservation, which allows a user to reserve a minimum rate of computation per a specified period. This mechanism provides a kind of firewall among CPU-intensive tasks and guarantees steady progress of real-time activities. The third program shows the effect of a dynamic control of QOS levels among the QuickTime player programs. The program demonstrates that a dynamic change of QOS is feasible and effective under a heavily loaded CPU.

All experiments are performed using a Gateway 2000 4DX2/66V, which has a 66-MHz Intel 80486DX2 processor and 16 megabytes of memory with an Alpha Logic's STAT! timer board to take measurements.

8.4.1 QTplayer: A QuickTime Movie Player

This QTplayer program can initiate several video sessions and one audio session using real-time threads and plays video with a specified frame rate or in a self-stabilizing fashion. By a self-stabilizing fashion, we mean that the player program tries to determine a stable temporal resolution (e.g., frames per second) under the available system resources. If the player's thread missed a deadline, it may adjust the length of period and deadline to be longer; similarly, when it satisfies its deadline, it may shorten the period and deadline.

We measured the average number of frames per second under the three cases where the program initiated one, two, and four video sessions simultaneously. We used a spatial resolution of 160 by 120 pixels wide with an 8-bit color QuickTime movie file, and the program read the image into memory first and then played. Figure 8.2 shows the results of the player with a self-stabilizing mode. The results indicate that under the one-session case, the player can achieve up to 23.5 fps and then drops to 12 fps and 6 fps under two and four sessions.

In order to check the jittering effect between frames, we also measured the interframe gap. Figure 8.3 shows the series of interframe gaps for 10 seconds of play. The result indicates that the interframe gap was also maintained at a stable level in each case.

The stabilization mechanism using the real-time threads worked well, and the player threads always reached a stabilized rate and provided the same frame rate among the threads. Figure 8.4 shows the frames per second and the interframe gap using a modified X11 server.

8.4.2 Processor Reservation

In this example, we demonstrate that a processor reservation scheme [17] can extend the time-sharing–based processor scheduling paradigm so that a thread can at least reserve a minimum rate of computation among competing activities.

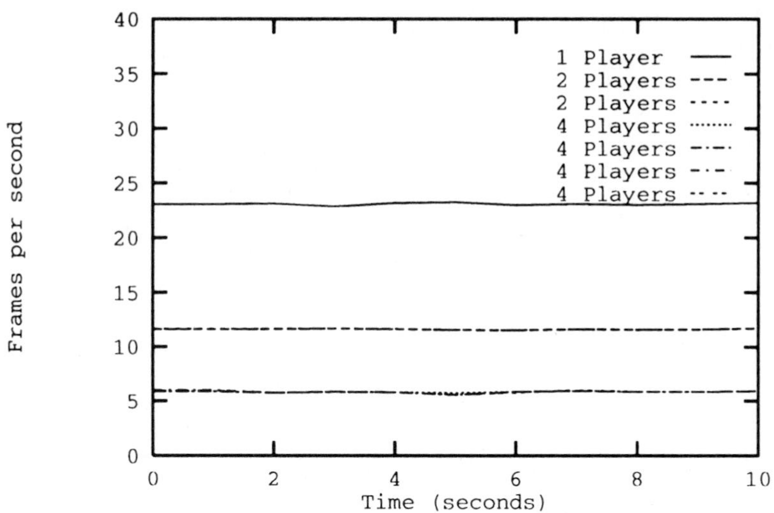

Figure 8.2 A QuickTime player with a self-stabilization scheme

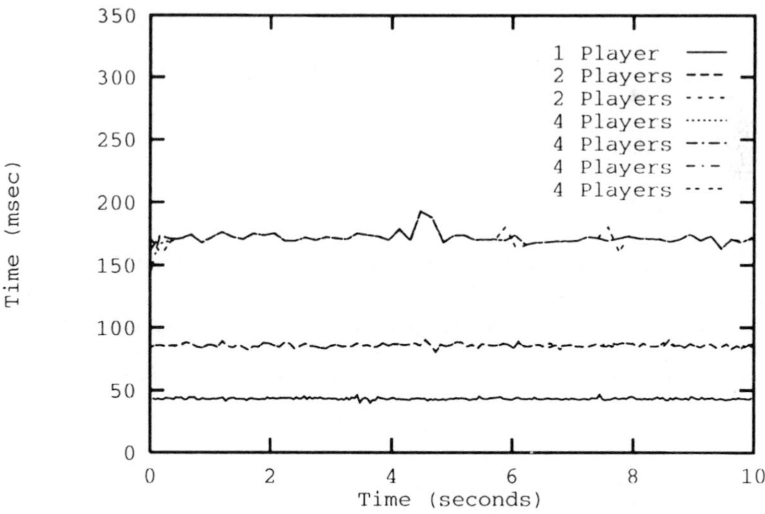

Figure 8.3 The interframe gap using the QuickTime player

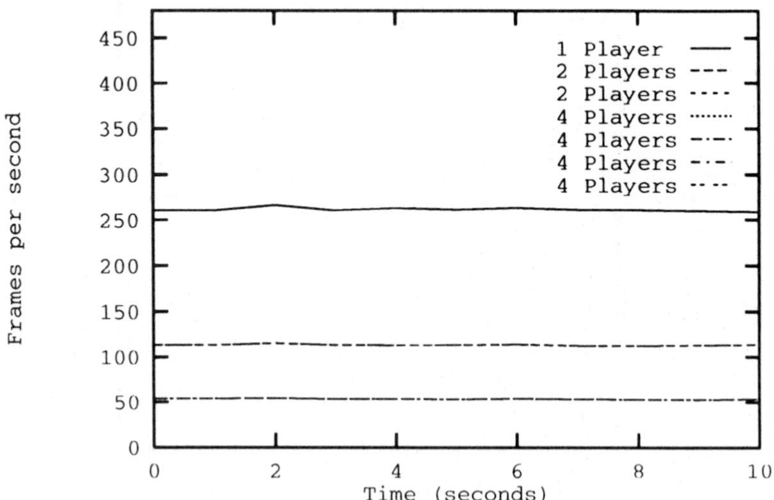

Figure 8.4a Frame rate using a modified X11 server

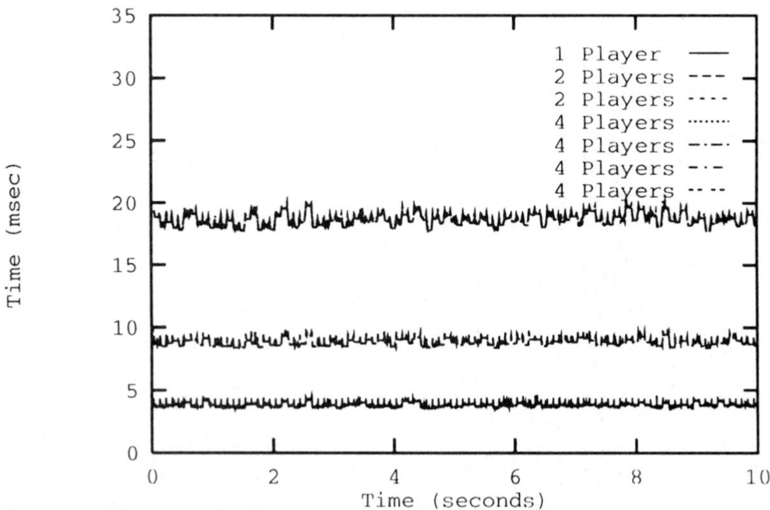

Figure 8.4b The interframe gap using a modified X11 server

Figure 8.5 shows the processor utilization of six threads under time-sharing scheduling policy. Because of a multilevel feedback queuing mechanism, each thread gets about 10 to 20 percent of processor cycles.

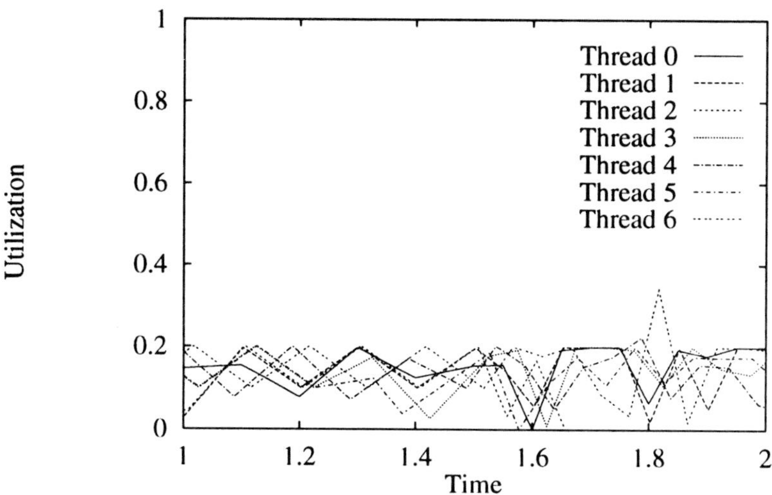

Figure 8.5 Process utilization for six threads under time-sharing scheduling policy

In Figure 8.6, we show the case where we enabled our reservation mechanism for Threads 0 and 1 with 20 and 30 percent reserves. The horizontal line at 20 percent and the line at 30 percent indicate that the utilization of these two threads is maintained. We note that a reservation ensures a lower bound on the usage for a thread which never blocks itself, and the increase in the usage of Thread 0 (reserved at 20 percent) jumps at time 1.95. This is a result of Thread 0's participation in the time-sharing scheduling pool.

This experimental work demonstrates the effectiveness of our processor reservation among CPU-intensive tasks, not I/O-intensive tasks. We are extending this scheme to support interrupt processing, DMA, paging activities, and networking activities as well.

8.4.3 Dynamic QOS Control

In this experiment, we created six player threads, namely players A through F, with different QOS requirements under a QOS manager. Under the QOS manager, the player threads are no longer independent and their rate of execution can be controlled by the manager. Each player must also submit a range of QOS levels (i.e., maximum and minimum of fps and spatial information) to the manager in order to create a video session.

In order to demonstrate the dynamic change of the temporal resolution, each thread used the same spatial resolution, namely 160 by 120 pixels wide

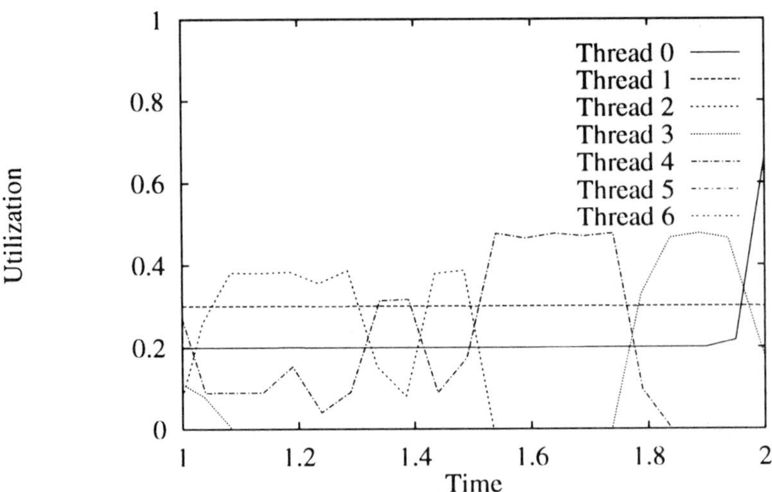

Figure 8.6 Time-sharing scheduling versus reserved scheduling. Process utilization for six threads under time-sharing scheduling policy with threads 0 and 1 given 20 percent and 30 percent reserve.

with 8-bit color. The following temporal resolutions are requested at the start time. Player A requests 6 to 10 fps, Player B is 5 to 5 fps, Player C is 1 to 1 fps, and Players D and E are stabilizing their temporal resolutions using remaining processor cycles, namely 0 to 30 fps. In this test, Players A, B, C, D, and E started at time 0. After five seconds, Player F started and created a new session with 4 fps resolution.

The execution result is shown in Figure 8.7. During the first five seconds, Player A executed with 10 fps, and other players' requested QOS levels were maintained. At time 5, Player F started and the QOS manager decided to degrade Player A's temporal resolution to 6 fps in order to accommodate F's request. The change of the temporal resolution of Player A was done by resetting the execution rate of the real-time thread. Because of explicit use of the timing attribute of real-time threads, it was simply done by changing the values of deadline and period of the thread.

8.5 CONCLUSION

In this chapter, we first addressed the limitations of workstation operating systems. We then discussed operating system support for multimedia computing from three different points of view: architectural support, resource management support, and programming support. An operating

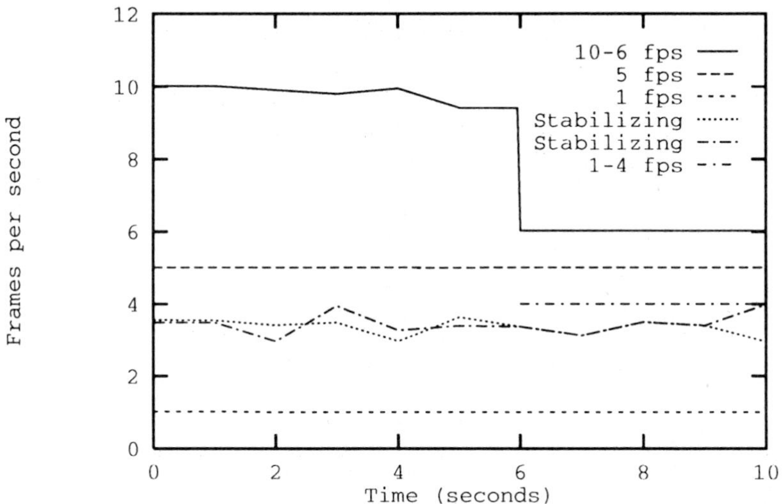

Figure 8.7 Dynamic QOS control with a QOS manager

system alone cannot build better distributed multimedia applications, but without this support the development of advanced multimedia applications would be very difficult.

The current performance of workstations has demonstrated enough ability to handle digital audio and video data within a single host environment. For distributed multimedia applications, however, it still lacks many system mechanisms which can guarantee a QOS level or resource usages such as CPU cycles, memory, and network bandwidth.

Under overload conditions or using less powerful machines, multimedia operating systems should support better QOS-based resource management with admission control and dynamic QOS control to provide QOS-guaranteed activities. Even with much larger and faster machines, operating systems should provide better timing control and time-based resource management.

8.6 ACKNOWLEDGMENTS

I would like to thank the members of the ART Project for their valuable comments. In particular, I thank Cliff Mercer and Stefan Savage for implementing the processor reservation scheme and Takuro Kitayama for measuring all data for the QTplay programs in Real-Time Mach. I also thank the editor, John Buford, for his technical and editorial comments.

8.7 REFERENCES

1. Tokuda, H., Tobe, Y., Chou S. T.-C., and Moura, J. M. F. Continuous Media Communication with Dynamic QOS Control Using ARTS with an FDDI Network. *Proceedings of ACM SIGCOMM '92*. August 1992.
2. Campbell, A., Coulson, G., Garcia, F., and Hutchison, D. A Continuous Media Tranport and Orchestration Service. *Proceedings of the SIGCOMM '92*. ACM Press. October 1992.
3. Herrtwich, R. G., and L. Delgrossi Beyond ST-II: Fulfilling the Requirements of Multimedia Communication. *Proceedings of the 3nd International Workshop on Network Operating System Support for Digital Audio and Video*. November 1992.
4. Nicolaou, C. A. A Distributed Architecture for Multimedia Communication Systems. Technical Report 220. Computer Laboratory. University of Cambridge. May 1991.
5. Tokuda, H., Nakajima, T., and Rao, P. Real-Time Mach: Towards a Predictable Real-Time System. *Proceedings of USENIX Mach Workshop*. October 1990.
6. Ishikawa, Y., Tokuda, H., and Mercer, C. W. Object-Oriented Real-Time Language Design: Constructs for Timing Constraints. *Proceedings Joint ACM OOPSLA/ECOOP '90 Conference on Object-Oriented Programming: Systems, Languages, and Applications*. October 1990.
7. Accetta, M. J., Baron, W., Bolosky, R. V., Golub, D. B., Rashid, R. F., Tevanian, A., and Young, M. W. Mach: A New Kernel Foundation for UNIX Development. *Proceedings of the Summer USENIX Conference*. July 1986.
8. Black, D. L., et al. Microkernel Operating System Architecture and Mach. *Proceedings of the Workshop on Micro-kernels and Other Kernel Architectures*. April 1992.
9. Golub, D., Dean, R., Forin, A., and Rashid, R. UNIX as an Application Program. *Proceedings of Summer USENIX Conference*. June 1990.
10. Cooper, E. C. and Draves, R. P. C Threads Technical Report. Computer Science Department. Carnegie Mellon University. CMU-CS-88-154. March 1987.
11. Sha, L., Rajkumar, R., and Lehoczky, J. P. Priority Inheritance Protocols: An Approach to Real-Time Synchronization. *IEEE Transactions on Computers*. September 1990.
12. Rajkumar, R. Synchronization in Real-Time Systems: A Priority Inheritance Approach. Kluwer Academic Publishers. 1991.
13. Tokuda H., and Nakajima, T. Evaluation of Real-Time Synchronization in Real-Time Mach. *Proceedings of USENIX 2nd Mach Symposium*. 1991.
14. Kitayama, T., Nakajima T., and Tokuda, H. RT-IPC: An IPC Extension for Real-Time Mach. *Proceedings of Workshop on Microkernel and Other Kernel Architectures*. September 1993.
15. Nakajima,T., Kitayama T., and Tokuda, H. Experiments with Real-Time Servers in Real-Time Mach. *Proc. of 3rd USENIX Mach Symposium*. April 1993.
16. Hoffert, E. et al. QuickTime: An Extensible Standard for Digital Multimedia. Digest of Papers. COMPCON Spring 1992. February 1992. pp. 15–20.
17. Mercer, C. W., Savage, S., and Tokuda, H. Processor Capacity Reserves: An Abstraction for Managing Processor Usage. *Proceedings of the Fourth Workshop on Workstation Operating Systems (WWOS-IV)*. October 1993.

CHAPTER 9

MIDDLEWARE SYSTEM SERVICES ARCHITECTURE[1]

This chapter presents an overview of the Multimedia System Services architecture proposed jointly by Hewlett-Packard (H-P), International Business Machines (IBM), and SunSoft [1]. The *Multimedia System Services* specification defines a standard set of services that can be used by multimedia application developers in a variety of computing environments. It was presented as a response to the Multimedia System Services Request for Technology [2], issued by the Interactive Multimedia Association.

Enabling multimedia applications in a heterogeneous, distributed computing environment has been chosen as the design center for the Multimedia System Services. This is an increasingly prevalent computing model, and a solution that meets the needs of this environment can more easily be scaled to stand-alone systems than vice versa.

1 This chapter is based on selected material from the document *Multimedia System Services Version 1.0*, June 1993, developed jointly by Hewlett-Packard Company, International Business Machines Corp., and SunSoft Inc. © Copyright 1993 by the Interactive Multimedia Association. Used by permission. For the complete specification of the Multimedia System Services, contact the Interactive Multimedia Association.

The complete *Multimedia System Services* document is organized in three major sections. The first section provides some motivation and introduction of concepts key to the Multimedia System Services. The second section provides an abstract definition of the Multimedia System Services interfaces, written in the Object Management Group's Interface Definition Language (IDL) [3]. The third section states the Multimedia System Services conformance with the RFT. This chapter is based on selected material from Section 1 of the document. In particular, sections on virtual devices, media format management, event handling, and detailed API and programming examples demonstrating the concepts have been omitted from the following excerpts.

9.1 GOALS OF MULTIMEDIA SYSTEM SERVICES

The primary goal of the Multimedia System Services is to provide an infrastructure for building multimedia computing platforms that support *interactive* multimedia applications dealing with *synchronized, time-based* media in a *heterogeneous distributed* environment. One can truthfully say that there are several products today that provide multimedia services that support *interactive* applications which deal with *synchronized, time-based* media. Most existing systems, however, operate only in a stand-alone environment. Thus, the major distinction of the Multimedia System Services described in this document is the ability to support such applications in a *heterogeneous, distributed* environment.

The Multimedia System Services is intended to address a broad range of application needs. It extends the multimedia capabilities of today's stand-alone computers to capabilities that are usable both locally and remotely. The Multimedia System Services gives applications the ability to:

- handle live data remotely
- handle stored data remotely
- handle both live and stored data simultaneously
- handle multiple kinds of data simultaneously
- handle new kinds of devices and media types

To provide support for remote media device control and remote media access that derive from the above application scenarios, the Multimedia System Services uses two distinct mechanisms. To support interaction with remote objects, the Multimedia System Services depends upon the Object Management Group's (OMG) Common Object Request Broker Architecture (CORBA) [3]. To support the media-independent streaming of time-critical data, the Multimedia System Services defines a *Media Stream Protocol* presented later in this chapter.

9.1.1 Summary of Multimedia System Services Functions

The Multimedia System Services is designed to satisfy the requirements put forth in the IMA Multimedia System Services Request for Technology and is broadly constrained by that document. As such, the Multimedia System Services constitutes a framework of "middleware"—system software components lying in the region between the generic operating system and specific applications. As middleware, the Multimedia System Services marshals lower-level system resources to the task of supporting multimedia processing, providing a set of common services which can be used by multimedia application developers on an industry-wide basis.

The Multimedia System Services encompasses the following characteristics:

- ☐ provision of an abstract interface for a media processing node, extensible through subclassing to support abstractions of real media processing hardware or software;
- ☐ provision of an abstract interface for the data flow path or the connection between media processing nodes, encapsulating low-level connection and transport semantics;
- ☐ grouping of multiple processing nodes and connections into a single unit for purposes of resource reservation and stream control;
- ☐ provision of a media data flow abstraction, with support for a variety of position, time, and/or synchronization capabilities;
- ☐ separation of the media *format* abstractions from the data flow abstraction;
- ☐ synchronous *exceptions* and asynchronous events;
- ☐ application visible characterization of object *capabilities*;
- ☐ registration of objects in a distributed environment by location and capabilities;
- ☐ retrieval of objects in a distributed environment by location and *constraints*;
- ☐ definition of a *Media Stream Protocol* to support media-independent transport and synchronization;
- ☐ use of industry standard CORBA technology as the basis for supporting distributed objects;
- ☐ provision of a local library to simplify the task of writing Multimedia System Services–based applications.

The next section of this chapter provides initial descriptions of the Multimedia System Services characteristics and shows how they cooperate to meet the goals outlined above.

9.2 SOME VIEWS OF THE MULTIMEDIA SYSTEM SERVICES ARCHITECTURE

The next few pages present several comprehensive views of the Multimedia System Services, which, taken together, represent a broad, architectural summary. These views include:

- an object interaction diagram, to characterize the dynamic relationships among instantiated objects and to illustrate client-visible interfaces;
- an interface inheritance diagram, to describe the inheritance hierarchy among IDL interfaces; and
- a discussion of a typical case.

Some of the more interesting features of the architecture will then be examined in further detail in subsequent sections.

9.2.1 Object Framework

Figure 9.1 summarizes the interactions between Multimedia System Services *framework objects* and the *client*; Figure 9.2 summarizes the interaction among framework objects. As seen in Figure 9.1, only a subset of the objects and interfaces are actually visible to a Multimedia System Services client. In particular, much of the interaction between the virtual connection and other objects in the framework is not client visible. This specification is concerned primarily with client-visible interfaces.

Figure 9.1 is suggestive, rather than realistic: The objects shown are *instances* of *abstract classes*, rather than concrete classes which would normally be instantiated. Also, object creation and destruction are not shown in this diagram.

In Figure 9.1, the client is communicating with a small data flow *graph*, comprised of two *virtual devices* and a *virtual connection*. A *group* object, which assists the client, is also shown. The client interacts with the objects indicated by the arrows. Each of these interfaces may be local or remote.

Each virtual device is a processing node in the data flow graph. The nature of the processing (capture, encoding, filtering, etc.) varies according to the specific object (and is implemented by *subclassing*). Associated with each virtual device is a *stream* object and one or more *format* objects shown by the boxes in the shaded areas. Virtual connections and groups also have an associated stream object and this association is represented similarly. These associations are referred to as *inclusion*. Although explicitly shown in the diagram, the client interacts directly with the included stream and format interfaces.

A stream object provides the client with an interface to observe media stream position in various terms (as a function of media transport, media

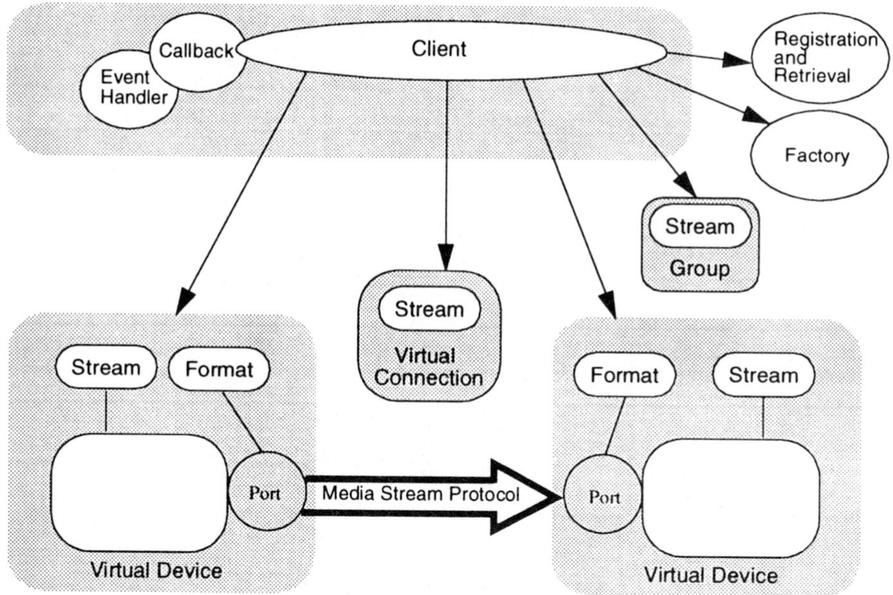

Figure 9.1 Multimedia system services client interaction

samples, or logical time). Some stream objects also provide an interface for controlling the flow of media data in a media stream and some stream objects provide synchronization interfaces.

In addition to a stream, a virtual device also contains one or more *ports*, describing an input or output mechanism for the virtual device. Ports are framework objects that do not have a client-visible interface; in the diagram, they are shaded to indicate this. Virtual devices do provide an interface to select a specific port, using an index as opaque handle.

Just as the stream object allows a media stream control abstraction, which is separable from media processing, the format object provides an abstraction of the details of media formatting, which is separate from both processing and flow control. For example, the details of a frame-dependent video encoding like MPEG, would be represented by a *subclass* of format.

The virtual connection provides an interface to create a connection between an output port of one virtual device and an input port of another, fully encapsulating low-level transport semantics. Virtual connections also provide support for multicast connections. An included stream object provides an interface for controlling the data flow on the virtual connection.

The group object, shown in Figure 9.1, provides assistance to the client to manage the data flow graph of the two virtual devices and the virtual connection. A group object provides a convenient mechanism for atomic resource allocation and specification of end-to-end *Quality of Service* (QOS) values for the whole graph. The group interface includes a stream object, through which the client can control data flow for the encapsulated graph.

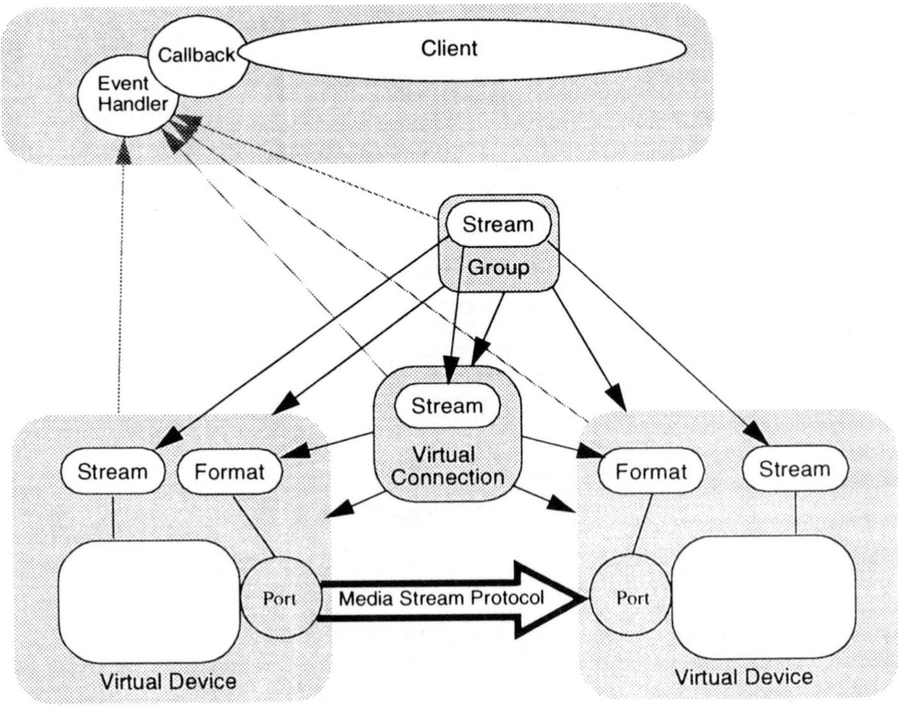

Figure 9.2 Multimedia system services internal interfaces

Multimedia System Services objects are instantiated by *factories*. A factory provides the client an interface to select among the various objects that the factory is capable of creating. A client can also use the *Registration & Retrieval Service* to find a reference to a factory capable of instantiating an object whose *capabilities* satisfy a list of *constraints*.

A client can register interest in receiving specific events produced by the various objects. The client can specify *callback* functions to handle these events received by an *event handler*.

Figure 9.2 shows the internal interfaces between Multimedia System Services objects. For the most part, the client is unaware that these interfaces exist, and this document will not focus on such interfaces. They are shown here to help explain the Multimedia System Services architecture. The primary purpose of most of the internal interfaces is to off-load work from the client. Note, for example, that the virtual connection interacts with the formats of both the source and target virtual devices. This allows the virtual connection to match those formats without client intervention. The group and the stream associated with the group provide similar assistance to the client; the group can assist in resource allocation, while the associated stream can assist in stream control. The shaded arrows show that the objects send events to the client via the event handler.

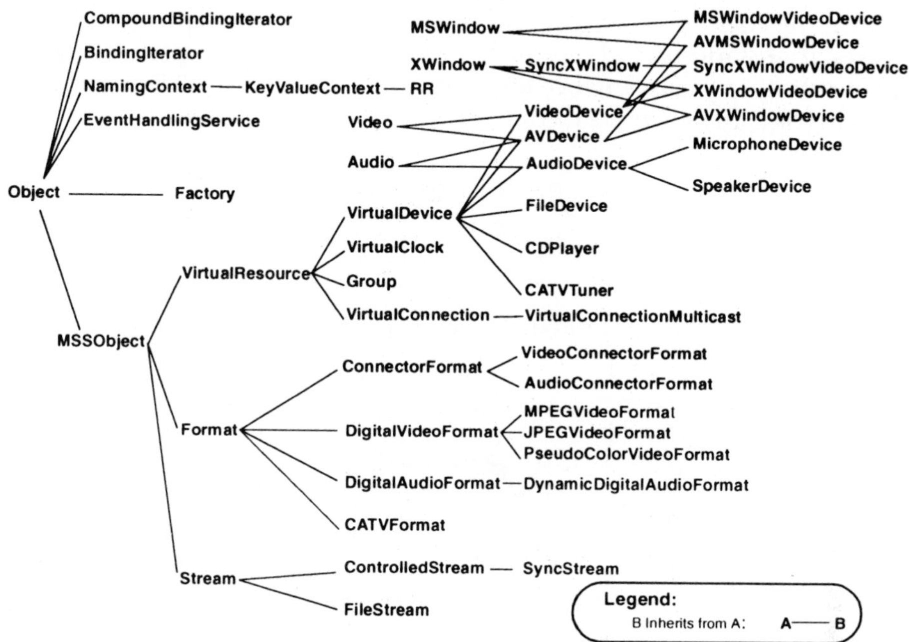

Figure 9.3 Interface inheritance diagram

9.2.2 Interface Inheritance

Another view of the Multimedia System Services architecture is given in Figure 9.3. This is an inheritance diagram for the IDL interfaces in the Multimedia System Services. It can be read like a class diagram, but specifies only interface inheritance; a specific implementation may mimic this diagram with a parallel class hierarchy, or it may use no inheritance at all.

9.2.3 A Typical Case

Here, the actions of a client using the Multimedia System Services to perform a simple distributed multimedia action—capturing audio with a microphone on one system and playing through a speaker on another system—are traced, in simplified form.

First, the client declares and initializes the Multimedia System Services client-side library.

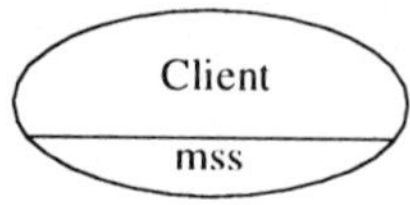

Now, the client builds a location-based constraint for a microphone and creates an instance of `MicrophoneDevice` on the correct system, using the client-side library convenience function `mss::new_object()`.This transparently invokes the `RR` and `Factory`.

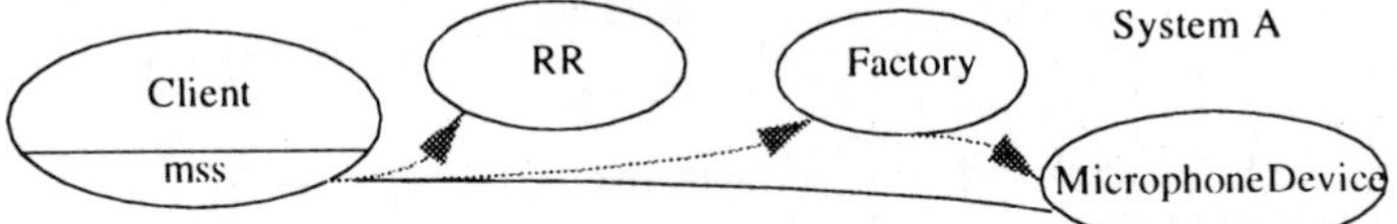

The client follows a similar process to create a `SpeakerDevice` on a different system.

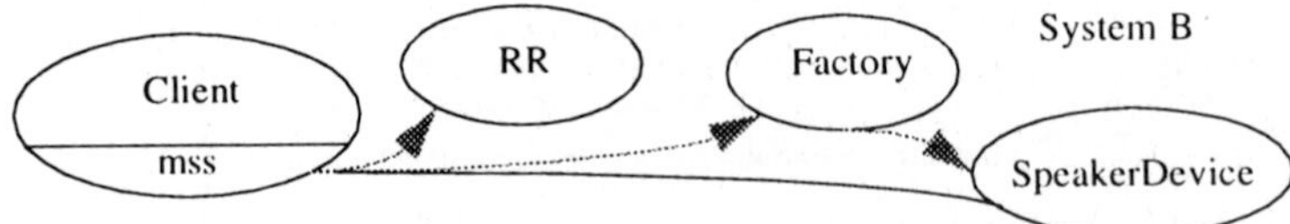

The client creates a `VirtualConnection` capable of connecting the two `VirtualDevice`s on the two separate machines.

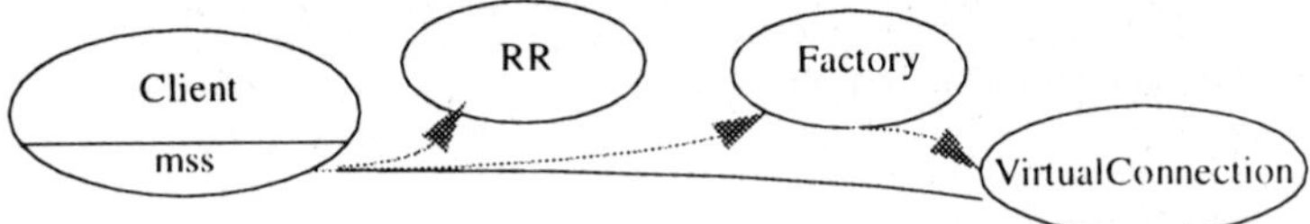

The client connects the two devices by sending a `VirtualConnection::connect()` request.

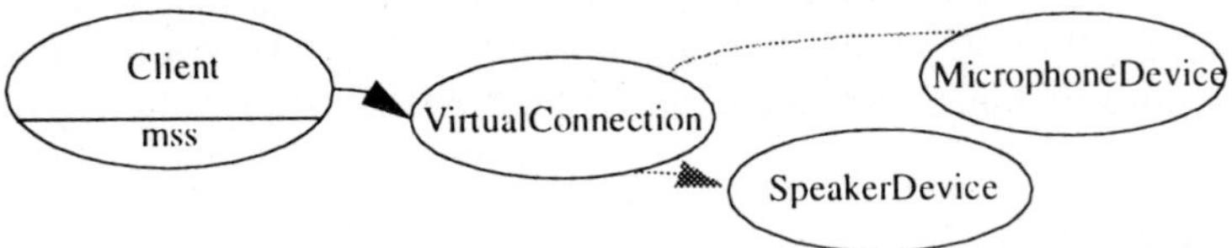

The client creates a `Group`, then adds all `VirtualResources` in the graph to the `Group` by sending the `Group::add_resource_graph()` request.

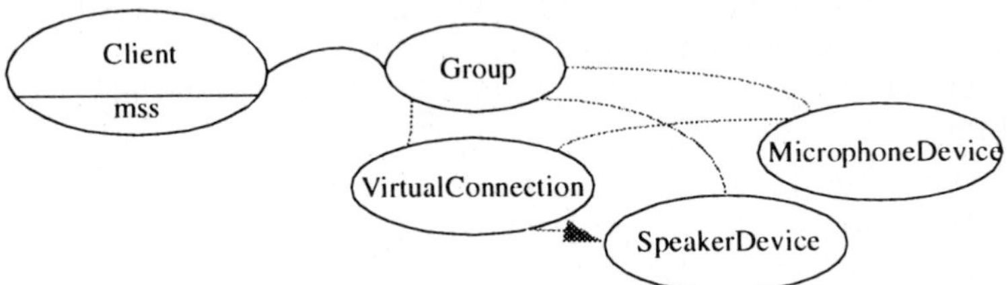

The client causes the `Group` to acquire resources by sending a `VirtualResource::acquire_resource()` request to obtain, for example, a reliable connection.

The client gets the `Stream` object for the `Group` by issuing a `VirtualResource::get_stream()` and then starts the stream.

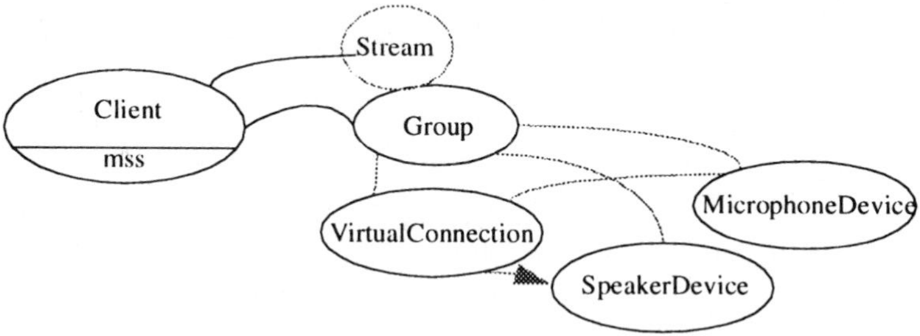

9.3 A CLOSER LOOK AT THE CLASSES AND OBJECTS

9.3.1 Multimedia System Services Object Concepts

Multimedia System Services objects have a set of characteristics that refine the definition of their behavior beyond that defined by the methods on their interfaces. Some characteristics are common to many Multimedia System Services objects, and others are particular to the interface class to which the object belongs. Examples of such characteristics are the location of an object (common to all Multimedia System Services objects) or the sample rate of digital audio (specific to the `DigitalAudioFormat` interface).

A *capability* of an object describes the *value* or *values* a characteristic may take on. Capabilities are specified as key/value pairs, where the key identifies the characteristic of interest, and the value is a discriminated union that can represent a variety of data types.

The client typically desires to obtain an object that satisfies certain requirements. For example, a client might be interested in an `AudioDevice` with specific capabilities, such as one that can process both "alaw" and "ulaw" encoded data at its input; it expresses this requirement by placing a constraint on the values that the `InputEncodingK` characteristic can take.

A *constraint* is a key/value/operator triple. The key is used to identify the characteristic of interest, and the value/operator pair is used to constrain that characteristic to a particular value or values. Operators include such things as `equal`, `greater_than`, `includes`, `prefix`, and so forth.

Events

An *event* is a message between objects in which the sender, not the recipient, defines the nature of the message. For other messages the recipient specifies the messages it is capable of receiving, but for events the sender specifies the events it is capable of sending. Clients interested in receiving events must register their interest in advance, so that the object generating the event knows whom to notify.

A simple event-handling scenario is depicted in Figure 9.4.

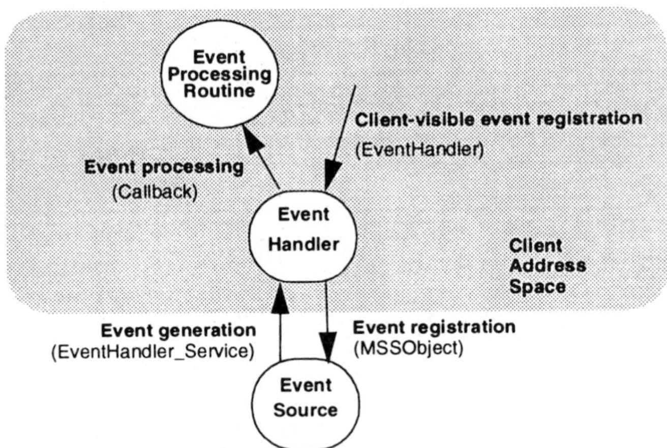

Figure 9.4 Event handling

9.3.2 Virtual Resource

A *virtual resource* is an abstraction of a physical resource that provides the client developer a consistent programming model, independent of the details of specific implementations. The notion of a virtual resource makes applications more portable across a variety of systems, while at the same time making the transparent sharing of physical resources possible.

The Multimedia System Services defines four basic kinds of virtual resources: virtual devices, which abstract media processors; virtual connections, which abstract connections between virtual devices; virtual clocks, which abstract time; and groups, which provide a convenient way to interact with a collection of virtual devices and connections.

Resource Acquisition and QOS

In order for a virtual resource to be useful, it must obtain the physical resources required for it to do its job. Resources include both system resources that are typically not multimedia specific, such as those provided by the CPU, memory, and network subsystems, as well as specialized multimedia resources such as audio and video devices.

Because the QOS that can be provided by many resources varies considerably, the client must also specify the desired QOS when requesting a resource.

Though QOS can take on many meanings, many of them media and device specific, the Multimedia System Services defines a core set of QOS attributes that can be used by a client to specify the QOS of interest. The core QOS characteristics defined by the Multimedia System Services are:

- ☐ guaranteed level: provides options for "Guaranteed" service, "Best Effort" service, or "No Guarantee" service

- reliable: the delivery of data is reliable or not
- delay bounds: the minimum and maximum delay
- jitter bounds: the minimum and maximum jitter (delay variance)
- bandwidth bounds: the minimum and maximum bandwidth

The client specifies the desired QOS when it requests that a virtual resource acquire its underlying physical resource(s). The QOS is specified as a key/value list. There is a unique key defined for each of the QOS variables defined above. This permits the client to specify only those QOS variables in which it's interested; any variables not specified are treated as "don't cares" by the virtual resource. This approach also allows new device or media-specific QOS variables to be introduced simply by defining new keys.

With the exception of having to explicitly acquire and release resources and potentially being notified of preemption, a virtual resource provides the client with the illusion that it is the only user of a physical resource.

Resource Management

Resource Manager When a virtual resource is requested to acquire resources corresponding to a particular QOS, one or more *resource managers*, which are responsible for managing the access to physical resources necessary to realize the virtual resource, get involved in the resource allocation process. Depending on the Multimedia System Services implementation, there may be one resource manager per managed resource, or there may be one resource manager per group of resources or per system.

When the `VirtualResource::acquire_resource()` method is executed, the `VirtualResource` object communicates with the appropriate resource manager(s) to request allocation to resources. The resource manager(s), which are contacted by the virtual resource, are dependent on the class of virtual resource and the Multimedia System Services implementation; typically virtual resources are created with the information necessary to contact the appropriate resource manager(s) at resource allocation time.

Some resource managers may have a generic interface for specifying resources, essentially providing a direct reflection of the `acquire_resource()` method. Other resource managers may provide a more specific interface appropriate to the resource being managed; virtual resources requesting the use of such resources would by their nature understand the necessary vocabulary for making resource requests.

The resource manager(s) may allow multiple virtual resources to share a given physical resource, so long as the desired QOS can be met. When a resource manager detects that it cannot satisfy the QOS requirements of its virtual resource clients, usually in response to a new request to share a physical resource, it may have to preempt a running virtual resource. When this happens, an event is sent to the virtual resource notifying it that it has lost access to the physical resource; the virtual resource, in turn, generates a `ResourceLostK` event, notifying the client that it has been pre-empted. At a later time, if the resource manager detects that it can meet the needs of a preempted virtual resource, it may send an event to the virtual resource notifying it that it has gained access to the physical resource; the virtual resource, in turn, generates a `ResourceAcquiredK` event, notifying the client that it has regained use of its resources.

The resource manager uses the QOS specified by `acquire_resource()`, together with the requirements placed on the virtual resource's characteristics, to determine resource allocation. For example, the requirement placed on an AudioDevice's sample rate parameter may affect the choice of audio hardware to be used to realize the `AudioDevice`.

Figure 9.5 depicts a possible resource management configuration.

Resource Policy Agent As depicted in Figure 9.5, resource managers may work in conjunction with a *resource policy agent,* whose job is to permit the user to get involved with the resource allocation decisions, much in the same way as a window manager allows the user to make window size and placement decisions in a window system.

When a resource manager has had a resource policy agent registered with it, resource management requests are redirected to the resource policy agent. The resource policy agent may get the user involved in the process and then resubmits a potentially modified request on the client's behalf back to the resource manager. This mechanism is similar in style to that used in the X Windows System.

When no resource policy manager is present, the resource manager typically uses some default policy when making resource allocation deci-

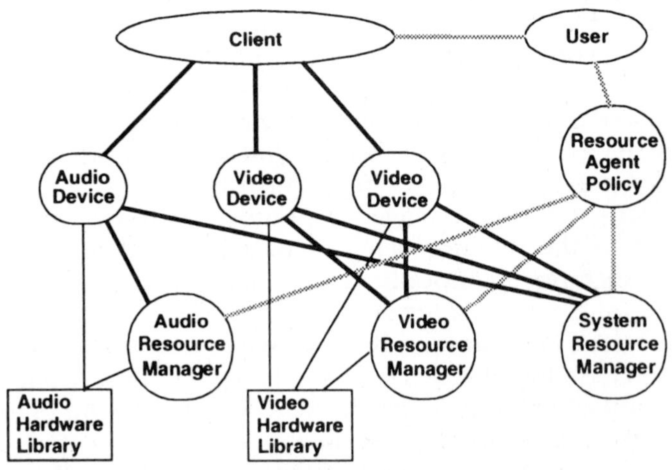

Figure 9.5 A possible resource management scenario

sions. Two examples of such a policy are "last requester wins" and "first requester wins."

Stream Control

Typically, virtual resources are involved in the generation, consumption, or transport of media data. The flow of media data through a device or across a connection can be thought of as a stream. In order to monitor or control the progress of the stream, the Multimedia System Services defines the `Stream` interface.

The `Stream` interface permits a client to determine the current position in the stream, to pause and resume the stream, and perform other functions related to the progress of a stream. The `Stream` interface provides a generic way to deal with stream control that is independent of the type of media data that comprise a stream.

9.3.3 Virtual Device

A `VirtualDevice` is a subclass of `VirtualResource` that abstracts media devices. These devices may be either hardware devices such as capture and display cards, or they may be software "devices" such as compressor/decompressors (CODECS). A virtual device may represent a resource internal to a system, such as an audio capture device, or it may represent a resource external to a system, such as a CATV tuner.

The virtual device abstraction is designed to provide a common way for clients to use a wide variety of physical devices in many kinds of operating environments. The construction of the Multimedia System Services `VirtualDevice` interface has been designed to address these considerations while providing an expressive, flexible framework into which a large spectrum of media devices may be cast. Figure 9.6 depicts the basic organization of virtual device components.

Connection Agreement

A virtual connection in Multimedia System Services constitutes an "agreement" on the following:

1. Media type to be transported between the two virtual device ports (including media master)
2. Type of connection
   - ☐ hardware
   - ☐ direct
   - ☐ local
   - ☐ network

   The virtual connection will determine the appropriate connection type.

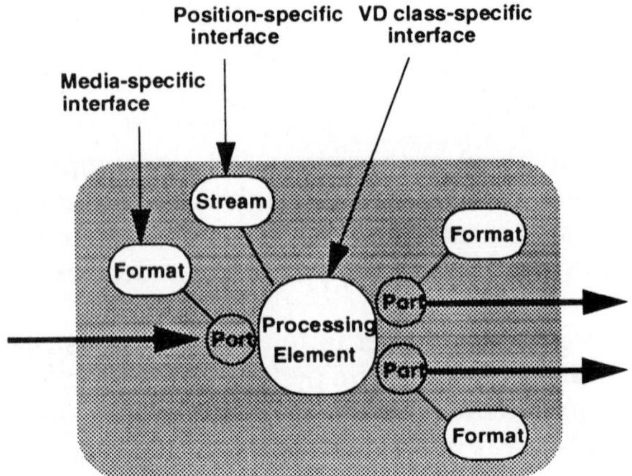

Figure 9.6 Virtual device construction

3. Quality of service
   - ☐ type (guaranteed, best effort, no guarantee)
   - ☐ reliability
   - ☐ delay max and min
   - ☐ bandwidth max and min
   - ☐ jitter max and min

   The connection will also constitute an agreement on the QOS. The QOS parameters are an integral part of the virtual connection and are a reflection of the expectations of the application.

4. Stream and synchronization capabilities
   - ☐ data exchange mechanism
   - ☐ time
   - ☐ synchronization mechanisms and policies

The virtual connection will determine if the virtual devices can agree on a common data exchange mechanism. The virtual connection will also determine the class of the stream object associated with each virtual device. Using this information, the virtual connection will, if necessary, instantiate the appropriate virtual connection adapters.

The Multimedia System Services provides two classes for virtual connections: *unicast* and *multicast*. This provides support for both unicast and multicast types of connections (Figure 9.7).

Virtual Connection Adapters

A *virtual connection adapter* is a framework internal object that the virtual connection will instantiate to transport the media between the two virtual

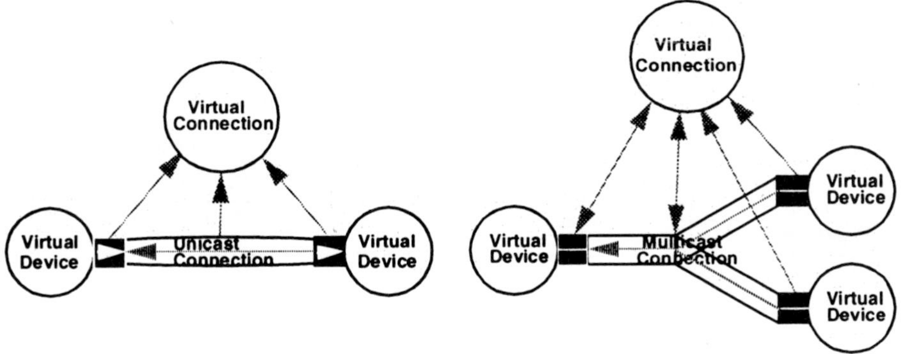

Figure 9.7 Construction of unicast and multicast connections

devices. This is required when the virtual devices are on separate systems or the virtual device ports are incompatible for direct media transfer. The virtual connection adapter is a private construct of the virtual connection and is not visible to the client.

For transport within a machine, it is up to the implementation to decide how data is moved.When the transport passes between machines, the Media Stream Protocol must be available. The virtual connection adapter is responsible for translating internal messaging formats to the Media Stream Protocol.

Figure 9.8 shows examples of how the virtual connections can be configured to support the types of connections. Note that the view to the application is the same in all cases. The client interfaces with the virtual connection and the virtual devices. Since both virtual connections and virtual devices are subclassed from `VirtualResource`, the interfaces are quite similar. A virtual connection contains a `ControlledStream` object for controlling the movement of the data.

The virtual connection is responsible for interfacing with the virtual connection adapter (including both parts when crossing system boundaries) and the virtual device as appropriate. When the client executes a `ControlledStream` method on the virtual connection (e.g., pause), this method will invoke the appropriate method on the `ControlledStream` object of the virtual connection adapter, virtual device(s), or all of them, to satisfy the client's request.

9.3.4 Group

It is often desirable to manipulate multiple resources as a group. When expressing QOS requirements, for example, the client often cares more about such things as end-to-end delay of a set of connected devices rather than the delay of individual elements. When controlling the movement of data through the set of connected devices, it is often more convenient to

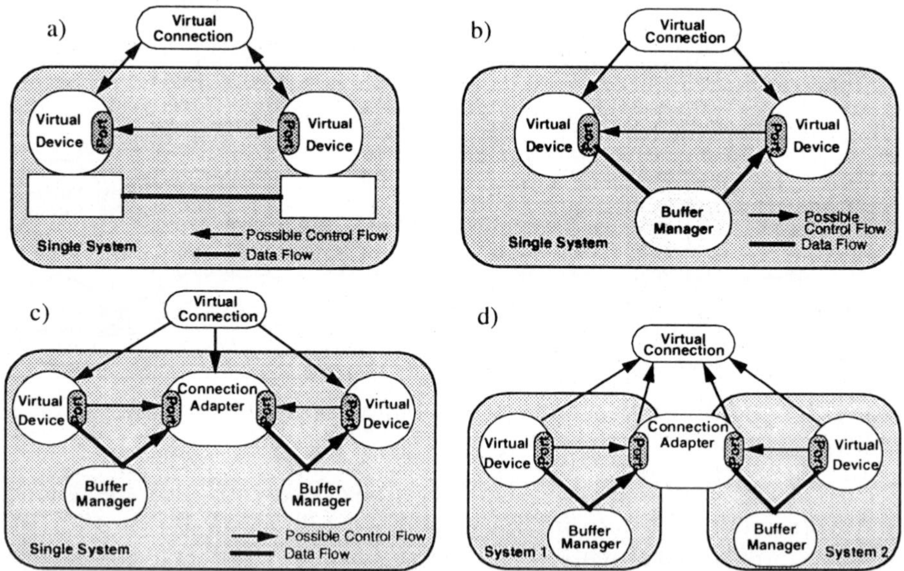

Figure 9.8 Example virtual connections: (a) hardware connection, (b) direct connection, (c) local virtual connection adapter, (d) network virtual connection adapter.

manipulate a single object, rather than having to manipulate the objects associated with each of the resources.

To address these and other problems, the Multimedia System Services provides a `Group` interface to allow grouping of `VirtualResource` objects. This supports the grouping of `VirtualDevice`s, `VirtualConnection`s, `VirtualClock`s, and `Group`s (i.e., hierarchical `Group`s are allowed).

The role of the `Group` interface is to perform the following operations:

- ☐ resource acquisition and end-to-end Quality of Service
- ☐ stream control

The current definition of the `Group` interface in the Multimedia System Services specification does not provide support for automatic synchronization of a group of `VirtualResources`. This functionality may be added to the `Group` interface in future revisions.

Resource Acquisition and End-to-End QOS

In a situation where the client has created and connected several virtual resources to perform a specific function, the resource acquisition and QOS specification procedures can be quite complex. While the ability to specify a (possibly different) QOS for each virtual device and each virtual connection is a very powerful feature, it also places a heavy burden on the client to understand the intricacies of each and to specify the QOS accordingly. In many situations, the client would like to specify only the end-to-end

QOS and have the system determine the necessary QOS at each node. The ability to group a set of virtual resources and specify a single QOS solves this problem for the client.

Once a set of virtual resources has been added to a group, the underlying physical resources required to realize the entire group can be obtained by calling the `VirtualResource::acquire_resource()` method of the `Group` interface. The specified QOS parameter is taken to be the desired QOS for the entire group. The group tracks the graph(s) that are contained within it, and the QOS parameter is taken to be the end-to-end specification for all graphs. The group does the work of allocating the QOS to individual objects to meet the overall QOS objective.

Other problems can occur when a client executes the `VirtualResource::acquire_resource()` method of each object independently. This can lead to resource deadlock or resource under-utilization. If the resources are acquired as a group, the system can help prevent these problems.

Stream Control

Since the `Group` interface is a subclass of the `VirtualResource`, it may have an associated `Stream` interface. The `Stream` interface provides the client progress information on the flow of data within the group. If the `Stream` object is a `ControlledStream` object, it gives the client a single point of control for manipulating the flow of data. This allows the client to call a single stream method, such as `ControlledStream::pause()` or `ControlledStream::resume()`, and have this command propagated to each of the stream objects of the members of the group.

The `Stream` objects of the constituent resources can be thought of as children of the (parent) group `Stream` object. Methods invoked on the group object are forwarded as appropriate to its children: Calling `ControlledStream::pause()` on a `Group`'s `ControlledStream` object causes all of its children to be paused. Methods invoked on the child `Stream` objects are not forwarded to the parent object; however, the parent `Stream` object or other child `Stream` object's state might change as a side effect. For example, pausing a child's `ControlledStream` object would not pause parent or sibling `Stream` objects, but these objects might enter the stalled state as a result of flow control.

9.3.5 Streams

The `Stream` interface and its subclasses provide a single point of focus for all inquiry and control of media stream progress in a media type independent way. `Stream` objects are never created in isolation; they are included objects of `VirtualResource` objects whose role is to monitor and control stream progress for the overall resource and in some cases for `VirtualDevice` ports. Figure 9.9 depicts the `Stream` class hierarchy.

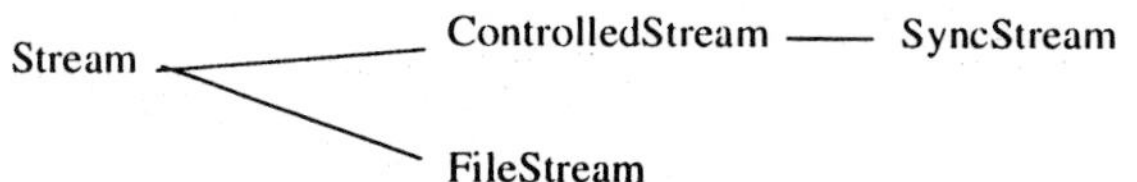

Figure 9.9 Stream class hierarchy

Stream Interface

The `Stream` interface provides methods to observe media position. A complication is that different objects require different concepts of position:

- transport aware object

  The object might understand transport packets, but not understand the structure of the media stream. The object can only report the stream address, that is, the byte count since the stream began to flow.

- stream aware object

  The object might understand media samples, but not how media samples translate into stream time. The object can report the stream sample count.

- time aware object

  The object understands how to extract stream time from the media stream. The object can report the stream time.

The `Position` data structure used throughout the Multimedia System Services specifies position in terms of an origin and a coordinate space. The `PositionType` element defines how to interpret the origin. The three values of `PositionType` are:

- absolute

  The origin is the beginning of the stream.

- relative

  The origin is the position at which the object receives the request. The client can invoke methods such as "pause 100 ms from now."

- modulo

  The origin is periodic. This convention is useful for events. The client can invoke methods such as "notify each time 100 ms transpire."

The coordinate space is specified by a key. A specific position is specified as a key/value or a list of key/values. The basic position keys are:

- stream byte count

  The position is the byte count from the origin.

- stream sample count

  The position is the sample count from the origin.

- ☐ stream media time

  The position is the stream time from the origin. The stream time is expressed in terms of seconds and nanoseconds.

The `Stream` interface allows the client to observe media position in terms of these keys. Depending on the type of object, the set of keys may vary.

The client can also ask to be asynchronously notified of stream position by asking for a position event. The client first registers for interest in position events and then specifies how it wants position events to be generated. The client specifies the position at which it wants the event to be generated; since this can be a modulo type, periodic events can be generated.

In addition, it may be useful to monitor stream progress by inserting markers into the data stream and waiting for events when they are detected. The client can register interest in marker detection events using the normal event registration method.

ControlledStream Interface

The `ControlledStream` interface supports stream control and time transforms. The interface provides five methods to control the advance of the stream (Table 9.1).

The `ControlledStream` interface provides methods to specify the transform between an object's *internal position* to its *external position*. An object's internal position is derived either as part of its basic function or through its input(s) (in the case of a `VirtualDevice` with input port[s]). An object's external position is that which is made available through the `Stream` interface and its outputs, if any.

Though the stream transform affects the interpretation of time by an object, it does not affect the sample rate or bandwidth being generated or

Table 9.1 Stream Object Methods for Stream Control

Stream Control Method	*Function*
`void pause(in Position a_position);`	object suspends execution
`void resume(in Position a_position);`	object resumes execution and stream position advances
`void prime(in Position a_position);`	preroll the object, filling internal buffers in anticipation of a resume
`void drain(in Position a_position);`	object drains its internal buffers
`void mute(in Position a_position);`	data flows into object but nothing flows out of object

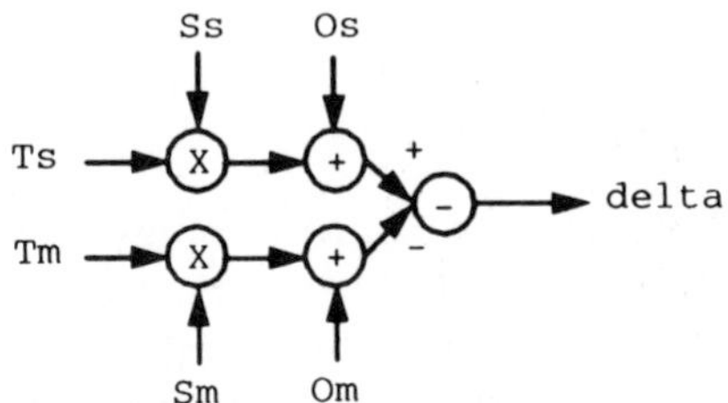

Figure 9.10 Stream alignment calculation

consumed. For example, a stream scale factor of 0.5 would direct a file virtual device to produce one second of output for every two seconds of input, that is, play forward at one-half speed. The sample rate produced at the file device's output is not changed. Position arguments and return values on methods related to the file device (e.g., on its `Stream` or `FileDevice` interfaces) would be in terms of the output time coordinate system.

SyncStream Interface

The `SyncStream` interface is designed to permit the synchronization of multiple media streams. The client specifies a second `Stream` object to provide a master position reference to the `SyncStream` object. The `SyncStream` object will attempt to synchronize its stream to that of its master. The `SyncStream` object may either poll the `Stream` object to determine its position or it may register interest in position events from the `Stream` object. The rate of position updates is determined by the synchronization precision set by the client (see below). It also can report information about the position relationship of the two streams.

The client describes both the stream time transform and master time transform. The master time transform specifies how the `SyncStream` object should transform the position coordinate space of its master before using those position values. The `SyncStream` object applies the transforms to calculate the alignment between its media stream and the master stream, as depicted in Figure 9.10.

Ts and Tm represent the `SyncStream` position and the master position, respectively. Ss and Sm are the stream and master transform scale factors, and Os and Om are the stream and master transform offsets.

Synchronization Reporting

The client can also create *synchronization event points* in terms of the alignment. This allows the client to register interest in events that are generated when the alignment between streams crosses these synchronization event points. This can be used by the client to detect synchronization exceptions.

The `SyncStream` interface provides the client with a variety of options with respect to setting up how synchronization is to be achieved. For example, a video display device can be synchronized with an audio display device by setting up the appropriate relationship between their associated `Stream` objects. Assuming the video device supports a `SyncStream` interface, the audio device's `Stream` object can be made the master of the video device's `Stream` object.

In another situation, the client may want to synchronize two displays to a common time reference. In this case, both displays would have to support the `SyncStream` interface. The client would make the `Stream` object associated with the time reference the master of the `Stream` objects associated with both the display objects.

9.4 MEDIA STREAM PROTOCOL

When a virtual connection determines that two virtual devices cannot be directly connected (often because they are on different machines), it creates a virtual connection adapter to transport media data between them. The virtual devices may reside in different implementations of the Multimedia System Services, so the virtual connection adapter must share a common protocol in order to interoperate.

The Multimedia System Services envisions one such protocol, the Multimedia System Services Media Stream Protocol (MSP), which runs over a number of network transports including NetBIOS, SPX/IPX, TCP(UDP)/IP, and RTP/ST-II. An interoperable implementation of the Multimedia System Services should provide a virtual connection adapter that implements the MSP over at least one network transport. Implementations are free to provide both additional transports for the MSP and complete alternatives to the MSP.

The purpose of the MSP is to convey media data along with the necessary information to do regulation, synchronization, and time-critical delivery of that data. To this end, the MSP defines a "media packet" that consists of media data and a media packet header (note that the media packet may be transmitted as any number of network packets).

The virtual connection determines the format of the media data, including its bit-level representation, by negotiation with the relevant `Format` objects and perhaps with client intervention. The MSP treats the media data as an opaque entity whose only visible attribute is its size. Neither the virtual connection adapter nor the underlying network transports know how to extract information from the media data; any information that is needed for data transport and regulation must be conveyed by the media packet header.

The MSP can convey the following information along with the opaque media data:

timestamp (monotonically increasing value from the start of the stream),

duration (for aperiodic media),

priority (importance of this media packet relative to others in the same stream),

dependency information. This allows virtual devices, virtual connections, or other nonframework objects to determine the structure of a stream, without knowledge of the media in the stream. An example use of this would be MPEG where the codes can be "I," "P," and "B." Given the dependency information one can decide that if for some reason (e.g., failures or lack of processing time) a "P" sample frame cannot be delivered, then the "B" frames are not useful and should not be delivered,

in-stream events, which can include markers and errors related to the media data,

sequence number,

checksum (for transports that require it),

length checksummed (for transports that require it),

length of the media (for transports that require it).

The checksum length is given as a separate field to allow checksumming of all the data, just the header, or no checksumming.

9.5 EXAMPLE: AUDIO AND VIDEO CAPTURE WITH SYNCHRONIZED PLAY

This example shows remote audio and video capture with synchronized local play as might be used for half of a LAN-based video conferencing system. Figure 9.11 shows the client-visible objects and data flows required for the example; to reduce complexity, the figure shows *only* the control paths of interest to the client. The figure also *does not* show the framework-visible objects and control paths. As shown in the figure, the client program is assumed to be on the same machine as the audio and video rendering devices, a speaker and a window.

The client-visible objects are:

- ☐ a `MicrophoneDevice`, which abstracts audio capture hardware with a microphone attached
- ☐ a `CameraDevice`, which abstracts video capture hardware with a camera attached

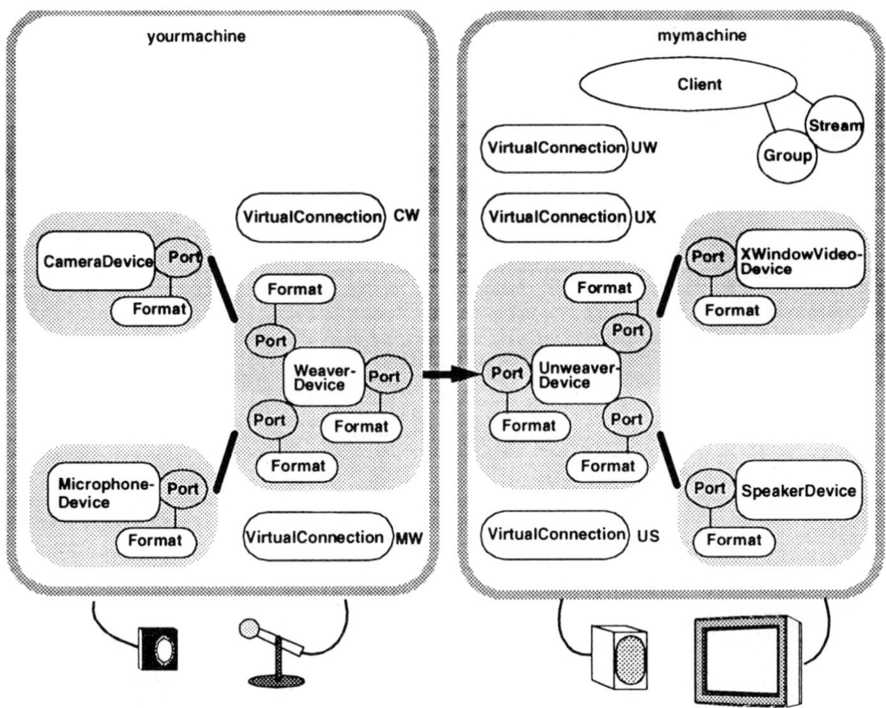

Figure 9.11 Audio/video remote capture example

- a `WeaverDevice`, which abstracts a device that "weaves" the audio and video streams into a single audio/video stream
- an `UnweaverDevice`, which "unweaves" the audio/video stream into an audio stream and a video stream
- a `SpeakerDevice`, which abstracts an audio render hardware with a speaker attached
- an `XWindowVideoDevice`, which abstracts the video display mechanism
- several `VirtualConnections`, which abstract the physical connections between the virtual devices
- a `Group`, which abstracts the device/connection graph as a single resource unit
- a `Stream`, associated with the `Group`, which abstracts the device/connection graph as a single control unit.

The detailed steps of how these objects are created and connected are given in [1].

9.6 ACKNOWLEDGMENTS

The following individuals, listed alphabetically by company, were the primary technical developers of Multimedia System Services Version 1.0:

Marty Picco (Cogent Technology)

Glenn Stewart (Hewlett-Packard)

Wayne Blackard (IBM Corp.)

Greg Flurry (IBM Corp.)

William K. Pratt (SunSoft,Inc.)

Jim Van Loo (Sun Soft, Inc.)

The complete version of the Multimedia Systems Services Version 1.0 document can be obtained electronically via ftp from node ibminet.awdpa.ibm.com (192.35.233.1) or by contacting the Interactive Multimedia Association.

9.7 REFERENCES

1. Interactive Multimedia Association. Multimedia System Services Version 1.0. (Hewlett-Packard, IBM, SunSoft). June 1993.
2. *Request for Technology: Multimedia System Services Version 2.0.* Interactive Multimedia Association Compatibility Project.
3. *Common Object Request Broker: Architecture and Specification.* Object Management Group document 91-12-1. 1991.

CHAPTER 10

MULTIMEDIA DEVICES, PRESENTATION SERVICES, AND THE USER INTERFACE

John F. Koegel Buford
University of Massachusetts Lowell

Multimedia applications differ from conventional applications in the use of new media types, complex temporal composition, object hyperlinking and annotation, and external multimedia devices. The challenge for developers of services and toolkits for multimedia user interfaces is to provide an extensible and efficient architecture as well as the appropriate programming abstractions. Concurrently, the application framework is evolving to include distributed object access, scripting languages, and multimedia interchange services. Integration with these additional facilities will require careful planning by application services designers. The state of knowledge regarding the use of multimedia in the user interface will grow dramatically as the technologies for constructing such interfaces become more pervasive.

10.1 INTRODUCTION

In a famous story of the ancient philosopher Plato, an imaginary lifelong cave dweller is brought out into the daylight for the first time, transforming the individual's preconceived notions of the nature of the world. Although perhaps not nearly as dramatic an impact, interactive multimedia interfaces do offer new dimensions of communication and interaction to computer applications. These benefits result from the natural richness of auditory and visual information to human perception.

Today, a number of toolkits exist for constructing user interfaces composed of buttons, text entry, scrollable areas, and other conventional interactors. As the technology for adding multimedia data types to applications progresses, the following presentation-related services will be needed by application developers [1]:

- Control of image presentation and continuous media streams such as digital audio and video
- Temporal composition and synchronization so that parallel and serial timing relations between different presentation steps can be easily expressed
- High-level control of multimedia peripherals and continuous media to hide device dependencies and low-level synchronization issues from the application
- Hyperlinking between two or more content objects to facilitate hypertext and hypermedia applications
- Support for new input technologies such as pen input and voice recognition
- Multimedia content interchange so that applications can exchange and share complex compositions in a heterogeneous environment
- Standardized multimedia-related interactors, such as a VCR-style panel, so that universal interaction paradigms will have a consistent look and feel

In the remainder of the chapter we discuss architecture and toolkit support for multimedia presentation services. Section 2 discusses the integration of multimedia services and the window system. Section 3 presents the integration issue from the client application perspective. Section 4 discusses device control, followed by a section on temporal coordination (Section 5). Section 6 reviews research and commercial toolkits for multimedia development. Section 7 discusses hyperapplication support. The final section summarizes the chapter.

10.2 MULTIMEDIA SERVICES AND THE WINDOW SYSTEM

Today's graphical user interfaces are built on an underlying window system. These systems were designed to provide a hardware-independent programming model for two-dimensional graphics. In the case of the X Window System [2,3] and NeWS [4], network transparency for GUI-based application programs has also been achieved. An application developer typically uses a

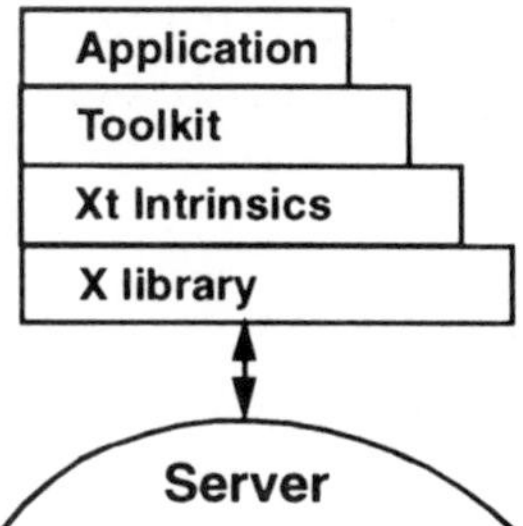

Figure 10.1 The X Windows System software architecture

software toolkit to create user interfaces that conform to a specific style or look and feel. Toolkits provide facilities common to many applications, simplifying the task of creating the interface, and offering a higher level of abstraction when compared with the 2-D graphics and window level. The components of the X Window System are shown in Figure 10.1. In the remainder of this section we use X as a vehicle for discussing the integration of multimedia services with a networked window system.

X uses the client/server model in which the application is the client and the local graphics device is managed by an X server, and defines a specific protocol by which clients and servers communicate. This protocol, mediated by the X library on the client side, was designed for networks in which the round-trip time between client and server is between 5 and 50 ms. Given this round-trip time, the X protocol was designed for asynchronous communication between client and server. One consequence of this is that an X client has no direct control on the timing of various requests that it issues to the server, an issue for future X servers which might provide playback and synchronization of continuous media streams. Another design philosophy of X is economy of functionality, and this is reflected in the avoidance of putting too much functionality in the server, for example, programmability.

10.2.1 Single Server versus Co-Servers

The integration of multimedia services with X requires that issues such as synchronization and server functionality be addressed. Different approaches to the architecture are possible, as shown in Figure 10.2. One way is to extend the X server so that it directly incorporates the multimedia functionality (Figure 10.2a). The X protocol would also be extended for the new functions, following standard guidelines for such extensions. This approach has been used for several video window extensions to X as well as the ACME continuous media server developed by Anderson et al. [5].

A second way is to provide a co-server that encompasses the multimedia functionality (Figure 10.2b). The co-server and its protocol can be designed

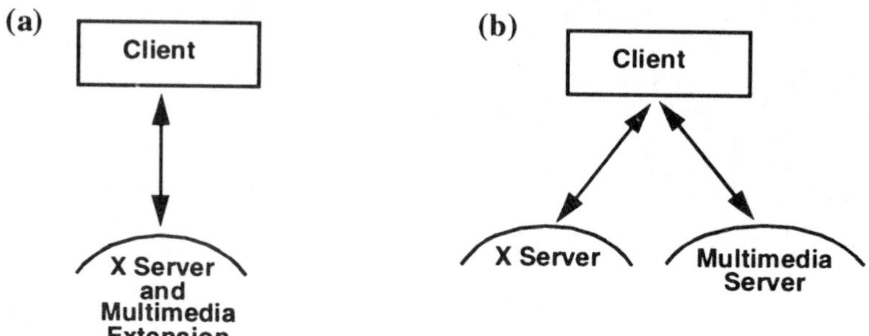

Figure 10.2 Two alternatives for extending the X Windows System to support multimedia: (a) extension of the X server, (b) a co-server specifically for multimedia.

specifically for multimedia presentation without impacting the X server or its protocol. Some resources must be coordinated between the two servers if this approach is to be effective. Access to the window hierarchy, colormaps, and certain event types is needed by the co-server in order for video to be presented properly in overlapping windows. MuX developed by SRI [6] is an example of a co-server architecture. Several digital audio interfaces have also been implemented as separate servers [7,8]. A variation of the co-server approach is to provide specific servers for each media type—an audio server, a video server, etc.

10.2.2 Multimedia Server and Window Server Coupling

The required coupling between the window server and the multimedia server is most stringent for video, involving window layering, colormaps, and the event stream. The video frame must be clipped in order to accommodate overlapping windows. For hardware-supported video, this can be done either by chroma keying or by having the hardware dynamically compute the clipping mask. In chroma keying, the window on which the video is drawn is assigned a unique color palette entry; this color is used to determine which part of the video signal is mixed into the graphics display. If the video hardware instead performs clipping, then the relevant window geometries must be available to the hardware on a dynamic basis. The window geometry information is directly managed by the window server, and any changes to the window hierarchy are computed by it.

For video which is written directly to the graphics frame buffer, window colormap management is necessary in order for the video to have the proper appearance. Color graphics frame buffers without true color 24-bit capability use color lookup tables (CLUTs) in which a fixed range of pixels can be mapped to a given color gamut. Depending on the size of the CLUT (the most common 8-bit color systems have 256 entries), it may be necessary for the colormap entries for each video window to be computed dynamically.

In this way, scene changes which require new color assignments can be supported. The X-Movie system developed by the University of Mannheim [9], for example, manages the colormap dynamically during playback of movie files. This system uses a gradual transition between different colormaps of successive video segments, eliminating unpleasant visual flashes that would otherwise occur when the colormap is modified in one step. X-Movie is a co-server architecture, communicating to the X server using a specially designed protocol. However, X-Movie clients communicate directly only to the X server.

10.2.3 Synchronization and Scheduling

A multimedia client specifies the synchronization requirements for time-dependent presentation of various media. The scheduling to achieve these requirements can be performed on the client side or the server side. In a co-server architecture, each server must be synchronized so that simultaneous actions can be coordinated. The ability of the operating system and network to support real-time scheduling and delivery determines which of these alternatives is practical. In systems in which little real-time support is available, a single server architecture performing the scheduling is the most effective. If the operating system provides real-time scheduling, then either single server or co-server architecture can be used. If the network provides real-time protocols, then client-side scheduling can also be done effectively.

10.2.4 Summary

As a network-based window system, X is a suitable vehicle for considering the issues of integrating distributed multimedia applications with the graphical user interface. Protocol design, degree of coupling between window server and multimedia server, synchronization, and scheduling are some of the key architectural issues to be faced. The client-side programming model is also crucial and is discussed next.

10.3 CLIENT CONTROL OF CONTINUOUS MEDIA

Presentation of individual media objects is a basic service that is typically provided as an extension to an existing graphical user interface toolkit. For image, animation, and video media, the application needs to be able to specify a viewport by which the object is presented and which may permit interactive zooming and panning. For continuous media, stream parameters such as position, direction, and rate are usually available to the application. The stream or track view of continuous media can be controlled using a player abstraction in the API.

For example, the following segment, based on the Fluency digital video object API[1] [10], creates a combined audio and video stream and processes requests to play, stop, and start recording.

```
/* Create an audio-video stream */
hwnd = DvoCreateAudioVideo(stream_name, x, y, w, h, ...);

/* Handle client request */
switch(type) {
    case IDM_PLAY:
        DvoPlayForward(hwnd); break;
    case IDM_STOP:
        DvoStop(hwnd); break;
    case IDM_RECORD_START:
        DvoRecord(hwnd); break;
}
```

The player abstraction is a natural way to control video and audio media. Notice that the stream media is distinct from the player and can be considered an opaque type. This is consistent with the view of continuous media applications programming in which data and control are separate. This not only frees the application program from the details of buffering the stream data, but it is also more efficient since the overall movement of data is reduced. As discussed in Chapter 8, data copying of continuous media data transfers from one device to another is a significant performance problem for conventional operating systems. Unless the application needs to process the continuous media data, client mediation of the data stream is unwarranted.

10.3.1 Stream Processing

For many cases, processing of the stream data is either unnecessary or can be handled by generic hardware or system software. For example, video compression levels, frame size, and frame rate are common hardware CODEC parameters. In other cases, in the absence of server support for processing operations, client-side processing is necessary.

The X Imaging Extension (XIE) is an example of a server integrated processing system for image data [11]. Figure 10.3 shows a high-level view of XIE. The Photoflo Manager is the computational engine which manages the image processing pipeline. The client controls the Photoflo Manager by specifying a directed acyclic graph (DAG), which represents the operations to be performed on the image. These operations include traditional image processing functions such as scaling, image arithmetic, convolution, filters,

---

1 Fluent Machines, developer of the Fluency API, is now Novell Multimedia.

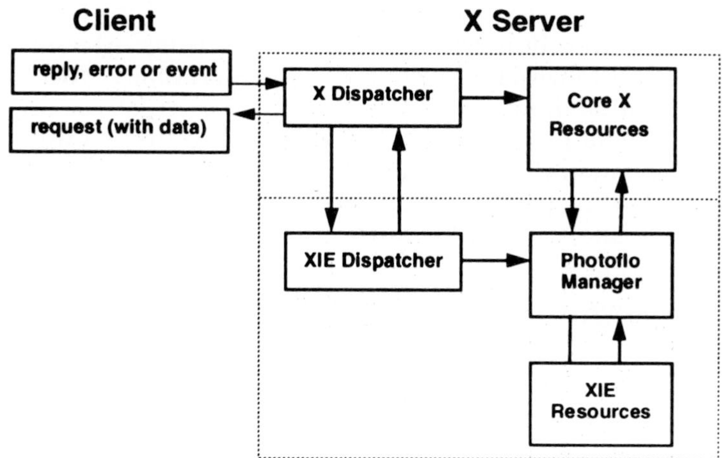

Figure 10.3 High-level view of X server with X Imaging Extension

and histograms. The client passes a compressed image stream to the server which carries out the operations specified in the Photoflo DAG. Since the client still handles the compressed image data in XIE, the benefits of separation of data and control are only partially achieved; however, only the server has to work with the uncompressed data, reducing client buffering requirements.

XIE is a server-based processing architecture for a specific media type. Such architectures for video and audio processing will likely result as research in these areas progresses [12,13].

10.3.2 Synchronization of Multiple Streams

In the Fluency API presented earlier, an audio stream and a video stream are treated as a unit for synchronization purposes. A more general approach is needed to allow arbitrary numbers of streams to be controlled in synchrony. For example, ACME allows an arbitrary collection of streams to be grouped for synchronization [5,14]. It implements such synchronization using a logical time system (LTS).

The ACME LTS is an independent clock with which various stream devices are associated. When the LTS is running, the clock value increases at the same rate as real time. Each stream is treated as a sequence of timestamped units. When the clock reaches time *t*, data units with timestamp *t* are processed by the associated devices.

An application creates an LTS and associates it with a device as follows:

```
LTS = create_LTS(mode, param);
bind(LTS, logical_device, start_time, max_skew, start_count);
```

The mode of the LTS is used to specify the reference for the LTS clock; it can be device-driven, connection-driven, or an external timer. The bind operation associates the LTS with the given device. The start time is the LTS time when device operation begins. The LTS will stop if a device falls behind by `max_skew` due to starvation. The start count is used to prime output devices so that a given amount of jitter can be tolerated.

Once the LTS is created and bound to the devices, the application controls progress using `start()` and `stop()` functions.

10.4 DEVICE CONTROL

Although the multimedia revolution is digital, the existing analog equipment base is still important for many applications. There are a large number of devices available today, which, under computer control, can be integrated with other desktop multimedia services. Available functions range from play and record to special effects and device-to-device connections. The technical problems of providing a device and media control service include:

- Identifying the correct device abstractions that cover many different device types
- Providing a model for device and media objects which permits applications to easily manipulate collections of such objects
- Controlling shared access to external devices

An an example of the concepts involved in an architecture for device and media control, we present a system developed at the University of Massachusetts Lowell called DMCS (Distributed Media Control System) [15]. DMCS was developed to provide an interim base for applications development; it has also been used in a commercial video-on-demand test. Distinctive features of DMCS include:

- Support for hybrid media (analog and digital)
- A routing layer for circuit-switch audio-video networks
- A connection management layer for conferencing applications
- Virtual objects which can be aggregated and provide an application level view of media objects

A number of other device control environments have been developed. Galatea and the Touring Machine are described in Chapter 15. The IMA Virtual Device model is shown in Figure 9.3 of Chapter 9.

DMCS consists of three layers (Figure 10.4) from lowest to highest. The Logical Media Control (LMC) layer provides a device-independent view of device functions. There are eight classes of devices, which include players, special effects, switches, speech generators, speech recognizers, and CODECs. The Media Connectivity Control (MCC) layer provides device

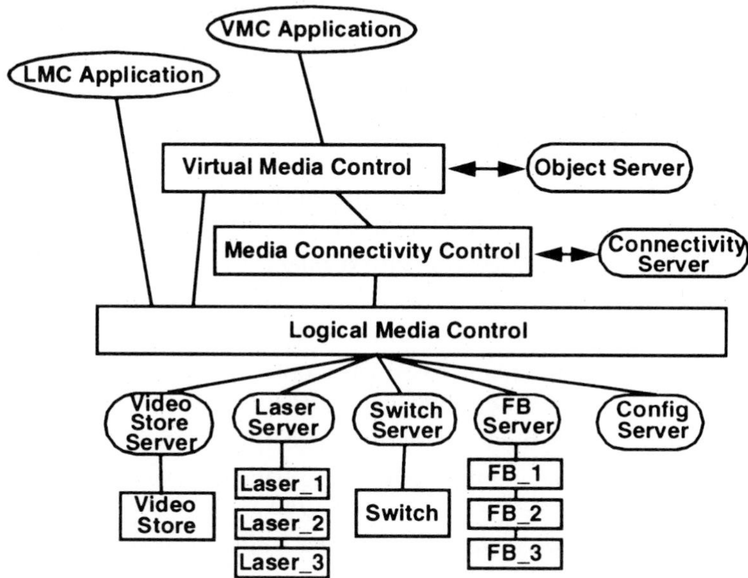

Figure 10.4 Distributed Media Control System layered architecture

connectivity for circuit switched interconnections as might be available through CATV and interconnected video switches. The Virtual Media Control (VMC) layer has an API for creating and managing persistent objects which represent one or more LMC-level media types. VMC objects can be manipulated using play, record, switch, and other functions. Additionally, the VMC layer has facilities for supporting audio-video conferencing using the session abstraction.

There is no single abstract device model that captures the range of equipment that can be interfaced to computers and interconnected today. Representative categories of devices are shown in Table 10.1. Some devices have combinations of functions and are typically decomposed into the corresponding logical classes.

The device control abstraction in DMCS allows the application to first (LMC layer) ignore any manufacturer-specific details within a device class and second (VMC layer) use an object API to create and manipulate virtual composite devices. The first goal is achieved by defining a logical view of eight categories of devices. These categories cover the current devices supported by DMCS, and each has a corresponding set of operations defined for it.

The second goal is implemented by providing a persistent object store in which virtual object definitions are created and stored. These virtual objects are referenced by the application by using a handle or name and are accessed by the VMC layer when a specific operation, such as playing an object, is performed.

Table 10.1 Examples of Different Multimedia Devices

Device	*Function*
Digital audio and video CODEC	Provides compression and decompression of a media stream
MIDI synthesizer	Generates musical tones and can be controlled using the MIDI protocol
Video effects	Combines two video segments in a transition such as a fade
Frame buffer	Stores a single still video image
Video store	Stores frame-based video on a secondary storage device for individual retrieval or sequential playback
Mixers (audio and video)	Combines two or more signals in a controllable ratio
DSP hardware	Programmable signal processing hardware which can be used to process digital audio, video, or images
Videodisc player	Plays analog video stored on an optical disk
Videotape recorder	Plays or records video from/to a magnetic tape, usually with time code for accurate frame addressing
Speech generator	Converts a sequence of words into an audio signal
Speech recognition	Converts digitized speech into a sequence of words
Switches	Multiport crossbar switches used to provide a computer-controlled patch panel

10.4.1 Routing in Hybrid Networks

Low-cost CATV and audio-video switches provide dedicated and broadcast circuits which allow devices to be interconnected. In stand-alone multimedia computing environments, devices will typically be available at the local workstation. In distributed environments, switching devices can be installed to share multimedia peripherals among a set of workstations. Such devices, which appear as an N by N crossbar switch for video and audio, can be interconnected to build hierarchical switching networks for greater sharing and, more importantly, audio-video conferencing. To permit video conferencing, a routing algorithm is needed to find multicast circuits.

The problem of finding a multicast circuit is equivalent to finding a Steiner tree (a variation of a spanning tree) in a graph. While the general problem is NP-complete, several algorithms exist that find trees which are no worse than twice the size of the optimal case [16]. The MCC layer implements a variation of one of these algorithms. It additionally allows reservation graphs to be stored in the route database. These reservation records are used by the VMC layer for allocating reserved connections.

The conferencing API provided by the VMC layer uses the notion of a session as the key abstraction. The session represents a multiparty call in which parties can range from human participants to any media stream source or sink. Sessions can be created, destroyed, and enlarged to include a new participant. Sessions can be reserved for later automatic scheduling. Connection abstractions are further discussed in Chapter 15.

10.5 TEMPORAL COORDINATION AND COMPOSITION

A time-based interface has a presentation or interaction sequence of steps in which time intervals between steps are specified. The use of the time dimension could follow from the inherent temporal nature of the information being viewed and manipulated, or it could be used as a device to achieve some secondary effect such as an animated icon. Toolkit facilities for time-based interfaces include abstractions for representing temporal relationships, schedulers for controlling and synchronizing the presentation sequence, and input objects for enabling the application user to create and manipulate time-based media. In this section we discuss a time-based interaction paradigm we call temporal coordination and provide a few general remarks about temporal composition, which is discussed in detail in Chapter 7.

10.5.1 Temporal Coordination

A temporally coordinated interface is one in which several time-based interaction or presentation areas must be synchronized to achieve some simultaneous effect. Simple cases of such coordination include synchronized playback of an audio track with an animation or video segment. More interesting cases arise when an arbitrary number of discrete and continuous media are involved and each medium has separate presentation controls. As the reference point of one medium is changed during user interaction, the reference point of the other presentation areas must be repositioned accordingly. The ability to control each presentation medium independently with a coordinated effect can be used to construct powerful integrated multiperspective interfaces.

Temporal coordination is a special case of synchronization in which a number of distinct time sequences, which are independently transformable and controllable, must be synchronized. Each sequence could be synthetically created or consist of some complex time-dependent structure. The media could be segmented such that when a segment boundary is reached, new content must be referenced. The content might be dynamically created during the presentation. Temporal coordination is an abstraction which is independent of the structure of the medium.

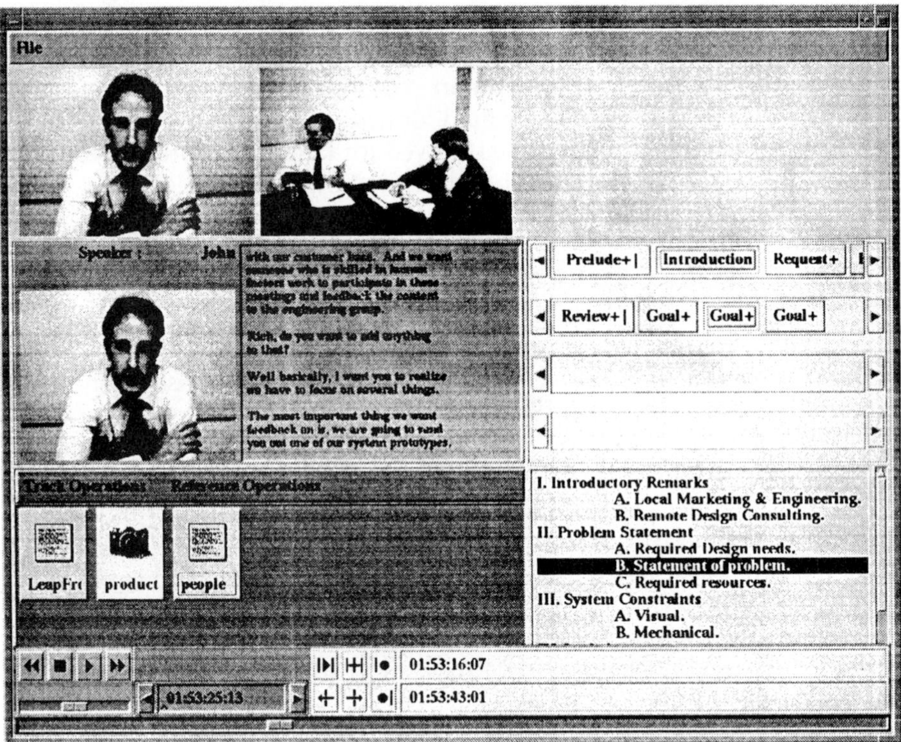

Figure 10.5 A temporally coordinated user interface for analyzing group meeting protocols.

Figure 10.5 shows an example of a temporally coordinated interface. The application is an editor for group meeting protocols [17]. The interface has areas for video segments from a given meeting, the meeting transcript, an outline of the meeting, materials referenced during the meeting, and a meeting protocol model. Each of these areas is time-based and is synchronized to a common clock.

10.5.2 Maintaining a Common Position

One of the first uses of temporal coordination as a user interface technique appears to be Dave Backer's movie repair manual [18] in which a video segment was synchronized with a rolling text display. The user could select portions of the accompanying text description and have the video segment automatically reposition to the corresponding point in the repair sequence. In order to perform this synchronization, the text of the repair manual must be indexed to the timeline of the video segment. This index must be determined manually and stored as a table of cross-referenced entries (frame number, text position), since the text has no inherent time base of its own and there is no linear mapping of the text to the video, either as characters or structured text.

Once the index table is constructed, user interaction with either the video controls or the text area causes a table lookup for the new position. Then the player functions for the video and text are restarted at the new positions. This illustrates a key issue with implementing a coordination mechanism: The relationships between the media are nonlinear so that coordination requires special indexing and cross-referenced structures that support multiway indexing.

10.5.3 A General Approach

The usual way to synchronize a set of time-based objects is to define one object as the reference object (Figure 10.6). As the position of the reference object changes, its position is used as an index to recompute the positions of the other objects.

In order to permit the user to independently control each object in a coordinated fashion, repositioning actions such as those shown in Figure 10.7 must be supported.

The temporal coordination mechanism ensures that synchronization can be established after repositioning of any temporal object. The operation of translating the position of one object to another is called mapping; the procedure to perform this operation is a mapping function.

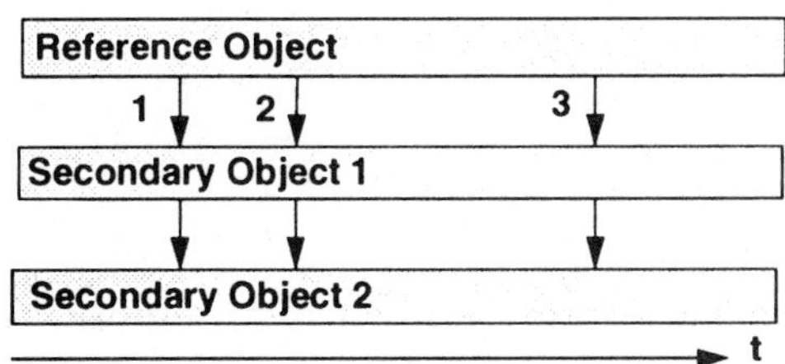

Figure 10.6 Reestablishment of reference position from reference object

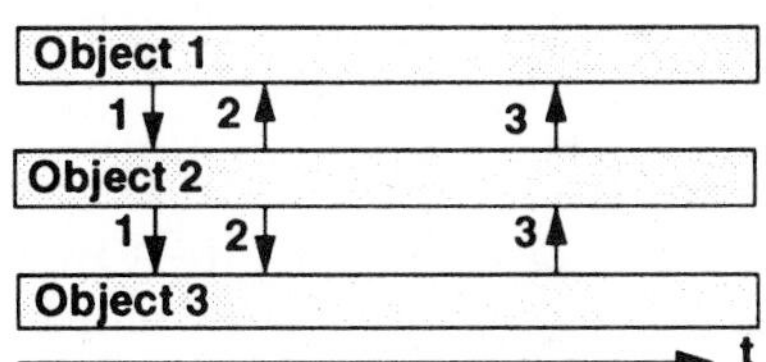

Figure 10.7 Reestablishment of reference position from any temporal object

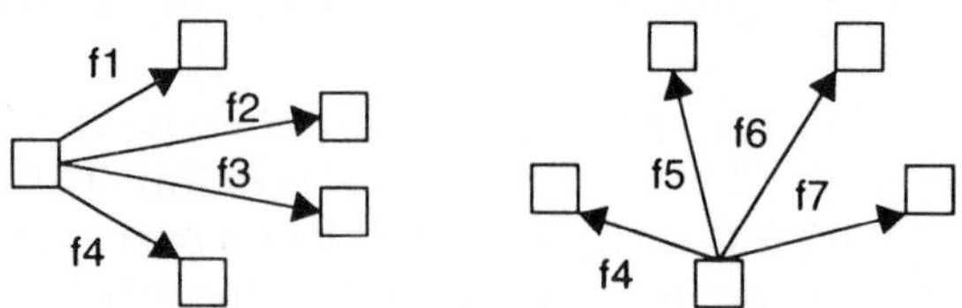

Figure 10.8 N-way remapping implies a fully interconnected graph of mapping functions.

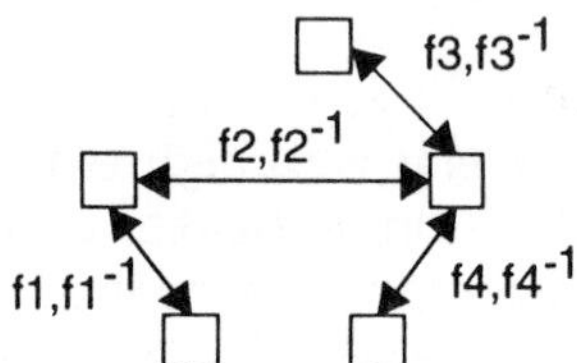

Figure 10.9 Because of transitivity, a spanning tree is sufficient for N-way remapping.

The coordination mapping functions support mapping of any object to all other objects, leading to the conceptual view of a fully interconnected graph of mapping functions (Figure 10.8), where the nodes are the objects and the graph edges are mapping functions. Since mapping is transitive, the mechanism only requires that the set of mapping functions forms a spanning tree (Figure 10.9). Then a change in any object's position can be propagated to all other temporal objects, and only 2(N-1) mapping functions need to be defined.

10.5.4 Temporal Composition

Temporal composition is the time analog of spatial composition in the user interface. A number of models have been proposed which correspond to some existing spatial model, such as temporal box and glue or temporal constraints. Several such models are described in Chapter 7.

10.6 TOOLKITS

10.6.1 Athena Muse

The Athena Muse multimedia construction set was developed by the Visual Computing Group of MIT's Project Athena [19,20]. Athena Muse can be viewed as a user interface management system (UIMS) with an integrated scripting language called EventScript (Figure 10.10). The design philosophy of Athena Muse is to provide a broad collection of paradigms from which the author or developer can select based on the requirements of the

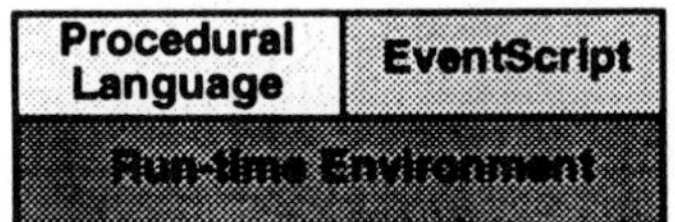

Figure 10.10 Architectural components of Athena Muse

application. As the authoring environment for Project Athena, Athena Muse is intended to support a range of educational computing applications, including hypermedia, simulation, navigation through visual databases, and surrogate travel.

Related materials (video, text, graphics) that comprise a segment of the presentation or interaction are grouped into a unit called a package. A set of packages can be organized as nodes in a directed graph, one of the four Athena Muse paradigms. The directed graph can be used in a variety of ways. For example, the edges can be used as hyperlinks between different parts of the application data, activated based on user input. Alternatively, the graph can be interpreted as a state diagram in which nodes are packages and edges are transitions. Transitions between nodes are made according to some change in the global state. The interpretation of the directed graph depends upon the application, and there are a number of additional paradigms that can be used to represent the control structure.

As the second paradigm, Athena Muse provides a multidimensional virtual space for applications to dimension and manage their data. Although the virtual space is in general specified by the application, an explicit time dimension can be used for synchronization. If several time-based objects are to be synchronized, they use a common timeline as their reference point. Another feature is the association of a viewport with a two-dimensional space for panning and zooming images, graphics, and video.

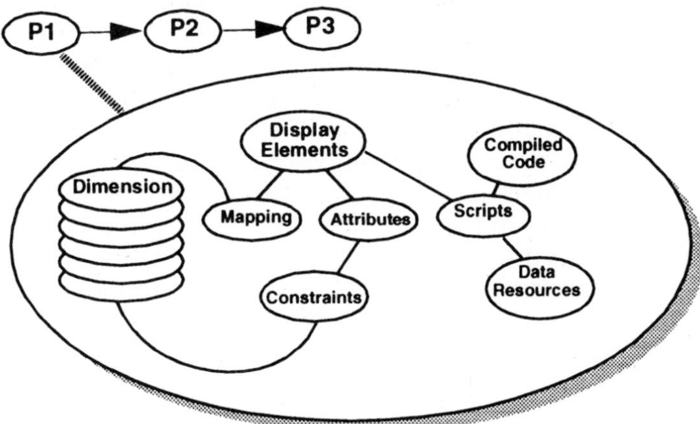

Figure 10.11 Components of an Athena Muse package

Dynamic behavior is represented by two additional paradigms: declarative constraints and procedural declarations. A constraint is a relation between two or more variables. When one of the variables in a constraint system changes, the constraint solver uses the relations on the set of variables to propagate the change to maintain a consistent set of values. In Athena Muse, constraints are either linear equalities (bidirectional) or assignments (unidirectional), which simplifies the design of the constraint solver. The constraints apply to dimensions and display element attributes. The advantage of using constraints is the high-level declarative style of programming provided. However, nonlinear constraints are typically not easy to solve, so Athena Muse provides a procedural language to augment the constraint representation.

The procedural language can be a simple functional call to perform an action on some entity or attribute. In more complex cases, an object-oriented scripting language called EventScript is used. EventScript is syntactically similar to HyperTalk. Scripting languages are discussed in Chapter 13.

The four paradigms in Athena Muse provide a general-purpose multimedia authoring and programming environment, which has been validated by a number of significant applications that have been developed. Athena Muse integrates these paradigms (Figure 10.11) so that there is flexibility for the author in choosing when to use a paradigm.

10.6.2 QuickTime

QuickTime is an Apple Computer system software architecture which was introduced in 1991 with a number of innovative features to support multimedia applications on the Macintosh platform. Two key aspects are its media-independent track model for multimedia data and a software-only video format that makes low-quality video playback possible without special hardware. The QuickTime architecture consists of four major components: system software, file formats, Apple compressors, and human interface standards.

The system software component of QuickTime incorporates three new pieces into the System 7 operating system: the Movie Toolbox, Image Compression Manager (ICM), and Video Compressor. Apple uses the term movie to denote dynamic data such as sound, video, and animation. The Movie Toolbox is a set of system software services that developers use to incorporate support for movies in their applications. Applications control media that are represented as tracks. Tracks of the same or different media can be grouped for synchronization, ordered in sequences, and joined in transitions. The track abstraction hides media-specific details from the application. Similarly, the ICM shields applications from the details of compression and decompression schemes.

QuickTime [21] provides a basic set of software compression/decompression schemes for still images, animations, and video. Included are compressors for JPEG, a run-length encoded animation format, and a digital video format. The Video Compressor allows digitized video sequences to be played from a hard disk or CD-ROM in realtime without additional hardware. Compression ratios ranging from 5:1 to 25:1 are possible. The video playback size is typically less than one-fourth of the computer screen size.

10.6.3 Object-Oriented Frameworks

Tactus [22] is a multimedia application toolkit which provides a continuous media player with scheduling controls for the application. Tactus combines three strategies for helping the application meet timing constraints in the absence of real-time scheduling by the operating system. First, the server precomputes the media stream to avoid access delays. Second, the server is located at the presentation workstation. Third, the server buffers the possible alternative media streams that would be valid responses to a user choice, reducing the turnaround time when a presentation change is made.

Researchers at NEC [23] have extended the InterViews C++ toolkit to include temporal composition of audio and video. The approach extends the TeX notion of spatial glue to the time domain.

Gibbs [24,25] has proposed an object-oriented framework for connecting various components of a multimedia presentation. In the current system [26], devices are categorized as either input, output, or transform components. Components can be connected in a data flow graph, a model convenient for visual programming of applications.

10.7 HYPERAPPLICATIONS

Hyperlinks are associations between two or more objects that are defined by the user or application developer. Hyperlinks are typically visible at the application interface and allow several types of use such as navigation, backtracking, and inspection of link labels. These connections are independent of the objects themselves; an object can have many such connections to or from other objects. Objects can be procedural, interactive, simple, or complex media types, located in the same or a different application. A hyperapplication environment allows objects in different applications to be linked together by the user for later navigation.

DEC LinkWorks is a hyperapplication environment (see Figure 10.12) which illustrates these ideas. Any application designed to run in LinkWorks has a link menu for the user to perform link operations. The application exports a link interface which can be activated by other applications. The application also provides a visual indicator of each link. Once a link is established, the user can traverse it to the corresponding application context. If the application is not running, it is automatically launched by LinkWorks and brought to the state which the link references.

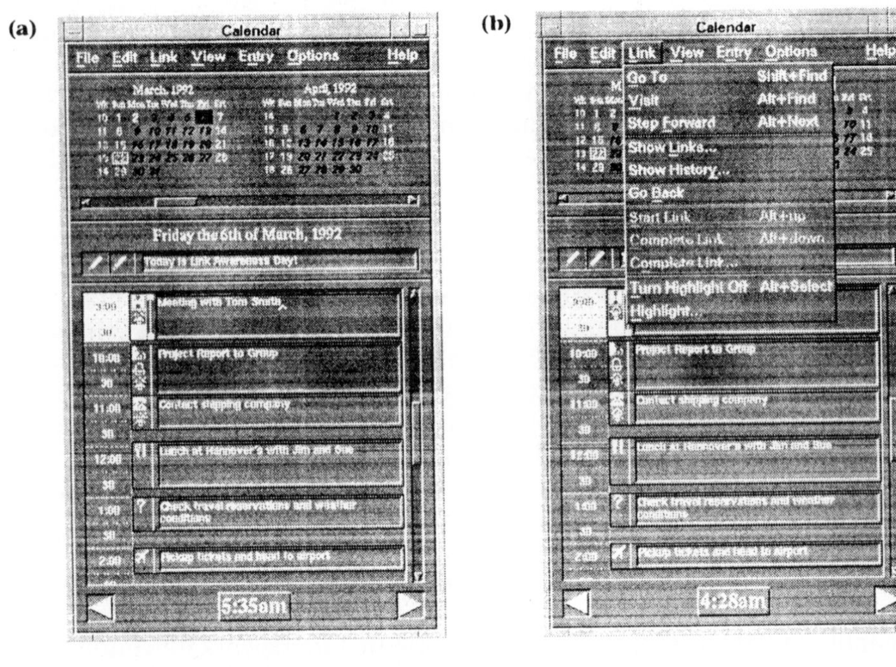

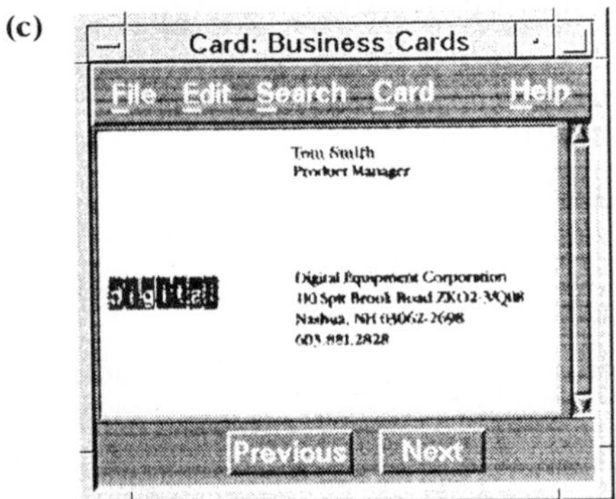

Figure 10.12 A sample DEC LinkWorks hyperapplication session: (a) calendar application showing lightbulb icons indicating presence of a link, (b) calendar application with link menu showing traversal options, (c) cardfile application which is linked to the 9:00 A.M. calendar entry.

An emerging distributed infrastructure supporting hyperapplications as well other types of distributed processing is a distributed object management facility (DOMF). DOMF is an object-oriented mechanism by which applications export functionality and data for use by other applications. The Object Management Group (OMG) standard for DOMF [27] permits all participating applications to access available services in a network-transparent manner (Figure 10.13). HB1 [28] is a prototype hyperapplication system that uses a semantic database to store links.

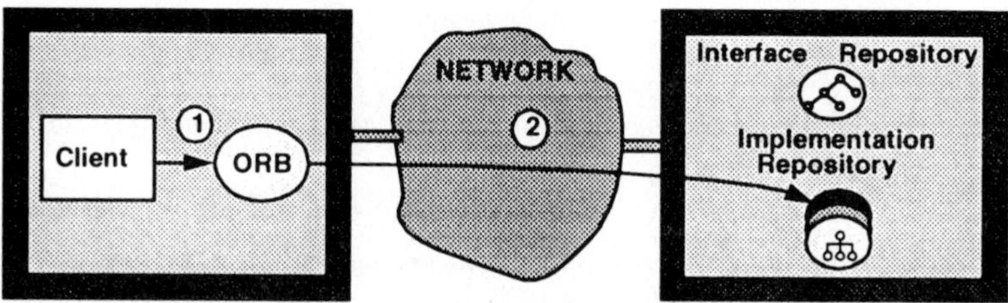

Figure 10.13 The OMG model for a distributed object-oriented application environment provides network-transparent object locating and invocation. The client requests a service by contacting the local object request broker (ORB). The ORB locates the service on behalf of the client and then invokes the appropriate method using the implementation repository.

10.8 SUMMARY

Multimedia applications will require a number of extensions to existing toolkits and servers used in the design of graphical interfaces. Multimedia interface design is still fertile ground, but the architectural components can be identified. The window system will be extended to support continuous media, device control, and scheduling. A variety of object-oriented toolkits are being developed to simplify the application development task.

The state of knowledge regarding the use of multimedia in the user interface will grow dramatically as the technologies for constructing such interfaces become more pervasive; recent research in this area is found in [29].

10.9 ACKNOWLEDGMENTS

Matthew Hodges and Ben Davis at MIT reviewed the Athena Muse description. Rita Brennan at Apple Computer provided information on QuickTime.

10.10 REFERENCES

1. Koegel, J., Keskin, C., and Rutledge, J. Toolkits for Multimedia Interface Design. *Xhibition '92*. vol. 2. 1992. pp. 275–285.
2. Scheifler, R. W., and Gettys, J. The X Window System. *ACM Trans. on Graphics* (5) 2. April 1986. pp. 79–109.
3. Scheifler, R. W., and Gettys, J. *X Window. System*. 3rd ed. Digital Press. 1992.
4. Sun Microsystems, Inc. *NeWS 2.1 Programmer's Guide*. 1990.
5. Anderson, D., Govindan, R., and Homsy, G. Abstractions for Continuous Media in a Network Window System. *Intl. Conf. on Multimedia Information Systems*. McGraw-Hill. 1990. pp. 273–298.
6. Rennison, E., Baker, R., Kim, D. D., and Lim, Y.-H. MuX: An X Co-Existent Time-Based Multimedia I/O Server. *The X Resource*. Issue 1. Winter 1992. pp. 213–233.
7. Angebranndt, S. et al. Integrating Audio and Telephony in a Distributed Workstation Environment. *Proc. Summer 1991 USENIX Conference*. 1991. pp. 419–436.

8. Billman, R. et al. Workstation Audio in the X Environment. *The X Resource*. no. 4. Fall 1992. pp. 137–158.
9. Lamparter, B., and Effelsberg, W. X-Movie: Transmission and Presentation of Digital Movies Under X. *Proc. 2nd Intl. Workshop on Network and Operating System Support for Digital Audio and Video*. November 1991.
10. Uppaluru, P. Networking Digital Video. *Digest of Papers COMPCON Spring 1992*. February 1992. pp. 76–83.
11. MIT X Consortium. *X Image Extension Protocol Reference Manual, version 4.12, Public Review Draft. The X Resource*. Special Issue C. January 1993.
12. Neville-Neal, G. V. Current Efforts in Client/Server Audio. *The X Resource*. no. 8. 1993. pp. 69–86.
13. Arman, F., Hsu, A., and Chiu, M.-Y. Image Processing on Compressed Data for Large Video Databases. *ACM Multimedia 93*. August 1993. pp. 267–272.
14. Anderson, D., and Homsy, G. Abstractions for Continous Media I/O Services. *Computer* (24) 10. 1991. pp. 51–57.
15. Koegel, J., and Syta, A. Routing in Hybrid Multimedia Networks. *SPIE Conf. on Multimedia Communications*. September 1992.
16. Kou, L., Markowsky, G., and Berman, L. A Fast Algorithm for Steiner Trees. *Acta Informatica*. vol. 15. 1981. pp. 141–145.
17. Koegel, J., Rutledge, J., Miner, R., and Krolak, P. Supporting Real-Time Analysis of Multimedia Communications Sessions. *Proc. SPIE*. vol. 1785. September 8–11, 1992.
18. Backer, D. Structure and Interactivity of Media: A Prototype for the Electronic Book. Ph.D. diss., MIT. 1988.
19. Hodges, M., Sasnett, R., and Ackerman, M. A Construction Set for Multimedia Applications. *IEEE Software*. January 1989.
20. Hodges, M., and Sasnett, R. *Multimedia Computing*. Addison-Wesley. 1993.
21. Apple Computer, Inc. *QuickTime Technical Backgrounder*. 1991.
22. Dannenberg, R., Neuendorffer, T., Newcomer, J., and Rubine, D. Tactus: Toolkit-Level Support for Synchronized Interactive Multimedia. *Third International Workshop on Network and Operating System Support for Digital Audio and Video*. November 1992.
23. Hamakawa, R., Sakagami, H., and Rekimoto, J. Audio and Video Extensions to Graphical User Interface Toolkits. *Third International Workshop on Network and Operating System Support for Digital Audio and Video*. November 1992.
24. Gibbs, S. Composite Multimedia and Active Objects. *OOPSLA '91*. 1991. pp. 97–112.
25. Gibbs, S. Application Construction and Component Design in an Object-Oriented Multimedia Framework. *Third International Workshop on Network and Operating System Support for Digital Audio and Video*. November 1992.
26. Mey, V. D., and Gibbs, S. A Multimedia Component Kit. *ACM Multimedia 93*. August 1993. pp. 291–300.
27. Object Management Group. The Common Object Request Broker: Architecture and Specification. December 1991.
28. Schnase, J. L., Leggett, J. J., Hicks, D. L., and Szabo R. L. Semantic Data Modeling of Hypermedia Associations. *ACM Trans on Information Systems* 11 (1). 1993. pp. 27–50.
29. Blattner, M., and Dannenberg, R. (eds.) *Multimedia Interface Design*. Addison-Wesley. 1991.

CHAPTER 11

MULTIMEDIA FILE SYSTEMS AND INFORMATION MODELS

John F. Koegel Buford
University of Massachusetts Lowell

The value of unstructured media forms such as images, audio, and video is that they represent certain types of information more effectively than other available means. Nevertheless, continuous media have traditionally been absent from information systems because of issues including storage capacity, bandwidth limitations, scheduling issues, lack of appropriate data models, and inadequate query support. This chapter surveys a number of the foundational issues related to future multimedia information systems. Recent results in multimedia file systems, multimedia document models, and content-based retrieval of unstructured data are discussed.

11.1 THE CASE FOR MULTIMEDIA INFORMATION SYSTEMS

The next generation of computer workstations will be hardware-enabled to support storage and presentation of compressed digital video and audio. In many applications, the new media forms available on the computer will provide richer, more natural, and more accessible representation. In numerous cases, materials such as pictures, video clips, and recorded speech can be easily obtained and communicate the desired information more effectively.

The support for these new media forms will impact all information processing services and applications in use today. Multimedia user interfaces, databases, authoring and presentation tools, interchange, and many others will become standard parts of the application framework. Today's information systems will evolve into multimedia repositories. Information that previously had to be stored and processed outside of the computer will now be accessible in the same context as the records and reports that make up the day-to-day information flow of the organization. All information, whether text, picture, audio, or video, will be integrated, easily accessed, and shared with others over the computer network.

The corporate information system will support rich information retrieval and organization communication. For example,

CAD drawings annotated with voice or video

Product simulations using animation and video

Marketing materials including videos and other documentation on competitive products

Requirements statements including video recordings of users, customers, and prior products

On-line manuals using videos of equipment operation

Product development teams sharing design information through application sharing over a wide area network

Multimedia mail containing video clips and/or pictures of proposed design changes and justifications

The ability to store and access all representations of information on-line solves the problem of disjoint information (Figure 11.1).

A few lines of research have pursued this combination of multimedia information systems and group communication. The early work by Doug Englebart to develop the Augment system [1,2,3] as well as his more recent Bootstrap project [4] have long articulated a similar vision. Ted Nelson's Xanadu is moving towards becoming a product [5]. More recently a number of researchers have worked on prototype multimedia database management systems.

More specialized applications of multimedia information retrieval include video-on-demand and multimedia-on-demand. Video-on-demand is an anticipated next-generation service to be offered by cable television and other telecommunication vendors. Subscribers access a remote video-on-demand server through a menu interface controlled by a hand-held device. The server stores a large number of digital compressed videos, which can be transmitted to a subscriber on request. The server is designed to act as a remote VCR player for each subscriber.

The multimedia-on-demand scenario is similar to the video-on-demand case except that the server stores complex multimedia documents that

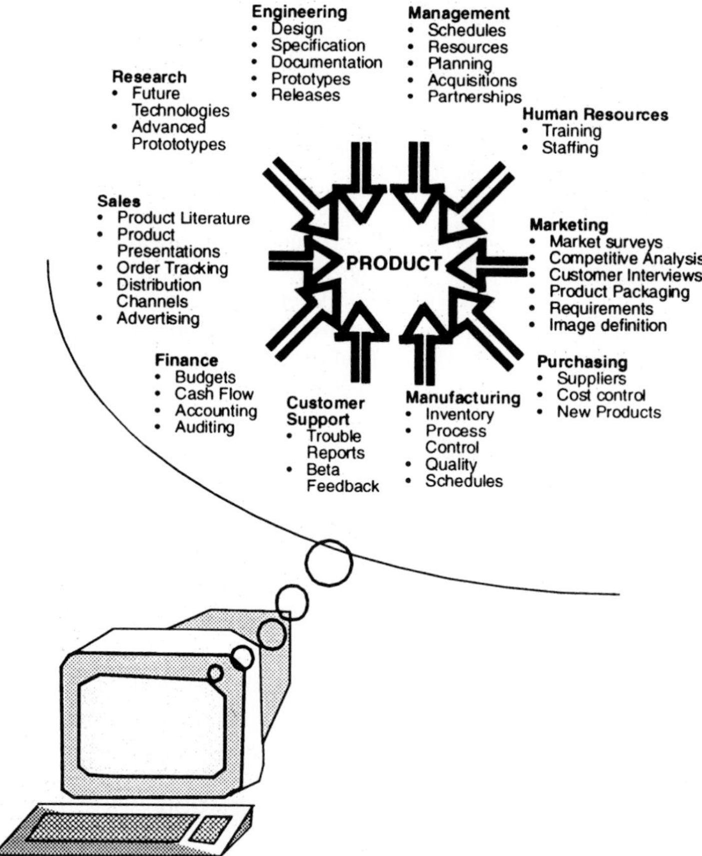

Figure 11.1 Computer-based information systems have become a primary tool in the multidisciplinary organizational efforts for product development. Multimedia information systems will allow all this information to be integrated on-line, eliminating the disjoint information base problem facing today's organizations.

include text, graphics, and images. Applications of multimedia-on-demand include news, education, and store catalogs.

The achievement of multimedia information systems faces a variety of technical problems, which are due in part to two characteristics of multimedia information: large amounts of data and stringent temporal constraints for both delivery and recording. Conventional file systems and database management systems are not designed to meet the performance requirements of multimedia information systems. Additionally, new data models for multimedia documents and new techniques for searching for multimedia content are needed.

This chapter surveys the current research results in multimedia information systems in the areas listed in Table 11.1. Since the area is very broad,

Table 11.1 Summary of the Issues Facing the Design of Multimedia Information Systems

Component	*Issues*	*Examples*
Physical Media	High-capacity and performance storage architecture	Disk arrays
File System	Layout	Contiguous versus scattered
	Admissability	Determinstic guarantees or nondeterministic guarantees
	Scheduling	Round-robin, quality proportional
	Semantics	Real time with minimum rate and buffering
Data Model	Document model	HyTime
	Temporal relationships	OCPN
Query Language	Search mechansims	Content-based retrieval
Application	Single or multiuser	VOD server
	Continuous media only or non real-time data	

the discussion is restricted to these areas, which are covered in the following sections:

File system support for continuous media

Data models for multimedia and hypermedia information

Content-based retrieval of unstructured data

11.2 FILE SYSTEM SUPPORT FOR CONTINUOUS MEDIA

Conventional file systems are unable to guarantee that clients can access continuous media such as digital audio or video in a way that permits delivery deadlines to be met under normal buffering conditions. Magnetic and optical storage devices have large seek and rotational latencies that can cause a continuous media client to starve if the continuous media stream is not buffered and coordinated with other service requests. Consequently, most research in this area has approached this problem by proposing solutions for one or more of the following interrelated areas:

Layout of continuous media files: How should blocks of continuous media files be positioned on the disk?

Buffer requirements: What are the minimum buffering requirements per stream that must be allocated, or, alternatively, how many simultaneous streams can be supported if the buffer allocation is fixed?

Admissibility criteria: When is it safe to accept an additional client to the current service set?

Scheduling of client requests in a service round: Given a set of client requests, how should these be ordered in a service round so that all client constraints are met and buffer resources are minimized?

We first look at the single stream as an illustration of the basic issues and typical approaches taken to support continuous media. We then survey research in the multistream cases.

11.2.1 The Single Stream Case

Gemmell and Christodoulakis [6] were the first to study the case of deterministic playback of a single continuous media stream and provide bounds on buffering. Consider Figure 11.2 as an illustration of the relationship between the disk read function $R(t)$ and the continuous media consumption function $C(t,t_0)$. Data are read from the disk in blocks starting at time 0 and ending at time t_r. Between blocks, no data are read so the slope of $R(t)$ is zero. During reads the slope may vary from one read to the next because of variable compression ratios of the media. At some time t_0 the client begins accessing the data in the buffer for playback. The difference between the disk transfer function and the consumption function is the buffer function $B(t,t_0)$; this function shows how much buffer space is needed versus time. In order to prevent the client from starving during playback, the buffer function must be greater than or equal to zero during the read interval $t_0 \le t \le t_r$.

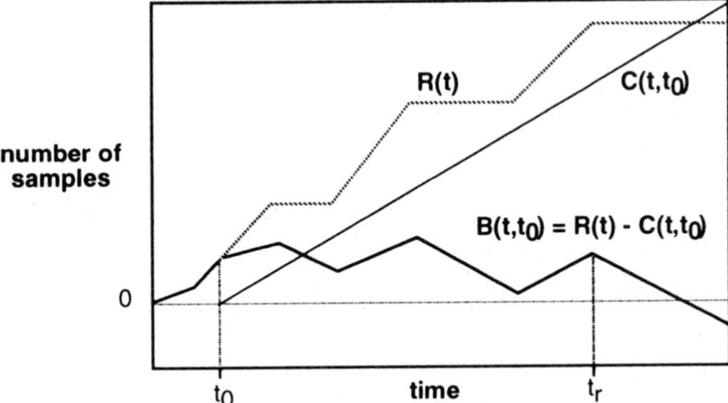

Figure 11.2 Relationships between the read function $R(t)$, the consumption function $C(t,t_0)$ and the buffer function $B(t,t_0)$. The read function has zero slope where no transfers occur; variations in slopes in periods of transfer represent different compression ratios of the stored samples. Based on [6].

It is desirable that buffer allocation be minimized. It can be shown [6] that the minimum buffer solution also is the solution with the earliest start time t_0. Therefore, finding the minimum start time guarantees the minimum buffer allocation. Starting before this time would cause the receiver to starve; starting after this time would increase the amount of buffer resources need. The procedure to find the minimum start time can be found graphically by changing t_0 so that $B(t,0)$ is minimized and still non-negative:

> The minimum value for t_0 may be found as follows. First consider $B(t,0)$. If this function is nonnegative for $0 \le t \le t_r$, then $B(t,0)$ is a solution, and the minimum value for t_0 is 0. Otherwise, let the minimum value for $B(t,0)$, in the range $0 \le t \le t_r$, be at time t_{min} with $B(t_{min},0) = -m$. The intersection of $R(t)$ and $B(t,0) + m$ is at the minimum value for t_0, yielding a workable playback.

The single channel model can be made more realistic to take into account delays between blocks of d_{max} as well as artificial delays d_{min} that might be necessary because of the consumption rate r_c being less than the transfer rate r_t. From [6] again, any algorithm that allocates a number of buffers independent of the record length must use a block size of at least

$$s_b \ge \left\lceil \frac{r_c\, d_{max}}{s_s} \left(1 - \frac{r_c}{r_t}\right)^{-1} \right\rceil$$

sectors (where s_s is the sector size) and must allocate at least

$$n_b \ge \left\lceil \frac{r_c}{s_s} \left(d_{max} + \frac{s_s}{r_t} + d_{min} \right) \right\rceil$$

sector-size buffers. These are upper bounds in which d_{max} is the maximum possible for a device access. The number of artificial delays of length d_{min} is limited to a constant k.

As an example, consider playback of digital audio with r_c equal to 12.8 Kbps from a drive with d_{max} equal to 40 ms, r_t equal to 1 Mbps, and a sector size of 512 bytes. Then the minimum block size s_b is about 1 sector (512 bytes), and the number of buffers needed is at least 1.

Gemmell has also investigated bounds on multichannel playback [7] under the following assumptions:

Channels may have different consumption rates

Playback for some channels may be paused while playback for others continues

The amount read for each channel is not fixed for each reading period (because of pauses, different consumption rates, variable rate compression, or different sample rates)

Operations during a reading period are buffer conserving; that is, the data read takes at least one reading period to consume

Operations during a reading period are nonstarving, the requirement that the reading operation keep up with the real-time consumption of data

The "no starvation" requirement implies that $r_c\Delta_{max}$ must be buffered between reads, where Δ_{max} is the maximum time difference between successive reads for a given channel.

Gemmell's model, which is intended to be a framework for describing arbitrary block placement and stream scheduling schemes in one common notation, is based on the use of sorting sets. Suppose that each channel is placed in a set $S_i = \{ c_1, c_2, ..., c_n \}$ where sets are always executed in a fixed sequence during a reading period. Within a set, reads are ordered to reduce seek time. If $T(S)$ is the maximum time to execute the reads for sorting set S, then the maximum length of the reading period for a channel c in sorting set j is:

$$\Delta_{max} = \sum_i T(S_i) + T(S_j - c)$$

This equation says that to prevent any channel from starving between reads, we must read enough to cover the reading of all the other sets as well as reading all other channels in the same set. It is the worst-case scenario, in which channel c is scheduled first in its set in one reading period and then last in its set in the next reading period.

Given this formula, then any particular policy for scheduling can be analyzed by providing values for $T(S)$ for each sorting set. Once Δ_{max} is known, then the minimum buffer requirements are $r_c\Delta_{max} + \beta$, where β is related to the cluster size. A detailed example of a construction of $T(S)$ for the preseeking sweep algorithm for different sorting sets and cluster sizes is given in [7]. The preseeking sweep algorithm orders the channels in each set according to physical disk order and does an immediate seek to the nearest endpoint of the set when the set begins.

11.2.2 Performance Guarantees for Continuous Media Access

Given the physical characteristics of the disk and the real-time requirements of the media delivery process, the remaining parameters available for the design of the file system are the file layout, scheduling of channel access, and admissibility criteria. There are two basic alternatives regarding performance guarantees: deterministic and statistical. Deterministic guarantees result in service reliability that can't be compromised by resource contention. Statistical guarantees provide service reliability with some probability; thus, there is the chance that resource contention could cause unpredictable delays for one or more channels. Whether statistical guarantees are acceptable depends upon the application. Deterministic policies have drawbacks as well. Most research dealing with deterministic guarantees makes worst-case assumptions about disk access and/or layout and ignores the variation in consumption rate due to variable rates of compression of the video or audio. Consequently, policies based on deterministic guarantees could lead to underutilized systems. Another problem with statistical guarantees is in the accuracy of the statistical model. Without an accurate model of the factors such as layout, compression rate, etc., statistical guarantees can't be made.

Much of the research on file system support for continuous media concerns deterministic guarantees. Approaches typically differ on whether the layout is constrained or unconstrained. Scheduling algorithms have been proposed, modeled, and evaluated so as to maximize the number of simultaneous channels or minimize buffer requirements. A number of examples are discussed next.

11.2.3 Continuous Media File System

The Continuous Media File System (CMFS) proposed by Anderson et al. [8] defines an API and provdes both deterministic and non-deterministic service classes. It uses the abstraction of a session to define the client interface for file operations. For example, the following function is used by a client to create a session prior to requesting read or write operations. The function `start_clock()` initiates the session logical clock.

```
ID = request_session(
      int direction;      // read or write
      File_ID name;
      int offset;         // position from beginning of file
      FIFO *buffer;       // buffer between disk and client
      TIME cushion;       // amount that client can read ahead
                          // of the logical clock for the stream
      int rate);          // the rate of the logical clock
                          // defining the consumption rate of
                          // the stream

start_clock(ID); // start the logical clock for the session
```

File operations are identified by session IDs, and session characteristics (buffer size, rate of consumption) are used in scheduling and admissibility tests. We discuss the following aspects of CMFS: disk layout, admissibility criteria, and disk access scheduling.

CMFS requires no specific layout policy. For a given disk configuration it is assumed that the time to read the next *N* blocks of data from file *F*, $U_F(N)$, and the time to read the next *N* blocks from file *F* starting at block *i*, $V_F(N,i)$, can be bounded. Using $U_F(\,)$ and $V_F(\,)$, the admissibility algorithm determines whether a static schedule, under worst-case assumptions, exists which includes the new session. The minimal static schedule for the operation set $\phi = <M_1, M_2, ..., M_n>$, where M_i is the number of blocks read for channel i in a service round, is determined as follows. The minimal operation set ϕ is one for which the length of the service round, denoted $L(\phi)$, is least for a given set of sessions.

1. We need the following definitions: Let D_i be the playback duration of one block of data for session S_i

   Let I_i be the interval (t_i, t_{i+1}), where $\{t_0, t_1, t_2, ...\} = \{ k_a D_a, k_b D_b, k_c D_c, ... \}$, k_i being integers

   Let $\phi_i = <\lceil R_1 t_i \rceil, ..., \lceil R_n t_i \rceil>$ be the operation set given the interval I_i and consumption rates R_i; that is, ϕ_i represents the amount that would be consumed per channel if the duration of the service round were in the interval I_i
2. Let $\phi_0 = <1, ..., 1>$. This is the operation set for which $D(\phi) \in I_0$.
3. Check if ϕ_i is feasible. $\lceil R_j t_i \rceil + Y_j$ is the amount of buffer space needed for channel j during the service round in order for ϕ_i to be feasible, where Y_j is the cushion specified when the session was created. If not, then stop; there is no feasible ϕ
4. If $L(\phi_i) \leq D(\phi_i)$, where $L(\phi_i)$ is the time needed to access ϕ_i in the worst case, using the function $U_F(N)$, stop. ϕ_i is the minimal feasible operation set.
5. Compute ϕ_{i+1}; go to step 3.

Various scheduling policies can be used for a given set of sessions. The *static* policy repeatedly uses the schedule in the order given by ϕ above, except that if a block transfer would cause a buffer overflow, the operation skips to the next session. Two other policies are *greedy* and *cyclic plan*, which depend upon the measures of workahead and slacktime. The workahead W_i for a session S_i is the amount of data buffered for that session in excess of the cushion. The slacktime H_i for a session S_i is the excess of workahead given that session S_i completes at time t_i in the current service round; that is, $H_i = W_i - t_i$. The slacktime estimate provide a window for service of non real-time traffic, as will be discussed shortly.

The greedy scheduling policy uses the slacktime to read ahead on the session with the smallest workahead. The cyclic plan scheduling policy schedules one additional block on the session with the smallest workahead. Slack time and workahead estimates are then updated, and the session with the smallest workahead is given the next one block workahead. This process is repeated until all slacktime is allocated. The cyclic plan policy involves significantly more overhead.

CMFS defines two non real-time service classes and uses slacktime to schedule these classes. CMFS introduces a hysteresis mechanism to improve efficiency. Measures for the hysteresis threshholds as well as CMFS performance measures for number of concurrent sessions, interactive session response time, and background throughput are provided in [8].

11.2.4 UCSD Multimedia-on-Demand Server

If the file layout is constrained, then it is possible to increase the number of simultaneous sessions. One constrained file layout policy is contiguous in which successive blocks are stored consecutively on a track. This policy is discussed by Gemmell and Christodoulakis [6]. The disk transfer rate and consumption rate may not be matched, and gaps between blocks can be used to provide the necessary delays to match the rates without requiring excessive buffering. Yu et al. [9] have studied merging techniques in which a pair of sessions are interleaved; Wells, Yang, and Yu [10] examine the merging of three patterns. This work assumes that the storage patterns of each channel are fixed in order to meet the constraints of playback of audio from optical disk.

Rangan and Vin [11,12] present a merging algorithm in which the constraints on the storage pattern for a given channel can be slightly altered to increase storage efficiency. The associated playback algorithm uses a staggered toggling technique to prevent channel starvation from occurring due to the storage pattern modification. The algorithm keeps track of channels which have only read a fractional amount of the required block during a "merge cycle" and periodically catches up when a merge cycle deadline is reached. The length of a merge cycle is the lowest common multiple of the lengths of the patterns of mergeable strands, where a pattern is represented by the pair *(M,G)*, *M* being the size of a data block and *G* being the gap between blocks. Techniques for both on-line and off-line merging are described. On-line merging of two strands is illustrated in Figure 11.3.

In [13], Vin and Rangan present admissibility criteria and scheduling algorithms assuming the same merging techniques as in [11,12]. Two scheduling policies for a given service round are described: round-robin and quality proportional. In a round-robin scheduling policy, where the number of blocks transferred per session in a service round is the same for each session, the maximum number of sessions that can be serviced is:

$$n^c_{\max} \le \frac{\eta_{vs}}{R^{\max}_{pl}} \left(\frac{R_{dr}}{M^{avg} + G^{avg}} \right)$$

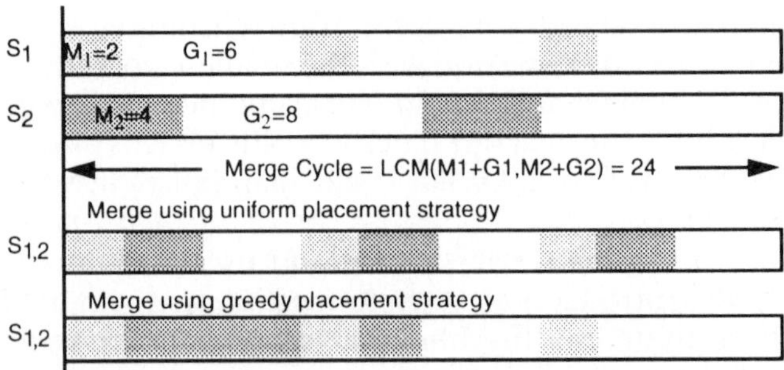

Figure 11.3 On-line merging of strand S2 with strand S1 [12]

where R_{pl} is the playback rate in display units per second, R_{dr} is the transfer rate of the drive in bits per second, G is the gap between blocks in bits, M is the block size in bits, and η_{vs} is the block size in display units. This indicates that under round-robin scheduling the maximum number of sessions that can be serviced is limited by the session with the maximum playback rate.

In the quality proportional servicing algorithm, the number of blocks transferred per session in a service round is proportional to the playback rate of the session. In this case the maximum number of sessions that can be serviced is:

$$n^{p}_{max} \leq \frac{\eta_{vs}}{R^{avg}_{pl}} \left(\frac{R_{dr}}{M^{avg} + G^{avg}} \right)$$

Given the constraints on placement, it can be shown that the quality proportional servicing algorithm results in the maximum number of simultaneous sessions.

11.2.5 Lancaster University

The Lancaster Continuous Media Storage Systems (CMSS) combines disk striping, a constrained disk layout, and round-robin scheduling [14]. CMSS assumes that a continuous media stream is consumed at a fixed data rate. The data block size of each stream is set to the same playback period. This avoids the problem described earlier with round-robin scheduling when streams have different playback rates. Consequently, during a round-robin sequence, streams with lower playback rates have smaller data blocks and take less access time and buffer space, while streams with high playback rates have larger data blocks and take greater access time and buffer space. Data blocks for a given stream are striped in sequence to the disk array, where the *nth* data block is stored on the *n mod m* disk, *m* being the total number of disks. Sessions can be scheduled as either hard guaranteed (deterministic) or soft guaranteed. Soft guaranteed streams are executed on a best-effort basis during the slack period of the hard guaranteed schedule.

11.2.6 Grouped Sweeping Scheduling

Chen, Kandlur, and Yu [15] evaluate Grouped Sweeping Scheduling (GSS), a variation of the traditional SCAN scheduling, in which the set of n sessions being serviced is divided into g groups. Groups are scheduled in a fixed order and sessions within a group are scheduled using SCAN. GSS is equivalent to SCAN when $g = n$ and is equivalent to fixed order when $g = 1$. GSS groups are assigned so that the amount of buffer space needed for each group is as similar as possible. Given this assignment, a procedure for minimizing buffer space is described.

11.3 DATA MODELS FOR MULTIMEDIA AND HYPERMEDIA INFORMATION

Although much attention has been given to file system support for individual continuous media streams, many applications will need to embed these media streams in complex documents. As described at the beginning of the chapter, examples of such use include multimedia annotations integrated with traditional text and graphic documents, electronic books with multimedia insets and rich interlinking, multimedia presentations, and large-scale hypermedia. The specification of multimedia/hypermedia documents includes relationships such as temporal synchronization, dynamic interactive behavior, and hyperlinking. The use of data models is required in order to formally define the structure of the information, to efficiently map the structure to storage, and to support information creation and retrieval.

Consequently, there has been a growing interest in modeling multimedia and hypermedia information. We will use the term multimedia document in the broad sense to include any structured document that involves two or more different media types. We distinguish multimedia and hypermedia in that hypermedia documents combine multimedia and hyperlinking.

A number of researchers have developed object-oriented models for multimedia databases. For example, Woelk and Kim [16] developed a multimedia information manager based upon the Orion object-oriented database. One contribution of this work was the definition of a class hierarchy to represent the presentation and capture semantics of multimedia applications. However, temporal and hyperlink relationships were not considered in this model.

11.3.1 Temporal Relationships

Formal modeling of temporal relationships has been done by Little and Ghafoor [17,18,19]. The Object Composition Petri Net (OCPN) [17] discussed in Chapter 7 can be used to construct a database schema which contains the synchronization information between components of a document. The presentation algorithm builds a process tree which corresponds to the OCPN defined for the document. The binary temporal relationships in [17] are extended to n-ary in [19]; additionally, reverse playback and other temporal access control functions are supported. The playback algorithm for the extended model is used in the Virtual Video Browser [20], a prototype video-on-demand retrieval system that includes content-based retrieval facilities.

Temporal models are the focus of Chapter 7 and will not be discussed further here.

11.3.2 Hypermedia Document Models

A common approach to defining hypermedia document models has been to extend an existing text document model such as Standard Generalized Markup Language (SGML) [21] or Office Document Architecture (ODA) [22] to include hypermedia. We discuss thee models here: MMV, an extension of the Compound Document Architecture (CDA); the Amsterdam hypermedia model; and HyTime, an extension of SGML.

MMV

Multimedia Viewer (MMV) is a prototype extension of DEC's CDA to support synchronization and multimedia objects [23]. CDA is a superset of ODA, an ISO standard document structuring model which includes both logical and presentation format structuring information. ODA extensions to support hypermedia are currently being pursued by ISO under the project HyperODA. MMV introduces the concept of a *cue* to support synchronization between media and interactivity. A cue object embedded in a document consists of the triple *(name?, boolean-expression?, operation)*, where "?" denotes an optional field. The boolean expression is constructed to match an input event from the user or a media timing event. Initially the cue evaluates to the value false. When the boolean expression is satisfied, the associated operation is invoked and the cue value is set to true. Giving the cue a name allows other cue objects to reference it within their boolean expressions. The cue model can be interpreted as a finite state machine in which transitions are triggered on evaluation of cue boolean expression becoming true.

The Amsterdam Hypermedia Model

The Amsterdam Hypermedia Model (AHM) [24] is a merging of the Dexter hypertext reference model proposed by Frank Halasz and the CWI multimedia model (CWIF). The Dexter model and recent use of it are described in [25]. The extensions to the Dexter model proposed by the AHM are shown in Figure 11.4. There are two basic changes. First, component objects, which are the atomic units of composition, are associated with CWIF *channels*. A channel is an independently controlled viewing area for a specified component. Second, composites can specify synchronization relationships between components; the components do not have to be in the same composite.

HyTime

HyTime [26,27] or Hypermedia/Time-Based Structuring Language is an ISO standard for representing hypermedia documents using SGML. HyTime

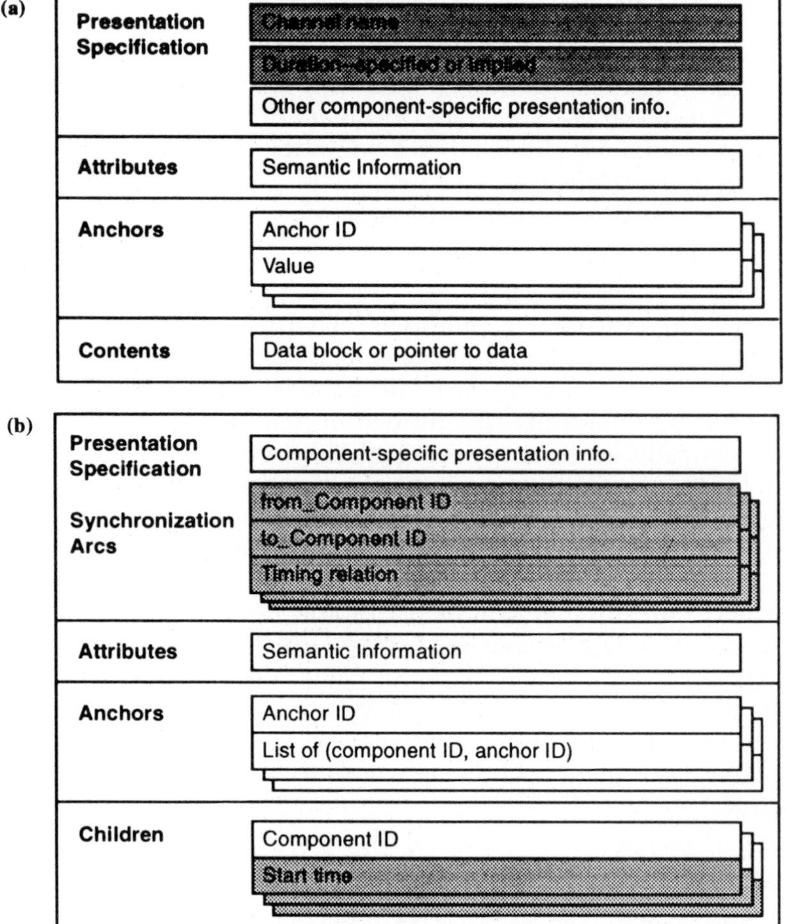

Figure 11.4 The Amsterdam Hypermedia Model extensions to the Dexter hypermedia model [24]; changes are highlighted. (a) component objects, (b) composite objects.

modeling concepts include the association of document objects with hyperlinks and the placement and interrelation of document objects according to coordinate systems which can represent space, time, or any quantifiable dimension. However, HyTime does not provide a model for interaction and, in keeping with the SGML philosophy, excludes presentation format modeling.

Hypermedia documents are not encoded in HyTime directly, but require a document type definition (DTD) which identifies the structural elements of the document. Thus, HyTime can be viewed as a meta-data model for defining an arbitrary number of multimedia document types, where each type would have its own DTD.

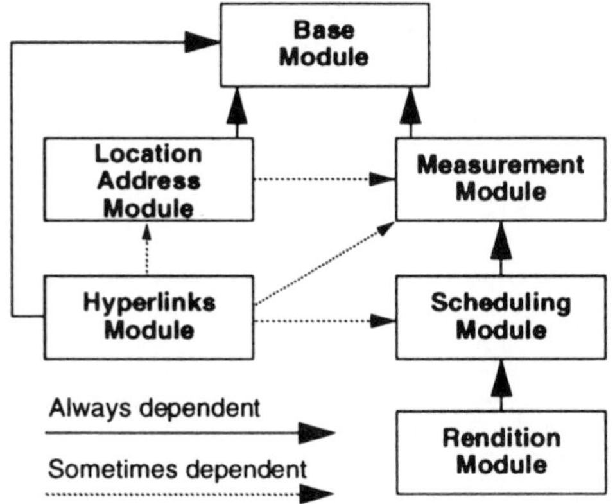

Figure 11.5 HyTime module interdependencies [27]

The HyTime architectural forms are grouped into seven modules (Figure 11.5). There is one required module, the base module. The **base module** specifies the architectural forms for specifying the root structure of the hyperdocument. The **measurement module** is used to represent concepts involving dimension, measurement, and counting. Dimensions can be defined which use particular units of measure, and document objects can be placed along these dimensions at particular locations.

The **location address module** provides a means of specifying locations in a hyperdocument which could not be specified by SGML. These include locating patterns in strings, specifying groups of objects as single locations, and locating objects with particular properties. The **hyperlinks module** provides two link templates for hyperlinking. The semantics of linking, link endpoints, and link types are controlled by the DTD designer and can be constructed using other HyTime facilities. The **scheduling module** places document objects in finite coordinate spaces (FCS), which are defined as collections of axes. Events are located on the axes of a finite coordinate space. The **rendition module** specifies how events in one finite coordinate space can be mapped to another finite coordinate space. For example, one FCS could represent a collection of document objects while the second FCS specifies the layout for a particular presentation of those objects.

The dependencies of the different modules are shown in Figure 11.5. An example HyTime DTD can be found in [28]. The architecture of a prototype retrieval engine for HyTime called HyOctane is shown in Figure 11.6. HyOctane stores the hypermedia document as a collection of objects in an object-oriented database. The first-level objects correspond to SGML elements and entities. The second-level objects correspond to the HyTime architectural forms. The top level stores the application objects as defined by the DTD. The HyOctane engine provides application services such as link management, location addressing, and scheduling.

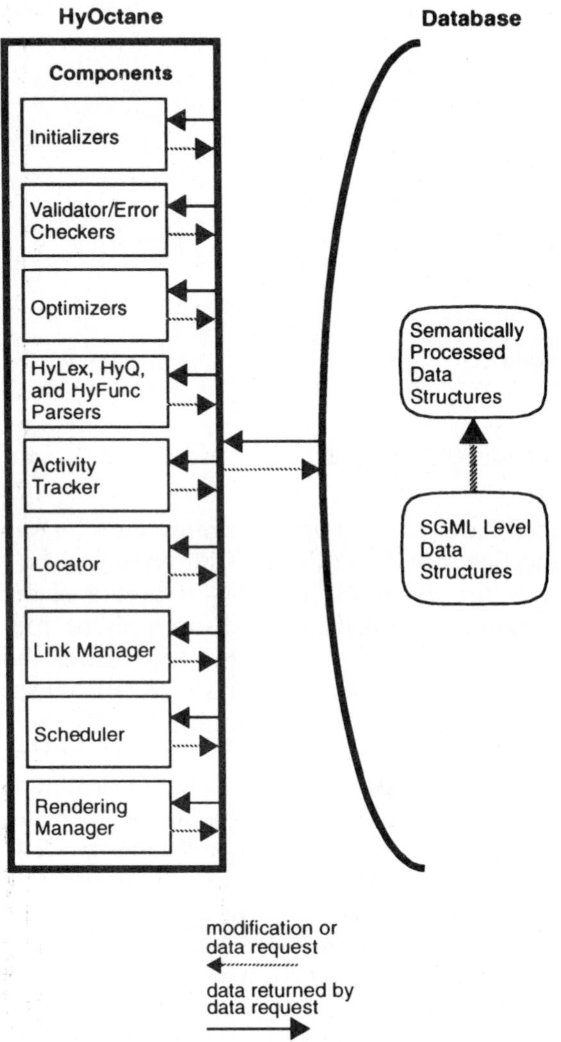

Figure 11.6 Architecture of the HyOctane HyTime engine [27]

11.4 CONTENT-BASED RETRIEVAL OF UNSTRUCTURED DATA

One of the advantages of storing multimedia documents in a database is the ease with which documents and their components can be associated with each other and shared with other users. Most databases and retrieval systems have powerful text search facilities, but current methods for searching content encoded using audio, image, or video are limited because of computational complexity and practical limits of knowledge representation techniques.

One approach is to use either manual methods or application-specific pattern recognition routines to extract text descriptions from the component media objects. These text descriptions can be stored in a database and can be incorporated into an existing information retrieval architecture. For example, [29] describes an approach to semantic modeling of multimedia documents in which multimedia content can be retrieved by searching the semantic model, logical model, or content. The Aegina system [30] integrates the FAIRS information retrieval system and the Athena Muse multimedia authoring environment. Search is performed on text information. Muse is used for constructing the user interface and supporting playback of multimedia content linked to text that has been matched in a query.

Another approach is to use Query-By-Example (QBE) techniques in which the user specifies graphical shapes or image characteristics. An extension to the MULTOS multimedia document system uses QBE for retrieval of graphical objects [31]. Queries can be entered by drawing the desired pattern in a graphical editor or text queries can be formulated through an application-specific interface. Hyperbook on Birds [32] is an electronic book, which has novel domain-dependent search facilities. A user can draw a silhouette of a bird to retrieve information about the bird families that match the pattern. A user can also provide a bird-call. The system uses the attributes sound power contour, fundamental frequency contour, and spectral changes to perform the match. Xenomania [33] is a face retrieval system, which allows the user to specify, via menu, facial attributes such as hair color and face shape which are then used to compute a similarity index with features that have been previously extracted by the image processing system.

11.5 SUMMARY

Current work on multimedia file systems has dealt with tradeoffs between the interrelated problems of disk layout, scheduling, buffering, and admissibility. A variety of configurations have been studied, principally with the goal of providing deterministic guarantees. The tradeoff between minimizing buffer space and maximizing the number of simultaneous sessions can also be seen. In addition to the experiment data that has been collected, at least one commercial system exists which validates many of these concepts [34]. The development of distributed multimedia information systems will require careful integration of the storage management system with network and presentation system resource management. This larger picture has not been discussed in this chapter, but is an active area of investigation [35,36,37,38].

The development of multimedia document architectures will have a strong interrelationship with authoring models. This interrelationship has not as yet received much attention. Practical content-based retrieval techniques for continuous media are likely to involve application-specific pattern recognition combined with application-defined content models.

11.6 ACKNOWLEDGMENTS

We appreciate the assistance of the following individuals in providing information used in the preparation of this chapter:

Richard Beckwith (University of London)

Thomas Casey (Cardiff Institute of Higher Education)

Kevin Daly (MCI)

Susan Howard (PictureTel)

11.7 REFERENCES

1. Englebart, D. C. A Conceptual Framework for the Augmentation of Man's Intellect. In P. W. Howerton and D. C. Weeks (eds.), *Vistas in Information Handling*. Spartan Books. 1963.
2. Englebart, D. C. and English, W. K. A Research Center for Augmenting Human Intellect. *AFIPS Conf. Proceedings. 1968 Fall Joint Computer Conference*. 1968.
3. Englebart, D. The Augmented Knowledge Workshop. *Proc. 1973 AFIPS National Computer Conference*. 1973.
4. Englebart, D. Knowledge-Domain Interoperability and an Open Hyperdocument System. *Proc. CSCW-90*. October 1990.
5. Berk, H. Xanadu. In E. Berk and J. Devlin (eds.), *Hypertext/Hypermedia Handbook*. McGraw-Hill. 1991. pp. 524–528.
6. Gemmell, J., and Christodoulakis, C. Principles of Delay-Sensitive Multimedia Data Storage and Retrieval. *ACM TOIS* (10) 1. January 1992.
7. Gemmell, J. Multimedia Network File Servers: Multi-Channel Delay Sensitive Retrieval. *ACM Multimedia '93*. 1993. pp. 243–250.
8. Anderson, David P., et al. A File System for Continuous Media. *ACM Trans. on Computer Systems* (10) 4. November 1992. pp. 311–337.
9. Yu, C., Sun, W., Bitton, D., Yang, Q., Bruno, R., and Tullis, J. Efficient Placement of Audio Data on Optical Disks for Real-Time Applications. *Communications of the ACM* (32) 7. July 1989. pp. 862–871.
10. Wells, J., Yang, Q., and Yu, C. Placement of Audio Data on Optical Disks. *Intl. Conf. on Multimedia Information Systems '91*. McGraw-Hill. 1991. pp. 123–134.
11. Rangan, P. Venkat, Vin, H. M., and Ramanathan, S. Designing an On-Demand Multimedia Service. *IEEE Communications Magazine*. July 1992.
12. Rangan, P. Venkat, and Vin, Harrick M. Efficient Storage Techniques for Digital Continuous Media. *IEEE Trans. on Knowledge and Data Engineering*. vol. 5, no. 4. August 1993. pp. 564–573.
13. Vin, H., and Rangan, P. V. Designing a Multiuser HDTV Storage Server. *IEEE J. on Sel. Areas in Comm.* vol. 11, no. 1. January 1993.
14. Lougher, P., and Shepherd, D. The Design of a Storage Server for Continuous Media. *The Computer Journal* (36) 1. 1993. pp. 32–42.
15. Chen, M.-T., Kandlur, D. D., and Yu, P. S. Optimization of the Grouped Sweeping Scheduling (GSS) with Heterogeneous Multimedia Streams. *ACM Multimedia 93*. 1993. pp. 57–64.
16. Woelk, D., and Kim, W. Multimedia Information Management in an Object-Oriented Database System. *Proc. 13th VLDB Conference*. 1987. pp. 319–329.
17. Little, T. D. C., and Ghafoor, A. Synchronization and Storage Models for Multimedia Objects. *IEEE J. on Sel. Areas in Communications*. vol. 8, no. 3. April 1990. pp. 413–427.
18. Little, T. D. C., and Ghafoor, A. Spatio-Temporal Composition of Distributed Multimedia Objects for Value Added Networks. *Computer*. vol. 24, no. 10. October 1991. pp. 42–50.

19. Little, T. D. C., and Ghafoor, A. Interval-Based Conceptual Models for Time-Dependent Multimedia Data. *IEEE Trans. on Knowledge and Data Engineering.* vol. 5, no. 4. August 1993. pp. 551–563.
20. Little, T. D. C., Folz, R. J., Reeve, F. W., Schelleng, D. H., and Venkatesh, S. D. A Digital Video-On-Demand Service Supporting Content-Based Queries. *ACM Multimedia '93.* August 1993. pp. 427–436.
21. Goldfarb, Charles F. *The SGML Handbook.* Oxford University Press. 1991.
22. Horak, W. Office Document Architecture and Office Document Interchange Formats: Current Status of International Standardization. *Computer.* vol. 18, no. 10. October 1985. pp. 50–60.
23. Herzner, W., and Kummer, M. MMV—Synchronizing Multimedia Documents: An Extension of CDA for Synchronization and Presentation of Mulimedia Documents. *Comput. & Graphics.* vol. 17, no. 3. 1993. pp. 229–241.
24. Hardman, L, Bulterman, D. C. A., and Rossum, G. V., The Amsterdam Hypermedia Model: Extending Hypertext to Support Real Multimedia. *Hypermedia.* vol. 5, no. 1. 1993. pp. 47–69.
25. Special Issue on Hypermedia. *Comm ACM.* January 1994.
26. ISO. ISO/IEC IS 10744, Hypermedia/Time-based Document Structuring Language (HyTime). August 1992.
27. Newcomb, Steven R. The "HyTime" Hypermedia/Time-based Document Structuring Language. *Communications of the ACM.* December 1991.
28. Koegel, J. F., Rutledge, L., Rutledge, J., and Keskin, C. HyOctane: A HyTime Engine for an MMIS. *ACM Multimedia '93.* August 1993. pp. 129–136.
29. Meghini, C., Rabitti, F., and Thanos, C. Conceptual Modeling of Multimedia Documents. *Computer.* vol. 24, no. 10. October 1991. pp. 23–32.
30. Chang, S., Phuah, V., Dediu, H., and Sasnett, R. A Distributed Multimedia Information Retrieval System. *International Conference on Multimedia Information Systems '91.* McGraw-Hill. 1991.
31. Constantopoulos, P., Drakopoulos, J., and Yeorgardoudakis, Y. Retrieval of Multimedia Documents by Pictorial Content: A Prototype System. *International Conference on Multimedia Information Systems '91.* McGraw-Hill. 1991. pp. 35–48.
32. Tabuchi, M., Yagawa, Y., Fujisawa, M., Negishi, A., and Muraoka, Y. Hyperbook: A Multimedia Information System That Permits Incomplete Queries. *International Conference on Multimedia Information Systems '91.* McGraw-Hill. 1991. pp. 3–16.
33. Bach, J. R., Paul, S., and Jain, R. A Visual Information Management System for the Interactive Retrieval of Faces. *IEEE Trans. on Knowledge and Data Engineering.* vol. 5, no. 4. August 1993. pp. 619–628.
34. Tobagi, F., Pang, J., Baird, R., and Gang, M. Streaming RAID™—A Disk Array Management System for Video Files. *ACM Multimedia '93.* August 1993. pp. 393–400.
35. Anderson, D. P., Homsy, G. A Continuous Media I/O Server and Its Synchronization Mechanism. *Computer.* vol. 24, no. 10. October 1991. pp. 51–57.
36. Little, T. D. C., and Ghafoor, A. Multimedia Synchronization Protocols for Broadband Integrated Services. *IEEE J. on Sel. Areas in Commun.* vol. 9. December 1991. pp. 1368–1382.
37. Ramanathan, S., and Rangan, P. V. Feedback Techniques for Intra-Media Continuity and Inter-Media Synchronization in Distributed Multimedia Systems. *The Computer Journal.* vol. 36, no. 1. 1993. pp. 19–31.
38. Blair, G. et al. A Network Interface Unit to Support Continuous Media. *IEEE J. on Sel. Areas in Communications.* vol. 11, no. 2. February 1993. pp. 264–275.

CHAPTER 12

MULTIMEDIA PRESENTATION AND AUTHORING

David S. Backer
Course Technology, Inc.

Easy-to-use tools for creating, manipulating, and presenting multimedia content will be an important factor in the utility of multimedia information. The digital representation of multimedia data simplifies many of the problems that have limited the use of analog audio and video editing systems to specialists. Yet interactive nonlinear time-based hypermedia data are still difficult and time-consuming to compose. The most powerful contemporary authoring tools use a programming paradigm to allow complex interaction and synchronization relationships to be defined. These programming facilities are typically provided through either a scripting language or an iconic visual programming interface. Individual media types are edited using separate media-specific editors. This chapter reviews the common approaches to multimedia authoring and presentation and discusses where future tools might be able to improve on the current tools.

12.1 OVERVIEW

Authoring and presentation systems are the software programs that allow people to create and deliver an experience for an end user (Figure 12.1). This experience can take many forms, from a computer-based training course to a room-sized presentation or a virtual-reality environment requiring head-

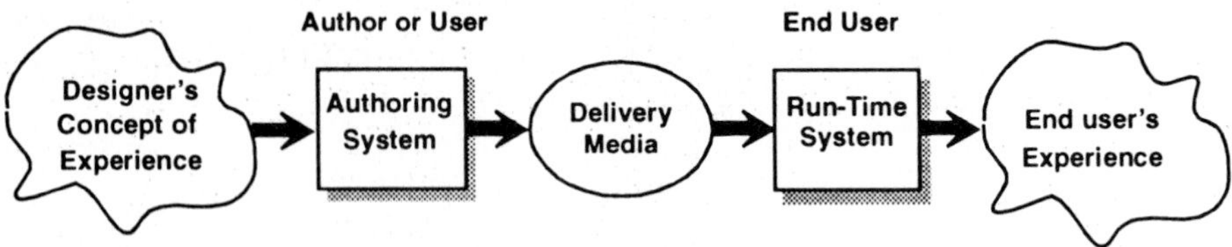

Figure 12.1 The authoring system versus the run-time system. The term "user" denotes the author or creator of the multimedia presentation, and the term "end user" denotes the consumer of the delivered presentation.

mounted displays and spatial input gloves. The common denominator across all of these forms is that the experience is an *interactive* one: The end user interacts with the programs on the computer by providing input (touching a screen, typing on a keyboard, or making a gesture in space, for example), which affects the output from the computer. This chapter surveys recent approaches to multimedia authoring and presentation that allow manipulation of diverse media forms through various modes of interaction.

Authoring and presentation systems are needed to create and present information on the computer because they provide an alternative to the custom programming of each end user experience, a process that is usually slow, complicated, and expensive. Although the range of options that can be created by custom programming may be greater than what can be created with authoring systems, the designers of the experience for the end user are less likely to be satisfied with the custom development process. Custom programming of an application requires that ideas for designs be translated and implemented by programmers, which is a rather indirect process, and one with a high probability for misunderstanding and frustration.

Authoring systems have been developed to give direct access to the tools for building an interactive experience to the designers who create the experience. Authoring systems provide ways to generate certain types of common interactions through the use of reusable templates or software modules, which can be customized by a designer for a particular objective. As an example, many training programs use a multiple choice question format. An authoring system can provide that format to a designer as a standard part of the system, which can be modified to produce many variations on the format.

There are differences between authoring and presentation packages because of the differences in their objectives and intended users. Authoring systems are designed to provide the tools for creating and organizing the data for a variety of media elements such as text, graphics, images, animations, audio, and video in order to produce an interactive application. Typically these applications are for education, professional training, public information kiosks, or retail marketing. The intended users of the software (the authors) are usually instructional designers—professionals who develop educational or marketing presentations—or graphic artists who make decisions about the graphic layout and style of interaction that the real end users (that is, students or individuals in the public) see and hear.

Authoring software is designed to support the creation of an interactive nonlinear experience in the sense that there are several pathways through the material, so the end user can make choices about where to go in the presentation, as well as how long to view each screen. The end user's choices are frequently referred to as *navigating*. Authoring software for training frequently supports testing of the end user, maintaining individual scores, and tracking the paths that users take through the material, known as courseware. There are often a variety of statistical reporting utilities included for the trainer as well. From a commercial standpoint, authoring systems tend to be more expensive than presentation systems, and often have one price for the full authoring environment plus a per copy or site license for a run-time playback-only module for each end-user machine.

Presentation packages are designed to suport the same media types, but without support for testing, scorekeeping, or tracking of end users. Some packages are intended for creation of simple linear presentations, which do not offer multiple pathways through the information. Presentation packages usually have a single price and simply offer different modes for creation and playback.

There are other software packages, which can be considered authoring systems in the broad sense of the term. Some [1,2,3] are intended for the creation of hypertext documents, the term coined by Ted Nelson [4] to mean nonsequential writing. These packages have certain features not necessarily found in training or presentation systems. These include the ability to make links from one place in a document to another, such as a reference to a textual term that can be activated as a hot button to take the reader to a full explanation of the term. Another feature is the capability to search all of the text in the entire document for all the occurrences of a specific word or phrase, known as indexed search.

New kinds of creation software are still being invented. Recent developments in the field called virtual reality[1] have produced systems that allow a user to interact with a simulated three-dimensional environment using computer systems that sense the user's position via cameras, gloves, or body-tracking devices. Three-dimensional modeling software, the authoring system for these environments, allows a developer to create the shapes, lighting, and behavior rules for the virtual environment. The end user navigates through the environment by spatial movement in real time.

Software also exists to manage a room-sized projection of a presentation containing text, graphics, audio, 35-mm slides, video from videodiscs, and input from a hand-held air mouse, all under computer control. While it is rare to find this type of equipment configuration, it illustrates the high end

---

1 Also artificial reality, coined by Prof. Myron Krueger.

of the presentation category, and the software required to orchestrate it is a type of presentation software as well.

There are so many software products on the market today that the distinctions between these categories has become somewhat blurred. All of these systems can be used to create similar experiences; the choice of which tool to use should be based on the characteristics of the experience that is to be created. There are also practical considerations in the decision, such as choice of computer platform(s), media types, and budget limitations for hardware and software.

The software and hardware technologies on which these systems are based span several markets and are all undergoing rapid change and advancement. The catalysts for their evolution are increasingly powerful personal computers and electronics for digital media, especially audio and video.

12.2 HISTORICAL EVOLUTION

Authoring systems for education and training have existed for many years. Early programs for creating educational materials on computers began in the 1960s with Control Data Corporation's mainframe-based Plato software and hardware. The Plato system spawned numerous descendants for mainframes and mini-computers. Many of the concepts still in use today are derived from these systems, though they have been changed significantly by the move to the personal computer. The inclusion of interactive video via analog videodisc for training courseware was an important part of the TICCIT (Time-shared Interactive Computer Controlled Information Television) instruction system, developed by the MITRE Corporation in conjunction with Brigham Young University in the early 1970s [5].

Software for the creation of presentations is relatively new compared to authoring systems. Early programs were developed in the late 1970s for creation of presentation slides or transparencies. Once the slides could be created with computer draw programs on desktop PCs, the presentation of the slides on the computer became possible, a technique that was made more practical by portable computers.

A problem that dogged early developers of multimedia, such as interactive videodisc programs, was a lack of standards. While the LaserVision videodisc itself had been established as a standard for several large manufacturers,[2] the interactive computer platforms required to use it were not

[2] Philips, Sony, Pioneer, Hitachi, and several other international manufacturers agreed on the LaserVison disc format, and discs created by one vendor would, in general, play on equipment made by another. There were and still are other incompatible disc formats.

standardized or even compatible. There were no standards to handle device control for developers who wanted to write device-independent software. There were no standards for handling computer graphics, color generation, or input devices; and there were no standards for the databases that developers created for courseware. A successful product on one platform had to undergo changes (sometimes extensive) before it could be delivered on another platform.

The standards problem was partially addressed over time as one vendor's approach became the de facto standard, such as IBM's InfoWindow videodisc system, and other vendors (such as Sony and Visage) developed emulator software to allow courseware designed for the de facto standard to operate transparently on their platforms.

The user interfaces for authoring systems have evolved in much the same way as the user interfaces for personal computers in the past decade or two. Initially, authoring systems were driven by text string input typed at a command prompt or into a data field. The process of constructing the structure and elements of a training course gradually became more menu-driven and then window-oriented until the mid-1980s when several systems pioneered an icon-based flowcharting approach (for example, Authorware and IconAuthor). Authors created the paths that a user could take by placing specific icon elements on a flow chart and linking them to other elements. This two-dimensional graphic design approach allowed authors to visualize and edit the course to match their designs. Individual screens were represented by elements in the flow chart (see Figure 12.2).

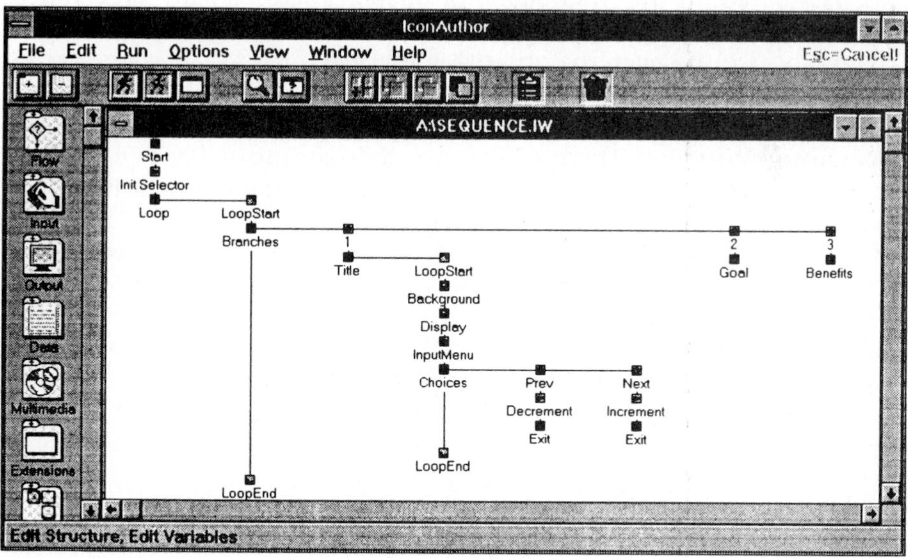

Figure 12.2 User interface for AimTech's IconAuthor, one of the first tools to provide an iconic flow chart or visual programming interface [6].

12.3 CURRENT STATE OF THE INDUSTRY

Authoring and presentation systems today provide a number of different models for developers to create and deliver experiences that use multiple media types.

12.3.1 Platforms and Recent Technologies

There are now three major computer platforms for the creation and delivery of multimedia applications: IBM PC compatibles running DOS, Microsoft Windows, or OS/2; the Apple Macintosh; and workstation-class computers with some variation of UNIX (Silicon Graphics, Sun, etc.). This set will expand with the introduction of new RISC-based PCs and other operating environments such as Microsoft Windows NT. The media display capabilities for all these platforms are improving very rapidly. In addition to support for the standard display types of text, graphics, and still images, there are new and powerful ways to create animations and to integrate sound and video (both analog and video).

12.3.2 IBM Compatibles

The largest percentage of the millions of personal computers in the field today are IBM PC compatibles. However, these are far from a uniform installed base of machines. The configurations range from high-performance PCs based on the Intel 80486 or 80386 processor with large system memory and hard disk capacity, to less powerful AT clones using the Intel 80286 processor, to even the original 8086-based IBM PC. The support for graphics, color, and sound varies tremendously.

The operating environment is largely DOS, but it is becoming dominated by Microsoft Windows. There is some growth in the use of IBM's OS/2. These factors have led to fragmentation in the industry that have made it difficult for developers to create multimedia applications.

An industry consortium known as the MPC Council was founded in 1991 in an effort to standardize the installed base. The council created a specification that defines a minimum feature set for a class of computers called the Multimedia Personal Computer or MPC. The members of the council[3] promote the manufacture of MPCs and the development of multimedia products that operate on MPCs. An MPC is defined to have at least the following features:

Intel 80386 SX processor

2 Mb system memory

---

[3] Including NEC, Tandy, Philips, Zenith, Olivetti, Fujitsu, and Microsoft.

30 Mb hard disk capacity and a high-density floppy disk drive
VGA graphics display and monitor
CD-ROM drive
Two-button mouse
8-bit digital audio input/output support
Microsoft Windows software

The MPC specification is important to users of authoring and presentation software because it wil guarantee that multimedia applications designed for the MPC platform will play successfully on *any* MPC machine. Recently an MPC-2 specification for a platform that supports video and audio has been published.

Apple Macintosh

The Apple Macintosh represents a significant portion of the installed base of personal computers. Like the IBM compatibles, these machines vary in configuration. But Apple has always had a well-unified development environment because of its control of the system software for its computers. It has also established a consistent baseline for multimedia developers through its QuickTime architecture, which provides a uniform interface for time-based media. Recent Macintoshes have had built-in support for 8-bit digital audio, high-resolution color graphics, and a mouse. Newer versions offer a built-in CD-ROM drive, and it is likely that 16-bit digital audio and digital video input and output will be supported soon.

Workstations

The workstation category covers numerous machines, most of which use a variant of UNIX and are based on a RISC microprocessor. There are different bus architectures and form factors. Although little has been done to standardize the hardware platform of these machines, several industry efforts such as COSE and the Interactive Multimedia Association are expected to lead to common system software and data exchange formats for multimedia.

Print-to-Videotape

Another means of delivery that has generated much activity is the ability to output computer screens as analog video or print-to-videotape. Analog videotape is an excellent means of publication and distribution because of the widespread availability of VCRs; however, the resulting presentation is of course **not** interactive. Nevertheless, the creation of videotapes for promotion and training is being transformed today in the same way that document publication was transformed by desktop publishing, by the personal computer and laser printers in the mid-1980s.

Presentation software packages can be used to create, control, and record all the various multimedia elements onto standard videotape at higher quality than has been previously available at desktop computer prices. This brings most of the tape development process to an individual's desktop and can decrease production costs considerably.

CD-ROM

The digital alternative to videotape is CD-ROM, which provides large random access storage for computer data for interactive presentations on personal computers. The cost of a CD-ROM drive has dropped dramatically. New-generation drives have also been improved to offer playback of CD-audio and higher data transfer rates, which are critical to the delivery of full-motion video from CD-ROM. As a result, the growth of CD-ROM titles intended for use via PCs has been dramatic in the past few years.

There are also low-cost CD-based delivery systems for consumer and home entertainment (see Chapter 2). Video game companies such as SEGA and Nintendo have also marketed CD-ROM-based systems. Each of these appliances has its own authoring tools and run-time software for playback of multimedia content. In some cases, such as the Tandy VIS system, the authoring software operates on a desktop PC.

12.4 DESIGN PARADIGMS AND USER INTERFACES

12.4.1 Authoring Systems

Many authoring systems are based on the model that one or more authors will create the design and enter the media elements for an experience with which an end user will interact. The result of the authoring process is a structure of elements, linked in various paths determined by the author(s). This structure appears to the end user as a series of screens containing information in various forms and interactive options available through buttons, icons or keystrokes.

This model is translated into separate and distinctly different interfaces for the author and the end user. The author's interface typically has a suite of on-screen tools available through menus, icons, text prompts, or other options, which can be invoked to create and place elements on the screen. The end-user's interface is defined by the elements that the author has invented. For example, a screen that includes text in paragraphs, a scanned image, and audio segments may have hot buttons or sensitive regions on the screen that the end user can select to interact with the screen elements, navigate to other parts of the presentation, or simply get help.

Implicit in this model has been the idea that the end user will not add to or modify the content of the experience and, in fact, will interact with it only on the terms set by the author(s). While this approach has been common, it does not necessarily provide the end user with the most effective experience. One of the trends in new software is the support annotation and personalization by the end user, especially for training.

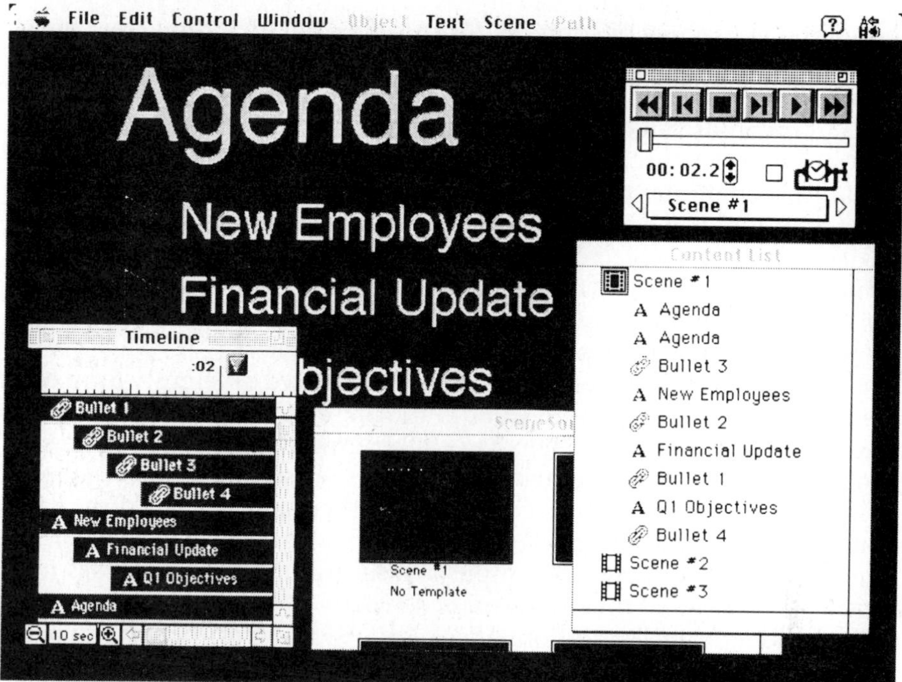

Figure 12.3 Creation environment for Macromedia Action!

12.4.2 Presentation Systems

Commercial presentation packages such as Aldus Persuasion and Lotus Freelance allow novice users to create presentations using text, graphics, scanned images, and animations with only minimal training. Presentations are typically linear sequences of information, so the interfaces for users have often been organized along the time dimension. However, presentations on the computer do not have to be limited to sequential display. Current presentation packages allow users to construct interactive, i.e., nonlinear, presentations that more closely resemble those produced by conventional authoring systems.

The requirement to deal more explicitly with the time dimension became even stronger as time-based media such as audio and video segments became available for presentations. New user interface metaphors were developed to allow users to organize their material along these lines. Packages such as Macromedia Director or Action! use a timeline metaphor with a read head for choreographing the elements in a display (Figure 12.3).

12.4.3 Power versus Ease of Use

For both presentation and authoring systems, there is a dilemma about how to balance the ease of use with power and flexibility. Making the software extremely easy to learn and use risks restricting an experienced author or limiting the interactive possibilities for the end user. Providing great flexibility and power risks making the software difficult to master. One of the solutions has been the combining of simple screen construction tools, similar to menu-driven draw programs with scripting languages. Scripting is a way of associating a script, a set of commands written in a form resembling a computer program, with an interactive element on a screen, such as a button. Some examples of scripting languages are Apple's HyperTalk for HyperCard, Macromedia's Lingo for Director, and Asymetrix' OpenScript for Toolbook (Figure 12.4). This combination allows novice users to begin working quickly on a presentation while allowing more advanced users to create sophisticated custom behaviors.

There are other basic issues that have been addressed differently from one system to another. For example, some authoring systems use two computer screens rather than one. This removes clutter from the presentation screen by moving the authoring activites to the second screen. It also requires switching attention from one screen to the other, and it adds to the cost and complexity of the authoring station.

Another issue is the means of input for the end user. Public kiosks rely almost exclusively on touchscreens or keypads. A mouse is simply not practical under normal conditions of use. Professional training systems may offer support for a mouse, a touchscreen, or even a tablet-and-stylus combination. Home entertainment systems such as Philips' CD-I machine provide a hand-held input device that combines the functionality of a

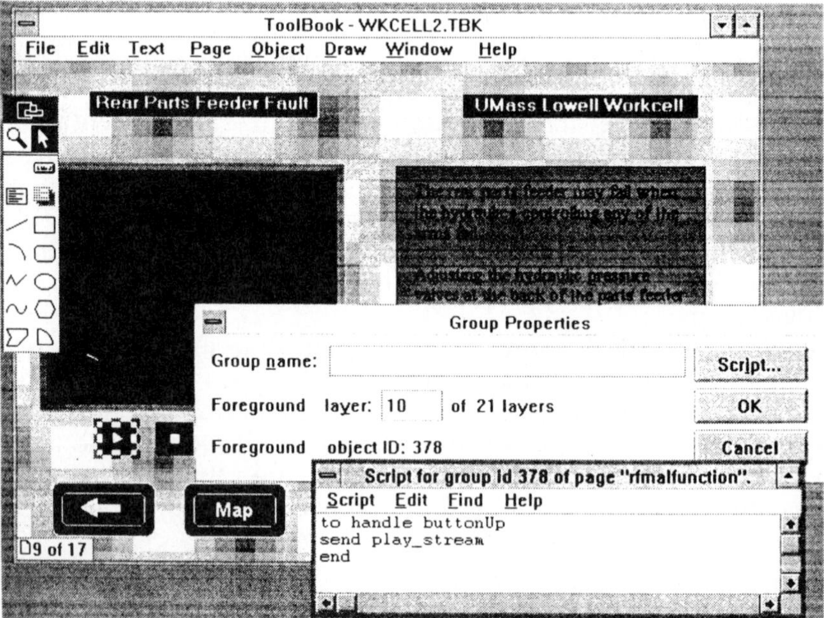

Figure 12.4 Toolbook OpenScript

remote control unit and a joystick. The best interface for a user is never an absolute, but a function of the intended user and operating platform.

12.4.4 Media Creation Tools

Creators of multimedia experience need tools to generate original data or import it from an external source for each of the media types supported by the system. In the mid-1980s a number of developers including MacroMind (now Macromedia) promoted the concept of domain editors[4]—applications for generating or capturing data of different types such as text, animations, audio, etc. In the past, these media editing tools were often proprietary and could only be used with one authoring system. The user interfaces and features varied widely from one vendor to another.

Today the trend is for authoring systems to allow authors to create and capture data using mainstream software packages and import the results into their presentation. For example, text can be entered and edited via a favorite word processor, then accepted by the authoring system. Still images can be scanned into the system using a variety of off-the-shelf hardware and software, then imported as standard elements in a presentation. There are many "paint" packages that can be used to create and import bit-mapped graphic images in the same way.

This importing approach allows authors to use familiar tools to reduce learning time and to promote the sharing of resources. It also relieves the developers of authoring systems from the effort of maintaining and enhancing dedicated (and usually hardware specific) tools in their own applications. Industry standards for media formats have also made it much easier for users to transfer material between tools.

There are other ancillary tools for creating presentation elements such as photographic retouching, animation, and video editing. Animation tools have raised designers' awareness of dynamic or temporal techniques and have led to new sets of design rules for choreographing multiple elements in time as well as in screen space. Industry standard programming interfaces for multimedia data types (such as Microsoft's Media Control Interface and Apple's QuickTime) are helping to make such tools commonplace.

12.5 EXAMPLE INTERFACES

12.5.1 Asymetrix Toolbook

Figure 12.4 shows an editing session in Toolbook to build a multimedia repair manual in which the end user can browse through video clips of fault

[4] Presentation by Marc Cantor, founder of MacroMind, at LaserActive Conference, Fall 1986, Boston, Massachusetts.

and repair sequences related to the problem at hand. The user of Toolbook constructs a "book," which consists of a series of pages. Each page may have one or more objects, such as buttons, graphics, and text. Interactivity is provided by associating a script with an object that the end user can select. The Toolbook scripting language, called OpenScript, is object-oriented in the sense that scripts are associated with a specific object and scripts are activated using message passing. Figure 12.4 shows a very small script associated with the selected play button. When a buttonUp event occurs, the script initiates a play video stream that has previously been initialized by another script.

Toolbook operates in two modes: author and view. While in author mode, objects can be created and edited using the Toolbook menus and tools. The Toolbook graphics tool is also shown in Figure 12.4. When in view mode, the author can execute the application and test its behavior.

12.5.2 AimTech IconAuthor

Figure 12.2 shows the editing interface for IconAuthor. The main work area contains a sample presentation flow chart. The icons in the flow chart are instances of the icons in the icon catalog on the left side of the editor. The parameters associated with an icon are editable via a dialogue box, which is displayed when the icon is selected. There are additional editors for creating text, graphics, and animations.

IconAuthor has no scripting language per se, but uses a visual programming approach to define interaction and flow of control. The icon set corresponds closely to actions found in conventional programming languages, with additional icons for media-specific presentation and interaction.

The graph in Figure 12.2 (partially expanded) represents a sequential presentation in which each screen or slide has a forward and backward button. The author interactively constructs the flow chart by dragging icons from the catalog to the work area and then editing the associated menus to define the appropriate parameters. Since the graph can become quite large, several ways to control the display of the graph are provided, including zooming and selective concealment of subgraphs.

The author can review the presentation by running part or all of the current graph.

12.5.3 Authorware Professional

Authorware Professional uses an iconic visual programming interface, which is noted for the small but powerful number of icons. Figure 12.5 shows a demonstration application provided with Authorware Professional (AP). Using the controls on the left, the end user can change the animation of the engine. This type of model-based presentation is difficult to construct because of the interdependency of the different parameters and the com-

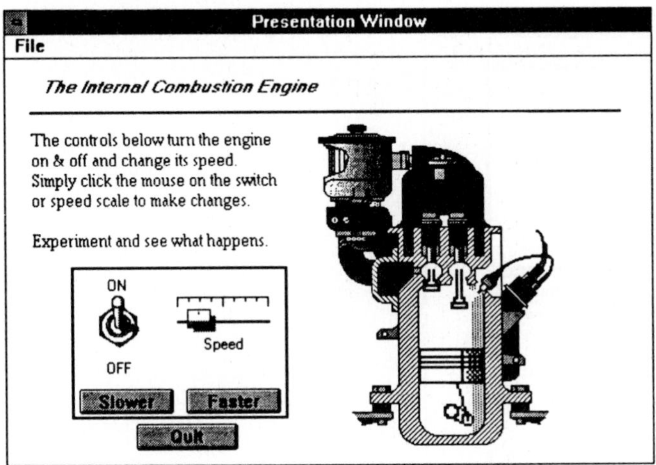

Figure 12.5 One of the Authorware Professional sample applications which shows the power of interactivity in teaching complex processes. The motion of the engine piston and valves is controlled by the user using the interaction area on the left.

plexity of the system being simulated. Figure 12.6 shows the graph and editing interface for this presentation. AP controls graph complexity by providing a small number of icon types and limiting the number of icons that can appear on a window. This latter technique forces the author to build the composition hierarchically. The resulting structured graph can be easier to navigate and understand than a flat single-level graph.

A detailed comparison of the visual programming approaches used by IconAuthor and Authorware Professional can be found in [6].

12.6 BARRIERS TO WIDESPREAD USE

In spite of recent advances in hardware and software technology, there are still substantial barriers to the widespread use and success of authoring and presentation systems. These issues are discussed in the following subsections:

Cost of acquisition, development, and delivery of multimedia material

Difficulties with production quality

Enforcement of intellectual property rights

Cost, availability, and ease of use of tools

Lack of standards for delivery and interchange

Lack of a clear vision for multimedia applications

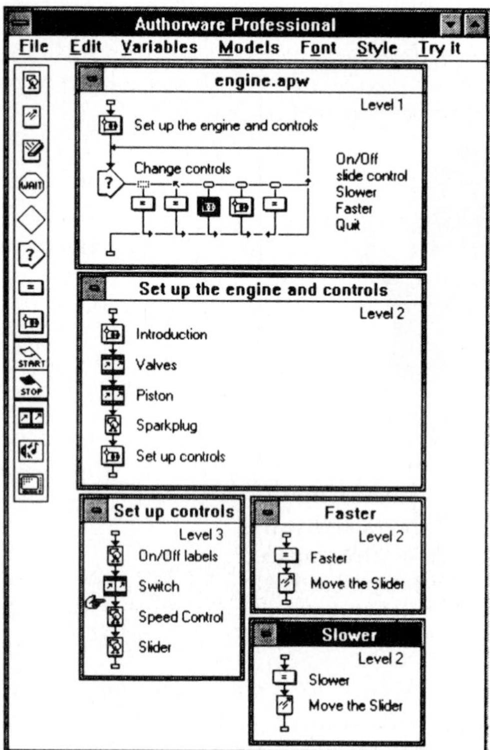

Figure 12.6 Flow chart graph corresponding to Figure 12.5. The graph is constructed hierachically. Level 1 icons expand to level 2 windows; level 2 icons expand to level 3 windows; etc. Each icon has an additional menu that is used to set parameters for the icon instance.

12.6.1 Cost of Acquisition, Development, and Delivery of Multimedia Material

Multimedia applications often require a number of different professionals and a range of content materials. The costs for planning, producing, and delivering these applications can be high. The primary factors are costs for labor (personnel) and production of graphics, video, and audio. Archival material owned by third parties is typically expensive. High costs for delivery are due to the equipment required at the end user's site and, to a lesser extent, the distribution media itself. Deployment of large multimedia applications such as interactive videodisc training systems may require customers to purchase large amounts of upgrade equipment or even entirely new computer systems.

Improvements have occurred in both production tools and delivery environments. Software applications are now available to help a developer plan, track, and integrate the multiple information types involved. These tools can boost productivity and help reduce the number of people and overall number of hours required for development. As certain products become industry standards, it is likely that developers can be found who are already familiar with the authoring tools selected for the project, reducing the time required for staff training. Similarly, as discussed in Chapter 2, platform costs have dropped while functionality and storage have increased. CD-ROMs can now be economically produced in-house using write-once CD-ROM technology.

12.6.2 Difficulties with Production Quality

A major issue related to cost of development has been that of production quality for multimedia materials. High-quality video or audio can be expensive because of the need for professional equipment and facilities (such as sound stages and editing suites) and contract employees to create the audio or video. If developers create the materials on their own without professional equipment or contract producers, the quality may not meet the users' expectations.

This situation is changing because of the technology. Equipment for recording high-quality video such as SVHS and Hi-8-mm camcorders is now much more accessible to developers. Digital Audio Tape (DAT) recorders can handle better than CD audio quality. Capture and edit tools for these media are available as off-the-shelf PC products today. Current development limitations include inadequate lighting and recording facilities.

12.6.3 Enforcement of Intellectual Property Rights

Due to the significant investment needed to obtain multimedia materials and the large potential value of such information, policies and mechanisms for enforcement of intellectual property rights are needed. Otherwise, owners of such materials will be reluctant to make them available for use in multimedia applications. The growing power of tools for manipulating digital media makes it easier for new content to be derived from existing content.

12.6.4 Cost, Availability, and Ease of Use of Tools

More software tools have become available for designing and delivering multimedia productions, but problems still exist. Some applications cost several thousand dollars to purchase, and many require substantial learning time for a developer to become a proficient and productive user. As noted earlier, the more powerful a tool is, the more difficult it is to become an expert. Ease of use will continue to be an important research issue, as discussed later in this chapter.

12.6.5 Lack of Standards for Delivery and Interchange

The same process that settled the standards issue for videodisc developers may solve the notable fragmentation of delivery platforms that exists today. As noted in Chapter 3, there are many activities underway, from formal standards organizations to industry consortia to vendor-driven. Without such standards, the fragmented market will make it harder to attract publishers of multimedia materials.

12.6.6 Lack of a Clear Vision for Multimedia Applications

Today there seems to be tremendous interest in all aspects of multimedia, and early adopters are creating prototypes and innovative products. However, there is still a need for better understanding of the potential of new interactive media in areas such as business communications and mass market entertainment, particularly with regard to the forms these new media need to take. The new products and services being developed today are causing the most important transition in the industry: the raised awareness of both developers and users of the power and importance of the new media.

12.7 RESEARCH TRENDS

12.7.1 WYSIWYG Multimedia Document Editing

As the new media types become better integrated into user interface toolkits and window systems (see Chapter 10), direct manipulation of all media types should become the norm for constructing the multimedia document. MediaView [7] is a prototype authoring system in which any media object can be inserted and edited into a document. These operations are achieved using drag-and-drop style of interaction.

12.7.2 Better Integration of Tools and Distributed Resources

Most commercial authoring systems, limited by the platforms on which they reside, access only local media. But sharing of content and multimedia equipment provides a number of advantages. MAEstro [8] is an example of an authoring environment in which a set of media editing tools have been integrated and which can access media resources located anywhere on a network. Underlying MAEstro's set of applications is a messaging system based on remote procedure calls (RPCs), which enables this distributed access.

GainMomentum is a high-end commercial authoring system, which is built on top of a distributed database management system. This type of coupling between the authoring system and the information system is necessary if multimedia information is to become the norm of organizations' operations.

12.7.3 Logical Structure of Presentation

Several researchers [9,10,11] have observed that today's authoring paradigms do not make the logical structure of the multimedia experience explicit except in trivial ways. The structuring paradigms are too closely related to programming models. The TRAIN-System [9] allows logical markup of hypermedia documents using an SGML-like syntax. The CMIF authoring environment [10] provides three simultaneous views of the authoring process: hierarchical structure editing, media control (channel) editing, and playback. The hierarchical structure editing allows the user to view the overall structure of the presentation; detailed timings are partially derived by the system and can be refined by the author later.

12.7.4 Integrated Rapid Storyboarding

The authoring process typically starts with a storyboard [11], which lays out the general organization and content of the presentation. The storyboard evolves as the media are collected and organized; new ideas and refinements to the presentation are added as the presentation takes shape. The author/artist replays parts of the presentation during this refinement process.

Current tools could be improved by providing an interface model which fits this authoring process. There are three conceptual levels in which an author works:

1. Storyboard
2. Media selection and layout
3. User input and flow of control

Each of these is parallel in time and could be represented as a parallel track in which time is in the horizontal direction. The storyboard track would permit freehand drawing of a series of panels for rapid prototyping of the story concept. The media layout track shows the corresponding presentation sections and is gradually populated by the author with pictures, video windows, text, graphics, and interaction areas as the story evolves. Typically, a storyboard panel would expand into a number of presentation panels. The control track could use a visual programming graph or a scripting language to define the input and link associations for the media layout track.

12.7.5 Tools for Constructing 3-D Virtual Worlds

Most authoring systems are limited to integrating 2-D time-based media. As 3-D graphics become more widely supported, techniques that simplify the construction of 3-D virtual worlds will be needed. One approach is to provide a set of 3-D icons to use as the building blocks of the world [12]. The user constructs the world by combining the icons in a script or graph and uses ancillary menus to parameterize the icons.

12.8 SUMMARY

Easy-to-use tools for creating, manipulating, and presenting multimedia content will be an important factor in the creation of multimedia materials by nonspecialists. The digital representation of multimedia data simplifies many of the problems that have limited the use of existing systems. The most powerful contemporary authoring tools use a programming paradigm to allow complex interaction and synchronization relationships to be defined. This approach will be supplanted by paradigms that are more visual in nature and which allow the author to focus on the conceptual level of the presentation. The concept of the multimedia document will likely also evolve as new interaction modes and media appear.

12.9 ACKNOWLEDGMENTS

Screen captures for Figures 12.6 and 12.7 were provided by Prof. Jesse M. Heines.

12.10 REFERENCES

1. Conklin, J. Hypertext: An Introduction and Survey. *IEEE Computer*. September 1987.
2. Akscyn, R., McCracken, D. L., and Yoder, E. A. KMS: A Distributed Hypermedia System for Managing Knowledge in Organizations. *Communications of the ACM* 7(31). 1988. pp. 820–835.
3. Halasz, F. Reflections on Notecards: Seven Issues for the Next Generation of Hypermedia Systems. *Communications of the ACM* 7(31). 1988. pp. 836–855.
4. Nelson, Theodor H. The Hypertext. *Proc. of the World Documentation Federation*. 1965.
5. Bennion, J. L. Possible Applications of Optical Videodiscs to Individualized Instruction. Tech. Report #10. Institute for Computer Uses in Education. Brigham Young University. February 1974.
6. Koegel, J. F., and Heines, J. M. Improving Visual Programming Languages for Multimedia Authoring. In H. Maurer (ed.), *Proc. of ED-MEDIA '93*. Assoc. for the Advancement of Computing in Education. June 1993. pp. 286–293.

7. Philips, R. L. MediaView: A General Multimedia Digital Publication System. *Communications of the ACM*. July 1991.
8. Drapeau, G., and Greenfield, H. MAEstro—A Distributed Multimedia Authoring Environment. *Proc. of USENIX Summer 1991*. June 1991.
9. Augestein, F., Ottmann, T., and Schoening, J. Logical Markup for Hypermedia Documents: The TRAIN-System. In H. Maurer (ed.), *Proc. of ED-MEDIA '93*. Assoc. for the Advancement of Computing in Education. June 1993. pp. 17–25.
10. Hardman, L., van Rossum, G., and Bulterman, D. Structured Multimedia Authoring. *Proc. ACM Multimedia 93*. August 1993. pp. 283–289.
11. Koegel, J. F., Rutledge, J. L., and Heines, J. Visual Programming Abstractions for Interactive Multimedia Authoring. *Proc. IEEE 1992 International Workshop on Visual Languages*. September 1992.
12. Lingua Graphica. *Proc. IEEE 1992 International Workshop on Visual Languages*. September 1992.

CHAPTER 13

Multimedia Services over the Public Network: Requirements, Architectures, and Protocols

Prodip Sen
NYNEX Science and Technology

13.1 Introduction

This chapter is primarily concerned with issues involved in offering advanced services over the public network to support multiuser, multipoint, and multimedia applications. Such applications have combinations of several unique characteristics: presentation of multiple media, management and transport of multiple media streams, distributed access to multiple media, large bandwidth requirements, low latency bulk data transfer, and multipoint communications. Should we address the problems by using end-stations with sophisticated capabilities and a "dumb" (but high bandwidth) network, or should we use "dumb" end-stations (the extreme example being a television and a phone) and an intelligent network? Discussions about these issues tend to get religious, but clearly there is no general answer. The choice should be dictated by the specific circumstances and is largely a business decision depending on issues such as cost and reliability of service. For any given situation, the real answer lies in-between these two extremes.

Network-based solutions seem to be most appropriate for a moderate size community of endpoints (users, data sources, as well as data sinks), where the connection requirements are dynamic. If we accept this, the next question that arises is whether the services required should be provided on private or public networks. Again, the decision depends on the circumstances, and the specific economics have to be considered. Where the set of user sites to be connected is dynamic and relatively large, and where organizational and institutional boundaries need to be crossed, public network-based solutions seem to be the most viable.

In reality, if experience with past and present communication is to be any guide, all the above arrangements have to be provided for. Recall the LAN/digital PBX/Centrex debate and many others like it. The public network has to provide a range of services and functionality to meet this goal. The development of network-based services in this environment is quite a challenge, since traditional networks have not been designed to address these issues. New architectures, protocols, and services are required. Some of these are emerging, though not all the issues have been worked out.

In the next section we list various industries where the demand for such applications is high. Next we consider a specific case study in the health-care industry. This case study is related to the NYNEX field trial for multimedia communications in healthcare, discussed in Chapter 1, and will be used here to discuss a set of detailed application requirements and the ensuing network service requirements. The subsequent sections will discuss network services, architectures, and protocols to support these.

13.2 APPLICATIONS

13.2.1 Application Requirements

The class of end-user applications we are considering include video-conferencing, multimedia information access, shared multimedia workspace, and collaborative design. The industries where such applications are being considered are as varied as healthcare, education, manufacturing, training, financial, and entertainment. The benefits of multimedia and broadband communications have been amply covered in the literature. For a discussion of the strategic benefits of broadband communications to some of these industries, see for instance [1].

We will focus on health-care applications to review the requirements that are imposed on the network services. Some typical applications in this field are: review of medical reports, medical report generation, teleradiology, remote pathology, surgical planning, and remote consultation. These applications readily lead to the unique characteristics mentioned in the introduction.

Review of Medical Reports: A typical medical report folder has text, images, charts, graphs, etc. If this is to be replaced by an electronic medical record, there is a need for simultaneous access to text, databases, images in various formats, and stored video (in case of cardiology and obstetric applications).

Medical Report Generation: This has much the same needs as the review application. The additional needs are access to audio (for report recording) and live video (sonogram applications).

Teleradiology: The main requirements here are that of high-speed large-image transfer (10–50 Mb/s) as well as access to audio.

Remote Pathology: Control channels are required for remote manipulation of image views.

Surgical Planning: This combines the needs of teleradiology and remote pathology.

Remote Consultation: Additional requirements in this case are the ability to share information among users, access to collaboration aids, and audio and/or video conferencing.

A view of these and other applications can be found in [2]. For a survey of a set of trials which NYNEX has pursued with various medical institutions over the last few years in the Boston metropolitan area, see [3].

13.2.2 Case Study: Report/Review/Consult

We shall use the Report/Review/Consult application system developed jointly by NYNEX Science and Technology and the Children's Hospital in Boston (as part of the trials mentioned above) to be the primary focus for a detailed discussion of the requirements below. We shall just touch upon the nature of the requirements. For details on the system that was implemented, see [4].

This system has to address the requirements of three main work processes at the hospital, namely:

Reporting: Creating a medical report based on the interpretation of an image-based examination;

Reviewing: Review of the medical report by other imaging specialists, clinicians, surgeons, etc.;

Consultation: Simultaneous review of the medical report by two or more physicians.

The following sections discuss the requirements for each of these processes in some detail.

13.2.3 Case Study: The Medical Reporting Process Requirements

The reporting process induces the following requirements.

Information Access: The reporting physician needs access to patient information such as demographics, identification, and referral notes. This information is stored in hospital or departmental databases. Access is required to images acquired during the examination being interpreted as well as images acquired in previous exams. (In the particular case under consideration these were nuclear medicine images.) Retrieval of images from examinations performed with other modalities (in the particular case these would be computerized tomography or magnetic resonance studies) is also highly desirable for diagnostic purposes. Such images are stored in a variety of file systems and formats, depending on the equipment used to acquire them. Thus, to summarize, access to databases, file systems, and imaging devices is required along with support for handling images in a variety of formats. In addition, there is a need to store and manage relationships between pieces of information, which are stored and managed in a distributed manner.

Information Presentation: Various image display modes are required. Examples are single and multiple image views, video view of image sequences, 3-D views, and support for display of varying resolution. The textual/database information described above has to be presented to the reporting physician. In addition, audio annotation and/or reports have to be available. There is clearly a need for mechanisms to transfer and coordinate the presentation of combinations of information in different media, with different granularities. The ability to handle large data chunks in short periods of time is also apparent—the smallest requirement being the retrieval of a set of thirty 128 by 128 pixel images with 8 bits/pixel, in one second. The ensuing bandwidth requirements vary from 4 to 126 Mb/s, depending on the image modalities to be supported. See, for example, the tables in [1] for details. Image compression may reduce these requirements a bit, but not significantly, since lossy compression is unacceptable for most medical scenarios and because of the low latency response time required. In most other application areas, however, compression is acceptable for both image and video transmission and will lead to significant reductions in the bandwidth requirements. This is especially the case in video conferencing.

Information Manipulation and Processing: Information manipulation and enhancement tools are required. Contrast enhancement and thresholding, image fusion between image sets, 3-D rendering from planar image studies, and the ability to support visual image directories, are some of the requirements on image manipulation. Text editing facilities, as well as audio record and playback facilities, are required for report creation. The audio needs to be stored in a manner that transcriptionists can access from the transcription system (via telephones). They can then transcribe the reports using word processing tools. The reports are then to be stored as part of the text report. (Future systems could involve voice recognition technologies to attempt this voice-to-text transfer.) State information of the reporting process as applied to the individual components (text, image, audio) of the report is required. Access to input and output facilities such as scanners and printers is also required. Apart from the need for end-station presentation tools, there is clearly a need for facilities to coordinate storage of the various media components and maintain automated transfer mechanisms between these. In certain cases there is a need for access to network-based processing facilities such as audio processing and computationally intensive processing (e.g., 3-D rendering).

13.2.4 Case Study: The Medical Reviewing Process Requirements

The reviewing process induces much the same requirements as the reporting process mentioned above. The differences have to do with restrictions on manipulation and view rights for the information components accessed. Security and confidentiality of information are of prime concern here.

13.2.5 Case Study: The Medical Consultation Process Requirements

In addition to the access, presentation, and manipulation requirements of the reporting and reviewing processes, the consultation process adds the following.

Conferencing: The consulting health-care professionals should be able to communicate with each other via audio and/or video in real time. The number of participants is typically two, but could be as many as three or four. If the preferred mode is audio, the end device should support this connection as well as regular telephony. Normally the video requirements of video telephony (64–128 Kb/s) should suffice, and the quality of voice is perceived as more important than the video quality. In special circumstances, however, for instance remote obstetrics (ultrasound), higher quality is required (TV quality or better, requiring tens of Mb/s).

Information Sharing: The information comprising a report has to be simultaneously accessible to the parties to the consultation. Changes in the presentation of the information by one party should be immediately communicable to the other participants. This includes image, text, and audio presentation. Examples in the image presentation are panning, image selection from a set, and changes in video display speeds of image sequences. Note that the information involved is not private information maintained by one party, but rather institutional information, stored and managed on an institutional or departmental basis. However, there are issues of ownership and access rights involved which have to be addressed.

Collaboration Environment: During consultation changes in the content of the information or other manipulation by the physician should be immediately communicable to the other participants. Examples are image enhancements and text and audio edits. Modification rights for users have to be maintained and used. In addition to these requirements is the availability of network-wide collaboration aids such as markers, pointers, and whiteboards.

13.2.6 Impact on Network Service Architecture

The detailed discussion of application requirements in the previous sections can be summarized as follows. End users need to access multiple media information, which is stored in a distributed manner on a variety of systems. They need access to large amounts of information in a timely fashion and require the ability to manipulate this information and have access to remote processing capabilities. They need to share this information with one or more users and collaborate with them using the shared information. Security and access control relative to the information are also needed.

Based on the details presented earlier, these applications typically require a network-based solution. An exception would be the simplest case of just two parties trying to communicate with private (i.e., noninstitutional) data stored on the end-stations. These can be special applications tailored to the individual organizations or communities of interest, as is the case for the health-care example considered above. Alternatively, they can be generic applications such as multimedia file transfer, multimedia conferencing, multimedia mail, and multimedia information retrieval services. They can be offered by special service providers or integrators or be provided (especially in the generic application case) by network providers as value-added services. The specific mix will depend on the specific instances, environments, and industries.

Irrespective of the specific choice made on how to offer these end-application services, the network has to offer a variety of underlying services and mechanisms to support them. The appropriate architecture is a layered, modular structure for the services together with an open architecture for the interfaces. This will allow access to various levels of service according to the specific application service arrangements. The following is a categorization which is derived from the NYNEX experience with the trials mentioned earlier.

Advanced call services: Services for collaboration; distributed access to multiple media; management and control of multipoint, multiuser, and multichannel connections; security and privacy control.

Access services: Services for user access to high bandwidth data transport mechanisms over wide area networks.

Transport services: The underlying transport and switching mechanisms within the network, to support the network access services.

The advanced call services and access services are also referred to as *teleservices* and *bearer services* in some of the international standardization activities. For a related view of such decompositions and rationales, as well as a discussion of application-induced requirements on network services, see [5].

The next section will discuss these layers in some detail.

13.3 NETWORK SERVICES

13.3.1 Architecture

In this section we will present a general service architecture for supporting the requirements of multimedia applications discussed in the previous section and discuss in detail the services. Figure 13.1 is a representation of this architecture. The end-user applications communicate with each other and with the application services from the Application Service Provider on a peer-to-peer basis. This layer provides the network applications such as multimedia conferencing, mail, file transfer, etc., to the end user. The Application Service Layer calls upon services from the teleservice and network access layers to perform its functions. The Advanced Call Services (Teleservices) Layer provides the control, data exchange, data access, and collaboration functions mentioned at the end of the previous section. There is peer communication at this layer across the transport network, as well as

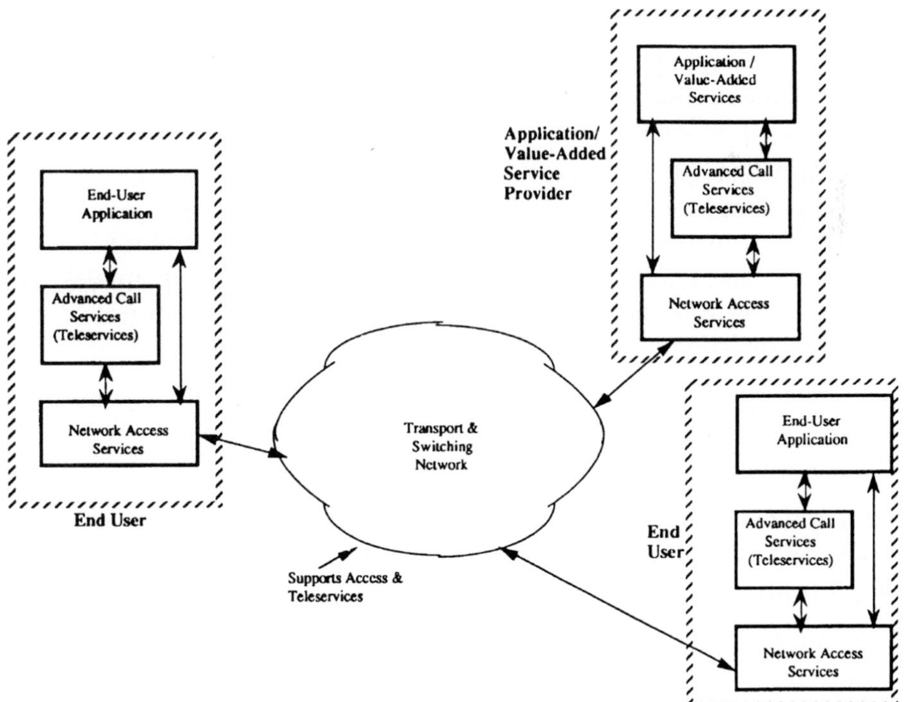

Figure 13.1 Architecture for network-based multimedia services

with entities within the network to provide these services. The Network Access Layer provides access to the appropriate data transport facilities. Again, there is peer communication at this layer across the transport network as well as with entities within the network to provide these services. The transport and switching network carries out data transfer, switching, and appropriate operations and management functions.

Note that the layering presented is a service hierarchy, not a protocol hierarchy. The complexity of the communication problem for multimedia forces us to an object-oriented approach. This is in contrast to the traditional protocol layer approach and procedure-based model for data communications as prescribed by the OSI model ([6], pp. 179–182). Each of the layers in Figure 13.1 could be considered as a set of objects, which provides a well-defined set of services and has an appropriately defined interface. The layers provide increasingly complex services, as we proceed from bottom up. The entities at the appropriate layer obtain services from any of the lower layers and are not restricted to service from the next layer below. As an example, data transfer with low delay requirements can take place between applications via the Access Layer directly, rather than going through the Teleservices Layer. The Teleservices Layer itself may have been used to provide control and call setup services for this same transfer.

This point will be discussed further in Section 13.4 on protocols.

13.3.2 Middleware and Mediaware

The Advanced Call Services (Teleservices) are those needed to allow applications to make effective use of the underlying transport services which are emerging. These include media and session services.

Media services: facilities for end-application collaboration, messaging and signaling; coordination of multiple media streams; distributed access to multiple media; and remote display and acquisition systems.

Session services: facilities for multicast exchange of diverse data streams; security and privacy control; management and control of multipoint, multiuser, and multichannel connections.

We refer to the software systems which implement the media services as *mediaware*. Software which provides the session services is gaining recognition as *middleware* [7].

Media Services

The Media Services can be further classified into Media Presentation and Media Control services.

Media Presentation: A layer of services to support access to distributed and multiple media information from heterogeneous customer premise equipment (CPE). These provide support for media data format conversion among different representations for a given media type and multimedia data synchronization to allow different types of media data to be presented with predefined spatial and temporal relationships.

Media Control: A layer of services to support sharing of and collaboration with multiple media information in multiuser communication. These include support for composite data management mechanisms for subscribers to compose documents consisting of different types of media; dynamic updates for shared data to update changes of shared composite data in a multiparty session; and arbitration and access control of shared data to provide arbitration and access control of shared composite data in a multiparty session.

Session Services

The Session Services can also be classified into two subgroups: one providing control functions and another providing advanced data exchange.

Session Control: A layer of services to establish and manage multipoint, multiuser, multinetwork (or channel) communication. These include facilities for multipoint session and multichannel session setup procedures allowing subscribers to create a session that consists of multiple channels and multiple endpoints; multichannel synchronization/coordination to synchronize the delivery of different types of media data being transported over different communication channels; dynamic session reconfiguration allowing subscribers to change the configuration of a session, such as adding or deleting parties within the session, without having to destroy and recreate sessions; and configurable call handling allowing subscribers to set up and change configuration preferences to allow for time-of-day and type-of-call–based call handling procedures.

Advanced Data Exchange: A layer of services to support advanced data exchange mechanisms. These include message passing facilities to send information to all the parties in a session (broadcast) and to a subset of the session members (multicast); remote procedure call facilities to support distributed information processing via a client and server model; transactional call handling mechanisms allowing subscribers to submit a sequence of call commands in a single transaction; data security/privacy/ownership support mechanisms to allow subscribers to protect the security of their data using various kinds of locking and encryption; and deadlock avoidance mechanisms to provide adequate arbitration schemes to avoid possible deadlocks and collisions in a multipoint communication environment.

Standards and Prototype Implementations

No general standard teleservices to support the above are available, and there is no attempt as yet to develop comprehensive standards for this layer of services. Various standards bodies such as ITU and ISO are focusing on specific capabilities [5]. Examples are the representation and coding for multimedia information objects, document architectures, and message systems.

Various proprietary prototype services, which implement some subset of the functions mentioned above, are being developed worldwide. A listing of projects being pursued as part of various European research initiatives such as RACE (Research and Development in Advanced Communications Technologies in Europe) and DELTA (Development of European Learning through Technological Advance) are available in [5]. The applications span many areas: banking, airline maintenance, education, and engineering design. A group teleworking system being developed in Japan is described in [8]. A system to address medical reporting and consultation is described in [4]. None of these are as yet open systems which could interwork with others.

13.3.3 Access

The Access Services (Bearer Services) provide end users access to high-bandwidth data transfer mechanisms to support the needs of multimedia applications over wide area networks. A number of these services are emerging. (The data rates specified below are approximate.)

BISDN or Broadband Services

Switched Multimegabit Data Service (SMDS): A connectionless cell-based (i.e., fixed-length packets) variable rate data service operating between 1.5 and 45 Mb/s

Cell Relay Service (CRS): A connection-oriented cell-based data service operating from 45 to 150 Mb/s

Continuous Bit Rate Service: A synchronous data service operating in the range 45 to 150 Mb/s (not standardized as yet)

Private Line Access Service (T3): A synchronous data service at 45 Mb/s

Wideband Services

Primary Rate ISDN: A channelized synchronous data service with 23 times 64 Kb/s channels and one 16 Kb/s channel, for a total of 1.5 Mb/s

Frame Relay Service (FRS): A connection-oriented frame-based (i.e., variable-length packets) data service operating up to 1.5 Mb/s

Private Line Access Service (T1): A synchronous data service at 1.5 Mb/s

See [9,10,11] for various discussions of SMDS and Frame Relay Service, and [12] for views on ISDN.

The above services can be provided in a variety of flavors. Using the private line access services results in static private networks. *Virtual private networks* are created by using permanent virtual circuit-based FRS and CRS (primarily in the form of LAN interconnect services [9,11]). Finally, on-demand switched broadband data transfer services are possible using SMDS, primary ISDN, or switched virtual circuit based FRS, CRS. Another flavor of access is via metropolitan area networks (MANs). In this mode, shared access token passing schemes can be used on top of services such as SMDS to provide a wide area network service.

Interworking

The current widespread presence of narrowband services, coupled with the emerging broadband service availability, gives rise to the question of interworking. We would like to stress that the services mentioned here are access services and as such live on the periphery of the network. There is no real incompatibility in allowing users to have simultaneous access, for instance, to narrowband ISDN and broadband continuous bitrate services. This is really a question of the availability of appropriate multiplexing and demultiplexing equipment and unified access to the network. An example of such systems is described in [13].

13.3.4 Transport, Switching, and Transmission

Data transport, switching, and transmission mechanisms, within the network, are required to support the network access services. Both private and switched network schemes are possible.

Private Networks

These can be provided by T-1 (1.5 Mb/s) and T-3 (45 Mb/s) access links, providing constant bitrate transport service over static private networks created with Digital Cross Connect switches (DCCS). The basic transmission services used are the standard digital hierarchies based on multiples of voice channel equivalents (64 Kb/s channels), in the bandwidth range 1.5 to 275 Mb/s (see for instance [6], p. 179, for North American and ITU standards).

Switched Networks

The Asynchronous Transfer Mode (ATM) service can be used to provide high bandwidth (155 and 600 Mb/s) data transport. This is a connection-oriented, asynchronous cell transport service [14]. The switching is provided by so-called fast packet switches or ATM switches—the speed being due to new switching fabrics, the fixed packet size, and the connection-oriented transfer [15]. The underlying digital transmission for these transport and switching mechanisms is the new optical transmission-based Synchronous Digital Hierarchy (SDH) with data rates from 52 Mb/s to 1 Gb/s [16]. The SDH is the emerging international standard for these data rates. It is based on the North American SONET (Synchronous Optical NETwork) standard initiated by Bellcore and adopted by the T1 Committee of the American National Standards Institute (ANSI).

Metropolitan Area Networks

Another form of transport network in the wide area environment is the so-called metropolitan area network configuration, where typically a logical ring/bus-type network is used with a token passing mechanism, using a protocol such as FDDI or IEEE 802.6. The bandwidths range from 10 to 100 Mb/s. Strictly speaking, this is an access arrangement, which would use underlying transport networks like that discussed above and in the Access subsection. An alternative is available where a physical fiber ring network is used to implement the transport itself.

13.4 NETWORK PROTOCOLS

13.4.1 The BISDN Reference Model

As already mentioned, the strictly one-dimensional layering of the OSI protocol stack is not appropriate for multimedia communications. The call and connection structures are fairly complex, multiple media streams have to be accommodated, and a more flexible structure is required, especially in the context of the public network. The BISDN reference model [17] (shown in Figure 13.2), with its multidimensional layering, seems to be the most appropriate to support these requirements and the architecture presented previously. We will discuss protocols in the context of switched networks. The case of private networks is simpler and will be omitted from this discussion.

Note that there are two service planes for user (or data) and for control, and two management planes for layer management and for plane management. The service planes are layered, while the management planes are not layered. The plane management plane provides the protocols for management messages and actions for coordination between planes. The layer management plane takes care of operations and maintenance communication for the layers. We will not consider the management aspects any

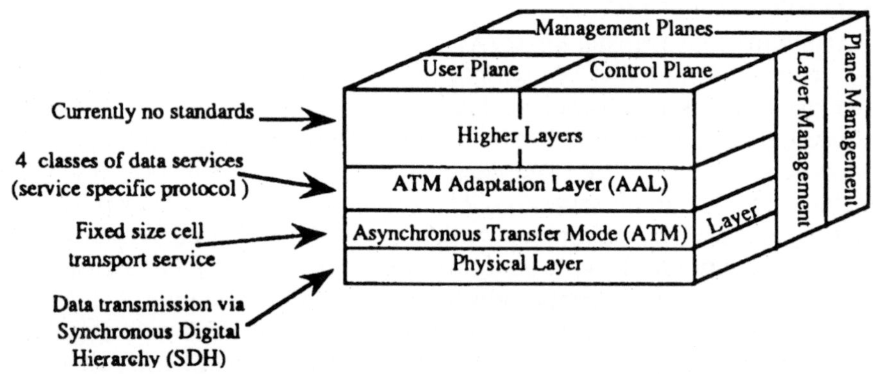

Figure 13.2 BISDN protocol reference model

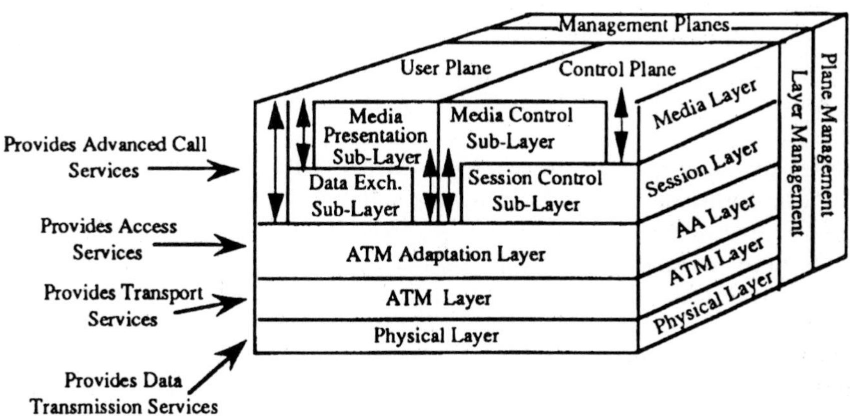

Figure 13.3 A protocol reference model for multimedia services

further here. Of more direct interest for the purposes of multimedia services are the control and user planes.

An expansion of the BISDN reference model is proposed here for true provision of broadband services. Figure 13.3 is the result of this expansion. We will use this model to discuss the implementation of the services described in Section 13.3.

13.4.2 Advanced Call Services

The Advanced Call Services/Teleservices are implemented by the Media and Session Layers, which have components in both the user and control planes. The services provided by the sublayers Session Control, Media Control, Media Presentation, and Data Exchange have been described. As mentioned above, no standard protocols exist for these layers.

A prototype implementation developed to address the requirements of the case study (Report/Review/Consult) discussed earlier is outlined in [4]. Capabilities within the Session Control and Media Control sublayers have been implemented on top of standard transport-level data protocols such as TCP/IP and private line access services. This implementation allows the establishment and management of multiparty, multistream sessions. It also allows for real-time sharing of data. The central concept here is of a session or workspace, defined in terms of the media streams available (voice, video, data), where users can be added to or deleted. Many open issues exist in terms of performance and scalability to a larger population of users.

Other partial implementations of these layers have been reported. For a description of a model and a protocol implementation for call management functions, which are within the purview of the Session Control sublayer, see [18]. The design is a distributed and object-oriented one, which seems quite suited to the nature of multimedia and broadband communications. The model is based on the notions of connections, which represent associations between endpoints, and access edges, which represent media streams. It is fairly complex, and has focused at present only on the call management aspects.

A related view of functions for the Session and Media Control Layers can be found in [19].

Very little has been reported on implementations of the functions in the Media Presentation and Data Exchange sublayers. Existing data protocols at the OSI transport layer, such as TCP, provide no support for connection management involving multiple parties, dynamic control of resources during communication, and the other functions we have discussed. Moreover, for data exchange itself, they may be unacceptable in situations of higher bandwidths and large distances (see [20]). This is due to the overhead in the traditional protocols, which were designed for high-speed processing, and low-speed communication channels—just the opposite of the situation here. Note that this does not imply that protocols such as TCP cannot be used at all. Rather, they become a component of the Data Exchange Sublayer.

13.4.3 Access Services Layers

The services offered by the ATM Adaptation Layer (AAL) of the BISDN model correspond to the Access Services we have discussed earlier. The Adaptation Layer is defined to provide four classes of service (there is a possibility that the standards will subsequently be extended to provide five classes). These are based on combinations of the requirements for connection-oriented versus connectionless transfer, constant versus variable bitrates, and maintenance versus nonmaintenance of timing between source and destination. The AAL is implemented in sublayers, the lower sublayers implementing functions generic to the class of service and the upper sublayers being service-specific implementations [14,21]. The access services mentioned previously—Switched Multimegabit Data Service (SMDS), Cell Relay Service (CRS), Frame Relay Service (FRS), and Continuous Bit Rate Service—are specific implementations of some of these classes. For MAN access arrangements, protocols such as FDDI or IEEE 802.6 are available.

13.4.4 Transport Service Layers

The Asynchronous Transfer Mode (ATM) Layer implements the standard connection-oriented, cell-transport service mentioned earlier as a uniform interface to underlying broadband and wideband networks. It provides high-bandwidth (approximately 155 Mb/s and 600 Mb/s) data transport [22]. The cells are of fixed size (53 bytes, including a 5-byte header), and the connections are based on combinations of Virtual Channels and Virtual Paths (bundles of Virtual Channels), which have to be set up before the data transfer takes place. The service is asynchronous but cell sequence integrity is maintained on a Virtual Channel. A cell priority mechanism allows for connections with different qualities of service based on cell loss in the network (including zero loss connections).

13.4.5 A Note

It should be noted that the protocol model allows for upper layers to bypass lower layers and obtain service from other entities as appropriate. This is inherently due to the fact that all layers above the ATM layer can provide different classes of service and functions, and multimedia applications often require a combination of services from various classes. For example, the AAL can provide services ranging from a continuous bitstream, which has sufficient functionality to be used directly by user applications, to a variable-size packet transfer service, which requires upper-layer mediation to be useful to applications. This is especially useful in multimedia applications that use different media streams simultaneously. This will be illustrated by the example in the next section.

13.5 THE MEDICAL CONSULTATION EXAMPLE

We now take the medical consultation application from before and present a sample implementation in the framework of the protocol reference model discussed above. Figure 13.4 shows four entities communicating over an ATM transport network: two end-user stations, an Information Server (IS), and a server for the advanced call services. The physicians who are engaged in the consultation use the end-stations to consult with each other over a video session. The medical information which they view simultaneously and collaborate with is provided to them by the IS. The Advanced Call Server (ACS) carries out all the necessary call and connection management functions discussed earlier. For simplicity we assume all the information under consultation to reside locally at the IS, though distributed data access can easily be supported in this framework. We also assume a consultation involving two physicians, though this can be generalized quite easily.

The communication scenario in this example is as follows. One of the end-stations uses the services of the ACS to initiate an information session with the IS. It then uses the ACS services to set up a video session with the other end-station. Next, the ACS services are used to manipulate the information from the IS, share it between the two users, and permit collaboration.

The ATM network carries three separate data streams in this example. A bidirectional constant bitrate stream is supported between video CODECs at the two user sites. Local video CODECs provide interfaces for the end-station video I/O devices. The underlying access service is the Constant Bit Rate Service (CBRS) provided by the ATM Adaptation Layer. A multicast multi-directional control data stream is supported between all the entities mentioned in the previous paragraph to provide all the session and media

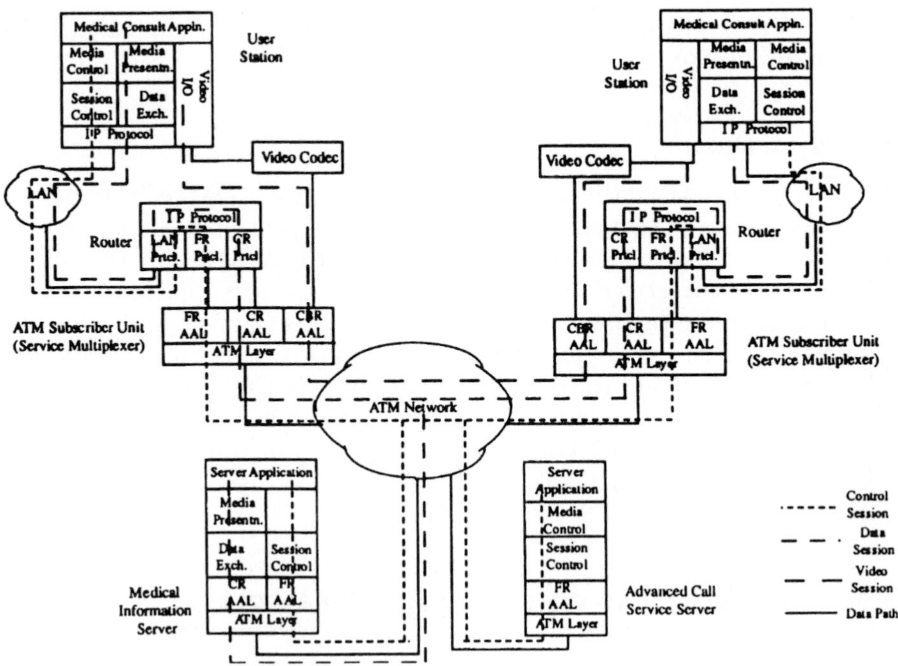

Figure 13.4 Example implementation of medical consultation application.

control interaction. The access to the ATM transport is via Frame Relay Service. A multicast media data stream is supported from the IS to the two end-stations. The underlying access service is the Cell Relay Service (CRS) provided by the ATM Adaptation Layer. CRS is used since the information in the consultation session involves medical images and requires high-bandwidth transfer.

The control and information streams are distributed locally at the end-user sites over Local Area Networks (LANs). For our discussion, the nature of the LAN is unimportant, though an FDDI LAN may be an appropriate choice to support the high-bandwidth, low-latency transfer of large medical images. At the end-user sites the ATM and AAL functions are implemented in Subscriber Units or Service Multiplexers, and routers provide interfacing between these and the LANs. The IP protocol is used as an example of an interworking protocol between the LANs and the ATM network. At the server sites the entire protocol stacks—ATM Layer through application—are implemented on the servers.

13.6 CONCLUSIONS

We have discussed the major issues which arise when multiuser, multimedia services are offered over the public network. Such services are most appropriate where the population to be connected is dynamic and relatively large and where connections across organizational and institutional boundaries are required. Traditional networks have not been designed for these environments, and new architectures and protocols have to be developed.

There has been considerable progress in broadband switching systems and transport networks to support such services in the recent past. Call management and control standards for broadband networks are rapidly developing. Specific requirements for multimedia are being incorporated. The same is true for access protocols. It is expected that preliminary versions will be available starting in 1994.

For the upper layers in the realm of middleware and mediaware there is much to be done. The Advanced Call Service capabilities discussed above need to be developed to offer true multimedia services which use the power of the evolving broadband network. Standards in services and protocols to support these are essential for effective end-to-end service. This is especially the case for public network–based services, which need to support large populations and interworking.

A large variety of services are being considered for public network offering. Many of these may be attractive only to special groups of subscribers. Thus, there is considerable uncertainty in the choice of specific services to be deployed and on their economic viability. This points out the importance of exploring other areas such as service-level performance and flexibility.

13.7 REFERENCES

1. Wright, D.J. Strategic Impact of Broadband Telecommunications in Insurance, Publishing, and Health Care. *IEEE JSAC*. vol. 10, no. 9. December 1992. pp. 1369–1381.
2. McGarty, T. P., Blaine, G. J., and Goldberg, M. (eds.), Special Issue on Medical Communications. *IEEE JSAC*. vol. 10, no. 7. September 1992.
3. Reis, H., Brenner, D., and Robinson, J. Multimedia Communications in Health Care, Extended Clinical Consulting by Hospital Computer Networks. *Annals of the New York Academy of Sciences*. vol. 67. December 17, 1992.
4. Treves, S. T. et al. Multimedia Communications in Medical Imaging. *IEEE JSAC*. vol. 10, no. 7. September 1992. pp. 1121–1132.
5. Armbruster, H., and Wimmer, K. Broadband Multimedia Applications Using ATM Networks: High-Performance Computing, High-Capacity Storage, and High-Speed Communication. *IEEE JSAC*. vol. 10, no. 9. Dec. 1992. pp. 1382–1396.
6. Stallings, W. *Data and Computer Communications*. 2nd ed. Macmillan. 1988.
7. King, S. S. Middleware—Making the Network Safe for Applications. *Data Communications*. March 1992. pp. 58–67.
8. Hoshi, T., et al. BISDN Multimedia Communication and Collaboration Platform Using Advanced Video Workstations to Support Cooperative Work. *IEEE JSAC*. vol. 10, no. 9. December 1992. pp. 1403–1412.
9. Cavanagh, J. P. Applying the Frame Relay Interface to Private Networks. *IEEE Communications*. vol. 30, no. 3. March 1992. pp. 48–65.
10. Ali, M. I. Frame Relay in Public Networks. *IEEE Communications*. vol. 30, no. 3. March 1992. pp. 72–79.

11. Clapp, G. H. LAN Interconnection across SMDS. *IEEE Network*. vol. 5, no. 5. September 1991. pp. 25–32.
12. Horn, R. W. (ed.), Special Issue on ISDN. *IEEE Communications*. vol. 30, no. 8. August 1992.
13. Verbiest, W., Van der Plas, G., and Mestdagh, D. J. G. FITL and BISDN: A Marriage with a Future. *IEEE Communications*. vol. 31, no. 6. June 1993. pp. 60–66.
14. Kawarasaki, M., and Jabbari, B. BISDN Architecture and Protocol. *IEEE JSAC*. vol. 9, no. 9. December 1991. pp. 1405–1415.
15. Denzel, W. E. (ed.), Special Issue on High-Speed ATM Switching. *IEEE Communications*. vol. 31, no. 2. February 1993.
16. Cheung, N. K. The Infrastructure for Gigabit Computer Networks. *IEEE Communications*. vol. 30, no. 4. April 1992. pp. 60–68
17. ITU Recommendation I.321, BISDN Protocol Reference Model and Its Application. Geneva. 1991.
18. Minzer, S. A Signaling Protocol for Complex Multimedia Services. *IEEE JSAC*. vol. 9, no. 9. December 1991. pp. 1383–1394.
19. Crutcher, L. A., and Waters, A. G. Connection Management for an ATM Network. *IEEE Network*. vol. 6, no. 6. November 1992. pp. 42–55.
20. La Porta, T. F., and Schwartz, M. Architecture, Features, and Implementation of High-Speed Transport Protocols. *IEEE Network. vol. 4, no. 2. May 1991. pp. 14–22.*
21. ITU Recommendation I.362, BISDN ATM Adaptation Layer (AAL) Functional Description. Geneva. 1991.
22. ITU Recommendation I.150. BISDN Asynchronous Transfer Mode Functional Characteristics. Geneva. 1991.

CHAPTER 14

MULTIMEDIA INTERCHANGE

John F. Koegel Buford
University of Massachusetts Lowell

Rita Brennan
Apple Computer

It is generally believed that a standard interchange format will play a crucial role in the growth of the multimedia application market. Today, several such formats are under development. In this chapter we first provide a survey of these current efforts, discussing goals, architecture, and abstractions of each format. An example of the use of the QuickTime movie file format is used as an illustration of the concepts.

Composition models are either track-oriented or object-oriented. This distinction can clarify differences in interobject referencing, compositionality, and access/presentation procedures. We use it as a basis for comparing the features of these formats.

Most formats are designed for file-based interchange, but formats will also be used in real-time delivery of multimedia materials from disk or across a network. We enumerate features that would enhance the ability of a format to support real-time interchange and conclude with an overview of an approach to quantitatively evaluate and compare such format models. This approach is based on a set of benchmark interchange cases and various parameters to be measured in a performance test.

14.1 OVERVIEW

In order for multimedia applications to work together and realize the benefits of distributed computing, a common interchange format for multimedia information is needed. It is not sufficient for the individual media formats to be standardized. The temporal, spatial, structural, and procedural relationships between the media components are an integral part of multimedia information and must also be represented. Today there is a growing realization that lack of a common format is a serious impediment to the development of the market for multimedia applications.

Without a representation that is widely adopted and is sufficiently expressive, multimedia content that is created in one application cannot be read or reused by another application. Further, without a common format, the sharing of multimedia information in a heterogeneous environment requires that an application-defined format have a converter on each platform.

Multimedia interchange formats are significant in several application contexts (Figure 14.1):

1. As a final storage model during the creation and editing of multimedia documents, for both the new composition and for archival materials which may be used in the editing process
2. As a format for delivery of final-form digital media, for example, by compact discs, to end-user players
3. As a format for real-time delivery from a server to clients connected via a network for training, information-on-demand, etc.
4. For interapplication exchange of data

In the architecture of multimedia computer systems, interchange appears in several different modes (Figure 14.2):

1. **Interapplication interchange:** Two or more applications exchange multimedia information using either an interchange API or a distributed object API. This service is accessed through an applica-

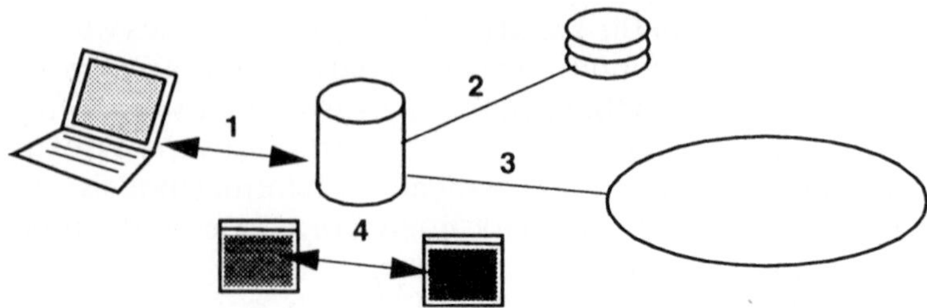

Figure 14.1 Example application contexts in which multimedia data interchange is used.

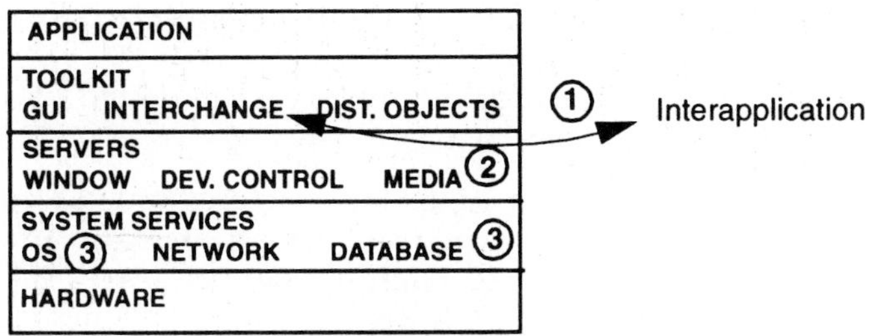

Figure 14.2 Multimedia interchange context from the perspective of the system architecture

tion toolkit. The application controls the interchange process and may also pass and receive the corresponding data. Enforcement of temporal relationships during the transfer is not important for this type of interchange.

2. **Media servers:** A media object server provides media objects to distributed clients for interactive playback and also stores and updates objects during authoring. The clients control presentation parameters through an API. The transfer of the data from the media server to the presentation system could employ a multimedia interchange format. Time dependencies in the composition must be maintained during retrieval and playback.
3. **Storage:** A process saves and/or accesses composite multimedia information through the file system or a DBMS using system calls or a query language. Time-dependencies may need to be enforced during read operations.
4. **Network:** Composite multimedia information is transmitted between two or more points across a network. The transmission may need to meet certain time constraints if the purpose is for playback.

The design of multimedia interchange formats can also be viewed in the context of the interchange format hierarchy (Table 14.1). In this diagram, lower levels correspond to increasing specificity. At the top level are general container formats. These formats are application independent. At the

Table 14.1 The Multimedia Interchange Format Spectrum

Category	*Examples*
General container	GDID, ASN.1, Bento
Multimedia document type	HyTime DTD
Final form multimedia composition	QuickTime Movie File, MHEG, OMFI
Monomedia and Script languages	MPEG, JPEG

bottom level are media-specific formats. These formats are optimized for a specific media type.

The major technical issues that must be addressed in the design of a multimedia interchange format include:

1. **Multimedia data model:** A data model for structured time-based interactive media (multimedia and hypermedia) must represent temporal relationships, synchronization, multiple media formats, addressing of media objects and composite media objects, hyperlinking, and an input model for interaction.
2. **Scriptware integration:** Many authoring tools integrate multimedia data with specialized procedural scriptware, which may be text based or iconic languages. These tools have a tight association of scripts with media objects and media composites, in particular associating input semantics of input objects with script input processing and allowing scripts to operate on object parameters dynamically. The interchange formats must retain the associations of the scriptware and the media objects. Further, scripts must be able to reference structured media objects for attribute control, retrieval, and presentation.
3. **Storage efficiency:** An encoding should be efficient for storage purposes, but the container is a small fraction of the information in a typical multimedia presentation.
4. **Access efficiency:** An encoding should be efficient for time-constrained and resource-limited retrieval. Enhanced functions for progressive and multiresolution delivery, flexible storage organization, media interleaving, index tables, and partial media referencing can support this goal.
5. **Portability:** GUI and platform architecture independence are essential, preferably without penalizing interchange on a single platform. Issues include look and feel independence, input architecture independence, file and object referencing, byte ordering, and data type encoding.
6. **Extensibility:** It should be possible to add new media formats, new media attributes, and other container extensions.

In the next three sections we survey current interchange formats, discussing goals, functionality, and abstractions of three important formats. This leads to an informal comparison in the following section in which the three formats are compared in various functional areas. The next section compares the track paradigm with the object-oriented paradigm. This is followed by a discussion of the role of interchange formats in supporting real-time interchange. Finally, we propose an approach for quantitative evaluation and validation of interchange formats.

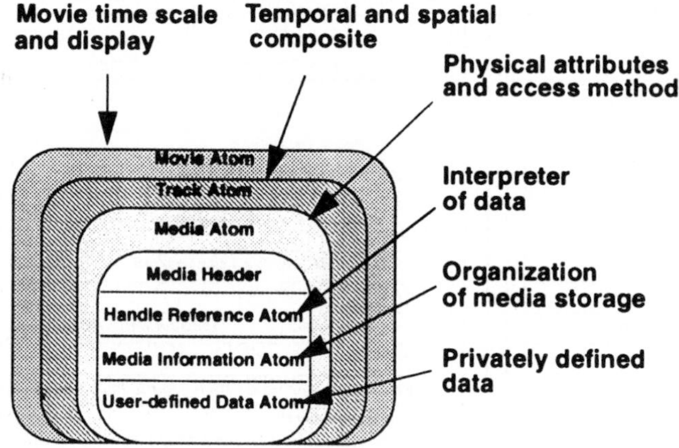

Figure 14.3 QuickTime™ abstract atom model

14.2 QUICKTIME MOVIE FILE (QMF) FORMAT

QuickTime is a multimedia extension for Apple's System 7 operating system for the Macintosh personal computer [1]. The QuickTime Movie File [2] is a published file format for storing multimedia content for QuickTime presentation. Several QuickTime players are available for other platforms. In this section we will only explore the file format part of the QuickTime architecture; more information on the QuickTime architecture can be found in Chapter 10.

QMF uses a track model for organizing the temporally related data of a movie (Figure 14.3). A movie can contain one or more tracks. A track is a time-ordered sequence of a media type; the media are addressed using an edit list (Figure 14.4), which is a list of the endpoints of digital media clips or segments.

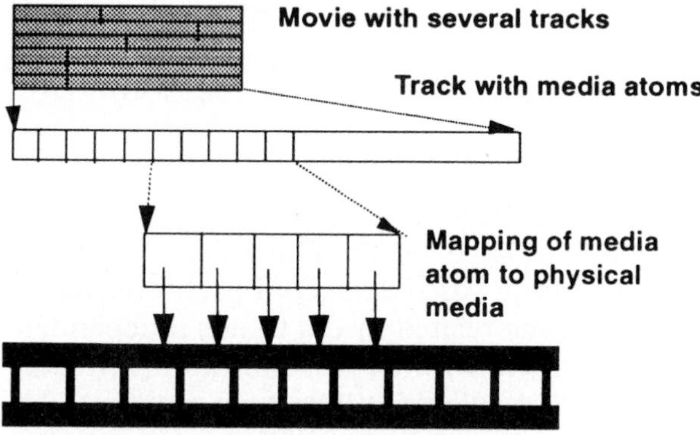

Figure 14.4 Components in QMF

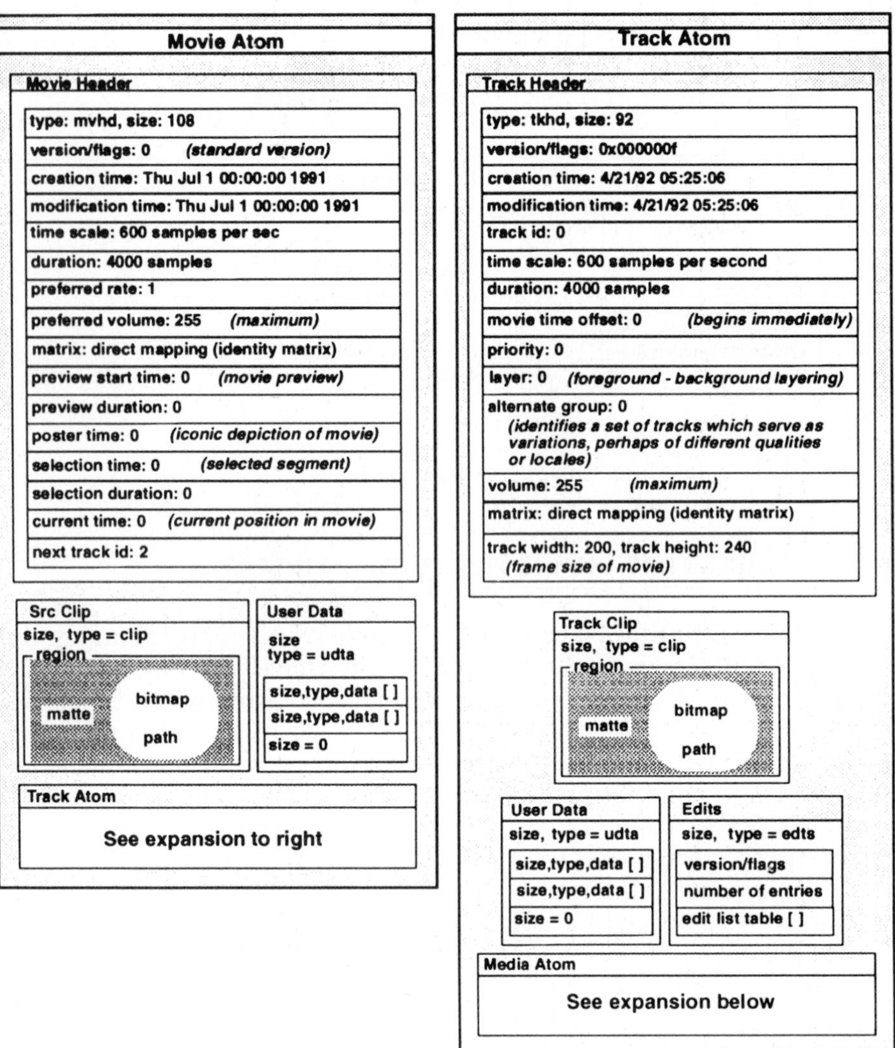

Figure 14.5a Anatomy of a QuickTime movie fragment—movie and track atoms

14.2.1 A QuickTime Movie File Example

QuickTime "movies" refer to all types of dynamic data, such as a presentation slide show or a dynamic graph of lab data. The QuickTime Movie File (QMF) format is a container for this time-based data. QMF presents a model for the storage and interchange of time-related media that is independent of a system's built-in timing and synchronization capabilities. QMF specifies a storage format and a model for media primitives such as time scales, spatial and aural information, image information, and text information.

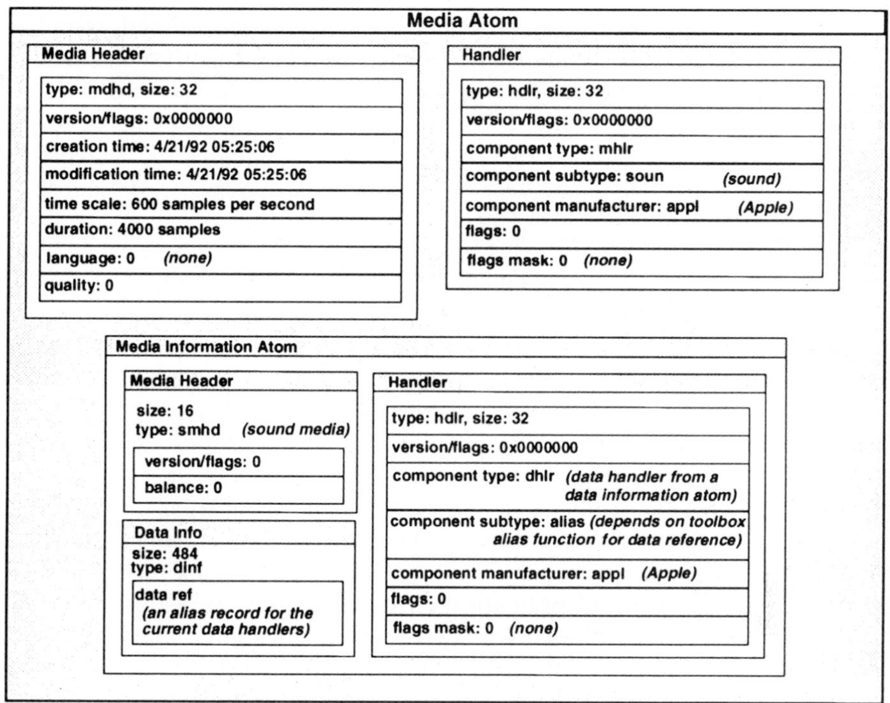

Figure 14.5b Anatomy of a QuickTime movie fragment—media atom.

As an example, Figure 14.5 shows the details of a fragment of a movie from a popular QuickTime application, Virtual Museum, developed by the Apple Advanced Technology Group. Virtual Museum is a HyperCard-based application which allows users to search and navigate interactively through electronic pictures and movies set in a synthetic museum space. A typical QMF data file taken from the Botanical section of the museum is shown in Figure 14.5.

The movie fragment in Figure 14.5 consists of a movie atom, a track atom, and a media atom. The media is a sound clip consisting of 4000 samples; at 600 samples per second the playback will occur in less than eight seconds. The bulk of the movie atom is the header, which provides descriptive information about the media such as creation date, preferred volume, and time scale. Video and animation media can provide a preview clip and a poster for use as an icon as well as the segment of the actual video. The movie "atom" is one of a number of atoms which are the building blocks of a QMF file.

The movie atom contains one or more track atoms. Each track in a movie atom consists of a single media type, which is represented by a media atom. The media atom encapsulates the details of the storage of the media.

The above "dump" chronicles the features of a movie in detail, whether it be media related, time related, or user/creator related. For further details on QuickTime movie files, refer to the QuickTime inside Macintosh documentation [3].

14.3 OMFI

The Open Media Framework (OMF) is an industry standardization effort being led by Avid Technology [4] to define a common framework and multimedia interchange format (OMFI). The OMF model is encoded using Apple Computer's Bento container format [5], a generic syntax for representing interrelated objects which are stored in a set of files. OMFI has been reviewed with respect to the Interactive Media Association's Data Exchange Request for Technology [6], and has been accepted by the IMA.

Like QMF, OMFI's primary concern is in representing time-based media such as video and audio, and similarly uses a track model as the composition paradigm. OMFI adds a number of features to the basic track model, which are particularly useful for applications involving video production. OMFI provides specific media objects for representing the source material counterparts of digital media—materials such as videotape and film. By including source material identification in the interchange format, it is always possible to identify the original source of any given media in case redigitization is needed. Further, in video production environments, final footage is frequently generated from the original video material so as to retain highest possible quality.

Figure 14.6 shows an example of the use of OMFI media objects (MOBs) to represent a composition of a scene in which the source materials are film and an audiotape. There are three files for this composition: the composition file (movieFile.omf) and the two digital media sample files (scene1Audio.omf and scene1Video.omf). The composition file contains the composition objects (MOB 104, 107), which identify tracks, segments, timing, transitions, and other attributes as created by the author of the material. Each MOB is given a unique identification (shown in simplified form in Figure 14.6).

The OMFI model has several other features which are particularly important in video production, including:

- Special track types such as Edge Code, Time Code, and Filler for storing SMPTE time code for a segment or, in the case of Filler, for representing gaps of no activity in a track
- A set of predefined transitions or effects, plus the ability for transitions to represent overlapping segments in which the overlap is needed to compute the effect
- Support for *motion control*, that is, the ability to play one track at a speed which is a ratio of the speed of another track

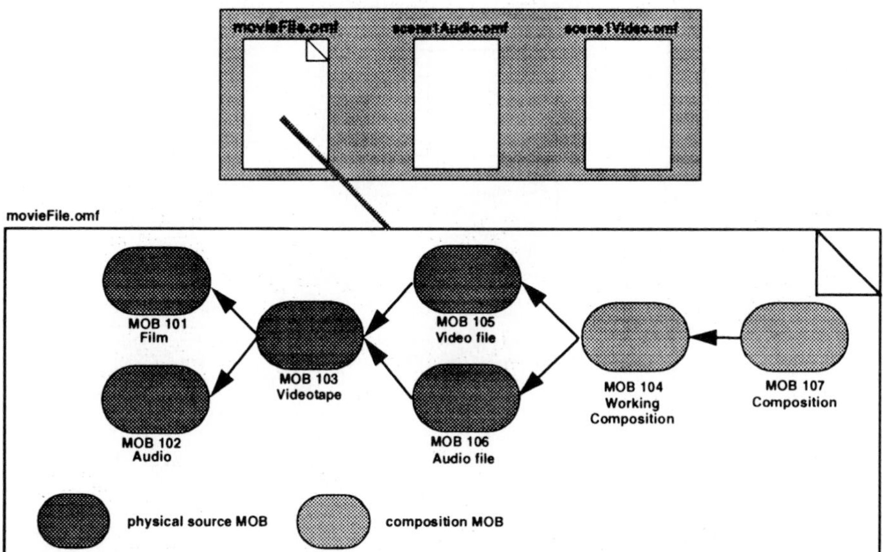

Figure 14.6 An example OMFI composition illustrating the use of media objects (MOBs) to represent both the composition and the source media, in this case Film and audio from which a video tape was derived. This was used in turn to create digital video and audio sample files.

The elements of the OMFI composition model are shown in the class hierarchy in Figure 14.7. Compositions are constructed using media objects (MOBs) which are subclasses of a track group object (TRKG). A media object groups a collection of related tracks (TRAK) which may be played in parallel, overlaid, or selected depending on the composition. A track can contain any kind of component, even another MOB, as shown in Figure 14.6.

Every OMFI interchange file contains a header (HEAD) which includes indices for objects contained by the file. Additionally, the OMFI class hierarchy can be extended by an application by including dictionary object references in the header. If an application needed a new type of track, for example, it could create a new track subclass and add the definition to the file using a dictionary object (CLSD).

14.4 MHEG (MULTIMEDIA AND HYPERMEDIA INFORMATION ENCODING EXPERT GROUP)

MHEG is an ISO working group that is defining an object-oriented model for multimedia and hypermedia interchange [7,8]. Like QMF and OMFI, MHEG is concerned with the composition of timed-based media objects whose encodings are determined by other standards. The scope of MHEG functionality is somewhat larger than either QMF or OMFI in that its representation model directly supports interactive media and real-time

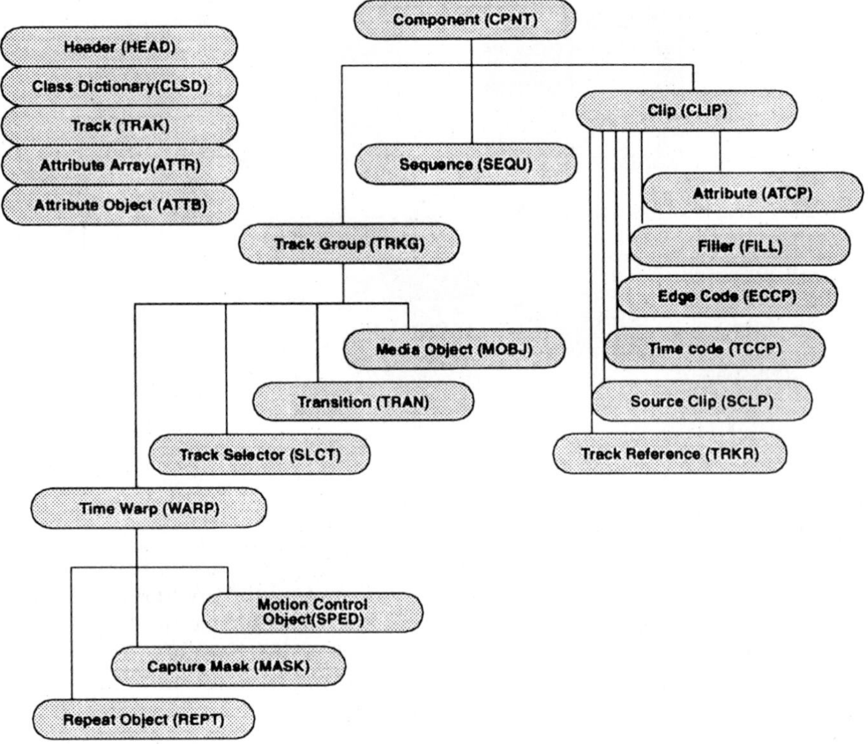

Figure 14.7 OMFI composition class hierarchy

delivery over networks. MHEG differs from document modeling formats such as provided by HyTime [9,10]. MHEG is a *final-form* representation in which the spatial and temporal relationships are retained but the logical model of the content is omitted.

MHEG supports the encoding of interactive multimedia presentations by defining a platform-independent set of interaction objects such as buttons, text entry, and scrolling areas. The look-and-feel aspects of interaction objects are controlled by the delivery environment. Input semantics are represented in one of two ways.

The first way of representing input semantics is intended for low-end platforms. A primitive set of input actions, which change the state of a display object, can be linked to an interaction object. When an interaction occurs, the MHEG system will invoke the associated actions. The second and more powerful mechanism involves the use of an embedded scripting language [11] (see Chapter 12 for a discussion of scripting languages). A typical use of this facility would be to associate script objects with the interaction objects. When an event of interest occurs, the script is interpreted to make the corresponding object state changes. MHEG itself does not define a scripting language; this is left to the application.

```
MH-Object
  Behavior
    Action
    Link
    Script
  Component
    Content
    Interaction
      Selection
      Modification
    Composite
  Descriptor
  Macro
    Macro Definition
    Macro Use
```

Figure 14.8 MHEG class hierarchy [10] in which indentation represents nesting in the class tree.

MHEG includes composition primitives for both space and time. Two binary temporal relationships are supported: serial and parallel. A macro facility [12] is available for simplifying the design of complex objects from the MHEG basic objects. Using a macro, an application can define a complex object as a template with parameters. The values for the parameters are substituted each time the macro is used. Macros can also enhance the efficiency of interchange. If an application defines several objects using the same macro, then once the macro definition has been interchanged only the specific parameters need to be retrieved for successive object instances.

MHEG is concerned with delivery of time-based interactive media over networks or on systems that have resource constraints. Although the interchange format only plays a supporting role in meeting the time constraints in the presence of resource limitations, MHEG does define features which could simplify the problem of time-based media delivery. The principles of real-time interchange support are described in Section 14.7. A number of these features are currently provided by MHEG [13].

The current MHEG class hierarchy is shown in Figure 14.8; the MHEG specification is still in development and is expected to be finalized in 1994. MHEG object encodings are expected to be available in several different notations. The base notation is ASN.1 (Abstract Syntax Notation) [14,15].

14.5 FORMAT FUNCTION AND REPRESENTATION SUMMARY

Each of the three formats described previously has been developed with different but overlapping requirements. The formats deal with a complex problem: how to efficiently represent and encode the broad range of multimedia compositions in a way that is not dependent on a particular approach to multimedia or a particular presentation platform. The format should be extensible to handle new requirements for multimedia content as they occur.

Table 14.2 shows a functional synopsis of the three formats. Each row identifies an area of functionality important to multimedia interchange. The table shows features which are common to the three formats as well as those which are unique to a particular format. With regard to unique features, MHEG includes an interaction model and object macros. OMFI provides a source media model and a dictionary object for extensibility.

Table 14.2 Functional Comparison of the Three Formats

Feature	*QMF*	*MHEG DIS*	*OMFI Version 1.0*
Model	Track	Object-oriented	Track
Encoding	Unique	ASN.1; others	Bento
Media object addressing	File name	Globally unique object ID	Globally unique object ID
Composition primitives	Movies, tracks, media	Composites, interactors, links	MOBs, tracks
Time composition	Serial and parallel	Serial and parallel	Sequence for serial, group for parallel
Component reference scope	Local for format units, global for media units	Global: all format units are objects and all have unique ID	Nested for format units, global for media units
Media source referencing	No	No	Unique physical MOB
Input model	None	Interactor and link objects	None
Link model	None	Use of link class	None
Scriptware objects	Yes if treated as media with own handler	Yes	None
Architecture independence	No: QuickTime and Macintosh System 7.0 dependencies	Yes: handles byte ordering, data types, and external references	Yes: handles byte ordering, data types, and external references
Extensibility	By Apple; user-defined atoms available	Yes: private data, private classes, private attributes	Yes: use of a dictionary object to define new classes
Macros or templates	No	Yes	No
File organization optimization	No specific features	Global object index Use of multiple media files	Global object indices Use of multiple media files

14.6 TRACK MODEL AND OBJECT MODEL

From the standpoint of media access, the composition model is a presentation list which defines the order in which media are accessed and displayed. In the track model, the primary access sequence is temporal. In an object model, the primary access sequence is through hierarchical descent of the tree; the ordering of the components in a composite would probably be based on display order. In the track model, multimedia presentation is viewed as a sequence of temporally oriented movie segments (Figure 14.9). In the object model, multimedia presentation is viewed as nonlinear hyperlinking between (temporally) composite object trees (Figure 14.10).

The object model has the feature that all format units (containers, media objects, etc.) are fully visible and addressable units. The track models presented provide addressing for media units but not for other container units. The tradeoff here is between the overhead of providing object IDs for

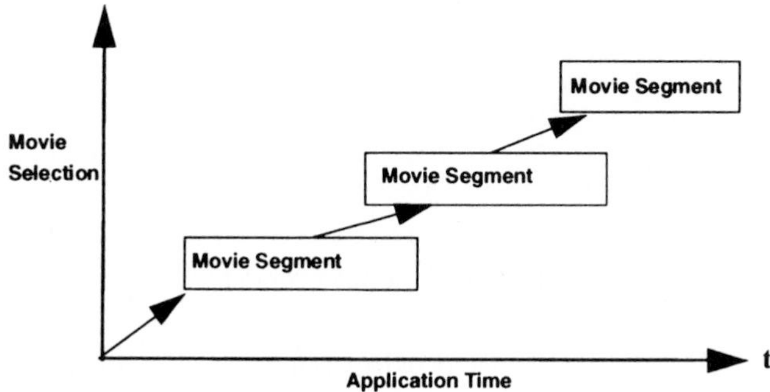

Figure 14.9 Multimedia presentation viewed as a sequence of temporally-oriented movie segments.

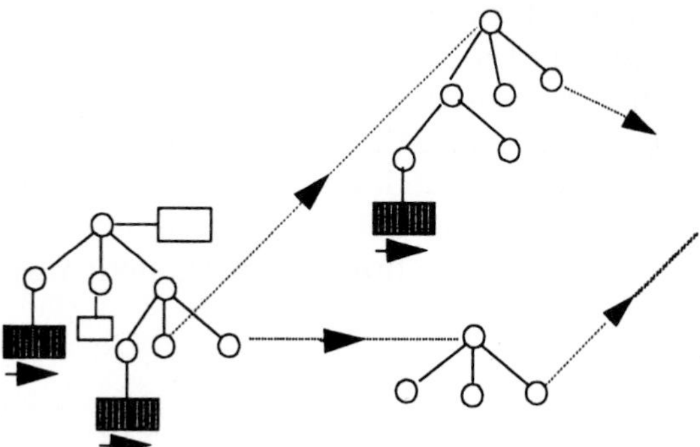

Figure 14.10 Multimedia presentation viewed as nonlinear hyperlinking between(temporally) composite object trees.

```
// Open
Initialize clock
Initialize movie, track, and media indices
Initialize handlers
// Players
Repeat
     Get next segment of media
     Call handlers
     Advance clock
```

Figure 14.11 Abstract presentation procedure for track model

```
// Open
Get table of contents, object tables
Initialize presentation processes
// Present
Repeat
     Repeat
          Get set of objects to be presented
          Invoke players for each object
     Until media event or input condition
     Pass input condition to application
      or script to interpret
     Identify next set of objects to present
Until exit condition
```

Figure 14.12 Abstract presentation procedure for object model

each format unit versus the possibility of reusing container structure by allowing it to be referenced from several places.

The implied presentation procedure for these two models differs as well (Figures 14.11 and 14.12). The two track formats do not model input, leaving interaction support to scriptware or the application. Then the presentation process can be seen as clock-based control of a collection of media players (Figure 14.11). In the object model, the input model allows some predefined input interpretation to be included in each composition, as well as providing links to the application and the script (Figure 14.12).

The object model presentation procedure includes both the presentation actions and the interaction interpretation. This allows the designer of an interchange engine to support a larger set of functionality in a generic way.

14.7 REAL-TIME INTERCHANGE

14.7.1 Definitions

For interchange during presentation to satisfy real time, the temporal nature of the systems, objects, etc., are delivered or executed in a way that follows the original time base as specified by the designer of the system. This implies that object retrieval, presentation, and response to user input must meet certain deadlines to be considered real time. However, minimal configurations are allowed to present subsampled time-based data (e.g., reduced rate video) and still satisfy this real-time criteria.

The interchange format can provide support for real time by providing file and data organization techniques which enable a delivery engine to have faster access to objects. Some selected techniques are listed below. Some of these techniques are independent of the format; all could potentially be available to the delivery system by preprocessing.

14.7.2 File Format Techniques for Supporting Real-Time Interchange

1. **Object Placement Optimization:** Objects are stored so that objects which are likely to be accessed simultaneously are adjacent from the standpoint of the access mechanism.
2. **Partial Object Retrieval:** Large objects can be retrieved in sections, since in many cases the entire content of such an object will not be presented at one time.
3. **Object Sequencing:** The order in which objects are expected to be presented is maintained for use by the access mechanism.
4. **Global Object Index:** A table of all objects and their position in the object set is provided to support fast lookup of objects.
5. **Object Interleaving:** Large objects which are to be retrieved simultaneously are interleaved so that large objects don't cause delays for other objects.
6. **Separate Retrieval of Object Description and Object Content:** The object description can be retrieved without necessarily retrieving the content. The system can use information about a set of objects to optimize the access for this set and so that resources needed for the access can be prepared.
7. **Progressive Access of Objects:** Images can be retrieved and presented in increasing resolution for systems in which presentation delay is significant. Scalable versions of objects can be represented and retrieved for systems with insufficient resources for full fidelity presentation.
8. **Resource Recommendations:** The resource requirements for retrieval and presentation by the target system are available by lookup rather than by derivation.

14.8 TOWARDS A PERFORMANCE MODEL

As observed previously, multimedia interchange will be needed in environments in which delivery systems have a range of presentation, storage, and network facilities. The data being delivered have temporal attributes which need to be met. A delivery mechanism is needed which is scalable across a broad range of systems and gracefully degrades in the presence of dynamic resource availability. This delivery mechanism depends in part on the format of the media being retrieved. Consequently, there is a need for quantitative performance metrics for systems which retrieve interactive time-based media stored using a given multimedia interchange format. Such metrics can aid system designers in optimizing the design of a delivery mechanism.

There are a number of ways that such formats can be evaluated:

1. **Representational power:** Define the composition, synchronization, media, interaction, and other primitives that are intrinsic to the domain and verify that each format can express these.
2. **Functional checklist:** Define a functional requirements list and identify which requirements are met by each format.
3. **Benchmarks**: Define configurations and usage patterns of representative multimedia compositions. Create sample multimedia documents corresponding to these. Use these benchmarks to compare the performance of interchange formats via both simulation and implementation.

14.8.1 Example Benchmarks

Test cases are needed in order to obtain quantitative results from a benchmark of the different formats. Test cases should naturally cover a broad range of the domain and should emphasize functionality that is most important. We briefly list several test cases as examples. Each of the following cases represents a distinct category from the perspective of the authoring environment and the composition characteristics. Each test case should be used in several different sizes.

1. **Edited video:** A sequence of video segments (analog and video) interspersed with various transitions and incorporating subtitles
2. **Hypertext:** A hypertext document with a large number of links; multiple links to and from specific objects
3. **Slide show–style presentation:** Simple branching structure with small number of media objects per screen
4. **Script-based interactive multimedia presentation:** A complex presentation, as in a model-based interactive lesson, controlled by a script

14.8.2 Measurements

The value of benchmarks rests in selecting performance measures that are relevant to the intended uses. The following list of measurements would most likely be performed across several platforms. For each test case, the following measurements can be made:

1. **Storage cost:** This measures the encoding efficiency.
2. **Retrieval cost:** For a presentation delivery sequence of accesses, what is the retrieval cost for accessing the necessary objects?
3. **Random access cost:** For a random sequence of object accesses, what is the cost to retrieve these objects?
4. **Update cost:** What is the cost of changing/adding/deleting an object or composition during an edited operation in terms of file reorganization?
5. **Conversion cost:** What is the cost of converting from/to one or more proprietary formats to/from the common format?

Measurements could be used to compare one format's performance versus another. Or measurements could be used to determine what file organization strategies are optimal for a given test case. Such strategies could be used by application developers to improve the performance of the end product.

14.9 SUMMARY

In this chapter we have given a comprehensive overview of the significant features of a number of current formats. Several of these formats are under design, and the description given here could change. We have summarized and compared the major contributions of each approach in a function checklist and discussed some differences between object-oriented and track models. Finally, an overview of various approaches for evaluating the design of such formats has been given.

14.10 ACKNOWLEDGMENTS

Much of this chapter is an updated version of [16] written by the first author.

14.11 REFERENCES

1. Ortiz, G. QuickTime 1.0. *Dialog*. Summer 1991.
2. Apple Computer. Proposal to Standardize a Temporal Media Movie Format. August 1991.
3. Apple Computer. QuickTime inside Macintosh. 1992.
4. Avid Technology. Open Media Framework (OMF) Interchange Specification Version 1.0. March 1993.
5. Moore, R. Bento Overview. Apple Computer. Unpublished document. February 1992.
6. Interactive Media Association. Request for Technology: Data Exchange. November 1993.
7. ISO/IEC. JTC 1/SC 29, Coded Representation of Multimedia and Hypermedia Information Objects (MHEG) Part 1, Committee Draft 13522-1. June 15, 1993.

8. Price, R. MHEG: An Introduction to the Future International Standard for Hypermedia Object Interchange. *ACM Multimedia 93*. August 1993. pp. 121–128.
9. ISO/IEC. IS 10744 Hypermedia/Time-Based Structuring Language (HyTime). August 1992.
10. Koegel, J., Rutledge, L., Rutledge, J., and Keskin, C. HyOctane: A HyTime Engine for an MMIS. *ACM Multimedia 93*. August 1993. pp. 129–136.
11. Koegel, J. Introduction of Script Objects. ISO/IEC JTC 1/SC 29/WG 12 N 92/ 462. November 1992.
12. Koegel, J. Macros. ISO/IEC JTC 1/SC 29/WG 12 N 93/507 and N 92/300. January 1992.
13. Koegel, J. MHEG and Real-time Interchange. ISO/IEC JTC 1/SC 29/WG 12 N 92/388. July 1992.
14. ISO/IEC. IS 8824 Specification of Abstract Syntax Notation One (ASN.1). 2nd ed. 1990.
15. ISO/IEC. IS 8825 Specification of Basic Encoding Rules for Abstract Syntax Notation One (ASN.1). 2nd ed. 1990.
16. Koegel, J. On the Design of Multimedia Interchange Formats. *Proc. Third Intl Workshop on Network and Oper. Sys. Support for Digital Audio and Video*. November 1993.

CHAPTER 15

Multimedia conferencing

John F. Koegel Buford
University of Massachusetts Lowell

Walter L. Hill[1]

The fundamental changes in telecommunications brought about by both multimedia and computer control will bring with them major innovations in how communication services are accessed and used. In sharp contrast to traditionally separate telecommunication services, it is expected that, in the future, control of communication services will be a general capability of computer systems and applications; dedicated communication applications will become the exception rather than the rule. At the same time, the very notion of communication medium is changing to include such things as shared windows and whiteboards and even shared virtual realities, which are enabled by distributed computing. These technologies require—and make possible—much better support for communications among more than two parties. Multimedia conferencing, as a technology for supporting communications with multiple parties and media, is more than an evolution of traditional specialized teleconferencing systems; it will play a more

[1] This chapter includes a description of work done at Hewlett-Packard Labs, Palo Alto, CA, by the second author, who may be reached currently at whill@netcom.com.

fundamental and pervasive role in daily life—in the workplace and in education and entertainment.

These changes in the relation between communications and computing require new software architectures and with them application programming interfaces (APIs), which will enable applications generally to access and control communications services. Recognizing the opportunity to develop a new architecture for multimedia communications, various proposals have emerged which share some common themes. In this chapter we are concerned with the abstractions for multiparty, multimedia communications and the implications of these abstractions on the underlying network architecture and system services. In presenting these ideas we will review results in traditional teleconferencing and, more recently, shared application architectures, which have played a motivating role in the development of these concepts.

15.1 TELECONFERENCING SYSTEMS

The practice of video teleconferencing over the past two decades can be characterized as the use of dedicated equipment and lines, specially-designed conference rooms, expensive proprietary CODECs, and a range of video qualities in which motion artifacts and audio delays were common. These systems were typically used by large organizations which needed to provide frequent interaction between a number of geographically distributed sites. The investment in conferencing equipment could be justified by the increased organizational interaction and the reduction in travel expenses.

Experience with such systems led to improvements in human factors, as system designers attempted to obtain a closer approximation to the experience of face-to-face meetings, a quality known as *telepresence* [1]. Techniques for camera positioning to get better eye contact, the use of displays in which the projected image appears life-size, the use of voice-controlled switching, and ancillary aids such as document cameras and electronic whiteboards became widely accepted [2,3]. System designers also introduced audio signaling techniques for anti-howling and echo suppression [4] and bridging for multisite conferences.

These systems were most frequently used for point-to-point conferences between predefined locations. Conferences were typically scheduled ahead of time. Participants went to specifically configured meeting rooms to attend the conference. Because of technology limitations and cost, these systems lacked the informality and accessibility of the typical phone call. Because of the dedicated nonstandard equipment involved, these systems became a "communication island" for organizations. These limitations have led to other approaches to real-time visual communications.

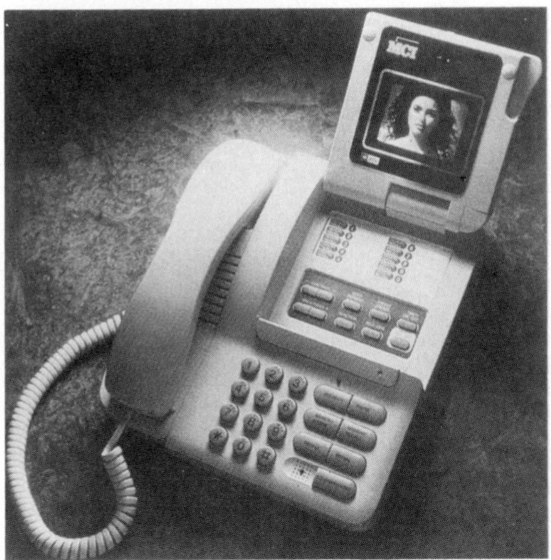

Figure 15.1 MCI's VideoPhone, one of several recent consumer-oriented videophones being marketed. (Courtesy of MCI. © Copyright 1993 MCI.)

15.1.1 Videophones

The affordable videophone is an appealing device for consumers as well as organizations. Unlike a dedicated video conferencing system, it has potentially global reach through the international phone system. However, like the conventional phone, it would be best suited for person-to-person conversations rather than group meetings. The video format supported by any widely adopted videophone will likely be a standard that other solutions would need to adopt. Recently, several consumer-oriented videophones have been announced (e.g., MCI's videophone in Figure 15.1). The price and quality of these devices will be important factors in their acceptance in the consumer market.

15.1.2 Multisite Video Conferencing

The creation of effective telepresence for group meetings has been another notable direction. A large-scale operational system developed jointly by British Telecomm and the University of London is particularly noteworthy for its achievements in this area [1,5]. The London University interactive education network (LIVE-NET) began operation in 1987 connecting seven sites of the university (Figure 15.2). Any five sites could be simultaneously viewable at each site during a video conference. This permitted a number

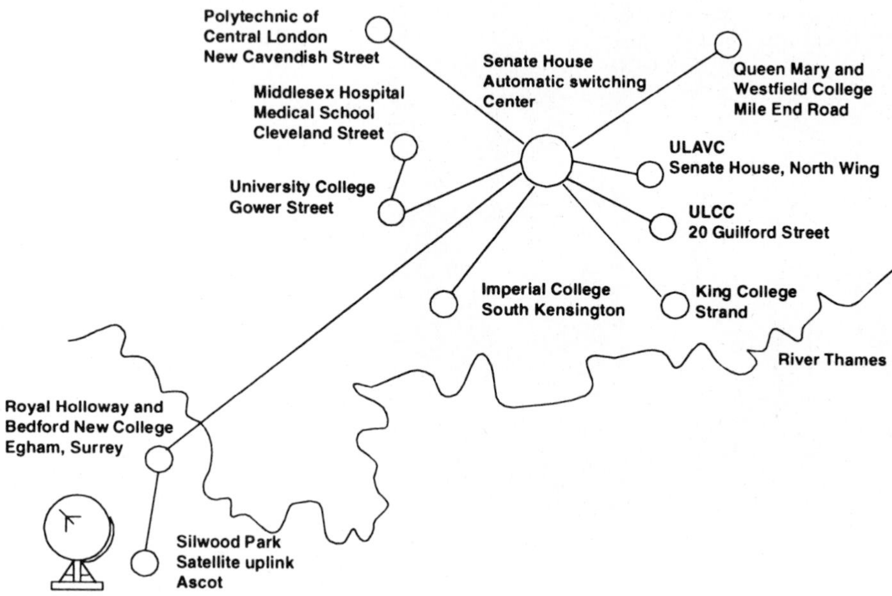

Figure 15.2 University of London's LIVE-NET in 1990.

of innovative uses in teaching, symposiums, and meetings, as will be described.

Each site is connected via fiber optic links varying in length from 1 to 40 km. The network topology is a star, with a crossbar switch located at the network hub. Four full-bandwidth video signals and a data carrier are simultaneously transmitted over each fiber. Consequently, since the network permits four incoming and four outgoing video signals, each party in a five-way conference can be continuously viewed by all participants.

An example use of this facility in the classroom context is shown in Figure 15.3. The lecturers sit at a table shown at the top of the diagram. Facing the lecturers is a camera and four monitors (shown at the bottom of the diagram). This allows the lecturers to see signals coming from four different sites, which typically would be four different classrooms located in the metropolitan area. The overhead camera is used to transmit drawings and can be switched in or out by the lecturer. Each classroom, both remote and local, has a set of five monitors viewed by the students. The monitors show the lecturer and the participants at the other four sites. Full-bandwidth video and audio is transmitted for each channel.

An example conference configuration is shown in Figure 15.4. The two side monitors show either full-screen or quad-sectioned views of incoming signals. An overhead camera on the table projects hardcopy visuals. The computer terminal to the right is used to schedule sessions.

The system is frequently used for team-teaching in which both instructors and students are located at several different locations of the university.

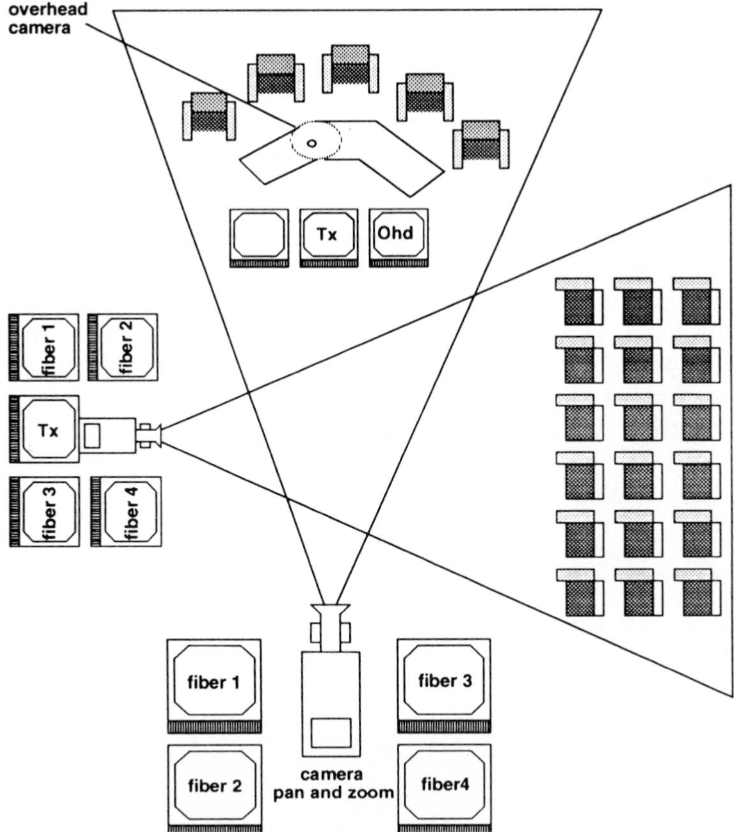

Figure 15.3 Example of a classroom configured for distributed teaching via LIVE-NET.

LIVE-NET is connected to an uplink satellite dish and has been used to broadcast conferences to other parts of Europe. Through its data channel, LIVE-NET also connects university LANs via bridges. It has begun experi-

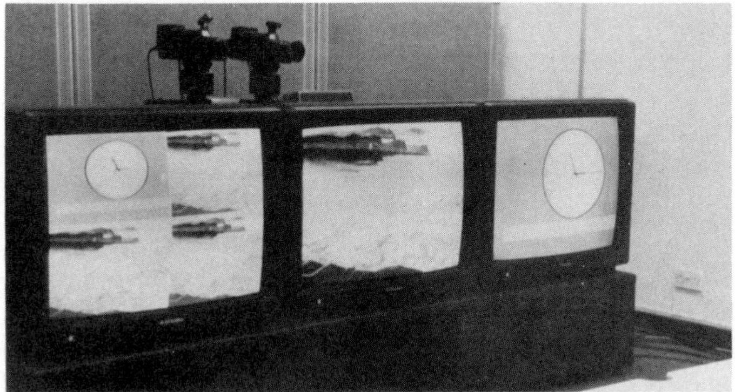

Figure 15.4 A LIVE-NET conference room with side monitors showing quad-split screen views.

menting with shared applications between workstations in parallel with the video communications.

15.1.3 Computer-Based Teleconferencing Systems

The development of lower-cost video CODECs and networks coincided with new software techniques for sharing applications between workstations. Such application conferencing permits two or more users to simultaneously edit, design, modify, and review computer-based materials of mutual interest. By bringing video teleconferencing to the desktop, conferencees can use the computer for presenting slides, taking notes, updating documents, and various other group work functions while participating in the meeting. The advantages of this type of collaboration has motivated much recent research and is the topic of Chapter 16. Further, products are now appearing which allow video conferencing over local and remote networks from the workstation (Figure 15.5).

15.1.4 Evaluation

The technology for teleconferencing is moving away from the limitations of the past. Video conferencing will no longer require dedicated equipment

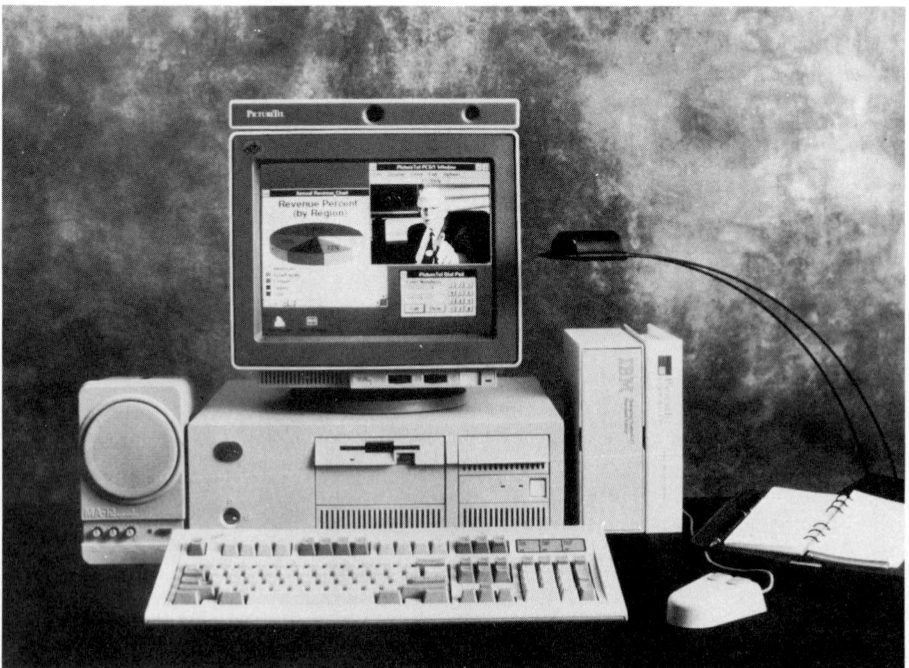

Figure 15.5 PictureTel's System 4000 (left), a stand-alone video conferencing station, and PCS/1 (right), a computer-integrated video conferencing station. (Courtesy of PictureTel. © PictureTel 1993)

operated as a communication island. Technologies for both group multisite conferences and personal video conversations are improving. By integrating communication devices with computing, communication is no longer limited to audio or video but can include all types of media. Additionally, new aplications and services for managing personal communications are now possible.

This *multimedia conferencing* is more than adding additional channels of connectivity between parties. As we will discuss in this chapter, the paradigm for controlling dynamic multiway multimedia connections is important as a unifying principle for the many disparate ways that humans, devices, and applications communicate today.

In the next section we present a perspective on the requirements for multimedia conferencing functionality, which has been important in our research. In the two following sections we describe architectures and issues for shared applications and workstation-based video conferencing systems, two important threads of research in this area. This leads to a discussion of underlying connection abstractions. A *call model* developed by the second author is described as a possible unifying abstraction. We conclude with a discussion of the implications of such a model on the system architecture.

15.2 REQUIREMENTS FOR MULTIMEDIA COMMUNICATIONS

There are a number of imaginative visions of how people will communicate for work and recreation in the future. Consider, as an example, one recently articulated by Larry Rowe [6] (slightly paraphrased):

> *Sue Smart is a manager at Big Bucks Software. Because of scheduling conflicts she is unable to attend a technical conference she is interested in. Fortunately, the conference is being broadcast over the Internet, so she is able to participate in the meeting remotely. During a morning conference session, her boss places a videophone call to Sue. Sue puts the conference session on hold and fields her boss's questions. After finishing the conversation with her boss, Sue returns to the conference session. The conference has just taken a break, so Sue replays the material that she missed, fast-forwarding over portions that are of less interest to her. Then Sue places herself on the "chance encounter" videowall at the workshop and does some social networking with conference attendees.*
>
> *Sue realizes that Steve Eagerbeaver should attend an afternoon session, so she calls him on videophone. Steve is not in his office, so she leaves him a videomail with a handle to the conference session so he can join it or review it later.*
>
> *After the conference, Sue prepares a report including video clips and her annotations. Several months later, while flying to her mother's home for a holiday, she "videos into" Kathy S. at the quilting video forum. Kathy also works for BBS and they talk about the conference. Sue calls up portions of her report for Kathy to see. Afterwards Sue settles back to watch the most recent Godzilla George movie in which participants get to . . .*

One basic feature of these types of scenarios is that the communication, no matter what device mediates it, involves connections between parties, documents, and applications and many of the operations on these connections resemble the familiar telephone ones—call, answer, forward, place on hold, hang up. There are other interesting features as well. First, a communication session has an identifier, which can be used to treat the session as a data object, i.e., one that can be shared with others, stored in documents, retrieved from directories, connected to, secured, etc. This leads to the need for a session abstraction.

Second, there is the expectation of seamlessness.[2] Through her video interface Sue connects directly to her boss (on a portable videophone), a conference audience (large-screen monitor), the chance encounter videowall (a shared multicast video "space"), her colleague's videomail device, and the videoplayers and recorders in her editing session. This seamlessness can be extended further. Connections do not need to be restricted to persons; a media player or recorder can also be treated as a *party* to a connection. Connections do not need to be restricted to "live" conversations; deferred in time communications such as electronic mail or fax can be treated as connections as well. The benefit is that the end user and the application can be less concerned with details of media and device interoperability.

Today there are many islands of communication: fax, electronic mail, voice mail, shared applications, video conferences, broadcast television and radio, etc. Architectures for *multimedia communications* can introduce unifying principles which avoid redundancy of common services (e.g., connection management, directory services) and reduce the number of devices and interfaces that the user deals with. Additionally, these multimedia communications services will support applications which interchange real-time multimedia information.

15.3 SHARED APPLICATION ARCHITECTURES AND EMBEDDED DISTRIBUTED OBJECTS

One distinguishing trend in the development of multimedia communications systems is the increasing use of computer mediation and integration. In this section we examine how applications and application objects can be "media" in a multimedia conference.

A shared application or application conferencing system permits two or more users at separate workstations to simultaneously view and interact with a common instance of an application and its content. For example, users collaborating on writing a report could collectively edit the document

---

2 Hiroshi Ishii and Naomi Miyake discuss the achievement of seamlessness further in Chapter 16.

by having a shared copy of the document editor at each workstation. Because the application is shared and permits a common view of the same document, any change made by one user can be immediately seen by the other participants. From the perspective of a multimedia conference, an application becomes another (interactive) presentation medium to be viewed by the conference participants.

This model can be further extended by recognizing that applications are not monolithic entities, but are hierarchies of interrelated objects, each of which could be associated with and connected to objects in other applications. This gives the user finer control over the application and access to many distributed services, but requires a mechanism for connecting and viewing such objects. Such a mechanism would share many features with those of other types of multimedia conferences.

We next look at shared application architectures and embedded distributed objects in more detail.

15.3.1 Shared Application Architectures

Although an application might be a medium in some future multimedia communications system, today's shared applications have been developed without such generality, primarily because the underlying window system itself supports a limited view of how an application can be used. Even in the case of networked window systems such as the X Windows System [7], shared applications were developed after the protocol, architecture, and toolkits were in place (see, however, a recent experiment in modifying the X protocol for multiuser applications [8]). Nevertheless, the architectures of such systems are important if shared applications are to be integrated with future multimedia conferencing systems. The following discussion surveys many of the issues involving shared applications in networked (client/server) window systems.

The two general approaches to application conferencing can be categorized as symmetric and asymmetric views. In the symmetric case each user has an identical synchronized view of the application. When any change is made by one user, the views of the other users are updated to maintain a consistent and identical state. In the asymmetric case, the application is specifically designed to give users different views of the common state. An example of an asymmetric shared application is a board game in which players compete; each player has a view of the game from his or her perspective. The symmetric approach fits well with existing single user application interfaces where users might wish to collaborate on a budget using a spreadsheet, a report using a technical publishing tool, or a schedule using a project management tool. Less is known about the design of asymmetric applications specifically for sharing. Such applications should correspond to and support some asymmetric group interaction such as a teacher and students or doctor and patient.

Table 15.1 Architectural Choices for Shared Applications

Shared Application State	*Coordination Point*
Centralized	Toolkit
Distributed/Replicated	Server

The architectures for shared applications vary in two dimensions (Table 15.1). First there is the choice of how the state of the shared application is distributed. The extreme cases are fully centralized and fully distributed (also called replicated) [9,10]. A centralized architecture maintains one instance of the application on some system on the network. The graphics command stream for the application is broadcast to the local window servers for each user. User input is sent from each user workstation to the application instance where it is synchronized with input from other users. The distributed architecture duplicates the application instance at each user workstation. Input and output are performed with the local instance, and changes to application state are propagated to the distributed copies in order to maintain consistency. (See Figure 15.6).

The second choice is where in the networked window system the coordination is performed. The extreme cases in this dimension are the toolkit level [11] and the window server level (see, for example, SharedX in [12]). The toolkit-level approach permits the application coordination to be represented at a higher level of abstraction since the server protocol is typically low-level graphics primitives. But a toolkit extension for application sharing requires that existing applications be reprogrammed for explicit sharing. A server extension can permit existing applications to be symmetrically shared without modification.

A number of other issues related to application sharing are discussed next.

15.3.2 Synchronization

Application sharing is fundamentally a problem of coordinating different users who are interacting with a shared resource—the application—at the same time. Unless synchronization is performed, users might attempt contradictory requests, leaving the application in an ambiguous or inconsistent state. While there are well-known synchronization techniques for both centralized and distributed systems, the implementation is complicated by the interaction level at which coordination is performed. In server-based implementations, the application updates are at a low level of input events and graphics updates. It is not possible to reconstruct the application-level object actions to determine where each critical section begins and ends. This is less of a problem at the toolkit level, where the semantics of the application are available.

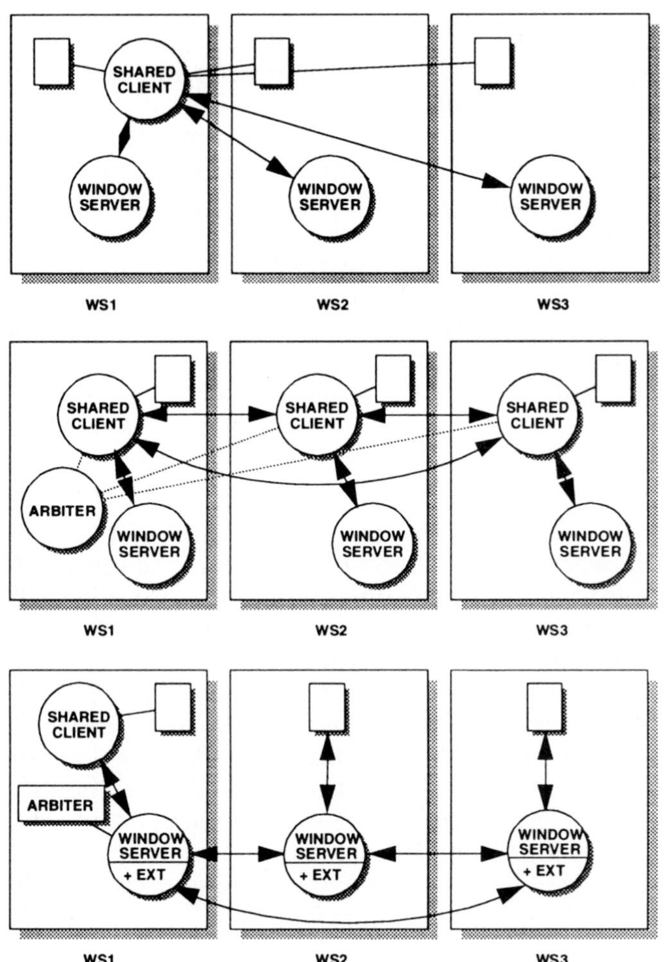

Figure 15.6 Different architectures for shared applications: (1) centralized—toolkit, (2) replicated—toolkit, and (3) replicated—server.

15.3.3 Latecomers

It is desirable to be able to add new parties to the shared application session after it is underway [13,14]. The current state of the application, whether centralized or distributed, may be insufficient to achieve this since in order to add the new user, a consistent screen state must be reconstructed. The screen state is dependent on the sequence in which window system objects were created and graphics commands executed. Contemporary window systems do not maintain this history. A backing store approach might be used, but this has translation problems in heterogenous environments with different graphics systems. Replaying a history log of graphics commands does work, however, in a heterogeneous environment.

15.3.4 Group Protocol Support

Whether the shared application follows a symmetric or asymmetric view, some mechanism to control the flow of the conversation is needed, particularly as the number of participants increases [12]. Such mechanisms are referred to as floor control. When a floor control policy is used, only one participant controls the application (i.e., has the floor) at a time. Only during possession of the floor can a participant change the state of the application. Various protocols for passing control of the floor from one user to the next are possible, such as round-robin or on-demand. It is generally agreed that selection of a protocol is a policy decision which should be controlled by the application or users; the architecture provides only the mechanism for implementing the different possible policies.

15.3.5 Performance

The response time of shared applications can suffer because of the additional communication overhead needed to update multiple screens. This overhead is a monotonic function of the number of participants, so that as the number of participants increases, response time increases. The use of multicast protocols is one possible remedy for this.

When sharing applications across platforms with different graphics capabilities and window systems, translation overhead may be incurred. These problems have been previously encountered by window system designers and include different color models, aspect ratios, fonts, and byte ordering. For cross-window system sharing, translation issues include different style conventions for layout and interaction.

Detailed performance measurements of different sharing mechanisms is given in [9].

15.3.6 Embedded Distributed Objects

The notion of embedded application objects developed from the desire to create documents which are active, that is, documents in which the displayed components are connected to content—in databases, files, or other applications—that can be independently manipulated. When the content changes, the views change as well. One common scenario used to illustrate this functionality is a spreadsheet object embedded in a document [15]. Rather than being just a static table, the embedded spreadsheet has all the functionality of a real spreadsheet. Additionally, the spreadsheet can be dynamically connected to data, so that if the stored data is changed, the change propagates to the spreadsheet view.

In order to generalize the notion of an embedded spreadsheet so that embedding of any application component in another application is possible, new mechanisms are needed for distributed application communication and presentation toolkits. At the same time, the application itself changes from monolithic and impenetrable to being a collection of interrelated objects which can export services to other applications.

Distributed object environments [16,17] are the infrastructure for providing application object connectivity in a distributed system. These facilities provide two key mechanisms: a directory service by which applications obtain access to objects in other applications and an API by which applications make connections. In the case of an embedded spreadsheet, for example, this infrastructure would be the means by which a document application would request a spreadsheet object provided by some other application to appear within a document.

At the presentation level, current user interface toolkits do not handle embedded objects well, although progress is being made in this direction [15,18,19].[3] A common approach is to distinguish between view objects (the presentation) and data objects (the information or state). For example, the Andrew Toolkit (ATK) uses this distinction to provide embedded objects [15], although there is no distributed object infrastructure for these objects to connect to. An embedded scripting language is available for "programming" connections between data and view objects. Rendezvous [21,22] uses the view-data distinction to provide asymmetric views of shared applications, but control over the connections between view and data objects is limited to the toolkit level.

15.3.7 Summary

Although application conferencing architectures have been developed independently of multimedia conferencing, communication notions such as multiparty connection management and shared views are prevalent and could be supported by a common mechanism. More research is needed to evaluate the features of embedded distributed objects from the perspective of a common connection model.

15.4 MULTIMEDIA CONFERENCING ARCHITECTURES

In this section, we will describe some of the important experiments in designing architectures for future multimedia telephony systems and some of the higher-level abstractions which they use. A discussion of underlying architectures for multimedia networking can be found in Chapter 13. While a complete discussion of APIs for communications would also need to include nonreal-time services, such as electronic mail, they are outside the scope of this chapter. An important topic for future research is how

[3] However, Microsoft OLE [20] does support embedded objects for applications on the same platform.

computer-controlled telephony, electronic mail, and other forms of communication such as publishing will interact with each other in the future, possibly giving rise to very different communication functionality and programming models.

The first pair of examples, VOX and Galatea, give client/server architectures, respectively, for remote audio and video services integrated with X Windows. Etherphone is a large distributed application for telephony using data networks. Some features of its highly innovative network application architecture could give rise to important APIs for general communication services. The last pair of examples, the Touring Machine and the Call System, are experiments in defining APIs for multimedia communications.

15.4.1 VOX

Although the VOX Project [23] at Olivetti dealt exclusively with audio and its integration with the user interface, its software architecture is significant for other media as well. The VOX architecture is based on the notion of an *audio server* which is analogous to an X Windows server, but supports audio in the user interface. Like an X Windows server, the VOX audio server can support multiple distributed clients. It manages shared resources for audio input and output and connections between those resources and clients. It also presents control interfaces (play, record, etc.) for a resource to clients.

A distinctive feature of the VOX software architecture is the notions of *logical device* and *device composition*. Hardware devices such as computer-controlled recorders, amplifiers, etc., are modeled in software. However, more complex devices can be modeled as composites built up from components. The control interface to a logical device is an event queue and devices use events to communicate with each other.

As an abstraction, a device models connection and control properties simultaneously. It is important to recognize that these could be separated to allow different subsystems to handle connectivity and control. However, it is sometimes convenient to have a single object to refer to for both purposes. Composite devices can be very useful for modeling complex devices such as answering machines. While device composition works well for VOX, there are many situations where it is not appropriate in a communications architecture. This is the case, for example, if components are subject to conflicting privacy or control restrictions, so that the composite could not be accessed or controlled. Such situations arise frequently in distributed systems. Device composition may also not be appropriate when device configurations change frequently, affecting both interface and implementation of a composite device.

15.4.2 Galatea

Galatea [24] is a system for distributed (analog) video device control. It is an extension to the Project Athena campus-wide distributed computing services at MIT. The Galatea server provides a programmatic interface for viewing images and motion video from remote sources over a switched analog network. It also manages shared resources. When there are multiple Galatea servers, one server can access resources of others, so that a client need only access a single server. A hierarchical client/server model thus simplifies the requirements for Galatea clients.

One of the interesting features of Galatea is its directory service ("Volume Table"), which abstracts multiple equivalent sources. If the same movie is available on multiple videodisc players, the client need only specify the movie; the server takes care of selecting a player, making appropriate connections, and presenting an appropriate movie control interface to the user.

Directory services are obviously a very important component of communications systems generally. There are large-scale efforts to define and establish directory service standards such as X.500. The information-hiding in Galatea's directory service is not unusual in conventional telephony where multiple agents can support a single phone number. Some of the more novel and challenging issues for directory services have to do with rapidly changing information to support, for example, active badge systems, and the integration of directory access with other forms of information access. Video-on-demand services, for example, will surely extend the functionality of traditional information retrieval systems. Requirements such as these suggest that directory services need to be broadly distributed rather than residing in a central source.

15.4.3 Etherphone

Etherphone [25] was the pioneering experiment at Xerox PARC in using Ethernet to transport and control digital audio communications, using the network to provide both traditional and flexibly extended telephony services. It is distinguished for the quality of its innovation in both networking and user services. Like VOX, Etherphone was an audio application. More recently, it has been extended to support video (analog so far) as well [26].

Etherphone connection services are provided by a central connection manager server which provides a range of services including a control interface to clients, user preference management, and call notification. The connection manager supports a notion of *party object*, which can represent both communication devices and users. Etherphone is thus able, for example, to support calling a user either using a phone number or via the user's party object, which may hold current information about the user's location. Etherphone now uses its connection management architecture to control transmission and switching of heterogeneous analog and digital media.

In its current realization, the Etherphone architecture introduces a notion of a *conversation*, which is "any connection between two or more users or between users and multimedia services." There is a conversation taxonomy, and connections for things like videophone calls and video conferences are different kinds of conversations. In [26], various design issues such as default conversation connection policies and support for multiple simultaneous conversations are discussed.

15.4.4 Touring Machine

The Touring Machine [27] project at Bellcore takes as its primary goal the design of a software platform for developing distributed applications controlling multimedia communications across multiple WANs. It is particularly concerned with identifying the higher-level services that such a platform needs to provide, and gives careful attention to the separation of general mechanisms from application-specific policies in designing such services. The Touring Machine architecture is based on a set of coarser-grained objects (station objects, session objects, resource managers, transport objects, resource objects, and name servers) together with fine-grained connector and endpoint abstractions used in controlling transport topologies of communication sessions. The current Touring Machine implementation controls an analog audio-video network supporting 100 users in two Bellcore locations 50 miles apart.

Touring Machine uses the term user to refer to users in the usual sense and also to producers and consumers of multimedia information within the system. Touring Machine supports communication among users who use (possibly multiple) applications which are Touring Machine clients communicating with a Touring Machine server. It is the Touring Machine server that supports the Touring Machine API. One of the most important Touring Machine abstractions is the session, which, like the Etherphone conversation, represents an instance of multiparty multimedia communication. The interface to a session supports adding and removing parties and media and using connectors to control connections among endpoints which map onto communications ports. Different Touring Machine sessions can support different policies, for example, for privacy of information about the session and permission for controlling the session.

Connection management within a session is effectively the representation of an abstract switch with logical endpoints specific to the session. These logical endpoints may be mapped to different ports at different times, while a single port may at different times have different endpoints in different sessions mapped to it. In effect, the endpoints provide an indirect reference to ports. It is thus possible to write applications that only depend on aspects of the structure of a session, but are independent of the session itself or how it is mapped onto ports. This is analogous to the effect of using local coordinates in windows in a graphical user interface. Using local coordinates, a graphics application can run in a window independent of the window's location on a display. The endpoints in a session represent a single medium and direction such as video-in. It would be possible to introduce a notion of composite endpoint to represent a set of media channels which are often used together. That would allow some connections to be expressed more simply at the expense of adding support for more fine-grained control when needed. It is important to note that the notion of endpoints introduces the kind of separation of connection and control mentioned above in discussing device abstractions. In the Touring Machine architecture, the media lines and control lines of a device such as a VCR are represented independently rather than through a unifying device abstraction.

15.5 A CALL MODEL FOR MULTIMEDIA COMMUNICATIONS

The Call System at Hewlett-Packard Laboratories [28] was originally designed as a component for a desktop video conferencing application, but has evolved into a high-level multimedia communications API. The system design is based on the ability to represent in software the well-known operations such as place, hold, forward, and hang up associated with a phone call. This operational approach gives rise immediately to call and party abstractions, which have simple, intuitive interfaces while supporting the communications needs of diverse applications. It seems possible that the call abstraction might play a role as fundamental for communications software architecture as the window abstraction does for user interfaces. Indeed, the Call System has many similarities (although it was developed independently) with Etherphone conversations and party objects, Touring Machine session objects and users, and other notions of call objects such as [29]. The Call System was designed to be implemented in a distributed object system so that calls and parties are realized as objects. The Call System can control multiple switches; while the original implementation was for control of switched analog audio and video, extensions are being developed for a telephony interface and for control of certain client/server applications which can be represented as logical switches. Some of the call operations applied to connections between clients and servers give rise to interesting new functionality in these systems and point the way to further integration of telecommunications with data communications and distributed computing.

One of the fundamental requirements for a general call abstraction is the ability to add and remove parties and media. To support this, the original implementation of call objects was remarkably similar to that of Touring Machine session objects. Calls are created by specifying a set of party objects and for each party object a set of media. Some of the design tradeoffs mentioned in the discussion of Touring Machine endpoints demand further investigation, but, in any case, the call interface needs to support connecting media as well as adding and removing parties and media. It is important to note that a call may or may not have a distinguished party, which is the "caller," and, indeed, may or may not have parties at all. In contrast to intuitions derived, for example, from network implementations, calls are not equivalent with a "state of the system." They are more like templates which can determine a state. Calls can be used, for example, to implement virtual meeting rooms that are not always inhabited. Making calls into objects which can be referenced and manipulated like any other data leads naturally to new ways of representing and managing communications. It becomes easy, for example, to create browsable collections of calls or associate a call with an element in a user interface such as an icon.

As recognized in both Etherphone and Touring Machine, it is useful for party objects to represent more than just human users. Indeed, in traditional phone services, it has been meaningful to call, for example, time and weather services which can legitimately be interpreted as parties. Those examples would suggest using party objects to represent all media sources. That is both feasible and desirable, since it promotes uniformity and hence simplicity in developing applications. In an object-oriented system, one can go further and recognize that any object can be viewed as a party as long as it supports the set of operations on parties. The party interface supports call placement and notification, holding and resuming connections, and maintaining the set of that party's calls. There is an important interdependency between party objects and directory services. Directory services provide access to directory information needed to make a connection to a party. In many cases, it seems most appropriate for such directory information to be provided by the party objects themselves. Both Galatea and Etherphone seem to lend themselves to this distributed directory approach.

While call and party objects play the central roles in the Call System, there are numerous supporting abstractions, including resource manager objects for managing shared resources and user preferences. There are also objects which represent media and connections in a spirit similar to Touring Machine's connectors and endpoints. But possibly the most interesting question, if a call system is to play as basic a role as a window system or file system, is whether there are other kinds of objects which, along with calls and parties, will be basic building blocks for developing future communication applications.

15.5.1 Call Model Example

To give an example of using call and party objects to represent communication tasks, we recall the scenario described at the beginning of Section 15.2. Figure 15.7 shows a snapshot of the logical connections controlled by call and party objects in the scenario. The snapshot is taken during the time when Sue Smart has put the conference call, represented by Call1, on hold and has accepted Call2 from her boss. While Sue's connection to Call1 is on hold, the conference is being recorded through a connection between Call1 and a party representing a video recorder. When Sue finishes her conversation with her boss, she hangs up Call2 and resumes her connection to Call1. At that point, she has access both to the live conference and to the video record. One of the advantages of the call system is that most of Sue's actions are supported directly by messages sent to the call and party objects which manage the underlying media connections transparently.

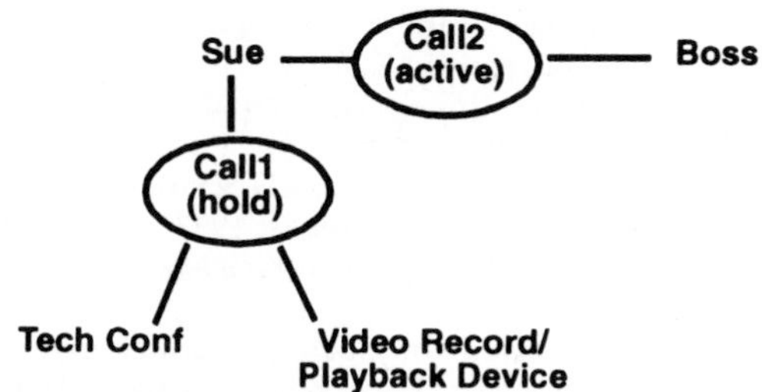

Figure 15.7 Snapshot of the top-level objects used by the Call Model in an example session.

15.6 SUMMARY

The concept of "session" in contemporary network architectures such as OSI and TCP/IP is too limited to support the type of communication transactions that will be possible with future multimedia communication systems. For example, the TCP/IP abstraction, the socket, is a bidirectional point-to-point connection which guarantees only arrival order. Features such as real-time delivery guarantees, multiparty communication, and QOS-based resource allocation are not directly provided.[4] The implications of such requirements on the network architecture are discussed in Chapter 13. The perspective of this chapter is that a call model abstraction should replace or extend the existing session abstractions used in today's networks. Further, such an abstraction is a unifying principle for the design of many communication applications which are today developed as independent systems.

In addition to the use of a common call model abstraction, services such as directory services, locators, and resource managers should be standardized and incorporated into the communications infrastructure. Standardization is necessary to support global communications, a powerful feature of today's phone system. Such services will facilitate the development of applications which help end users manage their personal communications.

15.7 REFERENCES

1. Powter, E. J., and Beckwith, R. C. LIVE-NET—An Interactive Switched Video Network for the University of London. *Intl. J. of Digital and Analog Cabled Systems* (1). 1988. pp. 19–28.
2. Kenyon, N., White, T., and Reid, G. Behavioral and User Needs for Teleconferencing. *Proc. of the IEEE* (73) 4. April 1985. pp. 689–699.
3. Elton, M. Visual Communication Systems: Trials and Experiences. *Proc. of the IEEE* (73) 4. April 1985. pp. 700–705.

---

4 As discussed in Chapter 3, new protocols such as RTP and CCP are being developed to provide these capabilities.

4. Watanabe, K., Murakami, S., Ishikawa, H., and Kamae, T. Audio and Visually Augmented Teleconferencing. *Proc. of the IEEE* (73) 4. April 1985. pp. 656–670.
5. Kirstein, P. T. and Beckwith, R. Experiences with the University of London Interactive Video Education Network. *Electr. and Comm. Engr. J.* February 1991. pp. 4–12.
6. Rowe, L. Multimedia Technology State of the Art. *ACM Multimedia 93 Workshop on Programming Abstractions for Distributed Multimedia Applications.* August 1993.
7. Scheifler, R. W., and Gettys, J. The X Window System. *ACM Trans. on Graphics* (5) 2. April 1986. pp. 79–109.
8. Borman, C., and Hoffman, G. Xmc and Xy-Scalable Window Sharing and Mobility, or, From X Protocol Multiplexing to X Protocol Multicasting. *The X Resource.* Issue 9. 1994. pp. 205–210.
9. Ahuja, S., Ensor, J., and Lucco, S. A Comparison of Application Sharing Mechanisms in Real-Time Desktop Conferencing Systems. *ACM Conference on Office Information Systems.* April 1990. pp. 238–248.
10. Lauwers, J., Joseph, T., Lantz, K., and Romanow, A. Replicated Architectures for Shared Window Systems: A Critique. *ACM Conference on Office Information Systems.* April 1990. pp. 249–260.
11. Crowley, T., Baker, E., Forsdick, H., Milazzo, P., and Tomlinson, R. MMConf: An Infrastructure for Building Shared Applications. *Proc. of CSCW '90.* 1990. pp. 329–324.
12. Greenberg, S. Sharing Views and Interactions with Single-User Applications. *ACM Conference on Office Information Systems.* April 1990. pp. 227–237.
13. Lauwers, J. C., and Lantz, K. Collaboration Awareness in Support of Collaboration Transparency: Requirements for the Next Generation of Shared Window Systems. *CHI '90 Conference Proceedings.* April 1990. pp. 303–312.
14. Chang, G., Jeffay, K., and Hussein, A.-W. Accommodating Latecomers in Shared Window Systems. *IEEE Computer* (26) 1. January 1993. pp. 72–74.
15. Palay, A. J. Toward an "Operating System" for User Interface Components. In M. Blattner and R. Dannenberg (eds.), *Multimedia Interface Design.* ACM Press. 1992. pp. 339–355.
16. Nicol, J., Wilkes, C. T., and Manola, F. Object Orientation in Heterogeneous Distributed Computing Systems. *IEEE Computer.* June 1993. pp. 57–67.
17. Soley, R. M. (ed.). *Object Management Architecture Guide.* Object Management Group TC Document 92.11.1. 1992.
18. Linton, M., and Price, C. Building Distributed User Interfaces with Fresco. *The X Resource* 5. pp. 77–88.
19. Price, C. Extending Xt to Support CORBA-Based Embedding. The X Resource. Issue 9. pp. 47–61.
20. Microsoft Corp. Object Linking and Embedding 2.0 Design Specification. 1992–1993.
21. Patterson, J. F., Hill, R. D., Rohall, S. L., and Meeks, W. S. Rendezvous: An Architecture for Synchronous Multiuser Applications. *Proc. of CSCW '90.* 1990. pp. 317–328.
22. Hill, R., Brinck, T., Patterson, J., Rohall, S., and Wilner, W. The Redezvous Language and Architecture. *Communications of the ACM* (36) 1. January 1993. pp. 62–67.
23. Arons, B., Binding, C., Lantz, K. A., and Schmandt, C. The VOX Audio Server. *IEEE 2nd International Workshop in Multimedia Communications.* April 1989.
24. Applebaum, D. I. The Galatea Network Video Device Control System. MIT Media Laboratory. 1989.
25. Swinehart, D. C. Telephone Management in the Etherphone System. *IEEE GlobeCom '87.* November 1987.
26. Vin, H. M., Zellweger, P. T., Swinehart, D. C. and Rangan, P. V. Multimedia Conferencing in the Etherphone Environment. *IEEE Computer.* October 1991.
27. Arango, M., Bates, P., et al. Touring Machine: A Software Platform for Distributed Multimedia Applications. *IFIP '92.* May 1992.
28. Hill, W., and Ishizaki, A. A Call Model for Distributed Multimedia Communications. Hewlett-Packard Laboratories Technical Report HPL-93-06. 1993.
29. Minzer, S. E., Signaling and Control for Multimedia Services. *IEEE Multimedia '90.* November 1990.

CHAPTER 16

MULTIMEDIA GROUPWARE: COMPUTER AND VIDEO FUSION APPROACH TO OPEN SHARED WORKSPACE[1]

Hiroshi Ishii
NTT Human Interface Laboratories

Naomi Miyake[2]
Chukyo University

16.1 INTRODUCTION

Groupware is intended to create a shared workspace that supports dynamic collaboration in a work group over space and time constraints. To gain some collective benefits of groupware use, the groupware must be accepted by a majority of workgroup members as a common tool. Groupware must overcome this hurdle of *critical mass* at first.

1 A previous version of this chapter was published in *Communications of the ACM*, December 1991 [1].

2 Naomi Miyake participated in the experimental and observational phase of this research.

People do a lot of their work alone, without computers, or using different tools on different computer systems, and have developed their own work practices for these situations. In order to get new groupware accepted, *continuity* with existing individual work environments is the key issue because users work in either individual or collaborative modes and frequently move back and forth. Groupware that asks users to abandon their familiar tools, methods, and even computer hardware and software, to learn a new system just to gain some benefits in communication or coordination, is likely to encounter strong resistance. Many case studies have shown that if the tools force users to change the way they work, then the tools are generally rejected [2].

Mark Stefik pointed out that the key idea for the next generation collaboration technology is the *seamlessness* between individual and group work.[3] He insisted that group tools (groupware) must merge with individual tools. However, it is not easy to develop a self-contained and wholly integrated environment over a variety of computer systems that supports both individual and cooperative work, because each member may have very different preferences on individual tools and working methods. A member may like organizing his/her thoughts with an outline processor running on a book-size computer, and another member may prefer drawing on a sheet of paper with his/her favorite fountain pen to represent his/her idea.

Even in a heavily computerized individual workplace, users often work both with *computers* and on the physical *desktop* and frequently move back and forth. Neither of them can replace the other. For example, printed materials such as books and magazines are still an indispensable source of information. Therefore, when designing real-time shared workspaces, depending on the task and the media of the information to be shared (paper or computer file), co-workers should be able to choose either computers or desktops and to switch between them freely. This choice should be *independent* of the other members' choices. Group members should be able to use a variety of *heterogeneous* sets of tools (computer-based and manual tools) in the shared workspace *simultaneously*. We call such a space the "open shared workspace." Figure 16.1 illustrates this concept.

One important feature of face-to-face collaborations is the role of the shared drawing space such as a whiteboard. Bly, Tang, Leifer, and Minneman pointed out that it plays a very crucial role not only in storing information and conveying ideas, but also in developing ideas and mediating interaction, especially in design sessions [4,5,6]. The open shared workspace should incorporate this shared drawing space concept and extend it by allowing the simultaneous use of both computer and manual tools. The shared workspace must support *direct interaction* among co-work-

---

3 Mark Stefik made this statement in the video that introduced the Colab project of Xerox PARC [3].

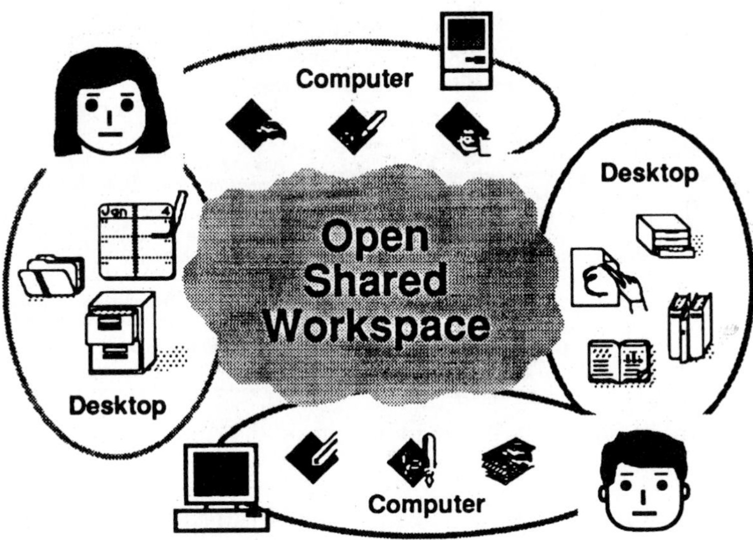

Figure 16.1 Concept of open shared workspace

ers by allowing any member to directly point to and draw on other members' workspaces in real time.

Current groupware has not effectively supported this concept of openness in shared workspaces. TeamWorkStation (TWS) solves this problem for real-time distributed collaboration. We chose video as the basic medium of TWS because it is the most powerful medium for fusing a variety of traditionally incompatible visual media such as papers and computer files.

This chapter introduces TeamWorkStation, which is designed to establish an open shared workspace by fusing distributed group members' workspaces, including both computers and desktops. First, the seams in the current CSCW environment are discussed and previous approaches to real-time shared workspace design are reviewed. Then the new fusion technique and architecture of TWS are introduced. Experience in the use of TWS for design and calligraphy sessions, and the results of an experiment in the remote teaching of machine operation are discussed. We identify the role of open shared workspace in the support of a broad range of dynamic collaboration activities that cannot be supported consistently by existing task-specific *highly structured* groupware.

16.2 SEAMS AND DESIGN APPROACHES

The new shared workspace is required to be open, in the sense that no new piece of technology should block the potential use of already existing tools

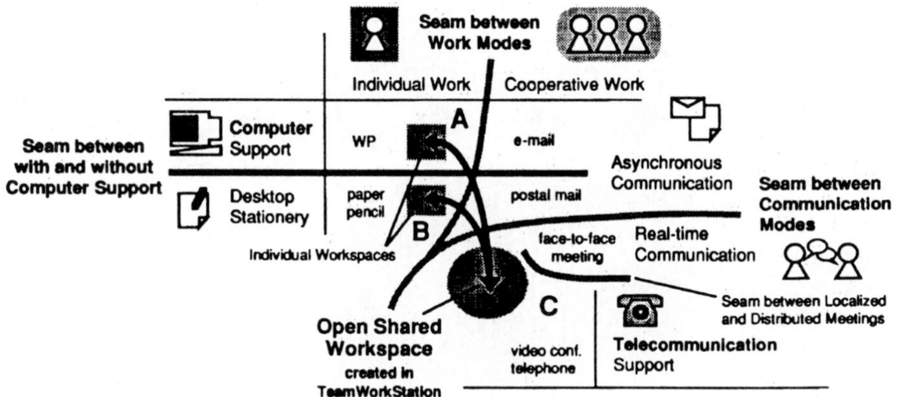

Figure 16.2 Seams in current CSCW environment

and methods. A new piece of technology inevitably introduces with it the burden of learning. It is also often coupled with the introduction of *seams* and *discontinuities* from the old work practices. The world is filled with many *seams*. The current variety of application programs running on the same or different platforms create seams of incompatible data formats and inconsistent human-computer interfaces. These seams increase the users' cognitive load.

Figure 16.2 illustrates a view of the major seams in the current computer- and communication-supported work environment. Some seams are easy to overcome, some are harder. For example, the seam between computer-supported work (A) (e.g., word processing) and the work supported by traditional desktop stationery (B) (e.g., writing with pen on a paper) is not easy to overcome because of the necessity of media conversion using special equipment such as image scanners, optical character readers, or printers.

The gap between computer support (A) and telecommunication support (C) is also difficult to overcome because of the differences in time characteristics (store and read versus real time), media (text and graphics versus live video and sound), and the support technologies (computer and LAN versus telephone and PBX).

Two major types of approaches, computer-based and video-based, have been proposed to realize real-time shared workspaces for distributed groups. Figure 16.3 illustrates these previous approaches and the fusion approach of TWS.

16.2.1 Computer-Based Approaches

Computer-based approaches try to bridge from A to C by enhancing computer programs so that data and programs can be used by a group in real-time collaboration.

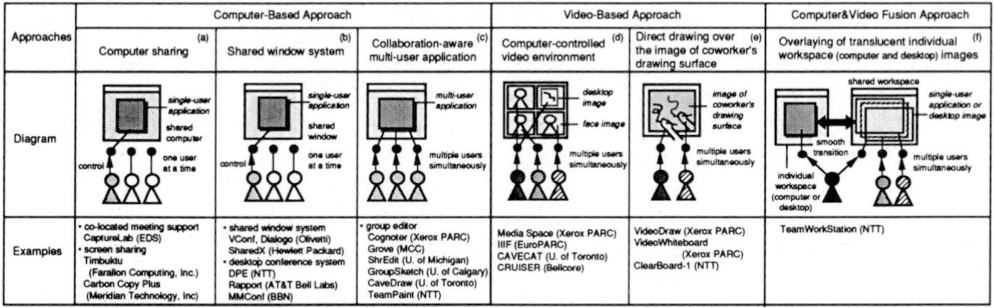

Approaches
Computer-Based Approach
Video-Based Approach
Computer&Video Fusion Approach
Computer sharing (a)
Shared window system (b)
Collaboration-aware multi-user application (c)
Computer-controlled video environment (d)
Direct drawing over the image of coworker's drawing surface (e)
Overlaying of translucent individual workspace (computer and desktop) images (f)
Diagram
single-user application
shared computer
one user at a time
control
single-user application
shared window
one user at a time
control
multi-user application
multiple users simultaneously
desktop image
face image
multiple users simultaneously
image of coworker's drawing surface
multiple users simultaneously
shared workspace
single-user application or desktop image
smooth transition
multiple users simultaneously
individual workspace (computer or desktop)
Examples
• co-located meeting support
CaptureLab (EDS)
• screen sharing
Timbuktu
(Farallon Computing, Inc.)
Carbon Copy Plus
(Meridian Technology, Inc)
• shared window system
VConf, Dialogo (Olivetti)
SharedX (Hewlett Packard)
• desktop conference system
DPE (NTT)
Rapport (AT&T Bell Labs)
MMConf (BBN)
• group editor
Cognoter (Xerox PARC)
Grove (MCC)
ShrEdit (U. of Michigan)
GroupSketch (U. of Calgary)
CaveDraw (U. of Toronto)
TeamPaint (NTT)
Media Space (Xerox PARC)
IIIF (EuroPARC)
CAVECAT (U. of Toronto)
CRUISER (Bellcore)
VideoDraw (Xerox PARC)
VideoWhiteboard
(Xerox PARC)
ClearBoard-1 (NTT)
TeamWorkStation (NTT)

Figure 16.3 Approaches to real-time shared workspace design

Computer sharing (Figure 16.3a) is a straightforward approach to allow co-located or distributed users to share a computer (screen and input devices) via network. Capture Lab™ [7,8], a computer-supported face-to-face meeting environment took this computer sharing technique to allow meeting participants to access shared application programs. Timbuktu™ [9] and Carbon Copy Plus™ are the commercial software which provide the function of remote screen sharing and remote control of the shared computer via network.

Shared window system (Figure 16.3b) provides a special window in which users can share an existing application program. VConf [10], Dialogo [11] and SharedX are the early examples of shared window systems. Shared window systems are incorporated in many desktop conference systems such as DPE [12], MMConf [13] and Rapport [14].

Both **computer sharing** and the **shared window system** allow users to execute existing single-user applications in a shared display or shared window. There is no need to modify existing single-user application programs for group use. However, all the users must use the same shared application programs, and usually only one user can control the shared application program or computer at a time.

Another approach is to implement new **collaboration-aware**[4] **multi-user application** programs for particular tasks (e.g., group editing) (Figure 16.3c). In this type of system, multiple users can control the editing cursors independently, and an access control mechanism for smaller grain size objects (e.g., words on a screen) can be provided. However, significant programming effort is needed to write new multiuser application programs. Discontinuity with existing single-user applications, and response delays caused by updating the collaborators' shared views can also be problems.

Group idea processor Cognoter [16], group outline processor Grove [17], group text editor ShrEdit [18], group drawing/painting editors GroupSketch [19], Commune [20], CaveDraw [21], TeamPaint [22], and group word processor Aspect™ [23] are the examples of collaboration-aware multiuser applications.

---

4 The word "collaboration-aware" was coined by Lauwers and Lantz [15].

All three of these computer-based approaches can handle only information stored in computers of a specific architecture. These approaches suffer from a lack of flexibility in that information outside the computers cannot be utilized. Users are still stuck with a rather large seam between the computer (A) and the actual desktop (B).

16.2.2 Video-Based Approaches

The second type of approach utilizes video communication technology that belongs to area C in Figure 16.2.

The **computer-controlled video environment**, Media Space [24,25] pioneered the use of video technology for the support of remote collaborations.[5] Media Space made video available as a work medium, and the video was used to see co-workers' face and drawing surfaces (Figure 16.3d). Recent development of computer-controlled video environment includes IIIF [27], CRUISER [28], and CAVECAT [29]. In these systems, since each member's workspace images are spatially separated in windows on a screen (or multiple screens), direct pointing and drawing over co-workers' workspace images is hard to achieve.

Tang and Minneman showed a new way to design shared drawing space in their VideoDraw [6] by allowing users to draw directly over the images of co-workers' drawing surfaces (Figure 16.3e). VideoDraw allows users to draw on a shared surface simultaneously and convey hand gestures without any time delay. However, VideoDraw restricted the targets to be shared to the images (e.g., hand-drawn images and hand gestures) on a special transparent sheet attached to the surface of a TV monitor. No papers or printed materials can be used in the collaborative session.

These video-based approaches successfully mediate dynamic interactions, and a group can share information on physical desktops (B) if the system provides cameras to capture desktop surface images. However, they suffer from a lack of flexibility in that information stored in computers (A) cannot be utilized directly. Although these video-based systems can be used in conjunction with a shared computer application, described in Figure 16.3a–c, video and computer are not integrated. Users still encounter a large seam between the video communication technologies (C) and computer technologies (A).

16.2.3 Fusion Approach of TeamWorkStation

TWS is designed to bridge gaps between personal computer (A), desktop (B) and telecommunication (C), as shown in Figure 16.2, and so realize the open shared workspace. The goal of TWS design is to provide distributed

---

[5] Our work was motivated by their Office Design Project [26] which utilized Media Space for collaborative building design by geographically distributed architects.

users with a real-time open shared workspace which every member can see, point to, and draw on *simultaneously* using *heterogeneous* personal tools.

In order to satisfy the requirements of open shared workspace, Ishii devised the key TWS design idea, **translucent overlay of individual workspace images,**[6] as illustrated in Figure 16.3f. This technique consists of superimposing two or more translucent live-video images of computer screens or physical desktop surfaces. The overlay function created with this video synthesis technique allows users to combine individual workspaces and to point to and draw on the overlaid images simultaneously. Therefore, the entire task-space is open to other members.

Figure 16.4 illustrates an overlay process in the remote teaching of calligraphy. The student uses MacCalligraphy[7] (a calligraphy simulation program), while the teacher uses actual brush, ink, and paper.

Figure 16.5a shows the appearance of the TWS prototype. The individual screen and the shared screen are contiguous in video memory. Two CCD video cameras are provided at each workstation: one for capturing live images of the member, the other for capturing the desktop surface images and hand gestures. For ease of use, the camera capturing the desktop image is mounted on a flexible desk lamp.

Figure 16.5b shows an example of a shared screen image. Two users are discussing the system architecture using a draw-editor, a handwritten diagram, pens, and hand gestures simultaneously. Face images can be displayed in windows on the shared screen. A speaker phone is used for hand-free face-to-face conversations in conjunction with these face windows.

Translucent overlay is a very simple and intuitive concept, but it is powerful because it has much more flexibility than the existing task and window-system specific groupware approaches. Overlaid video images provide users with rich semantics, which they can easily interpret. We find that users can differentiate up to three overlaid video images without much difficulty. The drawback of this overlay approach is that the results of collaboration cannot be shared directly. Another drawback is that the quality of overlaid video images is not as sharp as most computer displays. These problems are discussed in the following section.

"Shared workspace" is taken by many computer people to mean "data sharing."[8] However, we think it is not required that all the results of the

---

6 VideoDraw led Ishii to come up with the *translucent* overlay idea.

7 MacCalligraphy is the trademark of Enzan Hoshigumi Co., Japan.

8 Prof. J. Nievergelt commented on TWS that the vast majority of the literature on collaboration uses the term "shared workspace" to designate *shared data*, in the sense that the actions of all participants affect the single logical version of the data. Instead of "shared workspace," he proposed to use the term "shared visual space" to explain the essence of TWS. The authors acknowledge his thought-provoking comment.

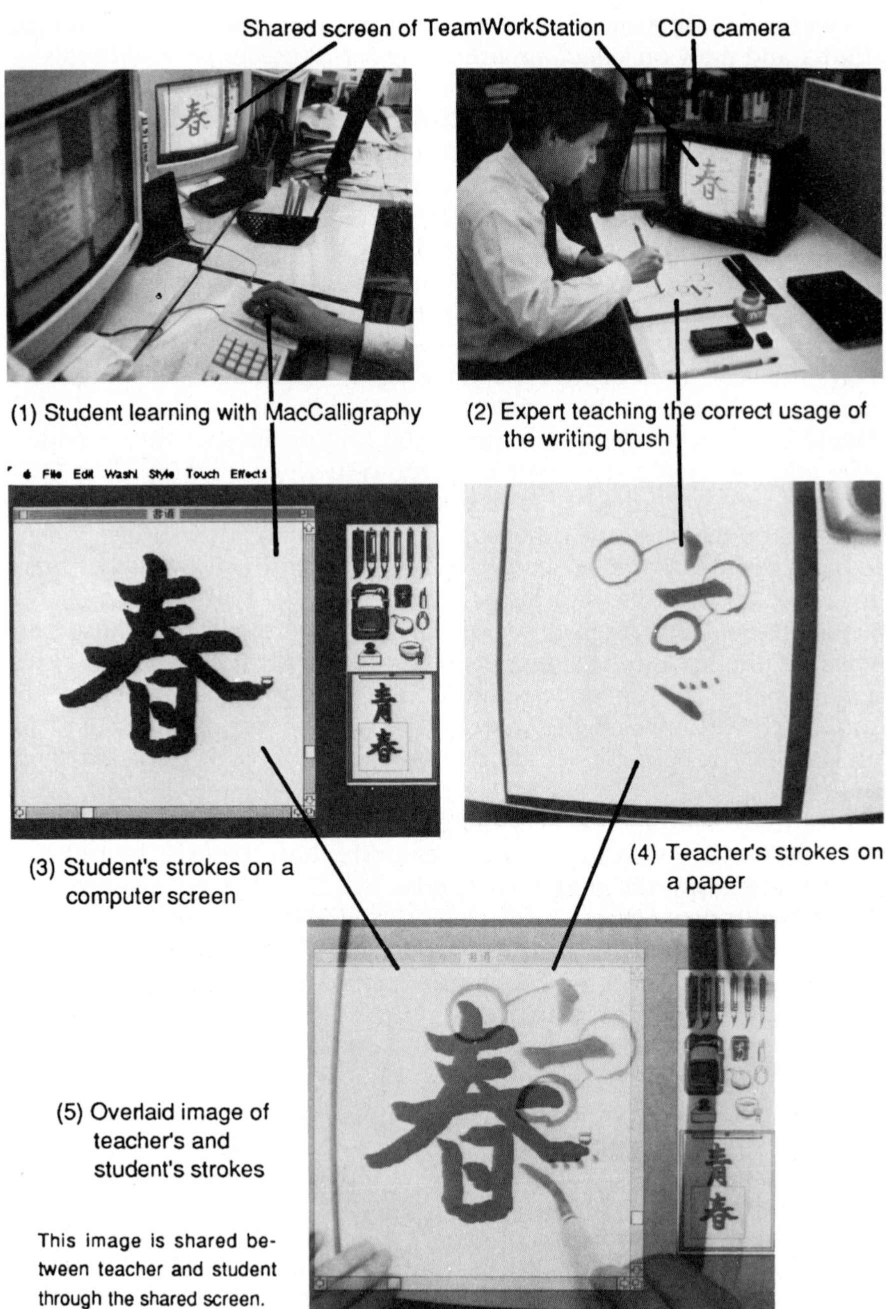

Figure 16.4 Translucent overlay process in remote teaching of calligraphy

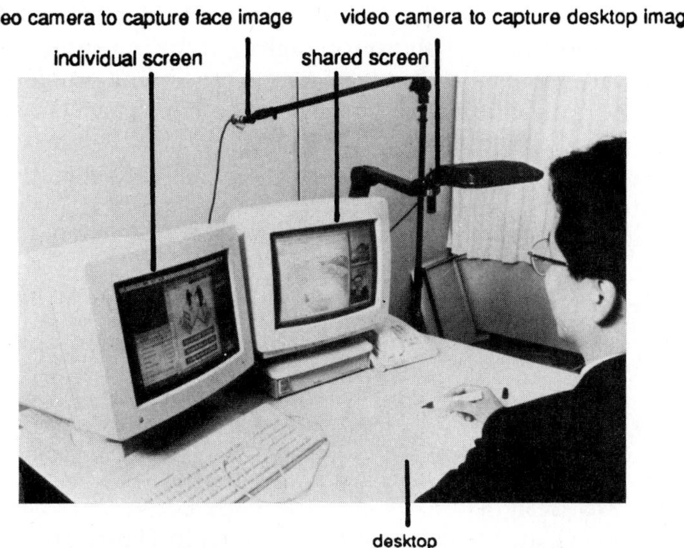

(a) Appearance of TeamWorkStation

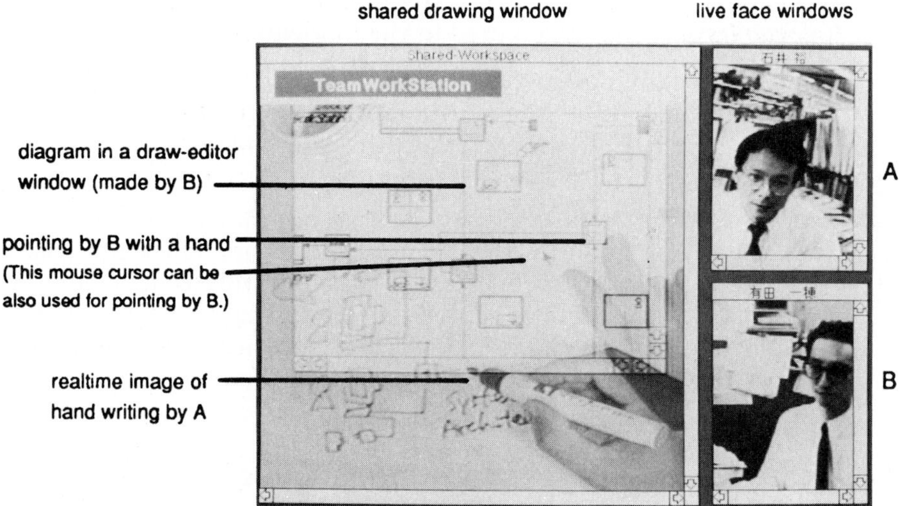

(b) A Shared Screen in Design Session

Figure 16.5 Appearance of TeamWorkStation and shared screen example

work-in-progress be directly manipulatable by all the participants. Psychological studies on collaboration highlight the important aspect of the shared task space. A detailed study of two-person joint problem solving indicates that the natural form of constructive collaboration is a type of *role division*: One member performs the complete task while the other monitors the progress [30]. The monitor does not get engaged directly in the work being done by the actor. They work on different layers: The actor works on the acting layer, and the monitor works one layer above on the monitoring layer. It is important that the monitor and the actor share the entire visual space, open to both perspectives. These observations support the overlay approach to create real-time shared workspaces.

16.2.4 Cognitive Seamlessness Achieved in TeamWorkStation

TWS was designed to bridge the gaps between personal computer (A), desktop (B), and telecommunication (C) in Figure 16.2. However, through the experimental use of TWS described below, we found Figure 16.2 shows just a superficial view of seams and TWS functions. We realized that the essence of the TWS approach is not the functional seamlessness but the *cognitive seamlessness* that is achieved in the following two points.

1. Since TWS allows users to keep using their favorite individual tools (in whatever form) while collaborating in a desktop shared workspace, there is no need to master the usage of new sophisticated groupware.
2. Because TWS's multiscreen architecture allows users to move any application program windows between the individual and shared screens just by mouse dragging, it is easy to bring the data and tools in each personal computer to the shared workspace. The information on paper and books can also be easily shared just by bringing them under the CCD camera attached to the desk lamp.

16.3 ARCHITECTURE OF TEAMWORKSTATION

TWS is designed to provide small workgroups (2–4 members) with the new medium of dynamic interaction. TWS provides users with a shared screen as the open shared workspace and live video and audio communication links for face-to-face conversation.

The present TWS prototype is based on Macintosh computers. The computer screens, individual and shared, are contiguous in video memory, as shown in Figure 16.6. Therefore, just by moving the window of any application program from the individual to shared screen, a user can transmit the application's window to all participants for remote collabora-

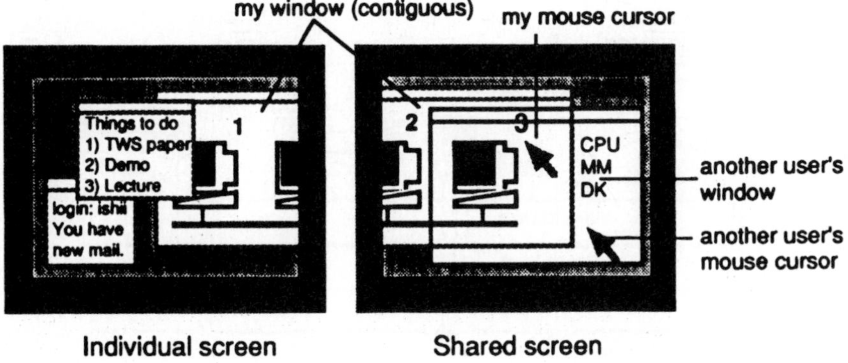

Figure 16.6 Contiguous multiple screens for smooth transition

tion. The shared screen of TWS is a strict implementation of the "WYSIWIS" (What You See Is What I See) design principle [31]. However, the combination of individual and shared screen relaxes the space constraints of WYSIWIS.

The system architecture of the TWS prototype is illustrated in Figure 16.7. In order to connect distributed workstations, a video network (NTSC and RGB) and an input device network were developed and integrated with existing data network (LocalTalk™ network) and voice (telephone) network. In the future, we will integrate these four networks into a multimedia LAN and BISDN, which are being developed by NTT.

The video network is controlled by a *video server,* which is based on a computer-controllable video switcher and video effector. The video server gathers, processes, and distributes the shared computer screen images, desktop images, and face images. Overlay of video images is done by the video server. The results of overlaying are redistributed to the shared screens via the video network. The basic architecture of this video network is similar to that of EuroPARC's IIIF[9] (Integrated Interactive Intermedia Facility) [27], except for the overlay functions of TWS's video server.

16.3.1 Modes in TWS

In addition to the "overlay" mode, this video network also provides users with two other modes: "tele-screen" and "tele-desk" modes. These modes are for the nonoverlaid remote display of individual screens and desktops, respectively. These modes are designed to show just the information within

---

[9] In the invited lecture of IFIP WG8.4 conference at Crete in September 1990, William Buxton talked about his design principle: "Let's do smart things with stupid technology today, rather than wait and do stupid things with smart technology tomorrow." Both IIIF and TWS share the same principle. The authors believe this principle is essential in pursuing new groupware technologies.

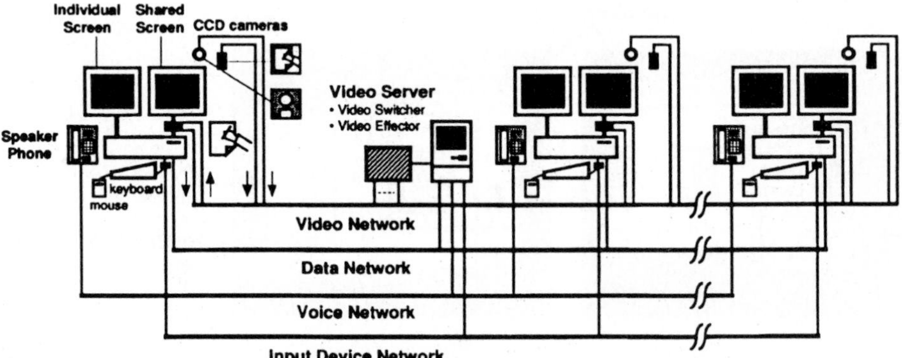

Figure 16.7 System architecture of TeamWorkStation prototype

a computer or on a desktop to remote users in a loosely coupled collaboration.

Another mode is "computer-sharing" (Figure 16.3a), for tightly coupled collaborations such as co-editing. The input device network was implemented for the computer-sharing mode. The computer-sharing mode allows collaborators to operate one computer by connecting their keyboards and mice to the computer whose screen is shared. The computer-sharing approach was taken by Capture Lab for the support of face-to-face meetings [8]. The same function has been implemented in software such as Timbuktu™ [9]. However, the software solution creates greater response delays. In this computer-sharing mode, TWS provides no special software or hardware embedded protocol for floor control, but relies on the informal social protocol agreed on by the collaborators via the face-to-face communication links.

TWS is designed to allow users to choose the most suitable mode and move from one mode to another according to task contents and roles played by the co-workers. For example, suppose user A starts to explain his/her plan by showing a diagram to user B using the tele-screen mode. (If his/her diagram was written or printed on a paper, the tele-desk mode would be used instead of the tele-screen mode.) If B wants to point to or mark a part of the diagram to ask a question, he/she can move to the screen-overlay or screen-and-desk-overlay mode and user B can point to the part of A's diagram by B's own pointer (mouse or pencil). If B felt it was necessary to directly change a part of the diagram, and if A agreed, they could move to the computer-sharing mode.

Since the pattern of collaboration changes dynamically, TWS's flexibility in shuttling between these collaboration modes is important in supporting the dynamic collaboration process. However, the tele-screen and tele-desk modes were seldom used in the experimental sessions described below because the overlay mode is more flexible and includes tele-desk and tele-screen functions. The overlay mode was used as the default mode in most collaborative sessions, and sometimes users moved to computer-sharing mode when they needed to edit the same document or data stored in a computer.

16.3.2 Use of Heterogeneous Computers

Although the TWS prototype uses Macintosh™ workstations, heterogeneous computers can also be used since overlaying is done at a standard video signal level. Indeed, screen-overlay and tele-screen functions have been successfully implemented between an NEC PC-9800™ series computer running MS-DOS™ and the Macintosh™ computers.

16.4 EXPERIMENTAL USE OF TEAMWORKSTATION

Since July 1989, TWS has been used by Ishii and two of his colleagues in NTT for daily work including refining the design of TWS itself.

16.4.1 Design Session

The major TWS usage has been discussion about the system architecture design. When Ishii and his colleague Arita redesigned and rebuilt the TWS prototype in July 1990, they used TWS to discuss the new architecture of video network for about 10 hours in total. The photograph in Figure 16.5b shows a typical shared screen image in our design session. The regular tools in our design sessions were drawing editors, an outline editor, a graphic computer,[10] and pen and paper.

Comments on the base diagram were exchanged mainly using *voice* with pointing and marking by *hand* in the overlay mode. The capability of this direct hand pointing to the co-worker's diagram by hand gave us a strong sense of sharing common task space. We found the hand was preferred to the mouse as a means of pointing and marking because hand gestures are much more expressive and because hand marking is generally quicker. Even in the situation where a user presents a diagram made and stored in computer, the user often overlaid his/her desktop over his/her computer screen image for explaining the points of the diagram by finger pointing and pen marking (Figure 16.5b is an example of this situation).

While using TWS, we noted that the face-to-face conversation link played an important role in the informal control of group interaction, especially for the coordination of the use of this limited workspace on the shared screen.

Also, we rarely used the computer-sharing mode. Most of our comments and discussion on diagrams were done in the overlay mode. We seldom felt the necessity of editing the other's diagrams directly. If a diagram was to be

---

10 "Graphic computer" is a painting tablet which generates the NTSC video output.

changed, usually the originator would change it according to the comments made by the other. Thus, we collaborated mostly in the *role-division* mode, as observed and explicated in Miyake's joint problem-solving study [30]. There were few occasions where we had to divide the entire task into subtasks and each had to be taken care of separately and in parallel. We used the computer-sharing mode only for such *subtask-division* modes.

One reason for this preference for *role-division* appears to come from the respect paid to the ownership of the diagrams. When a diagram is drawn, the drawer owns it. When I draw a diagram and someone else changes it, even with my permission, that is a challenge to my ownership. This is a very natural feeling, even in a close collaborative session. Through these design experiences, we recognized that the shared workspace does not always require the direct data sharing and editing function. The overlay solution provides us with a more comfortable environment, because the overlaid layers keep the person's own layer of work intact in the role-division mode.

16.4.2 Remote Teaching of Calligraphy

One of the important features of TWS is that all the collaborators can share not only the *results* of drawing or marking in the shared workspace, but also the dynamic *process* of drawing and pointing. One application that demonstrates the importance of process sharing is the teaching of calligraphy. The photograph in Figure 16.4 shows a snapshot of a calligraphy teaching session we conducted using TWS, where the student used MacCalligraphy™ and the teacher used an actual brush, ink, and paper.

In these sessions, first the student uses MacCalligraphy™ (or a brush with black ink) to generate a Chinese character on the shared screen (or a sheet of paper on his/her desktop). The instructor watches the student's real-time strokes via the shared screen and makes necessary comments by using a brush with red ink on the paper on his/her desktop. Here the real-time nature of the collaboration is extremely important. The instructor can make his/her comments directly over the student's strokes when the student deviates from the suggested forms, and the student gains the immediate feedback of the teacher (e.g., correct use of the wrist).

We also conducted other calligraphy sessions where both teacher and student used actual brushes on their physical desktops to evaluate the usability of TWS in teaching. Through these calligraphy experiments, we realized that the overlaid live video images of dynamic and three-dimensional gesture of drawing play a very important role in the teaching process.

We expect that TWS will be far superior to ordinary telephone or fax communication systems for the sharing of *process-oriented knowledge or skill* between remote experts and trainees. The fusion of live video images of each workspace in combination with voice and face communication is expected to enhance the quality and efficiency of remote consulting and training.

16.4.3 Problems of Overlay Approach

Through the experimental use of the overlay mode in TWS, we also found the following problems of the overlay approach based on the video synthesis technique.

- The results of collaboration cannot be shared directly. Since individual workspaces are overlaid as video images, the marks and the marked documents occupy different layers in the shared screens. They are actually stored separately in different places in different media (in computer files or on paper). We mainly used a video printer (to hard-copy), a video digitizer (to store in a computer file), and a videotape recorder to record the results and the process of real-time collaboration.
- The quality of overlaid video images is not sharp nor stable enough to support sharing detailed documents. When we needed to discuss such detailed documents, we often distributed copies of the documents by e-mail or fax in advance.
- Indirect drawing and pointing on the desktop by hand needs time and effort to get used to. (This is similar to the learning process needed for indirect pointing devices such as a mouse or tablet.) Since the desktop images captured by CCD camera are displayed on a shared screen after the image overlay operation, users must learn to control pencil or finger following the feedback from the screen.

  In contrast, VideoDraw [6] allows users to draw directly on the screen at the cost of less flexibility (unavailability of papers). Through the use of TWS in design sessions, we found the advantages of use of papers and books outweighed this disadvantage of indirect drawing.
- Especially when more than three users are co-working, identifying the owners of objects (such as cursor, draw object, window, marks on paper) on an overlaid screen is difficult. The use of a different color for each user's objects improves this problem slightly. To identify the objects, a user can also dim the video signal electrically or move the CCD camera a little.
- Since overlaid screen images are completely independent of each other, scrolling or moving a document in one layer breaks the spatial relationships with the marks made on other layers. Users must pay some attention to retain the consistency of spatial relations among layers.

16.5 EVALUATION OF OVERLAY IN REMOTE TEACHING OF MACHINE OPERATION

The key design idea of TWS is the overlay of individual workspace images. In order to clarify the effects of overlay quantitatively, we conducted an experiment using the remote teaching of machine operation with and without overlay.

16.5.1 The Experiment

Task: Using a digital video effector (Panasonic VW-VE300), instructors whose behavior was also the object of our observation were to teach students how to achieve two desired results by combining two input video images into one, in two different layouts, Task 1 and Task 2. The difficulty of the tasks was set to be equal, by equating the number of steps required to achieve the results.

Subjects: Two subjects who were knowledgeable in the use of the video effector served as instructors. Each instructor taught four students, two women and two men, who were all novices. There were thus eight students in all. They were recruited from adjacent labs for cooperative help, but none of them knew the experiment's objectives in advance.

Design: Each student was to carry out first Task 1 and then Task 2, one in the overlay mode and the other in the tele-desk mode. To counterbalance the practice effect, half the subjects started with the overlay mode, while the other half started with the tele-desk mode. Figure 16.8 shows the snapshots and schematic diagrams of this experiment in overlay and tele-desk modes. After the tasks, both the instructors and the students were briefly interviewed individually on what they liked and disliked about the tasks and the task environment.

Findings: For each task, the task completion time was measured from the end of the explanation of the objective layout till the moment when the instructor declared that the expected outcome was obtained. The overall results are shown in Figure 16.9. Every student completed the task in the overlay mode faster than in the tele-desk mode, regardless of the order. The time difference was statistically significant (F [1,5[= 58.40, $p < .01$). F values were calculated from the $2 \times 2 \times 2$ analysis of variance (mode difference as a within-subject variable, while instructor and mode-order type differences as between-subject variables). No other main effects, or interactions, were found to be statistically significant, though the instructor difference was almost statistically significant (F [1,5] = 15.57, $p = .01$). This instructor difference appears to have come from the different teaching styles of the two: One, who spent more time teaching, tended to explain why some action would work, while the other instructor limited explanations to issuing procedures.

In the post-task interview, the students generally preferred the overlay mode to the tele-desk mode. They commented that seeing the teacher's hand actually move over the effector made it easier for them to follow. Two students commented that things had been hard to see in the overlay mode.

Both of the instructors spontaneously commented quite favorably about the overlay mode. They often stated that the direct pointing, which was only possible in the overlay mode, had greatly relieved them from the

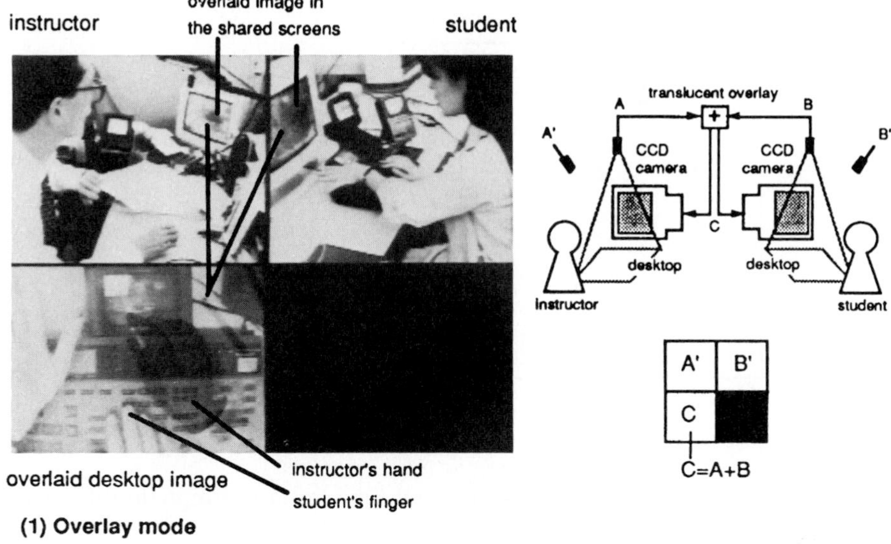

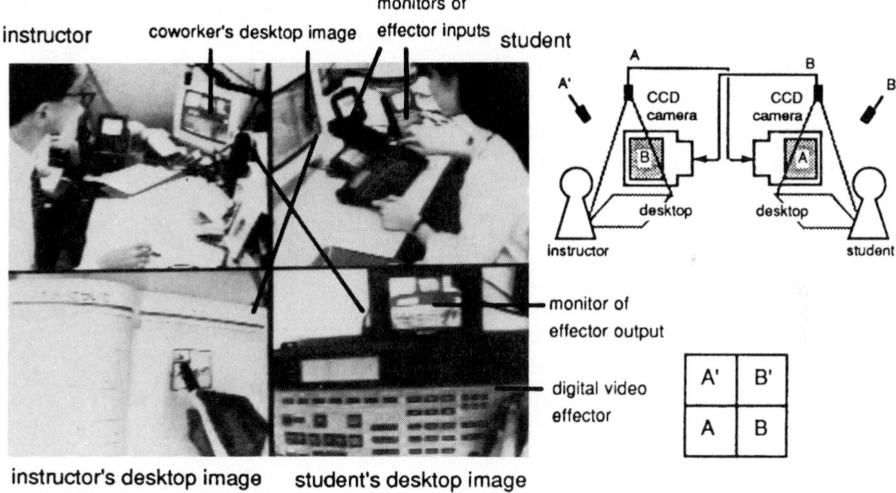

Figure 16.8 Experiment of remote teaching of machine operation with and without overlay

extraneous burden of either verbalizing the locations of the buttons or pulling out the manual to indirectly point to the locations on the drawings. In the post-task interview, they both said they felt that they had talked much less in the overlay mode. In fact, however, the actual numbers of units uttered in the two modes are roughly the same (on average, 68.3 utterance units per minute for the overlay mode; 52.7 units for the tele-desk

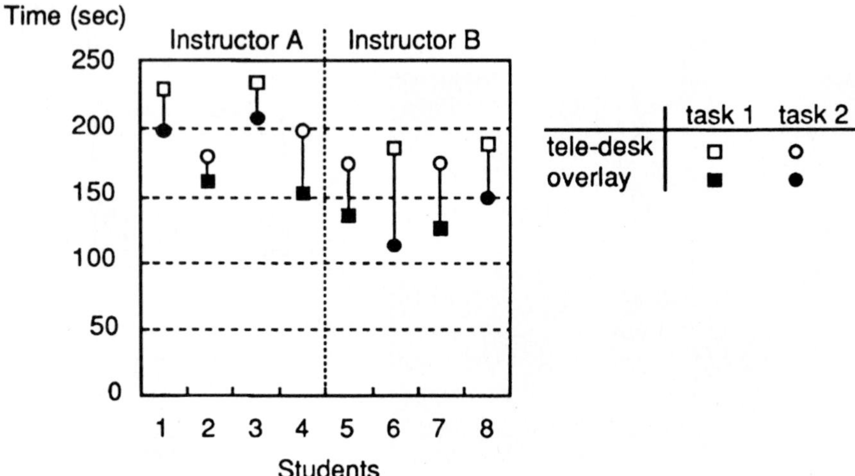

Figure 16.9 Results of experiment: Elapsed time for task completion in overlay and tele-desk modes by each pair.

mode). This implies that the relief felt by the instructors did not come from the less amount of actual verbal work; it might have come from the ease of superimposing instructors' monitoring view onto the actual "task-doing" view of the student. The time efficiency and the teaching ease realized by the overlay mode are two good indicators of the gains achievable in a seam-reduced collaboration environment.

16.6 CONCLUSION

Multimedia applications have been discussed mainly in the context of package media, such as an interactive multimedia book in a CD-ROM. The focus of research and development effort was on the representation of media-composite information in computer memory and the ways to interact with that information.

However, the emergence of CSCW (Computer-Supported Cooperative Work) as an identifiable research field has enabled us to shift our focus of multimedia applications from the traditional *package media* to dynamic *collaboration media*. Groupware has demonstrated a new view of computer interaction: We are interacting not *with* computers, but *through* computers.

TeamWorkStation was introduced in this chapter to illustrate the new direction of multimedia applications. TWS is a novel collaboration medium that approaches *seamless* CSCW fusing the two different types of media—video and computer. It effectively integrates two kinds of individual workspaces—*computers* and *desktops*—and provides distributed users with an *open shared workspace*. Its key design idea is the translucent overlay of individual workspace images. Because each co-worker can continue to use favorite application programs or desktop tools, there is only a *minor cognitive seam* between individual and shared workspaces. Using translucent video overlay functions, real-time information such as hand gestures and handwritten comments can be shared between co-workers as well as information contained in printed materials and computer files.

TWS was not intended to replace existing groupware approaches. Rather, we designed TWS in order to support a broader range of dynamic collaboration activities that range over several seams and cannot be supported consistently by existing task-specific structured groupware.

TWS will be tested with a larger variety of tasks and users to investigate the dynamic nature of collaboration and to enhance computer support by further reducing the seams. We expect that progress in BISDN and multimedia LAN technology will enhance the attractiveness of the TWS approach to realize the truly open shared workspace.

16.7 ACKNOWLEDGMENTS

The authors thank Masaaki Ohkubo at NTT for his contribution in building the first prototype of TWS in 1989, and Kazuho Arita at NTT for his contribution in the redesign and implementation of the new prototype system with extended video control functions in 1990. Discussions with these co-workers provided a lot of insight. In the experiments of remote teaching of machine operation, Kazuho Arita, Minoru Kobayashi, and other colleagues in NTT contributed as instructors and students.

Hiroshi Ishii thanks John Tang for insightful discussions on the design of shared drawing space and his detailed comments. He also thanks Keith Lantz for his very detailed and encouraging comments on the earlier version of this chapter, and thanks Takahiko Kamae, Takaya Endo, and Gen Suzuki of NTT Human Interface Laboratories for their encouragement.

The authors also thank Jonathan Grudin for his particularly helpful comments on the draft of this paper. Thanks are also due to Ellen Francik for her advice on the experiment design, and Morten Kyng and the anonymous reviewers for their comments on this manuscript.

16.8 REFERENCES

1. Ishii, H., and Miyake, N. Toward an Open Shared Workspace: Computer and Video Fusion Approach of TeamWorkStation. *Communication of the ACM (CACM)*. ACM Press. vol. 34, no. 12. December 1991. pp. 37–50.
2. Grudin, J. Why CSCW Applications Fail: Problems in the Design and Evaluation of Organizational Interfaces. *Proceedings of CSCW '88*. 1988. pp. 85–93.
3. Foster, G., and Tatar, D. Experiments in Computer Support for Teamwork—Colab (Video). Xerox PARC. 1988.

4. Bly, S. A. A Use of Drawing Surfaces in Different Collaborative Settings. *Proceedings of CSCW '88*. 1988. pp. 250–256.
5. Tang, J. C., and Leifer, L. J. A Framework for Understanding the Workspace Activity of Design Teams. *Proceedings of CSCW '88*. September 1988. pp.244–249.
6. Tang, J. C., and Minneman, S. L. VideoDraw: A Video Interface for Collaborative Drawing. *Proceedings of CHI '90*. April 1990. pp. 313–320.
7. Mantei, M. Capturing the Capture Concepts: A Case Study in the Design of Computer-Supported Meeting Environments. *Proceedings of CSCW '88*. 1988. pp. 257–270.
8. Halonen, D., Horton, M., Kass, R., and Scott, P. Shared Hardware: A Novel Technology for Computer Support of Face-to-Face Meetings. *Proceedings of COIS '90*. April 1990. pp. 163–168.
9. Farallon Computing Inc. *Timbuktu 4.0 User's Guide*. Farallon Computing Inc. 1991.
10. Lantz, K. A. An Experiment in Integrated Multimedia Conferencing. *Proceedings of CSCW '86*. 1986. pp. 267–275.
11. Lauwers, J. C., Joseph, T. A., Lantz, K. A., and Romanow, A. L. Replicated Architectures for Shared Window Systems: A Critique. *Proceedings of COIS '90*. April 1990. pp. 249–260.
12. Suzuki, T., Taniguchi, H., and Takada, H. A Real-time Electronic Conferencing System Based on Distributed UNIX. USENIX Conference. 1986. pp. 189–199.
13. Crowly, T., Milazzo, P., Baker, E., Forsdick, H., and Tomlinson, R. MMConf: An Infrastructure for Building Shared Multimedia Applications. *Proceedings of CSCW '90*. ACM Press. October 1990. pp. 329–342.
14. Ahuja, S. R., Ensor, J. R., and Lucco, S. E. A Comparison of Application Sharing Mechanisms in Real-Time Desktop Conferencing Systems. *Proceedings of COIS '90*. April 1990. pp. 238–248.
15. Lauwers, J. C. and Lantz, K. A. Collaboration Awareness in Support of Collaboration Transparency: Requirements for the Next Generation of Shared Window Systems. *Proceedings of CHI '90*. April 1990. pp. 303–311.
16. Foster, G., and Stefik, M. Cognoter, Theory and Practice of a Collaborative Tool. *Proceedings of CSCW '86*. 1986. pp. 7–15.
17. Ellis, C. A., Gibbs, S. J., and Rein, G. L. Groupware: Some Issues and Experiences. *Communications of the ACM*. Vol. 34, No. 1. January 1991. pp. 38–58.
18. McGuffin, L., and Olson, G. M. ShrEdit: A Shared Electronic Workspace. CSMIL Technical Report No. 42. 1992.
19. Greenberg, S., Roseman, M., Webster, D., and Bohnet, R. Issues and Experiences Designing and Implementing Two Group Drawing Tools. *Proceedings of HICSS '92*. IEEE Computer Society. 1992. pp. 139–150.
20. Minneman, S. L., and Bly, S. A. Managing a Trois: A Study of a Multi-User Drawing Tool in Distributed Design Work. *Proceedings of CHI '91*. ACM Press. 1991. pp. 217–224.
21. Lu, I., and Mantei, M. Idea Management in a Shared Drawing Tool. *Proceedings of ECSCW '91*. Kluwer. 1991. pp. 97–112.
22. Ishii, H., Kobayashi, M., and Grudin, J. Integration of Inter-Personal Space and Shared Workspace: ClearBoard Design and Experiments. *Proceedings of CSCW '92*. November 1992. pp. 33–42.
23. Group Technologies, Inc. Aspects: The First Simultaneous Conference Software for the Macintosh. *Aspects User's Manual*. Group Technologies, Inc. 1990.
24. Stults, R. Experimental Uses of Video to Support Design Activities. Xerox Palo Alto Research Center. 1988.
25. Harrison, S., Minneman, S., Stults, R., and Weber, K. Video: A Design Medium. *SIGCHI Bulletin*. ACM Press. January 1990. pp. 86–90.
26. Weber, K., and Minneman, S. The Office Design Project (Video). Xerox PARC. 1987.

27. Buxton, W. and Moran, T. EuroPARC's Integrated Interactive Intermedia Facility (IIIF): Early Experiences. *Proceedings of IFIP WG8.4 Conference on Multi-User Interfaces and Applications*. September 1990. pp. 11–34.
28. Root, R. W. Design of a Multi-Media Vehicle for Social Browsing. *Proceedings of CSCW '88*. September 1988. pp. 25–38.
29. Mantei, M., Baecker, R., Sellen, A., Buxton, W., and Milligan, T. Experiences in the Use of a Media Space. *Proceedings of CHI '91*. May 1991. pp. 203–208.
30. Miyake, N. Constructive Interaction and the Iterative Process of Understanding. *Cognitive Science*. vol.10, no. 2. 1986. pp. 151–177.
31. Stefik, M., Bobrow, D., Lanning, S., Tatar, D., and Foster, G., WYSIWIS Revised: Early Experiences with Multi-user Interfaces. *Proceedings of CSCW '86*. 1986. pp. 276–290.

CHAPTER 17

High Definition Television and Desktop Computing

Charles A. Poynton
Sun Microsystems Computer Corporation

Multimedia seeks to engage people through interfaces that provide visual and aural richness. Providing a rich visual environment demands a lot of pixels and a high refresh rate. High Definition Television (HDTV) represents the state of the art of image quality in motion image capture, recording, processing, and electronic distribution, and will be important to high-end multimedia applications.

Advanced Television (ATV) systems for the distribution of entertainment to consumers are being standardized and will begin to be deployed in about 1995. ATV technology will be used to distribute entertainment that will be produced primarily using film or HDTV studio technology. Consumer ATV receivers—and eventually VCRs and camcorders—will incorporate high-performance digital compression and decompression technology, and ATV equipment will benefit from the economy of scale of manufacture in consumer volumes. Cheap consumer hardware and components and the wide availability of program material in compressed digital form will cause ATV to be a significant influence on multimedia.

Emerging ATV standards have much in common with the ISO MPEG-2 standards, and it is likely that these standards will converge to the extent that common components could be used. This will benefit the computer and communications industries.

This chapter outlines the background of HDTV, describes the basic parameters of the 1125/60 production standard, discusses the features of proposed ATV systems, outlines potential application areas, and briefly describes standardization issues currently under discussion.

17.1 NOMENCLATURE—VIDEO VERSUS COMPUTING

17.1.1 Image Structures

A video system is denoted by the total number of lines in its raster (frame) and its field rate—in hertz, or fields per second—separated by a slash. Broadcast television in North America and Japan is denoted 525/59.94; the system used in Europe is denoted 625/50. These systems are colloquially called *NTSC* and *PAL*, but those terms properly denote color coding and not raster structure. Conventional television has a 4:3 picture aspect ratio and employs interlaced scanning (to be discussed later), which is implicit in the 525/59.94 notion.

The total number of lines in a raster is of less concern to the viewer than the number of lines that contain useful picture information. The number of *lines per picture height* (L/PH) is about 4 percent less than the number of total lines in a field—in an interlaced system, 8 percent less than the total lines in the frame—in order to accommodate vertical blanking interval overhead. For example, a 525/59.94 system has about 483 picture lines. (See Figure 17.1.)

Computer users denote scanning structures by their horizontal and vertical pixel counts only, and generally do not indicate field or frame rate. For example, a 1152×900 system may have 937 total lines and a frame rate of 65.95 Hz. Sometimes, scanning parameters are implicit in acronyms, for example, *VGA* implicitly has a "resolution" of 640×480. Figure 17.1 shows the parameters of several standard scanning systems.

17.1.2 The Definition of "Resolution"

Resolution refers to the capability of an imaging system to reproduce fine detail. As picture detail increases in frequency, the response of an imaging system generally deteriorates. For a given resolution, the perception of image quality depends in part on viewing distance. (See Figure 17.2.)

In film, resolution is measured as the finest pattern of straight, parallel lines that can be reproduced, expressed in *line pairs per millimeter* (lp/mm). A line pair contains a black region and a white region.

In video, resolution refers to the number of line pairs (cycles) resolved on the face of the display screen, expressed in cycles per picture height (C/PH) or cycles per picture width (C/PW). A *cycle* is equivalent to a *line pair* of film. In a digital system, it takes at least two samples—or pixels or scanning lines—to represent a line pair. However, resolution may be substantially less

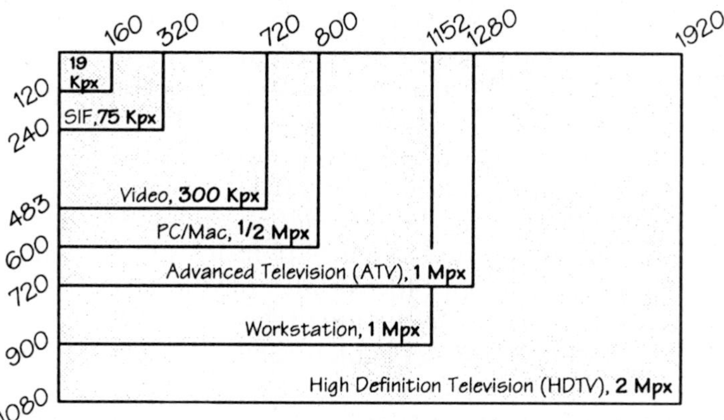

Figure 17.1 Image structures of various display systems are compared, showing the horizontal and vertical pixel counts of each. The smallest format shown here, 19 kilopixels, is representative of the image size typical of motion playback through current software decompressors. SIF resolution is used in today's MPEG-1 implementations. Direct-view CRT displays are available for all of the larger formats. HDTV has about six times the number of pixels as conventional video and about five hundred times the spatial and temporal resolution of today's software image decompressors.

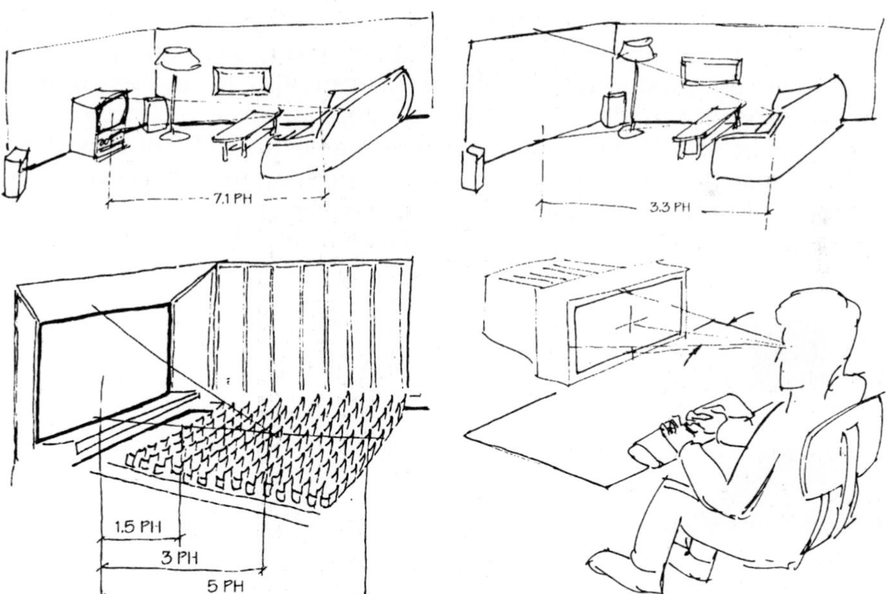

Figure 17.2 In the living room, television viewing is best when the viewer is located at a distance of about seven picture heights from the screen. Cinema offers a wide range of viewing distances, but about three times picture height is optimum. In the long term, consumer HDTV will bring the cinema viewing experience to the living room. A workstation user typically sits very close to his screen, but for a large display surface his viewing angle approximates that of HDTV.

than the number of pixel pairs due to optical, electro-optical, and electrical filtering effects. *Limiting resolution* is reached at the frequency where detail is recorded with just 10 percent of the system's low-frequency response. In consumer television, the number of scanning lines is fixed by the raster standard, but the electronics of transmission, recording, and display systems tend to limit bandwidth and reduce the horizontal resolution. Consequently, in consumer electronics the term *resolution* generally refers to horizontal resolution. Confusingly, horizontal resolution is expressed in units of lines per picture height, so once the number of resolvable lines is measured, it must be corrected for the aspect ratio of the picture. Resolution in *TV lines* is *twice* the resolution in cycles per picture width, divided by the aspect ratio of the picture.

In computer graphics, *resolution* refers simply to the number of discrete horizontal and vertical *picture elements*—or *pixels*—that are employed to represent an image in digital form. For example, a 1152 × 900 system has a total of about one million pixels (one megapixel, or 1 Mpx). Computer graphics has not traditionally been concerned with whether individual pixels can be discerned on the face of the display. In most color computer systems, an image comprising a one-pixel black and white checkerboard displays as a uniform gray. (See Figure 17.3.)

Computer graphics often treats each pixel as representing an idealized rectangular area independent of all other pixels. This notion discounts the correlation among pixels that is an inherent and necessary aspect of image acquisition, processing, compression, display, and perception. In fact, the rather large spot produced by the electron beam of a CRT and the arrangement of phosphor triads on the screen produce an image of a pixel on the screen that bears little resemblance to a rectangle. If pixels are viewed at a sufficient distance, these artifacts are of little importance. However, there is generally a strong economic incentive to have imaging systems that make the maximum perceptual use of the delivered pixels, and consequently we

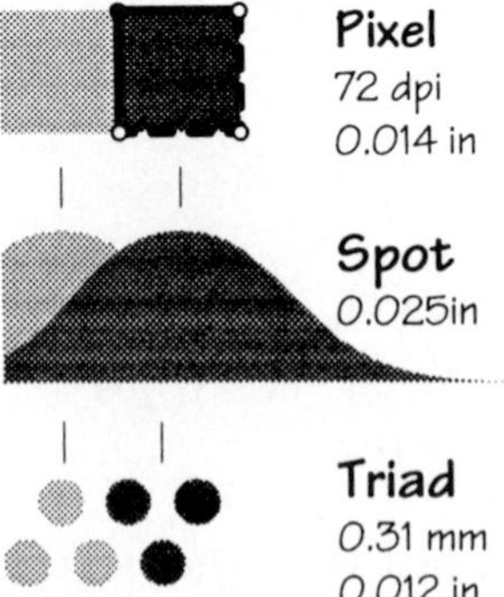

Figure 17.3 Computer graphics view of pixels compared with the electron beam spot shape and the arrangement of phosphor triads on the screen.

tend to view CRTs at close viewing distances. The distortions of nonideal pixels need to be compensated in order to achieve good image quality at close viewing distances. HDTV systems are designed to take these distortions into account. This concern with "image microstructure" is by no means unique to video and HDTV systems: The printing industry has for decades chosen screen frequencies, screen angles, and dot shapes to optimize for the conditions under which their products will be viewed.

Resolution refers to the capability of a system to reproduce spatial detail. Another important aspect of digital picture representation is the capability to reproduce intensity values. HDTV uses 8 bits for each of three components—red, green, and blue—but the transfer function and color interpretation are established with careful attention to the needs of human visual perception.

17.2 VIEWING CONDITIONS

The fundamental development work for HDTV was done at the Japan Broadcasting Corporation (NHK), after extensive psychophysical and perceptual research led by Dr. Takashi Fujio. Human viewers tend to position themselves relative to a scene such that the smallest detail of interest in the scene subtends an angle of about one minute of arc (1/60°), which is approximately the limit of angular discrimination for normal vision. For the 483 picture lines of 525-line television, the corresponding viewing distance is about seven times picture height, and the horizontal viewing angle is about 11°. For the 1035 visible lines of 1125-line HDTV, the corresponding viewing distance is 3.3 times screen height and the horizontal viewing angle is almost tripled to 28°. (See Figure 17.4.)

In order to achieve a viewing situation where a pixel subtends 1/60°, viewing distance expressed in units of picture height should be about 3400 divided by the number of picture lines. Computer users tend to position themselves closer than this—about 60 to 75 percent of this distance—but at this closer distance individual pixels are discernible.

$$\text{distance}_{PH} = \frac{3400}{\text{lines}}$$

The viewer of HDTV consequently does not perceive increased definition (resolution) for the same size picture compared to conventional television, but rather moves closer to the screen. Psychophysical research has shown that a viewer's emotional involvement in a motion picture is increased when the picture subtends a large viewing angle. Consumer HDTV should be called *wide screen television*, and this designation would probably be more appropriate to consumer marketing and product differentiation than HDTV. Figure 17.5 shows how some early studies made different comparisons of the aspect ratio difference between conventional video and HDTV.

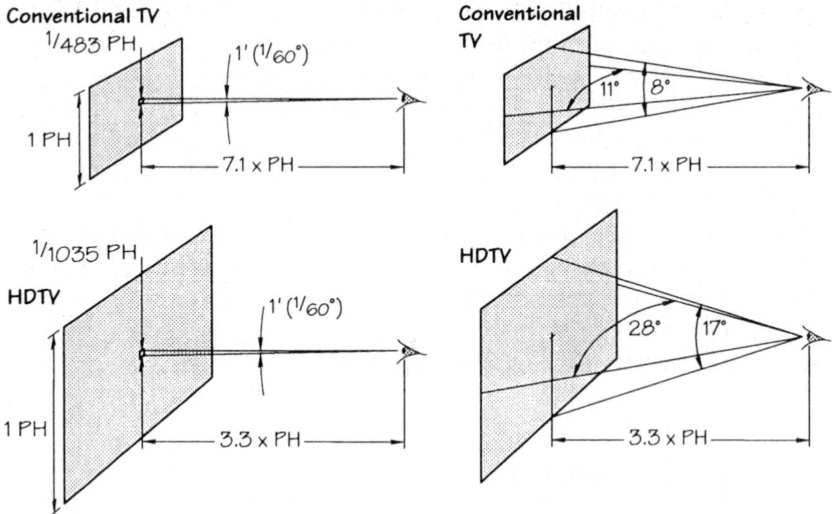

Figure 17.4a Viewing distance is established by the observer, who is positioned so that the smallest detail of interest in the scene—shown here as a pixel—subtends an angle of about one minute (1/60 degree) of arc, the limit of angular discrimination for normal vision. For the 483 visible lines of conventional television the corresponding viewing distance is about seven picture heights (PH). Closer than this distance, the scan lines are objectionable; farther away, the picture is unreasonably small. For HDTV with 1080 visible lines, the corresponding viewing distance is about 3.3 times screen height.

Figure 17.4b Viewing angle can be computed from viewing distance by simple trigonometry. Conventional television has a horizontal viewing angle of about 11 degrees. In HDTV, the increased pixel count and the increased aspect ratio result in the horizontal viewing angle being increased to about 28 degrees. The viewer of HDTV does not normally perceive increased "definition" (resolution) for the same size picture, but rather moves closer to the screen so as to experience a picture of similar spatial resolution to conventional video but which subtends a much wider field of view. Some argue that it would be more appropriate—and better for market differentiation—to call it "wide screen television" instead of "HDTV."

However, HDTV's capability for increased viewing angle is much more significant than just an increase in aspect ratio.

It is unnecessary to increase the vertical angle of view as much as the horizontal, and the aspect ratio of 16:9 has been standardized for HDTV, compared to 4:3 for conventional television. The HDTV aspect ratio, about 1.78:1, is almost the same as the most common cinema aspect ratio of 1.85:1.

NHK research has revealed that in combination with large viewing angles, high-quality stereo sound impacts the psychophysical response of the viewer to the picture. In particular, the viewer's eye-tracking response is

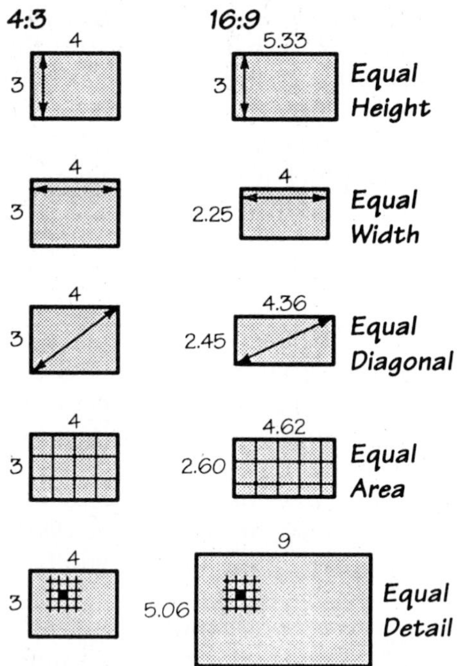

Figure 17.5 Picture size of HDTV, with its 16:9 aspect ratio, has been compared to conventional video with 4:3 aspect ratio on the basis of equal height, equal width, equal diagonal, and equal area. The first four rows of this diagram show graphical representations of these comparisons. These relationships have even been used in consumer preference testing for HDTV. But any comparison on aspect ratio alone disregards the most significant aspect of HDTV: its capability to reproduce picture detail. A comparison on the basis of equal detail is shown in the bottom row. The main goal of HDTV is to present—with roughly the same angular resolution as conventional television—a much larger picture.

dramatically different from conventional television. All HDTV systems include CD-quality stereo audio.

17.3 QUALITY

The picture quality of HDTV is superior to that of 35-mm motion picture film, but less than the quality of 35-mm still film. Motion picture film is conveyed vertically through the camera and projector, so the width—not the height—of the film is 35 mm. Cinema usually has an aspect ratio of 1.85:1, so the projected film area is about 21 mm × 11 mm, only three-tenths of the 36 mm × 24 mm projected area of 35-mm still film. In any case, the limit to the resolution of motion picture film is not the static response of the film, but judder and weave in the camera and the projector.

The colorimetry obtainable with the color separation filters and CRT phosphors of a video system is greatly superior to that possible with the photochemical processes of a color film system. There are other issues related to the subjective impressions that a viewer obtains from viewing motion picture film—the *film look*—that are still being explored in HDTV. For example, specular highlights captured on film have an appearance that is subjectively more pleasing than when captured in video.

17.4 HDTV, ATV, EDTV, IDTV

HDTV is defined as having about twice the horizontal and twice the vertical (linear) resolution of conventional television, a 16:9 picture aspect ratio, and at least 24-Hz frame rate. Under this definition, HDTV has approximately double the number of lines of current broadcast television, at approximately the same field rate. The doubled line count, combined with the doubled horizontal resolution and the increase in aspect ratio, causes an HDTV signal to have about six times the luma (Y) bandwidth of conventional television.

Advanced Television (ATV) refers to delivery of entertainment television to consumers at a quality level substantially improved over conventional television. Terrestrial (VHF/UHF) ATV requires a change in FCC broadcasting regulations. HDTV studio equipment will be used to produce programming for ATV distribution, but the standards used for these two areas need not be identical. My definition of ATV reflects the wide latitude of choices available in setting ATV standards. For example, the ATV proposals of Zenith and ATVA/MIT offer only 900 Kpx, substantially short of the two megapixels required for twice the vertical and twice the horizontal resolution of NTSC.

Enhanced Definition Television (EDTV) describes a 525/59.94 or 625/50 broadcast television signal that is originated with altered or augmented signal content, requiring broadcast regulation changes, that makes possible higher quality at consumer receivers.

Improved Definition Television (IDTV) describes receiver techniques that improve the quality of standard NTSC or PAL broadcast signals but require no emission regulation changes. A receiver is considered IDTV if it employs frame-rate doubling to eliminate interline twitter, although additional techniques such as noise reduction may also be employed. IDTV does not require changes in signal transmission standards and consequently can be implemented entirely at the receiver.

17.5 HDTV STANDARDS

Standards for motion pictures and video exist in three tiers: production, exchange, and distribution. *Production* is the shooting and assembling of

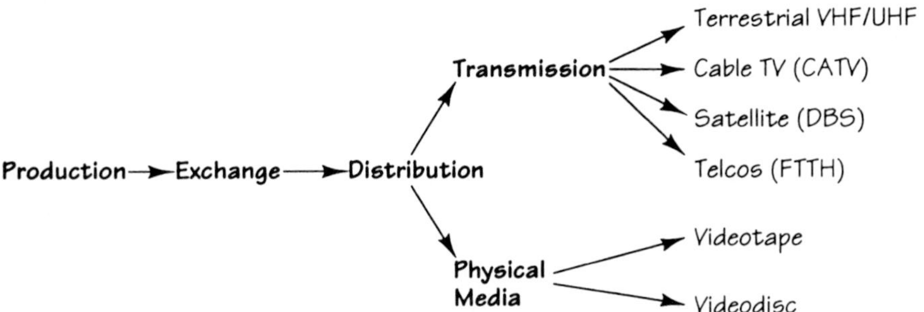

Figure 17.6 Standards for motion pictures and video exist in three tiers: production, exchange, and distribution.

program material. *Exchange* of programs takes place among program producers and distributors. *Distribution* to the consumer may take place using *physical* media such as videotape or videodisc, or through one of four *transmission* media: terrestrial VHF/UHF broadcast, cable television (CATV), direct broadcast from satellite (DBS), or telecommunications. (See Figure 17.6.)

The film production community will produce material in the electronic domain only if it can be assured the access to international markets afforded by 24 Hz, which translates easily to both 29.97 Hz and 25 Hz with minimal artifacts. Electronic origination at either 25 Hz or 30 Hz would introduce serious artifacts upon conversion to the other. It is my contention that a single worldwide standard for HDTV production is feasible only if it accommodates distribution of material originated at 24 Hz.

Broadcasters have recently made proposals to produce HDTV material in Widescreen-525 or Widescreen-625 production formats with a 16:9 aspect ratio. These proposals would use conventional video production equipment, modified for wide aspect ratio. This technique would allow broadcasters and perhaps even local stations to originate wide-aspect-ratio programming with minimum expenditure. However, programs would contain approximately the same amount of picture detail as conventional television; therefore, the viewer could not take advantage of the wide viewing angle and the increased sense of involvement, which is the key to consumer differentiation of HDTV.

17.5.1 SMPTE 240M: 1125/60 Production Standard

The technical parameters of the 1125/60 production system were standardized in SMPTE Standard 240M, adopted in February 1989. Disclaimers on this document indicate that it is applicable to HDTV production only, although the MUSE broadcasting system in use in Japan is based on 1125/60 parameters. SMPTE 240M applies to the 1125/60 analog signal. A digital representation of 1125/60 having a sampling structure of 1920 × 1035 and a sampling rate of 74.25 MHz has recently been adopted in SMPTE Standard 260M.

SMPTE 240M specifies RGB or YP_bP_r color components, with carefully-specified colorimetry and transfer functions. Luma (Y) bandwidth is specified as 30 MHz, about five or six times the bandwidth of current broadcast television. Not all currently available HDTV equipment meets this bandwidth, and most of the proposed transmission systems do not come close to the performance of the studio production equipment. (See Figure 17.7.)

Although the field rate of SMPTE 240M system is exactly 60 Hz—emphasized by the *60.00* notation in the document—certain organizations propose operating at a field rate of 59.94 Hz to maximize compatibility with existing NTSC equipment and production processes. Some current HDTV studio equipment is configurable for operation at either rate. There are several system problems with 59.94-Hz field rate. In 59.94-Hz operation with standard digital audio sampling frequencies of either 44.1 kHz or 48 kHz, there is not an integer number of audio samples in each frame. This, and the requirement for dropframe time code, imposes a penalty on operation at that rate. However, the production procedures for 59.94 Hz are, of course, well established for conventional 525/59.94 video, troublesome though they may be.

17.5.2 1125/60 Studio Equipment

Commercial hardware operating with the 1125-line system is now widely available. Professional studio equipment that is commercially available for purchase at the time of writing (January 1994) includes:

- Cameras
- Videotape recorder (analog, 1-inch open reel)
- Videotape recorder (digital, 1-inch open reel)
- Videotape recorder (analog "Uni-Hi," 19-mm cassette)
- Videodisc
- Telecine (film-to-video)
- Film recorders
- Video monitors
- Video projectors
- Still and sequence stores
- Up-converters
- Line doublers
- Cross-converters
- Down-converters
- Production switchers

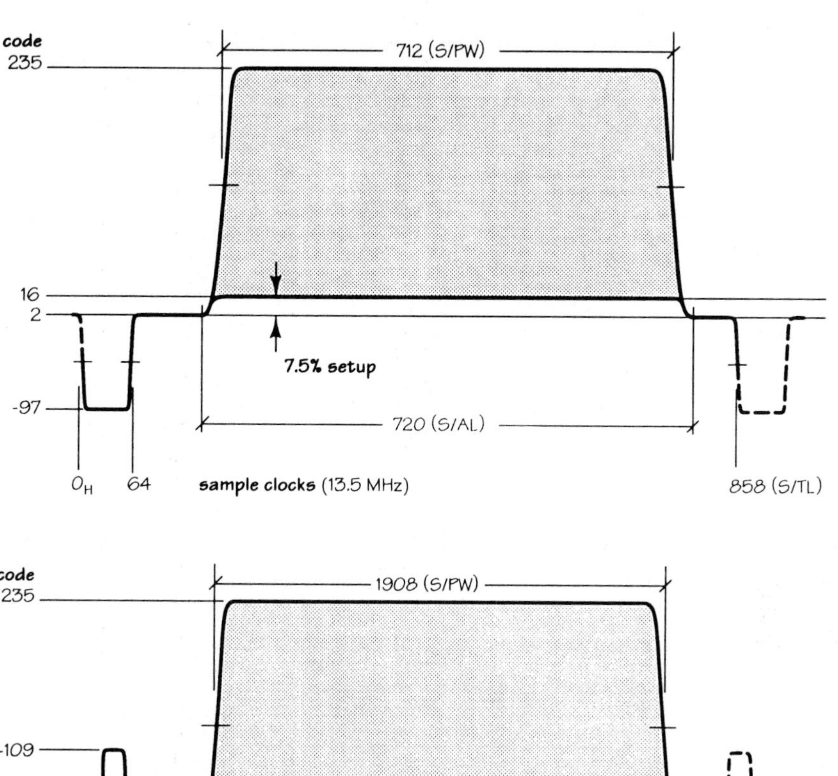

Figure 17.7 Video waveforms of a single scan line of luma information for conventional CCIR Rec. 601-1, 525/59.94 video (top) and SMPTE 260M, 1125/60 HDTV (bottom) are shown. HDTV has a bandwidth—or, in a digital system, data rate—about 5.5 times that of 525/59.94. Tri-level sync is used in HDTV to obtain the necessary high timing accuracy, and setup is eliminated to improve color reproduction.

- ☐ Graphics and paint systems
- ☐ Blue-screen matte (Ultimatte)
- ☐ Test equipment

Sony has demonstrated a fourth-generation 1125/60 CCD camera that has resolution, sensitivity, and noise performance comparable to the best film cameras and motion picture film.

A digital studio HD-VTR records a raw data rate of about 1.2 gigabits per second (Gbps); this is the state of the art for digital magnetic recording.

Real-time digital video effects equipment has been demonstrated by several manufacturers, but no commercial DVE is deployed in an independent commercial facility at the time of writing.

HDTV is being used for the production of material to be released on theatrical (cinema) film. Its acceptance as a production medium for cinema awaits the wider availability of HDTV production facilities and more knowledge of HDTV production techniques on the part of the film production community.

17.5.3 HDTV Exchange Standards

The de facto international television program distribution standard has been for the last 40 years, and continues to be, 35-mm motion picture film. In North America, film is transferred to video using *3-2 pulldown,* which involves scanning successive film frames alternately to form first three then two video fields. The film is run 0.1 percent slower than 24 frames per second to result in the required 59.94-Hz field rate. In Europe, film is run 4 percent faster, with *2-2 pulldown* to result in a 50-Hz frame rate.

Discussions of exchange standards are in an early stage, but there is general agreement that film "friendliness" will be important for ATV: It is certain that the primary origination medium for consumer ATV in any form will initially be 35-mm motion picture film, due to the vast amount of existing program material in that medium.

17.5.4 ATV Transmission Standards

All proposed transmission standards involve the reduction of transmission bandwidth by exploiting the statistical properties of typical images and the perceptual properties of the human visual system.

Terrestrial and satellite broadcasting requires spectrum allocation, which is subject to domestic and international political concerns. Broadcasting standards are agreed on by the International Radio Consultative Committee (CCIR), a treaty organization that is part of the United Nations. CCIR *Recommendations*—which you and I might call standards—are agreed unanimously and internationally. The CCIR started setting broadcasting standards well before the introduction of video recording, and the CCIR has inherited video production and exchange standards even though they do not (strictly speaking) involve the radio spectrum. The CCIR has adopted Recommendation 709 for an HDTV production system. HDTV colorimetry has been agreed, but the recommendation is in a half-finished state, reflecting the lack of international agreement on remaining parameters—particularly frame rate and raster structure.

Broadcasters in Europe and the United States have proposed transmission systems having 50-Hz and 59.94-Hz field rates, respectively, citing requirements for compatibility with local broadcast standards. No commercial equipment, and very little experimental equipment, exists for either of these standards.

It is now evident that there will be no single worldwide transmission standard for ATV, mainly for political and national industrial policy reasons. In the United States, adoption of SMPTE 240M as an ANSI standard was blocked by a legal challenge by the ABC television network, which cited "lack of industry consensus." This was the first time in history that a SMPTE standard was not endorsed by ANSI, and the ABC objection can be taken as evidence that U.S. television networks have little to gain and much to lose by consumer adoption of HDTV. The most obvious problem for the networks—and for local TV stations—is that HDTV promises huge capital equipment expenditures with little or no corresponding increase in revenue.

Distribution of high-quality material for consumers could take place using HDTV either through cable systems (in the manner of Home Box Office) or on consumer HDTV video cassette (for sale or rental), prior to the introduction of HDTV broadcasting in either North America or Europe. This approach to consumer HDTV may arise due to both the technical difficulty of HDTV broadcast (because of its large spectrum/bandwidth requirement) and the difficulties that the traditional broadcasting networks are likely to face in adopting HDTV.

Independent of the choice of transmission standard, it is virtually certain that consumer HDTV receivers will incorporate upconversion circuitry to display 525-line or 625-line signals at IDTV quality or better.

ATV Transmission in Japan

At the time of writing, the Japan Broadcasting Corporation (NHK) is broadcasting eight hours per day of ATV programming, using direct broadcasting from satellite (DBS) with the MUSE (Multiple Sub-Nyquist Encoded) system. MUSE is an ATV recording and transmission system based on the 1125/60 studio standard. MUSE decoders, videodiscs and videotape recorders suitable for consumer use have been demonstrated.

ATV Transmission in North America

In the United States, VHF and UHF spectrum is controlled by the FCC. The so-called "Grand Alliance" of proponents of ATV have asked the FCC to consider their system for adoption as the standard. The proposed system codes video, audio, and data into an ATV signal of about 20 Mbps. This is modulated for transmission in a 6 MHz terrestrial VHF/UHF channel, according to the current allocation plan and frequency spacing of NTSC service. Existing NTSC users will be serviced by simulcasting an NTSC signal in a separate channel, although simulcast will not commence immediately upon the introduction of ATV service. It is the FCC plan that transmission of NTSC VHF and UHF will cease 15 years after the commencement of ATV service.

The underlying technology of the Grand Alliance proposals is very similar to the MPEG-2 standard that is emerging from the international ISO/IEC JTC-1 standards effort that originated in the computer and telecommunications industries.

ATV Transmission in Europe

The standardization process in Europe is substantially different from the standardization process in North America. Most broadcasting organizations are state-owned. Standards are agreed upon by the European Broadcasting Union, whose only members are broadcasters. These meetings are closed; manufacturers (and other interested parties) attend only when invited.

Systems based on 1250/50 scanning, with a raster structure of 1920 × 1152, have been proposed by the Eureka-95 project in Europe. These proposals are HDTV extensions to the MAC system (HD-MAC). British and Swedish researchers have introduced a revolutionary broadcasting technology called *orthogonal frequency division multiplexing* (OFDM), which may accelerate the consideration of digital broadcasting in Europe.

The Europeans (and the Australians) had a strong political interest in basing HDTV on MAC. Receiver manufacturers include MAC decoders in their new receivers, but consumers must install set-top converters in order for old receivers to receive MAC. However, recent business failures associated with MAC make extension of the service to HD-MAC problematic, and the EC recently withdrew funding for HD-MAC research.

17.5.5 Commercial/Industrial/Scientific Applications

Current 525-line video systems have about 640 visible pixels per line and about 480 visible lines per frame for a total of about 0.3 megapixels. Current workstations have between 1 and 1.25 megapixels per frame (e.g., 1152 × 900 or 1280 × 1024). HDTV has approximately two megapixels per frame, or roughly twice the pixel count of current workstations. This pixel count, combined with a picture aspect ratio of 16:9, allows a display measuring 19 inches by 11 inches at 100 dots per inch. This is sufficient for two 8.5-by-11-inch (A4) pages side by side or an 11-by-17-inch (B-size or A3) engineering drawing, with a few inches left over on the side for menus and icons. Many computer workstation users today obtain a two-megapixel display by attaching two screens to one workstation; this "two-headed" configuration is also typical of computer animation and medical systems. This interim solution to increased pixel count will be remedied by HDTV displays.

Computer users have for many years been plagued by a wide variety of incompatible monitor interface standards. At one megapixel, the user doesn't particularly care whether the display is 1152 × 900 (Sun),

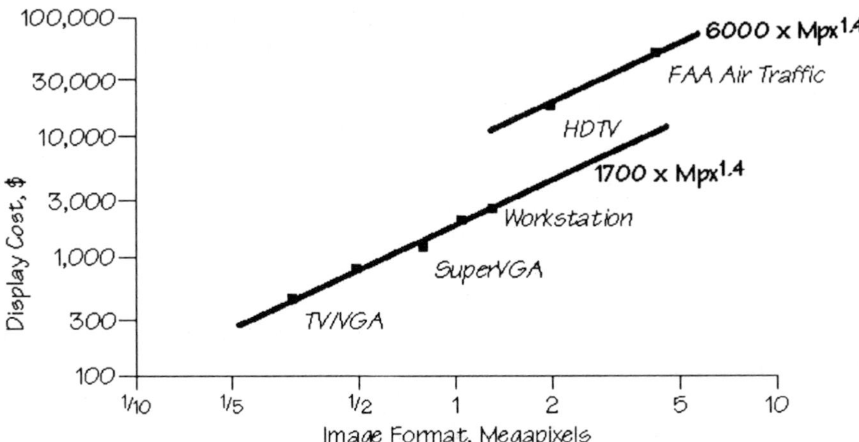

Figure 17.8 Display cost is related to the image format and to unit volumes. The points on the lower line represent displays currently being manufactured in high volume; the shaded line is the function $1700 \times Mpx^{1.4}$. The points on the upper line represent displays currently being manufactured in low volume; the shaded line is the function $6000 \times Mpx^{1.4}$. As HDTV displays approach consumer volumes, we can expect their prices to fall to the lower line.

1120 × 832 (NeXT), 1152 × 870 (Mac), or 1024 × 864 (DEC), but each manufacturer carries the burden of specifying its own unique monitors and monitor interface standards, and users have difficulty interfacing to peripheral equipment. HDTV offers a common scanning and interface standard for the next generation of workstations. This will simplify the interfacing of workstation to monitors, projectors, downconverters, film recorders, and other peripheral equipment. Figure 17.8 shows how the cost of a display is a function of both the image format ("resolution," in computer terms) and the manufacturing volume. It is the emergence of standards that enables manufacturers to invest in high-volume tooling; this in turn leads to lower costs.

Use of the HDTV production standard by the computer industry will open access to equipment for image capture, recording, transmission, distribution, and display. Interface to 525-line video equipment has been difficult due to the disparity in interface standards between computer graphics equipment and video equipment. Further, poor detail and color resolution in NTSC have precluded its use in application areas such as medicine and graphics arts. HDTV remedies those deficiencies by adopting component color coding (instead of composite coding as in NTSC), zero setup for accurate reproduction of blacks (instead of 7.5 percent setup as in NTSC and in EIA-343-A), a single well-characterized colorimetry standard (as opposed to the wide variety of phosphor chromaticity and white point values currently in use in computer graphics), and a well-defined transfer function that will allow accurate gamma correction.

In the past, many application areas have been forced to adopt proprietary display interface standards because the resolution or color accuracy available from standard workstation platforms has been inadequate. HDTV has a display quality that will meet the requirements of even the most exacting users, and this will allow the use of platform technology in place of proprietary solutions in applications such as printing and publishing. Quantel's HDTV Graphic Paintbox is optimized for printing and publishing applications and includes interfaces to prepress equipment. The Rebo Research ReStore offers access to HDTV through a Macintosh computer and thereby allows the use of HDTV imagery and equipment with commercially available Macintosh programs for retouching, presentation, color separation, and many other applications.

Obtaining motion in computer graphics has in the past required either very expensive graphics accelerator hardware or painstaking frame-by-frame nonreal-time animation. HDTV will allow easy access to video equipment designed to handle motion video and therefore will bring motion to the workstation world.

17.6 STANDARDIZATION ISSUES

17.6.1 Square Pixels

Current digital 1125/60 HDTV production equipment conforms to SMPTE 260M, which has 1920 samples per active line (S/AL), 1035 lines per picture height (L/PH), and conforms to the 16:9 aspect ratio of SMPTE 240M. This combination of parameters yields samples spaced about 4 percent closer horizontally than vertically, that is, a sample aspect ratio of about 0.96. This situation came about due to lack of a cohesive input from the computer industry during the standards development process. Some U.S. interests were buoyant at this development, perceiving that nonsquare pixels would deter the deployment of non-American HDTV equipment. Others were dismayed that since no American equipment was available, the effect of the standard would be to deter the computer industry from exploiting HDTV.

Unequal vertical and horizontal sample spacing, or *nonsquare pixels*, is very inconvenient to computer users. Although many rendering systems can utilize any pixel aspect ratio and geometric calculations are only moderately inconvenienced by unequal spacing, interchange of raster data is severely compromised by nonsquare pixels. If raster data at a sample aspect ratio of unity is to be utilized in a system with a different sample aspect ratio, spatial resampling is necessary. Resampling requires substantial computation. This computation takes time in nonreal-time applications or requires dedicated arithmetic hardware in real-time applications. Also, resampling introduces picture impairments that are unacceptable in certain applications, such as in graphic arts, where 90-degree picture rotation is a common operation that must be accomplished with no impairments.

Square pixels have a number of important properties that make geometric calculation straightforward. There exists a huge volume of image data that is already scanned and stored in square-pixel form. Adoption of a standard with square pixels assures easy access to this data. Many imaging devices (such as CCD sensors) and display devices (such as LCD and plasma screens) have inherently fixed geometry. Having these devices use square pixels would allow the same devices to be used for television and industrial applications.

The term *Common Image Format* (CIF) refers to an attempt to standardize the spatial sampling structure of an HDTV image, independent of its frame rate. Square pixels can be accommodated in a Common Image Format of 1920 samples per line and 1080 picture lines. This would result in just slightly less than two megapixels per frame, an arrangement that results in optimum utilization of DRAM and VRAM devices. There have been proposals for a 2048 × 1152 common image format, but its total storage requirement of 2¼ Mpx has poor utilization of power-of-two memory and multiplexer components. Unfortunately, it is in the interest of some organizations in the United States to delay the adoption of any HDTV standard, and, despite ATSC's endorsement of the 1920 × 1080 common image format, the United States took no official position on the matter at the 1990 international CCIR standards discussions.

17.6.2 Display Refresh Rate and Interlace

A scanned display must be operated at a field rate sufficient to overcome *wide-area flicker,* which is a strong function of ambient brightness level. Although 48 Hz is an adequate refresh rate in the dark environment of a movie theater, and 60 Hz is adequate for the average North American living room, a refresh rate of at least 70 Hz is necessary for the high-ambient-brightness environments typical of computer displays.

All 525/59.94, 625/50, and 1125/60.00 television systems currently utilize interlaced scanning. Interlace is a mechanism of reducing transmission bandwidth by half for a given wide-area flicker rate by transmitting a single frame as two fields whose scan lines intertwine. Interlaced systems reduce transmission bandwidth at the expense of introducing *interline twitter* in pictures with a large amount of vertical detail.

Interlace works reasonably well in television because the electro-optical filtering that is inherent in television image sensors (such as camera tubes) reduces vertical detail and consequently reduces interline twitter. Interlace causes objectionable twitter in pictures that have not been electro-optically or otherwise filtered, such as in synthetic computer graphic pictures that have large amounts of vertical detail or contain spatial aliasing components.

Aside from issues of interline twitter, interlace is undesirable for television production because of its inherent confusion of vertical detail and motion. Interlace is now generally seen by the HDTV production community as an expedient way to achieve a 2:1 bandwidth compression in order to permit economical camera and recording equipment in the short term. When technology permits, HDTV production equipment will utilize progressive scanning.

Although current-generation 1125/60 acquisition and recording equipment is universally 2:1 interlaced, there is general agreement that the industry will tend towards progressive (noninterlaced) systems for transmission and display. Zenith and ATVA/MIT have proposed transmission systems that rely on a 787.5/59.94/1:1 production standard with progressive scan. Essentially, these proposals take a factor of two penalty in spatial resolution—from 2 Mpx to 900 Kpx—in return for a factor of two increase in temporal resolution. The claim is made that these systems have better temporal resolution than interlaced systems, but the cameras that have been shown for 787.5/59.94 have relatively poor performance compared to the best available 1125/60 cameras, and to date no conclusive experiments on HDTV/ATV motion rendition have been conducted.

At the time of writing, the Grand Alliance have indicated that their system will accommodate both interlaced and progressive variants in the transmission channel. This scheme offers the maximum flexibility for program originators. This flexibility does impose a slightly increased complexity and, therefore, a slight cost increase in consumer decoders.

17.6.3 Handling 24-Hz Sources

Although a Common Image Format would be appealing in the absence of a single world standard, it ignores the most difficult issue of frame rate conversion. Frame rate conversion—temporal resampling—causes highly objectionable picture impairments. Also, the Common Image Format proposal does not address the desire for a common sampling frequency that would allow equipment commonality.

About 80 percent of prime time television in the United States originates on film at 24 frames per second. Film will undoubtedly provide the vast majority of initial program material for consumer ATV. These facts suggest that the ATV transmission system adopted in the United States should easily accommodate 24-Hz original material. Motion video compression relies heavily on accurate motion prediction to achieve good performance, and it has proven very difficult to perform motion-compensated DCT compression of a source image on film after it has been subjected to 3-2 pulldown. Certain ATV proponents advocate source coding at the native frame rate of the source for this reason. This technology may make it possible to encode in the channel a representation that can be decoded at different frame rates. For example, a consumer receiver could be designed to have a relatively fixed field rate of 60 Hz and perform the equivalent of 3-2 pulldown at the display in the case of a film source. A more sophisticated receiver could potentially display a 24-Hz source at three times that rate, 72 Hz, to achieve a higher-quality display.

The possibility of an electronic production standard at 24 Hz has been discussed. Images originated at 24 Hz would obviously be suitable for display at three times that rate, and 72-Hz refresh rate is appealing to computer users, who require refresh rates considerably higher than 60 Hz to avoid flicker in their work environments. 24-Hz origination has certainly proven to be adequate for motion rendition for the entirety of cinema film production, admittedly with the cinematographer's assistance as a temporal prefilter.

The Grand Alliance have indicated that film originals will be coded for transmission at their native frame rate of 24 Hz.

17.7 CONCLUSIONS

It is evident that ATV broadcasting will use different standards in different parts of the world. However, there is no reason that the computer community should continue to suffer a diversity of display standards that are functionally equivalent. HDTV offers a technology base for the next-generation computer display standard. With cooperation among computer manufacturers, computer users, and the entertainment production community, a single 1920 × 1080 standard is possible.

Producers of entertainment programming and future producers of multimedia titles wish to have access to a world market, not just a continental one. It is obviously advantageous to program producers to have a single production standard, preferably one that is computer friendly. If the computer graphics community participates sufficiently in HDTV standards efforts, a single HDTV production standard could serve entertainment, communications, and computing applications. If a standard is chosen for advanced television broadcasting that is incompatible with the needs of emerging communications technology, it is more likely to accelerate the demise of television than to deter the new applications.

It is difficult to imagine a world in which audio cassettes or compact discs could not be freely exchanged among the countries of the world. Why should we settle for less with pictures? Thirty years ago when the incompatible NTSC, PAL, and SECAM standards were adopted, there were political motivations to deter communication among the people of the world. Now, the walls between East and West have been torn down and the worldwide political situation is in favor of open communication. In the context of this world situation, HDTV represents not just a once-in-a-generation opportunity but a once-in-a-century opportunity to adopt a single worldwide stan-dard for the production and exchange of motion pictures in electronic media.

I have not yet given up hope that our generation can agree on a single world standard for HDTV. If ever there was a time to apply television technology to social ends, that time is now.

17.8 FOR FURTHER READING

1. Frenkel, K. HDTV and the Computer Industry. *Commun. ACM* 32, 11. November 1989. pp. 1301–1312.
2. Special Issue on High Definition Television. *IEEE Trans. on Broadcasting*. vol. BC-33. December 1987.
3. Special Issue on Advanced Television Systems. *IEEE Trans. on Consumer Electronics*. vol. CE-34. February 1988.

CHAPTER 18

KNOWLEDGE-BASED MULTIMEDIA SYSTEMS[1]

Jeannette G. Neal
Calspan Corporation

Stuart C. Shapiro
State University of New York at Buffalo

Multimedia systems hold the promise of great benefits in terms of increased productivity, efficiency, effectiveness, and information enjoyment. Multimedia systems promise to provide the needed increase in the bandwidth of information exchange between humans and computers, and to enhance human understanding of complex information through better presentation technologies and appropriate combinations of these technologies for information presentation. However, before these promises can be fulfilled, there are many problems that need to be solved. Many of these problems are in technology areas such as multimedia document authoring, multimedia information and document storage and management, search techniques, computer-supported collaborative work, and multimedia human-computer interaction. The field of artificial intelligence will help provide solutions to these problems.

---

[1] This research was supported in part by the Defense Advanced Research Projects Agency and monitored by the Rome Air Development Center under Contract No. F30603-87-C-0136.

This chapter discusses the possible role of artificial intelligence in multimedia systems. A concept for a multimedia system is presented that provides an integrated work environment with a human-computer interface designed as an intelligent agent with the ability to communicate and make presentations in coordinated multiple media/modalities. The objective is to integrate the various subsystems and functionality that a user needs in a workstation environment, to simplify operator interaction with sophisticated computer systems, and to minimize the time and effort spent by the user on manipulating the interface. A working prototype system, called CUBRICON (CUBRC [2] Intelligent CONversationalist), is also discussed.

This chapter also reviews some of the current research being conducted in the area of artificial intelligence applied to multimedia systems. Future directions are also presented.

18.1 INTRODUCTION

Multimedia systems hold the promise of great benefits such as increasing peoples' productivity, efficiency and effectiveness, and increasing the utility and enjoyment of our vast information resources. Multimedia systems promise to provide the needed increase in the bandwidth of information exchange between humans and computers, and to enhance human understanding of complex information through better presentation technologies and appropriate combinations of these technologies for information presentation. The extent to which these promises are fulfilled depends on continued improvement in hardware technology, development of much needed supportive software technology, and the growth of a community of trained multimedia authors and technologists.

The scope of today's multimedia systems is very limited, and the functionality of the different types of systems is not integrated to form a productive workplace. In fact, multimedia means different things to different people. To some it means video for conferencing, to others it means hypermedia documents, and to others it means multimedia human-computer dialogue. Also, some people view multimedia documents as static and fixed, and others view documents and data as "live." For example, Clark states that multimedia should be referred to as " 'interactive electronic presentation (IEP)' to describe a collusion of sounds and images elicited from a piece of (electromechanical) machinery by the user's persistent activity" [1, p. 75]. However, Clark's definition includes only the concept of self-contained multimedia "books" to be consumed by "readers" or "viewers," and he states that an IEP is closed and finite. On the other hand,

[2] Calspan—UB Research Center (UB is the State University of New York at Buffalo)

Boy [2,3] and Cornell, Suthers, and Woolf [4] stress that documents and data should be treated as "live" or dynamic.

Certainly the view of documents and data being static and fixed is inadequate for people engaged in productive activity or problem-solving tasks. People will need to be able to locate, retrieve, use, save, and possibly manipulate relevant multimedia documents/data in an environment that will support the accomplishment of their tasks, possibly in cooperation with others.

We take the position that multimedia does not simply mean self-contained static documents, nor does it simply mean that computer-based video is used to provide a "media space" to support cooperative work among co-located or remotely located people [5,6].

Our concept of a multimedia system is that of an integrated work environment with a human-computer interface designed as an intelligent agent with the ability to communicate and make presentations in coordinated multiple media/modalities. The objective is to integrate the various subsystems and functionality that a user needs in a workstation environment, to simplify operator interaction with sophisticated computer systems, and to minimize the time and effort spent by the user on manipulating the interface. The human-computer interface should have the ability to: conduct dialogue with the user; act as an intelligent assistant for accessing application systems; accept and understand input expressed in multimodal language; decide how information and responses are to be presented to the user, including the selection of media/modalities for information presentation, composition, and presentation of the output in multiple modalities; adhere to respected human factors guidelines for human-computer interaction and information presentation; and support cooperative work with others. This system concept is discussed in Section 18.3.

This chapter discusses the possible role of artificial intelligence in multimedia systems and some of the current research being conducted. We also present our concept of a multimedia system and discuss its architecture and functionality. Although necessary hardware is becoming widely available at reasonable cost, application software and trained personnel are in short supply. These related problems are discussed in Section 18.2. Our system concept and prototype are discussed in Section 18.3. Related research is described in Section 18.4. Conclusions and future directions are presented in Sections 18.5 and 18.6, respectively.

18.2 PROBLEMS FACING MULTIMEDIA SYSTEMS

Although great benefits are to be gained from multimedia systems, their incorporation into the workplace, school, and home is not an easy task. The requisite hardware is becoming widely available at reasonable cost, but other problems remain to be solved. These problems are primarily in two areas, personnel and technology:

1. Personnel
   - ☐ There is a lack of people trained in the development and management of distributed databases and document repositories, and
   - ☐ In the words of Grimes and Potel, "a fundamental problem afflicts multimedia authoring—not enough people have the necessary skills" [7, p. 25].
2. Technology
   - ☐ There is a lack of software designed to integrate, control, coordinate, manage, and adapt the various media for human-computer interfaces.
   - ☐ There is a lack of support software for facilitating the authoring, composition, and production of multimedia documents.
   - ☐ There is a lack of support technology in the area of multimedia data and document storage and manipulation.
   - ☐ There is a lack of search and pattern recognition capability for locating information and/or documents that are of interest in multimedia storage facilities.
   - ☐ There is a lack of software support technology for group decision making and cooperative work, especially in the application of multimedia technology to cooperative decision making and work.

All of the tasks listed above are difficult and provide good candidates for application of artificial intelligence technology to help solve the problem.

18.3 THE ANATOMY OF AN INTELLIGENT MULTIMEDIA SYSTEM

As mentioned briefly in Section 18.1, our concept of a multimedia system consists of an integrated work environment with a human-computer interface designed as an intelligent agent with the ability to conduct dialogue with the user in coordinated multiple media/modalities. The human-computer interaction is modeled on the manner in which two or more people naturally communicate in coordinated multiple modalities when working with graphics, video, and other devices at hand. The system should have the ability to:

- ☐ Conduct dialogue with the user:
  - — Adhere to respected principles of conversation [8], and

  - Adhere to respected human factors guidelines for human-computer interaction and information presentation, including maintaining the context of the dialogue and maintaining consistency in displays and presentations.

- ☐ Maintain knowledge and belief models to enable the system to understand user inputs and compose system outputs:
  - Track and model the dynamic focus of the dialogue in order to maintain context during the dialogue.
  - Model the user's task(s) and the state of the user's accomplishments and progress with respect to the task(s).
- ☐ Maintain knowledge bases of information about:
  - Modalities and user interaction,
  - World knowledge, and
  - Application-specific knowledge.
- ☐ Act as an intelligent assistant for accessing and using application systems, through such activities as:
  - Assisting the user in finding relevant information on topics of interest.
  - Assisting the user with finding, selecting, and accessing appropriate tools to apply to the task.
  - Assisting and guiding the user in the accomplishment of tasks.
  - Providing explanations and multimedia presentations to aid in user comprehension of relevant information.
- ☐ Accept and understand input expressed in multimedia language.
  - Provide the user with flexibility in the media that is selected and combined for expressing input to the system.
- ☐ Decide how information and responses are to be presented to the user:
  - Select modalities/media for information presentation.
  - Compose the output in multiple modalities.
  - Present the multimedia output in a coordinated manner.
- ☐ Manage the windows by intelligently performing the window operations (i.e., creation, placement, sizing/resizing, moving, iconization, retrieval, and destruction) to relieve the user of the burden of performing these chores.

18.3.1 Intelligent Multimedia System Design

Figure 18.1 provides an overview of our design for an intelligent multimedia system. An implemented system, called CUBRICON, has been developed as a proof-of-concept prototype as part of the Intelligent MultiMedia Inter-

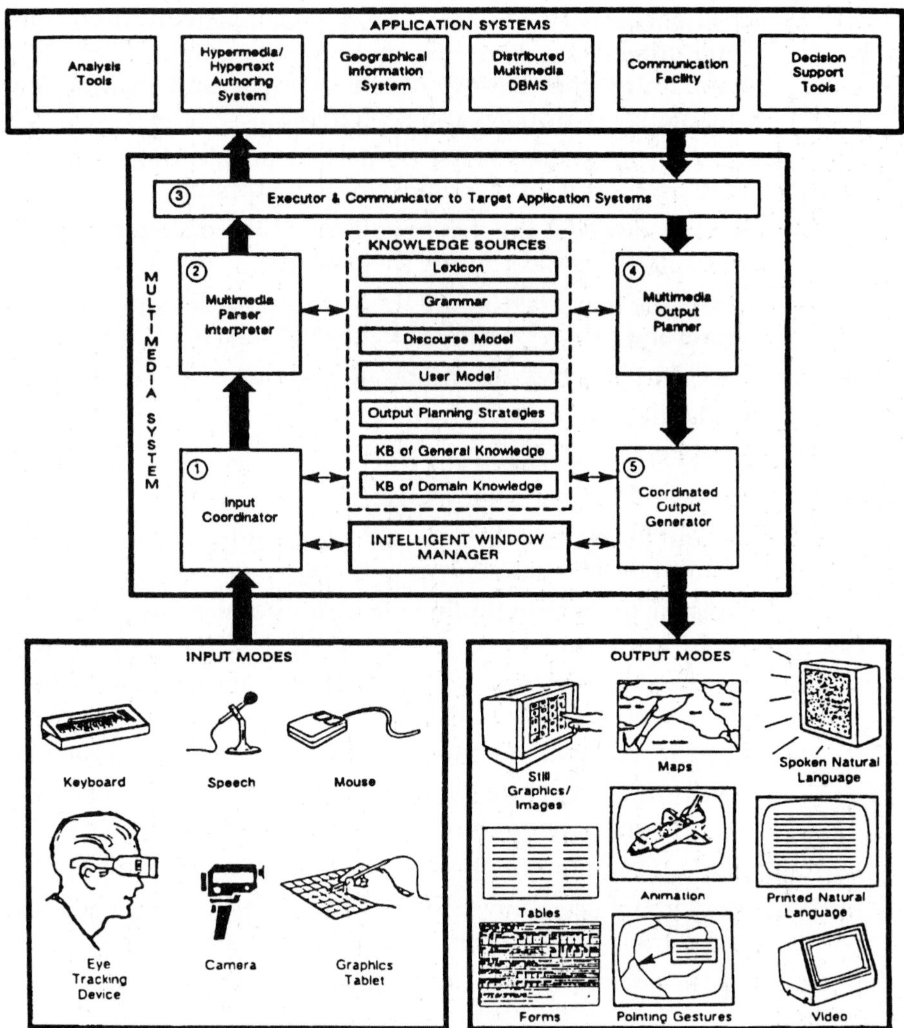

Figure 18.1 Multimedia system design

faces Project [9,10,11,12,13]. The CUBRICON prototype includes implementation of all the components shown in the box labeled "Multimedia System." The application used for the CUBRICON prototype was that of air force mission planning. The input modes that were implemented in the CUBRICON system were speech, keyboard, and mouse. All of the output modes shown in Figure 18.1 were implemented in the CUBRICON system except for video, and the implemented graphics and animation capability was fairly simple.

The CUBRICON system design is based upon an integrated use of communication modes or media, whether verbal, visual, tactile, or gestural. Human beings primarily communicate with each other via written and spoken natural language and gestures, supplemented with pictures, diagrams, video, and other sounds. The CUBRICON system design provides for the use of a unified multimedia language. Input and output streams are treated as compound streams with components corresponding to different media. This approach is intended to imitate, to a certain extent, the ability of humans to simultaneously accept input from different sensory devices (such as eyes and ears), and to simultaneously produce output in different media (such as voice, pointing motions, and drawings). The CUBRICON system includes: (a) language parsing and generation that processes and supports synchronized multimedia input and output streams, (b) knowledge representation and inferencing to provide reasoning ability, (c) knowledge bases and models to provide a basis for its decision-making ability, and (d) automated knowledge-based medium selection and formulation of responses.

CUBRICON possesses the following critical functionality. CUBRICON:

- accepts and understands multimedia input such that references to entities in a natural language sentence can be accompanied by coordinated simultaneous pointing to the respective entities on a graphics display:
  - is able to use a simultaneous pointing reference and natural language reference to disambiguate one another when appropriate;
  - infers the intended referent of a point gesture which is inconsistent with the accompanying natural language
- automatically composes and generates relevant output to the user in coordinated multimedia:
  - automatically selects appropriate output media/modalities for expressing information to the user, with the selection based on the nature of the information, discourse context, and the importance of the information to the user's task;
  - uses its media/modalities in a highly integrated manner including simulated parallelism;
  - judges the relevance of information with respect to the discourse context and user task and responds in a context-sensitive manner;
  - adheres to respected human factors guidelines for human-computer interaction and information presentation; these guidelines include: (i) maintain the context of the user/computer dialogue, (ii) maintain consistency throughout a display, and (iii) maintain consistency across displays.
- automatically performs the window manipulation operations (i.e., creation, placement, sizing/resizing, moving, iconization, retrieval, and destruction) so as to relieve the user of the need to manipulate the interface.

CUBRICON accepts input from three input devices: speech input device, keyboard, and mouse device pointing to objects on a graphics display. CUBRICON produces output for three output devices: high-resolution color graphics display, monochrome display, and speech output device. The primary path that the input data follows is indicated by the modules that are numbered in Figure 18.1:

1. Input Coordinator,
2. Multimedia Parser Interpreter,
3. Executor/Communicator to Target System,
4. Multimedia Output Planner, and
5. Coordinated Output Generator.

The Input Coordinator module accepts input from the three input devices and fuses the input streams into a single compound stream, maintaining the temporal order of tokens in the original streams. The Multimedia Parser/Interpreter is an augmented transition network (ATN) that has been extended to accept the compound stream produced by the Input Coordinator and produce an interpretation of this compound stream. Appropriate action is then taken by the Executor module. This action may be a command to the mission planning system, a database query, or an action that entails participation of the interface system only. An expression of the results of the action is then planned by the Multimedia Output Planner for communication to the user. The Output Planner is a generalized ATN that produces a multimedia output stream representation with components targeted for different devices (e.g., speech device, color graphics display, monochrome display). This output representation is translated into visual/auditory output by the Coordinated Output Generator module. This module is responsible for producing the multimedia output in a coordinated manner in real time (e.g., the Planner module can specify that a certain icon on the color graphics display must be highlighted when the entity represented by the icon is mentioned in the simultaneous natural language output).

The CUBRICON system includes several knowledge sources to be used during processing. The knowledge sources include:

- ☐ a lexicon,
- ☐ a grammar defining the language used by the system for multimedia input and output,
- ☐ discourse model,
- ☐ user model,
- ☐ a knowledge base of human-computer interaction knowledge, including output planning strategies to govern the composition of multimedia responses to the user,

- ☐ a knowledge base of information about generally shared world knowledge, and
- ☐ a knowledge base of information about the specific task domain of tactical air control.

These knowledge sources are used for both understanding input to the system and planning/generating output from the system. They are discussed in more detail later.

The CUBRICON system is implemented on a Symbolics Lisp Machine with a color graphics monitor, a monochrome monitor, and a mouse pointing device. Speech recognition is handled by a Dragon Systems VoiceScribe 1000. Speech output is produced by a DECtalk speech production system. CUBRICON software is implemented using the SNePS semantic network processing system [14,15,16], an ATN parser/generator [17], and Common Lisp. SNePS is a fully intensional propositional semantic network and has been used for a variety of purposes and applications [16,18,19,20,21]. SNePS provides:

- ☐ a flexible knowledge representation facility in the semantic network formalism;
- ☐ representation of rules in the network in a declarative form so they can be reasoned about like any other data;
- ☐ a bidirectional inference subsystem [22] which focuses attention towards the active processes and cuts down the fan-out of a pure forward or backward chaining;
- ☐ a simulated multiprocessing control structure [23];
- ☐ special nonstandard connectives [24] to model human reasoning processes.

18.3.2 The Multimedia

The CUBRICON design and implementation incorporates the following media or modalities: spoken natural language, typed or printed natural language, pointing gestures, geographical maps, color graphic pictorial displays, tables, and "fill in the blank" forms. This list does not exhaust the possibilities, of course, but provides a good variety with which to prove our concept and upon which to build. Other media, such as video and eye-tracking devices, were not used in the prototype but would be a natural extension of the system and are included in Figure 18.1.

One of the significant features of the CUBRICON system is that it not only generates output in multiple modalities, but also decides which modalities to use and how to use and combine them. CUBRICON modality

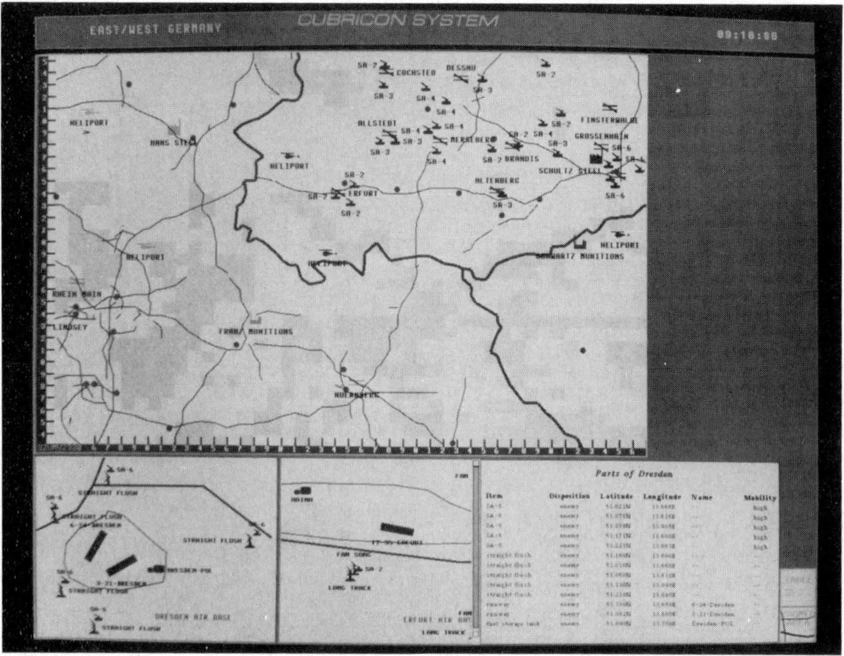

Figure 18.2 Example CUBRICON displays

selection is primarily based on the nature and characteristics of the information and the purpose for which the modality is being used. Our system design is based on the premise that graphic/pictorial presentation is always desirable. The following is a list of the CUBRICON modalities and a brief summary of the selection criteria.

1. **Color graphics:** Selected whenever the CUBRICON system knows how to represent the information pictorially.
2. **Geographic maps:** Selected when the information is geographically locative or has a locative attribute. An example is shown in Figure 18.2.
3. **Table:** Selected when the values of common attribute(s) of several entities must be expressed.
4. **Forms:** A predefined form is selected when the task engaged in by the user requires the form. An example modeled on one of the forms used by air force mission planners is shown in Figure 18.3.
5. **Animation:** Simple animation is used for information or objects that can be visually presented and which are temporally changing or moving.
6. **Deictic gestures:** Selected for emphasis or to call the user's attention to one or more objects on the screen(s).

PACKAGE WORKSHEET

PKG#	0026	Preparer's Name		Date Prepared		Priority	

OFFENSIVE COUNTER AIR MISSIONS

Mission	OCA#	Origin	TOD	#AC	AC Type	SCL	AC Pool
1	345	Rhein Main Air Base	05:45				49tfw-f-1
2	445		06:00				45tfw-Ef-
3							
4							

PRE-TARGET REFUELING

SVC#	STN#	Start	Dur.	Disbur.

TARGET STRIKE MISSION

Mission	Aim Point	TOT
1	6-24-Merseberg Runway	06:50
2	3-21-Dresden Runway	07:02
3		
4		

POST-TARGET REFUELING

SVC#	STN#	Start	Dur.	Disbur.
345	244	07:25	00:20	21968 lbs
445	244	07:45	00:20	20942 lbs

REFUELING MISSION

RFL#	345	TOD	07:00	AC Type	Kc-135	Load		Origin	Lindsey Air Base

Station	STN#	Start Time	Stop Time	Orbit Location
1	244	07:20	07:55	50.340 N Latitude, 11.692 E Longitude
2				

AIR ESCORT MISSIONS

Mission	AEM#	Origin	TOD	#AC	ACT	SCL	Remarks
1							
2							

SAM SUPPRESSION MISSIONS

Mission	SSM#	Origin	TOD	#AC	ACT	SCL	Target	TOT
1								
2								

=>> What are the aimpoints within the Erfurt airbase?
Look at the color graphics screen. The aimpoints within Erfurt are being presented.

The corresponding table is being presented on the color screen.
=>> What are the aimpoints within the Dresden airbase?
Look at the color graphics screen. The aimpoints within Dresden are being presented.

The corresponding table is being presented on the color screen.
=>>

Figure 18.3 The CUBRICON mission planning form

7. **Natural language:** Selected for the expression of a proposition, relation, event, or combination thereof, when the types of knowledge structures being expressed are heterogeneous. Natural language can be presented in either spoken or written form.

   Printed natural language (printed on the screen) is selected for longer technical responses that would strain the user's short-term memory if speech were used (see [25]).

   Spoken natural language is used in a manner that is designed to avoid overwhelming the user's short-term memory. It is selected for:

   - ☐ Dialogue descriptions to assist the user in comprehending the presented information. These include explanations of graphic displays or display changes and verbal highlighting of objects on the displays (e.g., "The enemy airbases are highlighted in red").
   - ☐ Warnings to alert the user of important events that have taken place or are about to take place (e.g., new critical information comes into the application system database and the system notifies user: "The XXX airbase has been damaged by enemy shellfire").
   - ☐ Informing the user about the system's activity (e.g., "I'm still working" when the user must wait for output from the system).

- Short expressions of relatively nontechnical information that can be remembered when presented serially (e.g., a "yes"/"no" answer to a user's question).

Most frequently, multiple modalities are desirable to present a body of information to the user. For example, to inform the user about the movements of a certain tank battalion, a desirable presentation might be an explanation delivered in combined spoken speech and coordinated drawing on a graphic map display showing movements of the battalion, as well as a printed textual summary with ancillary information on the monochrome display. The multiple modalities should be selected to complement and enhance one another. Andriole [26] has used graphic equivalence effectively using dual displays or split screens to present the same material in different forms to aid user comprehension and problem-solving performance. We are not restricting the system to presenting the *same* material in different forms, but, instead, our system presents related material or different aspects of a given event or concept in different forms/modalities (as appropriate based on the nature and characteristics of the information). We are also not restricted to graphic display presentations.

18.3.3 Knowledge Sources for Multimedia Interaction

The CUBRICON system includes several knowledge sources for use in multimedia language understanding and production. These knowledge sources are a lexicon and grammar; a discourse model; a user model; a knowledge base of human-computer interaction knowledge, including output planning strategies to govern the composition of multimedia responses to the user; a knowledge base of information about generally shared world knowledge; and a knowledge base of information about the application task domain used in this research effort, namely, tactical air control.

The Lexicon and Grammar

A lexicon is the collection of all the tokens or signals that carry meaning in a given language. The CUBRICON system's lexicon consists of words, graphic figures, and pointing signals. The grammar defines how the morphemes, tokens, and signals of the lexicon can combine to form legal composite language structures. An example of a multimodal language structure that is legal according to the CUBRICON grammar is a noun phrase. A noun phrase consists of the typical linguistic syntax (e.g., determiner followed by zero or more modifiers followed by a noun) accompanied by zero or more pointing signals (pointing to objects on the graphics display). The lexicon and grammar together define the multimodal language used by the system.

The Discourse Model

Continuity and relevance are key factors in discourse. Without these factors, people find discourse disconcerting and unnatural. The attentional discourse focus space representation [27,28,29,30] is a key knowledge structure that supports continuity and relevance in dialogue. CUBRICON tracks the attentional discourse focus space of the dialogue carried out in multimedia language and maintains a representation of the focus space in two structures:

1. a main dialogue focus model, which includes those objects and propositions that have been explicitly expressed (by the user or by CUBRICON) via natural language or by a pointing or direct manipulation gesture, and
2. a display model, which represents all the objects that are "in focus" because they are visible on one of the monitors.

CUBRICON is based on the premise that visual communication is an integral part of language, along with natural language and other forms of text and pointing. The CUBRICON system treats objects presented visually on the graphics displays as having been intentionally "expressed" or "mentioned." All objects on the graphics display are "in focus," and CUBRICON maintains a representation of all these objects in the display model. The display model consists of two levels: 1) a list of the windows on each monitor, and 2) a list of all the objects that are visible in each window. This display model is used in a manner that is analogous to the use of the main dialogue focus model.

When processing the user's input, the dialogue attentional focus space representation is used for determining the interpretation of anaphoric references [29] and definite descriptive references [31] expressed by the user in natural language. In the CUBRICON system, the main dialogue focus model is consulted in determining the referent of a pronoun. In the case of a definite reference, if an appropriate referent is not found in the main dialogue focus model, then CUBRICON consults the visual display model. The motivation for this is the fact that when a person expresses a definite reference such as "the airbase" with just one such object in view (as on a graphics display) and none have been verbally discussed, then the person most likely refers to the one in view even though he or she might know about several others.

The discourse model is used during output generation also. When CUBRICON composes a reference for an object as part of a natural language sentence, for example, it consults the discourse model. If the object is represented in the display model as being visible in one of CUBRICON's windows, then the system uses a deictic dual-media expression to refer to the object in the output sentence. The deictic expression consists of a phrase such as "this airbase" and simultaneously blinks/highlights the airbase as its means of pointing to the object. If the object is the most salient of its gender according to the main focus model, CUBRICON uses a pronoun to refer to the object.

The User Model

Many aspects of a user are highly relevant to human-computer interaction and user modeling is an active area of research [32,33,34,35,36]. Relevant aspects of the user include his or her level of expertise in the current task, perspective based on his or her role, value system, degree and nature of impairedness due to fatigue or illness, and preferences concerning mode of communication. To address all of these aspects of user modeling is, of course, beyond the scope of this chapter. The aspects of the user that seemed most relevant in our research and which are modeled in the CUBRICON user model are: 1) the degree of importance that the user attaches to the different object types as a function of task, which we call the user's *entity rating system*; and 2) the stage of the current task on which the user is currently engaged.

CUBRICON includes a representation of the user's entity rating system as a function of the task being addressed by the user. For a given task in the process of being carried out by the user, the entity rating system representation includes a numerical importance rating (on a scale from zero to one) assigned to each of the object types used in the application task domain. The numerical rating assigned to a given object type represents the degree of importance of the object to the user. Associated with the entity rating system is a *critical threshold* value: Those objects with a rating above the critical threshold are critical to the current task and those with ratings below the threshold are not. The CUBRICON design provides for the entity rating system representation to change automatically under program control in the following manner: 1) when the user's task changes, the system replaces the current entity rating list with the standard initial rating list for the new task; and 2) when the user mentions an entity whose rating is lower than the critical threshold, then its rating is reset to be equal to the critical threshold to reflect the user's interest in the entity and its seeming relevance to the current task from the perspective of the user. In the current implementation, CUBRICON performs the second function listed above, but the implementation of the first is not complete.

The user's entity rating system plays an important role in composing responses to the user: 1) the entity rating system representation is used in determining what information is relevant in answering questions or responding to commands from the user, 2) the entity rating system is used in selecting ancillary information to enhance or embellish the main concept being expressed and to prevent the user from making false inferences that he might otherwise make, and 3) the entity rating system is also used in organizing the form in which information is presented.

As an example of 1) above, if the user instructs the system to "Display the Fulda Gap Region," CUBRICON uses the entity rating system representation to determine what objects within the region should be displayed. If the user is a military mission planner, then displaying all the country cottages in the region, for example, is irrelevant. The objects to display are those that are relevant to the job of the mission planner. Thus, the objects that the system selects from its database for display are airbases, missile sites, targets, etc.

CUBRICON includes a representation of the current task in which the user is engaged. CUBRICON's mode of response to the user is affected by whether or not the user's task has just changed. The CUBRICON team is developing a task hierarchy: a decomposition of the user's main tasks into subtasks. This a priori task knowledge can be used by CUBRICON to help track the discourse focus, manage the displays, and anticipate the needs of the user.

Knowledge Bases: General and Application-Specific

The CUBRICON system includes knowledge bases containing general and application-specific information. General information includes world knowledge applicable across different task domains, while application-specific information is applicable to the particular task on which the user is engaged.

Crucial information included in the knowledge bases is information concerning the visual presentation or verbal expression of the objects/concepts known to the system. This information includes the words and symbols used to express an object, which symbols are appropriate under which conditions, and when particular colors are to be used.

An important component of the application-specific knowledge base is a representation of the different types of mission plans that the user would be engaged in constructing. The knowledge base includes a model or structure to represent each type of mission plan (e.g., Offensive Counter Air, Refueling) and the components of each type of plan (e.g., aircraft, airbase, temporal information, flight path), as well as specific instances of plans that have been developed by the user.

18.3.4 Multimedia Language Understanding

A user communicates with the CUBRICON system using natural language and gestures (pointing via a mouse device). Typically, the user speaks to the system, but keyboard input is just as acceptable. The use of pointing combined with natural language forms a very efficient means of expressing a definite reference. This enables a person to use a demonstrative pronoun as a determiner in a noun phrase and simultaneously point to an entity on the graphics display to form a succinct reference. Thus, a person would be able to say "this SAM" (surface-to-air missile system) and point to an object on the display to disambiguate which of several SAM systems is meant. The alternative, using natural language only, would be to say something like "the SAM system at 10.35 degrees longitude and 49.75 degrees of latitude" or "the SAM system just outside of Kleinburg." The use of pointing references combined with natural language is efficient, since the cognitive process of generating the dual-media reference would be much shorter than the generation of the reference using natural language only. The result is a reduction in the cognitive workload for the user.

The CUBRC team has developed a formal grammar defining the syntax of the multimedia language. The grammar is implemented in the form of a generalized ATN. The traditional ATN, which takes a linear textual input stream, has been modified so that it takes a multimedia input stream with components from the different input devices. Input from the devices is accepted and fused into a compound stream, maintaining the information as to which point gesture(s) occurred with (or between) which word(s) of the sentence. Each noun phrase or locative adverbial phrase can consist of zero or more words of text, along with zero or more pointing references to objects on the displays (there must be at least one point reference or one word). The pointing input that is a component of a noun phrase or locative adverbial can occur anywhere within the phrase: as the first token(s), between the natural language words of the phrase, or as the last token(s).

In the CUBRICON system, four types of objects can be referred to via pointing:

- ☐ Geometric points within any window (e.g., a map or graph);
- ☐ Objects represented by icons;
- ☐ Table entries; and
- ☐ Windows on the monitors.

CUBRICON accepts interrogative, imperative, and declarative sentences, although the most commonly used are interrogatives and imperatives. The following are illustrative examples. These inputs presuppose that a map is displayed on the color graphics screen with icons representing various objects. Each "<point>" represents a point to an object or location on one of the graphics displays.

INTERROGATIVE:

"Where is the 43rd Tank Battalion?"

"What is the mobility of this <point> SAM?"

"Is this <point> the base for these Troop Battalions <point>$_1$ <point>$_2$ <point>$_3$?"

IMPERATIVE:

"Display the East-West Germany Region."

"Display the aimpoints within this <point> airbase."

"Present the OCA1001 mission plan."

Use of such dual-media references entails certain problems, in that: 1) a point by the user can be ambiguous if he or she points to a location where two or more graphical figures overlap (one could be part of another as in the case of a hubcap being part of a car wheel) or two or more icons overlap (they could be closely located), and 2) the user can inadvertently miss the object at which he or she intended to point. CUBRICON uses semantically based techniques for resolving such issues. These problems and the CUBRICON solution techniques are discussed in [9,10,12,13].

An important feature of a multimedia system such as CUBRICON is that the user and the system have significant flexibility with respect to their manner of communication. To refer to a particular object such as an airbase, for example, one could use its proper name, refer to it by its location, or simply point to it on a map. Similarly, for intangible objects such as a mission plan: The plan could be described using paragraphs of text or by the use of a form such as shown in Figure 18.3.

Another important feature of the CUBRICON system is that it is a unified system in which various displays and presentations reflect a single integrated underlying reality. This underlying reality is represented in the CUBRICON knowledge base, which is central to the system. So, for example, as a user builds up an air force mission plan, he or she may input decisions verbally as in "Make Nuremberg the origin airbase of the OCA345 mission" or he or she may input such information via the form shown in Figure 18.3. The key central representation of information, such as the elements of the mission plan, is in the knowledge base. This knowledge base is updated when the user makes such inputs. Existing visual representations on the displays are updated also.

An interesting way for the user to input a plan decision such as the one mentioned above is to make a very terse, efficient spoken input with accompanying point gestures such as the following:

USER: "Enter this <point-map-icon> here <point-form-slot>.

This example illustrates that CUBRICON enables the user to use point gestures in conjunction with more than just one phrase of a sentence and that the point gestures may access different types of windows on different monitors. In this example, the user's first point gesture touches an object on a map display on the color graphics CRT (Figure 18.2) and the second selects a slot of the mission planning form on the monochrome CRT (Figure 18.3). One of CUBRICON's features that is critical to its ability to process this input is that its display model contains representations of the objects displayed visually in each of the windows of each CRT. The object representations in the display model are the same representations as in the knowledge base, so that each object has a unique representation and we avoid the problem of tracking and maintaining multiple representations of an object. The knowledge base is shared by all the modules of the CUBRICON system. If the <point-map-icon> selects the Nuremberg airbase on the map of Figure 18.2 and the <point-form-slot> touches the "origin airbase" slot on the mission planning form of Figure 18.3, CUBRICON builds the knowledge base structure which represents the assertion that Nuremberg is the airbase from which the particular mission will be flown. The visual version of the form seen by the user is also updated.

18.3.5 The CUBRICON Intelligent Window Manager

One of the important technologies in human computer interaction is the use of windows to enable the computer to help users manage and access several sources of information on one screen, much as office workers typically organize desk space into separate areas for organizing papers by use category [37].

The CUBRICON Intelligent Window Manager (CIWM) [12,38] was designed to automatically perform all window placement and manipulation functions within the CUBRICON system. The decision to automate window management functions was based on the premise that this would reduce the efforts required of the user for window management, and thus free the user's mental and temporal resources for task domain activities. As the problems and application tasks confronting computer users become more complex and information-intensive, the potential of this approach for improving overall human-system performance is enhanced. Bly and Rosenberg [39] found that, for a database management task, almost half of the user's time is spent in managing the window-based interface. If their findings are representative of all or most computer-based tasks that use windowing systems, the concept of automated window management offers great potential for increasing human-computer effectiveness on these tasks. In addition, automatic window management offers a critical capability for applications in which the user's hands and cognitive resources are not available, such as in the cockpit environment or other situations in which the person is performing simultaneous tasks.

The CIWM is a knowledge-based component that automatically performs window management functions on CUBRICON's color and monochrome screens, including window creation, sizing, placement, removal, and organization. These operations are accomplished by the CIWM without direct human inputs, although the system provides for user override of the CIWM decisions.

Important CIWM features, including window layout, placement, importance, sizing, and window iconization, are discussed briefly in the following paragraphs.

Window Layout: The CIWM combines tiled and overlapping layout approaches to form a hybrid window configuration management methodology, allowing CUBRICON to realize the advantages of both types of windowing systems, while minimizing the disadvantages. The CIWM always prefers tiled windows, but allows a window to overlap adjacent windows when necessary based on window contents and the task at hand.

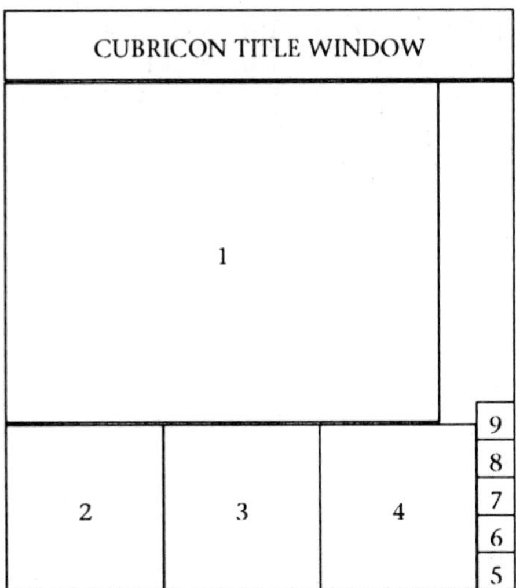

Figure 18.4 The CUBRICON preferred window positions

Window Placement: Window placement combines heuristics for each window type (e.g., prefer to place geographic maps on the color CRT, forms on the monochrome CRT, tables on the monochrome CRT) with placement logic that addresses the problem of placing a window within a given CRT screen. For a given CRT screen, placement of windows is based on window type and on relative importance and relationships among the displayed windows. In placing a window on one of the CRTs, the CIWM checks whether one of the four preferred predefined window positions shown in Figure 18.4 is available. If so, the CIWM puts the new window in the available position. If all the window positions are full, the CIWM removes (and iconizes) the least important window to make room for the new window.

Window Importance: The importance of each window is computed by an algorithm which is a function of:

time of creation,
contents,
recency of use,
time since last interaction,
frequency of use, and
context (or relation to the ongoing dialogue).

Window Sizing: The size of a map window is determined by a combination of its function and an algorithm that computes the minimum necessary size based on clutter analysis. (This algorithm may dictate a window size that results in the new window overlapping adjacent windows.)

Window Iconization: As the number of windows increases, a limited number of the most useful windows are kept open, while those of lesser importance are removed and transformed to labeled icons. Billingsley [40], for example, has discussed the use of icons to remind users of closed but available windows. This maximizes the visibility of available information and maintains an organized display. Animation is used to portray the window-to-icon transformation for the user.

The CIWM is discussed in more detail in [12,38] with interactive examples, evaluation results, and limitations and applicability of the research.

18.3.6 Multimedia Presentations for Space/Time-Dependent Activities

Just as it accepts multimedia input, CUBRICON generates multimedia output that combines spoken natural language, visually displayed natural language, graphics, simple animation, and deictic gestures. An important feature of the CUBRICON design is that the output modalities are composed and coordinated by a single generator providing a unified multimedia language with components (e.g., speech and graphics) synchronized in real time. CUBRICON uses a generalized augmented transition network (GATN) [17] for multimodal language generation. This GATN generates multimedia language "on the fly" from knowledge base structures or representations—that is, the presentations are not "canned." The knowledge base representations are based on generic structures and relations with generic "slot" names (e.g., subtype, supertype, subtask, supertask, name, property-name, property) so that the multimodal generation components can be applied and used with other applications. In this section, we focus on the multimedia presentation of space/time-dependent activities. Other aspects of CUBRICON's multimedia generation capability are discussed in [11,12,13].

CUBRICON's output generation component composes and produces multimedia presentations that are designed for the explanation and presentation of activities consisting of events with spatial and temporal attributes. The prototype implementation has been applied to the presentation of OCA (Offensive Counter Air) missions that include flight path traversals with related activities, such as the striking of targets and the airborne refueling of strike aircraft. This multimedia presentation component uses two critical concepts: *task hierarchy* and *granularity measure*. These are discussed in the next paragraphs, followed by discussion of discourse structure and output composition.

Task Hierarchy

CUBRICON's multimedia presentation component uses a knowledge base representation of a task hierarchy and the interrelationships and properties of the tasks. This information is used to define the concept of granularity in the CUBRICON system. For the mission planning application domain

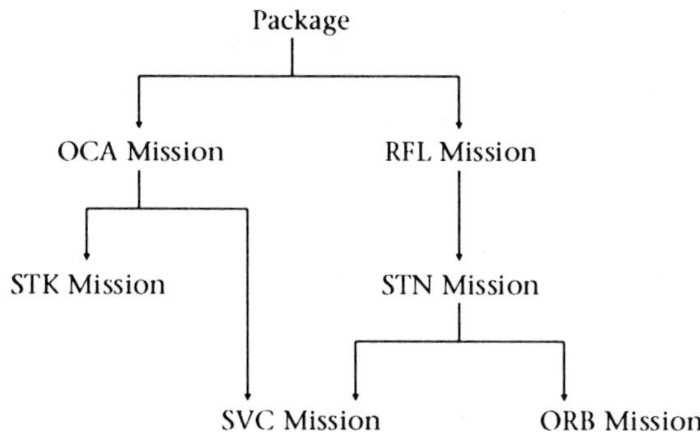

Figure 18.5 Hierarchy of mission types

used in this project, the tasks represented in the hierarchy in CUBRICON's knowledge base are tactical air force missions. This knowledge base includes information about the different types of missions and their interrelationships and properties. The primary mission types that are modeled in CUBRICON's current knowledge base are shown in the hierarchy of Figure 18.5. The dashed lines in this figure represent the relation of parent to child (or supertask to subtask). The knowledge base also includes information about mission details such as, for an OCA mission, the airbase from which the mission aircraft originate, the aircraft unit flying the mission, the type of aircraft used, the time of departure of the aircraft, and the target(s) of the mission.

An SVC (service) mission consists of the refueling of a strike aircraft by an orbiting refueling tanker. The properties of an SVC mission include the start time of the SVC, the length of time that the servicing takes (called the duration of the servicing), and the amount of fuel disbursed to the strike aircraft.

An RFL (refueling) mission consists of a tanker aircraft flying a certain route in order to service one or more strike aircraft.

An STN (station) mission consists of a tanker aircraft stationing itself, by orbiting for a certain period of time, at a certain location in order to service one or more strike aircraft.

An STK (strike) mission consists of a strike aircraft striking its target. Properties of the STK mission include the identifier of the target, target location, and the time of the target strike.

Granularity

If a system has a knowledge/database that contains a voluminous amount of information, the system must have a method of selecting the appropriate information to present in response to user requests if the response is not well constrained by the request itself. A factor that can play an important role in selecting appropriate information is that of granularity and, indeed,

Table 18.1 Granularity

Node Level	*Very Coarse*	*Coarse*	*Default*	*Fine*	*Very Fine*
Parents	name	name major	name major	name major	name major minor
Node	name	name major	name major minor	name major major	name minor major
Children		name	name	name major	name major minor

CUBRICON uses the concept of granularity for this purpose. The CUBRICON design includes two types of granularity:

1. Detail granularity: The first type is a measure of degree of detail and includes measures called "coarse," "medium," and "fine." The properties of each task type are divided into two groups: major and minor. These two groups roughy separate the properties into the more important properties of a mission and the less important properties, respectively. The name of a task is treated as special.

   Table 18.1 shows how the levels of detail granularity are defined in the current CUBRICON prototype. Each column of the table, other than the first, defines a granularity level or type. For each granularity type, the corresponding column shows the information to be presented about the parent tasks, the task itself, and the children tasks. For example, for coarse granularity and a task X, the name property and all major properties of the parent are presented, the name and major properties of X itself, and the names of the children tasks are presented.

2. Scope granularity: The second type is a scope concept and is measured on a scale of "local" to "global." For any task type, scope granularity is relative to the task node in the hierarchy. "Local" refers to information about a particular task node itself, and nonlocal granularity would include information about one or more child, parent, grandchild, grandparent, etc., nodes.

Multimedia Output Composition

This section discusses the CUBRICON generation component that composes multimedia output for *collections of compound space/time-dependent activities*. For the air force mission planning domain of this project, the compound activities are OCA missions. These missions are composed of sub-missions, with their flight paths forming *activity sequences*.

The presentation of a collection of compound activities is subdivided into two parts by the multimedia output grammar: an *introduction* and a *main body*. The introduction provides summary highlights of the activities, and the main body provides a detailed presentation of the activities. The main body of the discourse consists of the presentation of the main space/time-dependent activities and their related activities. The introduction uses *coarse granularity*, the main body of the presentation uses *medium granularity*, and ancillary activities are presented using *fine local-only granularity*.

For each OCA mission presentation, the main activity sequence is the flight path traversal. A path traversal sequence is composed of activities, each of which consists of traversing a leg (line segment) of the (polygonal) path. The arrival at the endpoint of the leg is an event. This terminology is similar to that of Activity-on-Edge Networks. We call the endpoints of each of the line segments "waypoints," the common military terminology. Each of these segment traversals takes place in both space and time: The waypoints of each segment have coordinates in terms of latitude/longitude, and each waypoint has an associated time at which the aircraft traversing the path is scheduled to reach the waypoint. The segments of each path are sequenced by their common endpoints; that is, the last (second) endpoint of line segment S is the first endpoint of line segment $S + 1$.

Important ancillary activities occur during the main space/time-dependent activity sequence. The ancillary activities are submissions or subtasks of the main OCA mission, including tasks such as the striking of targets and the airborne refueling of strike aircraft. After each leg (segment) of the path is presented, the multimedia generator determines whether there are any ancillary activities whose occurrence time or start time precedes the occurrence time of the next waypoint. If so, these ancillary activities are presented in order of their time of occurrence as represented in the knowledge base. Otherwise, the next leg or segment of the path is presented. Figure 18.6 shows the color graphics display after two flight paths have been presented as part of a multimedia presentation.

After each leg-transition activity is presented, the relevant and timely ancillary activities are presented. As indicated previously, for an OCA mission presentation these ancillary activities are the subtasks of striking the targets and the refueling of the strike aircraft. For each ancillary activity, local granularity is used to select the information to present. The information is generated in multimedia language.

The CUBRICON natural language generator composes and presents both spoken and written (on the CRT) natural language. As discussed in the previous section, when graphic gestures and expressions are used, spoken natural language is generated so that the natural language and graphics are temporally synchronized. The system also produces a written version of its natural language utterances. During the multimodal presentation of a collection of complex activities such as mission plans, the written version of the natural language is presented in special dynamic text windows (one per OCA mission) on the color graphics CRT.

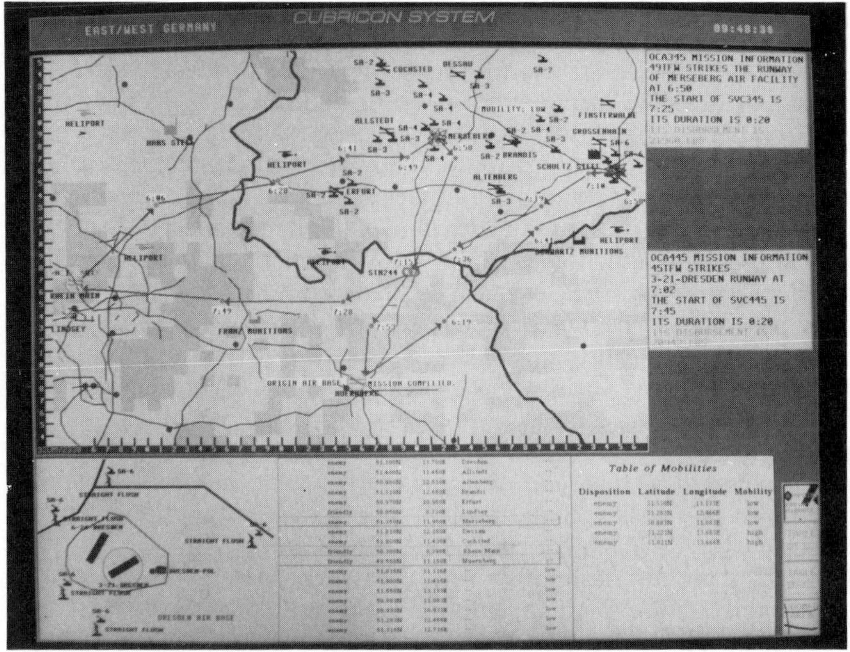

Figure 18.6 Color graphics display after presentation of missions

Figure 18.6 shows the color graphics display after the conclusion of a multimodal presentation of a collection of space/time-dependent activities, which are OCA missions in this application.

Spoken versus Visually Displayed Natural Language

An important feature of the CUBRICON system is that it distinguishes between the manner in which it generates spoken and visually displayed natural language. CUBRICON embeds deictic expressions with pointing gestures (e.g., "this SAM" with an accompanying pointing gesture to call the user's attention to the SAM system on one of the displays) in spoken output but not with NL printed to the screen, since a pointing or graphic gesture needs to be temporally synchronized with the corresponding verbal phrase, allowing for multiple deictic expressions within any individual sentence. The coordination between a pointing gesture and its co-referring verbal phrase is lost if it is embedded in printed text instead of speech, since it is difficult for a user to look in two places at the same time on the screen, that is, both at the natural language being printed to the screen and at a pointing gesture. When CUBRICON generates natural language to be visually displayed, definite descriptions are generated for noun phrases (with hopefully sufficient specificity to avoid ambiguous references) instead of simple demonstrative pronouns (with optional head nouns) and pointing gestures.

There are a number of different types of pointing gestures that CUBRICON uses, depending on the type of object being pointed to, the dialogue context, and the modality in which the object is visually presented. The primitives that CUBRICON combines for deictic expressions are speech, blinking, highlighting, graphic devices such as circling or boxing an item or region, "pointing text boxes," and flashing the border of a window (for pointing to a window).

Example Multimedia Presentation Summary

The multimodal presentation of a collection of OCA missions is fairly lengthy and complex. The following summarizes such a presentation from the perspective of what a viewer sees and hears. Figure 18.6 shows the color graphics display after the conclusion of this multimedia presentation.

1. As an introduction to the presentation, for each OCA mission, its ID number, its package number (a package is a set of related missions), the origin (departure) airbase, and the OCA's submissions (strike and refueling missions) are summarized in speech and written language (on the Natural Language Interaction Window), accompanied by temporally synchronized pointing gestures to the corresponding items (as they are presented) on the mission form, which is on the monochrome display. For each OCA mission, a mission information window is initialized on the color graphics display, next to the relevant map window. It is used during the rest of the presentation to summarize important information in a written form.
2. The startup of each mission flight is signaled by the presentation of information about the aircraft departing the origin airbase in spoken natural language, with accompanying deictic and graphic gestures shown on the map display. Other relevant information includes the location of the origin airbase, the time of departure, and the unit that is flying the mission.
3. One by one, the segments making up the different (polygonal) flight paths are displayed in an animated manner on the map window so as to simulate simultaneous flight path traversal. Each flight path segment is presented at its appropriate time according to the time on waypoint for its second endpoint. For each flight path, an aircraft icon moves from waypoint to waypoint as a directed line segment grows to represent the particular leg of the flight path. As the aircraft reaches each waypoint, the time on waypoint is printed next to it.
4. For each mission flight, when the target of the mission is reached, it is identified via spoken natural language with synchronized deictic gestures consisting of blinking/highlighting its icon on the map window, highlighting the information on the form window, and any tables that include the information. The time on target is also presented. The target information is also summarized in the mission information window on the color graphics CRT.

5. For each mission, when the refueling location is reached on the map window, information about the refueling mission is presented in spoken natural language with synchronized simultaneous deictic gestures pointing to the relevant information representations on the various windows (i.e., map, form, and tables). The information is also summarized in the mission information window.
6. For each mission, when the aircraft arrives back at the origin airbase, the completion of the presentation is announced using speech output.

18.4 RELATED RESEARCH

In this section, we discuss related research in which artificial intelligence is applied in the following areas: intelligent multimedia interfaces, multimedia authoring, multimedia information and document storage and retrieval, and multimedia conferencing and decision making.

18.4.1 Intelligent Multimedia Interfaces

Multimedia dialogue for human-computer interaction has been a focus for several research groups. We consider both input and output in the following paragraphs.

For the understanding of multimedia input, our CUBRICON project focused on the understanding of natural langauge accompanied by simultaneous coordinated pointing gestures, particularly the problem of referent identification. Related work includes the development of the TEMPLAR system [41] at TRW, XTRA [42,43] at the University of Saarbrucken, and the IMAGE system [44] at the ATR Communication Systems Research Lab. The TEMPLAR system seems to provide only for a pointing gesture to substitute for a natural language definite reference within a natural language sentence, rather than also allowing a pointing gesture to be used in combination with an NL reference. The CUBRICON approach is closer to that of Kobsa and colleagues with the XTRA system, in accepting dual-modality input and applying several knowledge sources for referent identification. The IMAGE system is an illustrated map guidance system with an interface that enables the user to use voice and hand pointing gestures for spatial layout and/or positioning during input. The IMAGE system uses a DataGlove for hand pointing gestures, instead of the mouse device used for pointing gestures in the other systems mentioned above.

The automated composition and generation of multimedia dialogue output and presentations from knowledge base representations has been addressed by several efforts: CUBRICON [10,11,12,13], Integrated Interfaces [45,46], COMET (Coordinated Multimedia Explanation Testbed) [47,48], WIP [49,50], SAGE [51], and Maybury [52]. The CUBRICON effort was discussed in Section 18.3. The Integrated Interfaces system is based on models of the objects of the application and the interface and their classes, relationships, behaviors, and behavior effects. The prototype is capable of producing presentations that include map graphics, natural language, menus, and forms for a navy situation database-reporting application.

The COMET, WIP, SAGE, and Maybury projects are addressing the issue of composing and generating coordinated graphics and text in such a way that they complement one another. Planning paradigms are responsible for deciding what to say and how to say it. The presentation planners can be considered to construct and organize presentation material to achieve communicative goals. COMET is designed to generate explanations for an expert system concerning how to carry out field maintenance and repair procedures for military radio equipment. Its architecture is based on separate communicating media generators for text and graphics. The SAGE system is designed to produce explanations of changes in quantitative models used in programs such as spreadsheets, database, and scheduling tools. Currently, the WIP system is being designed to generate instructions for a user to properly manipulate real-world devices, such as an espresso machine. In the WIP system, generation is controlled by a set of generation parameters such as target audience, presentation objective, resource limitations, and target language.

18.4.2 Multimedia Information/Document Storage and Retrieval

Information/document storage and retrieval issues are fundamental to multimedia document navigation and multimedia document authoring. First, since the components of a hypertext or multimedia document are linked, the lines between documents become blurred; that is, the information packets that comprise the chapters or sections of a multimedia document can be considered as separate documents or as components of the same (or several) document(s). Following a hypertext or multimedia document link while viewing or navigating a multimedia document is a simple form of associative information retrieval.

Second, a critical component of the multimedia or hypertext authoring process is the determination of what information to include in a multimedia document and what links to establish. Again, a key function that needs to be provided to support the multimedia author is the location and retrieval of relevant information, both from documents that the author(s) has (have) created or from the works of other authors.

Therefore, we review related research in the applications of artificial intelligence technology to multimedia information storage and retrieval in this subsection from the perspective of viewers (or readers or navigators) and authors (creators) of multimedia documents.

Limited forms of artificial intelligence technology have recently been incorporated into hypertext and multimedia document manipulation tools. For example, KnowledgePro from Knowledge Garden, Inc., is an expert system development tool for the IBM PC that includes a hypertext facility. The links provided by KnowledgePro can trigger rules that query the user and guide document navigation.

Researchers at the NASA Ames Research Center are addressing the problem of document management and maintenance in the design and development of their Computer Integrated Documentation (CID) system [2,3,53]. Their approach is to design and build an intelligent problem-driven context-sensitive tool that interacts with and learns from users, and uses interaction media including intelligent hypertext, multimedia, and virtual environments. The focus of this work is on combining conventional indexing, hypertext, and knowledge-based systems to develop semantic context-sensitive indexing and information retrieval. The objective is to improve the precision and recall for document retrieval. Their approach depends on the use of contexts which define mappings from descriptors to document referents. The NASA researchers call their documents with associated indexing knowledge "active documents," since they can be considered as knowledge-based systems in the sense that they can present relevant information in an appropriate format based on context knowledge.

Cooperative research by the NASA Ames Research Center and the Center for Design Research at Stanford University is focusing on the development of methods for capturing and storing design knowledge and a knowledge-based interface for information retrieval [54,55]. The goal is to facilitate the reuse of design knowledge and information.

Recent research in the application of artificial intelligence technology to document/data indexing and search methods include new approaches to text analysis for automating the key phrase indexing process [56], deductive hypermedia technologies [57], and expert system approaches to image classification and retrieval [58,59,60].

Research at the MIT Media Laboratory is addressing the problem of representing the content of multimedia information, with emphasis on the problem of data entry or video logging [61]. The representation of the information must be able to support all aspects of the process of video document authoring: logging the footage into the archive, displaying information about the footage, retrieving it, and inserting it into the new video document. An iconic user interface, called the Director's Workshop, is being developed to support the process of describing multimedia information for later retrieval and resequencing by automatic presentation systems.

18.4.3 Multimedia Conferencing and Decision Making

Computer-supported cooperative work (CSCW) [62,63,64,65,66] has attracted dramatically increasing attention during the past several years and is an area in which multimedia systems are being applied to support group conferencing and decision making [5,6,67,68]. Just as we have seen the application of artificial intelligence to the problem of providing single-user decision support systems, artificial intelligence is now being applied to the more difficult problem of supporting collaborative work by groups of decision makers. Systems supporting collaborative or group decision making are primarily distributed systems, and, therefore, much of the artificial intelligence research in this area is classified as "distributed artificial intelligence" [69,70].

Moulin, Chaib-draa, and Cloutier [71] are working on a multi-agent system in which several artificial and human agents are able to interact together and also work individually and/or jointly on a planned course of action. Their work is based on a model of speech acts and ordinary acts using communication/action structures. Decision spaces are used to model agents' states and their relations: effective states, potential states, intentions, and commitments. Each artificial agent includes three layers: an operational component which builds plans; a tactical component which reasons about the agent's motivations, intentions, and goals; and a strategic component which reasons about the agent's commitments in relation to other agents' beliefs and intentions.

Kaye and Karam [72] are designing and implementing a system to support office workers using an approach based on embedding office knowledge in a network of distributed cooperating knowledge-based "assistants" and servers. This distributed system incorporates both factual and procedural knowledge and is capable of making use of existing conventional office technology.

18.5 FUTURE DIRECTIONS

The development of hardware user interface devices is advancing rapidly, providing ever-more sophisticated 3-D graphics and animation systems, video manipulation and presentation systems, 3-D sound and speech production systems, speech recognition systems, DataGlove devices, Datasuits, eye-tracking devices, stereo goggles, machine vision systems to capture and interpret user body language and facial expressions, and other devices that will contribute to creating virtual realities for human-computer interaction.

The problems for the future lie in the integration and intelligent use and control of the various devices and media: the problems will be with software development, not hardware.

The critical areas of artificial intelligence technology in which future significant progress is needed include:

Self-adaptive systems: As systems become more complex with regard to their ability to use combinations of larger suites of communication modes and media, adapting, tailoring, and porting any given system to another user, user group, user environment, or application will become increasingly difficult. Therefore, it becomes increasingly important for systems to automatically adapt or modify themselves appropriately, while giving the user a feeling of control over the system and interaction process and providing a stable interaction environment.

Multimedia input understanding: Significant progress needs to be made in the coordination and interpretation of complex multimedia input, composed of media such as spoken natural language, facial and other body language expressions, eye-tracking information, and pointing gestures. Even combining two communication modes poses difficult problems, and the history of research into combining multiple input modes is relatively brief. Furthermore, computer understanding of some of the individual communication modes is still not satisfactorily accomplished. For example, after many years of research, natural language understanding is still a problem to which there is no general satisfactory solution, and it remains one of the most challenging fields within artificial intelligence.

Intelligent automated multimedia output generation: As the volume and types of information and presentation types become more numerous and varied, it will become increasingly important for computer systems to make automated knowledge-based decisions regarding information presentation to users. If we consider the status of the technology for composing and temporally and spatially coordinating information presentations using just two media, natural language and graphics, we find that the problem is difficult and the technology is just in its infancy. As more media and modalities are added to the presentation suite, the problems become more severe and the need for research becomes more significant.

Such intelligent automated multimedia information presentation has application in many areas, including multimedia or hypermedia document presentation, information retrieval from multimedia databases and knowledge bases, and explanation subsystems of user help facilities.

Some of the subproblems of multimedia output generation include:

- ☐ Selection of media and apportionment of information content among the media used for information presentation.
- ☐ Coordination of the media with respect to both space and time.
- ☐ Consistency of selection, composition, and generation across presentations.

Knowledge-based development tools for multimedia systems: As more media become viable and available for computer systems, the need for more sophisticated development tools becomes more critical. For example, high-quality authoring systems for hypermedia or multimedia presentation/document authoring are needed as well as development tools for multimedia human-computer interfaces. Generic intelligent automated multimedia composition and generation technology, mentioned above, could play an important role in alleviating some of the development problems.

Hypermedia document systems: As mentioned above, the area of hypermedia/multimedia document authoring and presentation systems requires better system development tools and intelligent automated multimedia presentation technology. Another area in which hypermedia document technology could benefit is in the area of "smart links," that is, hypertext/media links which have some decision-making ability to lead the viewer/reader to appropriate information based on factors such as what the system knows the viewer has already "read," the viewer's goals and objectives for viewing the material, and the viewer's background and level of expertise in relevant fields.

Intelligent interfaces: Systems are becoming capable of manipulating ever-more sophisticated object types because of increased variety in the storage media used in databases and knowledge bases. Research and development is already in progress in the area of intelligent interfaces, but the need for more highly intelligent interfaces will increase to relieve the user of the need to know the increasing capabilities of information manipulation computer systems.

Computer supported cooperative work: Collaboration is pervasive and complex, and it brings an associated suite of difficult problems to each of the collaborators in areas such as the decomposition of tasks into subtask assignments, scheduling, coordination, communication, planning, searching and retrieving information, sharing resources, integrating individual collaborators' products into group products, and understanding one another's goals, plans, activities, and accomplishments. This field will benefit significantly from the application of artificial intelligence research and development to CSCW systems. Artificial intelligent agents, for example, could provide assistance and guidance to their human counterparts and relieve them of their more mundane and time-consuming tasks.

18.6 SUMMARY

This chapter has focused on applications of artificial intelligence to multimedia systems. We presented a concept and design for a multimedia integrated workstation environment with a human-computer interface designed as a supportive intelligent agent with the ability to communicate and make presentations in coordinated multiple media/modalites.

The design and functionality for an implemented prototype system, called CUBRICON, was discussed. CUBRICON has several unique features:

- ☐ CUBRICON accepts and understands natural language input accompanied by simultaneous pointing gestures. CUBRICON allows a variety of object types to be targets of point gestures and accepts a variable number of multimodal phrases within any sentence. CUBRICON can also use natural language inputs to disambiguate corresponding point gestures, and vice versa. CUBRICON also handles certain types of ill-formed multimodal inputs.

- ☐ CUBRICON composes and generates relevant output to the user in coordinated multiple modalities. CUBRICON selects appropriate information to output to the user based on the user request, relevance to the user's task, relevance to the dialogue, and consistency of output displays. CUBRICON selects appropriate output media/modalities based on the characteristics of the information to be expressed as well as task and dialogue context. The output modalities are used in a highly integrated manner. Multimedia outputs, especially speech and accompanying graphics, are temporally synchronized. The system distinguishes between spoken and written natural language output and composes such natural language outputs appropriately.

- ☐ CUBRICON provides intelligent automatic management of windows in a dual-monitor environment. This includes a method for determining window importance that is used to decide which windows to remove when display space is needed for other windows.
- ☐ CUBRICON includes several knowledge sources to support its decision-making processes. These knowledge sources include a dialogue model, user-task model, and a knowledge base of interface and task-specific information.

Related research is being conducted at various institutions into the application of artificial intelligence to multimedia interfaces, multimedia authoring, multimedia information and document storage and retrieval, and multimedia conferencing and decision making. We reviewed some of the research in these areas.

The application of artificial intelligence to multimedia systems shows promise of significant future benefit in producing systems that provide a natural multimedia language for human-computer interaction, provide more assistance and support for users, relieve the user of the burden of managing the interface, and are adaptable to tasks, users, and context.

18.7 REFERENCES

1. Clark, D. R. The Demise of Multimedia. *IEEE Computer Graphics and Applications*. vol. 11, no. 4. 1991. pp. 75–80.
2. Boy, G. A. *Computer Integrated Documentation*. NASA Technical Memorandum 103870. 1991.
3. Boy, G. A. Semantic Correlation in Context: Application in Document Comparison and Group Knowledge Design. *Proceedings of the AAAI Spring Symposium on Cognitive Aspects of Knowledge Acquisition*. 1992.
4. Cornell, M., Suthers, D., and Woolf, B. Using "Live Information" in a Multimedia Framework. *Proceedings of the AAAI-91 Intelligent Multimedia Interfaces Workshop*. 1991. pp. 93–98.
5. Bly, S. A., Harrison, S. R., and Irwin, S. Media Spaces: Video, Audio, and Computing Environment. *Communications of the ACM*. vol. 36, no. 1. 1993. pp. 28–47.
6. Fish, R. S., Kraut, R. E., Root, R. W., and Rice, R. E. Video as a Technology for Informal Communication. *Communications of the ACM*. vol. 36, no. 1. 1993. pp. 48–61.

7. Grimes, J. and Potel, M. Guest Editors' Introduction: Multimedia—It's Actually Useful! *IEEE Computer Graphics and Applications*. vol. 11, no. 4. 1991. pp. 24–25.
8. Grice, H. P. Logic and Conversation. In P. Cole and J. L. Morgan (eds.), *Syntax and Semantics, vol. 3: Speech Acts*. Academic Press. 1975. pp. 41–48.
9. Neal, J. G., Bettinger, K. E., Byoun, J. S., Dobes, Z., and Thielman, C. Y. An Intelligent Multimedia Human-Computer Dialogue System. *Proceedings of the Workshop on Space Operations, Automation, and Robotics (SOAR-88)*. 1988. pp. 245–251.
10. Neal, J. G., Dobes, Z., Bettinger, K. E., and Byoun, J. S. Multimodal References in Human-Computer Dialogue, *Proc. AAAI-88*. 1988. pp. 819–823.
11. Neal, J. G., Thielman, C. Y., Dobes, Z., Haller, S. M., and Shapiro, S. C. Natural Language with Integrated Deictic and Graphic Gestures. *Proc. of the DARPA Speech and Natural Language Workshop*. 1989. pp. 410–423.
12. Neal, J. G., Shapiro, S. C., Thielman, C. Y., Lammens, J. M., Funke, D. J., Byoun, J. S., Dobes, Z., Glanowski, S., Summers, M., Gucwa, J. R., and Paul, R. *Final Report for the Intelligent Multi-Modal Interfaces Project*. RADC Technical Report TR-90-128. 1990.
13. Neal, J. G., and Shapiro, S. C. Intelligent Multi-Media Interface Technology. In J. W. Sullivan S. W. Tyler (eds.), *Intelligent User Interfaces*. Addison-Wesley. 1991. pp. 11–44.
14. Shapiro, S. C. The SNePS Semantic Network Processing System. In Findler, (ed.), *Associative Networks—The Representation and Use of Knowledge by Computers*. Academic Press. 1979. pp. 179–203.
15. Shapiro, S. C. *SNePS User's Manual*. The SNePS Implementation Group. Computer Science Deptartment, SUNY at Buffalo, NY. 1981.
16. Shapiro, S. C., and Rapaport, W. SNePS Considered as a Fully Intensional Propositional Semantic Network. *Proc. AAAI-86*. In G. McCalla and N. Cercone (eds.), *Knowledge Representation*. Springer-Verlag. 1987. pp. 278–283.
17. Shapiro, S. C. Generalized Augmented Transition Network Grammars for Generation from Semantic Networks. *AJCL*. vol. 8, no. 1. 1982. pp. 12–25.
18. Maida, A. S., and Shapiro, S. C. Intensional Concepts in Propositional Semantic Networks. In R. J. Brachman H. J. Levesque (eds.), *Readings in Knowledge Representation*. Morgan Kaufmann. 1985. pp. 169–190.
19. Shapiro, S. C., and Neal, J. G. A Knowledge Engineering Approach to Natural Language Understanding. *Proc. ACL*. 1982. pp. 136–144.
20. Neal, J. G., and Shapiro, S. C. Knowledge Representation for Reasoning About Language. In J. C. Boudreauz, B. W. Hamill, and R. Jernigan (eds.), *The Role of Language in Problem Solving*. Springer-Verlag. 1986. pp. 27–47.
21. Neal, J. G., and Shapiro, S. C. Knowledge Based Parsing. In L. Bolc (ed.), *Natural Language Parsing Systems*. Springer-Verlag. 1987. pp. 49–92.
22. Shapiro, S. C., Martens, J., and McKay, D. Bidirectional Inference. *Proc. of the Cognitive Science Society*. 1982. pp. 90–93.
23. McKay, D. P., and Shapiro, S. C. MULTI—A LISP-Based Multiprocessing System. *Conference Record of the 1980 LISP Conference*. Stanford University. 1980. pp. 29–37.
24. Shapiro, S. C. Using Nonstandard Connectives Quantifiers for Representing Deduction Rules in a Semantic Network. Paper presented at Current Aspects of AI Research, a seminar held at the Electrotechnical Laboratory, Tokyo. 1979.
25. Miller, G. A. The Magical Number Seven Plus or Minus Two. *Psychological Review* 63. 1956. pp. 81–97.
26. Andriole, S. J. Graphic Equivalence, Graphic Explanations, and Embedded Process Modeling for Enhanced Process Modeling for Enhanced User-System Interaction. *IEEE Trans. on Systems, Man, and Cybernetics*. vol. 16, no. 6. 1986
27. Grosz, B. J. Discourse Analysis. In D. Walker (ed.), *Understanding Spoken Language*. Elsevier. 1978. pp. 229–345.
28. Grosz, B. J. The Representation and Use of Focus in a System for Understanding Dialogs. In B. J. Grosz, K. S. Jones, and B. L. Webber (eds.), *Readings in Natural Language Processing*. Morgan Kaufmann. 1986. pp. 353–362.

29. Sidner, C. L. Focusing in the Comprehension of Definite Anaphora. In B. J. Grosz, K. S. Jones, B. L. Webber (eds.), *Readings in Natural Language Processing*. Morgan Kaufmann. 1986. pp. 353–362.
30. Grosz, B. J., and Sidner, C. L. Discourse Structure and the Proper Treatment of Interruptions. *Proc. of IJCAI*. 1985. pp. 832–839.
31. Grosz, B. J. Focusing and Description in Natural Language Dialogues. In A. Joshi, B. Webber, and I. Sag (eds.), *Elements of Discourse Understanding*. Cambridge University Press. 1981. pp.84–105.
32. Carberry, S. First International Workshop on User Modeling. *AI Magazine*. vol.8, no.3. 1987. pp.71–74.
33. Kobsa, A., and Wahlster, W. (eds.). *Computational Linguistics. Special Issue on User Modeling*. MIT Press. 1988.
34. Kobsa, A., and Wahlster, W. (eds.). *User Models in Dialog Systems*. Springer-Verlag. 1989.
35. Kass, R., and Finin, T. General User Modeling: A Facility to Support Intelligent Interaction. In J. W. Sullivan and S. W. Tyler (eds.), *Intelligent User Interfaces*. ACM Press/Addison-Wesley. 1991. pp. 111–128.
36. Wahlster, W. User and Discourse Models for Multimodal Communication. In J. W. Sullivan and S. W. Tyler (eds.), *Architectures for Intelligent Interfaces: Elements and Prototypes*. Addison-Wesley/ACM Press. 1991.
37. Malone, T. W. How Do People Organize Their Desks? Implications for the Design of Office Automation Systems. *ACM Transactions on Office Information Systems* 1(1). 1983. pp. 99–112.
38. Funke, D. J., Neal, J. G., and Paul, R. D. An Approach to Intelligent Automated Window Management, *International Journal of Man-Machine Studies*. 1993.
39. Bly, S. A., and Rosenberg, J. K. A Comparison of Tiled and Overlapped Windows. *CHI '86 Proceedings*. 1986. pp. 101–106.
40. Billingsley, P. A. Taking Panes: Issues in the Design of Windowing Systems. In M. Helander (ed.), *Handbook of Human-Computer Interaction*. Elsevier. 1988. pp. 413–436.
41. Press, B. The U.S. Air Force TEMPLAR Project Status and Outlook. *Western Conf. on Knowledge-Based Engineering and Expert Systems*. 1986. pp. 42–48.
42. Allgayer, J., Jansern-Winkeln, R., Reddig, C., and Reithinger, N. Bidirectional Use of Knowledge in the Multimodal NL Access System XTRA. *Proc. of IJCAI-89*. 1989. pp. 1492–1497.
43. Kobsa, A., Allgayer, J., Reddig, C., Reithinger, N., Schmauks, D., Harbusch, K., and Wahlster, W. Combining Deictic Gestures and Natural Language for Referent Identification. *Proc. of the 11th International Conference on Computational Linguistics*. 1986.
44. Takahashi, T., Hakata, A., Shima, N., and Kobayashi, Y. Unifying Voice and Hand Indication of Spatial Layout. *SPIE vol. 1198. Sensor Fusion II: Human and Machine Strategies*. 1989. pp. 346–353.
45. Arens, Y., Miller, L., and Sondheimer, N. Presentation Design Using an Integrated Knowledge Base. In J. W. Sullivan and S. W. Tyler (eds.), *Intelligent User Interfaces*. ACM Press/Addison-Wesley. 1991. pp. 241–258.
46. Arens, Y., and Hovy, E. H. How to Describe What? Towards a Theory of Modality Utilization. *Proceedings of the 12th Cognitive Science Conference*. 1990.
47. Feiner, S. K., and McKeown, K. R. Automating the Generation of Coordinated Multimedia Explanations. *IEEE Computer*. vol. 24, no. 10. 1991. pp. 33–41.
48. Feiner, S. K., and McKeown, K. R. Coordinating Text and Graphics in Explanation Generation. *Proceedings of the 8th National Conference on Artificial Intelligence*. 1990. pp. 442–449.
49. Wahlster, W., Andre, E., Graf, W., and Rist, T. Designing Illustrated Texts: How Language Production is Influenced by Graphics Generation. *Proceedings of the 5th Conference of the EACL*. 1991. pp. 8–14.
50. Wahlster, W., Andre, E., Bandyopadhyay, S., Graf, W., and Rist, T. WIP: The Coordinated Generation of Multimodal Presentations from a Common Representation. In A. Ortony,

J. Slack, and O. Stock (eds.), *A.I. and Cognitive Science Perspectives on Communication*. Springer-Verlag. 1991.

51. Roth, S. F., Mattis, J., and Mesnard, X. Graphics and Natural Language as Components of Automatic Explanation. In J. W. Sullivan and S. W. Tyler (eds.), *Intelligent User Interfaces*. ACM Press/Addison-Wesley. 1991. pp. 207–240.
52. Maybury, M. T. Planning Multimedia Explanations Using Communicative Acts. *Proceedings of the 10th National Conference on Artificial Intelligence*. 1991.
53. Mathe, N., and Boy, G. The Computer Integrated Documentation Project: A Merge of Hypermedia and AI Techniques. *Proceedings of SOAR '92*. 1992.
54. Baudin, C., Gevins, J., Mabogunje, A., and Baya, V. A Knowledge-Based Interface for Design Information Retrieval. *Proceedings of the AAAI-91 Intelligent Multimedia Interfaces Workshop*. 1991. pp. 133–140.
55. Baudin, C., Sivard, C., and Zweben, M. Recovering Rationale for Design Changes: A Knowledge-Based Approach. *Proceedings IEEE*. 1990.
56. Driscoll, J., Rajala, D., Shaffer, W., and Thomas, D. The Operation and Performance of an Artificially Intelligent Keywording System. *Information Processing and Management*. vol. 27, no. 1. 1991. pp. 43–54.
57. Parsaye, K., Chignell, M., and Khoshafian, S. *Intelligent Databases: Object-Oriented, Deductive Hypermedia Technologies*. John Wiley & Sons. 1989.
58. Ragusa, J. M., and Orwig, G. Expert Systems and Imaging: NASA's Start-Up Work in Intelligent Image Management. *Journal of Expert Systems*. vol. 3. 1990. pp. 25–30.
59. Ragusa, J. M., and Orwig, G. Attacking the Information Access Problem with Expert Systems. *Journal of Expert Systems*, vol. 4. 1990. pp. 26–32.
60. Ragusa, J. M. and Heard, A. Intelligent Multimedia Interfaces: Research Issues and Some Sample Applications. *Proceedings of the AAAI-91 Intelligent Multimedia Interfaces Workshop*. 1991. pp. 162–172.
61. Davis, M. E. Director's Workshop: Semantic Video Logging with Intelligent Icons. *Proceedings of the AAAI-91 Intelligent Multimedia Interfaces Workshop*. 1991. pp. 122–132.
62. Special Section on Computer-Supported Cooperative Work. *Communications of the ACM*. vol. 34, no. 12. 1991.
63. *CSCW '88: Proceedings of the Conference on Computer Supported Cooperative Work*. ACM Press. 1988.
64. *CSCW '90: Proceedings of the Conference on Computer Supported Cooperative Work*. ACM Press. 1990.
65. *CSCW '92: Proceedings of the Conference on Computer Supported Cooperative Work*. ACM Press. 1992.
66. Ellis, C. A., Gibbs, S. J., and Rein, G. L. Groupware: Some Issues and Experiences. *Communications of the ACM*. vol. 34, no. 1. 1991. pp. 38–58.
67. Ishii, H., and Miyake, N. Toward an Open Shared Workspace: Computer and Video Fusion Approach of TeamWorkStation. *Communication of the ACM*. vol. 34, no. 12. 1991. pp. 36–51.
68. Francik, E., Rudman, S. E., Cooper D., and Levine, S. Putting Innovation to Work: Adoption Strategies for Multimedia Communication Systems. *Communications of the ACM*. vol. 34, no. 12. 1991. pp. 52–63.
69. Bond, A., and Gasser, L. *Readings in Distributed Artificial Intelligence*. Morgan Kaufman. 1989.
70. Datta, A. Cooperative Problem Solving in Distributed Decision Making Contexts. *Proceedings of the 1991 IEEE International Conference on Systems, Man, and Cybernetics*. 1991. pp. 2085–2090.
71. Moulin, B., Chaib-draa, B., and Cloutier, L. A Multi-Agent System Supporting Cooperative Work Done by Persons and Machines. *Proceedings of the 1991 IEEE International Conference on Systems, Man, and Cybernetics*. 1991. pp. 1889–1893.
72. Kaye, A. R., and Karam, G. M. Cooperating Knowledge-Based Assistants for the Office. *ACM Transactions on Office Information Systems*. vol. 5, no. 4. 1987. pp. 297–326.

18.8 FOR FURTHER READING

1. *Communications of the ACM: Special Issue on HyperText.* vol. 31, no. 7. 1988.
2. Cheikes, B. A., and Webber, B. L. The Design of a Cooperative Respondent. In J. W. Sullivan S. W. Tyler (eds.), *Architectures for Intelligent Interfaces: Elements and Prototypes.* Addison-Wesley/ACM Press. 1990.
3. Conklin, J. Hypertext: An Introduction and Survey. *Computer.* vol. 20, no. 9. 1987. pp. 17–41.
4. Egan, D. E., Remde, J. R., Gomez, L. M., Landauer, T. K., Eberhardt, J., and Lochbaum, C. C. Formative Design-Evaluation of SuperBook. *ACM Transactions On Information Systems.* vol. 7, no. 1. 1989. pp. 30–58.
5. Hollan, J., Miller, J. R., Rich, E., and Wilner, W. Knowledge Bases and Tools for Building Integrated Multimedia Intelligent Interfaces. In J. W. Sullivan and S. W. Tyler (eds.), *Architectures for Intelligent Interfaces: Elements and Prototypes.* Addison-Wesley/ACM Press. 1990.
6. Kaplan, S. J. Cooperative Responses From a Portable Natural Language Database Query System. In M. Brady (ed.), *Computational Models of Discourse.* MIT Press. 1982.
7. Reithinger, N. Generating Referring Expressions and Pointing Gestures. In G. Kempen (ed.), *Natural Language Generation.* Nijhoff. 1987. pp. 71–81.
8. Shapiro, S. C. Generation as Parsing from a Network into a Linear String. *AJCL.* 1975. pp. 45–62. Microfiche 33.
9. Shepard, S. J. A New Approach to Hypertext: MINDS. *AI Expert.* vol. 4, no. 9. 1989. pp. 69–72.
10. Simmons, R., and Slocum, J. Generating English Discourse from Semantic Networks. *CACM* 15:10. 1972. pp. 891–905.
11 Sullivan, J. W., and Sherman, W. T. (eds.). *Architectures for Intelligent Interfaces: Elements and Prototypes.* Addison-Wesley/ACM Press. 1990.

INDEX

F

G

H

I

J

L

M

Q

R

S

Membership Information

This book is published as part of the SIGGRAPH Books Series with ACM Press Books—a collaboration among ACM SIGGRAPH, ACM Press, and Addison-Wesley Publishing Company. Founded in 1947, ACM is the oldest and largest educational scientific society in the information technology field. Through its high-quality publications and services, ACM is a major force in advancing the skills and knowledge of IT professionals throughout the world. From a dedicated group of 78, ACM is now 85,000 strong, with 34 special interest groups, including SIGGRAPH, and more than 60 chapters and student chapters.

For more than 25 years, SIGGRAPH and its conferences have provided the world's forum for the interchange of information on computer graphics and interactive techniques. SIGGRAPH members come from many disciplines and include researchers, hardware and software systems designers, algorithm and applications developers, visualization scientists, educators, technology developers for interactive visual communications, animators and special-effects artists, graphic designers, and fine artists.

For further information about ACM and ACM SIGGRAPH, contact:

ACM Member Services
1515 Broadway, 17th floor
New York, NY 10036-5701
Phone: 1-212-626-0500
Fax: 1-212-944-1318
E-mail: ACMHELP@ACM.org

ACM European Service Center
Avenue Marcel Thiry 204
1200 Brussels, Belgium
Phone: 32-2-774-9602
Fax: 32-2-774-9690
E-mail: ACM_Europe@ACM.org